Teaching Special Students
in General Education Classrooms

Teaching Special Students in General Education Classrooms

SEVENTH EDITION

Rena B. Lewis
San Diego State University

Donald H. Doorlag
Emeritus, San Diego State University

PEARSON

Merrill
Prentice Hall

Upper Saddle River, New Jersey
Columbus, Ohio

Library of Congress Cataloging in Publication Data

Lewis, Rena B.
  Teaching special students in general education classrooms / by Rena B. Lewis and
Donald H. Doorlag—7th ed.
    p. cm.
  Includes bibliographical references and index.
  ISBN 0-13-148635-7
  1. Inclusive education—United States. 2. Special education—United States.
  3. Mainstreaming in education—United States. I. Doorlag, Donald H. II. Title.

LC1201.L48 2005
371.9'046—dc22   2004059706

Vice President and Executive Publisher: Jeffery W. Johnston
Acquisitions Editor: Allyson Sharp
Development Editor: Heather Doyle Fraser
Editorial Assistant: Kathleen S. Burk
Production Editor: Sheryl Glicker Langner
Production Coordination: Jolynn Feller, Carlisle Publishers Services
Design Coordinator: Diane C. Lorenzo
Photo Coordinator: Lori Whitley
Cover Design: Bryan Huber
Cover Image: Corbis
Production Manager: Laura Messerly
Director of Marketing: Ann Castel Davis
Marketing Manager: Autumn Purdy
Marketing Coordinator: Brian Mounts

This book was set in Berkeley Book by Carlisle Communications, Ltd. It was printed and bound by Courier Kendallville, Inc. The cover was printed by Coral Graphic Services, Inc.

Photo Credits: Jim Cummins/Corbis-Bettmann, pp. 2, 378; Anthony Magnacca/Merrill, pp. 6, 27, 31,106, 138, 160, 184, 206, 210, 245, 251, 315, 339, 356, 383, 387, 399; Patrick White/Merrill, pp. 11, 89, 288, 341; Scott Cunningham/Merrill, pp. 21, 34,; Tom Watson/Merrill, pp. 24, 86, 128, 234; Leanne Temme/Photolibrary.Com, p. 56; David Napranik/Merrill, p. 62, 156, 296, 336, 386; Richard Hutchings/PhotoEdit, pp. 69; David Young-Wolff/PhotoEdit, pp. 78, 180, 272, 371; KS Studios/Merrill, p. 93; Charles Gupton/Corbis/ Bettmann, p. 113; Michael Newman/PhotoEdit, pp. 134, 394; Steve Lumb/Dorling Kindersley Media Library, p. 139; Ken Karp/Prentice Hall School Division, p. 146; Larry Hamill/Merrill, p. 166; Pearson Learning Photo Studio, p. 199; David Roth/Getty Images Inc.–Stone Allstock, p. 204; David Mager/Pearson Learning Photo Studio, pp. 228, 325, 388; Richard Hutchings/Photo Researchers, Inc., p. 234; Ellen Senisi/The Image Works, p. 260; Dennis MacDonald/PhotoEdit, p. 269; Mark Lewis/Getty Images Inc.–Stone Allstock, p. 280; Jan Sonnenmair/Aurora & Quanta Productions Inc., p. 305; Myrleen Ferguson Cate/PhotoEdit, p. 310; Bill Aron/PhotoEdit, p. 319; EyeWire Collection/Getty Images–Photodisc, p. 332; Modern Curriculum Press/Pearson Learning, p. 359; Karen Mancinelli/Pearson Learning Photo Studio, p. 365; Nancy Sheehan/PhotoEdit, p. 372; Rhoda Sidney/PH College, p. 406; Paul Conklin/PhotoEdit, p. 408.

Pearson Education Ltd.
Pearson Education Singapore Pte. Ltd.
Pearson Education Canada, Ltd.
Pearson Education–Japan

Pearson Education Australia Pty. Limited
Pearson Education North Asia Ltd.
Pearson Educación de Mexico, S.A. de C.V.
Pearson Education Malaysia Pte. Ltd.

10 9 8 7 6 5 4 3 2 1
ISBN: 0-13-148635-7

DEDICATION

With thanks for your support and encouragement through the years:
>   Jim Lewis
>   Deanne Doorlag
>   Wayne and Florence Douglas

With the highest hopes for the years ahead:
>   Dylan and Jeniffer Lewis
>   Kristi Doorlag
>   Scott Doorlag

About the Authors

Dr. Rena B. Lewis earned her Ph.D. at the University of Arizona, with a major in special education and minors in psychology and systems engineering. She began in special education as a teacher of children with mental retardation, although the majority of her work has been with students with learning disabilities. She is currently Associate Dean for Faculty Development and Research in the College of Education at San Diego State University.

A frequent contributor to the professional literature, Dr. Lewis is interested in instructional adaptations for students with special needs, classroom assessment techniques, and ways to use classroom technologies to improve literacy instruction. In addition to this book, she is co-author with Dr. James A. McLoughlin of *Assessing Special Students* (6th ed.). She was honored with an award by the International Reading Association for her report on research implications for teaching reading to students with learning disabilities. Her current research interests center around literacy interventions for highly gifted children from linguistically diverse families.

Dr. Donald H. Doorlag is now Professor Emeritus of Special Education. After receiving an undergraduate degree in secondary education, he worked as a teacher of students with emotional and behavioral disorders. He completed his doctorate at Michigan State University and joined the faculty at San Diego State University, where he chaired the Department of Special Education for a number of years. Among his numerous accomplishments at San Diego State were a certificate program for teachers of students with serious emotional disturbances and a combined training experience for prospective teachers interested in earning general and special education teaching credentials simultaneously.

Dr. Doorlag's most recent professional interests and activities have focused on the recruitment, retention, and training of special education teachers. In addition, he has worked with state agencies and professional organizations regarding the provision of educational programs for students with emotional and behavioral disorders and incarcerated youth with disabilities.

Preface

This book is about two things: Students with special needs and teaching. It is designed to prepare the professional educator to effectively teach the range of students found in the typical elementary or secondary classroom. It provides information about four groups of students with special needs: students with disabilities, gifted and talented learners, culturally and linguistically diverse individuals, and students at risk for school failure. In addition, it presents practical strategies for adapting standard instruction to meet the learning needs of all students in general education classrooms.

THE SEVENTH EDITION

The seventh edition has been thoroughly updated with the addition of several new topics and expanded coverage of others. Included are discussions of important areas such as these:

- The most recent federal law governing special education services for students with disabilities, the Individuals with Disabilities Education Improvement Act of 2004;

- Updates on federal reforms such as "No Child Left Behind";

- Changes in the nature and diversity of the U.S. population according to recent census data;

- Current information about the inclusion of students with disabilities in public schools and general education classrooms;

- A new chapter on strategies for teaching students with autism spectrum disorder;

- New information on differentiating classroom instruction to meet the special needs of gifted and talented learners;

- Expanded coverage of strategies for assessing the progress of students with special needs in the general education curriculum; and

- Information about the principles of universal design and classroom technology resources for general educators.

The seventh edition reflects current research in the fields of special and general education (more than 200 new references have been added), and there is information on the newest technologies available for use with special students in general education classrooms. Several of the "Spotlight on Technology" sections now feature software and assistive devices recommended for students with special needs. In addition, the "Window on the Web" feature introduces readers to websites that offer valuable information about special education, general education, or the teaching–learning process.

ORGANIZATION AND CONTENT

In organizing this book, we have attempted to maintain a noncategorical approach to instruction while acknowledging the differential impact of student characteristics on school performance. To accomplish this, the first eight chapters of the book (and the Epilogue) address the needs of all special students and their teachers. The chapters dealing with instructional methods (chapters 9 to 18), in contrast, are tied to specific populations of students and the types of school problems they most often encounter. However, the instructional strategies discussed in these chapters are relevant for any student with the same difficulties. For example, because students with learning disabilities are characterized by the problems they experience with mastering basic skills, the chapter focusing on this group includes techniques for teaching reading, written language, and mathematics skills. These techniques can and should be used with other students facing similar skill acquistion problems.

The 18 chapters of this book are divided into four major sections. The first part, "Introduction," identifies the purposes of inclusion, provides a rationale for a team approach to the solution of educational problems, and describes the major instructional needs of special students.

The second part, "Skills for the General Education Teacher," addresses the needs of the educator. Strategies are provided for achieving four basic instructional goals: adapting instruction, managing classroom behavior, promoting social acceptance, and coordinating the classroom learning environment. Also, information is provided on the effective use of computers and other technologies in the general education classroom.

In the third part, "Methods for Teaching Students with Disabilities," teaching strategies are suggested for a variety of different types of special students. These include students with learning disabilities, mild retardation, behavioral disorders, communication disorders, autism spectrum disorder, physical and health impairments, and visual and hearing impairments. This part also discusses interventions for individuals with three other types of disabilities: students with ADHD (chapter 9), severe disabilities (chapter 10), and traumatic brain injuries (chapter 14).

The fourth part, "Methods for Teaching Students with Other Needs in General Education," recommends instructional techniques for three other groups of students: gifted and talented students, culturally and linguistically diverse students, and students at risk for school failure.

A brief Epilogue, "Inclusion Today . . . and Tomorrow," ends the book. It examines past mistakes, current practices, and some of the promising approaches that will give new direction to the inclusion of students with special needs in school and society.

Although the chapters in this book are designed to be read in the order in which they appear, some instructors find other sequences more beneficial to their students. For example, some instructors prefer to proceed from Part I of the book directly to Parts III and IV, leaving the chapters on skills for teachers until after students have gained information on the special needs of various populations.

ANCILLARIES

The seventh edition has an enhanced instructor support package including a Companion Website, an interactive Inclusive Classrooms CD-ROM, an Instructor's Manual with Test Items, a computerized test bank and assessment software (Test Gen), and a video to accompany the text.

Companion Website

Located at *http://www.prenhall.com/lewis*, the Companion Website for this text includes a wealth of resources for both professors and students. The Syllabus Manager enables professors to create and maintain the class syllabus online while also allowing the student access to the syllabus at any time from any computer on the Internet. The student portion of the website helps students gauge their understanding of chapter content through the use of online chapter reviews, resources, and interactive self-assessments.

Inclusive Classrooms: Video Cases on CD-ROM

The CD-ROM that accompanies the seventh edition of the text provides immediate access to real classroom examples of teaching and learning strategies for inclusion. Each classroom case contains 9 video clips. These video clips give the preservice teacher a good picture of what inclusion looks like in a preschool, an elementary school, a middle school, and a secondary school. The CD-ROM is integrated into the text with end-of-chapter activities and an insert that explains more about each case and poses reflective and discussion questions for readers (see pages xxi–xxiv).

IM with Test Items and Test Gen Software

The Instructor's Manual (also available online at the Instructor's Resource Center, described below, at *www.prenhall.com*) is organized by chapter and contains summaries, objectives, terminology, presentation outlines, class discussion questions, application activities, CD-ROM activities, and test items (including multiple choice, true/false, short answer, and essay questions). The computerized version of these test items (Test Gen) is available in both Windows and Macintosh format, along with assessment software allowing professors to create and customize exams and track student progress.

Overhead Transparencies/PowerPoints

The transparencies—available in PowerPoint slide format by going to the Instructor's Resources Center, described below, at *www.prenhall.com*—highlight key concepts, summarize content, and illustrate figures and charts from the text.

Instructor Resource Center

The Instructor Resource Center at *www.prenhall.com* has a variety of print and media resources available in downloadable, digital format—all in one location. As a registered faculty member, you can access and download pass-code protected resource files, course management content, and other premium online content directly to your computer.

Digital resources available for *Teaching Special Students in General Education Classrooms,* Seventh Edition include:

- Text-specific PowerPoint Lectures
- An online version of the Instructor's Manual

To access these items online, go to *www.prenhall.com* and click on the Instructor Support button and then go to the Download Supplements section. Here you will be able to log in or complete a one-time registration for a user name and password. If you have any questions regarding this process or the materials available online, please contact your local Prentice Hall sales representative.

Video

Course instructors receive a complimentary copy of the Inclusive Classrooms Video which can be used to supplement and extend information and issues introduced in the text. The video features all of the clips from the interactive CD-ROM plus additional classroom footage on a VHS tape.

SPECIAL FEATURES

Throughout this book are several types of special features that enhance the readers experience and facilitate a better understanding of chapter concepts:

- **Student Stories.** This new feature introduces each chapter and includes information about typical students with special needs and the types of classroom adaptations they might need. A "Looking Ahead" section at the end of each case provides questions to aid in reader comprehension and further reflection.

- **Inclusion Tips for the Teacher.** These sections answer the questions teachers most often ask about inclusion and offer practical inclusion tips for the classroom.

- **Window on the Web.** This feature introduces readers to websites that offer valuable information about special education, general education, or the teaching-learning process.

- **Spotlight on Technology.** These sections provide information about the use of classroom technologies, featuring the most up-to-date software and assistive technology devices recommended for students with special needs.

- **For Your Information.** These boxes highlight important facts throughout each chapter and provide an aid for reader comprehension.

- **Things to Remember.** Each chapter ends with this feature—a brief summary of the major points of the chapter.

- **Application Activities.** These end-of-chapter activities are designed to help readers extend their understanding of the chapter by taking part in school observations, interviews with practicing professionals, perusal of the special and general education literature, and exploration of the World Wide Web.

- **Classroom Connections CD-ROM Activities.** These activities appear at the end of each chapter and connect chapter content to the cases depicted on the *Inclusive Classrooms CD-ROM* packaged with the text. The video

cases depicted on this CD-ROM show teachers engaged with students in various inclusive classroom settings (from pre-school to secondary classrooms) employing strategies featured in the text. Additional information about the cases on the CD-ROM appears in a special insert on pages xxi-xxiv.

CONTRIBUTORS

Revisions for the seventh edition were completed primarily by Rena B. Lewis, one of the co-authors of the first six editions. Donald H. Doorlag, now a Professor Emeritus, chose not to participate in the revision, although his contributions to previous editions continue to add to the strength of this book.

Three new authors helped with the seventh edition, and we thank them for their willingness to share their perspectives and expertise. They are Laura J. Hall, author of chapter 13, "Teaching Students with Autism Spectrum Disorder"; Kristina M. English, author of chapter 15, "Teaching Students with Visual and Hearing Impairments"; and Margie K. Kitano, author of chapter 16, "Teaching Students Who Are Gifted and Talented."

OUR THANKS

Our greatest debt is owed to our students and the special and general educators and educators-in-training who asked the difficult questions that prompted the writing of this book. We also wish to thank our editors, Allyson P. Sharp and Heather Doyle Fraser. Thanks also to our reviewers: Frank Kohler, Northern Iowa University; Rangasamy Ramasamy, Florida Atlantic University; Joseph R. Boyle, Virginia Commonwealth University; Moon K. Chang, Alabama State University; and Deitra A. Kuester, Purdue University. Third, special thanks to our colleagues at Merrill/Prentice Hall and Carlisle Communications who helped to birth yet another edition of this book. Last, but never least, Rena would like to thank Jim and the fabulous felines for continuing their support, understanding, and wondrous powers of distraction through yet another edition.

Rena B. Lewis

Donald H. Doorlag

Educator Learning Center: An Invaluable Online Resource

Merrill Education and the Association for Supervision and Curriculum Development (ASCD) invite you to take advantage of a new online resource, one that provides access to the top research and proven strategies associated with ASCD and Merrill—the Educator Learning Center. At **www.educatorlearningcenter.com**, you will find resources that will enhance your students' understanding of course topics and of current educational issues, in addition to being invaluable for further research.

HOW THE EDUCATOR LEARNING CENTER WILL HELP YOUR STUDENTS BECOME BETTER TEACHERS

With the combined resources of Merrill Education and ASCD, you and your students will find a wealth of tools and materials to better prepare them for the classroom.

Research

- More than 600 articles from the ASCD journal *Educational Leadership* discuss everyday issues faced by practicing teachers.
- A direct link on the site to Research Navigator™ gives students access to many of the leading education journals, as well as extensive content detailing the research process.
- Excerpts from Merrill Education texts give your students insights on important topics of instructional methods, diverse populations, assessment, classroom management, technology, and refining classroom practice.

Classroom Practice

- Hundreds of lesson plans and teaching strategies are categorized by content area and age range.
- Case studies and classroom video footage provide virtual field experience for student reflection.
- Computer simulations and other electronic tools keep your students abreast of today's classrooms and current technologies.

LOOK INTO THE VALUE OF EDUCATOR LEARNING CENTER YOURSELF

A four-month subcription to Educator Learning Center is $25 but is **FREE** when packaged with any Merrill Education text. In order for your students to have access to this site, you must use this special value-pack ISBN number **WHEN** placing your textbook order with the bookstore: 0-13-186209-X. Your students will then receive a copy of the text packaged with a free ASCD pincode. To preview the value of this website to you and your students, please go to **www.educatorlearningcenter.com** and click on "Demo."

Brief Contents

Contents

Disclaimer: We have devoted great time and energy to providing accurate and current information in this book. Nevertheless, in an environment as constantly changing as the Internet, it is inevitable that some of the information provided here will also change, and we cannot be responsible for these changes. Information provided at one Internet location may move to another, sometimes without any indication it has moved. If you notice changes to the Internet locations described in this book, please keep us informed so that we may update the links at the accompanying home page to this text (http://www.prenhall.com/lewis).

    Also, the authors and the publisher do not assume responsibility for errors or omissions with regard to the Internet resources identified in this book, nor do they assume liability for any damages resulting from the use of any information identified in this book or from links listed at sites that are described. As we state in this book, the best way to protect children from viewing inappropriate sites or receiving inappropriate messages is to implement a sound, acceptable use policy and to carefully monitor student use of the Internet in your classroom, at school, and at home.

Special Features

SPOTLIGHT ON TECHNOLOGY

WINDOW ON THE WEB

The *Inclusive Classrooms: Video Cases* CD-ROM packaged with this text provides immediate access to powerful, living classroom examples of teaching and learning strategies for inclusion. The CD contains four video cases. In each case, you will see the impact of inclusion on supporting students with challenging behaviors (preschool), classroom climate (elementary), assessment and planning (middle school), and partial participation and cooperative learning (high school).

As you use the video cases on the CD, you will see expert teachers in action. In each of the cases, you will be viewing classrooms in which children with learning disabilities, attention deficit hyperactivity disorders, and mild/moderate disabilities are successfully engaged in the classroom community and in learning. Because of the natural supports and inclusive stance of the teachers and schools featured, it may be difficult for you to identify which children have been identified as having disabilities or are in need of other accommodations.

ABOUT THE CASES

The video cases depicted on this CD-ROM show teachers engaged with students in various inclusive classroom settings and employing the strategies featured in the text. Each case has its own button on the navigation bar on the left of the screen. By clicking on the case of your choice, you move into the specific video clips and discussion for that case.

Nine video clips are featured for each of the four cases. The first clip in each of the three classroom cases shows the entire video segment from beginning to end. The other eight clips show specific teaching strategies employed by the teacher featured in the clips.

As you view these cases, remember that these are expert teachers, and no one begins work in inclusive classrooms at this level of proficiency. But you can practice the professional behaviors that they demonstrate. These teachers are not technicians; they are reflective professionals who may teach their students differently than you were taught.

Think back on your own experience as a student and recall a favorite teacher.

- What two or three core values did that teacher demonstrate?
- Do any of those values appear in these video cases?
- Can you articulate three important questions you have as a teacher? Are those questions answered in these clips?
- How do the teachers in the clips view the child? Do they see the child as someone to be fixed or are children approached as collaborators in a problem-solving process?
- How do you perceive yourself as a team member? What do you do when you need assistance?

Watching expert teachers in inclusive settings may make using these strategies look easy. Remember the amount of planning it takes to have a menu of tasks available so that every student can be successful. Think about the exhausting vigilance of monitoring young children and supporting your assistant teachers. Think about the details of planning a field trip to a construction site. Think about the voices of these teachers, as they communicate their absolute belief that every child can learn, and should have the opportunity to shine. We enjoyed seeing these students actively engaged in learning and these professionals in action, and hope you can find pieces of their work to use as you construct your own practice.

Inclusive Classroom Cases

CASE 1: Difficult Behavior in the Preschool Classroom

Jane Chambers, Early Childhood Teacher

Providing an inclusive environment for young children can be very complex. All young children are learning social and school behaviors. When students have disabilities, a wide range of behaviors may be seen in the classroom. In addition, these disabilities interact with specific settings, events, cultural issues, and language learning. As you view this case, consider these questions:

Discussion Questions

1. There are two assistants in this classroom. Observe both Ms. Chambers and the assistants. What are the key differences between the efforts of the teacher and those of the assistants?
2. How does Ms. Chambers interact with the children both verbally and nonverbally?
3. How do Ms. Chambers and the teaching assistants deal with challenging behaviors?
4. When Ms. Chambers interacts with a student regarding his or her behavior, she provides a rationale. Give an example.
5. What are some routines in place in this classroom?

Reflection Questions

1. Imagine yourself in a classroom full of active children. When you look around and listen to the activity, you become aware of the noise level. Suddenly you wonder if other teachers or the principal thinks your classroom is out of control. How would you explain your classroom environment and its sounds to an outsider?
2. Teachers need to step back on a regular basis and consider their classroom from various perspectives. They enter a discourse with themselves. How would you structure such reflection to make sure it happened for you on a regular basis?
3. Today's classroom is multicultural and, yet, we ourselves are from particular cultures. How do teachers become explicitly conscious of the values that drive their practice and allow those values to be shared with the cultural values of those individuals and families represented in our classrooms?

CASE 2: Classroom Climate of a Sixth Grade Class

Sally Schmitt, Sixth-Grade Social Studies Teacher

In an inclusive classroom, it is essential that all students feel as if they belong, that they are welcome and part of the group. Because the focus is on the tasks rather than the different personalities involved, collaboration and ensuring the success of every student becomes important. There are several ways to support this positive climate in inclusive classrooms. This case demonstrates a strong, positive classroom climate; however, this climate did not just happen. Ms. Schmitt worked hard to establish a setting in which there is mutual respect, engagement, and enthusiasm for learning. As you view this case, consider the following questions:

Discussion Questions

1. What are some of the actions and phrases that Ms. Schmitt uses to communicate her positive feelings toward the students?
2. The students report back about vocabulary words that they heard used over the weekend. What does this tell you about student engagement?
3. Is there a "front" to this classroom? What does this communicate to the students? How does Ms. Schmitt prevent the sense of a front and back of the classroom?
4. How are students given ownership in this classroom?
5. Can you identify the reprimand that occurs? What are the characteristics of this reprimand?

Reflection Questions

1. Setting up desk and chair arrangements is such an easy thing to do, yet this teacher has transformed this mundane task into a vehicle of ownership and responsibility for children. What can you do in your environment that would send clear messages to your students that this room is their classroom?
2. Whether it is a lesson about the ancient pyramids or the construction of the Empire State Building, a curricular topic can be organized and seen from several angles. The instructor can integrate writing, mathematics, and social studies into lessons. What are your strengths or areas of growth in the curriculum and how will that influence your planning and level of curricular integration?
3. One of the core values of this teacher is respect for the learner. She operationalizes this in respect to her approach to children. Gentle reprimands were done in the hallway, a slight touch on the shoulder brought a child back to focus on a project, she listened to children's need for control of the environment, and she provided earned incentives. Consider one of the core values that drives your practice. How would an observer know this value was important to you? What would the observer see you doing or hear children saying to become aware that this key value was operative in your classroom?

CASE 3: Assessment Planning in the Middle School

Steve Kroeger, Intervention Specialist; Christine Hamm, Reading Teacher; Andrea Comarata, Language Arts Teacher; Cathy Burton, Science Teacher; Beth Kouche, Math Teacher

Assessment is a team effort and drives planning. Identifying what a child can do in a content area assists the planning of the next proximal steps of development. Maintaining high standards and multifaceted instruction creates reachable expectations through various approaches and modes of learning. In this team meeting, a young man at risk for failing is discussed. Remarkably, he is described in very positive terms, and the emphasis is on helping rather than excluding. As you view this case, consider these questions:

Discussion Questions

1. The student being discussed is described as vulnerable. How is he vulnerable?
2. Why is a "C" a more appropriate goal than an "A"?
3. What is the purpose of this team meeting?
4. What is the impact of beginning with strengths? Is this typical of a problem-solving meeting?
5. What active listening skills do you see Steve Kroeger (the facilitator) using?

Reflection Questions

1. Meetings such as this are time intensive. Time is one of the most precious commodities of a teacher. If you have 135 students, how can you devote such critical amounts of time to an individual? What happens if you ignore such needs?
2. This team met with the parent and the child the previous day to discuss various issues. Based on their conversation,

can you describe several advantages of having the child present in such a meeting? Do you think the parent felt like he or she was an integral part of this team's proceedings?

3. Besides the curricular issues that were referred to in this team meeting, what were other key concerns that these teachers were addressing as integral for this student's growth? How would you develop a process of reflection among cooperative teachers to make sure you had time to address such concerns?

CASE 4: Support for Participation in the High School

Rog Lucido, Physics Teacher

One challenge in inclusive schools is that of limiting students' class choices to those in which they can fully participate. For some students, there could be very few selections. This brings us to partial participation—assisting students to participate in classes to the level they are able and making sure that they are viewed as true members of the class, but that everyone responds to the best of his or her ability. Without partial participation, students with disabilities may never engage in a discussion of ethics, social justice, or personal identity because these topics may be deemed "beyond them." Yet, in the classroom featured in this case, a diverse group of students is highly engaged in a complex physics activity. As you view this case, consider these questions:

Discussion Questions

1. How does the teacher communicate that each student's contribution is valued?
2. How do the students demonstrate ownership?
3. How do the students support each other?
4. How does the teacher bring physics to life for the students?

Reflection Questions

1. Providing a safe environment, physically and psychologically, is a significant part of preparing a learning environment. Everyone at the construction work site wore a hard hat and a reflective vest. The classroom was arranged for easy access to work spaces and computers. Considering the principles of universal design, what are the priorities that you will establish to provide safety and security in your learning environment?

2. Once a collaborative learning environment is created, peer assistance becomes a vital and affirming practice for learners. Can you describe specific and structured ways to train students on how to assist one another? What are the risks involved in peer assistance issues? What qualities must a teacher have to make this learning dynamic successful?

3. How is student choice exercised in this classroom? Can you brainstorm a variety of meaningful choices for learners in a project you might design for a classroom of high school students?

Introduction

Success for All Students in the General Education Classroom

CHAPTER 1

Tiffany

Tiffany is 8 years old and likes to swim, skate, and eat pizza. She and her two best friends, Jennifer and Sarah, walk to school together each morning. They are all in Ms. Cole's second-grade class. Tiffany likes school this year, but last year was very different. Tiffany is a student with special needs; she has learning problems. In first grade Tiffany had great difficulty with reading. This year she works with the resource teacher for a half hour each day, and she's beginning to make progress in reading. In her second-grade class she does well in math and handwriting, and she can keep up with her classmates in spelling. Tiffany is successfully included.

Josh

Josh is a high school student who is planning to attend college when he graduates. He wants to pursue a career in chemistry or physics. This year he's taking English, American history, biology, and geometry. Josh is a student with special needs; he has a physical impairment and travels by wheelchair. Josh rides a special bus to school and attends an adapted physical education class. Josh writes and types slowly, so he sometimes needs extra time to complete tests and assignments. His grades in all his classes are excellent, and he has many friends. Josh is successfully included.

LOOKING AHEAD

Later in the chapter we will take a look at portions of the Individualized Education Programs for Tiffany and Josh. Until then, think about these questions:

- What do you think is Tiffany's best subject in school?
- What types of assistance do you think Tiffany might need to succeed in the general education classroom?
- From what you know now, what are Josh's greatest strengths?
- If Josh were one of your students, what types of classroom adaptations do you think might be helpful?

To answer these questions online, go to the Students' Stories module in Chapter 1 of the Companion Website.

Behind each classroom door lies a world of diversity. In a typical class of students, there is a wide range of abilities. Some students learn easily; others require much assistance. Some are well behaved; others, mischievous. Some are friendly; others, ill at ease with their peers. In addition, students perform differently at various times and under different circumstances. The class leader may be overcome with shyness when asked to speak at a school assembly. The student who excels in science may write and spell poorly. Addition and subtraction problems may be easy for a student, but multiplication extremely difficult. Such variations contribute to the wonder of individuality.

When students with special needs are members of a class, the range of diversity increases. Students with disabilities, gifted and talented students, and culturally and linguistically diverse students are indistinguishable from their peers in most ways. However, their learning needs may be more serious or more compelling. Such students are individuals with different personalities, preferences, skills, and needs. Like all students, they present a challenge to the teacher.

This book is for teachers who wish to learn more about students with special needs. It is also about good teaching. All students, particularly those with special learning needs, deserve special care and special teaching. This book provides teachers with the skills needed to deal with the complex and often perplexing diversity that lies behind the classroom door.

INCLUSION IN TODAY'S CLASSROOMS

Many different terms have been used to describe the practice of educating students with special needs in the general education classroom. In the 1970s and 1980s, most professionals called this approach *mainstreaming*. In the 1990s, the terms *full inclusion* and *inclusion* became more popular. However, these terms differ somewhat in meaning, and it is important to understand those differences.

Mainstreaming*refers to the inclusion of students with special needs in the general educational process. Students are considered mainstreamed if they spend any part of the school day with general education class peers. In a typical mainstreaming program, special students in general education classrooms participate in instructional and social activities side by side with their classmates. Often they receive additional instruction and support from a special educator such as a resource teacher. That instruction may take place within the general education classroom or outside of it in a setting such as a resource room.

Special students are those with special learning needs. Because of these needs, they require instructional adaptations in order to learn successfully. This book considers four types of students special: pupils with disabilities, gifted and talented individuals, culturally and linguistically diverse students, and students at risk for school failure. Because of physical, cognitive, or emotional disabilities, some children and adolescents receive special education services in addition to (or, in some cases, in place of) the general educational program. Other special students may not be offered special programs in their schools, but their special learning needs soon become apparent to the general education teacher.

Integration of students with special needs into the mainstream of education differs according to the needs of the individual. The amount of time special students participate in regular class activities varies from student to student. For some, the mainstream is their full-time permanent placement; for others, mainstreaming occurs for only a portion of the school day. The activities in which mainstreamed students take part also vary. Some interact with typical peers primarily on a social basis; others are included in both social activities and classroom instruction. In the area of instruction, many participate in most of the general education curriculum, whereas others are mainstreamed only for selected subjects.

Mainstreaming is an educational program that varies with the needs and abilities of the student. It is characterized by the meaningful interaction of special and typical students in social activities and/or classroom instruction. Mainstreaming has been defined in many ways. In one early definition, mainstreaming is described as "temporal, instructional, and social integration" (Kaufman, Gottlieb, Agard, & Kukic, 1975, p. 5). Not only are students with special needs placed in an educational environment with typical peers for some specified amount of time (temporal integration), they participate meaningfully in the academic activities of the general education class (instructional integration) and are accepted as members of that class by their teacher and classmates (social integration). Integration to this extent is a real possibility for many special students, particularly those with mild learning and behavior problems. However, severe disabilities may prevent some students from full participation in all instructional aspects of the general education class.

Full inclusion, a more recent term than mainstreaming, was introduced by professionals interested in students with severe disabilities. The full inclusion movement calls for reform of practices that exclude and segregate individuals with disabilities (Stainback & Stainback, 1985; Thousand & Villa, 1990). Advocates of full inclusion maintain that the general education classroom is the most appropriate full-time placement for all students with disabilities—not only those with mild learning and behavior problems, but also those with more severe disabilities. In the purest form of this model, students do not leave the mainstream to receive special services; instead, support is provided within the regular classroom setting.

---

*Words appearing in **boldface** in the text are defined in the Glossary.

Many special education professionals disagree with the assumption that full-time mainstreaming is the only appropriate placement for students with disabilities (e.g., Kavale & Mostert, 2003). Many argue that other options, such as resource rooms, should be available so that educational programs can be tailored to the specific needs of individual students. This is the position of the Council for Exceptional Children (CEC), the major professional organization in special education. According to the *CEC Policy on Inclusive Schools and Community Settings* (1993b),

> CEC believes that a continuum of services must be available for all children, youth, and young adults. CEC also believes that the concept of inclusion is a meaningful goal to be pursued in our schools and communities. In addition, CEC believes children, youth, and youth adults with disabilities should be served whenever possible in general education classrooms in inclusive neighborhood schools and community settings.

As discussed later in this chapter, this position is consistent with current federal laws and their requirements for placement of students with disabilities in the "Least Restrictive Environment."

Inclusion is the term most often used today to describe the placement of students with special needs in general education. *Inclusion* is a more modern term than *mainstreaming* but unfortunately its meaning is imprecise. Sometimes inclusion is used as shorthand for *full inclusion;* at other times, it is a synonym for *mainstreaming*. It is important to determine what each speaker and writer means by the term *inclusion* because there are basic philosophical differences between the approaches of full inclusion and mainstreaming.

In this book, we use the term *inclusion* to refer to the meaningful participation of students with disabilities and other special needs in general education classrooms and programs. Although we believe that all students should be participants in the general education process, we also contend that the nature and extent of their participation should be determined on an individual basis. No one program, placement, or service arrangement meets the needs of all students.

Including students with special needs in general education programs is not a new idea. In the early days of education in the United States, classrooms served a wide variety of individuals, including some students with disabilities. The one-room schoolhouse with its range of ages and skills is an example. Kirk and Gallagher (1979) describe an inclusion program that began in 1913 for students with vision losses. Students spent part of their day in the regular classroom and part in a special "sight saving class."

Today, most special students begin school in general education and receive the majority of their education there. Many never leave the general education classroom. If their learning problems become apparent, some are identified as having a disability and receive special education services. Of these, few are served in special classes and special schools. Those who do attend special classes often join their regular class peers for social activities and for instruction in nonacademic subjects such as art, music, and physical education. However, most students with disabilities are educated in general education classes, with part-time special services provided if necessary. In the 1999–2000 school year, for example, the general education classroom was the primary educational placement for more than 75% of this nation's children and youth with disabilities ages 6 to 21 (U.S. Department of Education, 2002). Consider the stories of Tiffany and Josh at the start of this chapter. Tiffany and Josh are students with disabilities who participate fully in general education while receiving special assistance in problem areas. They are examples of successfully included students.

STUDENTS WITH SPECIAL NEEDS

Most discussions of inclusion concentrate on only one type of special student: children and adolescents with disabilities. Students who have a disability that negatively affects their school performance are served by special education, and federal laws uphold their right to a free, appropriate public education. In this book, however, we have expanded the concept of special students to include three other groups with learning needs significant enough to warrant special consideration. These are gifted and talented students (often served by special education but not protected by the laws for learners with disabilities), culturally and linguistically diverse students, and students at risk for school failure. The special needs of these students, like those of many students with disabilities, can often be accommodated within the general education classroom. Special students are a heterogeneous group. They may learn quickly and easily or with great difficulty. Their school behavior may be beyond reproach or frequently inappropriate. Some have sensory or physical impairments. Others stand out because of their speech, language, or culture. Despite their special needs, such students can and do learn. However, more than most students, they require good teaching to succeed in general education classrooms.

Students with disabilities may have special learning needs because of a cognitive, physical, sensory, language, or emotional disability. According to the Individuals with Disabilities Education Improvement Act of 2004 (IDEA 2004), students with disabilities include those with

> mental retardation, hearing impairments (including deafness), speech or language impairments, visual impairments

(including blindness), serious emotional disturbance (referred to in this title as "emotional disturbance"), orthopedic impairments, autism, traumatic brain injury, other health impairments, or specific learning disabilities. [PL 108-446, Sec. 602(3)(A)(i)]

Another disability, attention deficit disorder (ADD), is covered under other federal legislation and as one type of other health impairment under the IDEA.

Some of the terms that describe disabilities in federal laws are replaced or changed in common usage. For example, most special educators prefer *behavioral disorders* to *emotional disturbance*. Also, *orthopedic impairments* are often called *physical impairments*, and the term *ADD* may be changed to *ADHD* to include students with attention deficit hyperactivity disorder. The term *autism* is often replace by *autism spectrum disorder.*

Students with learning disabilities have adequate general intelligence and are able to succeed in many school tasks. However, because of specific disabilities in areas such as attention, perception, and memory, they experience difficulty in school. They may encounter learning problems in one or more, although usually not all, academic subjects. In contrast, students with mental retardation generally are delayed in most, if not all, academic subject areas. They are characterized by a slower rate of learning and difficulty with reasoning tasks.

Students with behavioral disorders may have adequate academic achievement despite poor classroom behavior, or their behavior problems may interfere with learning. Such students may be disruptive or withdrawn, they may experience difficulty controlling their own behavior, or they may lack the skills necessary for building and maintaining interpersonal relationships with peers and adults.

Communication problems are primary in students with speech and language impairments. As student's speech may be difficult for others to understand, or language development may be delayed. Students with autism spectrum disorder experience difficulty in socialization as well as in communication. With visual and hearing impairments, the disability is sensory. Individuals with visual impairments may be blind or partially sighted; those with hearing impairments may be deaf or hard of hearing. In either case, learning takes place through the senses still available to the student.

Students with physical and health impairments may participate fully in regular class activities. However, those with limited physical mobility, such as those who travel by wheelchair, may take a less active role. Some with chronic health problems may have special needs because of prolonged school absences. In general, students with physical and health needs can progress successfully in general education. For many of these special students, their physical problems have little effect on their ability to learn.

Two other groups of individuals with disabilities are often members of general education classes: students with traumatic brain injury (TBI) and those with ADHD. Most students with TBI are members of general education classes when the accident or other trauma that causes the injury to the brain occurs, and most return to that setting after hospitalization and rehabilitation. Students with ADHD typically remain in the general education setting while receiving assistance for problems in attention, impulsivity, and hyperactivity.

Like learners with disabilities, **gifted and talented students** are exceptional. Although they usually do not encounter school failure, their special abilities require special teaching. Gifted students are unusually bright; they may learn quickly and excel in all areas. They may be far ahead of their peers and thus require special attention and instruction. Some gifted students are creative; others may have special abilities in specific areas such as art, music, drama, and leadership. Opportunities for expression of creativity and talents can be provided within the general education classroom.

Culturally and linguistically diverse students present a different type of challenge. Although many students from diverse groups do not need special assistance to succeed in general education, some do. The customs, traditions, and values of their culture may set them apart from their peers and hinder their acceptance. Some students may be fluent speakers of English; others may be bilingual, speaking English and another language; and still others may be just beginning to acquire English language skills. If communication is difficult, learning problems may result.

Also posing a challenge to the teacher are **students at risk for school failure.** Although these students are not considered to have a disability under the law, their current performance and future welfare are threatened by a host of complex societal problems: poverty, homelessness, child abuse, and drug and alcohol abuse. They are the potential school dropouts, potential or actual delinquents, runaways, teenage parents, and suicide risks. Like other special students, students at risk have very real educational needs that must be addressed if the likelihood for school failure is to be reduced.

Students with special needs come to the attention of their teachers when they require instructional assistance in order to succeed in school. Their needs, however, are similar to those of their peers, although probably more serious and long standing. Every class, no matter how homogenous, has its bright and not-so-bright students, its troublemaker or behavior problem, and its student with a transitory physical impairment in the form of a broken arm or leg. Special students only enhance the range of skills and abilities within the general education classroom. To learn more about students with special needs, see the accompanying "For Your Information"

box. Boxes such as these, placed throughout the book, present facts of interest to teachers.

HISTORICAL PERSPECTIVES AND CURRENT PRACTICES

Today, most students with special needs are educated in general education classrooms. If identified as having a disability, being gifted, or in need of English language instruction, they may also receive part-time services from a trained specialist such as a special education teacher. In some cases, that professional provides support to students (or to the teacher) within the general education classroom; in others, students leave the classroom for brief periods to receive instruction in a resource room or other setting. In either case, students with special needs remain with their peers for all general education activities in which they can successfully participate.

Not all students with special needs spend the majority of the school day in the general education classroom. Special classes (and, in some locations, special schools) are available for students with more severe disabilities whose instructional needs are different from and more intense than those of their age peers. Although educated in separate programs, these students are included in general education nonacademic and social activities whenever feasible. Also, they may increase their level of participation in the general education program as they acquire new skills and/or as professionals become more proficient at providing them the support they need to succeed in the general education classroom. The door to the general education classroom remains open to all students with special needs. This has not always been so. Inclusion, as it is known today, has had a long developmental period.

For Your Information

Special Students

- Although students with special needs differ in the extent of instructional adaptation they require, most have mild learning problems. Only a small proportion have severe disabilities.
- Approximately 11% of the population ages 6 to 17 is identified as having a disability (U.S. Department of Education, 2002). In a typical classroom of 30 students, there may be 3 students with disabilities.
- Many people think of physical problems when they hear the term *disability*. However, physical, visual, and hearing impairments are the least common types of disabilities. Most

frequent are learning disabilities, speech and language impairments, behavioral disorders, and mental retardation.
- It is usually not possible to tell whether students are special from their physical appearance. Typical students may be indistinguishable from gifted students, students with learning disabilities, and those with speech impairments.
- It is possible for a student to have more than one special need. A young child with mental retardation may have poor speech and language skills, a talented adolescent may have a learning disability, and a student who is blind may be gifted.

The Past

In the early days of education in the United States, special students were placed in general education classes because this was the only placement available. Special services were virtually nonexistent. Students with special needs did not receive assistance from trained specialists; classroom teachers were left to cope with special students as best they could. Students considered difficult to teach, such as those with severe disabilities, were often excluded from public education.

With the growth of special education and other such services, changes occurred. Children and adolescents with severe disabilities, who had until then been denied an education, were provided with special schools. Regular class students with learning and behavior problems were removed from general education and placed in separate special classes. Because those students were having difficulty meeting the demands of the general education classroom, intensive full-time special education services were seen as the remedy. It was thought that the needs of students with disabilities could best be served by specially trained teachers in special situations, far from the general education mainstream.

Although the idea of providing special services to students with special needs was a worthwhile notion, serious problems grew out of the special class movement. It was soon discovered that full-time special education was not the answer for most students with disabilities. Many special students did not require full-day services. Many were able to participate in at least some general education activities; all could benefit from contact with their peers. But students in special classes were removed from the mainstream of education; special classes were often located in obscure places in the school building. Special class students were also segregated from their peers and often excluded from typical school activities such as assemblies. In addition, the labeling process set special students further apart from their peers. In order for students to qualify for special services, it was necessary to determine the existence of a disability. Students were tested and, often on the basis of inadequate assessments, were labeled brain injured, mentally retarded, or emotionally disturbed. Labels such as these did not provide useful educational information for the classroom teacher or the special educator; worse, they attached a stigma to special students.

Another major problem was the inappropriate placement of students in special classes. Students who spoke little or no English were tested in English and labeled retarded. Students from diverse cultures were compared with middle-class, Anglo American peers and were found different and, therefore, inferior. Such students were placed in special classes side by side with students with disabilities. And once removed from the general education setting, a student had little chance to return. Special class placement was virtually permanent.

These practices were soon recognized as problems. Parent groups, such as the Arc (formerly the Association for Retarded Children) and the Learning Disabilities Association of America (formerly the Association for Children with Learning Disabilities), became active in support of appropriate services for all special students. Leaders in special education began to speak out against special class abuses; the article "Special Education for the Mildly Retarded—Is Much of It Justifiable?" by Lloyd Dunn (1968) is an example. Researchers like Jane Mercer (1973) accumulated evidence that students from diverse groups were vastly overrepresented in special classes. *The Six Hour Retarded Child,* by the President's Committee on Metal Retardation (1969), found that many students acted disabled only in the school situation. Court cases were filed. The *Diana* suit (1970, 1973) attacked testing abuses with students who did not speak English; the *Larry P.* case (1972, 1979, 1984) pointed up abuses with students from diverse cultures.

As more and more information became available, the prevailing educational philosophy began to shift. With the report of the Project on Classification of Exceptional Children by Hobbs (1975, 1976), the disadvantages of labeling became apparent. Normalization, or the belief that individuals with disabilities have the right to as normal an existence as possible, became an accepted goal of special services (Nirje, 1969; Wolfensberger, 1972). The pendulum swung away from segregation of special students in separate special schools and classes and toward inclusion in the mainstream of education. This viewpoint was endorsed not only by parents and professional educators but also by state and federal laws such as Public Law 94-142, the Education for All Handicapped Children Act of 1975.

As the accompanying "For Your Information" box explains, PL 94-142 expanded the idea of normalization and applied it to school programs by requiring that students with disabilities be educated in the least restrictive environment— that is, alongside their peers without disabilities—whenever feasible. Congress enacted this law in 1975 for several reasons. At that time, 1 million children with disabilities had been excluded from the public school system. Also, large numbers of students in general education classes were experiencing failure because their disabilities had not been detected. Congress concluded that less than half of the students with disabilities in the United States were receiving appropriate educational services (PL 105-17, 1997). PL 94-142 has been updated several times since its passage in 1975. In 1990, it was given a new name: the Individuals with Disabilities Education Act (IDEA). Revised in 1997 and again in 2004, the most current version is called the Individuals with Disabilities Education Improvement Act. The "For Your Information" section also describes other pieces of federal legislation considered to be landmark civil rights laws for persons with disabilities.

For Your Information

Landmark Legislation for Persons with Disabilities

Federal legislation has had a dramatic impact on the lives of individuals with disabilities in the United States. Some of these laws regulate the education of children and adolescents with disabilities; others guarantee the civil rights of persons with disabilities of all ages.

Legislation Related to Education

Public Law 94-142, the Education for All Handicapped Children Act of 1975, guaranteed appropriate educational services to all school-aged students with disabilities. It also required that students with disabilities be educated with general education peers to the maximum extent appropriate. The major provisions of PL 94-142 are:

- All students with disabilities are guaranteed a free, appropriate public education.
- An Individualized Education Program (IEP) must be developed for each student with disabilities.
- Parents have the right to participate in planning their children's educational program.
- Students with disabilities are to be educated in the least restrictive environment, that is, with students not identified as having disabilities, whenever possible.
- Tests and other assessment procedures used with students with disabilities must not discriminate on the basis of race, culture, or disability.
- Due process procedures must be in place to protect the rights of students with disabilities and their parents.
- The federal government provides some funding to states to help offset the costs involved in educating students with disabilities.

Public Law 105-17, the Individuals with Disabilities Education Act. Amendments of 1997, introduced several key changes:

- allowed states to serve youngsters ages 3 to 9 as children experiencing developmental delays (rather than requiring identification of a specific disability);
- required that students with disabilities participate in state- and district-wide assessments, with accommodations as necessary, or in alternative assessments;
- expanded IEP teams to include both special and general education teachers, when appropriate;
- revised IEP requirements to include consideration of students' involvement with and progress in the general education curriculum; and
- added provisions related to discipline of students with disabilities for weapons, drugs, alcohol, and injury to self or others.

Public Law 108-446, the Individuals with Disabilities Education Improvement Act of 2004. (IDEA 2004), the current special education law, includes these provisions:

- brings special education into closer conformity with the No Child Left Behind (NCLB) Act by spelling out what makes special education teachers "highly qualified"
- continues the mandate for participation of students with disabilities in state and district assessments required by NCLB
- changes the criteria for identifying students with specific learning disabilities
- modifies IEPs by requiring research-based interventions (if available) and the inclusion of annual goals but not benchmarks or short-term objectives
- relaxes requirements for IEP meetings (e.g., team members can be excluded from meetings if parent and school agrees, meetings can be held via phone or video conference, multi-year IEPs allowable)
- permits parent and school to decide that reevaluation for special education is unnecessary
- allows schools to change the placement of students with disabilities who violate the student conduct code

Civil Rights Legislation

Section 504 of the Vocational Rehabilitation Act of 1973 applies to people of all ages. Known as the civil rights act for persons with disabilities, it provides that

> no otherwise qualified handicapped individual in the United States . . . shall, solely by reason of his handicap, be excluded from the participation in, be denied the benefits of, or be subjected to discrimination under any program or activity receiving federal financial assistance.

Section 504 forbids discrimination in employment, in admissions to institutions of higher education, and in the provision of health, welfare, and other social services (Berdine & Blackhurst, 1985). Also, it entitles school-aged children with disabilities to a free, appropriate public education.

Public Law 101–336, the Americans with Disabilities Act of 1990, or ADA, is a comprehensive law designed to "provide a clear and comprehensive national mandate for the elimination of discrimination against individuals with disabilities." To this end, the ADA prohibits discrimination in employment, public accommodations (e.g., restaurants, hotels, theaters, and medical offices), services provided by state or local governments, public transportation, and telecommunications.

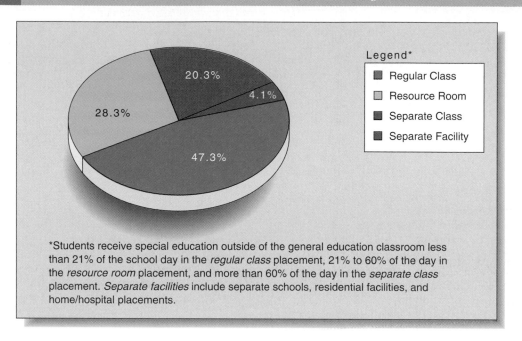

FIGURE 1-1   Educational Environments for Students with Disabilities, Ages 6–21, 1999–2000

*Students receive special education outside of the general education classroom less than 21% of the school day in the *regular class* placement, 21% to 60% of the day in the *resource room* placement, and more than 60% of the day in the *separate class* placement. *Separate facilities* include separate schools, residential facilities, and home/hospital placements.

The Present

Today, the inclusion of special students in general education is a reality. As Figure 1-1 shows, more than 95% of students with disabilities are educated in regular schools (U.S. Department of Education, 2002). These students receive instruction in general education classes, resource rooms, and separate classes. The majority (about 75%) are placed in general education and receive special education services for some portion of the school day (the regular class and resource room options). Approximately one-fifth are educated in separate classes within regular schools, and less than 5% are educated in separate facilities.

There are several important differences between current practices and those of several decades ago. First, today the general education classroom is not the only service available to students with special needs, although it is viewed as the most appropriate option for many. Second, rather than being allowed to flounder and fail in the mainstream, students with disabilities are provided with aid and assistance including, when necessary, individualized instruction from a specialist.

Third, general education teachers also receive assistance from specialists. Professionals such as resource teachers or special education consultants may aid in planning educational programs for students with special needs, provide suggestions for the modification of general education classroom activities, and supply special materials and equipment. As part of the team that serves students with special needs, the general educator contributes by sharing information and ideas with parents and specialists.

According to federal law, alternative placements must be available for students with disabilities whose educational needs cannot be met in general education classes. However, such students are encouraged to interact with general education peers in any way feasible. For example, in many districts students once placed in special schools are now members of special classes located within regular schools. This greatly enhances their opportunities to interact with age peers. In addition, special classes are not viewed as permanent placements; students may reenter the mainstream at some time in the future if they are able to benefit from the general educational program.

Although school districts typically offer a range of special education services for students with disabilities, services for other types of special students are less common. If available, programs for students who are gifted, talented, bilingual, or at risk for school failure are similar to those offered by special education. That is, students are educated in regular classes for a portion of their school day and receive individualized services from specialists as necessary. Most programs also provide assistance and support to the general education teacher.

BENEFITS OF INCLUDING SPECIAL STUDENTS

Many benefits accrue when students with special needs are members of general education classrooms. Special students remain with their peers; they are not segregated from the normal activities of the school. Labeling is de-emphasized. Students leave the classroom for special help, not to see the teacher of students with mental retardation or emotional disturbance. Resource room services have aided in decreasing the stigma attached to special education because resource teachers often serve students with many different types of special needs. In addition, research indicates that students with disabilities can achieve academic success in mainstream classrooms. Success is most likely when general education instruction is individualized and when support is available not only to students with special needs but also to their teachers (Leinhardt & Pallay, 1982; Madden & Slavin, 1983; Schulte, Osborne, & McKinney, 1990).

Current practices safeguard against the inappropriate placement of students in special education programs. Every effort is made to keep special students in general education situations, and those students in separate special programs are encouraged to participate in as many of the school's regular activities as feasible. For example, they should attend school assemblies, use the playground with other classes, and eat at the regular lunchtime.

General education students benefit from association with their peers with special needs. The inclusion of individuals with disabilities in school activities is a realistic introduction to U.S. society. As the "For Your Information" box shows, typical students learn about those different from themselves and have the opportunity to learn that the differences are unimportant.

Teachers and specialists also gain when students with special needs are included in general education. Special educators are able to serve more students. Special classes usually contain only 10 to 15 individuals, whereas resource programs may serve as many as 25 to 30 students. Also, specialists are able to concentrate on the special learning needs of the student and are not forced to duplicate the efforts of the general education classroom. General educators benefit, too, from collaboration with other professionals and in the support they receive in the team approach. Specialists provide special students with individualized help and are available to assist the teacher in meeting the needs of students placed in the general education classroom.

Of course, difficulties may occur in the inclusion process. General education teachers who have little experience with students with special needs may be reluctant to participate. Both typical and special students and their parents may be apprehensive. These problems are exacerbated when financial and personnel resources are reduced; there may be fewer services for special students and less assistance to teachers. Such difficulties are minimized when general education teachers are skilled in dealing with special students. One purpose of this book is to help teachers develop the necessary skills. See the "Inclusion Tips for the Teacher" box to learn about meeting the needs of special students as well as those of the other pupils in the classroom.

THE ROLE OF SPECIAL EDUCATION

According to federal laws, **special education** is instruction specially designed to meet the unique needs of students. That instruction can take place in a variety of settings (such as classrooms, homes, and hospitals), and it includes instruction in physical education. In his definition, Heward (1996) describes the type of instruction involved and its purposes:

> *Special education* is individually planned, systematically implemented, and carefully evaluated instruction to help exceptional children achieve the greatest possible personal self-sufficiency and success in present and future environments. (p. 47)

In a later work, Heward (2003) expanded this definition to include a more detailed description of the instructional methodologies used in special education:

> *Special education is individually planned, specialized, intensive, goal-directed instruction.* . . . Special education is also characterized by the use of research-based teaching methods, the application of which is guided by direct and frequent measures of student performance. (p. 38)

Special educators serve students identified as having disabilities: students with learning disabilities, behavioral disorders and emotional disturbances, mental retardation, speech and language impairments, autism spectrum disorder, physical and health impairments, traumatic brain injury, and visual and hearing impairments. Many states also provide special education services to gifted and talented students. Unless they

For Your Information

Students' Perceptions of Inclusion

Until quite recently, Jessica Rose attended a special school for students with multiple disabilities. Last fall, however, Jessica became a fifth grader; with support from a special education teacher, Jessica was included as a member of a grade 5 general education classroom located in a regular neighborhood school. Jessica's parents, Peggy and Tim, describe Jessica as a beautiful 9-year-old who is nonverbal, nonambulatory, and unable to feed, dress, or care for herself. Her fifth grade classmates have a somewhat different perspective. Read a sample of their responses (presented here in their original form) when they were asked at the end of the year to describe what it was like to have Jessica in their class:

- I feel that Jessica has changed my life. How I feel and see handicapped people has really changed. My friends used to make fun of handicaped children. When I saw Jessica I was scared and I didn't know what of. I used to think about handicaped people being really weak and if I would touch her I would hurt her but now I think diffrently.
- Whenever I'm around Jessica I feel very special. I feel lucky to be able to interact with her. When I look at Jesse and then look at myself I look back at how I used to be. I never used to look at a disabled person without staring at them. I've learned alot from Jesse. She taught me how to accept peopl's differences. Jessica is very special to me. She's a pleasure to be around.
- I feel like she is just a normal person. I though that I would not ever have a eperence with a handycaped but I do now. I feel lucky to have this experience. I use to feel unconferable but now I do not. I like her in our room now.

- I think it is great that Jessica is in our room. Jessica is very fun. She laughs and smiles a lot. Sometimes she crys but that is OK. I have learned that Handicapped people are just like the others. I used to say "ooh" look at that person but now I don't I have a big heart for handicapped because they are interesting they can do things that other people can't do. I think Jessica has changed because she is with lots of other kids.
- I like Jessica a lot and I enjoy it a lot when I hear her giggle. I feel just because she is in a wheelchair that doesn't mean she is bad. I have learned a lot about Jessica. Jessica will allways be my friend.
- I really like having Jessica in my class. Before she came I always had thought people in wheelchairs were real weak. I was wrong. Jessica is really quite strong. I never really thought that she could have feelings because she was handicapped. She can have feelings too. She can paint with guided help. I never thought she could paint. Having Jessi in my class has taught me stuff others might never know.
- I think that I used to be scared of handy caped people but now that Jessica came in I am not scared anymore. Because I think we should be treated equally. Because we are all the same.
- I really like Jessica in my class. Befor I met her I never really cared about handycapt people. Jessie is really nice and I like her alot. Jessica is almost like a sister to me. I like to spend my recess playing with her. I thought a handycapt kid would never be part of my life but now one and alot more are.

---

are also disabled or gifted, culturally and linguistically diverse students are not eligible for special education; instead, they may receive services from specialists in bilingual education or from teachers of English for speakers of other languages.

Special education services are available to both special students and their teachers. These services range from special consultation provided to the teacher of a student with disabilities, to special instruction delivered to a special student a few minutes per day by a special education resource teacher within the general education classroom or in the resource room, to full-day special classes for students with severe and comprehensive disabilities.

Several other **related services** may be provided to students with special needs if necessary. These include psychological services for assessment and counseling, transportation, speech and language services, special physical education, rehabilitation counseling, and physical and occupational therapy. Auxiliary services such as these are available

to help students with special needs derive the maximum benefit from special education.

Supplementary aids and services, in contrast, are supports provided to students with special needs to help them succeed in general education classes and other settings. Examples are special materials such as taped textbooks, equipment such as computer adaptations, and services such as peer tutors.

Many different professionals may provide service to the same student with disabilities. For example, Tiffany, the 8-year-old student introduced earlier in this chapter, receives instruction from her second grade teacher, Ms. Cole, and from the resource teacher. Josh, the high school student, attends four different subject matter classes, sees the adapted physical education teacher, and receives special transportation services. The resource teacher coordinates his program and provides assistance to his general education teachers as necessary. In addition, the assistive technology specialist will be working with Josh to find a computer adaptation to help increase his writing speed.

Inclusion Tips for the Teacher

Teaching Special Students *and* All the Others

As the teacher of a general education classroom, you are responsible for the education of your students. Each of the children or adolescents in your charge has specific learning needs; each is an individual. When students with special needs are members of your class, you may feel overwhelmed. Don't! Special students have specific learning needs, just like the other students in your class. They are individuals, just like their peers. Their differentness comes from the severity of their needs. They require more help in some areas than typical students do. In these areas they receive special education. In your classroom they participate in general education. Some adaptations of instructional procedures or the classroom environment may be necessary, but many "regular" students also need such changes.

Shortly after the passage of PL 94-142, Mills (1979) made several suggestions for teachers of general education classrooms. These suggestions are still good ones, and, although they deal specifically with students with disabilities, they are equally applicable to all types of students.

- Develop the necessary skills.
- Think positively.
- Know your own strengths and weaknesses.
- Insist on in-service.
- Seek assistance.
- Utilize parents.
- Prepare your class.
- Smile.

This last suggestion deserves more explanation. Mills elaborates:

> These are kids, too. They need the same love and warmth as do all children and may need a little assurance of the mainstream's desire to have them there. The other children won't accept the child with problems if the teacher isn't ready to do so. Be a leader in your own class; set the stage for a positive learning environment for all children. (p. 16)

A team approach is used to plan and deliver the educational programs of students such as Tiffany and Josh. That team is made up of the student's classroom teacher (or teachers), any specialists who work with the student, the parents of the student, and, when appropriate, the special student. Each of these individuals has an important role in planning and executing the inclusion experience. The team approach is critical in fostering communication, cooperation, and collaboration among those interested in the education of the special student.

One of the functions of the team is to plan the student's educational program. As soon as a student is found to be eligible for special educational services, the team meets to make several important instructional decisions. After the student's present level of performance in important educational areas is identified, the team plans the student's program for the next year and annual goals are established. The next decisions concern placement and services. The extent to which the student is able to participate in the general education program is determined, along with any supplementary aids and services needed to support the student's participation in general education. Special education and related services are provided to meet the remaining educational needs. In this way the student's needs determine the amount and kind of services and supports to be provided. Placement outside the general education class occurs only when absolutely necessary.

The educational plan devised by the team is called the **Individualized Education Program**, or IEP. It is a written plan agreed on by a team that includes the student's parents and often the student. An IEP is prepared for each student who receives special education services. The IEP is available to all team members and it is reviewed typically once a year.

A sample IEP form is shown in Figure 1-2. On this form, the team records information about the student's present performance and lists annual goals. Special education services are described, and the extent to which the student will participate in the general education program is noted. At the bottom of the form is a space for parents to indicate their approval of the educational program and placement.

Portions of the IEPs for Tiffany and Josh appear in Figure 1-3. Included for each student are present levels of educational performance, annual goals, and the persons responsible for helping each student achieve those goals. After that come descriptions of the educational services to be provided. Note that both special education services and the amount of general education participation are specified.

General education placement is considered optimal for student with disabilities if they are capable of making progress in the standard school curriculum. As Figure 1-4 illustrates, a range of special services is available, and many of these include at least part-time placement in the general education classroom. For example, a special educator may collaborate with the classroom teacher to identify appropriate instructional adaptations for one or more students or assist in the general education classroom by teaching lessons to a small group that includes a student with special needs. The array of special education service options is sometimes viewed as a continuum. The continuum extends from placement in general education with no special services or supports to options that serve small numbers of students with very severe needs, such as a school within a hospital for young children receiving treatment for cancer.

In selecting placements for students with special needs, it is necessary to follow the principle of **Least Restrictive Environment,** or LRE. The LRE for a student with disabilities is believed to be the appropriate placement closest to the general education classroom. As federal special education law states:

> To the maximum extent appropriate, children with disabilities . . . are educated with children who are not disabled, and special classes, separate schooling, or other removal of children with disabilities from the regular educational environment occurs only when the nature or severity of the disability of a child is such that education in regular classes with the use of supplementary aids and services cannot be achieved satisfactorily [PL 108-446, Sec. 612 (a)(5)(A)]

For students unable to function successfully in a general education class, placement in a special class within a public school is less restrictive (i.e., closer to the mainstream) than placement in a separate school or residential facility. This concept does not imply that students should be placed in less intensive settings simply to bring them closer to the mainstream. Their placement must be feasible; they must have a good chance of successful performance. The goal is the least restrictive and most appropriate placement possible. For most students with disabilities, this means the general education classroom with special services for the student and teacher.

CURRENT ISSUES AND TRENDS

Several important factors have begun to influence general education, special education, and their collaboration in the provision of services to students with special needs. The educational reform movement is one major trend. The 1980s produced a series of commission reports and recommendations aimed at improving the quality of U.S. schools. Best known among these is *A Nation at Risk: The Imperative for Educational Reform* (National Commission on Excellence in Education, 1983). This report and others calling for educational reform led to the excellence in education movement. Among

---

FIGURE 1-2   IEP Form

Date _____
❏ Initial IEP
❏ Annual Review
❏ Three-year Review
❏ Other _____

Orchard County Public Schools
Individualized Education Program (IEP)

Student Information
Name _____ Birth Date __-__-__
Male ❏ Female ❏ Age _____ Grade _____ Ethnicity _____
Social Security Number _____-___-_____ English Language Learner Yes ❏ No ❏
Home Language _____ Interpreter Required Yes ❏ No ❏
Address _____
School of Residence _____
School of Attendance _____
Rationale for placement, if other than student's school of residence:
_____

Parent/Guardian Information
Name _____
Address _____
Home phone _____ Work phone _____
Interpreter Required Yes ❏ No ❏

Assessment Information
Present Levels of Performance (include how disability affects involvement and progress in general curriculum)
_____
_____
_____
_____

Modifications needed in State and district wide assessment _____
_____

Why needed _____

IEP Information
Date of Next IEP _____ Date of 3-year Review _____
Primary Disability Category _____
Primary Placement _____
P.E. Type _____
Transportation _____

Special Education & Related Services; Supplementary Aids & Services; Program Modifications	Start Date	Duration	Frequency	Location

Extent to which student will not participate with nondisabled students in regular class _____
_____

Explanation _____

Annual Goals and Progress Measures
_____
_____
_____
_____
_____
_____
_____
_____
_____
_____
_____
_____

continued

FIGURE 1-2   continued

Parents/guardians will be informed of student's progress via _____
_____

As appropriate, the following factors were considered in the development of this IEP:
- ❑ For students whose behavior impedes learning, positive behavioral interventions, strategies, and supports
- ❑ For students with limited English proficiency, language needs
- ❑ For students who are blind or visually impaired, instruction in and use of Braille and appropriate reading and writing media
- ❑ Communication needs of the students
- ❑ For students who are deaf or hard of hearing, language and communication needs
- ❑ Assistive technology devices and services

Transition Services
- ❑ Transition service needs included in this IEP
- ❑ Transition service needs described in attached Individualized Transition Plan
- ❑ Student has been informed of his or her rights

Signatures
My due process rights have been explained to me.
- ❑ I consent to the IEP.
- ❑ I consent to portions of the IEP as described on the attached form.
- ❑ I do not consent to the IEP.

_____
Parent/Guardian's Signature   Date

_____
Student's Signature   Date

_____
Signature of Administrator/Designee   Date

_____
Signature of General Education Teacher   Date

_____
Signature of Special Education Teacher/Specialist   Date

_____
Signature/Title of Additional Participant   Date

_____
Signature/Title of Additional Participant   Date

_____
Signature of Interpreter   Date

Note: Developed by Tamarah M. Ashton, Ph.D., California State University, Northridge.

the results of this movement were an increased emphasis on content area subjects (as opposed to basic skills), longer school days and years, higher expectations and grading standards, and more stringent discipline requirements.

The next wave of reforms led to the school restructuring movement and efforts to increase the decision-making powers of educators through site-based management models. At the same time, the nation's governors, led by the first President Bush, agreed on six national educational goals (*America 2000*, 1990). Modified slightly, these goals became the framework for President Clinton's Goals 2000: Educate America Act of 1994. The goals for the new millennium included these:

- All children in America will start school ready to learn.
- The high school graduation rate will increase to at least 90 percent. . . .

FIGURE 1-3   Portions of the IEPs for Tiffany and Josh

Tiffany
Current Grade: 2
Present Levels of Educational Performance
- Tiffany is in good health with normal vision, hearing, and motor abilities. She is well adjusted and gets along well with her peers.
- Tiffany's listening and speaking skills are age appropriate. She performs at grade level in math and handwriting.
- Tiffany is able to say the alphabet and identify all letters. She knows most of the consonant sounds and the short sound of *a*. Her sight vocabulary is approximately 70 words. Tiffany reads on the primer level.
- Tiffany is able to spell most of the words in the first grade spelling text (although she cannot read them all). She receives passing grades in spelling in her second grade classroom.

Annual Goals
1. By the end of the school year, Tiffany will read at a beginning second grade level with 90% accuracy in word recognition and comprehension.
   Person responsible: Resource teacher
2. By the end of the school year, Tiffany will increase her sight vocabulary to 150 words.
   Person responsible: Resource teacher
3. By the end of the school year, Tiffany will know the short and long sounds of the vowels.
   Person responsible: Resource teacher
4. By the end of the school year, Tiffany will read and spell at least 70% of the second grade spelling words.
   Person responsible: Second grade teacher
5. By the end of the school year, Tiffany will successfully complete second grade requirements in math, handwriting, science, social studies, art, music, and physical education.
   Person responsible: Second grade teacher

Amount of Participation in General Education
- Tiffany will participate in the second grade class for all subjects except reading.

Special Education and Related Services
- Tiffany will receive special instruction in reading (Annual Goals 1, 2, and 3) from the resource teacher for 30 minutes daily.

Josh
Current Grade: 10
Present Levels of Educational Performance
- Josh is unable to move his legs and has difficulty with fine-motor tasks involving eye–hand coordination. He is able to travel independently by wheelchair.
- Josh's general health is good. His hearing and vision are within normal limits. He is well adjusted and friendly and appears to get along well with his peers.
- No academic problems are apparent. Josh received *A*s and *B*s in grade 9 classes and scored well above average in group academic achievement tests.
- Josh communicates better orally than in writing because of motor difficulties. His handwriting and typing are slow and require much effort.

Annual Goals
1. By June, Josh will successfully complete all 10th grade requirements, including physical education.
   Persons responsible: General education teachers, resource teacher, adapted physical education teacher
2. By June, Josh will increase his writing speed by using a computer with an adaptation such as word prediction or voice input.
   Persons responsible: Resource teacher, assistive technology specialist

Amount of Participation in General Education
- Josh will participate in regular 10th grade classes four out of five periods per day.

continued

FIGURE 1-3   continued

Special Education and Related Services
- Josh will receive special transportation services between his home and the school.
- Josh will attend an adapted physical education class one period per day.
- The assistive technology specialist will assess Josh to determine an effective computer adaptation.
- The resource teacher will provide consultation as needed to Josh's regular class teachers.

FIGURE 1-4   Placement in the Least Restrictive Environment

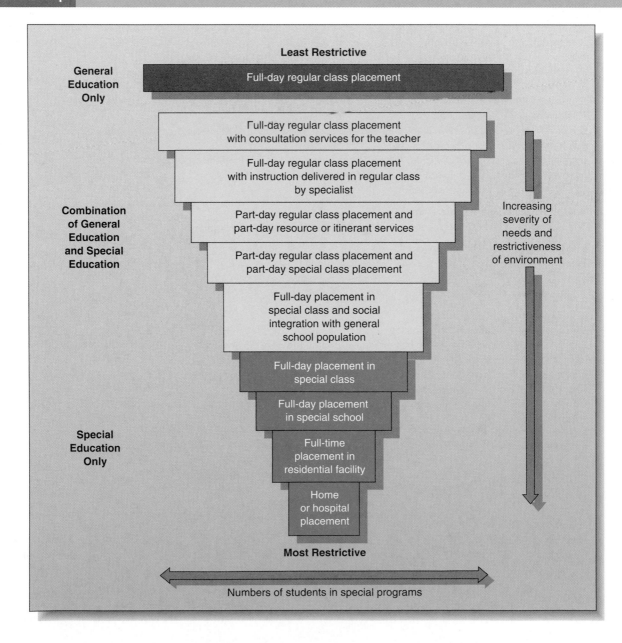

- United States students will be first in the world in mathematics and science achievement.
- Every adult American will be literate. . . .
- Every school in America will be free of drugs, violence, and the unauthorized presence of firearms and alcohol. . . . (National Education Goals Panel, 1997)

Goals 2000 called for a number of reforms such as drug-free schools and improved high school graduation rates. Math and science achievement was stressed, but attention was also given to universal literacy and readiness for school. In addition, "all students" was defined as including not only typical students and those who are academically talented but also students with disabilities, those from diverse cultural and ethnic groups, those with limited proficiency in English, and those who are disadvantaged. Progress has been made toward some of these ambitious goals (Manzo, 1996), although none had been fully met by the turn of the century.

Another important trend of the 1990s was the standards movement. Several national professional organizations established student standards or performance indicators in subjects such as mathematics, science, history, and English–language arts. In addition, virtually all states developed common academic standards for their students, and most states began to link student assessment to standards (American Federation of Teachers, 1996). The standards movement has not been without controversy as groups have attempted to achieve consensus about appropriate educational outcomes for students. Many questions also remain about how best to ensure that students with disabilities participate in standards-based assessments (National Research Council, 1997).

The direction of educational reform shifted in 2001 with the election of George W. Bush as president. His education initiative, "No Child Left Behind" (NCLB), continued the earlier focus on academic success for U.S. students but shifted emphasis to greater accountability along with more state and local authority and control. In Bush's words, the four major tenets of the initiative are as follows:

- *Increase Accountability for Student Performance:* States, districts and schools that improve achievement will be rewarded. Failure will be sanctioned. Parents will know how well their child is learning, and that schools will be held accountable for their effectiveness with annual state reading and math assessments in grades 3–8.
- *Focus on What Works:* Federal dollars will be spent on effective, research-based programs and practices. Funds will be targeted to improve schools and enhance teacher quality.
- *Reduce Bureaucracy and Increase Flexibility:* Additional flexibility will be provided to states and school districts, and flexible funding will be increased at the local level.
- *Empower Parents:* Parents will have more information about the quality of their child's school. Students in persistently low-performing schools will be given a choice. (Bush, 2001)

Of particular interest in relation to students with special needs is the move toward greater educational accountability. Federal special education laws require that students with disabilities participate along with their general education peers in state and local assessments of academic achievement. In many cases, testing accommodations or even alternative assessment procedures are required to enable students with disabilities to participate in this type of "high stakes" assessment. However, in a national survey by *Education Week* (Olson, 2004), a majority of teachers believed that students receiving special education would be unlikely to meet the same state standards as age peers. School districts are likely to remain concerned about how the test results of this group of students will affect their overall standing in relation to state and national expectations for performance.

A national trend that continues to influence education is the changing nature of the U.S. population. As reform movements lead to more rigorous educational standards, the student population is becoming more diverse and in some ways less able. Children under 18 are one of the poorest segments of the national population; in 2002, 16.7% of this group fell below the poverty line (U.S. Census Bureau, 2003). Several general population trends will have dramatic effects on the needs of students entering general education classrooms. The population of the United States continues to increase and with it the number of school-aged children. School enrollment reached an estimated 48 million in 2003, and it is expected to increase each year until it reaches a record high of 50 million in 2013 (U.S. Department of Education, 2004). The racial and ethnic composition of the United States is also changing, and by the start of the 21st century almost one-third of the country's population was African American, Hispanic, Asian, or American Indian (Grieco & Cassidy, 2001). This increase is mirrored in the public schools where 39% of all students were considered members of minority groups in 2000 (U.S. Department of Education, 2004). The U.S. Census Bureau (1997) reports that more than one-fourth of the children born in 1994 were born to unmarried mothers, and the number of single parents tripled between 1970 and 1994. In addition, the fastest growing segment of the U.S. population consists of persons with limited proficiency in English language skills (PL 108-446, 2004).

Changes such as these are likely to increase the number of students at risk for school failure. This suggests that educational reform efforts that divert funds away from remedial programs may be moving in the wrong direction. There is a need for more support for low-performing students and their teachers, not less (McLoughlin & Lewis, 2005).

Within special education, there has been much debate about full inclusion, the movement that calls for increased integration of students with severe disabilities. While some leaders advocate the full-time inclusion of all students (including those with severe disabilities) in general education classrooms in neighborhood schools, others disagree. Groups such as the Council for Exceptional Children (1993b), the Division for Learning Disabilities (1993), the National Joint Committee on Learning Disabilities (1993), and the Learning Disabilities Association of America (1993) maintain that one educational option is not sufficient. Instead, a variety of special education programs should be available to serve the diverse needs of students with disabilities. For example, the position statement of the Learning Disabilities Association of America (1993) emphasizes the need for individualization by starting that this organization "does not support 'full inclusion' or any policies that mandate the same placement, instruction, or treatment for ALL students with learning disabilities" (p. 594).

Another trend in special education is increased interest in preschool and postsecondary age groups. Federal laws focus attention on young children with disabilities and their families. States may offer programs for infants and toddlers with disabilities; with very young children, an Individualized Family Service Plan (IFSP) guides the delivery of services instead of an IEP. Federal special education laws also address the needs of adolescents and young adults with disabilities. For example, one requirement is a transition plan for students with disabilities beginning at age 16 in order to ensure coordination between school programs and postschool options such as vocational training, postsecondary education, employment, and adult services.

At present, the effects of educational reform movements and the changes in student demographics are becoming apparent in general education. Special education is directing some of its efforts to the early childhood years in an attempt to reverse or at least slow the effects of disabilities on young children's readiness for school. There is also debate about the relationship of special and general education and the most effective ways of promoting the social and instructional integration of students with disabilities. As this debate continues, it will become increasingly important for general and special educators to collaborate in the search for solutions to the educational problems facing all types of special students, not only those with identified disabilities.

GENERAL EDUCATION TEACHERS AND SPECIAL STUDENTS

General education teachers make several contributions to the success of special students. The teacher is often the first professional to identify the special needs of students and to initiate the referral process. The classroom teacher is also a source of valuable information about current school performance when students are assessed for possible special education services. As

For Your Information

People-First Language

Language is a powerful tool. When talking or writing about people with disabilities, professionals should make every effort to use language that reflects positive attitudes, not negative stereotypes. One important consideration is putting the person first, not the disability. Consider these examples from the California Governor's Committee for Employment of Disabled persons (1990):

DON'T SAY . . . "Mr. Lee is a *crippled teacher* and *confined to a wheelchair*. All of his students are *normal*."

BUT INSTEAD SAY . . . "Mr. Lee is a *teacher with a disability*. He is a *wheelchair-user*. All of his students are *nondisabled*."

The Research and Training Center on Independent Living (1996) provides several suggestions in its brochure *Guidelines for Reporting and Writing About People with Disabilities*. Here are examples:

- DO NOT USE GENERIC LABELS for disability groups, such as "the retarded," "the deaf." Emphasize people not labels. Say *people with mental retardation* or *people who are deaf*.

- PUT PEOPLE FIRST, not their disability. Say *woman with arthritis, children who are deaf, people with disabilities*. This puts the focus on the individual, not the particular functional limitation. . . .

- EMPHASIZE ABILITIES not limitations. For example: *uses a wheelchair/braces, walks with crutches*, rather than *confined to a wheelchair, wheelchair-bound*, or *is crippled*. Similarly, do not use emotional descriptors such as *unfortunate, pitiful*, and so forth.

The guidelines are updated periodically. To obtain a print copy of the latest version, contact the Research and Training Center in Independent Living, University of Kansas, 4089 Dole Center, 1000 Sunnyside Avenue, Lawrence, KS 66045-7555. Or view the brochure on the World Wide Web at *http://www.lsi.ku.edu/lsi/internal/guidelines.html*

part of the inclusion team, the teacher participates in planning the student's educational program and in developing the IEP.

The teacher's most important role is implementation of the special student's general education program. This process sometimes requires adaptation of classroom procedures, methods, and/or materials to guarantee success for the student with special needs. Classroom activities should be coordinated with the special services received by the student. And communication between parents and professionals is crucial.

In addition, the classroom teacher may help to evaluate the student's progress not only in the general education program but also in the areas served by specialists. Evaluation is a critical step in the educational process because it helps determine program modifications. Figure 1-5 presents the educational process, including the final step of evaluation. This diagram also provides a summary of the general education teacher's roles.

Even though these roles are not new ones for the teacher, special students may require special teaching skills. The first part of this book provides basic information about inclusion. Chapter 1 has presented the concept and some of the benefits of this approach, has introduced special students and special education, and has briefly described the roles of the general education teacher. Chapter 2 will acquaint the teacher with the team approach and the collaboration process. In chapter 3 the special needs of special students will be explored.

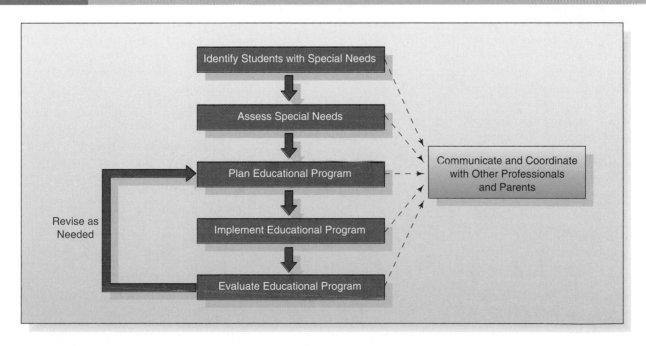

FIGURE 1-5   The Special Education Process

Identify Students with Special Needs

Assess Special Needs

Plan Educational Program

Implement Educational Program

Evaluate Educational Program

Revise as Needed

Communicate and Coordinate with Other Professionals and Parents

Part II focuses on the teacher's role in helping students with special needs to succeed in the general education classroom. Each of the chapters in that section deals with an important skill area: adapting instruction, managing behavior, promoting social acceptance, coordinating the classroom learning environment, and integrating computers and other technologies into classroom learning activities. In the third and fourth parts of this book, these skills are applied to each type of special learner.

Before turning to chapter 2 to meet the team, check your understanding of this chapter by consulting the section entitled "Things to Remember."

Things to Remember

- Most students with special needs can succeed in general education classrooms.
- Inclusion is the meaningful participation of students with special needs in the general educational process.
- Special students include students with disabilities (students with learning disabilities, behavioral disorders, mental retardation, speech and language impairments, autism spectrum disorder, physical and health impairments, traumatic brain injury, and visual and hearing impairments), gifted and talented students, culturally and linguistically diverse students, and students at risk for school failure.
- Inclusion in general education allows special students to interact with typical peers. It also reduces the effects of labeling.

- Most special students receive the majority of their education in general education classrooms. These students and their teachers are provided with aid and assistance to ensure their success.
- The general education teacher contributes to the success of students with special needs by participating in assessment, program planning and IEP development, placement decisions, and, most important, implementation of students' general education programs.

ACTIVITIES

Here are several activities that will help increase your understanding of the concepts presented in this chapter. Some are designed to acquaint you with the print literature or with resources on the World Wide Web. Others are explorations of current programs and practices in your local schools and community. You will find activities such as these at the end of each chapter.

1. Arrange a visit to an elementary, middle, or high school. Talk with the principal or one of the staff members about the special services at the school. What types of programs are available? Is there a resource teacher who provides part-time special services to students with disabilities? If possible, visit a general education class and observe the students carefully. Can you tell which are identified as having special needs?

2. Interview several general education teachers about their perceptions of inclusion. Have they taught students with special needs in their classrooms? If so, what special learning needs did these students have? What do the teachers believe are the advantages and disadvantages of inclusion?

3. Select one or two of the major educational journals in your field. Look for articles that present useful suggestions for adapting instruction for students with special needs. You may also wish to look at some of the journals in special education. Two that feature practical articles about educating students with disabilities are *Intervention in School and Clinic* and *Teaching Exceptional Children*. Despite its title, *Teaching Exceptional Children* includes suggestions for both elementary and secondary teachers.

4. Search the World Wide Web for information on mainstreaming. Then search for inclusion. (If you're unfamiliar with the World Wide Web or search techniques,

CD-ROM Activities

Inclusive Classrooms, the CD-ROM accompanying this book, introduces you to several classrooms serving students with special needs through a series of video case studies (also called video ethnographies). Begin your exploration of this CD-ROM by choosing one of the first two classrooms—Preschool or Sixth Grade—and looking at the first video clip. As you view this clip, think about how you would respond to these questions:

- *Can you identify which students in this classroom have special needs?*

- *What strategies is the teacher using to individualize the classroom experience for students?*

If you have difficulty navigating through the program, click on the Help button (the question mark at the bottom lefthand corner of the screen).

consult chapter 8 for an introduction.) Which search term produced the most results? Visit some of the sites to get an idea of what people are saying. Are any of the sites sponsored by elementary or secondary schools?

5. The major professional organization in special education is the Council for Exceptional Children. Many communities have local CEC chapters, and student chapters are often found at colleges and universities. The national CEC office is located at 1110 North Glebe Road, Suite 300, Arlington, VA 22201. Get in touch with your local or state CEC or contact the national headquarters to learn more about this organization. (See the "Window on the Web" feature for its World Wide Web location.) Is CEC concerned with all types of special students? Are all of its members special education teachers? How does it attempt to improve educational services for students with disabilities?

Window on the Web

The Council for Exceptional Children

http://www.cec.sped.org

The national headquarters of CEC maintains this website to provide information to its members and others interested in special education, students with disabilities, and gifted and talented students. The site offers information on professional development opportunities, CEC publications, careers in special education, and position openings. Also of interest is the Public Policy and Advocacy/Legislative Action Center section, a good source to consult to learn about bills now in Congress and recently passed laws.

Note: Courtesy of The Council for Exceptional Children.

For more information, go to the Web Links module in Chapter 1 of the Companion Website.

Collaboration and the Team Approach

CHAPTER
2

Marvin and Jake

Marvin and Jake are 15-year-old freshmen at Jefferson High. They have always been somewhat less-than-average students with minor problems in school, but they have never been considered for special education services. This year Mr. Morse, the boys' English teacher, has decided to ask that their school performance and progress be reviewed.

In English class Marvin is disruptive and uncooperative; he fails to complete most of his writing assignments. Those that are finished are usually late and of poor quality (Marvin's average grade on writing assignments is 38%). In addition, when bothered by Marvin's outbursts, the other students in the class retaliate by commenting on his poor achievement, which leads to arguments in class and in the hall after class.

Jake also is doing poorly on his assignments, often turning them in late (Jake's average grade on assignments is 59%). He is late to class several times a week and appears to be confused about assignments; he seldom asks questions and never participates in class discussions.

The Prereferral Team

The prereferral team at Jefferson High reviewed Mr. Morse's request for assistance and decided that they would like additional information about both students. Mr. Morse was asked to collect data on their academic performance and classroom behavior. He carefully recorded their daily grades and collected samples of their work. He also collected information on the frequency of Marvin's classroom disturbances and arguments and how often Jake was late to class and how often

LOOKING AHEAD

Mr. Morse worked with three different teams in his efforts to meet the needs of his students Jake and Marvin. You'll learn more about each of these teams in this chapter but, before going on, think about these questions:

- What types of classroom modifications did the prereferral team recommend for Jake?
- What other types of modifications might be possible for students with different types of needs?
- What information do you think the assessment team might have asked Mr. Morse to collect about Marvin's classroom performance?
- Mr. Morse, Marvin, and Marvin's mother all participated as members of Marvin's IEP team. What do you think each of these individuals was able to contribute?

To answer these questions online, go to the Students' Stories module in Chapter 2 of the Companion Website.

he participated in classroom activities. The special education resource teacher observed both of the students during their English classes and carefully reviewed samples of their work.

Jake: Modifications of the General Education Program

After the prereferral team's review of this information, the team decided that it was most appropriate for Mr. Morse to attempt to meet Jake's educational needs without referral to special education. The team suggested that Mr. Morse establish a reinforcement system to encourage Jake to arrive in class on time, write down directions for his English assignments and their due dates, complete the assignments, and participate in class. Mr. Morse was to continue to collect data on Jake's performance. The remedial English resource teacher was contacted for information about appropriate instructional materials for a student such as Jake. In addition, the special education resource teacher offered to provide periodic consultation services to Mr. Morse.

Marvin: Referral to the Assessment Team

The review of Marvin's case led to the determination that a formal referral should be submitted to the assessment team and a full-scale evaluation conducted. An assessment plan was developed by the team, the parents' approval obtained, and the assessments carried out. Mr. Morse collected additional data on Marvin's in-class performance. The school psychologist and the special education resource teacher assessed Marvin's overall academic performance and his general ability. The school counselor visited Marvin's parents to discuss home performance. The counselor also contacted Marvin's math, science, and history teachers to determine how he was doing in those classes.

The assessment team then met with the parent to review the assessment data. Results indicated that Marvin has good general ability and is able to read at grade level. His grades in subjects other than English are passing but low. Marvin's writing skills are very poor, particularly in the areas of spelling, grammar, punctuation, and capitalization. In addition, he lacks the social skills necessary for establishing interpersonal relationships; he experiences particular difficulty relating to peers. From these results the team concluded that Marvin was qualified for special education services and his case was forwarded to the IEP team.

Marvin's IEP Team

An IEP team—composed of the vice principal, the counselor, Mr. Morse, the special education resource teacher, the school psychologist, Marvin, and Marvin's mother—then met to develop the IEP. According to the plan agreed on by the IEP team, Marvin will continue to attend his regular academic classes, including English. He will also see the resource teacher one period per day for special instruction in written expression. In addition, the resource teacher will meet at least once a week with Mr. Morse to assist in adapting Marvin's writing assignments. The school counselor will work with Marvin to develop the skills Marvin needs to get along with other students. The counselor, resource teacher, and Mr. Morse will meet with Marvin to establish a contract system to reward successful completion of classroom assignments and appropriate classroom behavior.

The IEP is to be evaluated in 6 months. In the interim the school counselor will monitor Marvin's progress in all of his ninth-grade classes. Marvin and his mother agree with the IEP goals and the special services to be provided. Optimistic about Marvin's future, they believe that with help Marvin will succeed in the general education program.

The team approach is not new in education. Most professionals are aware of individuals who work together as a team to accomplish some common goal. Teams can be established at different levels within the educational system for a variety of purposes, such as selection of instructional materials, development of curriculum, and evaluation of educational programs. These school teams work to plan, evaluate, or improve various aspects of the educational system.

In special education, the team approach has traditionally been used to decide whether students should receive special services. Groups of specialists, often called *placement* or *child study teams*, met to determine whether students were eligible for special education services and, if so, to select the educational placement of most benefit to the student.

Today, not only special educators but also general education teachers and parents assist in making important decisions about the education of students with special needs. Moreover, the purpose of the team approach to serving special students goes beyond that of placement. Team members collaborate to plan and evaluate the general education experience for students with special needs, and the educators on the team work to implement the plan in the classroom.

It is important to remember that not all students with educational problems need special education services. Problems can often be resolved by modifying the student's current instructional program. The team approach can help here, too, when professionals work together to adapt instructional strategies to meet the student's educational needs within the general education classroom.

TEAMS SERVING STUDENTS WITH SPECIAL NEEDS

Teams serving students with special needs are established within a school to initiate, facilitate, supervise, and evaluate the participation of students with special needs in the general and special education programs. Teams are found at all levels of education, from preschool programs through high school. Teams serving students with special needs serve one or more of the following purposes: (1) assisting teachers in meeting the educational needs of special students within the general education classroom; (2) determining whether students are eligible for services such as special education; and (3) planning, monitoring, and evaluating the provision of special services.

Although the team approach is required by federal special education legislation, many variations are seen from district to district and from state to state in the names given to different teams and the responsibilities that these teams assume. As described in the "For Your Information" section on the Individuals with Disabilities Education Improvement Act, two types of teams are mandatory: the assessment team and the Individualized Education Program (IEP) team. When an educator or a parent submits a referral for a student who is a potential candidate for special education services, the assessment team is responsible for developing a plan for evaluating the student to determine whether he or she is eligible for special education services. This team is sometimes called the *special services committee*, *special education committee*, or *placement committee*. Once a student is found eligible, the IEP team is charged with planning and monitoring that student's IEP. The IEP team may be called the *IEP committee* or the *educational planning team*. In some districts, one team assumes both the duties of the assessment team and those of the IEP team.

The third type of team for students with special needs is designed to assist teachers to solve problems in the general education classroom, before referrals are made to special education or other types of special services. This prereferral team may be called the *teacher assistance team*, *student study team*, or the *prereferral committee*. Although not required by federal laws, such teams are mandatory in some states and districts.

This book advocates that general and special educators work together as a team when making educational decisions about all students with special needs, particularly those who are served in the general education program. The team should be concerned with not only students identified as having disabilities but also students being considered for special education and similar services. For students with disabilities, state and federal laws and regulations describe the purpose, responsibilities, and membership of the teams that make educational decisions. For other students with special needs such as gifted and talented individuals, culturally and linguistically diverse students, and students at risk for school failure, there may be no laws or regulations that require the team approach. However, this book will stress the importance of the role of prereferral, assessment, and educational planning teams in helping all students with special needs succeed in the general education program.

Teams serving students with special needs are composed of individuals directly involved with some aspect of delivering or supporting instruction. Included are general and special educators, some of whom may provide direct services to the student. Other professionals such as school psychologists, speech-language pathologists, and school nurses are involved as necessary. School administrators serve as resources to the team, and the parents of the student are an important addition. Although typically not professional educators, parents are able to provide information about the student and thus play a significant role in the educational decision-making

For Your Information

Important Provisions of the Individuals with Disabilities Education Improvement Act

The Individuals with Disabilities Education Improvement Act (IDEA 2004)* provides guidelines for many of the activities and procedures that take place in special education, including requirements for the assessment and IEP teams IDEA is the current version of the original federal legislation, Public Law 94-142, the Education for All Handicapped Children Act of 1975, that was initiated to ensure that children with disabilities and the families of such children have access to a free appropriate public education and to improved educational results. Check the explanations of the following terms to further your understanding of federal special education laws:

- *Assessment team.* The **local education agency** (LEA) or district is responsible for providing an assessment team composed of professionals who possess the appropriate training and experience to evaluate students referred for consideration for special education services. Although the professionals involved in each evaluation may vary according to the needs of the student, it is the responsibility of the team to consider referral information, develop a plan for the evaluation, obtain the permission of the parent(s) to conduct the evaluation, and then evaluate the student to determine (a) whether the student has a disability and (b) his or her educational needs. On completion of the evaluation, the professionals and the parents determine if the student has a disability, and the parents receive a copy of the evaluation and documentation that eligibility has been determined.
- *IEP team.* This group develops, reviews, and revises the IEP. Individualized Education Programs are written for all students with disabilities who receive special education services. Until IDEA 2004, it was required that IEPs be reviewed and revised at least annually. IEPs are permitted for a period of no more than 3 years. The IEP team is composed of the following members: (a) the parents of the student with a disability; (b) at least one of the student's general education teachers (if the student is, or may be, participating in the general education program); (c) at least one special education teacher or special educator who provides service to students with the type of disability being considered; (d) a representative of the LEA who is qualified to provide or supervise the provision of special education and is knowledgeable about the general curriculum and the availability of the LEA's resources; (e) an individual who can interpret the evaluation results if one is not already represented on the team; (f) at the discretion of the parent or the LEA, others with expertise regarding the student; and (g) the student with a disability, when appropriate. Among the changes under IDEA 2004 is the ability to excuse a team member from attending an IEP meeting if both the parent and the local educational agency agree.

- *Due process hearing.* If the school or the parents of a student with disabilities are not satisfied that the student is receiving an appropriate educational program, an impartial due process hearing can be requested. Hearings attempt to resolve disagreements regarding issues such as identification, evaluation, and educational programs and placements. Under IDEA 2004, parents and the school must meet in a resolution session to attempt to reach a settlement before a due process hearing can be held.
- *Child find.* Active programs are maintained by state and local education agencies to identify unserved students in need of special education.
- *Nondiscriminatory assessment.* Assessment is nondiscriminatory when it does not penalize students for their native language, race, culture, or disability.
- *Confidentiality.* The provisions of IDEA guarantee "confidentiality in the disclosure of information that may unnecessarily identify a student as having a disability" (Strickland & Turnbull, 1993, p. 261). Parents of students with disabilities must be informed of the confidentiality requirements for personally identifiable information (e.g., name, address) and must give consent before this information can be released to anyone outside the school district. The district must maintain confidential records of each student, and these records must be accessible to parents. Legally responsible parents and guardians have the right to examine all records maintained on their child by the school and to participate in meetings with respect to identification, evaluation, and placement.
- *Surrogate parent.* If a parent of a student with disabilities is not available to work with the school, a surrogate parent can be appointed. The surrogate parent approves the student's placement, works on the IEP team, and serves as an advocate for the student.
- *Transition services.* Under IDEA, transition services must be provided according to the individual needs of each student with disabilities. Transition services are a coordinated set of activities for a student with a disability that are designed (1) to support movement "from school to postschool activities, including post-secondary education, vocational training, integrated employment (including supported employment), continuing and adult education, adult services, independent living, or community participation" and (2) that include "instruction, related services, community experiences, the development of employment and other post-school adult living objectives, and, when appropriate, acquisition of daily living skills and functional vocational evaluation" [PL 108-446, Section 602 (34)]. By the age of 16, the student's IEP must include a statement of post secondary goals and the transition services needed to meet those goals.

process. If appropriate, the special student should be encouraged to participate.

Teams serving students with special needs are multipurpose in nature. Major duties are the planning, implementation, and evaluation of educational programs for students with special needs who are enrolled in general education classes. A prereferral team considers students experiencing difficulty in school and determines, first, whether the general education program can be modified to meet student needs. If these modifications are appropriate, they work to plan the modification, monitor its implementation, and evaluate its effectiveness. If this cannot be accomplished, students are referred to the assessment team to be evaluated to decide whether they are eligible for special education or another type of special service. Once a student is determined to have a disability, an IEP team then works to develop a specific educational program. Several IEP team members may be responsible for implementation of that program. For example, the special education resource teacher may assist the general education teacher in adapting classroom instruction for the student. Or the special education teacher may provide the student with part-time instruction in mathematics while the general education teacher takes responsibility for all other subject matter areas. At regular intervals (most typically yearly), the IEP team evaluates the student's progress and makes any needed programmatic changes.

Teams provide a vehicle for general and special educators to effectively carry out their shared responsibility for the education of students with special needs. They provide the opportunity for parents and professionals, who have a common concern for the education of students with special needs, to work together to share information and expertise.

In effective teams, there is open communication and cooperation among members. Communication is the sharing of information that will assist in providing a more appropriate education for students. Formal meetings establish a working relationship among team members that can then be continued and solidified by informal contacts. For example, team members may compare notes about a student's progress by chatting in the teacher's lounge, by telephone, or during a home visit with the family. The team works together, with each team member contributing a different viewpoint. Parents, teachers, and other professionals collaborate to provide the best education possible for the student with special needs. Review the stories of the two high school students, Marvin and Jake, who were introduced at the start of this chapter for a glimpse of such teams in action.

Three features set teams serving students with special needs apart from other typical education teams. First, these teams consider each student individually. When recommen-dations are made, they are specific in nature and have direct application to the student's educational program. This practice is different from the operation of many educational teams that consider the needs of groups of students. For example, teams may make general recommendations about all third-grade classes in the district or all basic freshman English classes at a certain high school. The teams serving students with special needs, however, focus their attention on one student at a time.

Second, teams serving students with special needs are composed of both general and special educators, other professionals as needed, and the student's parents. Team composition is truly multidisciplinary. In the past, each of these disciplines often worked separately to provide instructional services, and communication with others was minimal. This approach frequently led to poor coordination of educational programs, with overlap in some areas of the curriculum and neglect of others. Frequently the instructional strategies or other interventions used from setting to setting were inconsistent. The multidisciplinary team approach can reduce or eliminate this problem by developing an educational plan that clearly specifies the responsibilities of each team member and coordinates the activities of all individuals involved in its implementation.

Third, the membership of teams serving students with special needs varies according to the role of the team and the special needs of the student under consideration. Although a different special education teacher (or consultant) may be required for students with different needs, the same professional responsible for interpreting the evaluation results and the administrative designee may serve on all of the teams serving students with special needs within a school. The parents and general education teachers who participate will change as each new student is considered. Other professionals may become a part of the team as students with different needs are studied. For example, the school nurse may be a necessary team member for a student with a physical impairment but not for a student with learning disabilities.

In addition, one of the teams serving students with special needs, the IEP team, must include not only professionals but also the parents of the student with special needs and, if appropriate, the student as well. This is a radical departure from past practices. The parents and student now have the right to be active members of the IEP team and to provide input regarding instructional needs, goals, and programs. They have access to the information concerning the student and participate in making important decisions about educational placement and programming. Figure 2-1 summarizes the responsibilities of the different teams that typically serve students with special needs.

FIGURE 2-1   Responsibilities of Teams Serving Students with Special Needs

Prereferral Team
- Identify possible problem.
- Consider previous interventions.
- Design data collection procedures.
- Design prereferral interventions.
- Identify needed support/services to implement intervention plan.
- Coordinate implementation of prereferral interventions.
- Evaluate prereferral interventions.
- Modify interventions as needed.
- Initiate special education referral if general education interventions are not successful.

Assessment Team
- Review referral for special education.
- Review data on prereferral interventions.
- Identify team members needed to develop assessment plan.
- Design assessment plan.
- Provide assessment plan to parents and review plan.
- Obtain parents' permission to conduct assessment.
- Conduct assessment.
- Summarize assessment results.
- Conduct meeting with parents to determine eligibility.

Individualized Education Program (IEP) Team
- Identify IEP team membership needed for specific student.
- Review assessment results.
- Establish present levels of educational performance.
- Identify and select appropriate annual goals.
- Designate the appropriate placement in the Least Restrictive Environment (LRE).
- Develop plan for implementation of the IEP.
- Develop evaluation plan.
- Identify process for reporting student's progress to parents.
- Establish and monitor reevaluation plan.

ROLES OF TEAM MEMBERS

Teams serving students with special needs are made up of a variety of different members. Both special education and general education are represented. Teachers and administrators are included as well as specialists such as psychologists, physical therapists, and counselors. In addition, parents and special students themselves may participate in team deliberations. Each of these individuals plays an important role.

Building Principals

School principals or vice principals serve as key members of teams serving students with special needs. As administrators, they are responsible for the general education programs and often the special education programs housed within their buildings. In large elementary or secondary schools, the vice principal with supervisory responsibilities for the special education program may represent the principal on the team.

The principal often schedules and chairs the team's formal meetings. Although usually not directly responsible for implementing any portion of the student's IEP, administrators do influence the operation and effectiveness of the effort. They are the educational leaders of the school and, as such, are aware of the school's program and personnel resources. Their activities, the attitudes they convey, and the support they provide can help establish the necessary school climate for developing educational programs that serve a wide variety of learners and for building successful programs that provide appropriate services for students with special needs.

Special Education Administrators

Special education directors are responsible for supervising the provision of appropriate educational programs for all students with disabilities within a district. Their primary activities include the direction of special education programs as well as the provision of support services to special classes, resource programs, and consultants to general education teachers within regular school buildings. Frequently they are responsible for developing in-service training programs to help general education teachers work more effectively with students with disabilities.

On assessment and IEP teams, special education administrators assist in the review of assessment information and help the team examine appropriate special education placement options. In some districts, these professionals serve on the team only when students are likely to require placement in more intensive service options such as separate special classes.

General Education Teachers

The involvement of general education teachers is critical because they have firsthand experience with students with special needs in their classrooms. They share ideas with parents and other professionals, and they assist in devising strategies for successful programs to serve special students included in the general education program. If these teachers do not participate on the team, the effectiveness of the effort to include students with special needs in general education classes is compromised.

At the secondary level, students are served by a number of general education teachers, and the school counselor may be designated as the teachers' representative on teams serving students with special needs. The counselor collects information from each teacher about a student's classroom performance and reports to the team. The counselor is then responsible for conveying team decisions and recommendations to each of the student's teachers. Of course, it is possible (and often desirable) for secondary teachers to serve as members of the team, as in the example of Mr. Morse, Marvin's and Jake's ninth-grade English teacher (see "Students' Stories").

General education teachers who have worked with students being considered for special education services can provide the team with much information. They are aware of special strengths students may have, students' past responses to various instructional programs and procedures, and specific areas in which students may require the most assistance. The presence of these teachers on the team can ensure that all important classroom information is considered. In addition, their experience with individual students may temper the interpretation of assessment results or the recommendations made by the team.

General education teachers responsible for implementing a portion of the IEP should be involved in the team's discussion of assessment results and any other relevant information gathered by professionals or provided by parents. Teachers can describe their classroom programs and their perceptions of a student's ability to participate in activities in the general education class. They can also contribute to and benefit from the team's discussion of ways to adapt the general education program. As soon as the modified classroom program or the

IEP is initiated, the classroom teacher can inform the team of the student's progress in the general education class. This input helps the team evaluate the current program in order to make any changes needed to enable the student to meet the goals established by the prereferral or IEP team.

Special Educators

In addition to general education teachers, special educators also provide instructional services to students with disabilities. The special educators most likely to be on the teams serving students with special needs are those assigned to a classroom or office within the student's school. The special educator may be a teacher-consultant who provides assistance to general education teachers who have students with special needs in their classes. Or the special educator may be a resource room teacher who provides direct services to special students as well as consultation to their teachers. The special class teacher also may participate as a member of the team; this teacher serves students who require more intensive special education but who may be included in the general education program for selected activities.

Itinerant special education teachers who work with students with disabilities participating in the general education program also serve on the team as necessary. **Itinerant teachers,** who travel from school to school, may be specialists in the education of students with speech or language impairments, visual impairments, hearing impairments, physical or health impairments, or other special needs. One of the most common itinerant specialists is the **speech-language pathologist,** who serves students with communication disorders. These and other specialists serve on the team when a student likely to receive their specific services is being evaluated.

Special educators fulfill a variety of roles on the team. Often they are responsible for organizing the teams serving students with special needs, conducting the meetings, and monitoring the services provided to students with disabilities. They may observe a student in the general education class and conduct much of the educational assessment. Special education teachers explain the different types of available special services and describe in detail the support services for general education teachers. Also, these professionals help interpret assessment results and assist the team in formulating the educational plan. In the implementation of the IEP, they typically provide direct services to special students and consultant services to general education teachers.

The special educator most likely to provide instruction to a specific student should serve on the IEP team when that student's educational program is being planned. This involvement provides the special educator with the opportunity to meet the student and his or her parents and teacher(s). The special educator thus becomes familiar with the student's current performance and specific educational needs, as well as with the views of the student's general education teacher(s), the student's parents, and other professionals concerned with the student's education.

Parents and Students

At first, parents may be reluctant to participate in the activities of teams serving students with special needs, particularly if past contacts with the school have been primarily negative. They may also be apprehensive about becoming a member of a team composed mainly of professionals. Team members may need to give them a great deal of reassurance regarding the importance of their involvement.

Programs are more effective for students when parents are active participants. Parents can provide the team with information about the performance of the student with special needs outside the school setting. They are also able to assist in establishing appropriate educational goals. In addition, parents contribute to the team effort by specifying which aspects of the educational program can be supported or supplemented within the home. The parents' awareness of the specific program designed for their child and the resultant coordination between home and school can make an important difference for many students. Moreover, the team's concern for the needs of their child may win parental support for the effort to meet the child's educational needs. See the "Window on the Web" box for information about Family Village, a site on the World Wide Web with many resources for families that include a student with disabilities.

The team should make every effort to include the special student's parents as fully participating team members. If possible, conflicts between parents and professionals should be resolved at the team level. However, if parents do not agree with the recommendations made by the team, they may request a hearing to appeal the team's decisions. The school district also has the right to appeal if it believes that the parents are not acting in the student's best interests.

Students with special needs participate in the activities of the team when appropriate. As a general rule, students who have reached adolescence are the most likely to be included. In one recent survey (Martin, Marshall, & Sale, 2004), secondary grade students with disabilities attended 70% of IEP meetings. Students participating in team meetings should be encouraged to discuss their reactions and perceptions regarding possible educational goals and placements.

School Psychologists

School psychologists typically assist the assessment team in evaluating students referred for special education services. In addition to administering tests and other assessments, psychologists may observe the student in the general education classroom, interview the parents, or consult with other professionals

Window on t[he Web]

Wrightslaw

http://www.wrightslaw.com

The Wrightslaw website featu[res]
and advocacy efforts related t[o]

- Special Education/Educat[ion]
- Special Education Advoca[cy]
- Law & Legal Issues
- Free Flyers, Resources, Pu[blications]
- Training and Conferences
- Books, Newsletters, Web[sites]

There is also an Advocacy Li[brary in-]
cluding Autism, Behavior & [Discipline]
ents" of students with disabi[lities]

For more inform[ation...]

Window on the Web

Family Village

http://www.familyvillage.wisc.edu

The Family Village website provides resources for persons with disabilities and their families as well as for professionals. The site is organized like a village. Visit the Library to find information about all types of disabilities; visit the Shopping Mall to learn about assistive technology and adaptive products. The Coffee Shop is the place to go to access the Family Village discussion boards. The Post Office features parent-to-parent web boards organized by topic; for example, persons interested in ADHD, cerebral palsy, or Down syndrome can read messages written by others and leave their own messages with questions or comments. Teachers might be interested in the School, which provides information and resources for parents of school-age children as well as an extensive list of "youth-friendly" websites for students with disabilities and/or chronic health conditions. Other locations in the Family Village include the Hospital (for health-related information), House of Worship, Recreation and Leisure (for information about topics such as air travel, fitness, Special Olympics, and wheelchair sports), Community Center (for family resources), Bookstore, and University (for links to research programs and projects, statistics, and surveys).

For more information, go to the Web Links module in Chapter 2 of the Companion Website.

information is available to all e[ligible]
parties, such as parents and app[ropriate]

Anyone within the school [system]
for consideration for possible s[pecial...]
referrals originate with general [educators,]
come from parents, counselor[s, or]
physicians. Teams serving stud[ents]
set up clear referral procedu[res that]
should then be communicated [to staff in]
the building as well as to paren[ts who make]
referrals. However, it is impor[tant to examine]
options within the general ed[ucation before begin-]
ning referral procedures. Rese[arch shows that stu-]
dents are referred for special ed[ucation are likely]
to be assessed (92%) and ulti[mately placed in special]
education (Algozzine, Christen[son...]

Prereferral Interventions

Classroom teachers refer stud[ents for]
other types of support services [. Among]
the most common reasons we[re...]
difficulty in reading, and beha[vior that]
tiveness (Lloyd, Kauffman, Lar[sen...]
before a referral is made, the t[eacher attempts]
to solve the instructional probl[em. When at-]
tempted, these strategies are c[alled...]

Interventions undertaken [...often]
ten eliminate the need to refe[r...]

who have information about the student's recent performance. Their participation on the assessment and IEP teams also involves explanation or interpretation of assessment results.

School psychologists generally have training in counseling and classroom management. However, their responsibilities for assessing students, writing reports, and serving on several prereferral, assessment, or IEP teams throughout the district often consume most of their time. Because they are usually required to serve more than one school, they may not be available for consultation with a teacher who has an immediate concern.

School Social Workers

School social workers assist in collecting information from parents, coordinating the efforts of the prereferral or IEP teams with community agencies, and observing the student's interactions in settings outside the classroom. They are able to provide consultative services to parents, teachers, and students themselves.

School Counselors

Although counselors are most likely to be found at the secondary level, in some districts they are available for students of all ages. Counselors take on a number of roles on teams serving students with special needs and also provide direct services to these students. They assist in gathering information from teachers,

school records, parents, and community agencies (particularly when school social workers are not available). Students with special needs may receive counseling or educational guidance from these professionals. Counselors at the secondary level often coordinate the educational programs for students with special needs and assume responsibility for communicating each student's progress to teachers, parents, and the student.

School Nurses

The school nurse may collect appropriate medical information regarding special students; for example, nurses can screen students for possible vision or hearing problems. As team members, nurses assist in interpreting a student's medical records and reports and also can explain the educational implications of medical information. They may provide services to students with physical impairments, those with chronic illnesses, or others needing continued medical attention. In addition, they assist parents in obtaining medical services for their children.

Other Team Members

Other persons join teams serving students with special needs when their special expertise is needed. For instance, for students with physical impairments, professionals such as **physical therapists**, **occupational therapists**, and **adapted**

physical education teac
When young students wi
portant to obtain informa
familiar with their progres
programs to facilitate thei
For secondary students,
selors may be an impo
tribute to the team's un
medical personnel may a
pairments are being cons
cialists can advise th
acquisition, and use of
maintain, or improve the
with disabilities. Anothe
tional aide who has work

Although these profe
bers as needed, the effec
viduals who are nece
consideration of the stu
more than five to seven r
ductivity declines. As
should include the stud
and special education te

COLLABORATION I
AND PREREFERRAL

A primary function of
students with special ne
justments must be made

Inclusion Tips for the Teacher

Collaborating with Other Professionals During Prereferral

Special education consultants and teacher assistance teams provide prereferral services to general educators in order to resolve educational problems within the general education classroom. To make the best use of these services, consider the following suggestions:

1. The job of the consultant or team is to assist you in developing a plan for working with the "target" student. The consultant or team is not there to dictate what should be done for the student or to "take over" the student's educational program.

2. The student continues to be your responsibility and you are in charge of his or her educational program.

3. Establish an agreement as to your role and that of the team or consultant. It may not be necessary to have this agreement in writing, but it is important that everyone be aware of each other's expectations.

4. It is important that you and the consultant or team work together collaboratively. Although your training and experience may be different from that of special education professionals, you are responsible for the quality of the program in your classroom, you are aware of the needs of your students, and you can describe their history in your classroom. The team or consultant is there to assist you.

5. Try to keep the focus of the discussions on the problems the "target" student has experienced. Be as specific as you can in your statements, and don't digress regarding other problems.

6. Provide specific information on the behaviors of the student and on the interventions you have tried. Data on the number of times a behavior occurs or how long it persists, the performance of the student in problem academic or social areas, or the success of an intervention can assist the team or consultant in providing feedback to you. You may be asked some questions regarding this information to clarify the team's understanding of the problem.

7. The team or consultant may suggest that additional data on the problem behavior be collected. Attempt to collect these data, but if you are not comfortable with the type of data to be collected, how the data should be collected, or how much of your time will be required, share these concerns and resolve the specifics of the data collection process. Some teams or consultants can assist with the initial collection of data on students.

8. The team or consultant should help you develop more than one possible intervention for the problem behavior. Don't expect "one magic solution." Do expect to be actively involved in providing suggestions and developing possible interventions.

9. Implement the interventions in the way they were developed by you and the team or consultant. If you are not comfortable with the intervention or are unsure of the specifics, ask for clarification or assistance. The consultant or a team member may be able to demonstrate the intervention or inform you about other teachers who are using similar techniques so that you can observe the intervention being implemented.

10. Be sure that a plan is devised to evaluate the effectiveness of the intervention(s). This plan should specify the type of data needed for evaluation. It should also include the length of time the intervention should be attempted and the alternative interventions that should be attempted if the initial one fails. Set a date for you and the team or consultant to review the progress of the intervention and to consider next steps. If it later becomes necessary to refer the student for special education services, be sure to share the information you have collected on the student and the interventions attempted.

11. Consider your work with the team or consultant an opportunity to gain new skills in working with students with special needs. Once these skills are mastered, they will help you work with other students with similar problems.

12. Provide feedback to the team or consultant. This feedback will help improve the prereferral services provided to you and other teachers.

interventions that they have found effective for similar problems; current teachers can share their experiences with the student and their observations of his or her ability to cope with classroom demands. Parents, too, can provide information about the student. In some cases, simply making parents aware of the problem is an effective intervention. For example, if the problem concerns homework, parents may decide to increase their supervision of the student's study sessions or make a valued activity (such as watching television) contingent on the completion of all assignments.

In some districts, special educators such as resource teachers or teacher-consultants work with general educators to help them modify classroom programs to meet the needs of students not yet referred for special education services (Idol, 1993; Sugai & Tindal, 1993). In many schools, teachers can also seek assistance from teams of colleagues. These teams are known by several different names: teacher assistance teams, student study teams, prereferral assistance teams, and so on. They are typically composed of several general educators representing different grade levels or subject areas; other members may include an administrator such as the principal, a specialist such as a special educator, and parents. Their major role is to collaborate with teachers in solving instructional problems. The research on teacher assistance teams (Chalfant & Pysh, 1989) and consultation services (Doorlag, 1989a; Graden, Casey, & Christenson, 1985; Idol, 1993) indicates that these approaches are quite successful in solving problems at the classroom level, thereby reducing the number of referrals to special education (Buck, et al., 2003; Hocutt, 1996; Safran & Safran, 1996).

Idol and West (1991) emphasize the collaborative nature of the team approach. The teacher seeking assistance becomes a member of the team and participates fully in the problem-solving process, which involves six steps:

- Step 1: Entry/Goal Setting
- Step 2: Problem Identification
- Step 3: Intervention Recommendations
- Step 4: Implementation of Recommendations
- Step 5: Evaluation of the Action Plan and the Team Process
- Step 6: Follow-Up/Redesign (pp. 77–78).

For example, in step 3, the entire team (including the student's classroom teacher) brainstorms possible solutions to the instructional problem, evaluates the advantages and disadvantages of each solution, and then selects the most appropriate one. Consult the "Inclusion Tips for the Teacher" material to learn more about collaborating with prereferral or teacher assistance teams and special education consultants.

Team deliberations are most fruitful when the teacher is able to clearly describe the student's problem and any attempts to remedy it. The student intervention checklist shown in Figure 2-2 is one method for recording this information. The teacher begins by noting the area or areas of concern (e.g., academic achievement, classroom behavior) and the steps already taken to solve the problem (e.g., student or parent conference). He or she then describes the student's present performance and current classroom procedures. At the end of the checklist, the teacher identifies the type of assistance he or she is seeking, and there is space for the team to record the results of its deliberations and the outcomes of any interventions.

Classroom Modifications. A number of prereferral intervention strategies involve changes in the instructional program of the general education class. To improve student performance, modifications can be made in any aspect of the program: the classroom curriculum, how instruction is delivered, the learning activities in which students participate, how students are graded, the physical arrangement of the classroom, and strategies for managing student behavior.

Curricular adaptations are changes in the body of knowledge and skills taught to students. One option is to retain the standard grade-level curriculum but teach only a portion of it—those areas determined to be the most important. Another option is the substitution of an alternative curriculum. In the general education classroom, this usually involves teaching the prerequisite skills that students lack or using curricular materials from a lower grade level. For example, a fifth-grade teacher might use fourth-grade reading materials for some students in the class.

Instructional adaptions are the most common type of classroom modification. These changes may involve any part of the teaching–learning process: the teacher's instructional methods and strategies, learning activities and instructional materials, performance requirements for students, testing and grading procedures, and grouping arrangements. Examples are as follows:

- Providing additional instruction in areas where students experience difficulty,
- Structuring practice activities so that students have ample time to master one set of skills before moving on to the next set,
- Modifying task requirements so that students can listen rather than read or give answers orally rather than write,
- Giving students extra time to complete exams and assignments,
- Allowing students to use aids such as calculators and dictionaries,
- Reducing the number of problems students are required to solve or the number of paragraphs they must write, and
- Grouping students with similar needs for instruction and changing the composition of the groups, as needed.

Management adaptations are changes in the classroom behavior management system. The teacher may need to provide additional instruction to all students on the rules for classroom conduct. Or he or she may need to modify the standard classroom management system if several students begin to display inappropriate behaviors. In some cases, it may be necessary to begin a systematic behavior change program for one or more students with more severe behavioral problems. For example, the teacher and student might negotiate a behavioral contract in which the student agrees to reduce his or her inappropriate behavior, and in exchange the teacher promises to provide a suitable reward.

Environmental adaptations are changes in the physical environment of the classroom. For example, a teacher may modify the arrangement of student desks and the location of learning materials in order to make classroom activities accessible to a student who uses a wheelchair. Students with visual and hearing impairments may be seated near the front of the room, if that is where instruction typically occurs. Students who act out and those who have difficulty focusing their attention may also be seated near the teacher. The classroom itself may be arranged so that there are areas for several different activities including large- and small-group instruction, independent study, work at the computer, and so on.

General education teachers use several different techniques to modify instruction for students with special needs. However, although teachers consider many kinds of classroom modifications valuable, they are less positive about their feasibility

FIGURE 2-2   Student Intervention Checklist

Name _____ Age _____ Date _____
Teacher _____ Grade _____

1. **Area(s) of Concern**
   ____ academic   ____ language   ____ gross motor   ____ hearing
   ____ behavior   ____ speech   ____ fine motor
   ____ emotional   ____ physical   ____ vision

2. What kinds of strategies have been employed to resolve this problem?
   A. **Records Review and Conference**
      ____ student conference(s)   ____ review of educational records
      ____ parent conference(s)   ____ vision   ____ medical   ____ hearing
   B. **Environmental Modifications**
      ____ class seating arrangement   ____ group change   ____ other
      ____ individual seating   ____ teacher change
      ____ schedule modification   ____ teacher position in class
   C. **Instructional**
      ____ modifications in methods used with group or class
      ____ modifications in learning aids used with group or class
      ____ individual methods with regular materials
      ____ individual learning aids with regular materials
      ____ individual methods and materials different from group or class
   D. **Management**
      ____ modification in classroom management system
      ____ use of systematic group management techniques
      ____ use of individual behavior management techniques

3. What methods are currently employed to address the concern?

4. Where does this student stand in relationship to others in class, group or grade regarding systemwide tests, class average behavior, completion of work, etc.?

Student Behavior	Class or Group or Grade Behavior

5. Is the concern generally associated with a particular time, subject, or person?

6. In what areas, under what conditions, does this student do best?

7. Assistance requested (observation, materials, ideas, etc.):
   _____
   _____
   _____
   _____

Assistance provided:			
Dates	Nature of Assistance	Individuals Responsible	Outcome

Permission granted by the publisher for noncommercial reproduction.

Note: Reprinted with the permission of Prentice-Hall, Inc., from *Developing and Implementing Individualized Education Programs* (3rd ed.) by Bonnie B. Strickland and Ann P. Turnbull. Copyright © 1993 by Prentice-Hall, Inc.

(Johnson & Pugach, 1990; Ysseldyke, Thurlow, Wotruba, & Nania, 1990). In general, teachers are most likely to introduce interventions that they themselves can accomplish quickly and easily within their own classrooms (Ellett, 1993; Johnson & Pugach, 1990). Some of the most common strategies are modifying assignments so they are shorter or less difficult, allowing students to respond orally on tests, and offering preferential seating (Bacon & Schulz, 1991; Munson, 1986).

General Education and Community Resources.   In addition to making modifications in their own classrooms, teachers can draw on the resources of the general education program to assist students with school problems. Although different schools will have different resources available, all teachers have access to some level of support within their school, district, and community.

The use of students as instructional assistants is one example. Students act as tutors to other students, thereby increasing the amount of individualized instruction that takes place within the classroom. Peer tutoring programs are inexpensive in terms of both time and money, and research supports their effectiveness for increasing the skill levels of students with school achievement problems (Lloyd, Crowley, Kohler, & Strain, 1988). Parents, other family members, and community volunteers can also act as assistants within the classroom.

The general education program may offer a number of resources: school-wide peer tutoring or peer counseling programs, academic assistance in the computer lab, remedial programs for low-income students, reading and math labs or tutorial services, programs for students learning English, bilingual education, enrichment opportunities for students with special gifts and talents, and so on. The community may offer additional resources such as after-school programs with homework assistance, big brother and big sister programs, sports activities and clubs, or a homework hotline with telephone tutors. School and community resources such as these provide options that teachers should consider when they select prereferral interventions for students with special needs.

A recent national study of prereferral intervention practices in the 50 states (Buck et al., 2003) sheds some light on the recommendations that teacher assistance teams tend to make. These recommendations span a range of different types of interventions. The most common team suggestions were instructional modifications, behavior management procedures, curricular modifications, and counseling. Other options reported by various states were placement review and change, parent training, tutoring, mentoring, and summer school services.

COLLABORATION IN REFERRAL AND ASSESSMENT

In some cases, prereferral interventions do not solve the problems that students with special needs are experiencing in the general education classroom. When this happens, the next step is a referral to determine if the student has a disability and is eligible for special education services. An assessment team considers the referral information, including the data collected during the prereferral stage, and designs a plan for evaluating the student to determine his or her eligibility and educational needs.

Referral

When students are formally referred, specific time lines and notification procedures are followed, ensuring that each student is evaluated in a timely manner as required by state and federal laws. Good educational practice dictates that any identified need be considered promptly, without relegating the student to a waiting list (as often occurred in the past). Delays deny the student access to appropriate services and also frustrate the individual making the referral.

Many different individuals can refer students for consideration for special education. The general education teacher, however, is the primary referral source because classroom teachers observe students daily in the school setting, constantly monitoring their physical status, academic performance, classroom behavior, and social interactions. Classroom teachers are able to compare the performance of one student with that of current classmates as well as students from previous school years.

Classroom teachers differ in the number and type of referrals they make to special education. Some teachers refer a high

FIGURE 2-3   Prereferral Intervention Checklist

Appropriate activities on this checklist must be completed before referring a student for assessment for special education services. Place the date that activities were completed in the space next to the activity. This form must accompany the referral form.

1. _____ Reviewed student educational records to determine longevity of concern and previous interventions.
2. _____ Established that student has passed vision and hearing screening or referred student for vision and hearing screening.
3. _____ Met with student to discuss concerns and possible solutions.
4. _____ Met with parents to discuss concerns and possible solutions.
5. _____ Collected and analyzed recent examples of student's classwork.
6. _____ Collected specific information from records and performance regarding student's academic skills.
7. _____ Collected specific information from the record and class regarding student's behavior.
8. _____ Brainstormed with co-teachers to obtain strategies that have worked in other similar cases.
9. _____ Identified in writing the student's specific educational problem.
10. _____ Consulted with counselor regarding student's behavior.
11. _____ Consulted with resource teachers in school to discuss concerns and obtain strategies.
12. _____ Obtained observation by another teacher or school resource to obtain information regarding concern.
13. _____ Developed and implemented instructional strategies with assistance of other educators.
14. _____ Developed and implemented a behavior management plan with other educators.
15. _____ Obtained or developed instructional learning aids to address this student's problem.
16. _____ List any other modifications, interventions, or strategies you have attempted to maintain this student in the classroom.

_____

_____

_____

Teacher Signature _____ Date _____

Permission granted by the publisher for noncommercial reproduction.

Note: Reprinted with the permission of Prentice-Hall, Inc., from *Developing and Implementing Individualized Education Programs* (3rd ed.) by Bonnie B. Strickland and Ann P. Turnbull. Copyright © 1993 by Prentice-Hall, Inc.

percentage of their students; others refer none. This discrepancy may occur for a number of reasons. Teachers may not have a clear understanding of how serious a student's problems should be before special education services are considered. Some teachers may not be aware of the special programs or consultation services available; others may already be capable of adapting their classroom program to meet the needs of a wide range of students. Still others may be unfamiliar with the appropriate referral procedures, or they may feel that referrals reflect negatively on their ability as a teacher and classroom manager. Most classroom teachers fall somewhere between the two extremes. Generally, the more teachers know about dealing with students with unique needs—and about the special services available, criteria for special education, and referral procedures—the more accurate and appropriate their referrals.

The exact procedure for making referrals varies greatly from school to school and from district to district. It can involve completing a short form with a minimal amount of information, an elaborate checklist, or a report requiring detailed data on the student's current and past performance. As part of the referral process in many districts, teachers must document the steps they have taken to meet the student's educational needs within the general education classroom. Figure 2-3 provides an example of a prereferral intervention checklist that a teacher might be asked to complete.

Students are referred for special education if they have special needs that interfere with their school performance and if these needs cannot be adequately met within the general educational program. Blankenship and Lilly (1981) provide the following guidelines:

FIGURE 2-4	Referral for Special Education Services

Directions: Teachers or other individuals referring a student for special education services should complete all sections of this form. The completed form should be sent to the principal's office for processing. Complete and specific information will assist the assessment and IEP teams in determining the student's eligibility for special education and specific educational needs. Use behavioral descriptions whenever possible.

Teacher _____ Grade/Class _____ Report Date _____

Student _____ Age _____ Birth Date _____

1. What is the student's problem? How does it affect his or her ability to participate in classroom activities?

2. How frequently does the problem occur? (For example, once a week? Six times a week?)

3. What changes have occurred in the behavior during this school year?

4. What changes in classroom activities, assignments, procedures, and so on, have you made to try to solve the problem? What are the results of these changes?

5. What are the student's major strengths and talents?

6. What special interests, hobbies, or skills does the student have?

As a basic principle teachers should refer students when two conditions exist: (1) the student is experiencing significant difficulty in the classroom, and (2) the teacher is unsuccessful in solving the problem as it exists. Many students experience difficulty in learning and not all should be referred for special education. Individual teachers have strengths in dealing with certain types of learning and behavior problems, and are confident that they can handle these problems as they occur. If the teacher is handling a problem successfully, the student should not be referred. (p. 36)

Although students with special needs may exhibit a variety of problems, their needs generally cluster into one or more of the following areas:

- *Physical needs.* Difficulty with one or more of the senses, with mobility or motor coordination, or with physical activities requiring strength and stamina.

- *Academic needs.* Poor performance in relation to peers in one or more areas of the curriculum. These needs may be evident in the communication skills of listening and speaking, academic areas such as reading and mathematics, and/or content areas such as science and history.
- *Classroom behavior needs.* Difficulty in controlling inappropriate behaviors that interfere with other students, the instruction of the classroom, or the student's own study activities. Both acting-out and withdrawn behaviors may be considered inappropriate.
- *Social needs.* Poor ability to establish and maintain interpersonal relationships, either with peers or with adults.

Information on special needs such as these is reported in a referral form such as that illustrated in Figure 2-4. This sample form asks for specific information about the student's current performance and his or her reactions to any instructional adjustments made by the teacher. Members of assessment and IEP teams work hard to make careful eligibility and placement decisions and provide educators and parents with specific programmatic recommendations. To accomplish these tasks, specific, accurate, and objective data are needed. It is difficult for teams to provide assistance when given only general information, such as the student "is slow," "acts out in class," "never talks," or "works below grade level."

Specific statements that describe the current status of the student are much more helpful. Examples of pertinent information to include on referral forms include these:

- Correct answer and error rates on academic assignments and the level of academic performance as compared with that of other students in the classroom,
- The frequency with which inappropriate behaviors occur during the class period or school day, or
- The number of assignments completed by the student and an analysis of the student's errors.

Specific information on the success or failure of changes in classroom instruction or management is also extremely helpful. The more objective and complete the data provided in the referral, the more accurately the assessment and IEP teams will be able to determine what additional assessment information is needed, what types of special education services should be considered, and which educational recommendations are appropriate.

Assessment

When the assessment team has determined that a referred student may be in need of special education services because adaptations of the general education program have not resolved the student's problems, the team designs a complete plan for evaluating the student and presents it to the student's parents for their approval. The assessment plan indicates which tests and other assessment procedures will be used in the evaluation of the student. This process is designed to gather relevant functional and developmental information to determine whether the student has a disability and to determine the student's educational needs.

The assessments used with students suspected of having a disability must meet several criteria. They must not be discriminatory on a racial or cultural basis and they must be administered in the student's native language (when feasible) or other mode of communication (e.g., sign language). They must be technically sound, and they must be administered by trained personnel in conformance with the instructions provided by the producers of the assessment instruments. No single instrument can serve as the sole criterion for determining an appropriate educational placement for a student. Tests

and other evaluations should assess specific areas of educational need for each student; typical concerns are academic performance, classroom behavior, and social skills. The student should be assessed in all areas that are related to the suspected disability. In addition, the general education teacher can assist by providing curriculum-based assessment information relating to the student's past perofrmance in the classroom setting. The student shall not be determined to have a disability if the decision is based on a lack of instruction in reading or math or limited English proficiency. The most recent reauthorization of IDEA 2004, adds that instruction in reading must be scientifically based.

The assessment information, collected from various sources by the team and presented in a written report, indicates the student's present levels of performance. This information is used to determine whether the student has a disability and is eligible for special education services; if so, it serves as the basis for the IEP team to design an individualized educational program and determine the appropriate educational placement for the student.

Under federal laws, eligibility for special education services is determined by two criteria: It must be established that the student has a disability, and there must be evidence that the disability in some way adversely affects the student's educational performance. Satisfying one criterion but not the other is not sufficient. For example, many students with school problems do not meet eligibility requirements because they do not have a disability. Similarly, a student with a mild disability (e.g., a mild vision loss or physical impairment) would not qualify for special education services if he or she were not experiencing educational difficulties as a result of that mild disability.

COLLABORATION IN DESIGNING THE INDIVIDUALIZED EDUCATION PROGRAM

Once it has been determined that a student is eligible for special education, the next step is to design the Individualized Education Program. This written plan must be developed prior to the start of special education services. The IEP, which is typically reviewed and modified at least annually, must include several specific components. (See the accompanying "For Your Information" material for an explanation of the legal requirements.)

A review of the student's present levels of performance may indicate a variety of educational needs. It may not be appropriate, or possible, to deal with each of these areas in the IEP. Possible measurable annual goals should be determined by the team and then ranked in priority order. When the goals have been selected, the team determines how progress toward those goals will be measured.

For Your Information

Required Components of the Individualized Education Program (IEP)

The Individuals with Disabilities Education Improvement Act (IDEA 2004) mandates the components of the IEP. Because the requirements are very specific, it is important that educators carefully review the following excerpts from the proposed reauthorization of the law.

Section 614(d)(1)(A) INDIVIDUALIZED EDUCATION PROGRAM.

(i)   IN GENERAL. The term 'individualized education program' or 'IEP' means a written statement for each child with a disability that is developed, reviewed, and revised in accordance with this section and that includes

 (I)   a statement of the child's present levels of academic achievement and functional performance, including

  (aa) how the child's disability affects the child's involvement and progress in the general curriculum;

  (bb) for preschool children, as appropriate, how the disability affects the child's participation in appropriate activities; and

  (cc) for children with disabilities who take alternate assessments aligned to alternate achievement standards, a description of benchmarks or short-term objectives;

 (II) a statement of measurable annual goals, including academic and functional goals, designed to

  (aa) meet the child's needs that result from the child's disability to enable the child to be involved in and make progress in the general curriculum; and

  (bb) meet each of the child's other educational needs that result from the child's disability;

 (III) a description of how the child's progress toward meeting the annual goals described in subclause (II) will be measured and when periodic reports on the progress the child is making toward meeting the annual goals (such as through the use of quarterly or other periodic reports, concurrent with the issuance of report cards) will be provided;

 (IV) a statement of the special education and related service, and supplementary aids and services, based on peer-reviewed research to the extent practicable, to be provided to the child, or on behalf of the child, and a statement of the program modifications or supports for school personnel that will be provided for the child

  (aa) to advance appropriately toward attaining the annual goals;

  (bb) to be involved in and make progress in the general curriculum in accordance with subclause (I) and to participate in extracurricular and other nonacademic activities; and

  (cc) to be educated and participate with other children with disabilities and nondisabled children in the activities described in this subparagraphs;

 (V)   an explanation of the extent, if any, to which the child will not participate with nondisabled children in the regular class and in the activities described in subclause (IV)(cc);

 (VI) (aa) a statement of any individual appropriate accommodations that are necessary to measure the academic achievement and functional performance of the child on State and districtwide assessments consistent with section 612(a)(16)(A); and

  (bb) if the IEP Team determines that the child shall take an alternate assessment on a particular State or districtwide assessment of student achievement, a statement of why

   (AA) the child cannot participate in the regular assessment; and

   (BB) the particular alternate assessment selected is appropriate for the child.

 (VII) the projected date for the beginning of the services and modifications described in subclause (IV), and the anticipated frequency, location, and duration of those services and modifications; and

 (VIII) beginning not later than the first IEP to be in effect when the child is 16, and updated annually thereafter

  (aa) appropriate measurable postsecondary goals based upon age appropriate transition assessments related to training, education, employment, and, where appropriate, independent living skills;

  (bb) the transition services (including courses of study) needed by the child to assist in reaching those goals; and

  (cc) beginning not later than 1 year before the child reaches the age of majority under State law, a statement that the child has been informed of the child's rights under this title, if any, that will transfer to the child on reaching the age of majority under section 615(m).

In addition, several other factors must be considered when applicable to individual students:

Section 614(d)(3)(B) CONSIDERATION OF SPECIAL FACTORS. The IEP team shall

(i)   in the case of a child whose behavior impedes the child's learning or that of others, consider the use of positive behavioral interventions and supports, and other strategies, to address that behavior;

continued

continued

(ii) in the case of a child with limited English proficiency, consider the language needs of the child as such needs relate to the child's IEP;

(iii) in the case of a child who is blind or visually impaired provide for instruction in Braille and the use of Braille unless the IEP Team determines, after an evaluation of the child's reading and writing skills, needs, and appropriate reading and writing media (including an evaluation of the child's future needs for instruction in Braille or the use of Braille), that instruction in Braille or the use of Braille is not appropriate for the child;

(iv) consider the communication needs of the child, and in the case of a child who is deaf or hard of hearing, consider the child's language and communication needs, opportunities for direct communications with peers and professional personnel in the child's language and communication mode, academic level, and full range of needs, including opportunities for direct instruction in the child's language and communication mode; and

(v) consider whether the child needs assistive technology devices and services.

The sample IEP presented in Figure 2-5 outlines the student's present levels of performance and provides goals and objectives in the curriculum areas of spelling and written expression. Although the format used to present information may vary from district to district, the essential components should be present in all IEPs written for special students.

The IEP team is responsible for ensuring that the student's educational program is implemented as specified in the IEP. Instructional recommendations and service provisions called for in the IEP are to be followed unless the plan is modified by the team and the changes are approved by the student's parents.

FIGURE 2-5   Sample IEP

	Date __11/15/05__
	☐ Initial IEP
	☒ Annual Review
	☐ Three-year Review
	☐ Other _____

Orchard County Public Schools
Individualized Education Program (IEP)

Student Information

Name __Steven Cooper__ Birth Date __7-23-94__

Male ☒ Female ☐ Age __11-4__ Grade __6__ Ethnicity __white, nonHispanic__

Social Security Number __000-00-0000__ English Language Learner Yes ☐ No ☒

Home Language __English__ Interpreter Required Yes ☐ No ☒

Address __1400 Lilac Rd. Blanchard 00000__

School of Residence __Piper Middle School__

School of Attendance __Piper Middle School__

Rationale for placement, if other than student's school of residence:
__N/A__

Parent/Guardian Information

Name __Bob Cooper and Helen Downing-Cooper__

Address __same__

Home phone __555-5555__ Work phone __555-0000__

Interpreter Required Yes ☐ No ☒

Assessment Information

Present Levels of Performance (include how disability affects involvement and progress in general curriculum)

Steven has average performance in all areas except written language. He scores in the below average to low average range in spelling and written expression. Steven should be able to function well in general education with support in written language.

Modifications needed in State and districtwide assessment   in assessments requiring written expression, use of dictionary and thesaurus; time and a half to complete essays

Why needed   student requires support in written expression

IEP Information

Date of Next IEP 11/06   Date of Three-year Review 11/07

Primary Disability Category specific learning disability

Primary Placement regular class & resource room

P.E. Type regular

Transportation N/A

Special Education & Related Services; Supplementary Aids & Services; Program Modifications and Supports	Start Date	Duration	Frequency	Location
Resource Room	11/05	1 year	1 hour, 5 days/week	Rm. 5
Consultation to general education teacher	11/05	1 year	as needed	Rm. 7
Testing accommodations in regular class, State/district assessments	11/05	1 year	as needed	Rm. 7
Assistive technology assessment re: Adaptations for written language	11/05	as needed	as needed	Rm. 5, Rm. 7

Extent to which student will not participate with nondisabled students in regular class   one hour per day

Explanation   Steven will participate in spelling activities in the regular classroom and receive additional spelling instruction in the resource room. He will begin written expression assignments in the regular class and receive support in editing and revising in the resource room.

Annual Goals and Progress Measures

1. WRITTEN LANGUAGE. Steven will write a 5-sentence paragraph with (a) correct capitalization and punctuation and (b) topic, supporting, and concluding sentences.

2. SPELLING. Steven's spelling skills will improve as evidenced by his performance in weekly spelling tests in the regular classroom.

EVALUATION. Portfolio assessment of Steven's work samples. All writing assignments and spelling tests will be graded with the criteria used for general education students.

continued

FIGURE 2-5   continued

Parents/guardians will be informed of student's progress via   <u>monthly progress reports and regular report cards</u>

As appropriate, the following factors were considered in the development of this IEP:
- ❏ for students whose behavior impedes learning, positive behavioral interventions, strategies and supports
- ❏ for students with limited English proficiency, language needs
- ❏ for students who are blind or visually impaired, instruction in and use of Braille and appropriate reading and writing media
- ☒ communication needs of the student
- ❏ for students who are deaf or hard of hearing, language and communication needs
- ☒ assistive technology devices and services

Transition Services
- ❏ Transition service needs included in this IEP
- ❏ Transition service needs described in attached Individualized Transition Plan
- ❏ Student has been informed of his or her rights

Signatures
My due process rights have been explained to me.
- ☒ I consent to the IEP.
- ❏ I consent to portions of the IEP as described on the attached form.
- ❏ I do not consent to the IEP.

Helen Downing-Cooper	*11/15/05*
Parent/Guardian's Signature	Date
Steven Cooper	*11/15/05*
Student's Signature	Date
Marianne Kemp	*11/15/05*
Signature of Administrator/Designee	Date
Connie Hernandez	*11/15/05*
Signature of General Education Teacher	Date
Edward Johnson	*11/15/05*
Signature of Special Education Teacher/Specialist	Date
Marsha Humphries, Advocate	*11/15/05*
Signature/Title of Additional Participant	Date
Signature/Title of Additional Participant	Date
Signature of Interpreter	Date

Note: Developed by Tamarah M. Ashton, Ph.D., California State University, Northridge.

Annual evaluation of the IEP is most typical, but it may be necessary to determine the appropriateness of the IEP well before it is a year old. The IEP team should be open to reconsidering the special educational needs of a student if one of the team members believes that the IEP is in need of revision. Data should be systematically collected and presented to the team for its review prior to the actual team meeting. Any changes made in the IEP must be approved by the student's parents prior to implementation. The annual evaluation of the student's progress can be conducted in the same manner as that used for the initial assessment of the student. However, this is neither practical nor necessary with the majority of special students. The annual evaluation is much more specific; it is concerned with the student's progress toward the goals stated in the IEP. Much of the evaluation information required will have been collected on an ongoing basis during the school year by the general and special educators providing services to the student. The continuous collection of data allows teachers to make immediate modifications in the student's instructional program. Also, continuous data are more sensitive to the small

Inclusion Tips for the Teacher

IEP Responsibilities of General Educators

General education teachers have many questions about IEPs and their responsibilities in the IEP process. Some of the most commonly asked questions (and their answers) appear here.

- *Does the classroom teacher participate in the development and review of IEPs?* Under current federal law, general education teachers are required to serve on the IEP team when students they are (or will be) teaching are being considered for special education services or when their IEP is being reviewed. When students with disabilities receive both general and special education services, the teacher in the general education classroom is expected to aid in the development of the IEP. At the elementary level, the classroom teacher is required to participate because he or she is probably the only general education teacher working with the student. At the secondary level, however, a staff member such as the school counselor is often selected to serve as the classroom teachers' representative on the IEP team.

- *Is the IEP a contract? Are teachers legally responsible for meeting each of the goals on the IEP?* The IEP is a contract because schools and agencies are legally responsible for providing the services indicated on the IEP. However, teachers are not held legally accountable for accomplishing IEP goals and objectives. Nevertheless, teachers do have the responsibility for making good-faith efforts to assist the students in accomplishing the goals and objectives stated in the IEP (Strickland & Turnbull, 1993).

- *Do IEPs cover both special education and general education programs?* The IEP must state an explanation of the extent,

if any, to which the student will not participate in the general education program. Goals and objectives are written for only those portions of the school day in which students require specialized services. The IEP must also include information about supplementary aids and services and other supports and program modifications that will be provided in general education classes or other education-related settings to enable children with disabilities to be educated with nondisabled children to the maximum extent appropriate. If major adaptations are made in general education classroom procedures, then those will be reflected in IEP goals and objectives. However, for most students with special needs, general education goals are not needed.

- *Who is responsible for implementing the IEP?* The IEP states who is responsible for implementing the special education program to meet each of the annual goals. In most cases this will be the special educator. However, if the IEP contains general education class or even home goals, then the general education teacher or the parent may be named as one of the persons responsible.

- *Who may see the IEP?* Copies of the IEP are available to the student's parents and each of the persons responsible for implementing portions of the IEP. Many districts do not distribute copies of the IEP to all teachers working with the student because of the cost of copying and because IEPs are considered confidential documents that must be stored securely. To see the IEPs of students included in the general education program, teachers should contact the special educator or their school principal.

---

incremental changes in performance often observed with students with special needs.

Information should also be collected on a regular basis from the parents of students with special needs. It is important to continue their involvement with the team and elicit their perceptions of their child's progress in school and at home. When data are collected from parents, it is appropriate to share information with them about the school performance of the student.

The IEP is a formal instructional plan designed for and based on the specific individual educational needs of each student with disabilities. It should clearly communicate to all team members the exact nature of the student's educational program. The IEP coordinates the efforts of the team by specifying what the team is attempting to accomplish, who is responsible for implementing each component of the plan, which evaluation procedures will be used to determine the student's progress, and how parents will be regularly informed of progress. Development of the IEP requires the team to carefully review each student's needs. The time spent in this analysis helps to improve the quality and appropriateness of the educational expe-

riences provided for each student with special needs. See the "Inclusion Tips for the Teacher" section to learn more about the responsibilities of general educators in the IEP process.

TYPES OF SERVICES FOR STUDENTS WITH DISABILITIES

One of the most important components of the IEP is a statement of the types of services the student will receive to support his or her attainment of the instructional goals specified on the annual plan. Possible options include four different types of services: special education, related services, supplementary aids and services, and program modifications and/or supports for school personnel.

Special education is defined by law as "specially designed instruction, at no cost to parents, to meet the unique needs of a child with a disability." As the next major section of this chapter describes, special education programs range from full inclusion with specially designed instruction provided by a special educator within the general education classroom setting to part-time, specially designed instruction in resource room settings to more intensive instructional services in special classes or even special schools or residential programs.

Some students require more than special education services. To benefit from special education, additional **related services** may be needed. In the words of the law, related services are those supports "required to assist a child with a disability to benefit from special education." An obvious example is the related service of transportation. If a student who travels by wheelchair cannot board the regular school bus, he or she will not be able to benefit from the specially designed instruction that awaits at the school. Special transportation arrangements are needed to provide access to special education services.

There are many different types of related services, including these examples:

- Transportation,
- Speech-language pathology,
- Audiology services for students with hearing impairments,
- Psychological services,
- Physical and occupational therapy,
- Recreation (including therapeutic recreation services),
- Early identification and assessment of disabilities,
- Counseling services (including rehabilitation counseling),
- Orientation and mobility services for students with visual impairments,
- Diagnostic medical services,
- School health services,
- Social work services,
- Parent counseling and training.

Supplementary aids and services are another type of support for students with disabilities. According to the law, these are "aids, services, and other supports that are provided in regular education classes or other education-related settings to enable children with disabilities to be educated with nondisabled children to the maximum extent appropriate." Thus, while related services allow students with disabilities to benefit from *special* education, supplementary aids and services allow students to take part in *general* education. One good example of a supplementary support is the provision of assistive technology to students with disabilities who receive at least part of their education in the general education classroom. In the sample IEP that appeared in Figure 2-5, one of the services planned for Steven was an assistive technology assessment to determine if specialized technology could help him with classroom writing tasks. If that assessment shows that some type of assistive technology would be useful, that technology would be provided to Steven and he and his teacher would be trained in its use by the assistive technology specialist serving their school. Other examples of supplementary aids and services are peer tutors, taped textbooks for students with visual impairments, and

classroom desks that meet the needs of students who travel by wheelchairs.

The fourth type of services that can be specified on the IEP are **program modifications and/or supports for school personnel**. These options are not spelled out in the law, but their meaning appears quite clear. Program modifications are any type of change made in the general education program to support the successful progress of a student with disabilities. One example might be a shortened school day for a student with a chronic illness who lacks the stamina to complete the entire day. In contrast, supports for school personnel are services provided to teachers and other school employees. Possibilities include training for teachers in how to use special devices and equipment needed by students with disabilities and part-time assistance from an instructional aide or community volunteer to help supervise classroom or recess activities.

SPECIAL EDUCATION PROGRAM OPTIONS

Special education placement options vary in the opportunities afforded to students with special needs for participation in the general education program. Some programs permit students with disabilities to spend their entire school day in the general education classroom (least restrictive), whereas other programs exclude the students from any interaction with their general education class peers (most restrictive). The remainder of the programs fall between these two extremes. Each type of program is designed to serve students with disabilities with a specific type or intensity of educational need.

The IEP team is responsible for ensuring that each student receives educational services in the most appropriate setting that is also the Least Restrictive Environment (LRE). Although current federal law requires that the IEP attempt to meet the needs in a way that enables the student "to be involved in and progress in the general curriculum" with their "nondisabled" peers, the general education classroom is not the LRE for all students. If the educational needs of a student with disabilities cannot be fully met in the general education program, the IEP team is responsible for considering the appropriateness of other placement options. For some students with special needs, the special class or even a special school is the LRE. The majority of special students, however, can benefit from spending at least part of their school day in the general education classroom.

Professionals and advocates interested in specific disability groups often have divergent perspectives regarding the educational needs of students with disabilities. They also have different views regarding the services that general and special education programs should provide to meet these educational needs. On the one hand, advocates for students with severe disabilities are most concerned about the social outcomes for these students rather than their academic performance (Hocutt, 1996). They have much less of a concern regarding the students' meeting the academic expectations of the general curriculum and are primarily interested in improvements in (a) the social skills of the students with disabilities, (b) the attitudes of the nondisabled students toward those with disabilities, and (c) the development of positive relationships and friendships between students with disabilities and their nondisabled peers (Machado, Belew, Jans, & Cunha, 1996). These groups propose that the educational needs of students with disabilities can be met while they are fully included in the general education program.

Advocates for students with learning disabilities have a somewhat different outlook. They are concerned with the ability of these students to perform academic tasks and the need for access to a continuum of special education services that provides the IEP team with placement options to ensure that students develop their academic skills (e.g., Zigmond, Jenkins, Fuchs, Deno, & Fuchs, 1995). It is important that IEP teams consider these different perspectives when identifying specific goals for students with disabilities, choosing the appropriate education services and

placements for these students, and evaluating their progress. It is also important to note that the different perspectives present quite different instructional demands on the general education teacher (i.e., arranging and supervising socialization activities versus providing specific individualized academic instruction) that may influence the implementation of the IEP.

When the IEP team considers the appropriate placement for each student with special needs, it generally has a number of special education program or placement options available at the school or within the district. Options may vary from district to district, but those noted in chapter 1 (Figure 1-4) are typical for students in the K–12 school levels. They range in intensity from residential schools to full-time participation in the general education class. Other programs, such as home-based programs in which special educators work directly with parents, are available for infants and toddlers or preschool students; community-based vocational programs may be offered for older students with severe disabilities.

As Figure 2-6 illustrates, three major categories of placement options are available for students with disabilities. In

---

FIGURE 2-6   Program Options

the first, general education options, students with special needs are members of general education classes and the general education teacher takes primary responsibility for their instruction. These programs serve the greatest number of students with disabilities. In the second option, special class options, students are members of special education classes, and the special education teacher takes primary responsibility for their educational program. The third option, more restrictive options, serves the smallest number of students with disabilities. It is designed for the students with the most severe, comprehensive, and specialized needs.

General Education Class Options

General Education Class.   The general education classroom is the least restrictive of all the educational placement options. Students not currently identified as having special needs spend their entire school day in the regular classroom; neither the students nor their teachers receive any direct special education services. The majority of students with special needs begin their educational careers in this setting. For most students identified as having disabilities, the goal is to provide appropriate educational programs to assist in developing the skills necessary for returning to the general education classroom. For some students with more severe disabilities, this goal may not be realistic.

Indirect services that do not relate to any particular student with special needs may be provided to general education teachers and their classes. For example, in-service training opportunities may be offered to teachers by the special education staff in areas such as special education legislation, referral procedures, or techniques for working with students with learning or behavioral problems. Students enrolled in general education classes may participate in special assemblies that explain various types of disabilities and encourage the acceptance of all individuals, regardless of their unique needs. Special education teachers may visit elementary or secondary classes to discuss alternative communication systems, such as Braille, sign language, or electronic communication devices. Students in the general education class may be trained by special educators to serve as classroom assistants or cross-age tutors in general or special education classrooms.

Students placed in the general education class may have received special education services at one time but now be able to function appropriately without special services. For instance, a student with a hearing impairment may have received special education services in the past but is now fitted with an appropriate hearing aid, trained to use and care for it properly, and able to supplement the information received via the hearing aid with speechreading skills. A student with a visual impairment may now have appropriate glasses, magnification devices, or other devices or skills that permit independent functioning in the general education classroom. Students who have been identified as having special needs at one time do not necessarily require special services throughout their entire educational careers. Many acquire the skills needed to function in the general education program without special support.

General Education Class with Consultation to the Teacher.   In this placement option, the student with special needs spends the entire school day in the general education classroom and receives no direct special education services. Instead, the general education teacher receives services; a special educator provides consultation on the needs of special students included in the teacher's classroom.

Consultation services can take a number of forms. A specialist, such as a special education consultant or a school psychologist, may assist the teacher in designing and implementing a behavior management program for a student with classroom behavior problems. An itinerant teacher of students with visual impairments may furnish the teacher with large-print, Braille, or tape-recorded versions of class textbooks and provide information on how these materials can best be used. The special education resource teacher may help the teacher modify the regular reading or math program for a student with learning disabilities.

Specialists who provide consultation services typically have extensive experience in both general and special education settings. They are aware of the needs of general education teachers and special students. Their goal is to assist the teacher in gaining access to appropriate materials and developing the skills and confidence required to meet the students' educational needs, not to evaluate classroom instruction or management. General education teachers should feel free to call on special education consultants for aid in adapting instruction, managing behavior problems, and promoting social acceptance of students with special needs. Whereas the general education teacher has the primary instructional responsibility for students with special needs, the consultant can help ensure their successful inclusion in the general education program.

General Education Class with Instruction Delivered by the Specialist.   This type of service is a relatively recent innovation in most schools and districts. In this option, students with disabilities receive special education services within the general education classroom. Instead of leaving their classroom to visit a specialist, students remain where they are. The specialist comes to the students' class and delivers services there.

The special education services are provided in the general education classroom by a special educator working alone or with a trained assistant. These staff members "can support integrated special students in many ways, including (a) making adaptations when needed; (b) assisting the classroom teacher in working with a student; (c) coaching nondisabled peers; (d) providing direct instruction; and (e) facilitating positive interactions among students" (Hamre-Nietupski, McDonald, & Nietupski, 1992, p. 8).

The amount of support provided to students who are included full time in general education classrooms depends on the needs of each individual student. For students with mild learning problems, the specialist may visit the classroom for a brief period each day to deliver specialized instruction to target students and perhaps some of their peers with similar needs. For students with more severe disabilities, support may be needed throughout the entire school day. In many cases, the amount and nature of services required will change over the course of the school year. For example, the specialist may be able to reduce time spent in the classroom once a cadre of peer tutors or other volunteers has been trained to assist the special student. Or the general education teacher may feel that he or she has developed the skills necessary to work with the students with special needs, thereby reducing the need for specialist support.

The advantages of this program option have been described by educators concerned with a range of students with special needs, from those with milder disabilities (e.g., Wiedmeyer & Lehman, 1991) to those with more severe disabilities (Hamre-Nietupski et al., 1992). Benefits include the opportunity for students with disabilities to have continuous interactions with their general education peers, reduction of the stigma associated with having a disability and receiving special education services, increased opportunities for exposure to the general education curriculum, and greater probability that the skills learned will be useful in other "normalized" settings. These educators also note that the success of this type of program is dependent on continuous cooperative planning between general and special educators to ensure that the educational needs of all students in the classroom are met.

General Education Class with Co-Teaching.

A variation of the specialist teaching in a general education class is the co-teaching model. In this option, a general educator and a special educator co-teach a class composed of students with and without disabilities. For example, if the class includes 30 students, 20 may be typical students and 10 students may be identified with disabilities. The teachers share responsibility for all the students in the class, with the special educator providing specialized interventions for students

with special needs, as required. Walsh and Jones (2004) report that instruction in co-taught classrooms is more likely to reflect the general education curriculum and support the development of critical thinking skills than instruction in self-contained special education classes.

General Education Class and Resource Room or Itinerant Services.

In this service option, special education services are generally provided to special students in a setting outside the general education classroom. However, the students continue to spend the majority of their school day in the general education class.

The resource room is usually located within the student's regular neighborhood school. At a regularly scheduled time each day (or several times a week), students leave their general education classroom to participate in special instruction in the resource room. Resource programs, common in both elementary and secondary schools, may serve several types of special students (e.g., those with learning disabilities, physical impairments, mild mental retardation), or they may limit service to only students with one particular disability.

Most typically, resource room programs include different types of students with special needs. In these cross-categorical or multicategorical resource rooms, educators no longer rely on the idea that the student's disability determines the educational needs of that student. One resource teacher may provide educational programs for several groups of students, including those identified as having physical impairments, learning disabilities, behavioral disorders, and mild mental retardation. This capability exists because the educational needs of these students are often quite similar despite their different disabilities.

Consultation services, such as those described earlier, are often provided for the general education teachers of the students with special needs enrolled in a resource room program. These services can assist the teacher and help coordinate general education and resource instructional activities.

The services provided by itinerant special education teachers, who travel from school to school, are managed in somewhat the same way as those of resource programs. Students with special needs may spend the majority of their day in the general education classroom but leave the classroom daily (or several times a week) to receive the services of itinerant teachers, such as speech and language clinicians. Whereas resource room teachers generally serve only students with disabilities who spend the majority of their day in the general education class, itinerant teachers may also serve students enrolled in a special class.

Resource and itinerant teachers serve the majority of the students with disabilities receiving special education services today. They supplement and support the general education program by providing assistance to students with disabilities and their general education classroom teachers. Although students with special needs usually leave their general education classrooms to receive special education services, special educators (or their instructional aides) occasionally teach small instructional groups within the general education classroom. As noted in the previous section, in this service arrangement, the special student is considered to be fully included and receives all instruction, both general and special education, within the general education classroom.

Special Class Options

Special Class and General Education Class. Special classes are located within regular elementary or secondary schools. Students receiving service in this placement option spend the majority of their school day in the special class and some time each day in the general education classroom. Participation in the general education class can vary from approximately half a day to only a few minutes. This is the most restrictive of the educational environments in which the student still spends time in the general education program.

Students with disabilities placed in this program option need intensive special education services. The student's involvement in the general education program is planned in curriculum areas in which success is fairly certain. Participation in general education for such students is limited to the period of time in which they can function successfully without becoming frustrated or creating a disruption.

Special classes can be operated for students in any of the categories of special education (e.g., students identified as having mental retardation, physical impairments, or behavioral disorders). General education teachers working with students in this option generally have consultation services available to assist them in designing and implementing appropriate instructional programs.

Full-time Special Class and Social Integration. An increasing number of students with severe disabilities are being educated on regular school campuses at all levels of education. This trend provides educators with the opportunity to integrate these individuals with their typical age peers whenever appropriate. Even if students do not attend regular academic classes, it is possible for them to participate in social activities such as lunch periods, assemblies, or recreational activities. Such activities offer students with severe disabilities the opportunity to interact with other students and gain the skills needed to function independently. Some schools have a reverse inclusion program in which general education students participate in activities in the special class. These programs are particularly appropriate for preschool and early elementary students.

Full-Time Special Class. Students placed in this program option are no longer included in the general education program; instead, they spend their entire school day in the special class. Special class programs are generally available at both elementary and secondary levels for students with different types of disabilities. Special classes may have different focuses, but the main goal of all such classes is to provide an intensive program to develop skills that will prepare students for adulthood and, if possible, inclusion in the general education program.

Special classes for students with physical, language, visual, and hearing impairments may be concentrated at the lower elementary level. These students are readily identified at an early age, and providing intensive instruction in preschool or as soon as the students enter the elementary grades can enable their inclusion in the general education program at an earlier age. Special classes for these students at the secondary level are somewhat less common; by this time students have either acquired the necessary skills to function effectively in the general education program, or they have been placed in special school programs.

Special classes for students with behavioral disorders, mental retardation, and learning disabilities are most typically found at the upper elementary, middle school, and high school levels. As these students progress through school, the discrepancy between their performance and that of their peers becomes apparent, particularly if they do not receive appropriate educational services. The special class provides intensive services to students with serious educational needs that cannot be successfully met in the general education classroom.

At one time, special classes served as the primary special education program option between the general education class and the special school options. Their use has diminished as other less restrictive programs, such as the resource room and teacher consultants, have become popular.

More Restrictive Options

Special School. Special schools are generally the most restrictive placement option offered by the public school system. Students are placed in this option on the premise that they cannot currently benefit from inclusion in the general education program. This program typically serves students with more severe disabilities (e.g., those with multiple disabilities, severe behavioral disorders, severe mental retardation). In the past, one justification for the concentration of students in one special school was the centralization of specialized services. It was thought that when psychologists, social workers, and physical and occupational therapists were housed in one building, they would be available to assist special education teachers in meeting the educational needs of the students. However, concerns over the segregation of these students from their age peers have led to the mandated closing of many special schools and the distribution of the students into integrated regular school campuses (Pumpian, 1988; Sailor, Gee, & Karasoff, 1993).

Residential Program.   Residential programs primarily serve two groups of students with disabilities. The first includes those who need intensive services that cannot be provided in less restrictive special education settings within the general education program. Students in this group may be those with severe behavioral disorders, severe or profound mental retardation, and severe multiple disabilities. These students may require specialized educational services and medical care that cannot be provided either in public schools or by their parents at home. In the residential setting, the 24-hour program permits the coordination of medical, psychological, educational, and other services.

The other students served in residential facilities are those who reside in a sparsely populated area that cannot practically offer a special program to serve their educational needs. When schools are so far from home that students cannot travel to school on a daily basis, the placement becomes residential. Placements of this type are becoming much less frequent as communities continue to expand the special education services offered locally.

As school districts have assumed more responsibility for offering appropriate educational programs to all students with disabilities, the role of the residential school has changed. For example, a few years ago a residential school may have served all the students with visual impairments in a state. Today, the majority of these students attend local school programs. Fewer students live at a residential facility, and those who do have severe or multiple disabilities.

The residential setting is the most restrictive special education setting because the students do not have regular contact with typical peers. In many cases they are also restricted from normal community and home contacts. However, for some students with very special needs, this is the least restrictive placement in which they can function successfully.

Home and Hospital Services.   A relatively small number of students are provided their education at home or in a

hospital setting. This arrangement is generally not permanent, but it may occur for various periods of time each year depending on the needs of the particular students. These students may have physical impairments, health impairments, or emotional or behavioral disorders that interfere with their attendance in classes at school. Typically a teacher visits the student several times a week to provide instruction and furnish the educational materials needed by the student. If the students have been included in the general education program or are capable of completing regular class assignments, the general education teacher may be asked to assist in providing assignments and materials to the teacher of home/hospitalized students.

Programs for Infants and Preschoolers with Disabilities

Federal laws include provisions designed to ensure preschoolers (ages 3 through 5) receive appropriate special education services and to encourage similar services for infants and toddlers (birth through age 2). These services typically involve a multidisciplinary, interagency program that coordinates a wide variety of services for young children with or at risk for disabilities and their families. States design programs in which various education and human service agencies collaborate to provide services such as medical and educational assessment, speech and language intervention, physical therapy, and parent counseling and training. The early intervention services are identified and implemented according to an Individualized Family Services Plan (IFSP) that is developed by a multidisciplinary team that includes the child's parents. Key elements of these programs are (a) the early identification and resolution of problems that may contribute to developmental delays in order to maximize the child's potential for independent living in society and (b) the coordination of these efforts with the programs for school-age students to improve the transition of young children from early childhood to school programs.

Many program options are available to students with special needs. Districts provide a continuum of services ranging from the general education classroom to more intense separate programs. Most students with disabilities, however, are able to succeed in the general education program if provided with appropriate support services.

In chapter 3, we will look more closely at students with special needs, their learning needs, and the challenges they provide to general education teachers when they are included in their classrooms.

Things to Remember

- The goal of the various teams serving students with special needs is to ensure that students are provided an appropriate education based on their individual abilities and needs.
- Teams serving students with special needs are composed of school administrators, general and special education teachers, parents, students with special needs (when appropriate), and other professionals whose expertise relates to the needs of the student.
- Teams serving students with special needs identify and evaluate students with disabilities, develop the IEP, determine an appropriate placement, and periodically evaluate student progress. Teams also assist the general education teacher in meeting the educational needs of other students with special needs who may be experiencing difficulty within the general education classroom.
- Placement of the student with special needs must be in the LRE for that student.
- Individualized Education Programs include information about the student's current performance, the goals of the educational program, necessary special services and placement, an explanation of the amount of time the student will not participate in the general education classroom, and procedures for evaluating and reporting student progress.
- The IEP, including the student's placement, is typically evaluated at least annually. No placement should be considered permanent.

- The special student's disability does not indicate the appropriate program or placement. Each student's placement must be based on his or her special needs in the areas of academics, classroom behavior, and social performance.
- Consultation is generally available to teachers working with students with special needs in the general education program. Teachers should request this service if it is needed.
- Special education consultants and teacher assistance teams can help teachers develop the skills needed to provide interventions for students with problems; if the pre-referral interventions are successful, these students may not require special education services.
- Prereferral interventions include the collection of data to describe the learning problem, collaboration with colleagues and parents, classroom modifications, and use of available general education and community resources. The most common types of classroom modifications are curricular, instructional, management, and environmental adaptations.
- General and special educators share responsibility for the education of students with special needs included in the general education program.

ACTIVITIES

1. Visit a local school that provides services for students with disabilities. What are the school's teams that serve students with special needs called? Who serves on the teams? How often do they meet? Do they consider only students with disabilities? Gather information that will help you explain to another educator how these teams operate. If possible, obtain permission to observe a team meeting.

2. Interview two individuals from a local school who serve on the same team serving students with special needs. Select persons who represent different roles—for example, a parent and a special educator, a general education teacher and a psychologist, or a speech-language clinician and a counselor. Compare their opin-

ions of the operation and effectiveness of the team. You may want to ask questions such as these: What is the purpose of the team? Are all team members encouraged to participate in deliberations? Are assessment results explained so that all members can understand them? Are the IEPs that are developed appropriate to the needs of students with special needs? Is each student's progress reviewed periodically? Summarize your findings, noting whether there is agreement between the perceptions of the two team members.

3. Read two journal articles on collaboration, the team approach, or consultation as it relates to the education of special students. The journals *Exceptional Children* and *Remedial and Special Education* often address these

topics. Write a brief summary and evaluation of each article you read.

CD-ROM Activities

View segments of two video case studies on the CD-ROM Inclusive Classrooms. *In the case featuring the preschool classroom, view the video clip entitled "Team Collaborate." In the case featuring the middle school student, view the first video clip ("Introduce Team"). Answer these questions based on what you've seen:*

- *Identify the professionals who are collaborating on these teams. Are both special and general education teachers involved?*

- *Are there any professionals present who are not teachers? For example, are physical therapists, speech-language pathologists, or school counselors part of either team.*

---

4. Contact a local school district to find out what types of special education programs are offered. Are resource rooms, special classes, and all the programs described in this chapter available? How have program options changed in the past 5 years? Compare your findings with those of someone who has investigated another district. Explain why programs may vary from district to district.

5. Several organizations are designed to serve parents of special students. Two of the most prominent are the Learning Disabilities Association of America (LDA), whose national headquarters is at 4156 Library Road, Pittsburgh, PA 15234, and the Arc of the United States (formerly the Association for Retarded Citizens), located at 1010 Wayne Avenue, Suite 650, Silver Spring, MD 20910. Does your community have local chapters of these organizations? Contact a local or national office of LDA or the Arc to learn the purpose of these groups. Do they provide information about special students? Serve as advocates for parents? Work for better special education legislation? What should classroom teachers know about these organizations?

Special Students, Special Needs

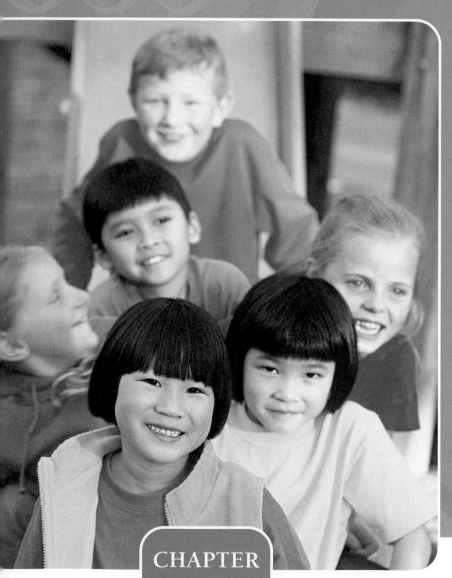

CHAPTER

3

- Jody's vision is limited; her textbooks, worksheets, and other reading materials are in large print.
- Luis has diabetes; he takes medication and must carefully monitor his diet and physical activity.
- George has poor reading skills; he uses taped textbooks for reading assignments, and he is learning to "take notes" in class with a tape recorder.
- Tom is impulsive and often leaves his seat, speaks out in class, and interrupts the work of other students; he and his teacher have set up a program to help Tom control these behaviors.
- Annette is very bright and academically far ahead of her peers; she works on special assignments in subjects that interest and challenge her.

LOOKING AHEAD

This chapter is all about the special needs of students with disabilities and others identified as possibly needing adaptations in the general education classroom. Before reading about these students, consider the questions that follow:

- Think about the students just described—Jody, Luis, George, Tom, and Annette. Which students have special needs in the area of academic performance?
- Which students have special emotional or classroom behavior needs? What about special social needs?
- Do any of these students show special physical needs?
- Do you think any of these students are gifted or talented? What evidence would you offer to support your opinion?

To answer these questions online, go to the Students' Stories module in Chapter 3 of the Companion Website.

Special students such as those described in the "Students' Stories" can succeed in the general education classroom with the assistance of the teacher and other members of the team. Because the educational needs of these students are not radically different from those of their peers, they can participate in many aspects of the general education program without special educational interventions. In areas where adaptations are necessary, support services are available to the student and to the classroom teacher. Special materials and equipment are provided, such as the large-print books needed by students with visual impairments and the tape recorders and taped texts needed by students with reading problems. The school nurse assists students with physical and health needs. The resource teacher works with the classroom teacher to set up behavior change programs for disruptive students and enrichment activities for advanced students. In this way the members of the team collaborate to meet the needs of special students within the general education classroom.

SPECIAL STUDENTS

Special students include those with disabilities, gifted and talented students, culturally and linguistically diverse individuals, and students at risk for school failure. Most special students have relatively mild learning problems and are thus able to succeed in the general education classroom.

Students with special needs make up a sizable portion of the school community. In a collection of 100 students, there may be 9 or 10 with disabilities and 3 to 5 who are gifted; depending on the community, any number of students may be from diverse groups. Learning disabilities, mild retardation, behavioral disorders, and speech and language impairments are the most common disabilities; physical, health, visual, and hearing impairments are relatively rare. Mild disabilities are much more frequent than severe disabilities. It is likely that at least 75% of the special education population has mild learning needs that can be met, at least in part, in a general education setting.

It is important to note that not all disabilities are equally represented in the general education classroom. As Figure 3-1 illustrates, students with more severe and comprehensive disabilities (such as mental retardation and multiple disabilities) are more likely to be placed in separate classes and other separate environments. In addition, even for groups such as students with learning disabilities and those with speech or language impairments for whom inclusion is the most common practice, some students require the more intensive, specialized services available in settings such as special classes.

Students with Learning Disabilities

Teachers often use the word *puzzling* to describe students with **learning disabilities.** These students are average, even bright, learners who encounter difficulties in specific school subjects. Because they seem capable and do learn some things quickly and easily, their failure to learn in other areas is perplexing.

Students with learning disabilities have adequate intelligence. Their learning problem is not due to hearing or visual impairments, physical or health impairments, or emotional disturbance. The reason for their poor school performance is much more subtle and elusive: They have difficulty processing information. **Information processing** (sometimes called psychological processing) refers to the way in which persons receive, store, and express information. Students with learning disabilities may have difficulty receiving information because of attention or perception problems, their memory may be poor, or they may have difficulty communicating information to others because of expressive language problems. Students with learning disabilities may use poor strategies for learning (Robinson & Deshler, 1995; Swanson & Cooney, 1996); for example, such students may be passive learners who fail to become actively involved in the learning task (Torgesen, 1977). When given a list of spelling words to learn or a textbook chapter to read, such students may simply stare at the page, or read and reread it, without actively studying its content.

Despite adequate general ability, students with learning disabilities experience school learning problems. They appear able to achieve, but their performance in school falls short of expectations. Even more perplexing than this discrepancy between expected and actual achievement is the variability of performance that characterizes individuals with learning disabilities. They are successful in some areas but have great difficulty in others. In addition, their performance may vary from day to day; teachers often comment that students with learning disabilities appear to know something one day but forget it the next.

Many different labels have been used to describe students with learning disabilities. Although the emphasis today is on educational terminology, it is still possible to encounter medical terms such as *neurologically impaired*. Labels such as this refer to the theory that learning disabilities are due to some type of damage to the central nervous system. There are also medical terms for common academic problems: *dyslexia* (difficulty in reading), *dyscalculia* (difficulty in math), and *dysgraphia* (difficulty in writing). More recent additions to the medical terminology associated with learning disabilities (and with behavioral disorders) are *attention deficit disorder* (ADD) and *attention deficit hyperactivity disorder* (ADHD).

Much debate has arisen over what constitutes a learning disability and how the condition should be defined. One widely accepted definition, which has been incorporated into several

| FIGURE 3-1 | Special Education Services for Students with Different Types of Disabilities |

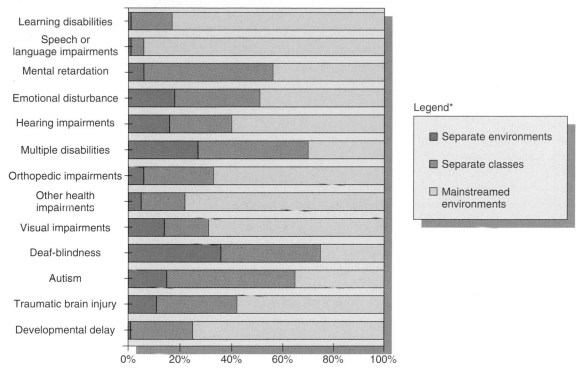

Mainstreamed environments include regular classes and resource rooms; *separate environments* include separate schools, residential facilities, and home and hospital services.

Note: From data provided in *Twenty-fourth Annual Report to Congress on the Implementation of The Individuals with Disabilities Education Act* by U. S. Department of Education, 2002, Washington, DC: Author.

state and federal special education laws, is that of the National Advisory Committee on Handicapped Children (1968):

A disorder in one or more of the basic psychological processes involved in understanding or in using language, spoken or written, which may manifest itself in an imperfect ability to listen, think, speak, read, write, spell, or to do mathematical calculations. . . . The term does not include children who have learning problems which are primarily the result of visual, hearing, or motor handicaps, of mental retardation, or of environmental, cultural, or economic disadvantage.

This definition, like most definitions of learning disabilities, excludes other disabilities and points to information processing deficits as the reason for poor school performance. In the general education classroom, students with learning disabilities may have special needs in the areas of academic, behavioral, social, and physical performance.

Academic Needs. Students with learning disabilities typically experience difficulty in one or more of the basic school subjects. Young children may enter school with poor listening or speaking skills. In the early grades, acquisition of language arts skills such as reading and spelling may prove difficult. For most elementary-aged students with learning disabilities, reading is the major stumbling block in academic achievement. However, some fare well in this area yet have specific disabilities in other subjects such as math or handwriting.

The basic skill problems of students with learning disabilities persist into middle school and high school (and beyond). These students may fail to acquire reading, writing, and perhaps math skills equal to those of their peers. Although able to cope with the content of secondary-level courses, many students with learning disabilities achieve poorly because of their inability to read texts and complete written assignments. Those with poor listening skills find lecture presentations a serious problem.

Behavioral Needs. Some students with learning disabilities, particularly in the elementary grades, are characterized by a high activity level. Such students may be constantly in motion and, as a result, may have difficulty paying attention to school tasks. Others who are not overactive may instead be impulsive and distractible; they, too, may have difficulty focusing their attention on appropriate aspects of the learning environment.

Older students with learning disabilities often have behavioral needs in the areas of classroom conduct and study skills. They may be unable to work independently (at least in part because of poor academic skills). Their attention span may continue to be a problem, and their organizational skills may be poor. In addition, some evidence exists of a link between juvenile delinquency and learning disabilities in adolescents (Leone, Rutherford, & Nelson, 1991a,1991b).

Social Needs.   The social arena is another area in which students with learning disabilities may perform poorly. Research indicates that some children and adolescents with learning disabilities have social perception deficits (Bryan, 1997; Bryan, Pearl, Donahue, Bryan, & Pflaum, 1983). That is, they may lack the skills needed for understanding and communicating appropriate social messages. Social communication requires not only speech but also an understanding of more subtle cues such as facial expression, vocal inflection, and body language; it becomes particularly important when students enter the peer-conscious world of the adolescent (Lerner, 2003).

Physical Needs.   Students with learning disabilities do not have obvious physical needs; in appearance they are indistinguishable from their peers. However, some students with learning disabilities have motor coordination problems. They may appear clumsy and may perform gross-motor skills, such as running and jumping, poorly. Fine-motor skills such as cutting, manipulating small objects, and mastering the use of pencils and pens may also be troublesome areas. In school, motor problems such as these become evident in physical education and art activities and in academic tasks requiring handwriting.

Special Services.   For students with disabilities severe and comprehensive enough to warrant placement in separate programs, many districts offer special classes. However, the majority of students with learning disabilities remain in general education throughout their educational careers and receive special services on a part-time basis from professionals such as resource teachers. Because students with learning disabilities have average ability and are able to perform as well as general education students in some areas, they are excellent candidates for inclusion.

Students with Behavioral Disorders

Behavioral disorders are a more obvious disability than learning disabilities. Students with behavioral disorders are often described by teachers as behavior problems or troublemakers. They may be rowdy, unruly, disruptive, and even aggressive. Some, whose behavior does not call attention to itself as readily, may appear withdrawn or depressed. All are characterized by inappropriate school behavior. Although most students with behavioral disorders have adequate intelligence as well as acceptable hearing, vision, and physical abilities, they often show poor achievement in academic skills. Some students, however, achieve satisfactorily despite inappropriate classroom behavior.

The term *behavioral disorders* includes a wide range of disabilities. The most severe are seen in students with serious emotional disturbances, such as individuals with psychotic behavior and childhood schizophrenia; such students generally require intensive special education services and are not included in general education instructional programs. However, most students with behavioral disorders have relatively mild problems that can be dealt with successfully in general education. In fact, the special needs of many of these students are virtually identical to those of the problem student found in every classroom.

Even though apparently obvious, the disability of behavioral disorders is difficult to describe and define. It is necessary to decide which behaviors are appropriate and which are not. The problem is further complicated by the fact that all students behave inappropriately at one time or another in their school careers. Kauffman (1977) sidesteps some of these problems by defining students with behavioral disorders as

> those who chronically and markedly respond to their environment in socially unacceptable and/or personally unsatisfying ways but who can be taught more socially acceptable and personally gratifying behavior. (p. 23)

This definition contains several important points. First, behavioral disorders are chronic and severe. The student's behavior must be inappropriate over time, not a one-time occurrence. The student's behavior problem must also be serious; it must in some way impair the student's ability to function in the school environment. Second, behaviors are judged to be inappropriate by either social or personal standards. This allows not only teachers and parents but also students themselves to determine problem behaviors. It also provides for inclusion of behaviors such as withdrawal that may be socially acceptable but are detrimental to the student. Third, Kauffman's definition recognizes that behavior is learned and that students with behavioral disorders are able to acquire more acceptable responses to their environment. This point is crucial for teachers who seek to change the behavior of their students.

The definition proposed by Bower (1969) is included in many special education laws. It describes students with behavioral disorders as those who show at least one of the following characteristics "to a marked extent" and "over a period of time":

1. An inability to learn which cannot be explained by intellectual, sensory, or health factors. . . .

2. An inability to build or maintain satisfactory interpersonal relationships with peers and teachers. . . .

3. Inappropriate types of behaviors or feelings under normal conditions. . . .

4. A general, pervasive mood of unhappiness or depression. . . .

5. A tendency to develop physical symptoms, pains, or fears associated with personal or school problems. (pp. 22–23)

A student need not exhibit all five of these characteristics to be identified as having a behavioral disorder; only one is necessary, although students may meet several of the criteria. This definition stresses the educational aspects of behavioral disorders by focusing on learning problems, student–teacher relationships, and school phobia problems. Like the definition of learning disabilities proposed by the National Advisory Committee on Handicapped Children, the Bower definition contains an exclusion clause: The learning problems of students with behavioral disorders must not be due to retardation, visual or hearing impairments, or health impairments.

The Council for Exceptional Children (1998) is critical of the definition found in current laws and recommends this revision:

Emotional disturbance refers to a condition in which behavioral or emotional responses of an individual in school are so different from his/her generally accepted, age-appropriate, ethnic, or cultural norms that they affect educational performance in such areas as self-care, social relationships, personal adjustment, academic progress, classroom behavior, or work adjustment.

According to CEC, this definition reflects current professional knowledge and research and is endorsed by mental health and education organizations, including CEC's Council for Children with Behavioral Disorders.

As Heward (1996) remarks, definitions of behavioral disorders "require a child's behavior, in order to be considered disordered, to differ markedly (extremely) and chronically (over time) from current social or cultural norms" (p. 286). In the general education classroom, this means that students with behavioral disorders may have special needs in the areas of social and academic, as well as behavioral, performance.

Behavioral Needs.   Children and adolescents with behavioral disorders are a heterogeneous group that exhibits a wide range of inappropriate classroom behaviors. These students may be disobedient, aggressive, or overly shy and retiring. One way to conceptualize this array of possible problem behaviors has been suggested by Quay (1979), who describes four typical patterns or dimensions of disordered behavior: conduct disorder, socialized aggression, immaturity, and anxiety-withdrawal.

Students with conduct disorders are aggressive, defiant, uncooperative, disobedient, and disruptive. Their behavior is judged socially unacceptable by teachers and others in authority. Students falling under the socialized aggression dimension also are perceived as behaving inappropriately. They are socialized in that they belong to gangs, but they participate in delinquent activities such as truancy and theft. Less obvious dimensions are immaturity and anxiety-withdrawal. Immature students appear delayed in development; they may be passive, have a short attention span, appear preoccupied, and daydream. Students characterized by anxiety and withdrawal appear fearful, timid, depressed, and lacking in self-confidence.

Students with behavioral disorders may have difficulty following classroom rules and meeting teachers' expectations for appropriate school conduct. Although aggressive students are the ones most easily and quickly identified by teachers, withdrawn and immature students also require special help. In middle school and high school, the truancy problems of predelinquent and delinquent students complicate their difficulties in meeting school demands.

Social Needs.   Students with behavioral disorders often have trouble establishing interpersonal relationships. Their inappropriate behaviors may make them unattractive to peers and to teachers. They may lack the social skills necessary to make and keep friends. In addition, the self-concept of students with behavioral disorders is often low, especially in individuals who are anxious and withdrawn. And the problem perpetuates itself. Students with poor social skills remain friendless, and their self-esteem suffers; students with low self-esteem are unwilling to risk interpersonal relationships.

Academic Needs.   Students with behavioral disorders, like those with learning disabilities, often experience difficulty with basic school skills (Whelan, 1995). Most studies of the academic achievement of students with behavioral disorders find poor performance in reading, math, and other subjects such as spelling and language (e.g., Rubin & Balow, 1978). Some evidence suggests that math achievement problems may be more serious than reading problems (Bower, 1969). The precise relationship between academic underachievement and inappropriate classroom behavior, however, is difficult to assess. Students may act out or withdraw as a reaction to school failure, or problem behaviors may interfere with successful school learning. In either case, most students with behavioral disorders require instruction in both behavioral and academic skills.

Special Services.   Some students with behavioral disorders require intensive special education services in special classes, special schools, and even residential facilities. Most, however, are able to participate in at least some aspects of regular classroom instruction. Some may spend part of their day in a special class and part in general education. Others take part more fully in general education class activities and receive only part-time special services. The general education classroom is generally the most appropriate placement for students with mild behavioral disorders, provided, of course, that necessary support services are available to students and teachers.

Students with Mild Mental Retardation

Students with mental retardation have comprehensive learning problems. Because of below-average intellectual ability, they may learn slowly and may appear delayed in most areas of school performance when compared with their age peers. Tasks requiring reasoning and abstract thinking may be particularly difficult for them.

Mental retardation is one of the oldest areas of study within the field of special education, and there is general agreement regarding the definition of this disability. According to the American Association on Mental Retardation (2002),

> Mental retardation is a disability characterized by substantial limitations both in intellectual functioning and in adaptive behavior as expressed in conceptual, social, and practical adaptive skills. This disability originates before age 18. (p. 8)

Less-than-average intelligence is central to the concept of mental retardation. Individuals considered retarded are those whose general aptitude for learning is impaired. Intellectual functioning is assessed by intelligence or IQ tests; these measures typically contain several types of verbal and nonverbal reasoning and problem-solving tasks. General ability level is established by comparing the performance of one student with that of others of the same age. Individuals who fall within the lowest 2% to 3% are considered retarded; that is, their intellectual performance is significantly subaverage in comparison to that of their peers. However, as Heward (1996) points out, measurement of intelligence is not an exact science, and it is possible for IQ scores to change significantly over time.

In addition to poor intellectual performance, students must show impaired adaptive behavior in order to be considered mentally retarded. Adaptive behavior, sometimes referred to as social competence, is "the effectiveness or degree with which individuals meet the standards of personal independence and social responsibility expected for their age and cultural group" (Grossman, 1983, p. 1). It is the way in which students meet the expectations of the total social environment, not merely those of the school. Expectations for adaptive behavior vary with the age of the student. Parents expect preschool youngsters to learn to walk, talk, and interact with family members; teachers expect school-aged children to learn to read, write, do math, and interact with peers; society expects adults to be gainfully employed and to get along in the community. Expectations also vary across cultures. For example, while American teachers expect their students to ask questions and participate in discussions, Asian parents may expect their children to be quiet and obedient and listen to adults without asking questions or challenging their authority (Cheng, 1991).

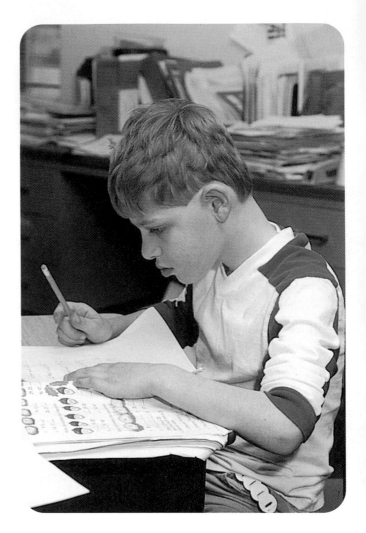

Thus, students with mental retardation are characterized by both below-average intellectual ability and deficits in adaptive behavior. A low IQ score alone is not sufficient to determine retardation; the student's learning problem must be substantiated in the home, neighborhood, and community. The problem must also become apparent during the developmental period (i.e., before age 18). Older persons whose intellectual abilities are impaired by an injury, accident, or illness are not considered mentally retarded.

Within the group of students considered mentally retarded are several levels of abilities. Students with mild retardation, as the term is used in this book, are those who are able to learn basic academic skills. The special needs of students with severe retardation are more serious and comprehensive. Students with severe disabilities may be educated in a full-day special class; such classes are typically located on regular school campuses to facilitate social interactions between students with severe disabilities and typical students. In some cases, however, students with severe disabilities are fully included in general education classes with support from special education personnel. Severe disabilities are discussed more fully in a later section of this chapter.

Many students with mild retardation are able to participate in at least some of the instructional activities of the regular classroom. The special needs of this group, which makes up approximately 80% of the population identified as retarded, are in the areas of academic, behavioral, social, and physical performance.

Academic Needs.   Students with mild retardation generally master academic skills at a slower rate than regular class students of the same age. Because they enter school somewhat behind their peers, they may not be ready to begin formal academic instruction immediately. Individuals with mild retardation are able to acquire basic school skills, but their achievement is below grade-level expectations. Nonetheless, most individuals with mild retardation acquire upper-elementary-level reading and math skills by the completion of their school careers (Kirk & Gallagher, 1979).

Some aspects of school learning are especially troublesome for students with mild retardation. They may have difficulty focusing attention, remembering, and transferring information and skills learned in one setting to another situation. Tasks involving abstract reasoning, problem solving, and creativity pose special problems. For example, students with mild retardation perform less well on arithmetic reasoning tasks than on straightforward computational problems.

In the elementary years, the discrepancy between the age of students with mild retardation and their achievement level is not great. In adolescence, the gap widens. At the secondary level, such students often participate in special programs that stress vocational training. Despite their evident learning needs, students with mild intellectual disabilities may be identified as retarded only during their school years. Outside the school environment, with its academic demands, many individuals with mild retardation do not have obvious needs.

Behavioral Needs.   As a group, students with mild retardation display more problem behaviors than their general education peers, perhaps because of their slower rate of learning. Their repertoire of classroom behavioral skills may be appropriate for their developmental level but not for their age group. Another possible factor is the low tolerance for frustration of many students with mild retardation. Repeated failure in school and social situations contributes to this decreased capacity for handling frustration.

Window on the Web

National Dissemination Center for Children with Disabilities

http://www.nichcy.org

The National Dissemination Center for Children with Disabilities was funded in 2003 by the U.S. Office of Special Education Programs to provide information to the nation on

- IDEA, the nation's special education law;
- No Child Left Behind (as it relates to children with disabilities), and
- Research-based information on effective educational practices.

The Dissemination Center takes the place of an earlier information service, the National Information Center for Children and Youth with Disabilities, but retains many of its features and is adding new resources.

Visit the site to learn about publications related to disabilities (e.g., Basics for Parents, Disability Fact Sheets, News Digests, Research Briefs), connections to research-based information sources, a state-by-state listing of resources, and in-depth information on federal laws. Users of the site with questions about specific topics can go to "FAQS" (Frequently Asked Questions), "A-Z Topics," or "Search for Information." In addition, the site features "En español," which provides resources for Spanish speakers, and "Zigawhat!," an activity area for children described as a "website for learning, connecting, growing, coping, and fun for young people with disabilities and their peers."

Note: Courtesy of National Information Center for Children with Disabilities

Companion Website

For more information, go to the Web Links module in Chapter 3 of the Companion Website.

Social Needs. Students with mild retardation may not be socially accepted by their age peers. Lacking social skills, they may be rejected or ignored. This difficulty in establishing interpersonal relationships may be due to the apparent immaturity of students with mild retardation. Their social skills are not well developed in comparison with those of their age peers, and their problem behaviors may make them unattractive. Also, the play and leisure interests of students with mild retardation may be inappropriate for their age.

Physical Needs. Not all individuals with mild retardation have special physical needs; indeed, some excel in the physical area. However, as a group, these students are somewhat deficient in motor skills. When compared with their age peers, they perform less well in tasks requiring agility, coordination, strength, and dexterity (Bruininks, 1977). In addition, youngsters with mild retardation show visual problems and hearing losses more frequently than do typical students.

Special Services. Students with mild retardation are educated in a range of settings. Some are placed in a special class but may attend general education programs for nonacademic activities. Others are members of general education classes for the majority of the day while receiving part-time special education services. As with all special students, decisions regarding the amount of inclusion for pupils with mild retardation must be made on an individual basis.

Students with Other Disabilities

Many general education classrooms include students with disabilities other than learning disabilities, behavioral disorders, and mild mental retardation. Among these are speech and language impairments, physical and health impairments (including traumatic brain injury), and visual and hearing impairments. Students with ADHD are also frequently served in general education settings. Students with autism spectrum disorder and those with other severe disabilities participate in general education programs in some districts; in others, they receive more comprehensive special education services. For more information about all types of disabilities, visit the National Dissemination Center for Children with Disabilities described in "Window on the Web."

Communication Disorders. Among the most common of all disabilities are **speech and language impairments.** According to Van Riper (1978), speech is considered abnormal "when it deviates so far from the speech of other people that it calls attention to itself, interferes with communication, or causes the speaker or his listeners to be distressed" (p. 43). Articulation disorders, or difficulty with the production of sounds, are the most typical speech problem, especially in young children. Other possible trouble areas include voice problems and disorders of fluency, such as stuttering.

Speech is the production of sounds for the communication of oral language. Oral language includes not only the expression of messages by speaking but also the reception of messages by listening. Students with language impairments may experience difficulty in either or both areas. Some students show an overall delay in language development. Others have particular difficulty with a specific component, such as grammatical structure (syntax) or the meaningful aspects of language (semantics).

In the general education classroom, students with speech and language impairments have special academic and social needs. In addition to receiving special help from speech-language pathologists, they may require instruction in listening skills, vocabulary, grammar, and oral expression. In the social area, students with communication problems may find interpersonal encounters stressful. Such students may need assistance in order to become full participants in classroom social interactions.

Physical and Health Impairments. This group of students is relatively small (less than 1% of the school-aged population) but extremely diverse. **Physical and health impairments** encompass a multitude of different conditions and disabilities that range from mild to severe and from invisible to obvious. According to Sirvis (1982), this group includes individuals with *functional limitations* "related to physical skills such as hand use, trunk control, mobility" (p. 384) and individuals with *medical conditions* that affect strength and stamina.

Students with physical impairments include those with missing limbs, spinal cord injuries causing paralysis, and conditions such as muscular dystrophy. Two of the most common physical problems are cerebral palsy and epilepsy. Cerebral palsy is a motor impairment caused by damage to the brain; it results in difficulty with coordination. Epilepsy is a convulsive disorder; students with epilepsy may have seizures during which they lose consciousness and motor control. Examples of health problems that may affect school performance are diabetes, cardiac conditions, asthma, hemophilia, and cancer.

In the general education classroom, students with physical and health impairments may encounter few difficulties; if special needs do arise, they are likely to be in the areas of physical, academic, and social performance. Special services may be provided by adaptive physical education teachers or other motor specialists; school nurses help with students needing special diets, medication, or activity restrictions. For students with physical mobility problems (such as individuals who walk with crutches or those who travel in wheelchairs), the physical environment of the school may need to be modified to allow access. Instructional materials are adapted for students whose physical problems make writing difficult. Although students with physical and health impairments are not poor achievers as a group, those with chronic medical conditions may miss much school and may fall behind their peers as a result. Social acceptance is another possible problem area, particularly for students with conspicuous disabilities.

Traumatic Brain Injury. **Traumatic brain injury** was recognized as a separate disability by the 1990 IDEA. The National Head Injury Foundation Task Force defines traumatic brain injury as

> an insult to the brain, not of a degenerative or congenital nature, but caused by an external physical force that may produce a diminished or altered state of consciousness which results in impairment of cognitive abilities. (as cited in Tucker & Colson, 1992, p. 198)

The most common causes of head injuries in school-aged individuals are motor vehicle accidents, falls, sports injuries, and, in some parts of the country, assaults (Mira & Tyler, 1991). Students with traumatic brain injury often have physical, academic, and social-behavioral needs. Such students receive educational services in hospital settings, at home, and in a variety of school placements, including general education classrooms.

Sensory Disorders. Another small group of students with disabilities includes those with **visual impairments** and **hearing impairments.** Many school-aged individuals are able to see and hear normally despite visual and hearing problems; their difficulties either have responded to medical treatment or are corrected by devices such as eyeglasses or hearing aids. Such students are not considered to have a disability. Only those whose senses remain impaired after treatment and correction are identified as having a visual or hearing impairment.

Students with visual impairments may be **blind** or may have **low vision**. Individuals who are blind receive so little information through the eyes that they must learn through their other senses; for example, they use the sense of touch to read Braille. Students with low vision, although visually impaired, are able to use their residual vision to learn. In the general education class, students with visual problems may have physical, academic, and social needs. They may require assistance in learning to move about the school and classroom environments; itinerant or resource teachers assist by teaching students basic orientation and mobility skills. These specialists also locate and provide any special materials and equipment needed for academic instruction; some examples are large-print books, Braille materials, raised or embossed maps, tape recorders and taped textbooks, magnification devices, and computers with "talking" word processing programs. In the social area, students with visual impairments may need encouragement to interact with sighted peers.

Students with hearing impairments may be **deaf** or **hard of hearing.** Individuals who are hard of hearing hear well enough to understand speech, usually with the assistance of a hearing aid. Students who are deaf, however, receive so little information through the ears that the sense of hearing is not useful for speech comprehension. In the general education classroom, students with hearing impairments may have special physical, academic, and social needs. Difficulty in speech and language development is one of the major educational problems associated with hearing loss. Students with hearing impairments may require classroom adaptations in order to use the skills taught by special educators. For example, sitting near the front of the classroom helps in hearing or speechreading the verbal instructions of the teacher.

Some students with hearing impairments communicate with speech; others use a manual communication system such as sign language. Interpreters may accompany some students who are deaf to the classroom, particularly at the secondary level; interpreters are hearing individuals who translate the spoken word into manual signs and vice versa. Students with hearing losses may be academically delayed in subjects related to language, such as reading, spelling, and written expression; they may receive special instruction from a resource or itinerant teacher in these areas. Speech and language problems may also inhibit the social interaction of students with hearing losses. If they communicate via speech, articulation problems may make them difficult to understand; those who use manual communication may be isolated from peers unless the peers have also acquired basic signing skills.

Attention Deficit Hyperactivity Disorder. Lerner, Lowenthal, and Lerner (1995) describe this disorder as a "condition characterized by developmentally inappropriate attention skills, impulsivity, and, in some cases, hyperactivity" (p. 4). In a recent definition of **attention deficit hyperactivity disorder** (ADHD), the American Psychiatric Association (1994) differentiated three subgroups: predominantly inattentive, predominantly hyperactive-impulsive, and combined (i.e., showing inattentiveness, hyperactivity, and impulsivity). ADHD appears to be quite common; a 1991 policy memorandum of the U.S. Department of Education estimated that 3% to 5% of the school aged population has significant educational problems related to ADHD. Students with ADHD may experience difficulty in academic achievement in addition to their behavioral problems.

Students with ADHD are served in both general and special education settings. Students with ADHD can receive adjustments in the general education program under Section 504 of the Rehabilitation Act of 1973 (U.S. Department of Education, 1991). In addition, IDEA includes students with ADHD under the disability category "other health impairment." According to the regulations for the 1997 reauthorization of IDEA, this category contains students with

> . . . limited strength, vitality or alertness, *including a heightened alertness to environmental stimuli*, that results in limited alertness with respect to the educational environment. . . .[italics added; *Federal Register,* 1999, Sec. 300.7(c)(9)]

Students with ADD or ADHD fit that portion of the definition related to "heightened alertness." Some students also meet eligibility qualifications for disabilities such as learning disabilities or emotional disturbance and receive special education and related services under those categories.

Autism Spectrum Disorder.   Kauffman (1997) calls **autism spectrum disorder** a "pervasive developmental disorder" because it affects all areas of functioning and is identified before a child reaches 3 years of age. Individuals with this disorder have difficulty engaging in interactions with other people; experience marked delays in language development; may use echolalic speech (i.e., instead of responding to a question, the person with autism echoes or repeats the question); and engage in behaviors such as tantrums, repetitive activities, and stereotyped movements (Kauffman, 1997; Lovaas & Newsom, 1976).

Experts often disagree about autism. Some maintain it is a severe behavioral disorder; others suggest it is a severe disorder of language or a type of health impairment (Heward & Orlansky, 1992). Because of this controversy, autism was designated as a separate disability under 1990 IDEA. Clearly, students with this disorder have special needs in all areas: behavioral, social, academic, and physical performance. These students are often served in special schools or classes. In recent years, some students with autism spectrum disorder have been placed in general education classes as part of the full inclusion movement. When that occurs, special education personnel must provide comprehensive support services in the regular classroom to assist the general education teacher and increase the probability that the student will benefit from the inclusion experience.

Severe Disabilities.   Students with severe disabilities have the most serious and comprehensive needs of all the individuals served by special education. Such students have severe mental retardation and/or show significant developmental delays; their cognitive disabilities are often accompanied by physical, health, communication, and sensory impairments. The U.S. Department of Education describes students with severe disabilities as those

> who because of the intensity of their physical, mental, or emotional problems, or a combination of such problems, need highly specialized educational, social, psychological, and medical services beyond those which are traditionally offered by regular and special education programs, in order to maximize their potential for useful and meaningful participation in society and for self-fulfillment. (*Federal Register,* 1988, p. 118, as cited in Heward, 1996)

In the past, students with severe disabilities were served in special schools and residential programs. Today, however, these students typically attend special classes in regular schools. Like students with autism spectrum disorder, students with severe disabilities are fully included in general education classes in some districts.

In working with special educators and others who serve students with disabilities, one of the first things that most general educators notice is terminology. Because special education is a technical field, many terms are used to describe disabilities. Abbreviations, designed as shortcuts in communication, are also used abundantly. However, statements like "Joel has been identified as having a BD and an LD, and his IEP says the RR is the LRE for him" certainly do not further communication. Translations of some of the common abbreviations used in special education are listed in the "For Your Information" feature.

Other Special Students

In addition to typical students, general education classrooms usually contain not only students with disabilities but also individuals with special gifts and talents. In many towns and cities, culturally and linguistically diverse students may also be class members. In addition, classrooms often include students at risk for school failure. Members of these three groups of students may have special learning needs.

Gifted and Talented Students.   These students, who are estimated to make up 3% to 5% of the school-aged population, may be exceptionally bright (i.e., gifted), have special talents in areas such as art or music, or be both gifted and talented. One definition of this group is found in federal law:

> The term *gifted and talented children* means children and, whenever applicable, youth who are identified at the preschool, elementary, or secondary level as possessing demonstrated or potential abilities that give evidence of high performance capabilities in areas such as intellectual, creative, specific academic, or leadership ability, or in the performing and visual arts. . . . (Section 902, PL 95–561, Gifted and Talented Children's Act of 1978)

Gifted students are characterized by above-average performance on measures of intellectual performance; they may excel academically in all subjects or be particularly advanced in one. Some have creative ability that allows them to produce unusual or novel solutions to problems. Talented students may excel in leadership, drama, art, music, dance, or other areas.

Many states provide special educational opportunities for this diverse group of students. Some gifted individuals are allowed to enter school early and accelerate quickly through the curriculum, perhaps skipping one or several grades. Others attend special schools or classes. Most common, however, is regular class placement with part-time special services either in a resource setting or through special enrichment activities such as seminars or after-school programs.

In the general education classroom, gifted and talented students may have special academic and social needs. Those who are advanced academically benefit from special learning projects and assignments to help them continue their development. Some, however, although bright, may achieve poorly in relation to their potential; for example, they may be unmotivated, lack prerequisite skills, become bored with what they perceive as elementary-level instruction, or fail to achieve because a disability interferes with their performance. Students who are creative and talented may be academically advanced or typical of individuals their own age; whatever

For Your Information

Making Sense of Special Education Abbreviations

Special educators are sometimes accused of speaking in jargon and "alphabet soup." Here are some of the abbreviations commonly used in discussions of students with disabilities. If you hear one that is not on this list and you fail to understand its meaning, stop the speaker and ask for an explanation. Remember that communication can occur only if the listener is able to comprehend the speaker's message.

ADA	The Americans with Disabilities Act of 1990
ADD	Attention deficit disorder
ADHD	Attention deficit hyperactivity disorder
BD	Behavioral disorder; often used synonymously with emotional disturbance (ED) or serious emotional disturbance (SED)
COHI	Crippled and other health impairment; an older term sometimes applied to physical and health disorders (Note: The term *crippled* is considered pejorative.)
DHH	Deaf and hard of hearing
ED	Emotional disturbance
EMR	Educable mental retardation; an older term that refers to mild mental retardation (MMR)
FAPE	Free and appropriate public education; refers to the basic guarantee of federal laws such PL 94-142, the Education for All Handicapped Children Act, and the Individuals with Disabilities Education Act (IDEA) and its amendments
HH	Hard of hearing
HI	Hearing impairment
IDEA	The Individuals with Disabilities Education Act of 1990
IDEA 2004	The Individuals with Disabilities Education Improvement Act of 2004
IEP	Individualized Education Program
LD	Learning disability; also called specific learning disability (SLD) and language and learning disability (LLD)
LLD	Language and learning disability
LRE	Least Restrictive Environment
MMR	Mild mental retardation
MR	Mental retardation
NCLB	The No Child Left Behind Act of 2002
OHI	Other health impairment; refers to health disorders
OI	Orthopedic impairment; refers to a physical impairment involving the skeletal system
PH	Physical handicap; an older term that refers to physical impairment
PL	Public Law, as in PL 94-142
POHI	Physical and other health impairment
RR	Resource room
SC	Special class, also called special day class (SDC)
SDC	Special day class
SED	Serious emotional disturbance; used in federal law to refer to emotional disturbance (ED)/behavioral disorders (BD)
SH	Severely handicapped; often used to describe individuals with severe retardation and/or multiple serious disabilities
SLD	Specific learning disability
TBI	Traumatic brain injury
TMR	Trainable mental retardation; an older term that refers to moderate and severe retardation
VI	Visual impairment

their academic ability, they require guidance to develop their talents. Some gifted and talented students have excellent social skills; others, especially those with extraordinary abilities, may need assistance in relating to their age peers. It is also possible for special populations to overlap. A culually diverse student with a disability may also be identified as gifted, and some gifted youngsters may be at risk for school failure.

Culturally and Linguistically Diverse Students.　Culturally diverse individuals are those reared in a culture that is at variance with that found in the school or different from the dominant culture in the United States. These students face at least two sets of expectations—those of the home and those of the school—and many times these expectations are discrepant. Included within this group are linguistically diverse students; these youngsters may speak languages other than English or be bilingual, speaking English and the language of the home. Some culturally and linguistically diverse students have special learning needs; others do not.

Students who speak little or no English are likely to be members of minority cultures. They are at an extreme disadvantage in school if both their language and experiential backgrounds set them apart from their peers. Many schools offer such students bilingual education, in which they develop English language skills while learning more about their own culture and the dominant culture of the United States.

Minority students include Native Americans and Alaskan natives, Asians and Pacific Islanders, African Americans, and Hispanics. African Americans and Hispanics are the two most prevalent minority groups in the United States today. Within the Hispanic group are individuals of Mexican, Cuban, Puerto Rican, or other Spanish culture or origin. Some minority students are bilingual, some may be considered culturally diverse, but many are English-speaking members of the dominant American culture.

Culturally diverse students are those whose background and experiences differ from those of their peers. Cultural differences must be defined in terms of local norms. For instance, a Christian student may be perceived as culturally different in a predominantly Jewish community; a student who speaks with a Boston accent may appear out of place among residents of the Deep South.

Students with ethnic, linguistic, and cultural backgrounds different from those of their peers add diversity and variety to the general education classroom. However, they may have special academic and social needs. Those still developing skills in understanding and speaking English may experience difficulty with academic instruction. Others may fail to meet teacher expectations because of different entry-level skills or different cultural values and motivational systems. Social acceptance may be withheld by peers unaccustomed to cultural variations.

Students at Risk for School Failure.   Students can be at risk for many reasons. They may live in an impoverished family with inadequate housing, poor nutrition, and little or no medical care; with their basic needs in jeopardy, such students often have few resources left to devote to school learning. Others may be slow learners who, although they do not have disabilities, learn at a pace that falls somewhat below grade-level expectations. Some students are unmotivated to achieve in school, and as a result their academic performance is less than satisfactory. Older students with a history of poor school achievement may become truant or contemplate leaving school. According to the National Coalition of Advocates for Students (1985), one of every four students who enters the ninth grade drops out before graduating from high school.

Every classroom contains students at risk for school failure, although it is difficult to determine precisely how many general education students fit within this category. Many types of students can be considered at risk. Among these are potential school dropouts, students with violent or suicidal behaviors, those who use or abuse alcohol or other drugs, teenage mothers, victims of child abuse or neglect, those with eating disorders, and delinquents.

At-risk students often have needs in the area of academic performance; they may fail to achieve, show little interest in instructional activities, or achieve at levels far below their potential. Some students may also show special needs in the area of behavior; they may exhibit inappropriate behavior in the classroom or begin to develop very serious problems such as drug and alcohol abuse, gang activity, and delinquency. Social acceptance may be a problem, particularly for students who fail to meet the school's expectations for achievement and the peer group's expectations for behavior. To learn more about these and other students with special needs, consult "For Your Information."

For Your Information

Special Needs

- A student may have a disability without being handicapped. A disability is some sort of impairment. It becomes a handicap only when it interferes with performance in some important area.
- Male students with special needs are more common than female students. No one knows exactly why this is so. It may be that males are more susceptible to the inheritance of learning problems and disabilities. Or it may be related to the cultural expectations for students of different genders.
- There is no relationship between physical impairments and intelligence. People with severe physical problems may be bright, and individuals with mental retardation may have no physical impairments.
- Most special students are not identified as disabled until they encounter difficulty in school. Children identified in the preschool years have serious or obvious disabilities or conditions that place them at risk for developmental delays.
- Given the right circumstances, any student could be considered culturally different. For example, a student who moves from Texas to New England will encounter new speech patterns, foods, social customs, and even sports activities.

SPECIAL NEEDS

It is common practice to divide students with special needs into separate groups or categories such as students with learning disabilities, those with mental retardation, and so on. In the classroom, however, the special needs of these students are often so similar that distinctions among categories become blurred. It also becomes difficult to differentiate between students with identified disabilities and some of their peers with similar learning problems.

Academic needs are common. The acquisition, mastery, and application of school skills proves difficult for many special students and for many of their classmates. Children are expected to enter school with listening, speaking, and other readiness skills. In the primary years (grades 1, 2, and 3), the basic skills of reading, writing, and mathematics are taught; at the intermediate level (grades 4, 5, and sometimes 6), students learn to use these skills to acquire information in content areas such as science and social studies. In middle school and high school, the focus of the curriculum shifts to these content areas; mastery of basic skills is assumed. For many students, this assumption is unwarranted; they are not able to read, write, and calculate at the level expected in the secondary grades. Those who have acquired rudimentary basic skills may fail to acquire content area knowledge and concepts. Still others may require alternatives to the general education curriculum; their major educational need may be career education with an emphasis on vocational training.

Classroom behavior needs frequently occur among special students and their general education peers. Elementary school students are expected to obey their teacher and others in authority, adhere to the rules of classroom conduct, and get along with their peers during instruction and in less structured situations such as lunch and recess. These expectations are also true for secondary students. In addition, however, they are assumed to have developed the study skills and work habits necessary for independent learning. Many students require assistance in meeting these expectations for classroom behavior.

Students may also have special *physical needs*. Children are expected to enter school with intact visual, hearing, and physical abilities. Those with sensory losses cannot participate in many classroom activities designed for sighted and hearing students. Many students, including those with physical and health impairments, cannot walk, run, or play games and sports as well as their general education peers. They have special needs in the area of physical development.

Special students and others often have *social needs*. Young children are expected to know how to make friends with their classmates. Instruction is often presented in group situations that require students to interact with both their teacher and peers. Many school activities are at least partly social in nature; personal interactions take place during lunch, recess, assemblies, and field trips and in clubs, organizations, and sports teams. Social skills become increasingly important as individuals approach adulthood; secondary students are expected to build and maintain friendships and begin establishing interpersonal relationships as preparation for courtship and marriage. Because they may appear to be different in some ways, special students may have difficulty gaining acceptance from their regular class peers. Students with poor social skills (whether they are identified as special or not) need instruction and training in this area.

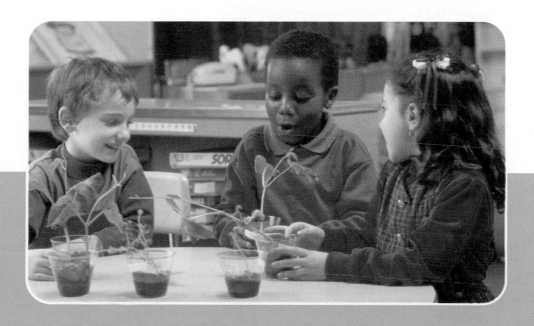

Most students require assistance in one or more of these areas at some time during their school careers. Special students are no exception. However, with special students it is possible to predict some of the areas in which they are likely to encounter difficulty. As shown in Table 3-1, it is probable that all will have special academic and social needs. Some may also have needs in the areas of classroom behavior and physical development. This table depicts only the typical needs of groups of students; it is certainly possible for students with speech and language impairments to display problem behaviors or for students with physical impairments to require no special academic assistance.

There are many similarities among special students and between special students and their regular class peers. This is

TABLE 3-1	Typical Needs of Special Students			
	SPECIAL NEEDS			
SPECIAL STUDENTS	**ACADEMIC**	**CLASSROOM BEHAVIOR**	**PHYSICAL**	**SOCIAL**
Learning disabilities	X	X	X	X
Behavioral disorders	X	X		X
Mental retardation	X	X	X	X
Speech/language impairments	X			X
Physical/health impairments	X		X	X
Visual/hearing impairments	X		X	X
ADHD	X	X		X
Autism spectrum disorder	X	X	X	X
Severe disabilities	X	X	X	X
Gifted/talented students	X			X
Diverse students	X			X
Students at risk	X	X	X	X

Inclusion Tips for the Teacher

Explaining Classroom Modifications to Peers

It is sometimes necessary to make changes in classroom activities so that students with special needs can succeed. For example, students with academic needs may be given special assignments or may be required to complete only part of the work assigned to the rest of the class. Those with behavioral needs may earn special rewards for good behavior. The rest of the class may become curious about why these students rate special treatment from the teacher.

Teachers can prevent problems from occurring by following these suggestions:

- Don't call undue attention to students with special needs. Treat them as you would any other student in your class.
- When special assignments are necessary, give them privately. Then, when the class is working on individual assignments, the student with special needs will not be conspicuous.

- Group students with similar learning needs together. If a student with a disability requires extra instruction in reading, set up a small group that includes peers with similar needs. If students with special needs have difficulty following class rules, consider beginning a behavior program for the entire class.
- When class members have questions, answer them promptly and honestly. Acknowledge that you are individualizing assignments and activities so that everyone in the class can learn successfully. A matter-of-fact response will usually satisfy curiosity and allay any feelings of resentment.

particularly true in relation to students with mild disabilities: learning disabilities, behavioral disorders, and mild retardation. These students make up perhaps 5% to 7% of the school population. They are physically indistinguishable from their regular class peers and are usually not identified as special until they experience failure in school. They begin school in general education classes and receive the majority of their education in mainstreamed situations. According to Hallahan and Kauffman (1976), students with mild disabilities cannot be differentiated by the causes of their learning problems, the methods found effective in their instruction, or their behavioral characteristics. All have academic, behavioral, and social needs that may require adaptations in general education classrooms.

When adaptations are made for special students, general education teachers often wonder how to explain these changes to the rest of the class. Students may wonder why others are receiving special treatment. Ideas for handling this situation are listed in the "Inclusion Tips for the Teacher" box.

CAUSES OF LEARNING PROBLEMS

For most special students, the cause, or **etiology**, of their learning problem is unknown. Although a host of causative agents has been identified, it is often impossible to state with certainty which was responsible for the disability of a particular student.

Causes can be classified according to when they occurred in the life of the individual: prenatal (before birth), perinatal (during the birth process), or postnatal (after birth). An example of a prenatal cause is rubella or German measles. If contracted by a woman during the first 3 months of her pregnancy, rubella can lead to hearing, visual, physical, and cognitive impairments in the fetus as it develops. Oxygen deprivation during the birth process is a perinatal cause, whereas a head injury sustained in an automobile accident at 3 years of age is a postnatal cause.

Another view of etiology is the dichotomy of hereditary and environmental factors. Some types of deafness are inherited, and there is some indication that reading problems tend to run in families. Environmental causes of learning problems include poor nutrition, lack of sensory stimulation, and inadequate instruction.

The causes of learning problems are of interest for two reasons: treatment and prevention. Medical research has developed treatments for some known etiologies and preventive techniques for others. For example, the Salk vaccine has virtually eliminated the crippling disease of polio in the United States, and progress is being made in the use of gene therapy for conditions such as muscular dystrophy. In education, the emphasis is on environmental causes of learning problems. Research indicates that providing appropriate early educational experiences for children with special needs may lessen or pre-

vent later learning problems (Casto & Mastropieri, 1986; White, Bush, & Casto, 1986). Education itself is one of the environmental influences on students, one that can precipitate learning problems. Poor or inappropriate instruction has been cited as a major factor in the development of school problems. Reynolds and Birch (1982) contend that "most pupil behaviors called learning disabilities and behavior disorders are best acknowledged as the consequences of failure to provide enough high quality individualized instruction" (p. 237).

ASSESSMENT OF SPECIAL LEARNING NEEDS

Assessment is the process of gathering information about students to make important educational decisions (McLoughlin & Lewis, 2005). In special education and other supplementary school services, it is necessary to determine whether students meet certain legal requirements before services can begin. In special education, for example, students are considered eligible for services only if they have a disability and if that disability has a negative effect on school performance. That is, students must experience difficulty in school, and that difficulty must be attributable to a disability.

Classroom Assessment

General educators play many roles in the assessment process. As discussed in chapter 2, the classroom teacher is typically the person who refers students for special education and other types of assessment. In addition, teachers collect all sorts of information about their students. Some of the assessment strategies that classroom teachers use most often are

- observations of students as they engage in academic activities and social interactions;
- analysis of students' errors and correct responses on work samples such as homework assignments, tests, essays, and math papers;
- administration of quizzes and exams to assess student progress toward instructional goals; and
- interviews with students to learn more about their attitudes, viewpoints, and the strategies they use to interact with classroom tasks.

These techniques are **informal assessment** strategies. Unlike formal, norm-referenced tests, their purpose is not to compare one student's performance to that of others of the same age or grade. Instead, they are considered **curriculum-based assessments** because they focus on students' mastery of the instructional goals addressed in the general education classroom.

Another example of an informal data collection technique is **portfolio assessment.** Portfolios are simply collections of student work gathered over time; however, students are responsible for selecting their best work for inclusion in the portfolio and for evaluating their own progress (Grady, 1992). Teachers evaluate the contents of a portfolio with the same informal techniques used to analyze other types of student work samples.

One major reason for the collection of data is to evaluate the effectiveness of instruction. When done systematically, this is called **clinical teaching** (McLoughlin & Lewis, 2005). First, the teacher gathers data about student performance on the task in question. Then, an intervention is introduced and data collection continues. Any of the informal assessment strategies described earlier can be used in clinical teaching: observation, analysis of student work samples, quizzes, and so on. The intervention is considered successful if results indicate that student performance has improved.

Curriculum-based measurement (CBM) is an informal assessment strategy used in special education to monitor student progress (Deno, 1985, 1987; Shinn & Hubbard, 1993). It is easy to use and sensitive to small changes in students' skill levels, which makes it a useful measurement technique for clinical teaching. In CBM, the teacher collects very brief samples of important student behaviors. For example, to assess oral reading skills, students read aloud for 1 minute while the teacher (or an assistant) records the number of words read correctly. This "probe" is administered frequently (e.g., two or three times each week), and results are graphed to provide a visual record of the student's progress. In clinical teaching, this graph is inspected to determine whether desired changes occurred when the new intervention was introduced.

Assessment for Program Eligibility

When students are referred for special education assessment, a multidisciplinary team is formed to plan the process of gathering information about the need for extraordinary services. **Norm-referenced tests** are typically used for this type of assessment. These tests provide information about a student's status in relation to other students of the same age or grade; this type of comparison is needed to determine whether a student's problem is severe enough to warrant special educational intervention.

The tests are administered by trained specialists to one student at a time. Group administration procedures are not used because they can depress the performance of students with special learning needs. Group tests require students to read, write, and attend to test tasks for a relatively long period of time. On individually administered tests, a student's knowledge of science can be separated from his or her reading skills because the tester reads the questions to the student; also, if the student's attention wavers, the professional can help the student refocus on the task at hand.

No matter what disability is suspected, the team will collect information on three major areas of functioning:

1. *Intellectual performance.* Tests of intellectual performance, sometimes called intelligence or IQ (intelligence quotient) tests, are used to assess the student's skills in reasoning and problem-solving tasks. These measures do not determine innate potential; instead, they assess a student's aptitude for academic tasks (McLoughlin & Lewis, 2005).
2. *Academic achievement.* At the beginning of assessment, tests that include several academic subjects (e.g., reading, spelling, composition, mathematics, content area knowledge) are administered to identify broad areas of need. Then, more specific measures (e.g., a test of reading skills) are used to pinpoint areas of difficulty.
3. *Area of disability.* In special education assessment, it is necessary to establish the existence of a disability. For instance, in mental retardation, the team will study intellectual performance and adaptive behavior. In learning disabilities, the focus is on information processing, and in behavioral disorders, severe and long-standing conduct disorders. Federal laws provide regulations for determining eligibility, and states and school districts supplement these with additional guidelines.

Figure 3-2 lists and describes some of the individually administered norm-referenced tests used most often in special education assessment. Included are measures of intellectual performance as well as academic achievement tests. Although classroom teachers do not administer tests such as these, test results are often discussed in the deliberations of the team.

To help teachers become better acquainted with the tests and other data collection procedures used in special education, common assessment tools and techniques are discussed throughout this book. However, this book places most of its emphasis on the types of assessment tools that teachers find useful in the classroom. These are typically informal assessments—measures and strategies devised by teachers to answer specific questions about the academic, social, physical, and behavioral needs of their students. The measures also tend to be curriculum based rather than norm referenced; that is, their purpose is to compare a student's performance to the demands of the local curriculum and the expectations in a particular classroom.

SKILLS FOR THE GENERAL EDUCATION TEACHER

General education teachers play an important role in the prevention and treatment of school learning problems. With appropriate instruction, students with disabilities and others with special learning needs can experience success in the general education classroom. The next chapters of this book fo-

FIGURE 3-2   Measures Used in Special Education

Measures of Intellectual Performance

Wechsler Intelligence Scale for Children–Fourth Edition—Contains 15 tests that assess several types of reasoning in students ages 6 to 17; results include a global IQ score (Full Scale IQ) as well as four index scores: Verbal Comprehension Index, Perceptual Reasoning Index, Working Memory Index, and Processing Speed Index. Called the *WISC-IV*, this is the most commonly used measure of intellectual performance in schools.

Woodcock-Johnson III Tests of Cognitive Ability—Estimates overall intellectual performance and provides measures of seven cognitive factors: Comprehension-Knowledge, Long-Term Retrieval, Visual-Spatial Thinking, Auditory Processing, Fluid Reasoning, Processing Speed, and Short-Term Memory; designed for ages 2 to 90+.

Stanford-Binet Intellectual Scales, Fifth Edition—Uses verbal and nonverbal subtests to assess five cognitive factors in persons from age 2 to adulthood: Fluid Reasoning, Knowledge, Quantitative Reasoning, Visual-Spatial Processing, and Working Memory. This test is the current version of the original IQ test devised in the early 1900s by Binet and Simon.

Measures of Overall Academic Achievement

Peabody Individual Achievement Test–Revised/Normative Update—Includes tests of General Information, Reading Recognition, Reading Comprehension, Mathematics, Spelling, and Written Expression for students in grades K–12.

Wechsler Individual Achievement Test–Second Edition—A newer measure with eight subtests that assess reading, mathematics, and written language as well as listening and speaking skills; designed for ages 4 through adult.

Woodstock-Johnson III Tests of Achievement—Contains more than 20 tests to assess Reading, Oral Language, Mathematics, Written Language, and Academic Knowledge for ages 2 to adulthood.

Wide Range Achievement Test 3—More limited in scope, the *WRAT3* assesses spelling, arithmetic, and reading recognition skills in students ages 5 through adulthood.

Measures of Specific Academic Skills

Woodcock Reading Mastery Tests–Revised/Normative Update—Used to identify strengths and weaknesses in Word Identification, Word Attack, Word Comprehension, Passage Comprehension, and reading readiness skills in K–12 and college students.

KeyMath Revised/Normative Update—Offers 13 subtests to assess mathematics skills in Basic Concepts, Operations, and Applications; normed for grades K–9.

Test of Written Spelling–4—A dictation spelling test for ages 6 to 19.

Test of Written Language–3—Identifies strengths and weaknesses in areas of written language such as vocabulary, spelling, and mechanics (e.g., capitalization and punctuation) in students ages 7 to 18; one part of the *TOWL-3* requires students to write a story describing a picture.

cus on the major skills needed by teachers to adapt instruction, manage behavior, promote social acceptance, and coordinate the learning environment of the classroom. These skills are simply good teaching procedures; they can be used with any student, special or not. Good teaching skills focus on the needs of the student (rather than any particular disability), and they are based on the following four assumptions about special students and the teaching–learning process.

All Students Can Learn. Despite any special needs they may have, all individuals are able to acquire new skills and absorb new information and attitudes. Students learn at different rates, and the same person may learn some things more quickly than other things. Although much is known about different types of special students and their disabilities, it is impossible to accurately predict the specific areas in which they will experience difficulty. However, we do know that they *can* and, with proper instruction, *will* learn.

Learning Is Determined by Changes in Behavior. Learning is a process of change. Students acquire new skills, become more proficient in previously learned skills, and learn to perform in certain ways. Teachers evaluate students' progress by their behavior; that is, they observe students' overt responses and infer that learning has occurred. Students demonstrate that they have learned academic, classroom conduct, and social skills in many ways; they may display new behaviors, a greater number of appropriate behaviors, or fewer inappropriate behaviors. Teachers monitor the learning process by noting what students say in class discussions, what they write on assignments and exams, and how they act in the many situations of the school day.

Teaching Involves Manipulation of the Environment. If learning is the change of student behaviors, then teaching is the arrangement of the learning environment to maximize the chance that desired behaviors will occur. In instruction, teachers have control over two important factors: the **antecedents** and **consequences** of student behaviors. An antecedent is anything that precedes or comes before a behavior; typical teaching activities such as lectures, small-group discussions, text readings, and written assignments are all instructional antecedents that can be manipulated to enhance learning. Consequences, or events that follow behaviors, include grades, teacher praise or scolding, and rewards (remember gold stars?) and punishments; these, too, are powerful tools that can be used to facilitate learning. Just as students learn at different rates, they also respond differently to instructional antecedents and consequences. Although there is no one sure-fire teaching method, material, or reward system, empirical evidence suggests that some instructional procedures are more effective than others. For example, direct instruction methods that focus on skill development have been found useful for teaching basic academic skills (Stevens & Rosenshine, 1981).

Data Collection Increases Teaching Efficiency.   Because the options to choose from in setting up an instructional system of antecedents and consequences are almost unlimited, it is important to approach the task systematically. After the desired student behavior is stated as precisely as possible, the most simple and straightforward strategy for teaching that behavior is tried. The teacher collects information about the behavior before instruction and also during the instructional intervention. If the behavior changes in the desired way, the intervention is considered successful; if it does not, the teacher proceeds to a more complex or intensive instructional strategy. In this way, instructional decisions are made on the basis of data rather than on guesses or hunches; teaching becomes more efficient, with the end result that students learn more. This data-based approach to instruction is particularly beneficial for special students and others who encounter difficulty in learning.

Turn to the next chapter to see how these assumptions about the teaching–learning process can be applied to the adaptation of instruction for special students and others in the general education classroom.

Things to Remember

- Both special students and their regular class peers may have special learning needs. Special needs occur in the areas of academic, classroom behavioral, physical, and social performance.

- Special students, as a group, typically experience difficulty in academic and social areas; some students also have special behavioral and physical needs.

- Information about special needs is more useful to the teacher than knowledge of the student's categorical label.

- Causes of learning problems are important if they help in treatment or prevention.

- Teachers use informal assessment tools to gather information for instructional decisions.

- Appropriate instruction can prevent some learning problems and help to overcome others.

- Teachers manipulate the learning environment to produce changes in the behavior of students.

- Data-based instruction is efficient and effective in teaching special students the behaviors needed to succeed in the general education classroom.

ACTIVITIES

1. Disabilities are not the same as handicaps. However, some disabilities interfere with the performance of tasks required by certain professions. For example, consider blindness for a painter or deafness for a musician. Are there any disabilities that would interfere in the profession of teaching? If so, what are they? What disabilities would a teacher be able to overcome? Be prepared to discuss your answers to these questions.

2. Interview two or more general educators about the students they teach. How many students with disabilities are included in their classrooms? What types of special needs do these students have? Do other children in the classroom have similar needs? What kinds of classroom modifications have the teachers made to accommodate the special needs of these students?

3. Many special education journals concentrate on one disability. For instance, the Council for Exceptional Children publishes *Behavioral Disorders*, *Education and Training in Developmental Disabilities*, and *Learning Disabilities Research & Practice*. Select one or two of these journals and look at several recent issues. Did you find any articles on the inclusion of students with special needs in general education?

4. Search the World Wide Web for information about one of the disabilities discussed in this chapter. What kinds of sites did you locate? Are they sponsored by professional organizations? Parent groups? Districts or schools? Individuals?

5. A person's culture affects many perceptions. Talk with someone from a culture different from yours, and compare your experiences. You might discuss foods, dress, manners, or traditional celebrations or holidays. Also, compare the ways in which different cultures view the birth of a child with a disability. Are persons with disabilities treated differently by different cultures?

CD-ROM Activities

Listen to the assessment team on the third video case study as they discuss Tommy, a student who is having difficulty in school. View the clips entitled "Identify Strengths" and "Identify Concerns," then respond to these questions:

- *What areas are strengths for Tommy? What areas are concerns?*

- *Do the concerns outnumber the strengths or vice versa?*

- *Create a new definition of the term special needs based the information provided by the members of this assessment team.*

Skills for the General Education Teacher

Adapting Instruction

CHAPTER

4

- Eleanor, a fourth grader, reads at the beginning third-grade level.
- Patrick can solve math computation problems with ease, but he has trouble with word problems.
- Erin's handwriting is barely legible, and the assignments he turns in are wrinkled, messy, and full of crossed-out words.
- Although Patty seems to understand the information presented in chemistry class, she has failed every quiz this semester.

- Ian's essays contain excellent ideas, but his spelling, grammar, and punctuation are atrocious.
- Billy is habitually late to class, and he often forgets to do his homework.
- Dan's vocational skills are good, but he'll have difficulty completing job applications.

LOOKING AHEAD

This chapter focuses on the academic difficulties faced by some students who are members of general education classrooms. As you read this chapter to learn about strategies to assist these students, think about the questions that follow:

- Each of the students just described has some sort of academic problem. In what school subject—or subjects—would you expect them to need assistance?
- What could you do to find out more about Patrick's difficulties with word problems? Erin's illegible handwriting? Billy's lateness to class and poor homework record?
- What adaptations might be useful to help Patty communicate her knowledge of chemistry? To help Ian better communicate his ideas?

To answer these questions online, go to the Students' Stories module in Chapter 4 of the Companion Website.

Students such as the individuals described in the "Students' Stories" have special needs in the area of academic performance. For them to succeed in the general education classroom, it may be necessary to adapt instructional procedures. To do this, teachers should be familiar with the typical **academic problems** of students with special needs and their peers, methods for gathering data about academic performance, and strategies for adapting instruction to meet the needs of all students.

ACADEMIC PROBLEMS IN THE CLASSROOM

Students can experience difficulty with academic instruction at any age and in any subject. Such students come to the attention of their teachers when their classroom performance does not meet teacher expectations. Elementary teachers often describe students with academic problems as "achieving below grade level" in one or more subjects. Secondary teachers, however, take note of students who receive poor or failing grades in specific courses, such as English 9, biology, American history, or woodshop.

School learning involves the acquisition of both information and skills. Students are expected to absorb vast amounts of information in academic subjects and to develop and sharpen their thinking and learning skills. Problems can occur in any one of the three stages of learning: acquisition, maintenance, and generalization. **Acquisition** is initial learning, **maintenance** is the recall of previously learned material, and **generalization** is the application or transfer of learned material to similar situations and problems. Students may require more time to learn new information and skills, have difficulty sustaining performance over time, or fail to apply old learning to new situations.

Teachers evaluate student responses to determine whether learning is occurring as expected. Students respond in the classroom in a number of ways: oral answers to teacher questions, participation in class discussions, in-class assignments and homework, and quizzes and examinations. Academic problems are suspected if one (or more) of the following response patterns is evident:

- *High number of incorrect responses.* The majority of the student's responses are incorrect, or the student's accuracy rate falls below the criterion set by the teacher. For example, George solves only 6 out of 10 subtraction problems correctly; the teacher's criterion is 90% accuracy.
- *Low number of responses.* The student fails to respond to a significant number of questions, problems, or activities. For example, Jack answers only 7 of the 15 questions at the end of the chapter.
- *Inconsistent responses.* The student's responses to the same question, problem, or activity vary in correctness from time to time. For example, Thelma writes all

20 spelling words correctly on the Wednesday practice quiz but scores only 40% on the test on Friday.

Of course, if many students show response patterns such as these, the first step would be to evaluate classroom instructional procedures.

Inappropriate response patterns can be seen in any school subject. One typical trouble spot is **basic skills;** listening, speaking, reading, writing, and mathematics often are difficult for students to acquire, maintain, and generalize. The written language skills of reading and writing are built on the oral language skills of listening and speaking. Students may have trouble with the reception of information (listening and reading), the expression of information (speaking and writing), or all aspects of the communication process. The development of basic skills is a high-priority instructional goal in the elementary grades. Special students may experience difficulty with the rote aspects of these skills (e.g., word recognition, handwriting, spelling, mathematics facts and computation) or with the more conceptual aspects (e.g., reading comprehension, written expression, mathematical problem solving).

At the secondary level, instruction centers on **content-area subjects** rather than basic skills. The academic curriculum is organized according to bodies of knowledge: English (including both composition and literature) and other languages; science (biology, chemistry, physics); higher math (algebra, geometry, trigonometry); the social sciences (history, social studies, geography); and other areas such as art, music, and physical education. However, academic problems in basic skills may persist; students may not have acquired or maintained adequate reading, writing, and mathematics skills, or they may be unable to apply these skills to the acquisition of new information. Students may also have difficulty learning the skills, information, concepts, and principles of particular content areas. Poor organizational and study skills may also interfere with student performance.

Preparation for the **transition** from adolescence to adulthood is another aspect of school learning in which academic problems can arise. Hasazi, Furney, and Hull (1995) define *transition* as a "series of purposeful activities designed to ensure that students have the skills, opportunities, and supports needed to locate and maintain employment, to pursue postsecondary education and training, to participate in the social fabric of the community, and to make decisions about their lives" (p. 420). Transition planning is required by federal law for students with disabilities; it is also an important concern for many other students with special needs. One aspect of transition planning is specific vocational training experience at the secondary level. Another is the application of basic skills and content-area information to the solution of daily life problems, such as reading menus, making change, and selecting appropriate items to purchase. Students may have difficulty in the acquisition of specific vocational skills, such as

Window on the Web

Educational Resources Information Center (ERIC)

http://www.eric.ed.gov

If you're looking for information on some aspect of education, ERIC is a good place to start. ERIC is the Education Resources Information Center, which, according to its website, is a "digital library of education-related resources, sponsored by the Institute of Education Sciences of the U.S. Department of Education."

The new online version of ERIC became available in September 2004. It includes a searchable database of more than 1 million ERIC entries dating back to 1966. Each entry contains information about author, title, and source as well as a brief abstract. An exciting new feature of this online service is access to full-text versions of recently published documents (excluding articles published in journals). This free service replaces the former system where users were required to purchase print or microfiche copies of ERIC documents or visit libraries who had already made these purchases.

For more information, go to the Web Links module in Chapter 4 of the Companion Website.

---

keyboarding, mechanical drawing, or welding. They may also have difficulty in the generalization of basic work habits, such as punctuality and task completion, and the application of school learning to job and community situations.

Because academic instruction is one of the major goals of U.S. education, academic problems are a concern to classroom teachers at all levels. However, as Montgomery (1978) points out, not all variations in student performance are learning problems:

> Johnny reads with his book turned sideways, or kneels instead of sitting on his chair, or wears his jacket in class. Do we "fix" him or let him be? Before we can answer that question realistically we must ask, "Is it a problem for Johnny— or for us?" Does it hamper Johnny's learning, or do we see it as a problem because of our own preoccupation with things being normal, with Johnny acting like everyone else? (p. 112)

PRINCIPLES OF INSTRUCTION

Students with special needs have the necessary skills to participate in many classroom activities. They may take part in all instructional aspects of the general education program, or they may be included only for selected subjects. The decision is made on the basis of three factors: the student's skills in the subject area, the amount of instructional support required to ensure the student's active participation, and the usefulness or functionality of the academic subject for the student. When students are included only for those subjects that are useful to them and in which successful performance is probable, the general education curriculum is appropriate; that is,

what is taught need not be modified by the classroom teacher. However, it is often necessary to alter instructional procedures, that is, *how* skills and information are taught to special students.

Much is known today about what teachers can do to have positive effects on student performance. This knowledge comes from a large body of research on teaching behaviors, sometimes known as the teacher effectiveness literature (Brophy & Good, 1986; Medley, 1982; Rieth & Evertson, 1988; Rosenshine & Stevens, 1986; Weil & Murphy, 1982). The major factors found to have a positive influence on student achievement are listed here (Weil & Murphy, 1982):

- Teachers maintain an *academic focus* in selecting classroom activities and directing classroom work.
- Teachers maintain *direction and control* in the management of the classroom learning environment.
- Teachers hold *high expectations* for the academic progress of their students.
- *Students are accountable* for the satisfactory completion of classroom work.
- Students work together, showing *cooperation* rather than competition.
- The affective climate of the classroom learning environment is *not negative*.

Among the most critical concerns in fostering student achievement are the quantity and pace of instruction (Brophy & Good, 1986). Both concerns are related to an opportunity to learn. Learning increases when more time is devoted to academic pursuits and when students are actually engaged in learning during that time. Learning also increases when students move through the curriculum at a brisk pace, provided that students maintain a high rate of successful performance.

Both quantity and pace of instruction can be enhanced by active teaching. According to Brophy and Good (1986), in active teaching "the teacher carries the content to the students personally rather than depending on the curriculum materials to do so" (p. 361). The teacher directs the learning experience, and students "spend most of their time being taught or supervised by their teachers rather than working on their own (or not working at all)" (p. 361). Active teaching has been called many things including **direct teaching,** direct instruction, and, most recently, **explicit instruction** (Spear-Swerling & Sternberg, 2001). In direct teaching, the teacher demonstrates appropriate strategies for the performance of the learning task, allows maximum opportunity for students to respond, and provides systematic and frequent feedback on their task performance (Archer, Gleason, Englert, & Isaacson, 1995; Archer, Gleason, & Isaacson, 1995; Lewis, 1983).

Lloyd and Carnine (1981) call this *structured instruction,* or the "carefully organized manipulation of environmental events designed to bring about prespecified changes in learners' performance in skill areas of functional importance" (p. viii). It is **individualized instruction,** designed to meet the needs of each student. This does not mean that instruction must be individual, delivered by one teacher to one student. Stevens and Rosenshine (1981) view instruction as individualized when a high proportion of student responses is correct. Good instruction can occur in large groups, small groups, or one to one; the criterion is student success.

Differentiated instruction is the term currently used to describe individualization within the general education environment (Tomlinson, 2000; Wormeli, 2003). Tomlinson identifies four aspects of classroom instruction that teachers can differentiate in an attempt to meet the needs of more learners:

1. Content—what the student needs to learn or how the student will get access to the information;
2. Process—activities in which the student engages in order to make sense of or master the content;
3. Products—culminating projects that ask the student to rehearse, apply, and extend what he or she has learned in a unit; and
4. Learning environment—the way the classroom works and feels.

As shown in Figure 4-1, instruction takes place in a series of steps involving both teacher and student(s) and progressing from the active direction of the teacher (teaching) to the active involvement of the student(s) (learning). There are five steps: curricular choice, presentation, practice, mastery, and application.

1. *Selection of the learning task.* To make this curricular decision, the teacher considers the scope and sequence of the general education curriculum, the skills and information already acquired by the student, and the student's current interests and learning needs. The learning task represents the goal of instruction, and successful performance of this task is the desired student behavior.
2. *Presentation to the student of the material necessary for task performance.* The teacher uses procedures such as lectures, in-class activities, and reading assignments to provide the student with the skills and information required for the task. The teacher may model or demonstrate the skill or explain new information by presenting rules, principles, and examples. Then the teacher gives directions for the performance of the task. The student's role at this stage is to give adequate attention to instruction and feedback to the teacher if instruction is unclear.
3. *Practice of the learning task.* The student first performs the task under the close supervision of the teacher (guided practice). Gradually the teacher's guidance is withdrawn, and the student performs independently (independent practice). The teacher's role is to monitor student performance and provide feedback to the student regarding the adequacy of task performance. In guided practice, feedback is immediate, whereas in independent practice, it is delayed. If a high proportion of student responses is incorrect, the teacher returns to the presentation step. Presentation and practice lead to the acquisition of skills and information.
4. *Mastery of the learning task.* At some later time, the student performs the task independently, and the teacher monitors student responses. If performance is not adequate, it may be necessary to return to the practice steps or even to the presentation steps. Mastery is determined by maintenance of previously acquired learning.
5. *Application of previous learning.* The student performs tasks similar to the original learning task. If the teacher notes poor performance at this step, it may be necessary to reteach the original task through presentation and practice or to devise a new instructional sequence in which generalization of skills or information is taught directly. Application generalizes previous learning.

The teacher directs instruction by selecting the desired student behavior, arranging instructional antecedents, and providing consequences such as feedback regarding performance accuracy. Even though the teacher is the instructional manager, student factors that influence learning must also be considered. Several of these are described in

FIGURE 4-1   Instruction

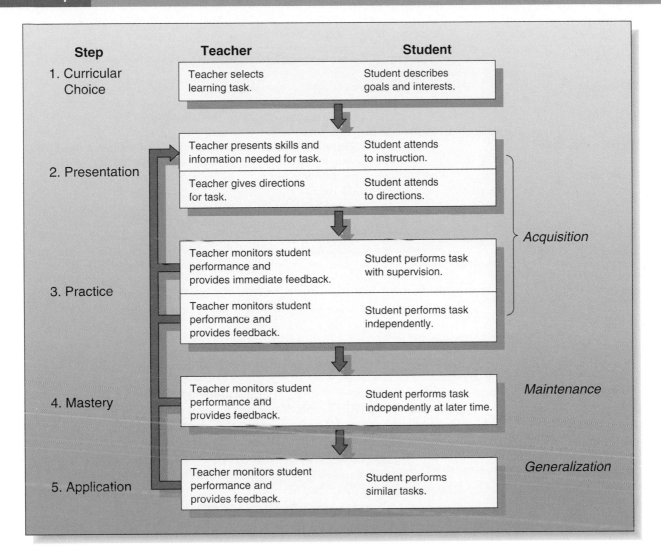

Table 4-1. In addition, the principles of teaching discussed in the following sections should guide the instructional process.

Before proceeding, it is important to differentiate between direct (or explicit) instruction and an alternative approach, **discovery learning**. In discovery learning, information and skills are not taught directly. Instead, the teacher arranges the learning environment and students explore that environment as they attempt to discover the facts, concepts, principles, and skills that make up the school curriculum. Discovery approaches are considered constructivist because students are expected to construct their own knowledge by building on the prior knowledge they bring to the learning task (Cegelka, 1995a). For example, many proponents of the whole-language approach to reading and writing

instruction recommend discovery learning (Gersten & Dimino, 1993; Keefe & Keefe, 1993; Mather, 1992). Students are expected to become proficient readers and writers by "exposure to and participation in many experiences involving written language" (Richeck in Lerner, Cousin, & Richeck, 1992, p. 227), not through direct teaching.

Unfortunately, some students do not succeed in programs in which discovery learning is the norm (Adelson, 2004; Gersten & Dimino, 1993). In fact, Mayer (2004) asserts that "there is sufficient research evidence to make any reasonable person skeptical about the benefits of discovery learning" (p. 14). Students with mild disabilities and others at risk for academic learning problems are more likely to succeed when instruction is presented using the principles of direct teaching (King-Sears, 1997; Vergason & Anderegg, 1991). As Morsink

TABLE 4-1   Facilitating Learning

FACTOR	PRINCIPLE
Meaningfulness	A student is more likely to be motivated to learn things that are meaningful to him or her.
Prerequisites	A student is more likely to learn something new if he or she has all the prerequisites.
Modeling	A student is more likely to acquire a new behavior if he or she is presented with a model performance to watch and imitate.
Open communication	A student is more likely to learn if the medium used in the learning situation is structured so that the teacher's messages are open to the learner's inspection.
Novelty	A student is more likely to learn if his or her attention is attracted by relatively novel presentations.
Active appropriate practice	A student is more likely to learn if he or she takes an active part in practice geared to reach an instructional objective.
Distributing practice	A student is more likely to learn if practice is done in short periods over time.
Fading	A student is more likely to learn if instructional prompts are withdrawn gradually.
Pleasant conditions and consequences	A student is more likely to learn if the instructional conditions are pleasant.

Note: From "General Principles of Learning and Motivation" by N. A. Carlson, 1980, *Teaching Exceptional Children, 12,* pp. 60–62. Copyright 1980 by The Council for Exceptional Children. Adapted by permission.

and Lenk (1992) point out, effective instruction of students with special needs can take place in any setting, general education or special, if teachers "(a) engage in teacher-directed instruction, (b) provide students with opportunities for active academic responding, (c) use high rates of contingent reinforcement, and (d) adapt teaching strategies to accommodate individual differences" (p. 36).

One of the cornerstones of the No Child Left Behind Act, the current federal education law, is that schools employ proven educational methods. According to the ED.gov website, "*No Child Left Behind* puts special emphasis on determining what educational programs and practices have been proven effective through rigorous scientific research" (*NCLB, Proven Methods,* n.d.). In special education, there is a substantial body of research on instructional methodologies (Mainzer, Deshler, Coleman, Kozleski, & Rodriguez-Walling, 2003). Vaughn, Gersten, and Chard (2000) synthesized this body of research and drew these conclusions:

> . . . instructional practices that are visible and explicit, interactive between students and teacher and between students and students, controlled for task difficulty, and include strategies to guide student learning result in the greatest student achievement. (Cited in Mainzer et al., p. 8)

Research findings on instruction in general education are less definitive, although the U.S. Department of Education is attempting to rectify this. One of the first steps is the establishment of the What Works Clearinghouse described in the "Window on the Web" feature.

Select Appropriate Learning Tasks

Selection of the learning task is a critical instructional decision. No matter how excellent the teaching procedures, instruction will not be effective if the task selected is inappropriate for the learner. Task selection is even more critical for students with special needs because they may learn new information and skills more slowly than their peers. The teacher should choose the most important portions of the general education curriculum as target behaviors. In making these decisions, priority should be given to skills and information that are useful both now and in the future. Special educators often use the term *functional* to refer to such learning tasks, whereas general educators talk about *authentic* tasks.

In addition, tasks should be described as precisely as possible. Some, such as Mager (1984), advocate the use of instructional objectives, which are statements of the desired student behavior in specific, observable terms. They spell out the conditions under which the behavior should occur and the criterion for successful performance of the behavior. Objectives help clarify the goals of instruction. Unlike broad goals such as "Students will become better readers," instructional objectives are stated with precision: "When presented with a 100-word passage from a book or story written at the grade 3 level, students will read the passage aloud with no more than 5 word recognition errors."

After the desired student behavior is identified, the teacher chooses instructional activities to present the skills and information required for task performance. Most teach-

Window on the Web

What Works Clearinghouse

http://www.w-w-c.org

The What Works Clearinghouse is a web-based resource for persons interested in effective educational interventions. According to the website, the "What Works Clearinghouse was established in 2002 by the U.S. Department of Education's Institute of Education Sciences to provide educators, policymakers, researchers, and the public with a central and trusted source of scientific evidence of what works in education."

The What Works Clearinghouse selects current educational practices of interest, gathers the research that has been conducted on these approaches, and determines which studies meet the standards for adequate scientific research. According to the clearinghouse, the most appropriate research designs are those that employ "randomized controlled trials." That is, the students or others who are research subjects are randomly assigned to either an experimental or control group, and subjects in the experimental groups receive the educational intervention under investigation.

As of the beginning of 2005, the clearinghouse website provided information about the effectiveness of only one approach: middle school math curricula. Among the next topics scheduled for review are

- beginning reading,
- character education,
- dropout prevention, and
- English language learning.

For more information, go to the Web Links module in Chapter 4 of the Companion Website.

---

ers use commercial programs and supplement them with teacher-made materials and activities. The teacher must be sure that ready-made programs present all necessary skills and information and do not include extraneous or irrelevant material. The teacher must also consider current performance level when placing a student in a program sequence. For example, grade 9 texts may not be appropriate for ninth graders who read at the seventh-grade level. Students should be placed in educational programs at a level at which they can succeed, that is, at their instructional level.

Break the Learning Task into Teachable Subcomponents

Tasks often require several skills or many different kinds of information for successful performance. Sometimes, particularly with commercial education programs, **task analysis**—the breaking down of tasks into smaller subtasks—is necessary. When the components of the task are identified, they can be presented to students in a systematic fashion.

First, the prerequisites for learning the task should be considered. For example, students who have not learned to solve multiplication problems will encounter difficulty when trying to calculate the area of a room. If necessary prerequisite skills are not present, instruction should begin with them. Next, the learning task is divided into subtasks. The subtasks may be a series of sequential steps or a collection of important subskills. An example of a task that can be broken into steps is addition of three-digit numbers; first the numbers in the ones column are added, then the numbers in the tens column, and finally the numbers in the hundreds column. Other tasks made up of a sequence of subtasks include building a model and locating a reference in the library. Writing a friendly letter is a task that can be divided into component subskills: handwriting (or keyboarding), spelling, capitalization, punctuation, and paragraph writing. Other such tasks are telling time, making change, and reading with comprehension.

The identification of subtasks and subskills allows the teacher to make decisions about the order in which skills and information will be presented. With tasks that are sequential in nature, subtasks are generally taught in the order in which they occur. With tasks made up of several components, the easier subskills are presented first. For example, in cursive writing instruction, simpler letters, such as lowercase *u* and *o*, are taught before more difficult letters, such as uppercase *F* and *G*.

Inclusion Tips for the Teacher

Writing Instructional Objectives

An objective, according to *Webster's New Collegiate Dictionary*, is "something toward which effort is directed; an aim, goal, or end of action." In education, objectives clearly state the aim of instruction. Their purpose is to direct the teacher in the selection of instructional activities.

Writing clear and useful instructional objectives is not an easy task. One common mistake is confusing objectives with goals. Goal statements are less specific than objectives; they generally describe only the behavior of interest and the direction in which the behavior should change.

  Goal: By the end of the school year, Jaime will increase his sight word vocabulary.

  Goal: Next semester Susie will be absent from school fewer days.

Instructional objectives, in contrast, are much more detailed. They include specific information about the exact behavior in question, the conditions under which the behavior should occur, and the criterion for successful performance of the behavior (Mager, 1984).

  Objective: When given a simple job application form,
                         (conditions)

          Jack will write his complete name and address
                        (behavior)

in legible handwriting with no errors in spelling.

             (mastery criterion)

One of the most important (and most difficult) steps in writing objectives is stating student behaviors in observable and measurable terms. The statement "Louise will write her name" is observable, but "Henry will know the meaning of all new vocabulary words" is not. Look at the lists of words below. The "observables" are action verbs; you can easily see whether someone is writing or walking. The "nonobservables" cannot be seen; it is not possible to see whether someone is understanding, knowing, or appreciating.

Observables	Nonobservables
Write a letter	Understand subtraction
Point to the answer	Know state geography
Say the alphabet	Appreciate sculpture
Read aloud from the text	Realize the importance of budgeting
Raise a hand to volunteer	Differentiate hand tools
Look at the teacher	Attend to class lectures
Name the U.S. presidents	Perceive the main idea
Draw a triangle	Draw conclusions

Use Systematic Instructional Procedures

Effective instruction follows the demonstration–prompt–practice model. After the teacher presents a demonstration or explanation of the skills and information necessary for performance of the learning task, students attempt to perform the task with prompts or assistance from the teacher. Students then practice the task independently. In other words, presentation is followed by guided practice, then independent practice.

In **demonstration,** the teacher may model the performance of new skills. If factual information is being presented, the teacher may simply tell students the new material. For example, in mathematics instruction, teachers can model appropriate performance by stating a fact or a rule, performing a task as students watch and listen, or asking one student a question while others observe (Lloyd & Keller, 1989). When information is conceptual, principles and examples are used to aid in explanation (Kameenui & Simmons, 1990). In one method (Close, Irvin, Taylor, & Agosta, 1981), the teacher presents new concepts directly, then cites relevant examples; guided practice is provided when students answer direct

Inclusion Tips for the Teacher

Direct Teaching

If you wish to teach spelling skills, here is one direct instruction method you can use. Be sure to select words that the students know the meaning of and can read. Then teach spelling.

Teacher: Let's spell the word *avalanche*. Watch me. (Teacher writes a word on the board and says letter names.) *A-v-a-l-a-n-c-h-e, avalanche.* Everyone say that with me.

Teacher and students: *A-v-a-l-a-n-c-h-e, avalanche.*

Teacher: Right. *Avalanche* is spelled *a-v-a-l-a-n-c-h-e.* Now, everyone, write *avalanche* on your paper.

Students: (Students write word.)

Teacher: Did you write *a-v-a-l-a-n-c-h-e, avalanche?* Good! Everyone say it with me.

Teacher and students: *A-v-a-l-a-n-c-h-e, avalanche.*

Teacher: *Avalanche* is spelled *a-v-a-l-a-n-c-h-e.* Now, turn your paper over and write *avalanche*.

Students: (Students write word.)

Teacher: Did you write *a-v-a-l-a-n-c-h-e, avalanche?* Good spelling.

This presentation requires only 2 or 3 minutes. In this short time the teacher has modeled the spelling of the word for the class once by writing it and five times orally. Students have spelled the word twice orally, have written it twice, and have been provided with immediate feedback each time. In just a few minutes each student in the class can be provided with several response opportunities.

---

questions, and then the teacher repeats and summarizes the original presentation.

In the prompt or **guided practice** stage, students are given opportunities to perform the task under the supervision of the teacher. This should occur before independent practice to ensure that students do not practice incorrect responses. In guided practice, the teacher gives immediate feedback to students regarding the accuracy of their responses; correct responses are confirmed, and incorrect responses are corrected. This step can be done individually, with small groups, or with the entire class. For example, the teacher can present new material to the class and then conduct a short question-and-answer session with all students. Stevens and Rosenshine (1981) recommend this technique and advocate the use of factual questions and whole-group unison responses.

In **independent practice,** the teacher continues to provide students with feedback or knowledge of results. Because this form of practice usually takes place in individual work sessions in class or as homework assignments, the time delay between student performance and feedback from the teacher is greater.

Direct teaching is another important feature of effective instruction. Skills are taught directly, and teaching activities are designed to be as close to the instructional goal as possible. For example, if the goal is for students to read words aloud, the teacher does not include activities such as matching words with pictures, looking up words in the dictionary, or writing sentences using the words. Instead, the teacher models, and students practice, reading words aloud.

Two other major considerations are maximizing the number of student responses and monitoring the accuracy of student performance. First, because students learn by responding, it is important to maximize the number of response opportunities available to each student. The goal is as many student responses as possible within given time limits. Second, because students learn by receiving information about the quality of their responses, it is important to monitor student performance by the frequent collection of data. Teachers (and students themselves) should collect information about the number and accuracy of student responses; this should occur frequently, even daily, but at a minimum once a week. This information provides feedback to both students and teachers. If the total number of student responses or the proportion of correct responses becomes low, the teacher can modify the instructional procedures.

Effective instructional strategies can be incorporated into any type of teaching situation for any age learner. Rosenshine and Stevens (1986) suggest that teachers should follow six fundamental steps in the instructional sequence:

1. Review, check previous day's work (and reteach, if necessary)
2. Present new content/skills
3. Guide student practice (and check for understanding)
4. Feedback and correctives (and reteach, if necessary)
5. Independent student practice
6. Weekly and monthly reviews. (p. 379)

This sequence is based on the demonstration–prompt–practice model; it is easily adapted to any subject matter area and is equally appropriate for elementary and secondary students. For more information about the specific procedures for each step, consult Figure 4-2.

FIGURE 4-2   Steps in Instruction

1. **Daily Review and Checking Homework**
   Checking homework (routines for students to check each other's papers)
   Reteaching when necessary
   Reviewing relevant past learning (may include questioning)
   Review prerequisite skills (if applicable)
2. **Presentation**
   Provide short statement of objectives
   Provide overview and structuring
   Proceed in small steps but at a rapid pace
   Intersperse questions within the demonstration to check for understanding
   Highlight main points
   Provide sufficient illustrations and concrete examples
   Provide demonstrations and models
   When necessary, give detailed and redundant instructions and examples
3. **Guided Practice**
   Initial student practice takes place with teacher guidance
   High frequency of questions and overt student practice (from teacher and/or materials)
   Questions are directly relevant to the new content or skill
   Teacher checks for understanding (CFU) by evaluating student responses
   During CFU teacher gives additional explanation, process feedback, or repeats explanation—
   where necessary
   All students have a chance to respond and receive feedback; teacher insures that all students participate
   Prompts are provided during guided practice (where appropriate)
   Initial student practice is *sufficient* so that students can work independently
   Guided practice continues until students are firm
   Guided practice is continued (usually) until a success rate of 80% is achieved
4. **Correctives and Feedback**
   Quick, firm, and correct responses can be followed by another question or a short acknowledgment of correctness (i.e., "That's right")
   Hesitant correct answers might be followed by process feedback (i.e., "Yes, Linda, that's right because . . .")
   Student errors indicate a need for more practice
   Monitor students for systematic errors
   Try to obtain a substantive response to each question
   Corrections can include sustaining feedback (i.e., simplifying the question, giving clues), explaining or reviewing steps, giving process feedback, or reteaching the last steps
   Try to elicit an improved response when the first one is incorrect
   Guided practice and corrections continue until the teacher feels that the group can meet the objectives of the lesson
   Praise should be used in moderation, and specific praise is more effective than general praise
5. **Independent Practice (Seatwork)**
   Sufficient practice
   Practice is directly relevant to skills/content taught
   Practice to overlearning
   Practice until responses are firm, quick, and automatic
   Ninety-five percent correct rate during independent practice
   Students alerted that seatwork will be checked
   Students held accountable for seatwork
   Actively supervise students, when possible

---

6. Weekly and Monthly Reviews
   Systematic review of previously learned material
   Include review in homework
   Frequent tests
   Reteaching of material missed in tests
Note: With older, more mature learners, or learners with more knowledge of the subject, the following adjustments can be made: (1) the size of the step in presentation can be larger (more material is presented at one time), (2) there is less time spent on teacher-guided practice and (3) the amount of overt practice can be decreased, replacing it with covert rehearsal, restating and reviewing.

Note: From B. Rosenshine and R. Stevens, "Teaching Functions," from *Handbook of Research on Teaching*, Third Edition, Merlin C. Wittrock, Editor, pp. 376–391. Copyright © 1986 by the American Educational Research Association. Reprinted by permission of the publisher.

Archer and Gleason (1989) suggest that lessons based on the demonstration–prompt–practice model be divided into three important components:

1. *Opening of the lesson.* The teacher gains the attention of the students and reviews any skills or knowledge areas critical to the content of the lesson. Then, he or she states the goal of the lesson and tells why the skill to be learned is important and when and where it will be used.

2. *Body of the lesson.* The teacher models the new skill and provides two types of guided practice: prompt and check. First, the teacher uses prompting to assist students in performing the new skill. Second, the teacher checks the students' progress by having them perform the new skill without assistance. According to Archer and Gleason (1989), with simpler skills, "MODEL, PROMPT and CHECK can occur in quick succession (e.g., 'This word is against. *Say the word with me. What word?*')" (p. 5).

3. *Close of the lesson.* The teacher ends the lesson by reviewing the critical information presented and providing a preview of the next lesson. Then students are assigned work for independent practice.

Consider Both Speed and Accuracy

In selecting and describing learning tasks, teachers should determine whether the instructional goal is rapid or accurate performance. This decision influences both presentation and practice.

For most learning tasks, particularly those that involve skills, both speed and accuracy are desired. The teacher demonstrates rapid, accurate performance; students practice for accuracy first and then speed. It is imperative in skill acquisition to provide practice that ensures that students acquire both accuracy and speed. If skills such as reading and writing are performed slowly, their usefulness decreases.

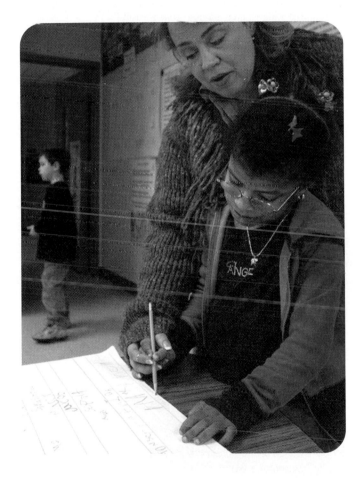

In skill acquisition, initial practice activities emphasize accuracy. Research suggests that students should achieve a 70% to 90% success rate during guided practice and at least a 90% success rate during independent practice (Englert, 1984; Rieth & Evertson, 1988; Rosenshine & Stevens, 1986). However, instruction should not stop with achievement of accuracy; further guided practice stressing speed should be given. This approach helps develop automatic responses that are both quick and accurate and also helps prevent students from acquiring slow response habits.

Maximize Engaged Time

Engaged time refers to the minutes and hours during which students are actively involved and participating in instruction. During that time they are "on task," whether that means listening to the teacher, watching a science experiment, answering the teacher's questions, reading, or writing. As engaged time increases, learning increases.

Students are engaged in learning for only certain portions of the school day because many noninstructional activities intrude. Even during time allocated for instruction, student attention may be directed elsewhere (Bulgren & Carta, 1992). In one study (Karweit & Slavin, 1981), actual instruction in elementary mathematics classes accounted for only 81% of the scheduled instructional time, and students were found to be engaged during only 68% of the time scheduled for instruction. Student inattention accounted for the greatest loss of learning time.

Similar results are reported by other researchers. In a study of general education classrooms, although 78% of class time was allocated to instruction, students with special needs were actively engaged only 63% of that time (Rich & Ross, 1989). Christenson and Ysseldyke (1986) compared regular classes and resource rooms and found that, regardless of the setting, students with learning disabilities and their peers spent less than 30 minutes of a 95-minute instructional period actively responding to academic tasks.

Student engagement can be increased in several ways. First, teachers should make full use of scheduled instructional time. Other activities such as clerical and housekeeping chores should not be done during the time allotted to teaching and learning. Make every minute count!

Second, teachers should emphasize instruction rather than independent practice. Research indicates that students show much higher engagement rates in teacher-led activities than in seatwork tasks (Rieth & Evertson, 1988).

Third, instruction should be designed to engage student attention. Materials and activities should be selected so that they are attractive, interesting to students, and at an appropriate level of difficulty. The length of the lesson should be neither too short nor too long; if the lesson is too long, student interest and attention may decline. The pace of instruction should be brisk. While not rushing students, the teacher should ensure that instruction proceeds at an energetic tempo with few pauses, hesitations, interruptions, or opportunities for boredom.

Fourth, engagement increases when students are required to respond. Students should be provided with as many response opportunities as possible; students actively involved in asking and answering lesson-related questions are engaged in learning. Maximum response opportunities that result in high proportions of correct responses are basic to successful instruction.

Group responding is one way to increase the number of active student responses. In **choral responding**, all of the students in the group respond in unison to questions posed by the teacher. Heward, Courson, and Narayan (1989) recommend including several brief (5- to 10-minute) choral response sessions throughout the school day for different academic subjects. The questions asked should require short answers (no more than three words), and only one correct response should be possible.

Response cards are another method to promote group responding (Heward et al., 1996). Instead of answering orally, students hold up a card with the response they believe to be correct; for example, students might choose between a true card and a false card or among cards saying *carnivore, herbivore*, or *omnivore*. A variation is the "pinch card" (p. 5). The card contains several responses (e.g., 25%, 50%, 75% and 100%), and the student pinches or points to the location of one of those responses. A third technique is group writing. The teacher asks a question or poses a problem (e.g., "What does the word *democracy* mean?"), and each student writes his or her response. Class members then discuss their answers and make corrections, as needed.

Englert (1984) presents several suggested ways to increase the amount of class time allocated to learning and methods for promoting student engagement during allocated learning time. The teacher checklist shown in Figure 4-3 summarizes these suggestions. For instance, teachers should spend at least 80% of class time in instructional activities and interact with 70% or more of their students each hour.

Give Clear Task Directions

For students to succeed, the directions for the learning task must be clearly stated and understandable. Before giving directions, the teacher should be sure that students are paying attention. Directions can be presented orally, in written form, or both. If directions are complicated and contain a number of steps, they should be broken down into subsets. For example, teachers who say, "Get out your math book and a sheet of paper, turn to page 46, do the even-numbered problems in Section A, the odd-numbered problems in Section C, and the first three story problems at the top of page 47" will likely find that their directions are not followed.

Directions can be simplified by presenting only one portion at a time and by writing each portion on the chalkboard as well as stating it orally. When using written directions, the teacher must be sure that students are able to read and understand the words and comprehend the meaning of the sentences. Also, directions should be presented immediately preceding the learning task (Rosenkoetter & Fowler, 1986). Students beginning an assignment at 10 A.M. are not likely to recall or follow the directions given by the teacher at 9:30 A.M.

Teachers can determine whether directions are clear by attending to feedback from students. Puzzled expressions and

FIGURE 4-3	Are You Making Optimal Use of Class Time?

Respond to each item in terms of the extent to which it describes yourself: (1) not at all descriptive, (2) descriptive to a small extent, (3) descriptive to a moderate extent, (4) descriptive to a large extent, (5) descriptive to an extremely large extent.

Competencies

Allocated Time

		Performance Evaluation
1.1	Maximizes time in instruction by continually scheduling students in direct instruction (e.g., interacts with 70% or more of the students per hour).	1 2 3 4 5
1.2	Minimizes time in non-instructional activities (e.g., spends 80% or more of class time in instructional activities).	1 2 3 4 5
1.3	Keeps transition time between lessons short (e.g., no more than 3 minutes between change of students and activity; no more than 30 seconds when a change of activity only).	1 2 3 4 5
1.4	Established procedures for lessons that signal a clear beginning and end.	1 2 3 4 5
1.5	Gains all students' attention at the beginning of the lesson and maintains student attention during lesson at 90% level.	1 2 3 4 5
1.6	Prepares students for transitions in advance by stating behavioral expectations and informing students that lesson is drawing to a close.	1 2 3 4 5

Engaged Time

2.1	Maintains students' attention during seatwork at 80% levels or higher.	1 2 3 4 5
2.2	Monitors seatwork students continuously through eye scanning.	1 2 3 4 5
2.3	Circulates among seatwork students between lessons to assist students and to monitor progress.	1 2 3 4 5
2.4	Maintains seatwork accuracy at 90% level or higher.	1 2 3 4 5
2.5	Tells rationale for seatwork and communicates the importance of the assignment.	1 2 3 4 5
2.6	Provides active forms of seatwork practice clearly related to academic goals.	1 2 3 4 5
2.7	Sets seatwork and assignment standards (neatness, accuracy, due dates).	1 2 3 4 5
2.8	Uses tutoring (e.g., peer, volunteers, aides) and other specialized instructional technology to increase opportunity for active academic responding during seatwork.	1 2 3 4 5
2.9	Establishes procedures for early finishers, students who are stalled, and those seeking help.	1 2 3 4 5
2.10	Schedules time to review seatwork.	1 2 3 4 5
2.11	Requires that students correct work and make up missed or unfinished work.	1 2 3 4 5
2.12	Gives informative feedback to students in making written or verbal corrections.	1 2 3 4 5

Note: From "Measuring Teacher Effectiveness from the Teacher's Point of View" by C. S. Englert, 1984, *Focus on Exceptional Children, 17*(2), p. 9. Copyright 1984 by Love. Reprinted by permission.

failure to follow the directions are immediate cues that directions are unclear. If students are asked to repeat the directions to the teacher, misunderstandings become apparent. Clear directions are an important part of effective instruction, and clarity is one of the teacher characteristics most valued by students. Figure 4-4 presents a checklist for students to use when assessing their teachers' clarity.

Provide Consequences for Successful Task Performance

In most classrooms, a variety of consequences are available for the teacher's use. Successful task performance may be followed by teacher attention, praise, special privileges, or awards. Unsuccessful performance, however, may result in the loss of teacher attention and praise or other unpleasant consequences. Because behaviors followed by pleasant consequences are more likely to occur again, teachers should make a systematic effort to reward successful task performance.

One powerful consequence is feedback to the student or **knowledge of results**. The student responds, and the teacher comments about the accuracy of the response; correct answers are confirmed, and incorrect answers are corrected. Students provided with information about the acceptability of their responses tend to modify their performances to increase the number of correct responses. Eventually they begin monitoring their own performances rather than relying on teacher feedback. Suggested ways of providing feedback are listed in the "Inclusion Tips for the Teacher" material on page 93.

In addition to knowledge of results, other consequences can be used. Teachers can reward successful task performance with attention, praise, and compliments; with letter or number grades; with recognition of the student's accomplishment before peers or parents; and with awards, privileges, and special activities.

FIGURE 4-4   The Clear Teacher Checklist

As your teacher I hope I am clear. In order to improve my ability to be clear I need your help. Below are 28 statements that describe what clear teachers do. Read each statement and place a check mark in the column that tells how often I perform the behavior that is described. In that way I'll know what I do well and what I need to improve.

(Put a check ✔ in one box after each statement.)

As our teacher, you:

	All of the time	Most of the time	Some of the time	Never	Doesn't apply to our class
1. Explain things simply.					
2. Give explanations we understand.					
3. Teach at a pace that is not too fast and not too slow.					
4. Stay with a topic until we understand.					
5. Try to find out when we don't understand and then you repeat things.					
6. Teach things step-by-step.					
7. Describe the work to be done and how to do it.					
8. Ask if we know what to do and how to do it.					
9. Repeat things when we don't understand.					
10. Explain something and then work an example.					
11. Explain something and then stop so we can ask questions.					
12. Prepare us for what we will be doing next.					
13. Give specific details when teaching.					
14. Repeat things that are hard to understand.					
15. Work examples and explain them.					
16. Give us a chance to think about what's being taught.					
17. Explain something and then stop so we can think about it.					
18. Show us how to do the work.					
19. Explain the assignment and the materials we need to do it.					
20. Stress difficult points.					
21. Show examples of how to do classwork and homework.					
22. Give us enough time for practice.					
23. Answer our questions.					
24. Ask questions to find out if we understand.					
25. Go over difficult homework problems.					
26. Show us how to remember things.					
27. Explain how to do assignments by using examples.					
28. Show us the difference between things.					

"The Clear Teacher Checklist" is based substantially on research findings contained in the article by Kennedy et al. in *Journal of Educational Research*, Sept./Oct. 1978.

Inclusion Tips for the Teacher

Providing Students with Feedback

- When students respond correctly, tell them! A simple "Yes," "Right," "Good," or "Correct" lets a learner know that the answer was on target.
- If a student's response is correct but hesitant, the teacher should provide process feedback. The response is confirmed and the teacher explains why it was correct. For example, the teacher might say, "Yes, John, that's correct. The first word in every sentence begins with a capital."
- If students give incorrect responses, again they should be told. The teacher can say "No" or "Not quite." If the teacher believes a student answered incorrectly because he or she did not understand the question or was not paying attention, the question should be repeated.
- The next step is the use of a correction procedure. After making the student aware that the response was incorrect, the teacher should help the student produce the correct answer. The teacher can model the correct response.

Teacher: Spell *this*.
Student: T-h-e-s.
Teacher: No, *this* is spelled *t-h-i-s*. Spell *this*.
Student: T-h-i-s.
Teacher: Right!

With some learning tasks a prompt can be given.

Teacher: Read this word: *shut*.
Student: *Cut*.
Teacher: Not quite. The first sound is *sh*. Read it again.
Student: *Shut*.
Teacher: Good reading.

Or the task can be made easier.

Teacher: Who was the first president of the United States?
Student: Lincoln.
Teacher: No. Was it George Washington or Thomas Jefferson?
Student: Washington.
Teacher: Correct.

Knowledge of results is a powerful tool for helping students learn. However, when students make errors, feedback alone is not sufficient. To help students learn the correct response, correction procedures must also be used.

Consequences, like instructional antecedents, are powerful tools for promoting successful classroom performance, and their use will be described in more depth in the next chapter. However, consequences must be used systematically. They should follow behaviors as closely in time as possible, especially when students are in the acquisition stage of learning. Consequences should also be used consistently. Behaviors confirmed as correct and rewarded on one day should receive the same consequences on the next day.

Check for Maintenance and Generalization

The majority of the time spent in instruction is devoted to acquisition of skills and information. However, if students are to use what they have learned in later school and life situations, maintenance and generalization are also important. Teachers cannot assume that tasks performed successfully today will also be performed successfully next week, next month, or next semester. Acquisition does not guarantee maintenance. Skills and information, particularly those that are verbal in nature, are forgotten if not practiced. To enhance

FIGURE 4-5   Mistakes in Instruction

Inappropriate Instructional Strategy	Example
Instructional content is presented sporadically, rather than sequentially and systematically over time.	The teacher presents an exercise demonstrating syllabication of words. He provides a verbal description of the process and written exercises which he scores. The next day a different concept is taught. Observation shows that syllabication activities are taught again 2 weeks later; the same procedure is used.
Well-written instructional activities are followed by nonspecific evaluation.	Although the teacher develops written lesson plans complete with behavioral objectives and teaching procedures, the evaluation component generally consists of such global statements as "It seems to go pretty well" or "I should make the material more relevant."
Conditions for independent seatwork are not stated clearly.	The teacher initiates and leads a group. Five minutes later Ruthie approaches the teacher and asks for help with her seatwork. The teacher excuses herself to help Ruthie. An observer notes that reading is resumed but is interrupted five more times in the 15-minute reading session.
Reading activities are geared to frustration rather than to comprehension level.	The teacher asks Dotty to read a three-paragraph (64-word) selection during an individual instruction session in a resource room. An observer's record shows that the teacher supplied (read) 22 words that Dotty failed to read.
Children's error rates are consistently high.	Tommy hands in a math exercise, and the teacher says, "OK." Observation reveals that he made 7 errors in the set of 15 problems. A question elicits this response: "Oh, he knows that; it's just sloppy work." No data are available to confirm or deny the statement.
Additional learning trials are presented after criterion has been met.	Mark, a 10-year-old member of a [special] class . . ., proudly reads his primer to an observer. A question reveals that he has been reading it without error for the last 2 weeks.

Note: From "A Teacher's Guide to Instructional Programming" by J. W. Tawney, C. G. Kruse, P. T. Cegelka, and D. L. Kelly, 1977, *Teaching Exceptional Children, 10*, pp. 2–6. Copyright 1977 by the Council for Exceptional Children. Adapted by permission.

maintenance, task performance should be monitored over time, and practice should be provided when necessary.

Generalization cannot be assumed, either. Students may perform quite well on one task but be unable to transfer their learning to a similar task. For example, words spelled correctly on a spelling test may be misspelled in a book report or essay. Generalization is crucial because there is insufficient time to teach all the possible situations in which particular skills and information may be needed. Teachers can promote transfer by evaluating its occurrence; if necessary, the teacher can demonstrate how skills and information are used in many different situations and then provide students with practice in generalization.

If Change Is Needed, Try the Least Intrusive Intervention First

Data on student performance may indicate the need for a change in instructional procedures. Student responses may be infrequent, inconsistent, or less accurate than desired. To increase the likelihood of successful performance, the learning task should be made easier—by changing teaching procedures, modifying materials and activities, or altering task requirements. Several ways of accomplishing this are described later in this chapter.

However, unsuccessful performance should not result in the immediate substitution of an alternate task. First, the original task should be modified in an attempt to increase response accuracy. The simplest, least dramatic changes should be tried first; for instance, task failure may be due to insufficient practice or poor understanding of the directions. Intense interventions such as radically different instructional procedures, new materials and activities, or abandonment of the original task should be used only when all other options have been exhausted.

The principles of instruction presented here apply to learners of all ages and all ability levels. The instructional technique used to help you learn these principles has been direct presentation with occasional examples. Another appropriate technique is the use of nonexemplars, or examples of noninstances. In teaching colors, we show students several examples of red and then introduce the concept of nonred by showing blue, yellow, green, and pink objects. See Figure 4-5 for nonexemplars of effective instructional strategies.

It is possible for teachers to use effective instructional techniques but to apply these techniques unequally with different groups of students. Research indicates that teachers treat high achievers and low achievers quite differently. For example, in one study (Alves & Gottlieb, 1986), general education teachers interacted less frequently with students with disabilities than with their classmates without disabilities. Students with disabilities also were asked fewer questions by their teachers and received less feedback on their performance. For instruction to be truly effective, it must address the needs of all students within the classroom.

METHODS FOR GATHERING DATA

Information about student performance helps the teacher make instructional decisions. For example, data are gathered to determine the student's current level of academic performance before instruction begins. Such information aids in planning the educational program and placing the student in the correct portion of the instructional sequence. During instruction, data are used to evaluate student progress and to explore reasons for poor performance; this information helps to determine whether instructional adaptations should be made.

Although many types of assessment techniques are available, in most cases informal assessment rather than formal testing is the method of choice for gathering information about a student's classroom performance. One approach to informal assessment is **curriculum-based assessment** (CBA), defined as "a procedure for determining the instructional needs of students based on the student's ongoing performance in existing course content" (Gickling & Thompson, 1985, p. 206). That is, the curriculum of the student's classroom is used as the yardstick by which to measure educational progress. Results of such assessments have immediate instructional applications (Pemberton, 2003). Skills that the student has not yet mastered become the next goals in the instructional sequence. The sections that follow provide principles for gathering useful information about student performance.

Determine the Student's Current Levels of Performance

Before beginning instruction, teachers are interested in determining what skills have already been acquired by the student. The group achievement tests given routinely to students in many school districts are one source of this information. Measures such as the Metropolitan Achievement Tests, the California Achievement Tests, and the Stanford Achievement Tests provide information about the level of performance in basic skills such as reading and mathematics. For example, results may indicate that a sixth-grade student is performing at a fifth-grade level in reading comprehension, a sixth-grade level in mathematics, and a fourth-grade level in written language.

Because student achievement levels change over time, only recent achievement test results are of interest. However, even recent test data should be considered with caution because test tasks may differ from classroom learning tasks. Also, some students—particularly those with special needs—do not perform to the best of their ability on tests administered in group settings. In general, standardized measures such as group achievement tests are not the best source of information about current levels of performance for this group of students. In fact, federal law requires that test modifications be made whenever necessary for students with disabilities who participate in the group achievement tests administered on district-wide or statewide basis to their general education peers. A later section of this chapter discusses principles for making test accommodations for these students.

Teachers can utilize the results of group achievement tests to identify students who may need interventions such as special education. Stone, Cundick, and Swanson (1988) recommend using the 5th percentile as a cutoff point. Percentile rank scores indicate the percentage of a test's norm group that a particular student's performance equals or exceeds. Thus, a student scoring at the 5th percentile would show achievement equal to or better than 5% of norm group peers (and worse than 95% of that group). Reynolds, Zetlin, and Wang (1993) recommend a somewhat different procedure, "20/20 Analysis." Results of group achievement tests are studied to identify two groups of students who benefit from adaptations of the general education program: (a) students with learning problems, defined as students who fall in the lowest 20% (i.e., below the 20th percentile); and (b) high achievers, defined as students who fall in the highest 20% (above the 80th percentile).

Informal measures such as placement tests, inventories, and criterion-referenced tests provide the most useful information about current levels of student performance. For example, the placement tests found in many commercial educational programs and textbook series assess the student's skill levels and provide information about where in the educational program the student should begin. If these measures are not available, the teacher can devise informal assessments such as inventories and criterion-referenced tests.

FIGURE 4-6   Handwriting Inventory

Print your name on the line below.

- -

Fill in the missing letters.

a cd fg ij l no qr tu w y

Print the uppercase (capital) letter that goes with each of the lowercase (small) letters below.

a A

b ____   f ____   d ____

g ____   r ____

Copy this sentence in your best printing.

Foxes and rabbits are quick, but turtles are slow.

_____

Write your name in cursive on the line below.

- -

Finish writing the cursive alphabet.

_abc_____

Write the following words in cursive.

dog ____   like _____   and ____   the ____

Write this sentence in your best cursive handwriting.

At the zoo you can see lions and tigers,
elephants, bears, and monkeys.

_____

_____

Inventories are measures that sample a variety of different skills and information within a subject matter area. They are designed to estimate the approximate level of student functioning. For instance, an informal math inventory would not assess all aspects of a mathematics curriculum. However, it might include a range of problems sampling knowledge of basic number facts, skills in basic operations (addition, subtraction, multiplication, and division), and ability to solve problems requiring regrouping. Student performance on this inventory would give the teacher some information about which skills have been acquired and which have not. An informal handwriting inventory appears in Figure 4-6; this measure provides general information about current levels of performance in the skill area of handwriting.

FIGURE 4-7	Observations of Academic Performance

Student: ___Juan___
Subject: ___Science 9___
Task: ___Homework Assignments___

Day	Number of Questions	Number of Responses	Number of Correct Responses	Percentage of Correct Responses
Monday	7	7	3	43%
Tuesday	9	9	4	44%
Wednesday	6	6	3	50%
Thursday	10	10	5	50%
Friday	8	8	3	38%

For more specific data, more precise measures are necessary. **Criterion-referenced tests** assess whether students have mastered the educational goals stated in instructional objectives. The teacher selects an objective, sets up the necessary conditions, and determines whether students are able to perform well enough to meet the criterion for acceptable performance. For example, to determine mastery of the objective "Students will write the names of at least 45 of the states with no errors in spelling," the teacher simply directs students to write the names of each of the states. Responses are acceptable if they are state names and if they are spelled correctly. Students with fewer than 45 correct responses have not yet met the objective and should receive further instruction.

Evaluate Progress

Information about student performance during instruction provides the teacher with feedback about the effectiveness of teaching procedures. Before instruction begins, it is important to pretest students to establish a performance baseline. This initial performance then becomes the reference point for evaluating progress in the instructional program.

Systematic observation is a useful technique for monitoring pupil progress. As chapter 5 will explain, observation is a flexible technique that can be used with a variety of student behaviors. In academic instruction, observation generally focuses on the number of responses made by the student and the proportion (or percentage) of correct responses. Figure 4-7 presents an example in which the teacher observed Juan's performance on science assignments for a 1-week period. Although Juan answered all the questions, the proportion of correct responses never rose above 50%. Thus, the teacher will modify instruction in an attempt to increase response accuracy.

As discussed in chapter 3, curriculum-based measurement is an effective strategy for monitoring student progress (Deno, 1985, 1987; Fuchs, 1986, 1987; Howell, Fox, & Morehead, 1993). Deno and Fuchs (1987) describe the procedures needed to establish a system of curriculum-based measurement in the classroom. The teacher decides what to measure and how to measure it, then formulates a specific instructional goal and objective. In the example provided by Deno and Fuchs, the goal is as follows:

In 19 weeks, when presented with stories for 1 minute from Level 2-SRA series, Michael will read aloud 80 words with no more than 6 errors. (p. 13)

The accompanying objective is to increase the number of words Michael reads correctly by an average of 2.6 words per week.

The teacher assesses this student's progress by having him read randomly selected passages from his reading text for 1-minute periods. These data are collected frequently, at least twice a week. The student's performance is graphed (see Figure 4-8), and his progress is compared with the aimline, a diagonal line extending from his baseline performance to the instructional goal (marked with an X on the graph).

Another approach to monitoring student growth is the use of **rubrics** to determine progress toward curricular standards. Airasian (1996) explains that rubrics are "brief, written descriptions of different levels of student performance" (p. 154). These levels can be indicated by numerical values (e.g., 1 through 5) or by descriptive labels such as *excellent, very good, good, average*, or *needs improvement*. The teacher (or other rater) evaluates the student's work and determines where within the descriptive framework that work falls. Figure 4-9 shows two sections of a rubric for evaluating student essays, the sections on Writing Conventions and Organization. In using this rubric, the teacher would need to decide which descriptions are most accurate. For example, a student's work might make

FIGURE 4-8   Curriculum-Based Measurement

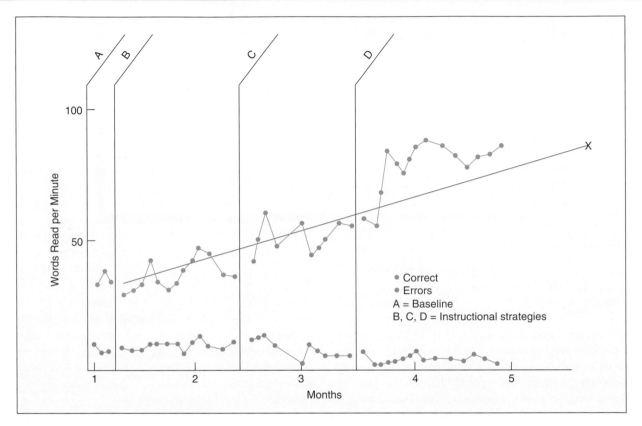

Note: From "Developing Curriculum-Based Measurement Systems for Data-Based Special Education Problem Solving" by S. L. Deno and L. S. Fuchs, 1987, *Focus on Exceptional Children, 19*(8), p. 15. Copyright 1987 by Love. Reprinted by permission.

sense (a rating of 4 in the Organization section), but show errors in the use of writing conventions (a rating of 2).

Analyze Reasons for Task Failure

When task performance is unsatisfactory, the student's responses can be analyzed to help locate problem areas. Called **error analysis,** this technique involves scoring each response as correct or incorrect and then looking for error patterns. For example, a student may solve only 8 of 22 addition problems correctly; by systematically analyzing the student's responses, the teacher may find that all errors involved problems requiring regrouping and that the student was using an inappropriate strategy, such as failing to carry:

$$\begin{array}{r} 4\ 2 \\ +3\ 9 \\ \hline 7\ 11 \end{array}$$

If student performance is poor (few responses are made, or most of the responses are incorrect), analyzing the task rather than the specific student errors may be helpful. With

task analysis, the task is broken down into component parts, and then students are asked to perform each of the parts. In this way, the subtasks that are causing the most difficulty can be identified, and instruction can begin with those areas.

STRATEGIES FOR ADAPTING INSTRUCTION

When students have difficulty acquiring skills and information, the teacher adapts instruction to better meet the students' needs. Teachers can modify instructional materials and activities, change teaching procedures, or alter the requirements of the learning task. Several of the specific strategies for instructional adaptations appear in Figure 4-10. These should be used in an attempt to improve student performance before more involved modifications are made. Note that the strategies are arranged in numerical order from 1 to 10. Number 1 should be tried before number 2, number 2 before number 3, and so on. Of course, before these methods are used, teachers should be sure that the learning task is at an appropriate level of difficulty for the student.

FIGURE 4-9	Excerpts from a Rubric for Evaluating Student Essays

Writing Conventions

Rating	Description
5	The use of writing conventions is very effective. No errors evident. These conventions are fluid and complex: spelling, punctuation, grammar usage, sentence structure.
4	The use of writing conventions is effective. Only minor errors evident. These conventions are nearly all effective: spelling, punctuation, grammar usage, sentence structure.
3	The use of writing conventions is somewhat effective. Errors don't interfere with meaning. These conventions are somewhat effective: spelling, punctuation, grammar usage, sentence structure.
2	Errors in the use of writing conventions interfere with meaning. These conventions are limited and uneven: spelling, punctuation, grammar usage, sentence structure.
1	Major errors in the use of writing conventions obscure meaning. Lack of understanding of spelling, punctuation, grammar usage, sentence structure.

Organization

5	Clearly makes sense.
4	Makes sense.
3	Makes sense for the most part.
2	Attempted but does not make sense.
1	Does not make sense.

Note: Reprinted with permission from *Authentic Assessment in the Classroom* (p. 176) by M. Tombari and G. Borich. Copyright © 1999 by Prentice-Hall, Inc., Upper Saddle River, New Jersey.

FIGURE 4-10	Adapting Instruction

IF students experience difficulty in task performance,
TRY these adaptations of . . .
Materials and activities:
  1. Clarify task directions
  2. Add prompts to the learning task
  3. Teach to specific student errors
Teaching procedures:
  4. Give additional presentation of skills and information
  5. Provide additional guided practice
  6. Make consequences for successful performance more attractive
  7. Slow the pace of instruction
Task requirements:
  8. Change the criteria for successful performance
  9. Change task characteristics
  10. Break each task into smaller subtasks
BEFORE selecting an alternate task.
IF NECESSARY, substitute a similar but easier task or a prerequisite task.

Modify Materials and Activities

The first type of adaptation to try is modification of instructional materials and activities. The learning task remains the same; what is changed is the way in which the necessary skills and information are presented to the student. Three possible strategies are the clarification of task directions, addition of prompts to the learning task, and correction of specific student errors (items 1, 2, and 3 in Figure 4-10).

Clarify Task Directions. Students may perform tasks poorly if the directions for the task are unclear. Several changes can make directions more understandable:

- Give directions both orally and in writing.
- Restate oral directions in simpler language.
- Give only one or two oral directions at a time.
- Be sure students are able to see directions written on the chalkboard.
- Keep written directions on the student's reading level.
- Explain any new or unfamiliar terms.

After giving directions, the teacher should demonstrate task performance and then answer any questions students may have.

Add Prompts. *Prompts* or *cues* are any features added to learning tasks that assist students in task performance. Prompts can be verbal, visual, or physical and can either call attention to the cues already available in the learning task or introduce an artificial cue system.

Prompts are often used to make critical features of the learning task more noticeable. For example, if students confuse addition and subtraction symbols, teachers might circle the symbols, make them larger, write them in red, or remind students to "check each problem to see whether you add or subtract." If students read aloud without attending to punctuation, punctuation marks can be underlined, highlighted, or color coded to make them stand out.

Artificial prompts can also be added to learning tasks. In handwriting instruction, for instance, guidelines are provided to assist beginning writers. Another example is the use of underlining; teachers who underline important words and phrases on the board are providing prompts. Teachers can also give verbal prompts or reminders; for example, before students begin to write a paragraph, the teacher might say, "Remember to begin each sentence with a capital letter."

Any learning task can be made easier by the use of prompts. However, as students learn, it is important to withdraw the prompts from the task, fading them gradually (as shown in Figure 4-11) to maintain successful student performance.

Teach to Specific Student Errors. If students make consistent errors that affect overall task performance, the teacher should focus on the correction of those errors. This approach is effective if a few types of errors account for the majority of incorrect responses. For example, if a student writes the cur-

sive alphabet correctly with the exception of the letters *m* and *n*, these letters should be singled out and taught directly. Or if oral reading is characterized by frequent repetitions ("I want . . . I want to go to the . . . I want to go to the store . . . I want to go to the store to buy . . . "), the teacher should attempt to correct this error. However, if task failure is due to several types of errors (or too few responses), it is probably necessary to modify the procedures used in teaching.

Change Teaching Procedures

If modification of instructional activities and materials does not result in successful performance, the next step is to adapt the teaching procedures. Strategies include giving additional presentations, providing additional practice, changing the consequences, and slowing the pace of instruction (items 4, 5, 6, and 7 in Figure 4-10).

Give Additional Presentation of Skills and Information. An additional presentation of the skills and information necessary for task performance may be appropriate. With this strategy, the teacher demonstrates skills and explains information. A repetition of the original presentation may produce the desired results. However, the teacher must usually provide a more complete (or simpler) explanation, additional examples, or several instances in which the skill is modeled.

Provide Additional Guided Practice. Poor task performance may be improved by additional guided practice. The teacher can increase the amount of practice by requiring more student responses, lengthening practice sessions (although not to the point of student fatigue), or scheduling extra sessions throughout the school day. To make practice more effective, teachers can increase both the amount and the quality of their feedback to students. To increase the amount, feedback can be given after every response rather than after every third or fifth answer. To increase the quality of feedback, the teacher can describe important features of the student's behavior in addition to telling the student whether the task was performed correctly. The statement "That's right. You remembered to put a period at the end of the sentence" tells the student that the response was accurate and points out the specific behavior for which praise is given.

Make Consequences for Successful Performance More Attractive. This strategy involves changing the consequences of the behavior rather than its antecedents. Consequences for successful performance include knowledge of results and rewards supplied by the teacher. To increase the effect of knowledge of results, teachers can improve the quality of feedback, as previously described. In addition, students become more aware of their performance if they are involved in data collection procedures. They can place an *X* or a check mark beside each correct response on their assigned papers and then plot their performance on a graph.

FIGURE 4-11 Fading Prompts from the Learning Task

Faded visual prompts in the instruction of one-digit–plus–two-digit addition with carrying

$$\begin{array}{r} \cancel{0}\;3\,|4 \\ +\;\;|8 \\ \hline \end{array} \quad \begin{array}{r} \cancel{0}\;3\,|4 \\ +\;\;|8 \\ \hline \end{array} \quad \begin{array}{r} \cancel{0}\;34 \\ +\;\;8 \\ \hline \end{array} \quad \begin{array}{r} \cancel{0}\;34 \\ +\;8 \\ \hline \end{array} \quad \begin{array}{r} 34 \\ +\;8 \\ \hline \end{array}$$

Faded visual prompts used in the instruction of one-digit into two-digit division

$$4\overline{)52} \quad 4\overline{)52} \quad 4\overline{)52} \quad 4\overline{)52}$$

Faded visual prompts used in the instruction of one-digit–times–two-digit multiplication

$$\begin{array}{r} \cancel{0}\;4\,|2 \\ \times\;|7 \\ \hline \end{array} \quad \begin{array}{r} 4\,|2 \\ \times\;|7 \\ \hline \end{array} \quad \begin{array}{r} 4\,2 \\ \times\;7 \\ \hline \end{array} \quad \begin{array}{r} 4\,2 \\ \times\;7 \\ \hline \end{array} \quad \begin{array}{r} 4\,2 \\ \times\;7 \\ \hline \end{array}$$

Faded visual prompts used in the instruction of two-digit multiplication

$$\begin{array}{r} 32 \\ \times\;24 \\ \hline \end{array} \quad \begin{array}{r} 32 \\ \times\;24 \\ \hline \end{array} \quad \begin{array}{r} 32 \\ \times\;24 \\ \hline \end{array} \quad \begin{array}{r} 32 \\ \times\;24 \\ \hline \end{array}$$

Note: Reprinted with permission of Merrill, an imprint of Macmillan Publishing Company, from *Teaching the Mildly Handicapped in the Regular Classroom* (2nd ed., p. 107) by J. Affleck, S. Lowenbraun, and A. Archer. Copyright ©1980 Merrill Publishing Company, Columbus, Ohio.

The reward system in use in the classroom may also need to be altered. Students may require incentives to begin or complete a task. And teachers may need to reward approximations toward successful task performance (e.g., 60% accuracy, then 70%, etc., until the criterion is achieved). The nature of the rewards used by the teacher may also require modification; things perceived by teachers as rewards may be less attractive to students.

Slow the Pace of Instruction. If changes in antecedents and consequences do not produce acceptable performance, slowing the pace of instruction may be necessary. The learning task and the time allotted for instruction remain the same, but less material is presented and practiced. For example, the

teacher may demonstrate telling time to the hour and to the half hour in two separate sessions rather than one. If this strategy is unsuccessful, the teacher should consider altering the requirements of the learning task.

Alter Task Requirements

The learning task itself can be modified to enhance student success. Possible strategies are changing task criteria, changing task characteristics, and breaking the task into smaller subtasks (items 8, 9, and 10 in Figure 4-10).

Change the Criteria for Successful Performance. The criteria for successful performance generally address three aspects of the task: quantity, speed, and accuracy. The requirements for each can be reduced. The number of questions, problems, or activities to be performed can be reduced. The time limits imposed can be increased so that speed demands are relaxed, or a lower accuracy rate can be accepted. However, the teacher should maintain reasonable accuracy requirements to ensure that the student is learning the task.

Change Task Characteristics.   Task characteristics include the conditions under which the task is performed and the nature of the behavior itself. If the task requires students to perform from memory without aids and assistance, the teacher might allow the use of aids. For example, students may be able to solve multiplication problems if they can use an aid such as a multiplication table or a pocket calculator. Presentation and response modes can also be changed. A task's presentation mode is the way it presents information; for example, many classroom tasks require reading skills. Instead of reading, students might listen to lectures and tapes or watch television and videos. Response modes can also be modified. Instead of writing, students might type, answer orally, tape-record their responses, or dictate them to a peer.

Break Tasks into Smaller Subtasks.   If alteration of task characteristics and criteria does not produce success, the task is probably too complex and should be broken into smaller subtasks. For example, if writing (or dictating or tape-recording) an essay is overwhelming to a student, the teacher can set up a series of smaller tasks: selection of a topic, preparation of an outline or organizational map, writing the title, formulation of the topic sentence for the first paragraph, and so on. This strategy is the last in a series of instructional modifications; the next step is to substitute an alternate task.

Select an Alternate Task

When student performance remains poor despite instructional adaptations, the teacher should consider replacing the learning task with an alternate task. Two choices are possible: a similar but easier task or a prerequisite task.

Substitute a Similar but Easier Task.   The teacher can select an alternate task similar in nature to the original task but easier for students to perform. For example, if students are unable to cope with the history textbook (even in taped form), the teacher can substitute another text that covers the same material but in less depth and at a lower reading level. This allows students to proceed at their own levels and rates while remaining in the same general subject area as their peers.

Substitute a Prerequisite Task.   The most drastic intervention available to the general education teacher is replacement of the original learning task with a prerequisite task. For example, if students with poor basic skills are unable to solve algebraic equations (even with the aid of a calculator), the teacher may substitute instruction in math facts and the operations of addi-

tion, subtraction, multiplication, and division. This strategy should be the last employed in the general education classroom because it involves the most radical change from typical classroom procedures. Students whose needs cannot be met with this strategy are candidates for special education services.

The most comprehensive instructional modification that can be made is change of the curriculum. This often occurs when students with severe disabilities are included in general education classes as part of their special education program. In most cases, the educational goals for students with serious learning needs address areas such as socialization and communication skills, rather than academic performance. For students such as these, instructional adaptations usually include the substitution of an alternative curriculum. For example, a student with severe disabilities might participate in the same lesson on volcanoes as others in the class, although the instructional goal for that student relates to learning to work with others, rather than science. Chapter 10 provides more information about instructional and curricular adaptations for students with serious learning needs.

MAKING TEST ACCOMMODATIONS

When students with special needs are members of general education classrooms, it is often useful to consider adapting not only instruction but also the procedures used to assess student learning. Adaptations are particularly important when students with disabilities participate alongside their general education peers in statewide or district-wide tests of academic achievement. These "high-stakes" tests, usually administered on an annual basis, are part of the national movement toward higher performance standards for students and greater accountability for schools, districts, and state educational agencies.

Federal special education law requires that IEP teams address how students with disabilities will participate in statewide or district-wide measures of academic achievement. Three options are possible. First of all, students may simply take the same tests as their grade-level peers under identical conditions; no changes or modifications are made. Second, students with disabilities may participate in the same assessments as their regular class peers but with one or more changes or accommodations to increase the probability of success. One common example of a test accommodation is an increase in the amount of time allowed to complete a particular section of a test. The third and most drastic option open to the IEP team is to determine that the general education achievement test is not appropriate for a student and that his or her educational progress should instead be measured by an alternate assessment procedure. That alternate assessment is then selected or developed by the IEP team.

The second option, test accommodations, is likely the most common for students with disabilities who are included in general education classes. Elliott, Kratochwill, and Gilbertson (1998) define testing accommodations as "a change in the way that a test is administered or responded to by the person tested" (p. 10). Because of the many types of accommodations possible, several attempts have been made to come up with category systems to simplify discussion of the possibilities.

For example, Erickson, Ysseldyke, Thurlow, and Elliott (1998) and Landau, Vohs, and Romano (1998) describe similar systems. Each addresses four basic types of test accommodations:

- Timing and/or scheduling accommodations,
- Setting accommodations,
- Presentation accommodations, and
- Response accommodations.

Timing/scheduling modifications involve extending time limits for a test, allowing a student to take frequent breaks, or scheduling the test over several days rather than one. Setting accommodations include changes such as administration of the test to a small group rather than a large group or a change in the location of the test. Presentation accommodations include modifications such as providing test materials in a different format (e.g., large print, Braille) and reading the test aloud to a student. In contrast, when the test's response mode is changed, students may be allowed to answer orally rather than write on an answer sheet.

Although many different types of accommodations are available, states and districts vary in the modifications they permit for students with disabilities. The most typical types of changes, allowed by more than half of the 50 states (Statewide Assessment Programs, 1998), are as follows:

- *Presentation.* Large print, Braille, sign language;
- *Setting.* Small-group administration, separate testing session; and
- *Timing/scheduling.* Flexible scheduling, extra time, multiple testing sessions.

Less common were alterations in response mode. Only 12 states allowed students to tape-record their responses and 21 permitted the use of word processors. A more recent review of state policies for test accommodations revealed a similar pattern with one exception. Forty-three states allowed dictation of responses to a scribe, an alternate response mode (Bolt & Thurlow, 2004; Thurlow, House, Boys, Scott, & Ysseldyke, 2000). It is hoped that restrictions on types of accommodations in high-stakes testing will continue to become less stringent as states and districts become more familiar with the process of making assessment modifications.

Students with special needs are more likely to succeed in general education classrooms when teachers adapt instruction and make accommodations in assessment. These accommodations make sense not only for statewide and district-wide testing but also for the types of assessments used routinely in classroom situations. Table 4-2 lists ideas for adapting assessment procedures in the general education classroom.

The next chapter discusses typical behavior problems and presents strategies for managing the classroom behavior of regular class students, including those with special needs.

TABLE 4-2	Strategies for Making Assessment Accommodations

TYPE OF ACCOMMODATION	EXAMPLES
Directions/instructions	Use simpler language when providing directions; repeat the directions as needed by the student.
Demonstrations	Show the student what to do before he or she is required to do it.
Time limits	Extend the time limits or remove them altogether.
Presentation mode	Change the way in which information is presented; for example, students could listen to a question rather than read it.
Response mode	Change the way in which answers are given; for example, students could answer orally rather than write.
Aids	Permit students to use aids such as paper and pencil or calculators.
Prompts and cues	Provide prompts during assessment; for example, begin the first task for the student or remind him or her to complete all parts of the question.
Feedback	During assessment, confirm to students that answers are correct; indicate which answers are incorrect.
Positive reinforcement	Praise students for attending to the assessment task; reward them for correct answers.
Physical location	Have the student work in a different part of the classroom or in a different room altogether.

Note: Adapted with permission from *Assessing Students with Special Needs* (6th ed., p. 112) by J. M. McLoughlin and R. B. Lewis. Copyright 2005 by Prentice-Hall, Inc., Upper Saddle River, New Jersey.

Things to Remember

- Students may experience difficulty in the acquisition, maintenance, and generalization of basic skills, content-area information, and transition training.
- Academic problems are indicated by a high number of incorrect responses, a low number of responses, or an inconsistent response pattern.
- Instruction is individualized when a high proportion of student responses is correct.
- In systematic instruction the learning task is selected, material necessary for task performance is presented, and practice is provided; skills are taught directly and the demonstration–prompt–practice technique is used.
- Increasing student engagement by increasing the response rate accelerates learning.
- Student performance data provide information about current levels of functioning, rate of progress, and reasons for task failure.

- When student performance is unsatisfactory, teachers introduce the least intrusive instructional modification first.
- Materials and activities are modified by clarifying task directions, adding prompts, and correcting specific student errors.
- Teaching procedures are changed by providing additional presentations and practice, making consequences more attractive, and slowing the pace of instruction.
- Task requirements are altered by changing the criteria for successful performance, changing task characteristics, and breaking the task into smaller subtasks.
- Substitution of an alternate learning task, the most drastic instructional change, is used only as a last resort.
- Students with special needs benefit from not only adaptations in instruction but also from accommodations in assessment procedures.

ACTIVITIES

1. Visit the two sites described in the "Windows on the Web" features in this chapter: the Educational Resources Information Center (ERIC) website and the What Works Clearinghouse website. After reading about the types of information each provides, browse each site looking for strategies for adapting instruction for students with special needs. Which site would you recommend to your colleagues?

2. Arrange to observe in a special or general education classroom. Explain to the teacher that you are interested in seeing how much of the school day is actually spent in instruction. Observe and keep a log of the teacher's activities for an hour or so. How much time is spent in large-group instruction? Small-group instruction? Supervision of students' independent work? Noninstructional duties?

3. Task analysis is used to break tasks into teachable subcomponents. Select one of the tasks that follow, and list all of the steps necessary to complete the task. Check your analysis by trying to do the task using only the steps you have listed.
   - Brushing your teeth
   - Looking up a number in the phone book
   - Boiling an egg
   - Making a bed
   - Writing a check

4. Ways of adapting instruction include changing the characteristics of the task and the performance criteria. Try your hand at modifying this objective:

   When given a page of 25 math problems, the student will write the correct answers to at least 20 problems within 5 minutes.

CD-ROM Activities

View the fourth video case study showing the high school physics class. Pay particular attention to the video clips entitled "Multiple Goals" and "Multi-level Assignments." Think about the strategies this teacher uses for adapting instruction:

- *Are all the students working on the same project? Does this mean that the instructional goals for all students are the same?*

- *How are student teams used to differentiate instruction?*

- *How does the teacher explain the differences in assignment sheets for different students?*

Describe how you would alter the task for each of the modifications listed here; the first one is done for you.

Modification	Altered Task
Reduce quantity	Give student only 20 problems
Reduce speed	
Reduce accuracy	
Change presentation mode	
Change response mode	

5. Explain why substitution of an alternate learning task should be the last instructional modification attempted.

Managing Classroom Behavior

CHAPTER

5

STUDENTS' STORIES

Classroom behavior problems such as those described in the following "Students' Stories" are not rare occurrences. They are a sampling of the problem behaviors that teachers face daily in a general education classroom.

- Henry is late for class at least 2 days each week.
- Maxine hasn't completed an assignment this semester.
- Several times each day, John interrupts the teacher's lecture by talking and making noises.
- Pablo argues and fights with other students in the classroom.

- During independent study time, Lisa looks around the room and watches other students or writes notes to her friends.
- Sue doesn't ask questions in class; in fact, the only talking she does is at lunch with her two close friends.
- Willie is seldom in his seat; he seems to be constantly on the move, and he holds the class record for the longest round-trip to the pencil sharpener.

LOOKING AHEAD

Behavior problems are one of the most common difficulties students with special needs experience in general education classrooms. Before reading about strategies for addressing these problems, think about the questions that follow:

- Each of the students described above appears to be having difficulty meeting classroom behavioral demands. Would you predict that these students also have special needs in the area of academic performance?
- Which students exhibit behavior that is likely to interfere with classroom instructional activities and disrupt their classmates' learning?
- Which students show behaviors that are likely to interfere only with their own learning?
- Do you think students such as John, Pablo, and Sue would have difficulty making friends? What evidence would you offer to support your opinion?

To answer these questions online, go to the Students' Stories module in Chapter 5 of the Companion Website.

BEHAVIOR PROBLEMS IN THE CLASSROOM

Behavior problems are exhibited by typical students and students with special needs of all ages and at every grade level. Some students call attention to themselves only in the classroom; others also experience difficulty at recess, in the school lunchroom, on the way to and from school, at home, and in the neighborhood.

The behavior problems of students frequently contribute to their placement in special education programs. When students with special needs return to the mainstream, teachers in general education are often concerned that their problem behaviors will interfere with the operation of the classroom. In addition, such behaviors may hinder the special students' academic achievement and may have a negative effect on their acceptance by others.

Two major types of behavior problems are of concern to the teacher: inappropriate classroom behavior and poor study skills. Behaviors that interfere with classroom instruction, impede social interaction with teacher and peers, or endanger others are considered **classroom conduct problems.** Examples of inappropriate classroom behaviors are talking out, fighting, arguing, being out of one's seat, swearing, and avoiding interactions with others. Immature and withdrawn behaviors also fall under this category. Behaviors that interfere with students' academic performance or the teacher's ability to assess academic progress are considered **study skill problems.** Typical study skill problems include failure to complete assignments, poor attention during lectures or class discussion, failure to follow directions, and poor management of study time.

Problem behaviors are exhibited in one of three ways: low rate of appropriate behaviors, high rate of inappropriate behaviors, or absence of the appropriate behavior from the student's repertoire. Different management strategies are linked to each type of problem behavior.

- *Low rate of appropriate behaviors.* Students exhibit appropriate behaviors but not as frequently as expected or required. For example, a student may be able to complete homework assignments but chooses to do so only 10% to 20% of the time. Also, students may behave appropriately in one setting but not in another. For instance, a student with disabilities may work well in the resource room but may find it difficult to work in a small-group setting in the general education classroom. To alleviate these problems, the teacher sets up a systematic program to increase the occurrence of appropriate behaviors or to help students generalize behaviors from one situation to another.
- *High rate of inappropriate behaviors.* Inappropriate behaviors that are troublesome to teachers occur frequently or for long periods of time. Examples include students who are out of their seats 30 to 40 times per day, those who talk during 50% to 60% of the class lecture, and those who use profanity 5 to 10 times in one class period. To overcome these high rates of inappropriate behavior, teachers attempt to decrease the frequency or duration of the undesired behavior by increasing appropriate behaviors that are incompatible. For instance, to decrease running in the classroom, the teacher can work to increase the frequency of walking.
- *Absence of the appropriate behavior from the student's repertoire.* Students may not yet have learned the appropriate behavior for social interaction or classroom functioning. The age or grade level of a student is not an accurate predictor of behavioral competence; it is necessary to consider each student individually. For instance, sixth graders may not know how to start a conversation or how to organize their time to ensure completion of assignments. To remedy this, the effective teacher directly teaches the new behavior (conversation skills or time management), provides instruction on when and how the behavior is to take place, and carefully builds practice and review opportunities into the instructional sequence (Cullinan, 2002; Emmer, 1981; Olson & Platt, 1996).

Behavior problems do not occur in isolation. The way in which the classroom learning environment is arranged and the actions of others can promote, initiate, or reinforce inappropriate behaviors. If classroom behavior problems are to be understood and managed, not only the behavior of the target student but also that of the teacher and peers must be examined. For example, a sarcastic comment from a teacher can initiate a verbal retort from the student. Classmates who laugh at the clowning or wisecracks of their peers ensure that similar behaviors will recur.

Students show inappropriate behavior when they have not learned correct responses—or when they have found that acting inappropriately is more rewarding than acting appropriately. Such behavior problems *do* respond to instruction. According to one point of view, behavior problems belong to the teacher, not the student. This viewpoint holds that it is not the students who fail; instead, educators have failed to develop acceptable student behaviors. Opinions on and results of research into student behavior in the schools are presented in the accompanying "For Your Information" feature. Figures 5-1 and 5-2 provide checklists of both teacher and student behaviors to consider as possible factors contributing to student misbehavior in the classroom.

PRINCIPLES OF MANAGING BEHAVIOR

Students who exhibit inappropriate behaviors require a classroom management system that is systematic, consistent, and concerned with both the prevention and cure of problem be-

Behavior Problems

- In a recent national survey (Rose & Gallup, 2003), the general public identified lack of discipline as the second biggest problem faced by schools today. The only problem considered more pressing was lack of funding.
- According to *Education Week's* 2003 National Survey of Public School Teachers as described by McCabe (2004), almost 70% of teachers believe that schools should focus on teaching behavioral and emotional skills to most special education students.
- On the subject of school safety, "students, teachers, parents and principals report that making the school safe is the most important part of a principal's job, but fewer than half of students describe their school's atmosphere as safe" (*The MetLife Survey of the American Teacher,* 2003, p. 7).
- Bullying is common in schools. A recent study by the UCLA/RAND Center for Adolescent Health Promotion (2003) concluded that more than 20% of 12-year-old students are bullies, or victims of bullies, or both.

- One older study (Rubin & Balow, 1978) reported that 60% of elementary school children are identified by at least one of their teachers as having a behavior problem.
- In effective classrooms, the teachers provide instruction in both academics and social behavior to maximize the time students spend on learning tasks, increase student achievement, and decrease the need to focus primarily on classroom management (Kauffman, 2001; Pacchiano, 2000; Sutherland & Wehby, 2001).
- Students with poor social behaviors do not achieve as well academically as peers with appropriate social skills. Improving performance in personal interactions and task-related social skills increases both academic performance and social acceptance (Cartledge & Milburn, 1986; Gresham, 1984; Zirpoli & Melloy, 2001).
- The behaviors that are appropriate in the classroom are determined by the teacher, the policies of the school, and the beliefs of the community. An inappropriate behavior for one teacher may be totally acceptable to another.

---

haviors. This system should provide for group management yet be flexible enough to allow individualization for the problems of one specific student.

Behavior management follows many of the same principles used in adapting academic instruction. Teachers state precise goals, break behaviors into teachable subcomponents, institute systematic management procedures, and collect data to monitor student progress. Whereas instruction (as discussed in chapter 4) deals primarily with academic skills, behavior management is concerned with classroom conduct and study skills; in both, the teacher arranges the classroom environment to produce changes in student behavior. The following paragraphs present principles to follow in setting up a systematic behavior management program.

Remember That Behavior Is Learned

Problem behaviors are learned behaviors that have developed from the student's experiences and reinforcement history. Sometimes called **operant behaviors,** they are under the voluntary control of the individual. Because behavior is learned, students can acquire new ways of acting; present behaviors can be replaced or supplemented. The learning of new behaviors occurs at different rates for different students, and instructional procedures affect individuals differently. This

individuality is particularly important for students with special needs, who may require extra time or additional practice. They are certainly capable of acquiring new behaviors but may need a more systematic management program than their typical general education peers.

Consider Both the Antecedents and the Consequences of Behavior

As suggested earlier, behaviors do not happen in isolation. The occurrence of a behavior is affected by the events that precede it and the consequences that follow it. Antecedents and consequences are both important in the management of behavior. New skills can be taught, or current behaviors can be modified, by either altering antecedent events or conditions or by manipulating consequences. As a general rule, if antecedents are contributing to the behavior, teachers should first alter the antecedent conditions and then consider changing the consequences. For example, if students fail to follow directions, the first step may be to alter the directions. A change from "Get back to your seat!" to "Would you please return to your seat?" may produce the desired behavior.

It is also possible to modify both antecedents and consequences at the same time. According to Walker (1995):

> Simultaneous manipulation of antecedent(s) and consequences is probably the most effective method for changing

FIGURE 5-1   Possible Contributions to Misbehavior: A Checklist of Teacher Behavior

- *Am I consistent in responding to children's behavior?* If your response to children's conduct—good or bad—is unpredictable, children will have difficulty learning how they are to behave. Your students should know what the consequences of appropriate behavior and misbehavior will be. Give clear directions; hold firm to your expectations; and be consistent in following through with rewards and punishment.
- *Am I rewarding the right behavior?* Children who present difficult management problems often are ignored when they are behaving appropriately. Often, about the only time they receive attention is when they are criticized or reprimanded for misbehavior. Sometimes teachers make the mistake of praising them (for something else) or making physical contact with them (in attempts to offer loving correction) when they misbehave. Make sure that children are receiving your attention primarily when they are behaving appropriately. You must make certain that desirable conduct receives a hefty amount of recognition and the misbehavior does not.
- *Are my expectations and demands appropriate for children's abilities?* When expectations are too high, children feel too much pressure and experience too much failure. When expectations are too low, children become bored and may feel resentful. Make certain that your expectations fit each child's ability level so that the child is challenged while his or her progress is obvious.
- *Am I tolerant enough of children's individuality?* Children have as much right as adults to express their individuality. Many children rebel against teachers who demand strict uniformity and regimentation or are unwilling to encourage appropriate individuality. Make certain that your rules and expectations allow sufficient room for harmless preferences and idiosyncrasies.
- *Am I providing instruction that is useful to children?* People do not learn quickly or happily when they see no point in what they are doing. First, you must make sure that you have chosen the most important things to teach. When children do not see the importance of what you are teaching, you must point out to them the value of what they are learning. If they still do not understand, you must find a way to make the material interesting or worth their while—perhaps by offering meaningful rewards or privileges for learning.
- *Are children seeing desirable models?* Children are great imitators of their teachers and their high-status peers. Make certain that if children are imitating you, they are behaving appropriately. Monitor your own behavior, and change it if necessary. Call attention to the desirable conduct of children's peers. Point out the kind of behavior you want to see.
- *Am I generally irritable and overreliant on punishment as a control technique?* Teachers set a tone in their classrooms by their general attitudes toward persons and events. A teacher who is easily upset, frequently short-tempered, quick to punish minor misbehavior, and hesitant in expressing approval is virtually certain to foster irritability and defiance in students. General irritability and a focus on punishment suggest depression; and a teacher's depression may contribute to children's depressive behavior.
- *Am I willing to try a different tack on the problem or to seek the help of colleagues or consultants?* A teacher who resists the suggestions of others, who insists on "going it alone," or who discards any different approach as useless or doomed to failure is not likely to be successful for long. Teaching today presents complex behavior management problems for which even the most competent teacher needs consultation. An attitude of openness and a willingness to look outside oneself are essential to success.

Note: From "Classroom Management: Teacher-Child-Peer Relationships" by J. M. Kauffman, P. L. Pullen, and E. Akers, 1986, *Focus on Exceptional Children, 19*(1), p. 3. Copyright 1986 by Love. Reprinted by permission.

behavior. A simple example of the manipulation of both an antecedent and consequences would be in the case where a teacher carefully defines classroom rules and then allows children to accumulate minutes of free time for following them. (p. 59)

Reduce Behavior Management Problems with Careful Organization of the Classroom

The physical organization of the classroom, the procedures established for movement within the classroom, and the quality of the instructional program all play important roles in determining the frequency of behavior problems. Careful arrangement of such things as physical space, student seating, storage of instructional materials, and student traffic patterns can greatly reduce the potential for disruptions of instructional activities and the occurrence of behavioral problems. Appropriate instructional programs and streamlined classroom procedures are also likely to reduce behavior problems. Chapters 4 and 7 provide specific suggestions for adapting instruction and coordinating the classroom learning environment.

Increase the Occurrence of Behaviors by Reinforcement

Behaviors followed by reinforcers are more likely to occur again. A student who receives praise from the teacher for raising her hand to speak in class is more likely to raise her hand

FIGURE 5-2	Possible Contributions to Misbehavior: A Checklist of Student Behavior

- *Is the child overdependent on you?* Children who cannot work independently are a constant source of interruption of the teacher's work and their peers' concentration. Their frequent demands for help, or their refusal to work without the teacher's constant oversight, are wearing on the teacher and may trigger rivalry from peers.
- *Does the child have difficulty concentrating and paying attention?* Learning requires focused attention. A child's lack of attention to task requires additional teacher effort, provides an inappropriate model for peers, raises the probability of disruptive behavior, and lowers the probability of academic success.
- *Does the child become easily upset under pressure to achieve?* The world contains many sources of pressure for productive activity and achievement. Therefore, a classroom without any pressure whatsoever for achievement is an unrealistic and debilitating environment. Children's resistance to expectations for performance is a source of frustration for the teacher and for peers who are striving to achieve.
- *Is the child's work sloppy?* Reflective, careful work is needed in the workplace, and it should be expected in the classroom. Teachers are justified in requiring reasonably neat, thoughtful responses. Teaching is difficult and progress is slow when the child has not learned good work habits and impulse control.
- *Does the child tease, annoy, or interfere with the work of other students?* Annoyance or hassle by neighbors or coworkers is a common and sometimes serious source of stress for adults and children. A child who interferes with the lives of others becomes a source of bad feelings and a sinkhole for the energies of teachers and peers.
- *Is the child negative toward schoolwork, self, teachers, or peers?* Faultfinding, whining, and criticism—whether directed toward others or oneself—induce negative responses in others. These characteristics often are indicative of depression, and they tend to make others feel depressed.
- *Does the child have poor personal hygiene or habits of self-care?* People, young or old, who are dirty or smelly are less likely to be approached socially or to be befriended by others than are those who maintain good hygiene and self-care. Teachers will have difficulty being positive toward children whose odor or appearance is offensive.
- *Is the child usually withdrawn or reticent?* A withdrawn or reticent child is easily overlooked by teachers and peers. A child with those characteristics is unlikely to be drawn into positive, reciprocal social exchanges without special intervention.
- *Does the child engage in self-stimulation or self-injury?* Excessive or socially inappropriate self-stimulation is incompatible with learning and social acceptance. Self-stimulation and self-injury usually are off-putting to others and inhibit normal psychological and physical development.
- *Is the child aggressive toward teachers or peers?* Aggression in the form of verbal threats, intimidation, extortion, or physical attack heightens anxiety and stress in all parties involved. An aggressive child can be expected to induce hostility and counteraggression in others.

Note: From "Classroom Management: Teacher-Child-Peer Relationships" by J. M. Kauffman, P. L. Pullen, and E. Akers, 1986, *Focus on Exceptional Children, 19*(1), p. 5. Copyright 1986 by Love. Reprinted by permission.

the next time she wishes to contribute something. This is an example of **positive reinforcement**; the behavior is followed by the presentation of a pleasant (or positive) event that makes the behavior more likely to recur. This is a constructive procedure that helps students feel better about themselves. Examples of positive reinforcers are praise, special privileges, positive notes to students and parents, early dismissal for lunch, and special awards. Positive reinforcement is a powerful tool for managing and changing behavior.

Although less favored, negative reinforcers also increase the probability that behaviors will recur. In **negative reinforcement**, the behavior is followed by the removal of an aversive (unpleasant or punishing) event or condition. A student who completes his homework to stop the nagging of his teacher and parents is being negatively reinforced; that is, the desired behavior, finishing the assignment, is followed by the removal of the aversive event, nagging, and is thus more apt to recur in

the future. The student who stops talking to classmates and begins working to stop the frown of the teacher is also being negatively reinforced. Negative reinforcement should not be confused with punishment; negative reinforcers increase the occurrence of a behavior by removing something that is aversive. However, because it is a negative approach, negative reinforcement may produce avoidance, escape, or aggressive behaviors on the part of the student (Zirpoli & Melloy, 2001).

Reinforcement is most effective when the reinforcer is clearly associated with the specific behavior and is presented closely following that behavior. The effect of reinforcing a student with immediate praise for entering class on time is much greater than complimenting the student at the end of the day. Reinforcement should be immediate, systematic, realistic, and meaningful to students in order to be effective. Table 5-1 gives examples of reinforcement procedures that influence the strength of a behavior.

TABLE 5-1	Procedures to Change Behaviors		
LEARNING CONCEPTS	*EDUCATIONAL PROCEDURES*	*EFFECTS ON BEHAVIOR*	*EXAMPLES OF POSITIVE OR AVERSIVE EVENTS PRESENTED OR REMOVED*
Positive reinforcement	Behavior is followed by positive event	Increase in strength of behavior	Smile, approval, affection, task completion, money, special privileges, recognition, passing grade
Negative reinforcement	Behavior is followed by removal of aversive event	Increase in strength of behavior	Frown, criticism, poor grade, threat of restriction of use of car, rejection, nonattention
Extinction (of behavior previously strengthened by positive reinforcement)	Behavior is not followed by positive event associated with previous occurrence	Decrease in strength of behavior	Smile, approval, affection, peer attention, bonus, special privilege
Extinction (of behavior previously strengthened by negative reinforcement)	Behavior is not followed by removal of aversive event associated with previous occurrence	Decrease in strength of behavior	Criticism, rejection, threat of loss of privileges, poor grade
Punishment: Presentation of aversive events	Behavior is followed by aversive event	Decrease in strength of behavior which results in the aversive event	Criticism, poor grade, rejection by peers, threat of dismissal from club
Punishment: Removal of positive events through time-out or response cost	Behavior is followed by temporary or permanent loss of positive events	Decrease in strength of behavior which results in loss of positive events	Smile, approval, affection, money, privilege, group membership

Note: From *Learning and Behavior Characteristics of Exceptional Children and Youth: A Humanistic Behavioral Approach* (p. 210) by William I. Gardner, 1977, Boston: Allyn and Bacon. Copyright 1977 Pearson Education. Reprinted by permission of the publisher.

Decrease the Occurrence of Behaviors by Removing Reinforcers or Introducing Aversive Events

The strength of a behavior decreases when it is followed by an aversive event or when it stops being followed by a reinforcer. The student who no longer receives laughs and snickers from peers for muttering profanities will generally decrease this activity. Tardiness will decrease if students lose privileges (such as time in the game center) for each minute they are late; the same is true for students who lose the use of the family car because they come home after curfew.

Extinction is the removal of reinforcers that have previously followed the behavior. If the objective is to decrease an inappropriate behavior that has been reinforced in the past, the reinforcer is withheld. For example, the teacher may wish to decrease the number of times Mike talks out in class. If the teacher has been reinforcing Mike's out-of-turn responses by attending to them, this positive reinforcer must be withdrawn; the teacher should ignore Mike's comments until he raises his

hand. Although extinction procedures will reduce and eliminate a behavior, their use may be somewhat frustrating. A teacher may be unable to identify or control all classroom reinforcers. In addition, the effect of extinction procedures is not always immediate; the student's undesirable behavior may even increase temporarily before it decreases. For example, the frequency of Ann's tantrums might increase until she realizes the teacher's attention can be gained only by exhibiting appropriate behaviors.

Some inappropriate behaviors should be ignored from the outset (e.g., occasional calling out, brief whispering). Behaviors falling into this category are (1) those of short duration that are not likely to spread or persist, (2) minor deviations from classroom rules, and (3) behaviors in which a reaction from the teacher would interrupt a lesson or draw undue attention to the behavior. Procedures that decrease behaviors more rapidly (such as punishment or overcorrection) should be considered if the behavior to be reduced is harmful to others (such as fighting) or if it causes a major disruption of the classroom (such as yelling or stealing).

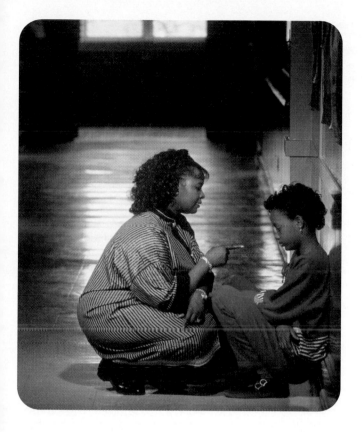

The presentation of an aversive event following a behavior is called **punishment.** Examples of punishers are verbal reprimands, criticism, and low grades. Two of the milder punishment procedures often used in the general education classroom are response cost and time-out. In **response cost,** an inappropriate behavior is followed by the loss or withdrawal of earned reinforcers or privileges. In **time-out,** the student is removed from an event that is reinforcing, or reinforcement is withdrawn for a specified period of time. Time-out may involve contingent observation (viewing from the "sidelines"), exclusion time-out (excluding students from observing or participating in activities without leaving the room by, for example, turning their chair toward the wall or placing it behind a screen), or temporary removal from the room. Time-out is effective only if it is carefully planned and systematically implemented and if its effects are carefully evaluated and documented (Cuenin & Harris, 1986).

Punishment is a negative procedure that can rapidly decrease a behavior. However, it should be used only if more positive approaches are not appropriate or feasible. Before punishment is used with students with special needs, teachers should carefully check district and state policies and regulations. In addition, the permission of parents should always be obtained because punishment can harm students' self-concept and can produce avoidance, escape, or aggressive behaviors.

Punishment is most effective if it is combined with positive reinforcement. This combination will bring about more rapid and effective changes than the use of either procedure alone (Walker, 1995). For example, a student who runs in the classroom will learn appropriate behavior more quickly if he or she receives both positive reinforcers (such as praise and extra recess time) for walking and also punishers (such as loss of earned free time or verbal reprimands) for running.

Identify Consequences That Are Meaningful to Students

To have the desired effect on behavior, consequences must be meaningful to the student. This is true for both positive and negative consequences. A consequence that is positive for one person may be negative for another. For example, going to the library is positive for the book lover but not necessarily so for the sports addict; watching a football game may be a negative activity for those who like to play tennis or visit museums. In addition, the effect of a specific consequence on an individual can change under different conditions. Earning a dessert for completing classwork is reinforcing to a student under most conditions; however, an offer of a banana split for doing the dishes would not be appealing even to the most avid dessert lover who had just eaten a huge meal.

Educators often assume that students are motivated by grades; however, for many students with special needs, grades are aversive. They have received poor grades that resulted in ridicule from their peers and negative feedback from their parents and teachers. For them grades are no longer positive consequences, and other reinforcers must be found.

It is possible to misinterpret the potential effects of a consequence. A teacher may use verbal reprimands as an aversive consequence for inappropriate behavior. However, the teacher's attention may be a positive reinforcer for the student, regardless of the nature of the attention. Also, verbal praise from a teacher may have the effect of a punisher; for instance, to adolescents, praise from a teacher may be distasteful if given in front of their peers.

Consequences must have meaning to their recipients. For instance, most teachers would soon tire of receiving grades instead of paychecks for their work. Pay is not bribery; it is the presentation of a meaningful reinforcer for hard work. Because the paycheck is negotiable, teachers can choose which secondary reinforcers they wish to purchase.

Beware of Noneducational Interventions

Periodically, methods that claim to bring about dramatic changes in the behavior of students appear in the field of education. Many of these are noneducational treatments and interventions. For example, special diets, medication, and therapies (e.g., relaxation therapy) may claim to solve academic and social problems. Teachers should exercise extreme caution when

Inclusion Tips for the Teacher

The Use of Drugs in Managing Hyperactivity

Authors such as Axelrod and Bailey (1979), Kauffman (2001), and Walker (1995) have discussed the concerns frequently raised about the effectiveness of drugs in managing hyperactivity and other inappropriate student behaviors. These experts have noted the need for continuing research in this area and indicate that teachers should approach the medical management of behavioral problems with due caution. Axelrod and Bailey suggest the following guidelines for the use of drug treatment in school settings:

1. Physical examinations should be prerequisites to commencing and continuing drug treatment. This is necessary not only to monitor possible physiological problems, but also to determine whether physical anomalies might be causing problem behaviors.
2. Drugs should be considered only when there is a demonstration of inordinately inappropriate behavior. . . . The mere claim from a parent or teacher that a child's behavior warrants drug treatment is insufficient.
3. Before drug treatment is implemented, behavior modification procedures or other remedial techniques should be attempted.
4. Children who receive drugs should be exposed to two different dosage levels, a baseline phase, and a placebo

condition. Whenever possible, drug and placebo conditions should be conducted in a double blind manner.
5. A continual, preferably daily, record of a child's behavior should be maintained. This should be done not only when attempting to determine a child's appropriate drug treatment, but throughout treatment.
6. The effects on at least one behavior that should increase and one behavior that should decrease should be monitored.
7. Minimal goals for each behavior of interest should be specified in advance. Only when drug treatment meets the prespecified goals should the treatment be continued.
8. During the course of drug treatment, the child should periodically be drug free. If the child's behavior again becomes disorderly, it may be concluded that the drugs were responsible for the previously noted improvement. If the child's behavior remains appropriate, it may be possible to permanently discontinue drug use.
9. Drug treatment should not be considered a permanent solution to a youngster's problems. When drug therapy is considered necessary, it might be combined with more standard educational procedures. As the package of techniques improves a student's behavior, it may be possible to wean the student from drug treatment. (pp. 547–548)

---

considering such approaches. Most are medical-type interventions; many have little empirical evidence to support their usefulness (Silver, 1987; Woolston, 1999) although an increasing amount of information indicates that the use of medications may be an important component of treatment programs for students with behavioral problems such as ADHD (e.g., Forness, Kavale, & Crenshaw, 1999; Kollins, Barkley, & DuPaul, 2001). Information about the use of drugs to manage hyperactivity and other behavior problems is presented in the "Inclusion Tips for the Teacher" box.

If questions arise, the teacher can consult the school nurse, counselor, special educator, or principal. Noneducational procedures should not be used with students with special needs unless the use of a particular procedure for a particular student has received the full endorsement of the team of professionals working with the student and the parents have given their informed consent.

METHODS FOR GATHERING DATA

Gathering data on the classroom behavior and study skills of students is an essential component of a behavior management program. Typically called **functional assessment** (or *functional behavioral assessment*), this systematic process is aimed at providing sufficient information to educators to al-

low them to (1) understand the factors contributing to the problem behavior and (2) plan the positive behavioral interventions necessary to bring the problem behavior under control (McLoughlin & Lewis, 2005; Walker, 1995).

It is important to note that functional assessment focuses not only on the student's behavior but also on the reasons for and factors influencing that behavior. Ryan, Halsey, and Matthews (2003) suggest that educational teams consider not only the environment in which the behavior takes place but also the functions that behavior serves for the student. Important aspects of the environment are the antecedents and consequences of the behavior as well as setting events (i.e., events that take place earlier in time) (Ryan et al., 2003); the two primary functions of problem behavior are "(1) to obtain something or produce a desired effect, or (2) to escape or avoid something" (Walker, 1995, p. 78). Ryan et al. provide the example of Johnny, a student who screams obscenities when given a writing task. This happens most often when Johnny has had little sleep (the setting event). The consequence for Johnny is that he is sent to the hallway, thereby avoiding the writing task.

Many different types of informal methods are used in functional assessment to gather information about problem behaviors. McLoughlin and Lewis (2005) explain:

Two techniques are always included: direct observation of the student in order to fully describe the behavior in ques-

TABLE 5-2	Example of a Sequence Analysis		
TIME	**ANTECEDENT**	**BEHAVIOR**	**CONSEQUENCE**
9:05	Teacher asks the class a question.	John raises hand.	Teacher calls on Bill.
9:07	Teacher asks question.	John yells answer.	Teacher reprimands John.
9:11	Teacher asks question and reminds students to raise hands.	John raises hand.	Teacher calls on John and compliments him for raising his hand.

tion, and interviews with persons knowledgeable about the student and the behavior. In some cases, other techniques are also used. Examples are record reviews (e.g., medical and educational histories), task and work sample analyses, and curriculum-based assessments. . . . (p. 161)

General education teachers may take part in functional assessment by participating in interviews and providing the educational team with samples of student work. However, even more important is the teacher's role in the collection of classroom observational data. Teachers use such data to determine students' current levels of performance, identify antecedents and consequences that may influence behavior, identify settings in which the behavior is likely to occur, determine the effectiveness of the intervention program, and communicate progress to students and parents. Knowledge of progress can be a strong reinforcer for students.

Direct Observation of Behavior

The most useful method for gathering information on classroom behavior and study skills is the direct observation of student behavior. Observations are usually conducted in the classroom setting by the teacher, an aide, or a trained volunteer; in some cases, students can be trained to collect information on other students or on their own performances.

Although teachers observe students every day, such observations are usually not systematic or precise; general impressions do not provide enough information for planning intervention programs. Instead, direct observations should be carefully planned and should follow the steps outlined in the following paragraphs.

Specify the Behavior to be Observed. The first task is to specify the behavior of interest to the teacher. This behavior must be described as specifically as possible. If it is stated clearly, two or more observers will be able to agree on whether the student has produced the behavior. Imprecise descriptions of behaviors make them difficult to observe and measure. The statements "Jack is hyperactive," "Mark is nasty," "Judy is restless," and "Sam has poor study habits" lack specificity and leave

much to the interpretation of the observer. Descriptions such as "Louis hits other students," "Wen-Chi leaves her seat frequently," "Candy talks out without raising her hand," and "José doesn't turn in his homework assignments" are more precise.

At times, teachers may wish to collect data on the overall performance of a student in order to identify specific problem behaviors. Sulzer-Azaroff and Mayer (1977) suggest narrative recording or sequence analysis for this purpose. In **narrative recording,** the observer describes all the behaviors displayed by the student during the observation period; this record is then analyzed to determine whether there is any pattern in the student's behaviors. **Sequence analysis** is more systematic; the observer describes each behavior and attempts to identify its antecedent and consequence. Table 5-2 presents a portion of a sequence analysis of John's behavior during instruction. Examination of the events that precede and follow a behavior yields much more information than is obtained in a simple observation.

However, narrative recording and sequence analysis may not be practical ways for the general education teacher to collect data. The teacher may be unable to undertake a detailed observation such as this while managing all of the activities of a regular classroom. One solution is to have someone other than the classroom teacher conduct the observation; this person could be an instructional aide, an adult volunteer, a special education teacher or consultant, or even a peer tutor. Another technique is to develop a simpler observation system. In any event, when the task is to identify problem behaviors, it is important to consider not only the behavior itself but also the effect of antecedents and consequences on it.

Select a Measurement System. As soon as a behavior has been identified and specifically described, the system to observe and measure the behavior can be selected. There are several different types of behaviors, and their nature influences the kind of measurement system chosen. One type is that of permanent products such as completed assignments, worksheets, and essays, which are available for review at a later time. Other behaviors are more transitory; they must be observed at the time of the occurrence. Examples include fighting, verbal outbursts, stealing, and being out of one's

TABLE 5-3	Measures of Behavior		
MEASURE	**DERIVED FROM**	**EXAMPLE**	**APPLICATION**
Percent	Number of units correct out of number of total units recorded	8 math problems correct out of 10 total math problems: $\frac{8}{10} \times 100 = 80\%$ accuracy	When a measure of accuracy is of concern without regard for time or proficiency
Frequency	$\dfrac{\text{Count of behavior}}{\text{Obsrevation time}}$	12 handraises in a 6-minute observation period: $\frac{12}{6} = 2$ handraises per minute	When it is desired to know how often a distinct behavior occurs within a period of time
Duration	Direct measures of length of time	A child tantrums for 15 minutes	When the total length of time a continuous behavior occurs is desired
Intervals	Number of fixed time units in which behavior occurred or didn't occur	Children are observed for 30 seconds, then the observer records whether or not behavior occurred during the interval. Observers then repeat the process. Usually data is expressed in terms of percentage of intervals during which behavior occurred. $\frac{5 \text{ intervals}}{10 \text{ intervals total}} \times 100 = 50\%$ of intervals	When total duration is not possible and an estimation of the occurrence of continuous behavior is desired

Note: From "An Applied Behavioral Analysis Research Primer for Behavioral Change Personnel" by M. A. Koorland and D. L. Westling, 1981, *Behavioral Disorders*, 6, p. 166. Copyright 1981 by the Council for Children with Behavioral Disorders, The Council for Exceptional Children. Reprinted by permission.

seat. These behaviors may be discrete (i.e., like writing and talking, they have a definite beginning and ending), or they may be continuous (e.g., studying). Some transitory behaviors can be converted into permanent products if they are audio- or videotaped for later study.

Several methods of recording data are possible during an observation:

1. *Permanent product or work sample analysis.* A sample of the student's work is evaluated, and information such as the number of problems correct is recorded.
2. *Event recording.* The number of times a behavior occurs within a time interval is noted; for example, the teacher counts the number of times a student leaves her seat during one class period.
3. *Duration recording.* The length of time a behavior occurs is recorded; for example, the teacher times how long a student takes to complete an assignment.
4. *Interval recording.* The occurrence or nonoccurrence of a behavior is noted within a specific time interval; for example, the teacher might observe that Bill was reading his science book during only two of the five 3-minute observation periods.

Which method to use depends on the type of behavior and the kind of data that will be most useful to the teacher. Also, the system must be easily implemented by the observer. Table 5-3 describes several kinds of information that result from the different recording systems: percentage, frequency, duration, and interval data.

Permanent product recording and **event recording** produce frequency data that can be converted into percentage data. Percentages and frequencies are appropriate measures for academic, classroom, and study skills behaviors. A teacher might be interested in the percentage of words read correctly or the percentage of time students spent on a task. Frequency data indicate the number of occurrences of a behavior. To compare frequencies, the teacher should be sure that observation periods are equal in length and that the student has the same opportunity to produce the behavior during each observation period. For example, results would be misleading if a student's questioning behavior during the teacher's lecture were compared with that student's questioning behavior during a discussion period.

Frequency data gathered during unequal observation periods can be more easily compared if they are transformed into rate information, which is simply the number of times a

FIGURE 5-3   Observations Using Momentary Time Sampling

Student(s) observed: Entire class

Behavior observed: Number of students on task, working on independent assignment or actively participating in assigned group activity

Measurement system: Momentary time sampling (observer determines the number of students on task at the end of each interval)

Length of interval: 5 minutes

Time of measurement: Reading instruction time (9:00–9:52 a.m.)

Data recorded: Number of students on task/Number of students in class (percentage can be calculated for each observation or for the entire period)

Results: Over the entire time scheduled for reading instruction, 62% of the students in the class were on task. However, the percentage of students on task decreased as the class progressed.

Observation Time	Data	Observation Time	Data
9:05	24/30 = 80%	9:30	18/30 = 60%
9:10	27/30 = 90%	9:35	15/30 = 50%
9:15	24/30 = 80%	9:40	12/30 = 40%
9:20	21/30 = 70%	9:45	15/30 = 50%
9:25	21/30 = 70%	9:50	9/30 = 30%

Class totals: 186/300 = 62%

behavior occurs within a certain period (e.g., 8 times per minute; 17 times per hour). Examples of rate data are the number of math problems completed correctly per minute or the number of tantrums per day. Rate and percentage data are easy to compare. For instance, it is possible to compare the percentage of correct responses or the rate of reading words from one day to the next even if the student does not read the same number of words per day.

Duration recording is useful if the length of time the student engages in a behavior is of interest. For example, teachers might note the amount of time students require to line up for lunch or the time a student takes to begin work after the teacher gives directions. Duration can be reported in actual time units (e.g., "Katie cried for 14 minutes"; "Elijah now starts his work within 15 seconds after the teacher gives his group the assignment") or as a percentage (e.g., "Ralph was out of his seat 10% of the school day").

Interval recording is particularly useful for the teacher of a general education class because it does not require that students be observed continuously. McLoughlin and Lewis (2005) describe several of the different interval recording systems:

With these techniques, the observer determines whether a behavior occurs during a specified time period. The class day, period, or activity is broken down into short intervals of a few minutes or even a few seconds, and a record of the presence or absence of the target behavior is kept for each interval. These techniques can also be used with discrete behaviors if a complete record of every occurrence is not necessary.

Several variations of interval recording and time sampling are available:

- *Whole-interval recording.* The student is observed for the entire interval, and the observer notes if the target behavior occurs continuously throughout the interval. Observation intervals are very brief, usually only a few seconds.
- *Partial-interval time recording.* The student is observed for the entire interval, but the observer notes only if the behavior occurred at least once during the interval. Again, time intervals are very brief.
- *Momentary time sampling.* The student is observed only at the end of each interval; at that time, the observer checks to see if the behavior is occurring. Intervals are usually longer—3, 5, or even 15 minutes—making this a more convenient method for classroom teachers. However, it is less accurate than [whole- or partial-] interval recording techniques because much of the student's behavior goes unobserved. (pp. 126–127)

Figure 5-3 provides an example of the use of momentary time sampling with an entire class. In this example, the teacher was interested in determining what percentage of the class was on task during reading instruction. The same observation system could also be used with individual students or small groups.

Decide Who Will Observe and How Often Observations Will Occur. Observers must be able to record data accurately and consistently. If the teacher is the only adult in the classroom, the kind and frequency of observations that are possible may be limited. However, the teacher can record data while conducting instruction or while assisting students; devices such as clipboards, data sheets, stopwatches, and counters are helpful. Some behaviors can be self-recorded if students are monitored by the teacher and reinforced for accurate recording. For more information about conducting observations in the general education classroom, see the suggestions in the "Inclusion Tips for the Teacher."

The frequency of observations depends on several factors, including the availability of the student, the type of behavior being observed, the observation system, and the availability of the observer. Data collection should occur frequently, but observations usually require only a short period each day. The observation must be long enough to obtain an accurate picture of the student's behavior. The time of day or the length of the observation should be adjusted if the teacher believes that this sample of behavior is not typical. Observations that occur for shorter periods over several days provide more accurate data concerning student behavior than monitoring efforts that occur over one or two longer time periods (Walker, 1995).

Collect and Graph Baseline Data.   Before any intervention is begun, baseline data are collected under the natural conditions of the classroom. Baseline data are generally gathered for at least 5 days to ensure that the extremes of the behavior have been established. These data, recorded on a graph, are used to determine the rate or magnitude of the problem, to suggest possible interventions, and later to set the standard for evaluating the effectiveness of instruction. Baseline data may indicate that the behavior believed inappropriate is not as frequent or intense as hypothesized; if so, a behavior change program is not necessary. When the teacher is sure that the desired behavior is not part of the student's repertoire or when a behavior is injurious to the student or others, baseline data need not be collected.

Graphing of data permits the teacher and student to easily see the behavior and its rate of occurrence. Graphs can present baseline data, progress during intervention, and later the maintenance of behavior after intervention has been discontinued. Graphs are an excellent way to communicate progress to parents and other educators. Figure 5-4 presents an example of a graph that could be used in the classroom.

Inclusion Tips for the Teacher

Techniques for Conducting Observations in the General Education Classroom

One typical concern of general education teachers is that they do not have time to set up and run behavior management programs. They are busy teaching 30 or more students and cannot drop everything to systematically observe the behavior of a specific pupil. However, several techniques allow the teacher to conduct observations while carrying on regular instructional activities. It is not necessary to stop teaching to observe; in fact, it is almost impossible to teach without observing! Try the following suggestions for integrating observations into your classroom procedures:

1. Carry a small card such as an index card; on it list the names of one or two target students and the problem behaviors you wish to observe (e.g., hitting, being out of their seats, talking to others). Place a tally mark on the card (and possibly the time of the behavior) each time the behavior occurs. Start this system with one or two students and gradually expand it as your skills improve.

2. Require students to record on their in-class work their starting and finishing time. This approach permits the calculation of rate as well as frequency and accuracy data. Students can also note the times they leave and return to their desks; then the total amount of time in-seat each day or each period can be calculated.

3. Carry a stopwatch to measure the duration of behaviors. For example, start the watch each time Maynard leaves his seat, and stop it when he returns. Continue this (without resetting the watch) and time each occurrence of the behavior. At the end of the observation period, note the total amount of time recorded.

4. To count behaviors without interfering with the operation of the class, use wrist counters (golf counters), supermarket counters, paper clips moved from one pocket to another, navy beans in a cup, and other inexpensive devices.

5. Have a seating chart in front of you as you talk to the class. Place a tally mark by a student's name for each target behavior, such as asking a question, talking out, or answering a question correctly.

6. Recruit volunteers to observe in the classroom. Older students, parents, senior citizens, college students, or other students in the class can be excellent observers. If the teacher has developed a method to record the data and clearly stated the behavior to be observed, a nonprofessional should be able to conduct the observation.

Collect Data During Interventions. Data collected during the intervention phase help the teacher determine whether the intervention is having the desired effect on behavior. The teacher can then decide whether the intervention program should continue as originally developed or be modified to improve its effectiveness.

Intervention data should be gathered for a minimum of 5 days. Longer data collection periods permit a more careful evaluation of the program's effectiveness. Figure 5-4 shows information collected by the teacher about Elsie's completion of assignments. During the intervention phase, Elsie was rewarded with 3 minutes in the game center for each assignment

FIGURE 5-4   Graphing Baseline and Intervention Data

Behavior observed: Assignments completed by Elsie

Intervention: 3 minutes in the game center for each assignment completed

Student: Elsie

Inclusion Tips for the Teacher

Explaining Special Behavior Programs to General Education Peers

Differential treatment of students is often a concern to teachers. However, no teacher is able to treat all students exactly alike, and students themselves realize that some may require a different type of instruction or additional attention from the teacher. In an individualized classroom, special interventions designed to improve the behavior of one or two target students should draw little attention. Try the following suggestions when implementing behavior change programs in the classroom:

1. If questions do arise, explain that each student has different needs, and some may need special help, special reinforcers, or other program modifications to enable them to learn appropriate social and academic skills.

2. Do not expect to place every student on a different special program. Instead, design programs for the entire class. For example, class members might earn points for assignments completed, books read, and so on. This type of system can be easily adjusted so that one or two students can earn additional reinforcers for accomplishment of special target behaviors.

3. An intervention program should interfere as little as possible with the operation of the class. Teachers can provide students with reinforcers without interrupting classroom activities and without calling attention to the student in question. However, it is essential that the student being reinforced knows it! The teacher can make a mark on the chalkboard, give the student a silent signal, write on a card at the student's desk, or place poker chips or other tokens in a jar.

4. Include other students in the program. Rewarding nearby classmates when the target student is successful often contributes to the effectiveness of the program and the classmates' attitudes toward the special student.

5. Teachers using programs that base decisions on data and careful manipulation of antecedents and consequences find that the benefits of the approach far outweigh its disadvantages.

---

she finished on time; this was the only way Elsie could earn time in the game center, an activity she enjoyed very much. After 1 week, Elsie's teacher decided that the intervention was working and that it should be continued.

POSITIVE STRATEGIES FOR MANAGING AND IMPROVING BEHAVIOR

Teachers can use several strategies in the management of classroom behavior and the development of study skills. Most effective are intervention programs based on student performance data; these programs help students learn new behaviors, increase or maintain appropriate behaviors, and decrease inappropriate behaviors. Because classroom and study skills are learned behaviors, many of the principles of instruction presented in chapter 4 remain applicable.

The goal in behavior management is to establish a learning environment in which students are accepted as individuals but in which there are definite guidelines for acceptable classroom conduct. This goal is communicated most effectively to students by positive behavior change approaches. Students understand the need for guidelines and accept them if they are applied fairly, equally, and consistently. However, questions may arise when behavior change programs are used with some students but not with others. See the accompanying "Inclusion Tips for the Teacher" material for ideas on how to handle this situation.

Managing and improving classroom behavior is a systematic process of identifying expected student behaviors, analyzing student performance to see whether it meets expectations, and implementing interventions when necessary. Figure 5-5 presents the step-by-step process followed by the teacher to plan, develop, implement, evaluate, and revise interventions.

The need for intervention can be reduced through preventive planning. Expectations for behavior should be communicated to students; students who meet expectations should receive positive reinforcement. If intervention is needed, the least intrusive approach should be attempted first; often a change in seating, a careful explanation of class rules, a demonstration of the expected behavior, or a mild reprimand in private can eliminate the problem. Intensive behavior change programs should be used only when less dramatic methods have proven to be unsuccessful.

Establish Behavioral Expectations and Communicate Them to Students

Students are often unaware of the behavioral expectations for a specific classroom situation. Although more able students are capable of interpreting expectations from environmental cues (e.g., teacher signals, behavior of other students), students with behavior problems often do not interpret these cues. They need specific direction and instruction to know how they are expected to act. Effective classroom managers

FIGURE 5-5	Systematic Behavior Management Model

1. State the behavioral expectations for all students.
2. Determine whether students meeting expectations are receiving reinforcement to encourage maintenance of these behaviors.
3. Determine whether some students do not meet expectations. If so, do they know and understand the expectations? Do they have the prerequisite skills for the behaviors?
4. For students with inappropriate behaviors, identify target behaviors to be achieved.
5. Select an observation system, and collect baseline data on each behavior.
6. Analyze data to determine the need for an intervention program.
7. If data indicate the need for an intervention, determine whether the target behavior needs to be learned, increased, or decreased.
8. Select (or design) the intervention that uses the most positive approach.
9. Implement the intervention.
10. Collect data on student performance.
11. Analyze the data to determine the need to continue, modify, or terminate the intervention. Take required action.
12. When the behavior is at the desired level and is no longer dependent on the intervention, continue to collect maintenance data and return to step 4.

have been found to be particularly skilled in establishing classroom rules and procedures that communicate behavioral expectations to students (Doyle, 1986). Research results suggest that effective teachers take the following measures:

1. *Establish classroom rules and procedures at the start of the year.* Effective managers do not wait until problems occur; they anticipate potential problems prior to the beginning of school.
2. *Introduce rules and procedures on the first day of the class.* When rules and procedures are communicated to students immediately (from the beginning of the first day of school), they need not guess what the expectations are. Information overload is avoided by introducing the most essential rules and procedures first and presenting others as they are needed. The rules are posted or given to students as a handout, and new students are immediately oriented to the classroom expectations when they arrive in class.
3. *Explain rules and procedures clearly and teach them deliberately to students as part of a system for classroom operation.* A rationale is provided and instruction continues until the students have the rules and procedures mastered.
4. *Make rules and procedures concrete, functional, and explicit so that they contribute to the accomplishment of work and the order of the classroom.* The statements should be few, clear, and plainly stated. They should indicate the desired behavior (e.g., "Work quietly at your desk," "Respect other people's property") rather than all the undesired behaviors (e.g., "Don't talk when you are working at your desk," "Don't write on the desks").
5. *Associate rules and procedures with clear signals that indicate when students are to carry out or stop specific behaviors or activities.* For instance, the teacher may use a specific phrase (e.g., "Please close your books and straighten your materials") to indicate that it is time to stop the current activity and quietly prepare to move to the next class or activity. In addition, the teacher may need to remind students about acceptable conduct prior to activities that are likely to elicit inappropriate behaviors (e.g., "You may sharpen your pencil but remember not to talk to others").
6. *Demonstrate or model rules and procedures and then allow students to rehearse them.* The teacher demonstrates both the correct and incorrect forms of the behavior (e.g., sitting at a desk, getting to the pencil sharpener). The demonstration enables the students to discriminate the dimensions of the behavior. Students are then given an opportunity to practice the required behavior. Mastering rules and procedures is similar to learning academics; it requires teacher instruction and feedback combined with student practice.
7. *Design rules and procedures to anticipate possible classroom interruptions or problems and to manage these situations.* For example, students may be expected to continue working when classroom visitors enter the room or to stop all activities immediately and line up quickly and quietly when there is a fire drill. Although these events may occur infrequently, expectations should be established and practiced.
8. *Monitor closely how well students follow rules and procedures.* Appropriate behavior is reinforced, and inappropriate behavior is stopped promptly. The teacher must be able to enforce the rules and procedures that are specified; failure to do so diminishes or eliminates their effectiveness. Rules should be modified or eliminated if they prove to be ineffective, unenforceable, or no longer needed. Specific teacher practices for monitoring and enforcing rules and classroom behaviors are presented throughout this chapter.

Prevent Inappropriate Conduct by Monitoring Behavior and Providing Feedback

To prevent behavior problems from occurring, teachers must be constantly aware of the behavior of their students and provide them with feedback regarding their performance. This process is as important in developing and maintaining appropriate classroom conduct and study skills as it is in providing academic instruction.

Two important skills related to preventing behavior problems have been identified by the research on effective teaching: (1) the ability to simultaneously monitor one or more groups while directing the activities of another and (2) the ability to direct the activities of those students who are not involved in the lesson being conducted by the teacher (Englert, 1984). The first skill requires that teachers position themselves to permit continual visual scanning of the entire class so that they can observe and make eye contact with students not involved in the lesson. The second skill involves more than observation; it requires that the teacher respond to the observed behavior with verbal or nonverbal signals (e.g., frown, finger point, head nod) that will redirect the student to the assigned task. Effective managers do this without interrupting the lesson they are conducting.

The combination of providing positive attention for appropriate behavior and ignoring inappropriate behavior is frequently advocated for decreasing behavior problems. However, it is more effective to use positive attention for appropriate behavior together with the careful use of **negative attention** (i.e., a verbal or nonverbal response indicating disapproval) for inappropriate behavior (Jones & Eimers, 1975; Jones & Miller, 1974). This combination can be implemented without interfering with the activities of the classroom if teachers follow certain guidelines:

1. *Identify potentially disruptive behaviors at an early stage.* The teacher anticipates the need to act by observing student actions that are likely to lead to inappropriate behaviors.

2. *Develop a repertoire of quick, low-intensity gestures and verbalizations that signify that a student is not following the accepted guidelines.* For example, the teacher may say "John" (student's name) or "That's all" to get the student's attention and identify the current activity as inappropriate.

3. *Establish physical proximity to the disruptive student and orient yourself toward the student.* This strategy may involve the teacher moving closer to the student and facing him or her to signal that the teacher is aware of, and does not approve of, the student's behavior. At the same time, the teacher maintains direction of an instructional group. Teacher movement around the room and a tight horseshoe arrangement of desks faciliate the use of this procedure.

4. *Promptly respond to inappropriate student behavior.* The teacher uses negative attention to interrupt the student's disruptiveness before it can produce approval or attention from peers.

5. *With negative attention, use a facial expression and tone of voice that is consistent with disapproval.* It is important to communicate to the offending student that the teacher is registering disapproval.

6. *After negative attention, provide immediate reinforcement and attention when the student displays the appropriate behavior.* This identifies the accepted behavior and reaffirms that appropriate behaviors are reinforced and inappropriate behaviors are punished.

7. *If necessary, use prompting to elicit the desired behavior, and then reinforce the student immediately.* Effective teachers actually require misbehaving students to practice the appropriate behavior until they have exhibited it at the established criterion level; these teachers often drill students until they perform the behavior automatically.

Reinforce Appropriate Behavior

It would be wonderful if all students behaved appropriately in school because their teachers expected them to or because it was intrinsically rewarding. However, this expectation is simply not realistic for many students. Teachers need to help students learn that accomplishments themselves can be rewarding. To do this, a powerful tool—reinforcement—is available.

When appropriate behaviors occur, they should be rewarded. To be effective, the reinforcer should follow the desired behavior. Rewards should not be provided when students promise to exhibit the behavior at some time in the future. Only performance is rewarded. If the student behaves appropriately, then the reward will occur. Appropriate behaviors should also be reinforced immediately. Reinforcers are most effective when delivered immediately after the occurrence of the behavior. For example, if the target behavior is completion of assignments, the student should be reinforced when handing in his or her paper. The reinforcer would lose its effect if it were delivered several hours later, after the teacher had corrected the paper.

When students are learning new behaviors, each occurrence should be reinforced. Continuous reinforcement rewards an appropriate behavior every time it happens. This is the most effective schedule for establishing a new behavior or for increasing the occurrence of an infrequent behavior. As soon as the behavior has become established, the reinforcers can be delivered according to one of the intermittent schedules described in Table 5-4; intermittent reinforcement requires less attention than the continuous schedule. If reduction in reinforcement is gradual, the student will eventually maintain the desired behavior with little reinforcement. Schedules of reinforcement should move from continuous to fixed interval/ratio and then to variable interval/ratio. With variable schedules, students are less able to predict when re-

TABLE 5-4	Properties of Four Types of Intermittent Schedules of Reinforcement		
		EFFECTS ON BEHAVIOR	
NAME OF SCHEDULE	*DEFINITION OF SCHEDULE*	*SCHEDULE IN EFFECT*	*SCHEDULE TERMINATED (EXTINCTION)*
Fixed Ratio (FR)	Reinforcer is given after each X responses.	High response rate.	Irregular burst of responding. More responses than in continuous reinforcement, less than in variable ratio.
Variable Ratio (VR)	Reinforcer is given after X responses on the average.	Very high response rates; the higher the ratio the higher the rate.	Very resistant to extinction; maximum number of responses before extinction.
Fixed Interval (FI)	Reinforcer is given for first response to occur after each X minutes.	Stops working after reinforcement; works hard just prior to time for next reinforcement.	Slow, gradual decrease in responding.
Variable Interval (VI)	Reinforcer is given for first response after each X minutes, on the average.	Steady rate of responding.	Very resistant to extinction; maximum time to extinction.

Note: From *The Acting-Out Child: Coping with Classroom Disruption* (2nd ed., p. 127) by Hill M. Walker, 1995, Longmont, CO: Sopris West. Copyright 1995 by Hill M. Walker. Reprinted by permission.

inforcement will occur because reinforcers are given after an average period of time (interval) or after an average number of responses (ratio). For example, a variable ratio of 1:10 may deliver the reinforcer after 8 responses, then 7, then 13, as long as the average is 1 reinforcer for every 10 responses.

Provide Reinforcers That Are Valued by Students

Reinforcers of little value to students soon lose their effect. The simplest method of finding out what students perceive as rewarding is to ask them. Figure 5-6 is an example of an inventory that can be used to discover students' reinforcement preferences. Another method of gaining this information is to observe how students use their free time.

It is also important to use a variety of reinforcers. Of the many types available, those that have strong effects on behavior are preferred. Following are several types of reinforcers found to be useful in the classroom:

1. *Social reinforcement.* Social attention or interaction with teachers and peers is a strong reinforcer for most students. It is easy to deliver and is naturally available in the school environment. It can be provided immediately after the occurrence of the desired behavior, and the effects can be generalized to other settings. When social reinforcement is provided, the teacher should tell the student the reason for the reward. The teacher can say (or write on the student's paper), "Good reading," "Nice job on the assignment," "I like the way you lined up for recess," or "Your handwriting is very easy to read." The teacher can also try smiles and, for younger students, hugs; these and other forms of positive attention are easy to give, free, and the supply is unlimited.

2. *Activity reinforcers.* Activities are also strong reinforcers. Any activity that the student enjoys can serve as a reward for the performance of a less desired task. This approach is known as the **Premack principle.** If Joe finishes his math, then he can feed the gerbil; or if the class works quietly all morning, then they will get to see a movie after lunch. Other examples of activity reinforcers are spending time in the listening center, watching television, reading comics or magazines, and helping the teacher. These reinforcers are readily available in the school and involve minimal cost.

3. *Tangible reinforcers.* Objects such as certificates, notes to parents, toys, and school supplies can also serve as reinforcers for students. However, tangible reinforcers should be used only after social and activity reinforcers have proved too weak to support the occurrence of the behavior. When tangible reinforcers are delivered, they should always be accompanied by a social reinforcer; over time, the tangible reinforcer can be gradually faded so that it is replaced by just the use of the social reward. Disadvantages of tangible reinforcers include their cost (in terms of money or time to prepare) and a possible loss of effectiveness if they are provided too frequently. In

FIGURE 5-6   Reinforcement Inventory

1. If you could do anything you wanted to do this afternoon, how would you spend your time? _____
_____

2. Name your three favorite television shows: _____
_____
_____

3. What is your favorite thing to do in each of these seasons:
   summer _____   fall _____
   winter _____   spring _____

4. If someone gave you $5 today, how would you spend it? _____

5. What is the best movie you ever saw? _____

6. Who is the adult you like the best? _____

7. Name your three favorite foods: _____
_____
_____

8. If you could play a quiet game with anybody in this school, who would you play with? _____
_____

9. What are your three wishes? _____
_____
_____

10. What do you like to read about? _____

Finish these sentences:
11. When I'm alone, I like to _____

12. It makes me really happy when my teacher _____
_____

13. When I grow up, I _____

14. The most fun at home is when _____

15. If I could take home something from school, I would take home _____

16. If I were the teacher in this room, I would
_____

Note: Reprinted with permission of Merrill, an imprint of Macmillan Publishing Company, from *The Resource Room* (p. 62) by M. F. Hawisher and M. L. Calhoun. Copyright 1978 Merrill Publishing Company, Columbus, Ohio.

addition, many parents and educators disagree with their use. Because they are not universally available, their effects may not generalize to other school settings.

4. *Edible reinforcers.* The use of edibles should be considered only if social, activity, and tangible reinforcers have been found ineffective. Edibles have disadvantages similar to those of tangible reinforcers. If edibles are used, their presentation should always be paired with the delivery of a social reinforcer.

5. *Negative reinforcers.* Unlike other forms of reinforcement, negative reinforcers are removed when the desired behavior occurs. For example, the teacher can eliminate 2 math problems for each 10 that are completed correctly. Or the teacher's frown can disappear when students begin working. Like the more positive reinforcers, these have a place in the classroom. When negative reinforcers produce the

desired behavior, the student should be rewarded. For example, when the student begins to work, the teacher can stop frowning and praise the student for working.

The variety of reinforcers available in the classroom is limited only by the teacher's imagination. Additional examples are listed in the accompanying "Inclusion Tips for the Teacher" box. Remember, though, that social, activity, tangible, and edible reinforcers are rewards only if they are valued by the student.

Use Token Economies to Deliver Reinforcers

In a **token economy**, students are presented with tokens rather than reinforcers after the occurrence of a desired behavior. Such a system can be used with one student, small groups, or the entire class. Students collect the tokens—such

Inclusion Tips for the Teacher

Classroom Reinforcers

Here are several examples of different types of reinforcers appropriate for use in school settings. Social and activity reinforcers have special appeal since they are usually available at no cost to the teacher.

	SOCIAL	ACTIVITY	TANGIBLE	EDIBLE
Elementary-aged students	Smile Hug Positive comments: "Good job," "I like the way you raised your hand," "You really pay attention" Pat on the back	Helping teacher Popcorn party Being team leader Reading with a friend Time in the computer center Choosing game for P.E. Extra minutes of recess X minutes of free time Cleaning the chalkboard Eating lunch with teacher	Toys Crayons Pencils Erasers Paper Art materials Books Stars Good note to parents	Cereal Fruit Cake Nuts Popcorn Ice Cream Sandwich Milk
Adolescents	Signal or gesture of approval Handshake Positive comment on appearance Positive comments: "Great job," "Best work I've seen," "Great to see you working so well"	Field trip Free time Early lunch Choosing class activity Listening to tape for X minutes Attending a concert	Pens Paper Rental of tapes/CDs School supplies Sports equipment Magazines Posters Positive note home	Teacher buys lunch Popcorn Chips Juice Candy Fruit Soft drinks

as poker chips, gold stars, or points—and later trade them for backup reinforcers listed on a **reinforcement menu**. Tokens should be delivered as soon as the desired behavior has occurred and should always be paired with a social reinforcer. In setting up a token economy, the teacher should

- specify and define the behaviors that earn tokens;
- use tokens that are appropriate for the students;
- develop and post a menu that includes a variety of reinforcers and a wide range of costs—students should be able to "cash in" for either high- or low-cost reinforcers;
- allow students to help in developing the menu;
- revise the menu regularly to ensure variety;
- use a record system that is clear and cannot be sabotaged by students (who might add points or take the tokens of others);
- give students frequent opportunities to cash in (daily or at least several times per week);

- set up a cash-in system that takes a minimal amount of time and does not disrupt the operation of the class;
- provide clear rules to staff for distribution of tokens; and
- gradually reduce the value of the tokens to increase reliance on more natural reinforcers.

Token systems have been shown to be effective with general education students and students with special needs (Smith, Finn, & Dowdy, 1993), and they are easily understood by teachers and students. The menu allows students to select their own rewards. Also, token systems accommodate students who have difficulty waiting for their reinforcers; they can cash in when they want to. When the token economy is first set up, students tend to cash in frequently; however, as they grow accustomed to this system, they are able to wait for longer periods. Figure 5-7 presents a reinforcement menu that can be used in a token economy.

FIGURE 5-7   Reinforcement Menu

Reinforcers	Points
Apple	10
Cookie	10
Pencil	10
Popcorn	10
Small candies	15
Large candies	45
Gum	45
Viewing educational videotape or DVD (10 minutes)	50
Viewing entertainment videotape or DVD (10 minutes)	100
Pen	100
Grab bag	100
Listening to cassette tape or CD (15 minutes)	150
Tokens for video games	150
Hamburger at fast-food restaurant	500
Free time	500
Time with the computer	500
Time for game with a friend	700
Lunch with the teacher	750
Blank cassette tapes or computer disks	1,000
Music tapes	1,500
CDs	2,500
Price as marked:	
Paperbacks of your choice	___
Magazines (Motorcycle, Car, Autocross, etc.)	___
Movie tickets/passes	___
DVD	___
Computer software	___
Field trip	___

With Older Students, Use Contingency Contracts

Contingency contracts are written agreements between the student and teacher that indicate what the student must do to earn a specific reward. These agreements, like most contracts, are negotiated; both parties must accept the terms. Because they involve negotiation and require students to assume responsibility for fulfilling their part of the bargain, contracts are probably best for older students.

Homme, Csanyi, Gonzales, and Rechs (cited in Blankenship & Lilly, 1981) provide the following rules for developing contracts in the classroom:

1. The contract payoff (reward) should be immediate.
2. Initial contracts should call for and reward small approximations.
3. Reward frequently with small amounts.
4. The contract should call for and reward accomplishment rather than obedience.
5. Reward the behavior after it occurs.
6. The contract must be fair.
7. The terms of the contract must be clear.
8. The contract must be honest.
9. The contract must be positive.
10. Contracting as a method must be used systematically. (p. 235)

A sample contract form, providing space for recording the agreement that has been negotiated between the student and the teacher, is shown in Figure 5-8. A good contract identifies the responsibilities of both parties and the consequences if the terms are not fulfilled.

Teach Behaviors by Shaping

Shaping is the reinforcement of successive approximations or small, progressive steps toward the desired behavior. The technique of shaping is used to teach new behaviors or increase the occurrence of behaviors exhibited infrequently. For example, shaping can be used with a student who completes only one

FIGURE 5-8	Contingency Contract

Official Contract

Effective Dates: From _____ to _____

This contract involves an agreement between _____ and
                                                                                    (Teacher/Parent)

_____ . This agreement will be reviewed on the following
        (Student)

date(s) _____ and can be renegotiated at any time by
agreement of both parties.

When _____ (Student) does the following: _____

_____

_____

then _____ (Teacher/Parent) will: _____

_____

_____

According to this agreement the teacher/parent will provide the agreed-upon reinforcers to the student only if he or she fulfills his or her part of the contract. If the
student does not fulfill his or her part of the agreement, the reinforcers will be
withheld.

Teacher/Parent Signature _____   Date _____
Student Signature _____   Date _____

---

or two assignments per week, when the desired behavior is eight assignments per day. First, a target of one completed assignment per day is established. This is reinforced until the student regularly finishes the daily work. Then the target is raised to two, then three assignments, and so on, as the student progresses toward the ultimate goal of eight assignments per day. For the student who completes no assignments, the beginning target might be a few problems or items of each assignment; this goal would be gradually increased toward the classroom goal of eight completed assignments per day.

Use Modeling to Improve Student Behavior

Modeling involves the reinforcement of another individual, the model, for exhibiting the desired behavior in the presence of the target student. The target student is then reinforced when he or she imitates the modeled behavior. For example, the model seated near the target student might be reinforced for studying; the teacher clearly identifies the reason for the reinforcement by saying, "I like the way you are working quietly in your seat." When this behavior is imitated by the target student, he or she is also rewarded.

Consider Involving Peers in Behavioral Programs

Involving class members in implementing programs designed to improve student behavior can be effective. Students can of-

ten provide strong reinforcers for the behavior of their peers, and in many cases they are able to monitor and respond to behaviors that the teacher might miss. The use of peers can involve either individual or group programs.

Group contingencies involve establishing a criterion level for the entire group, and the distribution of reinforcement to individual class members is based on the performance of the entire group. For example, a teacher concerned with the high number of talk-outs (average of 45 per day) could establish a system in which the entire class earns 5 minutes of extra recess if there were no more than 20 talk-outs the previous day. As the students improve, the teacher can gradually reduce the number of talk-outs accepted (e.g., they might be reduced by 1 each week).

Team-based contingencies involve grouping students into teams that compete against each other. As with group contingencies, individual students can help or hurt their team. A teacher wishing to increase the amount of homework completed might establish a prize based on the percentage of assignments completed for the week. The prize (i.e., consequence) could be awarded in one of several different ways: (1) Only the team with the highest percentage wins, (2) each team wins that reaches a percentage higher than a preset criterion (e.g., 95%), or (3) the prize earned by each team is based on the percentage of assignments completed by that team (e.g., a team completing 50% of the assignments earns 30 minutes in the computer area, whereas the team that completes 100%

earns 1 hour). Greater changes are usually achieved by dividing groups into teams than by concentrating on whole groups.

Another way of involving peers is to have group members share in the consequences earned by a particular student. A rather withdrawn student in a general education class might earn points for each social interaction with a peer. Peers might seek to increase their interactions with that student if the entire class receives an extra minute of recess for every 10 points earned by the student. Similarly, a student who is easily distracted might experience fewer interruptions from classmates if they are all earning reinforcers for increases in the student's on-task behavior.

Peers can be trained to reinforce students such as the withdrawn or distractible students described earlier. They might provide the reinforcement for such students, especially if they earn reinforcers for the other student's performance. They might also be used to record the other student's performance (e.g., actual interactions or the amount of on-task behavior); these data may be more accurate than teacher-collected data.

Although such programs can be effective, teachers must consider several factors before involving peers in interventions. First, all the students involved must be able to perform the desired behavior. Otherwise, students may be subjected to potential physical or verbal abuse. Second, individual students should not be able to subvert the efforts of the group. Third, students should not be able to do the work required of others in order to improve the performance of their group. The interactions resulting from these programs can be very reinforcing to the students involved, and they often lead to improved transfer of behaviors and to positive interactions

outside the typical classroom setting. As with other interventions, careful planning increases the likelihood of success.

Involve Students in Managing Their Own Behavior

Students can be directly involved in managing their own behavior by (1) participating in setting goals, (2) self-monitoring, or (3) assisting in the intervention itself by evaluating their own performance and rewarding themselves for appropriate behavior (Davies & White, 2000; Graham, Harris, & Reid, 1998; Prater, 1994; Reid, 1996). If they learn techniques that help improve their behavior in one setting, they can often transfer those skills to other settings.

Teachers can identify several areas in which students need to improve their behavior. The students themselves, especially those at the secondary level, can help to set goals for improvement in these areas, or they can choose other areas of need. Assisting in identifying goals increases students' active involvement in improving their own behavior.

Self-monitoring can take a number of forms. Students may simply be required to judge whether they are "working" at the end of each 5- to 10-minute segment of the class period or at the time a teacher-set buzzer rings. They might also record and graph their daily spelling performance, the number of times they leave their desk, or the length of time they are away from their desk each day. In addition, the number of talk-outs or the number of social interactions they initiate can be recorded by the students. Self-monitoring needs to be supervised by the teacher, with reinforcement provided for accuracy; reinstruction should be provided if the data are not consistent with those collected by the teacher. Self-monitoring decreases the demands on the teacher for collecting data, and it also makes students acutely aware of their own behavior.

A variety of interventions can be self-administered by students. They can learn to evaluate and self-reinforce their own performance in class. For example, they might give themselves points or check marks for improving their spelling performance or for reducing the amount of time they are out of their seats during a day. Self-punishment might involve deducting points for talking out in class or failing to complete a homework assignment. Other approaches might involve teaching students a strategy to use in resolving various kinds of problems they encounter. Students might be taught to ask specific questions or to make specific self-statements (i.e., **self-instruction**) to help themselves develop problem-solving skills (e.g., "What am I supposed to do? What is my plan? How do I do it?"). A combination of these various approaches (e.g., self-instruction followed by self-reinforcement) can actively involve students in improving their own behavior. It also increases the chance of the intervention's success and the generalization of newly learned skills to other situations.

Involve Parents in Behavior Management Programs

Parents are often willing and helpful participants in behavior management programs. They can provide continuation of the intervention program at home; for instance, parents can reinforce students for time spent doing homework. They can also assist by providing reinforcers for the school behavior of their children. For example, if students earn a certain number of points in school, parents can provide a special activity, such as a camping trip, or a gift, like a baseball glove or doll.

Positive notes to parents from teachers can be reinforcing both for students and for parents. Many parents of special students have received few good reports from school. A note from a teacher praising the accomplishments of a student can increase the level of praise that the student receives at home.

Before involving parents in intervention programs, teachers should be sure that the parents are willing and able to implement procedures consistently. If home and school programs are not well coordinated, the effectiveness of both may decrease. Consistency can be improved by providing some parent training or with frequent communication between parents and teachers. Englert (1984) provides several suggestions for improving classroom behavior management techniques. The checklist in Figure 5-9 summarizes these suggestions.

Techniques for promoting the social acceptance of students with special needs included in the general education classroom are discussed in the next chapter. Thank you for reading to the end of this chapter. When you complete your review of "Things to Remember" and the activities that follow, you may want to reward yourself with a short break or a favorite beverage.

Things to Remember

- To be successful members of the general education classroom, students may need to increase some behaviors, decrease others, and learn new ways of acting.
- Classroom behavior problems interfere with instruction and social interactions; study skills problems affect a student's academic performance.
- Intervention may be necessary if there is a low rate of appropriate behavior, a high rate of inappropriate behavior, or an absence of the appropriate behavior from the student's repertoire.
- Behavior is learned and can be taught; it is increased by reinforcement and decreased by the removal of reinforcers or the introduction of aversive events.
- Behaviors do not occur in isolation; their antecedents and consequences must be considered.

- Direct observation of student behavior provides the most useful data for classroom teachers.
- Class rules and procedures make students aware of the expectations for behavior.
- Methods of using reinforcers to change behavior include token economies, contingency contracts, and group contingencies.
- Preventing behavior problems involves careful monitoring of students, reinforcement of appropriate behaviors, and use of negative teacher attention for potentially disruptive behavior.
- Students can participate in self-management of behavior by setting goals, monitoring their own performance, or implementing interventions such as self-reinforcement or self-instruction.
- Effective reinforcers are those valued by the students.

FIGURE 5-9   Are You Managing the Classroom Effectively?

Respond to each item in terms of the extent to which it describes yourself: (1) not at all descriptive, (2) descriptive to a small extent, (3) descriptive to a moderate extent, (4) descriptive to a large extent, (5) descriptive to an extremely large extent.

Competencies

Classroom Set-up and Organization

1.1	Arranges physical space and instructional materials to minimize disruptive movement around classroom and to facilitate easy access to high-use materials.	1	2	3	4	5
1.2	Establishes and implements minimally disruptive traffic patterns and procedures.	1	2	3	4	5
1.3	Establishes and implements procedures for nonacademic class business (e.g., tardiness, material use, movement in and out of room, distributing materials, talk among students, bathroom breaks).	1	2	3	4	5
1.4	Establishes and implements procedures for academic business (e.g., seatwork procedures, obtaining help, volunteer behavior during small group, learning centers, set-up and takedown of lessons).	1	2	3	4	5

Teaching Rules and Procedures

2.1	Communicates clearly what behavior will be tolerated and what will not.	1	2	3	4	5
2.2	Gives behavior reminders and statements of desired behavior in advance of activity.	1	2	3	4	5
2.3	Clearly introduces rules, procedures, and consequences at beginning of school year and whenever needed.	1	2	3	4	5
2.4	States rules, posts rules, and provides discussion of rules at the time of their introduction.	1	2	3	4	5
2.5	Presents examples and non-examples of rules and procedures.	1	2	3	4	5
2.6	Requires student rehearsal of rules and procedures.	1	2	3	4	5
2.7	Monitors rule compliance and provides specific behavioral feedback.	1	2	3	4	5
2.8	Consequates rule noncompliance by stopping inappropriate behavior immediately and requiring students to practice the procedure until it is performed automatically.	1	2	3	4	5

Maintaining Rules and Procedures

3.1	Positions self in the room to provide high degree of visibility (e.g., can make eye contact with all students).	1	2	3	4	5
3.2	Scans constantly and makes eye contact with all students on an equal basis.	1	2	3	4	5
3.3	Detects disruptive behavior early and cites rule or procedure in responding to disruptive behavior.	1	2	3	4	5
3.4	Reinforces appropriate performance through specific praise statements (e.g., states specific behaviors).	1	2	3	4	5
3.5	Administers praise contingently.	1	2	3	4	5
3.6	Includes students in the management of their own behavior.	1	2	3	4	5
3.7	Uses nonverbal signals to direct students when teaching other groups of students.	1	2	3	4	5

Note: From "Measuring Teacher Effectiveness from the Teacher's Point of View" by C. S. Englert, 1984, *Focus on Exceptional Children,* *17*(2), p. 5. Copyright 1984 by Love. Reprinted by permission.

ACTIVITIES

1. Collect observation data on an individual (friend, student, teacher) during five separate observation periods. Be sure you have identified a specific behavior to observe (such as being on task). Record and graph the data using a format similar to the one presented in this chapter. When you are finished, show your graph to another individual; can that person interpret your data? Can you speculate about what antecedents and consequences contribute to the observed occurrence of the behavior? Describe an intervention you might use if you wished to change the behavior.

2. Interview both a special educator and a general education teacher. Obtain information about the approaches they advocate for managing students in the general education classroom. What do they consider to be problem behaviors? According to the teachers, are special techniques needed for students with special needs, or are the behavior problems of all students managed in generally the same way? Ask the teachers to describe how they use student performance data in behavior change programs. Do they collect data before beginning a program? During the program? How do they decide when a program is working? When it needs to be changed?

3. Develop a set of rules for a classroom you have recently observed. Describe the class and establish five to eight rules using the guidelines stated in the chapter. Explain specifically how you would implement these rules at the beginning of a school year. Identify potential problems you might experience in implementing your rules, and describe how you would deal with these problems.

4. Read and summarize two articles that discuss token economies, contracting, or one of the other techniques described in this chapter. Journals such as *Remedial and Special Education, Journal of Applied Behavior Analysis, Education and Treatment of Children,* and *Behavior Modification* often feature articles on these topics.

5. Consider different viewpoints on classroom discipline. Contact local school districts to learn about their policies. Also, get in touch with a national teachers' organization, such as the American Federation of Teachers or the National Education Association (see "Window on the Web"). Compare the policies of local districts with those of the professional organization you contact. What changes would you make in these policies? Why would you make these changes?

6. Develop a reinforcement menu for a school-aged student. Begin by interviewing the student using the inventory presented in Figure 5-6. You may want to add questions and observe the student in different situations. Then develop a menu that includes at least 10 items, ranging in cost (points) from cheap to expensive. Describe how a general education teacher could use this menu when implementing a behavior change program.

CD-ROM Activities

All of the teachers featured in the video case studies are very proficient in classroom management. For specific examples (and to answer the questions that follow), look at the clip entitled "Structure Routines" in the preschool classroom and the clip entitled "Clear Expectations" in the sixth grade classroom.

- *In the preschool classroom, what types of positive support does the teacher use to encourage the young boy to put away the materials? Do you see any instances of positive reinforcement?*

- *In the sixth grade classroom, what role do clear expectations play in helping students learn how to manage their behavior? How might classroom rules play a part in promoting appropriate behavior?*

Window on the Web

American Federation of Teachers and National Education Association

The American Federation of Teachers (AFT) and the National Education Association (NEA) are national professional organizations for teachers, and each sponsors a website with information for educators and others interested in education.

http://www.aft.org

The AFT website provides information about the organization, the latest news, AFT publications and reports, legislative action updates, and resources tailored for parents and for specific groups of professionals (e.g., teachers, paraprofessionals, and school-related personnel). Also available is information about "hot topics" such as charter schools, discipline and safety, National Board certification, No Child Left Behind Act, and the importance of high-quality reading instruction.

Note: Courtesy of American Federation of Teachers.

http://www.nea.org

The NEA website provides access to current education news in the Press Center; help for parents; NEA publications and multimedia; the legislative action center of this organization; and position statements on issues in education such as accountability and testing, class size, school safety, and special education and the Individuals with Disabilities Education Act. Also available is a link to OWL.org, a website full of resources for NEA members.

Note: Courtesy of the National Education Association.

Nonmembers can access some (but not all) of its features. Among the resources available to everyone are current education news stories, Works4Me tips for teachers from teachers, and informative articles for new teachers (e.g., "What Does It Mean to Be Smart?"), parents and community members (e.g., "Anti-Bullying Campaign"), and education support professionals (e.g., "Para[professional] Quality: Not So Simple Anymore").

Companion
Website

For more information, go to the Web Links module in Chapter 5 of the Companion Website.

Promoting Social Acceptance

CHAPTER

6

STUDENTS' STORIES

- Juan has been included in a general education class for a month and still eats lunch alone.
- Jackie, who travels by wheelchair, is the only girl in her fifth-grade class who hasn't been invited to a birthday party yet this year.
- June dislikes talking in class because the other students make fun of her speech.
- Even though Matt's classroom behavior has improved, his teacher is reluctant to have him join the class for assemblies and field trips.
- Maria's American history teacher wants her to read the text like everyone else rather than listen to special tapes.

- The school janitor is irritated because Hank's crutches leave marks on the floors of the classroom, halls, and bathroom.
- Mike attends a class for students with severe disabilities that was moved to the campus of the neighborhood school last month. Although members of his class eat in the lunchroom, attend assemblies, and use the playing fields and the gym for physical education, students in the general education program avoid social or verbal interactions with Mike and his classmates.
- Several of the parents of Tim's classmates are concerned about his mild seizures; they wonder whether Tim's condition is contagious.

LOOKING AHEAD

Consider the questions that follow as you read this chapter about helping students with special needs become socially included in the general education classroom.

- Sometimes students need help to make friends with their classmates. What suggestions could you offer to the teachers of Juan, Jackie, and Mike?
- Sometimes students are not accepted because their peers, teachers, or other adults have limited understanding of their special needs. How would you go about rectifying that situation for Maria, Hank, and Tim?
- How could you help June feel more comfortable about speaking in class? Would your plan include working with June's classmates?
- What ideas could you share with Matt and his teacher so that Matt could participate with his class in school assemblies and field trips?

To answer these questions online, go to the Students' Stories module in Chapter 6 of the Companion Website.

Students with special needs participating in general education programs often suffer rejection during their school years. They may be rejected by their general education peers, their teachers, or the parents of their classmates. This lack of acceptance has a negative effect on both their self-concept and their school performance (Heron & Harris, 2001; Schumaker & Hazel, 1984). To be truly effective, a general education program that includes students with special needs must make provisions for improving the social skills of these students and enhancing their social integration (Allsopp, Santos, & Linn, 2000; Hughes, 1999; Maag & Webber, 1995). This holds true not only for students with disabilities who enter the general education class from a special program but also for those who have never left the mainstream setting.

SOCIAL PROBLEMS IN THE CLASSROOM

Many students with special needs encounter difficulty when interacting socially with general education peers and teachers. One source of this difficulty can be the behavior of the special student. However, at least equally important are the attitudes and feelings of the general population. Many people have little accurate information about students with special needs, and this lack of knowledge can create fear and prejudice.

Students with special needs may fail to conform to the expectations of school and society. They may not look or act the same as other students. For teachers and peers unfamiliar with special students, these differences can create apprehension, distrust, and even hostility. The abilities, talents, and needs of the student with special needs are frequently overlooked.

Some students with special needs can be easily identified; their appearance or their actions are visibly different. One example is the student who travels by wheelchair. Others have no observable signs but stand out when their performance falls below expectations. For instance, students with learning disabilities are indistinguishable from their peers until they are asked to read or write or do math.

Throughout their school careers, students with special needs encounter failure. When placed in the general education classroom, they may be apprehensive about attempting activities. This fear of failure and feeling of incompetence may cause them to withdraw. This withdrawal can contribute to their rejection and make it difficult for even the most effective and creative teacher to provide an appropriate learning situation (Gresham, 1984; Meisgeier, 1981; Pavri & Luftig, 2000).

Students with special needs can be as delayed in their social development as they are in other areas (Leffert & Siperstein, 2003; Odom, McConnell, & Chandler, 1994). Thus, poor social skills can be another factor in their rejection (Hollinger, 1987). Many students with special needs are not as capable as their general education peers of initiating and

sustaining appropriate social relationships. For example, the research of Tur-Kaspa and Bryan (1994) found that students with learning disabilities were lacking in the language skills necessary for effective social communication. Students with disabilities may fail to develop appropriate social skills because they have fewer friends and are rated significantly lower in sociometric status than their peers (Asher & Taylor, 1981; Drabman & Patterson, 1981; McIntosh, Vaughn, & Zaragoza, 1991; Ray, 1985). Or it may be that they have difficulty using social cues; some misperceive their social standing and feel that they are better accepted by peers than they actually are (Heron & Harris, 2001). According to Bryan and Bryan (1977), students with learning disabilities exhibit more aggressive or negative behaviors, are less accurate in interpreting nonverbal communications, and "emit a lot [of] nasty statements to their peers" (p. 142). Drabman and Patterson describe students with special needs as "opposing peers, displaying disruptive behavior and exhibiting withdrawal behavior" (p. 48). It is difficult to determine the cause of the problem: Friendless students have little opportunity to develop social skills, and those with poor skills are unlikely to form friendships.

These problems may increase at the secondary level. In adolescence, social interaction with peers becomes extremely important. For students with disabilities who have spent the majority of their educational careers segregated from age peers, the transition to the general education environment can be hazardous. Students with disabilities may not only lack a common experiential background with general education students but also be delayed in the acquisition of important social skills. These obstacles, combined with the barriers to acceptance in the general education class, magnify the difficulty of promoting the social acceptance of secondary students with special needs.

Research indicates that general education students and teachers do not consistently accept the student with disabilities (e.g., Bryan, 1997; Drabman & Patterson, 1981; Gans, 1985; Pavri & Luftig, 2000; Sabornie & Kauffman, 1985; Sale & Carey, 1995). Teachers and peers are more likely to ignore social interactions initiated by students with disabilities. And teachers are more critical of their behavior, provide fewer praise statements, and consider them less desirable as students (Cook, 2001; Heron & Harris, 2001); this is especially apparent if the students are boys (e.g., Schlosser & Algozzine, 1980; Slate & Saudargas, 1986; Stitt et al., 1988).

One factor that influences teacher attitudes is labeling. When students are identified by a negatively perceived label (e.g., learning disabilities, mental retardation), teachers are less able to objectively observe, rate, and plan appropriate interventions for their behavior (Campbell, Dodson, & Bost, 1985). Although the effects of labeling on social acceptance have not been consistently supported by research (Gottlieb & Leyser, 1981), evidence is adequate to caution against reliance on labels for educational information. For instance, Gillung and Rucker (1977) found that teachers expected less from students who were labeled than from unlabeled students with identical behaviors. Alves and Gottlieb (1986) reported that teachers involved students with disabilities in fewer academic exchanges; these students were asked fewer questions and were given less feedback than their peers without disabilities. In a study conducted by Reschly and Lamprecht (1979), students' labels lowered the initial expectations of teachers; however, as teachers spent more time with special students and observed their behavior, expectations became more realistic. Thus, labels can be misleading and can have a negative effect, at least on the initial acceptance of students with special needs by their teachers.

Another factor that can contribute to the rejection of students with disabilities by general education teachers and administrators is a lack of special training and experience (Heron & Harris, 2001; Maag & Webber, 1995; Martin, 1974). Some teachers are afraid that they do not have the skills necessary for teaching students with special needs. Others may feel that working with these students is not as gratifying as working with typical individuals. Teachers with negative attitudes toward special students can convey these feelings to all the individuals in the class and thereby further reduce the chance for successful programs that include students with disabilities (e.g., Garrett & Crump, 1980; Heflin & Bullock, 1999; Heron & Harris, 2001).

A portion of the problem related to the attitudes toward students with special needs can be attributed to former special education practices. For some time, special classes were virtually the only special education service available for students with disabilities. Special educators advocated that these students be removed from the mainstream and entrusted to the care of a specialist in a separate class setting. As a result, general education teachers were not encouraged to attempt to meet the needs of students with disabilities within the mainstream setting. At present, however, a variety of part-time special education services are available for both students with special needs and their general education teachers. In addition, mainstreaming and inclusion are now common practices, and training programs for general education teachers often require some level of preparation in dealing with the needs of students with disabilities ("Special Needs, Common Goals," 2004). One important aspect of effective special education programs is ensuring that the collaboration and consulting role of the special educator helps teachers in general education classes realize that students with disabilities can successfully participate in general education settings for a portion of the school day that is appropriate for each student.

The parents of students with disabilities can also contribute to the social problems of their children. Parents can be overly protective and restrict a student's involvement in normal social activities, which thereby reduces the opportunities for acquiring friends and fosters a limited experience base. Parents reluctant to allow their child to experience failure can actually be increasing the probability that failure will occur in future social interactions. In addition, the parents of general education students can influence the acceptance of students with special needs. Some may resist inclusion of students with special needs in the general education program if they believe that it will reduce the quality of their children's education. Other parents may discourage their children from interacting with the students with disabilities in the class. These negative attitudes are often based on limited information about, and limited experience with, students with special needs.

PRINCIPLES FOR ENHANCING SOCIAL ACCEPTANCE

When rejected by general education teachers and peers, students with special needs may perform more poorly, both socially and academically. The self-concept of rejected students can be affected. In addition, because they are not encouraged to participate in classroom activities, rejected students may fall further behind in all skill areas. Simply including students with disabilities in general education classes does not guarantee their social acceptance or their acquisition of improved social skills (Guetzloe, 1999; Heflin & Bullock, 1999; Miller, 2003; Sale & Carey, 1995; Vaughn, 1995). In most cases, the general education teacher must participate in developing and implementing a systematic program designed to improve the students' social skills and to increase their social integration. Effective mainstreaming and inclusion programs require that educators pay attention to the social needs as well as to the academic, behavioral, and physical needs of their students (Gresham, 1984; York, Vandercook, MacDonald, Heise-Neff, & Caughey, 1992). The principles described in the following paragraphs assist in planning and implementing a successful program for social acceptance.

Change Attitudes with Information

Attitudes are extremely important. The attitudes of the teacher have a significant effect on the attitudes of the students within the class; negative feelings toward students with disabilities can be communicated by the teacher (Cartledge, Frew, & Zaharias, 1985; Garrett & Crump, 1980; Simpson, 1980). Teachers should realize that their words and actions provide a model for students; they should attempt to convey a positive attitude that encourages acceptance of the student with special needs. Attitudes are affected by information. When students and adults increase their knowledge about students with special needs, their attitudes improve (Donaldson & Martinson, 1977; Handlers & Austin, 1980; Simpson, 1980). Information dispels misconceptions and clarifies misunderstandings; prejudice and fear decrease. Teachers and peers in the general education class become more accepting as they learn more about the abilities and problems of students with special needs (Fiedler & Simpson, 1987; Simpson, 1980).

Knowledge about students with disabilities can be gained in many ways. Students and teachers can read or view films, videotapes, and television programs about special students. Also, simulations of disabilities can be used to increase understanding. Visits to special education settings can be arranged, or students and adults with disabilities can be interviewed or invited to the general education classroom. Even higher levels of exposure can be gained if teachers volunteer to accept students with special needs in their classes or if general education students are encouraged to work as peer tutors with special students. As more is learned about individuals with disabilities, they appear less different, more familiar, and more acceptable. See the "Inclusion Tips for the Teacher" box for some suggestions on how to get to know individuals with disabilities.

Recognize the Similarities Between Special and General Education Students

Teachers and students may form opinions about the abilities of a student with special needs solely on the basis of physical appearance, labels, or occasional behaviors. Assumptions made by teachers are extremely important because they may influence instructional expectations for the student. A student's looks or assigned label is an insufficient database for programming decisions or for predicting the characteristics of his or her personality. Although it is easy to jump to conclusions, more information is necessary before educational plans and predictions can be made. What is needed is specific assessment information about the student's skills and abilities and an opportunity to observe the student in the classroom. Knowledge that a student has a visual impairment, for example, can raise the anxiety level of the teacher. More pertinent is information that, although the student reads Braille materials, she is able to participate in class discussions, benefit from lectures, and interact socially with her classmates. When the team determines that students are able to benefit from placement in the general education classroom, those students do not need to be protected by the teacher. They should be included in as many activities as feasible and treated like any other student in the classroom—that is, as individuals.

Teachers often talk about the behaviors and characteristics of the students with disabilities in their classrooms. However, in most cases the academic problems and inappropriate behaviors of students with special needs are also evident in many of their "normal" peers. If teachers were to list the typical behaviors, traits, and concerns of general education students, they would find that these are also typical of students with special needs. Special students are children and adolescents with identified needs; despite these needs, however, they remain individuals. As Turnbull and Schulz (1979) state, "A difference is only a difference when it makes a difference. . . . [C]hildren [with disabilities] have far more similarities than differences with the [children without disabilities]" (p. 48).

Inclusion Tips for the Teacher

How to Get to Know People with Disabilities

Have you ever wondered about how to interact with a person with disabilities? Here are several suggestions:

- Converse with an individual with disabilities in spirit, content, and approach as you would with anyone else.
- When you think someone with a disability may need assistance, ask, "Do you need help? How should I help you?"
- Do not shout at blind persons. They have lost their *vision* not their hearing.
- Do not "talk over" or provide the words for someone who stutters or speaks with difficulty. Be patient and listen, and let the person speak for himself.

- *Always FACE* a person with a hearing impairment. Be sure the person can see your lips; speak clearly without exaggerating lip movements.
- Speak directly to a person with disabilities. Do not direct your conversation to an attendant, assistant, or nearby companion as if she did not exist.
- Do not call special attention to a person with disabilities. Approach her as another person who happens to have a disability—not as a disability that belongs to a person.

Note: From "Some Social Tips for Non-Disabled Folks," *Report from Closer Look,* Spring 1981, p. 5. Adapted by permission.

Prepare Students in the General Education Class for the Inclusion of Students with Disabilities

Students in the general education program are often isolated from any contact with students with disabilities. Consequently, general education students may never have met a person with a disability unless an individual with special needs is among their family, friends, or neighbors. This limited knowledge and experience can lead to the development of prejudice and nonaccepting attitudes and a natural discrimination against individuals who are different. Evidence

suggests that "discriminatory responses may exist as relatively normal patterns of behavior" (Simpson, 1980, p. 2).

The attitudes of students in the general education class can be improved and their acceptance of students with disabilities increased (Donaldson, 1980; Fox, 1989; Guralnick, 1981; Johnson & Johnson, 1984; Richardson, 2000; York et al., 1992). Before students with disabilities are placed in the general education class, activities should be conducted to provide information and skills to general education students. For example, students can learn about disabilities and gain skills in assisting students with special needs in the classroom. Such experiences also benefit students with disabilities who never leave the general education classroom. This training can be provided by general educators or general and special educators working together.

Prepare Students with Disabilities for Inclusion

One of the reasons for rejection of students with disabilities is their frequent lack of social skills. In most cases, students with disabilities should be provided with specific training in the social skills needed to function successfully in school and the community (Brady & McEvoy, 1989; Cartledge et al., 1985; Gresham, 1984; Hollinger, 1987; Schumaker & Hazel, 1984; Weiner & Harris, 1997). Students with special needs are able to acquire appropriate social behaviors; however, this is not likely to occur if students are only provided with opportunities to interact with peers and adults. Specific instruction, including modeling, imitating, coaching, and practice, is usually necessary (Allsopp et al., 2000; Elliott & Gresham, 1993; Lane, 1999) and can be provided in either the special or the general education classroom. In fact, the most successful social skills interventions are those that are structured for individuals or small groups and designed to be conducted over long-term periods (McIntosh et al., 1991).

Prepare Parents for the Inclusion of Students with Disabilities

Parents of both typical students and those with disabilities can make important contributions to the social acceptance program. The attitudes they convey to their children influence their children's viewpoints, the teacher's efforts, and the school program. Parents often have concerns about students with disabilities being involved in the general education program because they are uncertain about the effects on their children. Informing parents about the needs of students with disabilities, the purpose of the program, and the impact on their children will help gain their support. It is important for parents to realize that after students leave school, they will all be intermingling in the community. The school program helps prepare them for this involvement.

METHODS FOR GATHERING DATA

Data collection is just as important in promoting social acceptance as it is in instruction and management of classroom behavior. Assessment information can determine the current attitudes and social behaviors of students and teachers. If the effectiveness of a social acceptance program is to be evaluated, data should be collected both before and after the program is implemented. In addition, continuous monitoring of progress is necessary so that program modifications can be made.

Information about social skills and acceptance can be gathered from many sources: general education students and those with special needs, general and special education teachers, other professionals, and parents. Various methods are used in assessment. Sociometric measures provide information about how students with special needs are perceived by general education peers. Teacher opinions can be obtained in interviews or teacher ratings or rankings of class members. Self-concept measures, such as those appearing in Figure 6-1, are used to see how students with special needs feel about themselves. In addition, the observational techniques described in chapter 5 assist in identifying the types of social behaviors exhibited by students with special needs and their social interactions with teachers and peers. McLoughlin and Lewis (2005) describe a variety of assessment devices useful in a social acceptance program. These include measures of self-concept, attitudes toward school, interactions with teachers, and peer relationships.

One of the most popular methods for gathering data about acceptance and rejection of students with special needs is the **sociometric measure.** Sociometric devices, which measure the attitudes of group members toward one another, are often recommended for determining how well students with special needs are accepted by peers (Kauffman, 2001;

FIGURE 6-1   Assessing Self-Concept

Adjective Checklist
Directions: Put an X by each word that describes you.

_____ 1. smart	_____ 7. quarrelsome	_____ 13. bothersome
_____ 2. funny	_____ 8. fidgety	_____ 14. cranky
_____ 3. tired	_____ 9. energetic	_____ 15. eager
_____ 4. happy	_____ 10. friendly	_____ 16. honest
_____ 5. blue	_____ 11. shy	_____ 17. lazy
_____ 6. busy	_____ 12. sad	_____ 18. selfish

Behavioral Checklist
Directions: Put an X by each description that fits you.

_____ 1. makes friends easily	_____ 6. seems to lack confidence
_____ 2. not as smart as most kids	_____ 7. is a good leader
_____ 3. likes to be alone	_____ 8. enjoys school
_____ 4. is fun to be with	_____ 9. feelings are easily hurt
_____ 5. laughs a lot	_____ 10. daydreams a lot

Note: Reprinted with permission of Merrill, an imprint of Macmillan Publishing Company, from *Teacher Diagnosis of Educational Difficulties* (2nd ed.) by R. M. Smith, Copyright © 1982 Merrill Publishing Company, Columbus, Ohio.

Polloway & Patton, 1993). Results can serve as an overall index of the social skill development of students with disabilities (Cartledge & Milburn, 1995; Luftig, 1989). These devices are relatively simple, quick to administer, and easy to interpret. However, it is important to note that although they provide an overall measure of the acceptance of students, they do not identify specific behaviors or skills that require intervention (Foster, Inderbitzen, & Nangle, 1993).

As shown in Table 6-1, several different types of sociometric measures are used. Students can be asked to nominate favorite peers, rate their classmates, or choose between pairs of students. The nomination method tends to be a measure of friendship, whereas rating scales tend to assess the student's level of acceptance. General acceptance of students with special needs by their peers is probably a more appropriate instructional goal than an increase in the students' number of friendships. This point should be considered when selecting a sociometric device (Asher & Taylor, 1981).

Before using sociometric methods to gather data about social acceptance, teachers should consider school and district policies. These methods involve the collection of confidential information, and some schools allow their use only with parental permission. Results should be treated with caution; when students are asked to rate other students, they should be encouraged to keep the nature of their responses confidential. Also, it is important that teachers not share overall ratings with students, particularly those who may already have a poor self-concept (McLoughlin & Lewis, 2005). Sociometric devices also tend to lose their sensitivity to changes in the behavior of children over 10 years old. Finally, they provide little diagnostic information regarding which social skills should be taught, and, if used too frequently, they may actually contribute to the rejection of some students (Schumaker & Hazel, 1984).

Direct observation techniques are helpful in assessing and monitoring the specific social skills exhibited by students with special needs (e.g., Prasad, 1994) and the

TABLE 6-1 Sociometric Methods

METHOD	DESCRIPTION	EXAMPLE	SCORING	COMMENTS
Nomination	Requires students to name classmates who fit a particular sociometric criterion. Can be based upon positive or negative criteria.	Name three classmates whom you would like to have sitting near you (positive). Name three classmates whom you would not like to have sitting near you (negative).	A student's score is the total number of nominations received from classmates. (Tally those with positive and negative criteria separately.)	Scores are generally stable over time. Not as stable for very young children. Ratings are obtained on only those students nominated.
Rating scale	All students in the class are listed, and a rating scale (e.g., 1 = low and 5 = high) is provided. Each student in the class is rated.	Circle the number which best indicates your opinion. I would like to study with . . . Not at all / A lot. Joe 1 2 3 4 5. Mary 1 2 3 4 5	Each student's score is an average of [his or her] ratings from all students.	All students are rated by all other students in the class. Has high test–retest reliability.
Paired-comparison	The most preferred classmate is chosen from all possible pairings of students in the class.	Circle the classmate in each pair with whom you would most like to study. 1. John or Martha 2. John or Sam . . . 40. Martha or Sue	A student's score is the number of times he or she was chosen by other students in all the possible pairings.	All students are rated by all other students. Has high test–retest reliability. Administration and scoring take more time than other methods.

Note: From "Social Outcomes of Mainstreaming: Sociometric Assessment and Beyond" by S. R. Asher and A. R. Taylor, 1981, *Exceptional Education Quarterly*, 1(4), pp. 13–30. Copyright 1981 by PRO-ED, Inc. Adapted by permission.

behaviors of teachers and peers toward these students. Direct observation can take place in analogue settings (i.e., simulated situations, such as role playing or a contrived play setting) or a natural environment. This functional behavioral assessment technique attempts to identify factors that predict, trigger, or maintain particular behaviors by examining what is occurring in the setting and the antecedent and consequent factors that contribute to the occurrence of the behavior. This information is essential in developing appropriate interventions (Sugai & Lewis, 1996). Frequent data collection is important to ensure that the initial assessment is valid and to evaluate interventions to provide a measure of the timeliness of program modifications. Data can be recorded on a graph to allow analysis of behavioral changes over time. Examples of appropriate targets for direct observation include the frequency of positive statements made by the teacher to the student with special needs or the number of social interactions between the student with disabilities and a peer in general education.

Rating scales and checklists are also useful in collecting information about a student's performance. Typically, these measures list specific behaviors that are likely to occur in a particular setting. The teacher completes the checklist or rating scale following an observation of the student. For example, a student may be observed participating in an instructional group and then rated on a number of classroom behaviors (e.g., "The student attends to the teacher's instructions? The student raises his or her hand before responding? The student maintains eye contact when talking with the teacher?"). The teacher can simply check the items that describe the student's behavior or rate the quality of the behaviors observed (i.e., from Inappropriate to Appropriate on a five-point scale).

Behavioral rating scales may also offer a broader set of items that provide more general descriptions of behaviors (e.g., "The student participates appropriately in an instructional group"). A person who knows the student well (a teacher, parent, peer, or even the student in question) reads each description and then rates the student on a numerical scale (e.g., from 1 to 7). Checklists and rating scales permit the collection of consistent information from several different observers to assess the skill level of the student, identify problem behaviors, or assess the student's progress.

Parents can aid in gathering data by reporting on the special student's social interactions in the home, neighborhood, and community. They can also keep a record of the comments the student makes about school or self. This information can reflect changes in the student's self-concept or attitudes toward school.

Figure 6-2 presents a checklist for evaluating the social environment of the classroom. It can be used to assess not only teacher behavior but also peer behavior and the curriculum. Use this measure to find out about the social climate of your classroom.

STRATEGIES FOR PROMOTING ACCEPTANCE OF SPECIAL STUDENTS

Teachers can use several methods to increase the likelihood that students with disabilities will be socially accepted. These methods are directed toward students and teachers in general education, parents, and students with special needs themselves. Whereas general educators are typically responsible for implementing these strategies, special educators are available to provide the necessary assistance.

Inform General Education Students About Disabilities

Increasing their knowledge about individuals with disabilities improves the attitudes of general education students and teachers (e.g., Donaldson, 1980; Fiedler & Simpson, 1987; Handlers & Austin, 1980; Schultz & Torrie, 1984). Students should be informed about disabilities, preferably before students with special needs enter the general education classroom. Instruction can take many forms. Teachers can present information directly to younger students; more advanced classes can conduct some of their own research. Some teachers may develop texts and workbooks to use with their students (Schultz & Torrie, 1984); others may use commercially developed materials. Special educators such as the resource teacher can direct general education teachers and students to other sources of information about disabilities. For example, many books, films, instructional materials, websites, and even television programs discuss various types of disabilities.

The goal of instruction is to increase awareness of both the abilities and the problems of students with disabilities. The teacher can introduce the concept of individual differences and point out that each person is unique, with a distinct array of strengths and weaknesses. At the same time, the similarities between general education students and students with special needs should be emphasized (Schulz & Turnbull, 1983). Typical disabilities should be identified and discussed; students should learn why some individuals require special assistance. It is also possible to describe typical special education services and compare these with the general education program. The lives of famous people with disabilities, such as Helen Keller and Franklin D. Roosevelt, can be studied. Class discussions provide the opportunity for students to exchange information, experiences, and feelings about people with disabilities. Teachers should direct these discussions and clarify or correct any misperceptions or misinformation.

FIGURE 6-2   Social Environment Checklist

Teacher's Behavior

Direct Influence
- Can the teacher specifically state both appropriate and inappropriate student classroom behaviors he/she would like to increase or decrease?
- Does the teacher frequently follow appropriate behavior with encouragement and praise?
- Does the teacher refrain from punishing and criticizing students and rather consistently withdraw his/her attention following inappropriate behaviors?
- Does the teacher objectively record (tally, tape-record, use counter) and evaluate the frequency and consequences of his/her behaviors to document the effects they have on student behavior?
- Does the teacher clearly specify the classroom guidelines, responsibilities, and limitations for students?

Indirect Influence
- Has the teacher continued to grow by adapting teaching plans to meet the needs of each group of students?
- Is the teacher aware of any personal, social, racial, or mental prejudices and does she/he attempt to overcome these through objective teaching and evaluation methods?
- Has the teacher devised a method of getting the students' perceptions and feedback on the teacher and the class (questionnaire, suggestion box)?
- Does the teacher encourage and reinforce self-expression and participation from all the members of the class?

Peer Behavior
- Can the teacher identify the classroom leaders, followers, and isolates?
- Can the teacher identify the peer-group norm base and stereotypes that are held by the class?
- Can the teacher identify and redirect inappropriate peer attention (laughing at a class clown, picking on a . . . child [with a disability]) to promote more constructive activities?
- Does the teacher attend to the problems of the quiet, withdrawn children as much as to the acting-out problem children?
- Does the teacher use concrete activities and arrangements to maximize the social acceptance and participation of all the children?
- Do the classroom physical arrangements (seating plan) and group activities consider both the elimination of behavior problems and enhancement of social relationships?

Curriculum
- Does the curriculum encourage high levels of student independence and initiative?
- Does the curriculum present a balanced emphasis on students' personal social development and academic skill development?
- Does the curriculum provide challenging new ideas that require students to develop skills in analytic and evaluative thinking?
- Is the curriculum enhanced with a motivational system that guarantees that each child will have a successful learning experience?
- Does the curriculum require participation and interaction from the teacher and students?
- Does the curriculum encourage interaction and cooperation among the students?
- Is the subject content relevant to the interests and backgrounds of the students?
- Is an effort made to meaningfully relate the concepts covered in class to everyday experiences?
- Does the curriculum provide ample opportunity for student enrichment by frequently introducing new and different ideas and problems?
- Is motivation enhanced through liberal use of teacher praise and encouragement?
- Are students with special skills allowed or encouraged to share their expertise with their classmates?
- Is an attempt made to incorporate student ideas and suggestions into the instructional program?

Note: Reprinted with permission of Merrill, an imprint of MacMillan Publishing Company, from *Evaluating Educational Environments* (pp. 120–125) by R. M. Smith, J. T. Neisworth, and J. G. Greer, Copyright © 1978 Merrill Publishing Company, Columbus, Ohio.

Window on the Web

Kids on the Block

http://www.kotb.com

Kids on the Block is a disability awareness organization that began in 1977, shortly after the passage of the Education for All Handicapped Children Act. It develops programs for children and adults related to disabilities, medical and educational differences, and social and safety concerns. Among the topics are cerebral palsy, childhood cancer, learning disabilities, gifted and talented children, sexual abuse prevention, AIDS, and children of divorced parents. These programs are brought to life by large puppets, the "Kids." Community groups, schools, hospitals, and other organizations form puppet troupes that bring the Kids to audiences across the United States and in several other countries.

Visit the Kids on the Block website to learn more about this organization, the puppets it creates, and its programs. The site also provides links to Kids on the Block puppet troupes and a newsletter, *Keeping Up with the Kids*.

For more information, go to the Web Links module in Chapter 6 of the Companion Website.

AN EDUCATIONAL PUPPET TROUPE

Note: Courtesy of
The Kids on the Block, Inc.

Provide General Education Students with Experiences with Individuals with Disabilities

Attitudes of general education students are also affected by meeting and interacting with individuals with disabilities. One way to provide this experience is to invite adults with special needs to the classroom; students can listen to the viewpoint of the person with disabilities and then ask questions. Another method is to visit special education programs such as the resource room or special class located within the school. Older students can also be given assignments to interview an adult with disabilities. The teacher should guide all of these experiences by ensuring that students prepare appropriate questions prior to visits, interviews, and discussions.

Simulation is another way of experiencing disabilities. Simulations assist general education students in understanding the problems experienced by individuals with special needs and thereby improve the general education students' level of acceptance (Aiello, 1979; Handlers & Austin, 1980; Israelson, 1980). Some possible simulation activities are traveling around the school in a wheelchair, wearing a blindfold during lunch or art, using earplugs to limit hearing, and attempting to communicate without speaking. For younger children, puppets with various disabilities provide a type of simulation; students can talk with the puppets or become the puppeteers (Binkard, 1985). See the accompanying "Window on the Web" feature for a description of an innovative approach to disability awareness using puppetry. All simulations should be carried out in a business-like manner. Following

the activities, students should write or talk about their experiences to ensure that they have no misconceptions.

Literature can also be used to provide experience with people with special needs. A wealth of fiction, biography, and autobiography about individuals with special needs is available; much is appropriate for students to read or listen to. The accompanying "Inclusion Tips for the Teacher" material provides several suggestions.

Structure Interactions Between Typical Students and Students with Disabilities

Classroom and other interactions between general education students and students with disabilities have a greater chance for success if teachers provide guidelines. If the general education student's initial contact with a peer with disabilities is purposeful and occurs in a well-structured situation, positive attitudes are more likely to develop. Four techniques that may be helpful in structuring interactions are cooperative learning experiences, group rewards, special friendship programs, and peer or cross-age tutoring programs.

In **cooperative learning**, general education students and students with special needs work together as a team to complete activities or assignments (Maag & Webber, 1995). These teams, which operate in mainstream settings, are small groups of students with a range of abilities (i.e., low-, moderate-, and high-achieving individuals). According to the research reviewed by Gottlieb and Leyser (1981) and

Inclusion Tips for the Teacher

Children's Literature About Disabilities

Children's literature is one way for students to learn more about disabilities and other special needs. The books listed below are organized by general disability areas, and recommended ages appear at the end of each brief description. For more suggestions, see Ashton-Coombs and James (1995), Dyches and Burrow (2004), and Orr and others (1997).

Learning Disabilities, Learning Differences, and Attention Problems

The Don't-Give-Up Kid and Learning Differences by J. Gehret (Fairport, NY: Verbal Images Press, 1990). The story of Alex, a young boy with reading problems who wants to become an inventor. (primary grades)

Little Monster at School by M. Mayer (Green Frog Publishers, 1978). Little Monster has school friends including Yally. Yally isn't good at reading or math but he can draw better than anyone else. (primary grades)

Shelley, the Hyperactive Turtle by D. M. Moss (Rockville, MD: Woodbine House, 1989). Shelley, unlike other young turtles, cannot sit still. (primary grades)

Eagle Eyes by J. Gehret (Fairport, NY: Verbal Images Press, 1991). Ben's attention problems interfere with his life at school and home. (primary grades)

Josh, a Boy with Dyslexia by C. Janover (Burlington, VT: Waterfront Books, 1988). Josh, a boy with a learning disability, begins fifth grade in a new school. (intermediate grades)

Trouble with School: A Family Story about Learning Disabilities by K. B. Dunn and A. B. Dunn (Rockville, MD: Woodbine House, 1993). Allison and Allison's mother take turns telling the story of how Allison's learning disability was identified in second grade. (primary/intermediate grades)

When Learning Is Tough: Kids Talk about Their Learning Disabilities by C. Roby (Morton Grove, IL: Albert Whitman & Company, 1994). Eight young people discuss their lives, learning disabilities, and triumphs. (intermediate grades)

What Do You Mean I Have a Learning Disability? by K. M. Dwyer (New York: Walker, 1991). Jimmy, a 10-year-old, learns that he is not stupid and that he can succeed in school. (intermediate grades)

Mental Retardation and Severe Disabilities

Where's Chimpy? by B. Rabe (Niles, IL: Albert Whitman & Company, 1988). Misty, a young girl with Down syndrome, has lost her favorite toy, her stuffed monkey. (primary grades)

Making Room for Uncle Joe by A. B. Litchfield (Niles, IL: Albert Whitman & Company, 1984). Uncle Joe, an adult with Down syndrome, comes to live with Amy, Beth, and Dan. (intermediate grades)

I'm the Big Sister Now by M. Emmert (Niles, IL: Albert Whitman & Company, 1989). Michelle Emmert tells the story of her older sister Amy, a teenager with severe disabilities. (intermediate grades)

Physical and Health Problems

Books Featuring Heroes and Heroines Who Travel by Wheelchair:

Nick Joins In by J. Lasker (Chicago: Albert Whitman & Company, 1980). (primary grades)

Howie Helps Himself by J. Fassler (Chicago: Albert Whitman & Company, 1975). (primary grades)

Arnie and the New Kid by N. Carlson (New York: Viking, 1990). (primary grades)

Princess Pooh by K. M. Muldoon (Chicago: Albert Whitman & Company, 1989). (primary grades)

Grandma's Wheelchair by L. Henrod (Chicago: Albert Whitman & Company, 1982). (primary grades)

Our Teacher's in a Wheelchair by M. E. Powers (Chicago: Albert Whitman & Company, 1986). (primary grades)

Books About Specific Disorders:

Even Little Kids Get Diabetes by C. W. Pirner (Chicago: Albert Whitman & Company, 1991). (primary grades)

Alex, the Kid with AIDS by L. W. Girard (Chicago: Albert Whitman & Company, 1991). (primary/intermediate grades)

There's a Little Bit of Me in Jamey by D. M. Amadeo (Chicago: Albert Whitman & Company, 1989). The story of Jamey, a young boy with leukemia. (intermediate grades)

How It Feels to Live with a Physical Disability by J. Krementz (New York: Simon & Schuster, 1992). (intermediate grades/middle school)

Visual and Hearing Impairments

Handtalk Birthday by R. Charlip, M. B. Miller, and G. Ancona (New York: Aladdin Books, 1991). A storybook in words, photos, and sign language that includes the signs for numbers. (primary grades and up)

A Cane in Her Hand by A. B. Litchfield (Chicago: Albert Whitman & Company, 1977). The story of Valerie, a young girl with low vision who learns to use a cane to help her travel from place to place. (primary/intermediate grades)

I'm Deaf and It's Okay by L. Aseltine, E. Mueller, and N. Tait (Chicago: Albert Whitman & Company, 1986). A young boy tells about his life and the problems he experiences because he is deaf. (primary/intermediate grades)

Words in Our Hands by A. B. Litchfield (Chicago: Albert Whitman & Company, 1980). Michael, Gina, and Diane's mother and father are deaf. Michael tells about the family's move to a new town. (intermediate grades)

Johnson and Johnson (1980), cooperative learning is superior to both competitive learning and individualistic learning. In competitive situations, students attempt to outdo each other; in individualistic situations, the achievement of each student is unrelated to that of any other student. Cooperative learning increases the special student's opportunity to experience success (Slavin, 1995; Snell & Brown, 1993), it provides practice in school skills (Foyle & Lyman, 1990), and the social interactions involved promote the development of the social skills of the student with disabilities (Andersen, Nelson, Fox, & Gruber, 1988; Fad, Ross, & Boston, 1995; Goodwin, 1999; Johnson & Johnson, 1989) and their acceptance by peers in general education (Slavin, 1987; Slavin, Madden, & Leavey, 1984).

The teacher plays an important role in establishing and guiding the cooperative learning approach. Gottlieb and Leyser (1981) outline the following steps:

a. teacher specifies the instructional objectives;

b. selects the group size most appropriate for the lesson;

c. assigns students to groups and assures that the small groups are heterogeneous with students [with and without disabilities] in the same group;

d. specifies a structured role within the cooperative groups for the . . . students [with disabilities];

e. makes the requirements for the . . . child [with disabilities] reasonable;

f. provides appropriate materials to the groups;

g. explains the task and the cooperative goal structure;

h. trains . . . [all students] in helping, tutoring, teaching, and sharing skills; and

i. observes interactions. (p. 67)

It is important to consider that learners with disabilities may require some additional special preparation or support to allow them to participate effectively in cooperative learning activities (Johnson & Johnson, 1989). The student with special needs may require preparatory coaching or instruction in the social or academic skills required to participate in a group. Other students may need instruction on how to best teach or encourage their group member with disabilities. Descriptions of various methods of using cooperative learning in the classroom, plus highlights of research findings, are provided in Figure 6-3.

A second method of structuring interactions is to use group rewards (discussed in chapter 5). The teacher sets up a system in which students can earn classroom reinforcers when (1) general education students interact positively with students with disabilities, (2) a student with special needs performs a desired behavior, (3) class members reinforce a student with behavior problems for an appropriate behavior, or (4) class members ignore a student's inappropriate behaviors. Class members pool their earnings, and the entire class is rewarded. These approaches lead to an increase in the number of positive interactions with students with special needs and thereby help to improve the attitudes of general education students (Heron & Harris, 2001; Salend, 1987).

A third technique is to encourage the development of friendships through communication, social interactions, and recreational activities involving typical students and students with disabilities (Searcy, 1996). As friends, students are encouraged to provide support and assistance to others. For example, this support may involve assisting students with physical or visual impairments in their travels around school or providing a student with severe disabilities the opportunity to learn and practice age-appropriate skills while participat-

FIGURE 6-3 Cooperative Learning Approaches

Cooperative learning methods are aimed at reducing student isolation and perceived hostile climates that exist in highly competitive classrooms, and at increasing students' ability to interact and work with other students toward common goals.

The most widely used cooperative learning methods include

- **Student Teams-Achievement Divisions** (STAD)—Students assemble in teams of four or five members mixed according to achievement level, gender, and ethnicity to master the material covered in a lesson just presented by the teacher. Subsequently, they individually take a quiz on that material. The team's overall score is determined by the extent to which each student *improved* over his or her past performance. The team demonstrating the greatest improvement is recognized in a weekly class newsletter.
- **Teams-Games-Tournament** (TGT)—The procedure in TGT is the same as that used in STAD, but instead of taking quizzes, the students play academic games in tournaments with other members in the class whose past performance was similar to their own. The team score is also based on individual improvement. The balance[s] of the groups involved in the tournament are maintained by weekly adjustment of group members based on their performance.
- **Team Assisted Individualization** (TAI)—Teams of elementary or middle school math students are established and evaluated in the same manner as in STAD and TGT. This procedure uses placement tests to determine each student's individualized level and they proceed at their own rate. Teammates check each other's instructional work and help each other with problems. Student performance is based on individual tests and team rewards are based on the number and accuracy of units completed each week. TAI is based on a specific set of materials and its individualized features make it very appropriate for heterogeneous groups.
- **Cooperative Integrated Reading and Composition** (CIRC)—A comprehensive program for teaching reading and writing that involves pairs of students from different reading groups using basal readers and working on decoding, vocabulary, writing, spelling, and comprehension activities. Teacher instruction is provided to a team while others are working on individual activities and is usually followed by team practice, preassessments for the team, and tests. Tests are not taken until the team members determine their teammate is ready.
- **Jigsaw**—Students meet in five- or six-member teams. The teacher gives each student an item of information which the student must "teach" to the team. Students are then individually tested for their mastery of the material. **Jigsaw II** is the same, except that students obtain their information from textbooks, narrative material, short stories, or biographies. The class is then quizzed for individual and team scores.
- **Learning Together**—After the teacher has presented a lesson, students work together in small groups on a single worksheet. The team as a whole receives praise and recognition for mastering the worksheet.
- **Group-Investigation**—This is a more complex method, requiring students to accept greater responsibility for deciding what they will learn, how they will organize themselves to master the material, and how they will communicate what they have learned to their classmates.

These methods share four positive characteristics. (1) The cooperation required among students prevents one student from doing most of the work for the others. (2) In spite of the cooperative nature of the groups, each student must learn the material in order to improve his or her own score and the team score. (3) Even low achievers who may not contribute greatly can receive recognition since scores are based on individual improvement, however small, over past performance. (4) Students are motivated to cooperate since they receive not just a grade on a piece of paper, but public recognition from the teacher and the class.

Cooperative learning methods have positive effects in several areas. They contribute significantly to student achievement—to an equal extent in both elementary and secondary schools; in urban, suburban, and rural schools; and in diverse subject matter areas.

Schools with racially or ethnically mixed populations do not necessarily have better intergroup relations based solely on student proximity. However, when dissimilar students work together in small groups toward a common goal and are allowed to contribute equally, they will learn to like and respect one another.

Cooperative learning methods also increase acceptance and understanding among students with disabilities and their nondisabled classmates. They also have a positive effect on student self-esteem.

Students who participate in cooperative learning like school more than their peers who are not allowed to work together; they are better able to interact appropriately with others and to understand another person's point of view.

Note: From Slavin, R. E. (1981), "Synthesis of Research on Cooperative Learning." *Educational Leadership, 38,* p. 659. Used by permission of the Association for Supervision and Curriculum Development. Copyright 1981 by ASCD. All rights reserved. Adaptations based on *Cooperative Learning: Theory, Research, and Practice* (2nd ed.) by R. E. Slavin, 1995, Boston: Allyn & Bacon. Copyright 1995 by Pearson Education. Reprinted by permission of Allyn & Bacon.

Inclusion Tips for the Teacher

Enhancing Social Acceptance

- Be open and honest with your students. Don't avoid answering questions.
- Discuss disabilities with your class.
- Invite guest speakers—parents of children with disabilities or adults with disabilities.
- Read books to your class about people with disabilities.
- Hold class discussions. Allow students to ask questions and explore feelings.
- Emphasize how much alike we are, rather than how different we are.
- Take the mystery away from adaptive aids such as wheelchairs, braces, and hearing aids by exposing children to them and providing explanations of how they work.

- Try simulation exercises such as a blind walk or a soundless movie.
- Encourage a buddy system.
- Arrange for students without disabilities to work with special students as helpers or tutors.
- Look for ways to capitalize on the strengths of the student with disabilities and provide status and recognition through athletics, drama, the school newspaper, chorus, or as peer tutors.
- Locate and view media—filmstrips and films—on individuals with disabilities.

Note: From *Teaching Handicapped Students in the Mainstream* (2nd ed.), by A. L. Pasanella and C. B. Volkmor. Copyright © 1981 by the University of Southern California and by Macmillan College Publishing Company, Inc.

ing in games or verbal interactions with others (Falvey, Grenot-Scheyer, & Bishop, 1989).

Programs designed to promote friendships vary greatly in their structure. Teachers may reinforce natural interactions, provide students with information or skills related to their interactions, or establish more structured programs that actually provide training for general education students in how to assist and develop interactions with students with disabilities (Campbell, 1989; Perske & Perske, 1988). These programs may build peer support by (1) fostering proximity of students with disabilities with their general education peers, (2) encouraging the development of support and friendship, (3) teaching support and friendship skills, (4) fostering respect for individual differences, and (5) providing a positive model for appropriate interactions (Searcy, 1996; Stainback, Stainback, & Wilkinson, 1992). The implementation of programs that encourage friendships becomes especially important as more students with disabilities spend increasing amounts of time in general education programs.

The use of students as tutors is a fourth approach. General education students can help students with disabilities as peer tutors (working with age-mates or classmates) or cross-age tutors (working with younger tutees). General education students gain in experience and information by working with students with special needs, and students with disabilities benefit from the instruction and the model provided by the general education tutor. Tutoring programs have demonstrated their effectiveness in many situations (Gumpel & Frank, 1999; Heron & Harris, 2001; Jenkins & Jenkins, 1985; Krouse, Ger-

ber, & Kauffman, 1981; Maag & Webber, 1995; Maheady, Sacca, & Harper, 1988; Strain, 1981a, 19811b). Students have been found to be effective teachers with individuals who are withdrawn, students with acting-out behaviors, and those with academic needs. Tutors should receive specific training prior to their service, be provided with structured and carefully prescribed lessons, meet frequently with their tutee, and be continually monitored with needed reinforcement and reinstruction provided by the teacher. In addition, peer tutors should be warned that they may be rejected at first but that this response will most likely diminish as instruction proceeds (Doorlag, 1989a; Gable, Strain, & Hendrickson, 1979).

Students with disabilities can also serve as peer or cross-age tutors. These experiences can provide the student with special needs with new status, increased acceptance by other students in the school, opportunities to develop social skills, and practice and improved performance in academic skill areas (Cochran, Feng, Cartledge, & Hamilton, 1993; Tournaki & Criscitiello, 2003). For instance, a student with special needs may help a classmate practice spelling words, or a sixth-grade student with learning disabilities may enjoy practicing third-grade math if this occurs during the tutoring of a third-grade student. Students with disabilities serving as tutors should be provided the same type of training and assistance suggested for other tutors. These students often benefit more than their tutees from this educational experience (Osguthorpe & Scruggs, 1986). See the "Inclusion Tips for the Teacher" box for more ideas about how teachers can help general education students accept their peers with special needs.

Improve the Social Skills of Students with Disabilities

For many students with special needs, the development of appropriate social skills improves their chances of gaining social acceptance and succeeding when they are included in the general education program (Heron & Harris, 2001; Leffert & Siperstein, 2003; Maag & Webber, 1995; Nelson, 1988; Sugai & Lewis, 1996; Zaragoza, Vaughn, & McIntosh, 1991). Drabman and Patterson (1981) say that "it is important that integrated exceptional children display as many positive characteristics as they can to facilitate acceptance by nonexceptional peers" (p. 54). Social skills are best developed through direct instructional procedures, following the same principles as academic instruction and provided as a regularly planned component of the instructional day (Maag & Webber, 1995; Sugai & Lewis, 1996; Sugai & Tindal, 1993).

Initially, the teacher describes why the skill is needed, how the skill is performed, when it is to be used, and what its specific components are. Appropriate social behaviors are modeled for the student with special needs by the teacher and peers or by videotapes and films. The student is then questioned about the skill and the steps involved in it and is provided with the opportunity to practice the new behaviors. It is important that the teacher make use of prompts, praise, and corrective feedback during each step of the instruction. Providing multiple examples of how the skill is used and opportunities to practice in other settings improves the chance that the skills learned in the classroom will generalize to other settings (Cartledge & Milburn, 1995; Doorlag, 1989b; Elliott & Gresham, 1993; Farmer & Cadwallader, 1999; Maag & Webber, 1995; Sugai & Lewis, 1996; Winget & Kirk, 1991).

Instructional materials are available to assist in the teaching of social skills. Examples of programs designed for elementary-grade students are listed here:

- *Skillstreaming the Elementary School Child: New Strategies and Perspectives for Teaching Prosocial Skills*, by McGinnis and Goldstein (1997)
- *The Walker Social Skills Curriculum: The ACCEPTS (A Curriculum for Children's Effective Peer and Teacher Skills) Program*, by Walker and others (1983)
- *Getting Along with Others: Teaching Social Effectiveness to Children*, by Jackson, Jackson, and Monroe (1983)

Meisgeier (1981) describes a program for students with special needs who are included in general education classes in the secondary grades. Designed for adolescents, *The Social/Behavioral Curriculum* covers four major areas: responsibility, communication, assertiveness, and problem solving. Other programs designed for older students—*Skillstreaming the Adolescent: New Strategies and Perspectives for Teaching Prosocial Skills* (Goldstein & McGinnis, 1997), *Life Skills Counseling for Adolescents* (Schinke & Gilchrist, 1984), *The Prepare Curriculum: Teaching Prosocial Competencies* (Goldstein, 1999), and *The Walker Social Skills Curriculum: The ACCESS (Adolescent Curriculum for Communication and Effective Social Skills) Program* (Walker, Todis, Holmes, & Horton, 1988)—provide teachers with guidelines and activities for teaching social skills at the middle and high school levels.

Programs such as these typically cover several social skills areas. They often include checklists or rating scales designed to assess student behavior and identify appropriate areas in which to begin social skills instruction. For example, the *ACCEPTS* program offers a placement test that is designed to assess the five areas covered in the program: classroom skills (e.g., attending to teachers, following rules), basic interaction skills (e.g., maintaining eye contact, speaking in a moderate tone), getting along skills (e.g., sharing, assisting others), making friends skills (e.g., being clean and neat, complimenting others), and coping skills (e.g., appropriately expressing anger, ignoring teasing). This program includes specific lesson plans and scripts for the teacher to follow for each of the skill areas taught. Optional videotapes provide both positive and negative examples of the student behavior taught in each lesson, or the teacher can reenact these scenes from the description provided. The advantages of programs such as *ACCEPTS* and *ACCESS* are that their structured lessons permit them to be implemented readily by the teacher with a minimal amount of preparation because the lessons have been designed and field tested by individuals with experience in teaching social skills. Others, such as the *Skillstreaming* programs, are more flexible; they provide less structured guidelines for lessons, behavioral steps for each skill, a general lesson format, and suggested learning and homework activities.

Another method for developing social skills is the use of **cognitive training** approaches. These methods focus on improving behavior by changing the thinking strategies of the student in order to develop skills that can be used in a variety of settings with a minimum of external support. Students are involved as active participants in the program—they are aware of the behaviors targeted for change, receive training in how the change program will operate, and are actively involved in the intervention (Graham, Harris, & Reid, 1998; Henker, Whalen, & Hinshaw, 1980).

Cognitive training programs teach students strategies such as how to (1) use a sequence of steps to deal with a problem (self-instruction), (2) consider several solutions to a situation (problem solving), (3) collect and record data on their performance and evaluate the consequences of each alternative used (self-monitoring/self-evaluation), or (4) reinforce themselves for acceptable performance (self-reinforcement). It is important for the students to be provided with adequate instruction and practice in the use of cognitive training approaches; implementation of this type of program requires that teachers reward students for accurate evaluation of their own behaviors (Zirpoli & Melloy, 2001).

Cognitive training is an efficient approach because it allows teachers to train students to become responsible for portions of their instructional program; the teacher then assumes a monitoring role. A typical cognitive training program to teach social problem solving includes

- problem definition (specifically define the problem),
- goal statement (identify what you want to accomplish),
- delay response (determine ways to stop and think before you act),
- determine alternatives (identify as many solutions to the problem as possible),
- consider consequences (evaluate the different consequences that may follow each alternative solution),
- decision making/implementation (implement the alternative selected as most appropriate),
- review results (provide a self-evaluation and correct errors in strategies used in order to improve results in the future), and
- provide reinforcement (provide yourself a "pat on the back" for improving).

Introduce Students with Disabilities to the General Education Program According to Their Individual Needs

Adjustment can be made easier for the student with special needs who is entering the mainstream (and for the teacher and students in the general education class) if inclusion is carefully planned and occurs gradually. For instance, the first step can be an informal meeting between the student with disabilities and the general education teacher. Then the student can visit the classroom when general education students are not present. The next approximation can be participation in a nonacademic activity, such as music or art. These first steps are important because they allow the student to become acquainted with the new teacher, students, and classroom before academic demands are made. They also help the teacher learn about the new student and begin to plan effective instructional and social acceptance programs. It is important to note that not all students with disabilities require a gradual introduction into the general education program; this must be determined on an individual basis as part of the planning for the implementation of the student's Individualized Education Program (IEP).

Upgrade the Teacher's Information and Skills

At present, some but not all of the states require teachers to complete course work related to the inclusion of students with disabilities before they receive a teaching certificate or credential ("Special Needs, Common Goal," 2004). Because of this, some teachers have limited knowledge of and experi-

ence with students with special needs. Their teacher preparation program may have provided only a minimal amount of training in working with these students, and they may not have had the opportunity to learn about students with special needs through in-service training.

Because of the strong relationship between attitudes and information, teachers should be sure they have adequate knowledge about students with disabilities and the appropriateness of different educational interventions (Gable, Laycock, Maroney, & Smith, 1991; Heflin & Bullock, 1999). The strategies recommended for informing general education students about disabilities (e.g., visitations, simulations, readings, films, websites, discussions) are also appropriate for teachers. For example, several films have featured characters with disabilities: *Scent of a Woman, My Left Foot, Forrest Gump, Lorenzo's Oil, Philadelphia,* and *Rain Man* (Smith, Polloway, Patton, & Dowdy, 1998). Educators can direct their own study or request assistance in getting this information and training from resources available in their district or region.

Although teachers often have support available from special educators, it is "essential that the [general education] teacher assume primary 'ownership' and accept responsibility for the education of a student with disabilities, just as he/she does for all students on the class list" (Putnam, 1992, p. 132). To carry out this responsibility effectively, teachers should strive to upgrade their own skill levels. For example, research indicates that teachers make more negative comments to students with disabilities, ask them fewer questions, and provide them with less feedback. This affects the attitudes of students in the general education class as well as the self-concept and achievement of the student with special needs. Because it is important to provide positive support for the appropriate behaviors of students with disabilities, teachers should assess their own behavior. They can count the different types of statements they make (e.g., positive, negative, instructional) and determine which are made most frequently to students with special needs. Teachers can collect these data by self-recording while the class is in progress or by using observers or tape recorders.

Communicate with and Involve Parents

Parents should be informed of the purpose of implementing inclusion programs and the effects these programs will have on their child's education. Parents of students with disabilities may be concerned that their child will be rejected by students and teachers in the general education program. They also may regret the loss of the special attention and services provided in the special education program. In addition, they may fear that their child will experience failure when included in the mainstream. However, parents of typical students in the general education class often believe that students with disabilities require a great deal of the teacher's attention and that the amount of instruction their children receive will be reduced. They may also be concerned that the behavior of a student with special needs will have a negative effect on the behavior of their children.

Many of the apprehensions of parents can be eliminated if they are provided with accurate information concerning the inclusion of students with disabilities in the general education program. For example, the parent–teacher organization can feature programs on the needs of special learners, pamphlets explaining inclusion can be sent to all parents, and the acceptance of students with special needs can be a topic of discussion at parent–teacher conferences. Parents of students with disabilities will receive specific information at the meeting of the IEP team. Students in the general education class can assist by communicating accurate information about students with special needs to their parents.

Teachers should communicate regularly with parents to ensure that they remain informed. Parents of students with

disabilities often hear from the school only when their children behave inappropriately; they receive limited information about accomplishments and successes. In addition, students with special needs may convey distorted reports of classroom occurrences to their parents; for example, they may say that "all" the students in the general education class pick on them. Parents of general education students also need direct communication from the teacher; they may have misconceptions about inclusion because their children talk about only the negative acts of students with special needs. Parents of all students should be informed that they are important to their children's program and should be encouraged to visit the classroom if they have questions (Heron & Harris, 2001).

According to Kroth (1981), parents should be recognized as their children's major teachers, with professionals considered consultants to the parents. The Mirror Model of Parental Involvement advocated by Kroth (see Figure 6-4)

FIGURE 6-4   Mirror Model of Parental Involvement

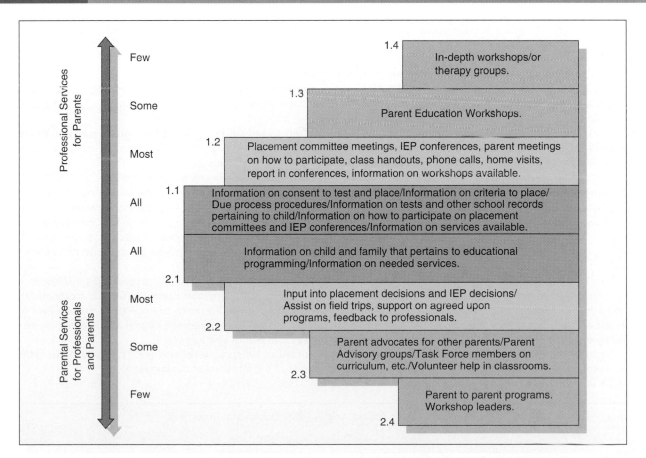

Note: Reprinted with permission of Merrill, an imprint of Macmillan Publishing Company, from "Involvement with Parents of Behaviorally Disordered Adolescents" by R. Kroth. In *Educating Adolescents with Behavior Disorders* (p. 129) by G. Brown, R. L. McDowell, and J. Smith (Eds.). Copyright © 1981 Merrill Publishing Company, Columbus, Ohio.

suggests that, even though professionals may provide parents of students with disabilities with information and skills, those parents also are able to aid professionals and other parents. With appropriate assistance, parents can improve their skills in working with their children, help professionals assist the students at school, and aid students and other parents in understanding and working with their special children (Binkard, 1985).

Edgar and Davidson (1979) recommend that communication with parents include information about specific events and activities. Professional terms such as *inclusion*, *mainstreaming*, and *Least Restrictive Environment* should be avoided; educators should use words everyone understands. Communication should occur on a regular basis so that parents keep in touch with the program, are informed of current events, and begin to accept and support the inclusion of students with disabilities. Figure 6-5 presents the opinions of the parent of a student with special needs about issues that teachers should consider when working with parents. Although the original statement was directed to special education teachers (Roland, 1989), it contains information that all individuals working with the parents of students with special needs should contemplate.

In this chapter, several techniques for promoting the social acceptance of students with disabilities in the general education classroom have been described. Consult the checklist in Figure 6-6 to review factors important in preparing to serve students with special needs. Next, you will learn about coordination skills for management of the total learning environment. Before proceeding, however, check "Things to Remember" to review ways to enhance social acceptance.

FIGURE 6-5   A Parent of Special Students Speaks to Educators

The following recommendations to teachers about working with parents of students with special needs were written by Peggy Roland, who is "the mother of a 12-year-old daughter with education difficulties" (Roland, 1989, p. 3). While the statement was originally directed to special education teachers, it contains concerns and advice that should be considered by others working with special students and their parents.

I'd like to express a few thoughts on behalf of the parents of your students.

Please be frank and *honest* with us. We need the information you have to share and we respect your professional advice and expertise. It may be painful for us to listen to what you have to say but inside we feel relief just hearing something. Our path has been, and always will be, long, but knowing you are there helps.

Please respect us, our children, our families, but above all, the feelings and thoughts that we have shared with you. You may believe we are unrealistic, opinionated, or guilty of ignoring the obvious, but it is probably the best we can manage at the moment. Tomorrow, perhaps even an hour from now, we may express very different feelings.

"They laugh so as not to cry." Such true words! Tears come easily and frequently and they are as much a surprise to us as they are to you. Don't be embarrassed or feel guilty when we cry. Take it as a sign of our humanness and feelings of safety that we react so when we're with you. Many people in the outside world understand neither our laughter nor our tears.

The same is true when we lash out or act defensive. Anger comes with the pain. That anger has no focal point so you may bear its brunt very undeservedly. For that we apologize. Do try to understand that it is usually not directed at you personally but rather at a situation which makes us feel very helpless and, often, very alone. Lashing out may be our overreaction to knowing we can't change the way things are.

Your work and continuing efforts on behalf of our disabled children mean more to us than we can ever explain. Without you, our children would not have achieved the sense of self-worth, the academic and physical success, the societal acceptance they have achieved. Without you, our families would be in more upheaval and distress. Please try to understand that our lives may be just a little different from the average; we have learned to take life one day, sometimes one hour at a time and to be aware and appreciative of the smallest steps while still maintaining our sense of humor and balance.

We are part of this vast thing called life and you are a most important and integral part of our lives. Thank you for being there and helping us establish and maintain a quality of life appropriate for *all* the members of our family.

We look forward to another year of working together!

Note: From "A Parent Speaks to Special Educators" by P. Roland, August 1989, *Exceptional Times*, p. 3.

FIGURE 6-6   A Checklist to Evaluate the Readiness of the Mainstream for a Special Student

Teachers and parents must be committed to carrying out the least restrictive alternative concept for children with disabilities. If individuals with disabilities are ever to be fully accepted in our society, this integration should occur as early and widely as possible. Educators should be willing to put forth their best efforts to make a general education class experience rewarding and enriching for students with disabilities. Special class teachers can do much to make these successes happen when students are included in the mainstream program.

The key to a successful experience in the mainstream is preparation. The checklist below can serve as a guide for the special class teacher in preparing not only the students with disabilities, but also the other people who must support the effort to include these students in the mainstream. Before placing each student with disabilities in a mainstreamed setting, the teacher should examine and work on each element of the checklist, until most, if not all, of the "yes" boxes can be checked.

1. Student with disabilities:

   Yes   No
   ____ ____   Is familiar with rules and routine of the general education classroom?
   ____ ____   Follows verbal and written directions used in the general education classroom?
   ____ ____   Remains on-task for adequate time periods?
   ____ ____   Has expressed a desire to participate in the general education class setting?
   ____ ____   Reacts appropriately to teasing, questions, criticism, etc.?
   ____ ____   Student's IEP objectives match instructional objectives in the general education class?

2. General education teacher:

   Yes   No
   ____ ____   Has been given rationale for activities related to including student with disabilities in the mainstream and asked to cooperate?
   ____ ____   Has information about the needs, present skills, and current learning objectives of the student with disabilities?
   ____ ____   Has been provided with special materials and/or support services as needed?
   ____ ____   Has prepared class for including student with disabilities in the mainstream?
   ____ ____   Has acquired special helping skills if necessary?
   ____ ____   Will be monitored regularly to identify any problems that arise?

3. Typical general education peers:

   Yes   No
   ____ ____   Have been informed about the participation of the student with disabilities and about his/her disability(ies) (if appropriate) with the opportunity to ask questions?
   ____ ____   Have been asked for their cooperation and friendship toward the student with disabilities?
   ____ ____   Have learned helping skills and praising behaviors?

4. Parents of the student with disabilities:

   Yes   No
   ____ ____   Have received verbal or written information about plan to include student with disabilities in the mainstream?
   ____ ____   Have been asked to praise and encourage child's progress in the general education and special education class(es)?

5. Parents of the typical general education peers:

   Yes   No
   ____ ____   Have been informed about the plan to include student with disabilities in the mainstream at PTA meetings, conferences, or through other vehicle, and asked for their cooperation?

6. School administrator:

   Yes   No
   ____ ____   Has been informed about specifics of plan to include student with disabilities in the mainstream?
   ____ ____   Has indicated specific steps she or he will take to encourage and support these activities?

Note: From "Helping Teachers Integrate Handicapped Students into the Regular Classroom" by J. C. Dardig, 1981, *Educational Horizons, 59,* pp. 124–130. Copyright 1981 by *Educational Horizons.* Adapted by permission.

Things to Remember

- Because rejection can damage both self-concept and academic performance, programs designed to include students with disabilities in general education should emphasize the social acceptance of these students.
- Students with special needs may be rejected if they do not look or act like their peers; another contributing factor is that some students with disabilities have poor social skills.
- Attitudes are very important; the attitudes of teachers influence the attitudes of their students.
- Attitudes are affected by information; the more teachers and peers know about students with disabilities, the more likely they are to accept them.
- General education students, students with special needs, and parents should be prepared for programs that include students with disabilities in the mainstream.
- Sociometric measures are often used to find out how students with special needs are perceived by their peers.

- Functional behavioral assessment and behavioral rating scales and checklists are used to help assess a student's social skill performance, identify problem areas that may require instruction, or assess the student's progress.
- Instruction about disabilities, experiences with people with special needs, and structured interactions with students with disabilities can be provided to help general education students (and teachers) gain information.
- Students with special needs can learn appropriate social skills; however, it is usually necessary to provide specific instruction in this area.
- Parental support for the inclusion program can be increased by explaining the purpose of the program, letting parents know how it will affect their children, encouraging parents to participate, and keeping parents informed through frequent communication.

ACTIVITIES

1. Visit a general education classroom that includes students with disabilities. Select one student with special needs and one general education peer to observe. Watch each of these students for approximately 30 minutes, and collect information about the number of times each of the following interactions occurs: The student talks to other students, the student talks to the teacher, other students talk to the student, the teacher talks to the student. Compare your results for the two students. Do you find any differences? Does one seem to be better accepted by the peers and teacher than the other?

2. Interview a student with disabilities who spends part of the school day in a general education setting. How does the student feel about the inclusion experience? Does he or she feel comfortable in the general education class setting? How positive does the student perceive the attitudes of the teacher and general education class peers to be? Does he or she feel accepted or rejected? Summarize your findings, and use them to prepare a list of questions you might use to interview another student.

3. Select two articles that discuss social acceptance of special students. Journals such as *The Exceptional Parent*, *Journal of Special Education*, and *Teaching Exceptional Children* would be good places to look. Read the articles to find suggestions for promoting the social acceptance of students with disabilities within the general education classroom.

4. Talk with special and general education teachers from two different schools about ways to improve the social acceptance of students with disabilities. What suggestions can they offer? What have they tried in the past that has worked? Ask about activities for teachers, students, parents, and staff members such as secretaries, custodians, and bus drivers.

5. Design a classroom activity that you could use to help general education students be more accepting of students with special needs. First, decide on a specific goal, and then describe the methods you would use to reach this goal. Include ideas about how you would go about implementing this program in your classroom and how you would evaluate its effectiveness.

CD-ROM Activities

View at least a portion of each of the three case studies that feature classrooms: the preschool, sixth grade, and high school videos. As you watch, pay special attention to social factors so that you can answer these questions:

- *Would you describe these classrooms as warm, friendly, and welcoming? What evidence can you present to back up your conclusions?*

- *Were you able to identify children who were not accepted by their classmates? What strategies did the teachers use to promote social acceptance.*

6. Locate one of the social skills training programs mentioned in the chapter (e.g., *ACCEPTS*, *Skillstreaming the Adolescent*) and use the program to teach a lesson on a specific skill to one or more of your friends, colleagues, or students. Write a short report on your experience, and describe specifically how you would use the lesson (or its techniques) with a student with disabilities included in a general education classroom.

Coordinating the Classroom Learning Environment

CHAPTER

7

- Karen is blind. She uses a cane for mobility and carries a portable Braille notetaking device with her to each of her ninth-grade classes. In some classes, the desks are too small to hold all of her materials.
- Axson is a middle schooler who travels by wheelchair. His teacher wonders where he'll be able to "park" when there are assemblies in the school auditorium.
- Susie is quite shy. Her classroom is arranged in neat rows and she chooses to sit in the last seat in the last row.

- Peter is very distractible and has trouble paying attention to his work in his noisy classroom.
- Louie wants to be in the same reading group as his best friend Herman but Herman's far ahead of him in reading.
- Sergio can't resist talking to the other third-grade boys as they pass his desk to turn in their work.
- Every day, Benjamin looks forward to working with Gramps, his class's Volunteer Grandfather.

LOOKING AHEAD

Think about the following questions as you read this chapter to learn more about coordinating the classroom learning environment.

- The physical environments of schools and classrooms can help or hinder learning. What suggestions could you offer to the teachers and principals of students like Karen and Axson?
- How classrooms are arranged can affect achievement, opportunities for social interactions, and disruptive behavior. What seating arrangement would you recommend for a shy student like Susie? Distractible students like Peter and Sergio?
- Community volunteers, like Benjamin's Gramps, are an important classroom resource. Peers tutors are another. What types of classroom duties do you think would be most appropriate for adult volunteers? Peer tutors?

To answer these questions online, go to the Students' Stories module in Chapter 7 of the Companion Website.

In general education classrooms, teachers adapt instruction, manage behavior, and promote the social acceptance of students with special needs. In addition, the teacher is responsible for the arrangement, management, and coordination of the total learning environment.

COORDINATION SKILLS FOR THE TEACHER

As managers, teachers structure the physical environment in which learning takes place and within these physical surroundings set up the instructional environment. To do this, teachers coordinate many different resources: time, people (including both students and instructional personnel), and educational materials and equipment. Management skills aid in the successful coordination of the general education classroom.

Classroom management is "what teachers do to help make student life in the classroom pleasant, meaningful, safe, and orderly" (Stephens, 1980). Stephens outlines six classroom management elements that teachers should consider:

> *Demographics,* the group's composition
>
> *Physical environment,* the use of the room and its furnishings
>
> *Time,* the amount of time available in the class and the teacher's and students' use of it
>
> *Student encouragement,* ways that students are reinforced for performance
>
> *Provisions for interacting,* among the students and with teachers
>
> *Differentiating instruction,* the extent to which and how the instruction is individualized. (p. 4)

The management skills of the teacher have been found to be related to the amount of student learning; good managers are more able to adapt instruction to student needs, particularly in heterogeneous classes (Evertson, Sanford, & Emmer, 1981). This chapter describes several of the factors to consider in managing the total learning environment. Included are principles for arranging the physical environment, organizing the instructional environment, using educational technologies, and coordinating time and other resources.

The teacher can structure the learning situation in many different ways. He or she receives a room, students, curriculum guidelines, and some standard instructional materials (such as grade-level textbooks); all other factors are under the teacher's control. Because there is a great deal of freedom in the selection of options, teachers should be aware of the reasons underlying their choices.

Figure 7-1 is a learning style questionnaire based on the work of several persons (Dunn & Dunn, 1978; Gartner & Riessman, 1977; Lewis, 1980; Pasanella & Volkmor, 1981; Renzulli & Smith, 1978; Schubert, Glick, & Bauer, 1979). Read this survey and determine which conditions you favor for learning. Consider your tolerance for environmental variations (noise, distractions, physical surroundings), your personal work habits (time of day, attention span, closure, rate), and your favorite learning methods (other learners, structure, presentation and response modes, activities, reinforcement). Then compare your preferred learning style with your present teaching style.

Many teachers, in arranging the physical and instructional environments, select options that reflect their own preferences as learners. Depending on the needs of the students in the classroom, this approach may or may not be successful. Teachers should be familiar with many different ways to structure the learning environment so that management decisions can take into account not only the preferences of the teacher but also those of the students.

ARRANGING THE PHYSICAL ENVIRONMENT

The **physical environment** is made up of the classroom and its furnishings. The nature of the physical environment and its arrangement have an effect on the behavior of both teachers and students (Smith, Neisworth, & Greer, 1978). For example, environmental constraints make it difficult to teach running skills in a closet, demonstrate cooking and food preparation techniques in a gymnasium, or supervise small-group discussions in a large auditorium with fixed seats. Environment exerts the greatest influence on the nonacademic performance of students. Reviews of research conclude that classroom characteristics affect attitudes and social behavior but have little impact (with the exception of seating arrangements) on student achievement (Doyle, 1986; Weinstein, 1979). In the following paragraphs, several principles are offered for consideration in arranging the physical environment of your classroom. Keep in mind that some aspects of the physical environment, such as classroom seating arrangements, are easy to modify; others, such as the size of the classroom and the colors of its walls, are less amenable to change.

Ensure a Safe and Barrier-Free Environment

A primary concern with any environment is the safety of its inhabitants. Although this is important for all students, students with physical and sensory impairments require special precautions. For example, books, other objects, and clutter on the classroom floor are hazards for students with balance problems or poor eyesight. Students with limited mobility

FIGURE 7-1   What Is Your Learning Style?

When do you work best? What type of learning environment do you prefer? Is the learning environment that *you* prefer the one you provide for students? If so, please reconsider. Your goal as a teacher is to meet the needs of the students!

Factor	Preference
Noise	Do you work best in absolute silence? in a quiet room? with music playing? with television on? with others talking?
Distractions	Are you able to work with many visual distractions (e.g., interesting pictures, bulletin boards, objects)? Can you work near a window? with people moving about? Do you work best with your desk or table clear?
Physical surroundings	Do you work best sitting upright in a straight-backed chair? an easy chair? on the floor? Do you prefer a desk or table for writing? A computer? Can you work anywhere at all? Do you work best if it is warm? cool? Are the best conditions those where you can eat? drink? move about at will?
Time of day	Is early morning the best time for you to learn? midmorning? midday? afternoon? evening? late at night? When are you most alert?
Attention span	Are you able to concentrate only a few minutes? a half hour? for long periods of time? until the work is done? How often do you need to take a break? Are you able to get back to work immediately after a break?
Closure	Do you want to finish a task once you've started it, or can you stop working at any point in the task? Do you like to take breaks in the middle of tasks? have work interrupted before it's completed? have to stop before you have finished?
Rate	Are you a fast or slow worker? Do you spend the most time planning? doing the task? checking your work?
Other learners	Do you like to work alone or with others? with peers or adults? If you work one-to-one, should the other person be the teacher? another student? Do you enjoy working in small groups? teams? committees? large groups?
Structure	Are you most comfortable when all task requirements are clearly spelled out for you? when you can make some choices? when you have complete freedom?
Presentation mode	In learning about something new, would you rather read about it? hear someone talk about it? see it in pictures? watch a videotape? listen to an audiotape? Interact with a computer program? watch someone demonstrate it? try it yourself? try explaining it to someone else?
Activities	Which of the following instructional activities help you learn: lecture? discussion? projects? drill? peer teaching? independent study? games? programmed instruction? simulation? role playing?
Response mode	Do you like to show what you've learned by writing reports? taking exams? telling others? demonstrating how to do it? expressing it artistically?
Reinforcement	Do you need incentives to do a good job? peer approval? praise and recognition from the teacher? tangible rewards? grades? pay? satisfaction that you did your best?

may need help to move out of the school quickly during fire drills; students who are deaf may need visual cues in order to react in emergency situations.

Another major consideration is **access** to the school and classroom. Many of the newer school buildings are designed to be barrier free; that is, **architectural barriers** are avoided, to allow individuals with disabilities entry to and use of the facility. Buildings have elevators and ramps, stairs have handrails for persons with crutches or canes, doorways are wide enough to allow wheelchairs to pass through, and bathroom facilities are specially designed. Drinking fountains, lockers, vending machines, trash cans, towel dispensers, and telephones are installed so that they can be easily reached by a person in a wheelchair. In older schools that do not have these features, it may be necessary to make modifications to allow access to students with disabilities.

The environment of the classroom should also be barrier free. The room should be arranged to allow easy travel between desks and tables. Instructional materials should be placed within reach, and storage space should be provided for special equipment such as magnification devices, crutches, and adapted keyboards for computers. In addition, bookshelves, chalkboards, whiteboards, and bulletin boards should be conveniently located and low enough to permit their use by students in wheelchairs.

Make the Working Conditions Pleasant

A pleasant physical environment is one that is both comfortable and attractive. The comfort of students and teachers depends on factors such as temperature, ventilation, lighting, and noise level. Classroom temperature should be moderate; hot or cold environments may hinder performance. Ventilation should be adequate so that the room is not stuffy. All work areas should be well lighted and free from glare; some students with visual impairments may require special lighting. Windows permit natural illumination but may offer distractions to students; these distractions can be avoided by building windows above eye level or by temporarily drawing the drapes. Noise can also distract students from their work or interfere with their ability to hear others speak. Soundproofed walls, carpeting, acoustical ceiling tiles, and drapes all help to decrease unwanted environmental sounds (D'Alonzo, D'Alonzo, & Mauser, 1979). Although some aspects of the physical environment are difficult to change (e.g., a poor heating or cooling system), it is possible to make classrooms more comfortable by additions such as heaters, fans, and lamps for additional lighting (Murdick & Petch-Hogan, 1996).

The attractiveness of the learning environment is important. Attractive classrooms help improve attendance, participation, and attitudes toward instruction (Weinstein, 1979). One aspect of aesthetic appeal is the use of color. Smith et al. (1978) caution against dark or bright colors for classroom walls; they say that "wall surfaces should be light in tone and subdued though not drab in hue, so that they can better func-tion as a pleasant background for whatever is placed on them or occurs in front of them" (p. 134). The room decor also affects its attractiveness. Furnishings, bulletin boards, pictures, posters, mobiles, and displays of educational materials and equipment all contribute to visual appeal. These stimuli should be interesting and enjoyable to look at without being sources of distraction.

Obtain Appropriate Furniture and Special Equipment

Classroom furniture should be comfortable, attractive, durable, and functional. The primary furnishings of most classrooms (with the exception of specialized classes such as auto mechanics and home economics) are chairs and tables or desks. Chairs should be the correct size; students should be able to sit comfortably with their backs supported and their feet on the floor. Tables and desks should be level and should provide adequate writing space and leg room. Special tables and desks may be needed by persons in braces or wheelchairs.

Students with visual, hearing, and physical impairments often require special classroom equipment. Students may bring with them some types of special equipment: wheelchairs, canes, braces, crutches, hearing aids, and eyeglasses. Other types are furnished by the special education teacher. For example, students with visual impairments may use a Braille notetaker or a slate and stylus to write, an abacus or talking calculator for math, and optical aids and magnifica-

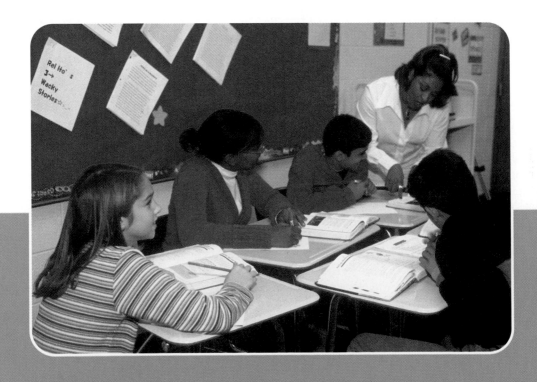

tion devices. Those with hearing losses may need amplification equipment. Students with physical impairments may require lapboards for writing, automatic page turners for reading, or special standing tables. Chapters 14 and 15 describe the special equipment needs of students with sensory and physical impairments.

Arrange Space Functionally

Classroom space should be divided into performance areas or zones to accommodate routine activities and tasks (Berdine & Cegelka, 1980; Mercer & Mercer, 2005). Stowitschek, Gable, and Hendrickson (1980) suggest that, in planning the room arrangement, teachers consider typical student groupings, storage needs for materials and equipment, and procedures for distribution and collection of materials and student work.

When the room is divided into separate areas, one essential consideration is space for instruction. Usually at least two areas are needed: one for large-group instruction and another for small-group instruction. As shown in Figure 7-2, desks and chairs can be arranged in many different ways for large-group instruction. Typical patterns are straight rows, clusters of desks, and configurations in the shape of horseshoes,

FIGURE 7-2 Arrangements for Large-Group Instruction

Straight Rows

Clusters

Horseshoe (or Crescent)

Circle (or Square)

X denotes the teacher.

FIGURE 7-3   Small-Group Arrangements

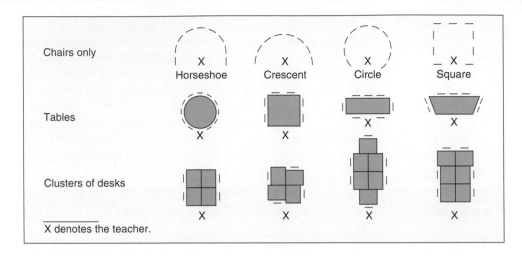

X denotes the teacher.

crescents, circles, and squares. Some arrangements for small-group instruction are shown in Figure 7-3. Arrangements can use chairs only, both tables and chairs, or clusters of desks.

In some classrooms, small-group instructional areas are set up for specific subjects or activities. For example, in classrooms that use learning centers or stations, separate areas may be set up for math, language arts, and science. These areas can be used by the teacher for direct instruction or by students for independent study or self-instructional activities. Mercer and Mercer (2005) recommend a separate area for each subject. This is appropriate even at the secondary level; for example, a classroom in which English is taught could be divided into writing, literature, free reading, and listening areas.

In addition to instructional areas, each student should have an individual work space. Usually the student's desk is the space where he or she works independently and takes part in large-group instruction. Students should have storage space in their desks or, if tables are used instead of desks, in cupboards, cabinets, or bookcases. Care should be taken to ensure that individual work areas are relatively quiet and private. Some students may benefit from separate work areas. Cubicles, carrels, booths, and partitions can be used to set up private office areas for students who are easily distracted or who have difficulty sustaining attention.

Teachers also need a work and storage area, which is usually the teacher's desk. Some teachers do not use their desks as a work area during school hours; they may move from place to place throughout the classroom or station themselves in one of the small-group instructional areas. The classroom should be arranged so that the teacher can visually monitor students' activities throughout the school day. Stain-

back, Stainback, and Froyen (1987) say that "the teacher should be able to make a visual sweep of the room and detect when students need assistance and what social interactions are occurring" (p. 12).

Other areas can be incorporated into the classroom if desired. A separate storage location may be needed if materials and equipment are not housed in learning centers. Some teachers set up a specific location at which students pick up their work for the day and return completed assignments. Classroom computers may be placed at the back or side of the room, so that students can interact with instructional programs without disturbing the work of others. Another option is a free-time or recreational area with games, tapes, books, and other types of reading materials. Time in this area can be used as reinforcement for appropriate behavior, completed work, or accurate performance.

The plan for an elementary grade classroom in Figure 7-4 includes areas for several types of activities. Student desks are clustered for either large- or small-group instruction. There are listening centers and study carrels, a partitioned area for quiet study or games, and a small carpeted area with beanbag chairs. Three tables are available for small-group work, and storage space is ample and conveniently located. Many possibilities for flexibility exist; the placement of desks and tables can be easily changed and the portable chalkboard can serve as a temporary partition.

The relationship among the different areas within the classroom should be carefully planned. According to Doyle (1986), the major concerns are provision of separate areas for different instructional purposes, careful design of classroom traffic patterns, and minimization of density. It is also important to arrange classroom space to encourage smooth and

FIGURE 7-4   Classroom Plan

Quiet Study, Game Area, and Peer Teaching (with cardboard partition)

Listening Stations and Study Carrels

Language Materials

Spelling and Reading Materials

Seatwork and Small-Group Instruction

Chairs

Desks

Teacher

Door

Chalkboard

Bulletin Board

AV Materials

Shelves

File Cabinets

Rotating Interest Centers

Carpet

Record Player

Table

Portable Chalkboard

Math Materials

Handwriting or Subject Materials

Beanbag Chairs

Note: Reprinted with permission of Merrill, an imprint of Macmillan Publishing Company, from *Teaching Students with Learning Problems* (3rd ed., p. 85) by C. D. Mercer and A. R. Mercer. Copyright © 1989 Merrill Publishing Company, Columbus, Ohio.

quick transitions between instructional activities (Rieth & Evertson, 1988). Among the factors to consider are these:

1. *Sound.* Separate quiet areas from noisy areas.
2. *Convenience.* Store equipment, supplies, and materials near where they are used; locate instructional groups near the chalkboard.
3. *Student traffic patterns.* Make traffic patterns direct; discourage routes that lead to disruptions (e.g., students distracting others when turning in assignments or moving to new activities). Also, make sure that traffic areas are uncluttered and wide enough to accommodate the flow of student traffic, particularly during transitions from one activity to another (Stainback et al., 1987).
4. *Teacher mobility.* Use an open room arrangement so that the teacher can move quickly and easily to any location. This allows the teacher to "respond to student needs as well as to potential behavior problems" (Cegelka, 1995b, p. 139).
5. *Flexibility.* Ensure that all classroom activities can be accomplished; make areas multipurpose or use different arrangements for different tasks. Stainback, Stainback, and Slavin (1989) recommend classrooms with "areas that can be opened, closed, or screened off depending on the needs of students when working on different tasks" (p. 140).
6. *Density.* Arrange student seating so that personal space is preserved; avoid crowding. High density can reduce attentiveness and increase dissatisfaction and aggressiveness (Doyle, 1986; Zentall, 1983).

When arranging classroom space, the teacher should not consider it permanent. New arrangements should be tried as often as necessary to increase the effectiveness of the learning environment. As Polloway and Patton (1993) comment, "every teacher should periodically review why the room is arranged as it is. There is no one best way to arrange a classroom, but some ways are clearly superior to others" (p. 59).

Consider Educational Goals in Making Seating Arrangements

How students are arranged in relationship to each other can affect their academic performance, classroom behavior, and social interactions. Weinstein (1979) concludes from a review of research studies that achievement is related to seat position: in classrooms arranged in rows, students sitting in the front center seats participate more, are more attentive, and spend more time on task. This finding may be due to the availability of more cues from the teacher (e.g., increased eye contact, better reception of nonverbal messages) (Doyle, 1986). It may also be due to self-selection if students choose their own seats or to the tendency of teachers to seat low achievers farther away from the teacher's desk than high achievers (Alves &

Gottlieb, 1986). However, according to Heron and Harris (1993), low achievers improve academically as their seats are moved from the back to the front of the classroom. This improvement is attributed to closer proximity to the teacher and the stimuli to which they should attend.

Seating also influences classroom behavior. Axelrod, Hall, and Tams (1972) found that study behaviors improved when students were seated in rows rather than in groups around tables. To prevent behavior problems, inattentive or disruptive students are placed near the teacher; those who argue or fight are separated. Disruptive students improve their behavior when grouped with well-behaved students (Stainback et al., 1987). In some cases, teachers may move students to separate areas, away from their peers. Students who act out or display serious inappropriate behaviors may be removed to a time-out area. Those who are easily distracted can be seated in individual study carrels or booths. However, teachers should consider all possible alternatives before physically isolating students from others in the classroom.

Social interaction can be facilitated by seating arrangements. Smith et al. (1978) note that interaction increases when students are seated close to each other or opposite one another. Heron and Harris (1993) observe that verbal communication tends to move across tables rather than around them. They recommend seating a low-verbal student across from a high-verbal student to enhance performance. In this arrangement, the low-verbal student is better able to receive the verbal messages and the facial and gestural cues of the peer model.

The physical environment of the classroom can be arranged in many ways to promote successful student performance. The environmental checklist in Figure 7-5 summarizes several important concerns. In addition, Prater (2003) suggests that teachers evaluate their classrooms to determine if visual or auditory distractions are present. Overton (2004) adds that it is important to make sure that the materials students use are easily accessible.

ORGANIZING THE INSTRUCTIONAL ENVIRONMENT

The **instructional environment** of the classroom includes the procedures, routines, materials, and equipment used by the teacher to increase student performance. The teacher organizes the curriculum, groups students, and sets up delivery systems for the presentation and practice of skills and information. This structure directly affects nonacademic performance as well as student achievement. Students actively involved in appropriate instruction are less likely to exhibit problem behaviors and more likely to feel good about their competence. Several principles are important to consider in arranging the instructional environment.

FIGURE 7-5 Physical Environment Checklist

Physiological Effects

Illumination
- Is there adequate light for reading and other demanding visual tasks?
- Is the lighting throughout the classroom varied and home-like?
- Is lighting used to help define the different activity areas of the room?
- Is the lighting warm yet not glaring?

Temperature
- Can adequate air movement be obtained when needed?
- Is there an adequate supply of fresh air?
- Are temperatures controlled within a comfortable range (68–74° F)?
- Are children assisted in making necessary clothing adjustments for the room temperature?
- Is humidity adequate year round?

Noise
- Can windows be opened without interference from outside noise?
- Is the noise level of each classroom controlled so that the activities of the other classrooms are not disturbed?
- Is the teacher rarely asked to repeat what he/she has said?

Color
- Are the colors in the classroom pleasantly varied?
- Is color used to define areas of the room and to attract attention to important educational displays?
- Are the colors in the room subdued, mellow, and pleasing?

Materials
- Does the classroom contain furnishings, materials, and displays in addition to typical institutional furnishings?
- Do teachers and students bring in a variety of materials and displays related to current assignments?
- Are learning materials and displays well organized by topics or learning area?
- Have excessive, unorganized materials been removed to eliminate confusion or distraction?

Spatial Effects
- Are related compatible activities arranged together and unrelated, incompatible activities separated within the classroom?
- Have an appropriate time and place been designated and assigned for all activities?
- Is there a variety of places where different-sized groups can meet and work?
- Are there special places that individual children can go (a) for isolation, (b) for rest and quiet, (c) to let off steam, (d) to reward themselves, (e) for private instruction, (f) to work independently, (g) to be disciplined privately?
- Can children enter, leave, clean up, and dress, etc. without disturbing others?
- Can children space themselves as they need or desire?
- Do the relative amounts of space allocated to various activities reflect their importance in the teaching program?

Physical Effects
- Is the environment kept clean?
- Are the furnishings (desks, displays, etc.) moveable to provide a variety of groupings and areas within the room for different learning tasks?
- Can the teacher control visual distractions between groups of children (by separating groups, raising room dividers, etc.)?
- Are storage facilities accessible to the students for getting out and putting away materials which they are allowed access to?
- Have high physical barriers been eliminated so that the teacher has visual access to the entire room?

Setting Effects
- Can the teacher identify an "overcommitted" setting (one in which most children are observers rather than performers and leaders) and then attempt to create new, smaller work or activity groups?
- Have physical barriers to children with disabilities been removed?
- Does the teacher periodically change the environment to improve the teaching program?
- Does the teacher systematically observe and evaluate the effects of the environment on the social behaviors and learning of the class?

Note: Reprinted with the permission of Macmillan College Publishing from *Evaluating Educational Environments* by R. M. Smith, J. T. Nersworth, and J. G. Greer. Copyright © 1978 Macmillan College Publishing Company, Inc.

Organize Curricular Skills and Information

Although the scope and sequence of the general education curriculum are usually well specified, the teacher does have the opportunity to arrange the skills and information in different ways. The traditional organization follows academic subjects; this is most apparent at the secondary level, where the curriculum is broken down into separate courses. At the elementary level, skills and information can also be divided into different subjects, such as language arts, mathematics, social studies, and science.

An alternate way of organizing the curriculum is the unit approach, which cuts across subject matter areas (Polloway & Patton, 1993). In this approach, content is organized around **thematic** or **instructional units.** Meyen (1981) describes unit teaching as a generic instructional approach that integrates instruction "on academic and social skills, with information structured around a common theme building on the previous experience of students" (p. 3). Topics of interest and importance to students become the vehicle for teaching academic skills. For instance, Meyen (1981) suggests experiential themes, such as transportation, the community, leisure time, and the newspaper. The teacher organizes the unit around a central theme and includes activities in each of the core areas: communication skills, math, social competencies, safety, health, and vocation.

Many teachers use thematic units as a supplement to the standard curriculum. While continuing instruction in specific academic subjects, they also introduce activities related to a special topic or interest area. Examples are space travel, February holidays, contributions of African Americans, and endangered species. This approach is more common at the elementary level but can also be adapted for secondary-aged students.

If units are carefully planned to ensure the inclusion of several important academic skills, they become a valuable addition to the instructional environment. Units include a variety of different activities, and the teacher can tailor instruction to the needs of the individual students within the classroom. In addition, the use of themes that interest and motivate students can increase their willingness to participate in academic activities.

Another method of organizing curriculum is the blending or integration of academic subjects. For example, at the elementary level, the whole language approach integrates the language arts of listening, speaking, reading, and writing (Lapp & Flood, 1992). Skills are taught in the context of authentic communication tasks, not as separate (and isolated) subjects (Westby, 1992). Writing across the curriculum is another example. In this approach, secondary students are expected to practice their writing skills in all subjects, not just in English classes.

Group Students for Instruction

Before presentation of skills and information can begin, the teacher must decide how to group students. Two factors must be determined: group size and group type. The number of students per group can vary from one (in a tutoring situation) to the entire class. Class size is a factor in instruction; it has been noted that student achievement increases as the number of students in the class decreases (Glass & Smith, 1978). However, this does not necessarily mean that classes of 30 or more students should always be broken into several groups for instruction. Using the whole class as a group is an efficient way of presenting new material, if that material is appropriate for all of the students (Brophy & Good, 1986). Also, providing guided practice for the entire class at once is an effective use of time. For instance, if the time allotted for mathematics is 1 hour, the teacher can spend only 2 minutes with each of 30 individual students or can devote the entire period to the class as a whole.

When it is necessary to present different material to different students, small groups are appropriate. According to Brophy and Good (1986), small groups are necessary in beginning reading instruction and in highly heterogeneous classes. Also, smaller groups can lead to greater student participation (Mercer & Mercer, 2005). Small groups generally range in size from three to seven or eight individuals. For some students, individual instruction is needed; this can be presented by the teacher or other instructional personnel, such as peers, aides, and volunteers.

The criterion used to group students often determines the size of the group. The most typical criterion is homogeneity: Students of similar ability, at similar levels, or with similar skills are placed in one group. For example, a placement test might be given to pinpoint each student's current instructional level and the results used to form instructional groups. A **skill-specific group** is made up of students requiring instruction in the same skill area. This type of homogeneous grouping, although temporary because skill needs change, is the most effective means of individualizing instruction.

Heterogeneous grouping can also be used for instruction. In this type of group, lower functioning students are provided with models (Smith et al., 1978); for example, students with articulation problems can benefit from hearing the more appropriate speech of their peers. Also, heterogeneous grouping can be used to promote the development of social skills (Bossert & Barnett, 1981). In groups with a range of skills represented, Affleck, Lowenbraun, and Archer (1980) recommend individualizing by using the same task to develop different skills. For example, having students read a short story can be used for instruction in several types and levels of comprehension skills.

Flexible grouping is the practice of using several kinds of grouping formats at different times; this allows all students to interact with one another (Schubert et al., 1979). Although skill-specific grouping remains the most effective for the purpose of instruction, several of the other methods suggested by these authors may be appropriate for nonacademic and social activities. Examples are grouping by common interests, grouping by choice, proximity grouping, alphabetical grouping, and grouping by counting off.

Set Up Systems for Monitoring Practice

Opportunities for practice are provided after new material is presented. During practice, student performance is monitored, either directly by the teacher or through the use of **self-instructional learning materials**. With self-instructional materials, students receive feedback from the materials themselves and thus are able to practice independently without the assistance of the teacher. This approach frees the teacher for other activities, such as direct instruction.

Among the different forms of self-instruction are self-correcting materials, programmed learning, and mediated instruction. Self-correcting materials are those that provide the student with the correct answer so that responses can be checked for accuracy. For example, math fact flashcards with the problem on one side and the answer on the other allow immediate feedback. Teachers can also prepare answer keys for independent practice activities and encourage students to check and correct their responses. Mercer and Mercer (2005) point out that this works well with students who have a history of academic failure because they are able to make (and correct) mistakes privately. See the "Inclusion Tips for the Teacher" material for more information about self-correcting materials.

Programmed instruction is another method that allows students to monitor their own practice. Figure 7-6 describes and illustrates this approach. The learner covers the answers on the right-hand side of the page and attempts to answer the questions; each response can then be checked immediately. Heron and Harris (1993) note that programmed instruction allows learners to progress at their own rate through small, incremental steps that build on previous learning.

Mediated instruction is any procedure that includes the use of media. For example, many computer software

---

FIGURE 7-6	Programmed Instruction

Programmed instruction does three things:

    First, it breaks learning tasks down into small steps. These small _____ help learners avoid making mistakes. That, then, is the first purpose of programmed instruction—to break material into small steps to help learners avoid making _____ .   steps   mistakes

    Second, programmed instruction requires that students make active responses while they work. These active _____ are often made by filling in blanks in the programmed material.   responses

    Third, as you respond actively by filling in each _____ , you can check immediately to see whether you made a correct response. This immediate knowledge of correct response is the reinforcement built into the program. When you see that you gave the correct response, that knowledge is your _____ .   blank   reinforcement

Note: From *Individualizing Instruction* (2nd ed., p. 241) by C. M. Charles, 1980, St. Louis, MO: C. V. Mosby. Copyright 1980 by C. V. Mosby. Reprinted by permission.

Inclusion Tips for the Teacher

Self-Correcting Instructional Materials

With instructional materials that are self-correcting, students receive immediate feedback on the accuracy of their responses. Some of the most common teaching tools contain self-correcting features. For example, at the end of many textbooks are the answers to all or some of the questions and problems.

Teachers can also design self-correcting materials to meet the needs of specific students. One example of an easy-to-make device that can be used for almost any school subject is suggested by Mercer and Mercer (2005):

Strips are cut in one side of a manila folder, which then is laminated. Worksheets containing problems and answers are inserted into the folder so that only the problem is presented. The student uses a grease pencil or a felt-tip pen to write the responses under each problem. Then the worksheet is pulled upward, and the answers appear in the strip.

Note: Reprinted with the permission of Merrill from *Teaching Students with Learning Problems,* 7th ed., by Cecil D. Mercer and Ann R. Mercer (p. 65). Copyright © 2005 Prentice-Hall, Inc.

programs provide programmed instruction or practice activities with immediate feedback and correction of errors. Another example is the use of audiotapes for self-instruction. As de Grandpre and Messier (1979) suggest, teachers can develop self-instructional tapes to aid secondary students in reviewing material before exams. The student listens to a tape-recorded question, stops the tape, writes an answer, and then continues the tape to find out whether the response is correct. The tape directs the student to correct any errors immediately.

A **learning center** is a common way to organize self-instructional materials for independent classroom practice. According to Berdine and Cegelka (1980), a learning or interest center is "an area especially designed for auto-instructional use by the student" (p. 212). Centers provide independent work for one or several students in one or several skill areas. A typical arrangement is by academic subject;

for example, many elementary classrooms contain centers for language arts, mathematics, science, and social studies.

Learning centers should be based on specific instructional objectives, house all necessary media and materials, and provide clear and simple directions for student activities. Pretests allow students to select appropriate activities; several kinds and levels of activities should be included in each center. Another important component is a record-keeping system; for example, checklists can be used to note which activities each student has completed. Student progress is measured by post-tests or other evaluation devices.

Learning centers can be constructed so that practice activities are individualized. Centers promote independence, free the teacher for other duties, and encourage students to work cooperatively. Like other types of self-instructional systems, they also provide students with immediate feedback on the adequacy of their performance during practice.

Flashcards are another example of a self-correcting material. The question or problem appears on one side of the card and the other side contains the answer. Like the folder device, flashcards are easy to make and can be adapted for many different subjects. Also, students can use flashcards for independent practice or for review with a peer.

When students use self-correcting materials for class assignments, teachers often ask how to prevent them from merely copying down the correct answers. Here are three ways to avoid this problem:

- Within each activity or assignment, include a few questions or problems for which the answer is not provided. These items serve as probes to determine whether students can transfer skills to questions for which the answers are not supplied.
- Have students correct each other's work. Students can trade assignments, or one or two individuals can be selected to be graders for the period or the day.
- Distribute answer keys only after students have completed their work; be sure, however, that the feedback occurs as soon after completion of the assignment as possible.

Provide Guidelines for Student Behavior

Classroom rules and routines help structure the learning environment. Many students need guidelines for behavior and benefit from consistently enforced rules. As noted in chapter 5, rules for classroom conduct are helpful for students of any age. Madsen, Becker, and Thomas (1968) recommend that classroom rules be short and to the point, few in number, and phrased positively (e.g., "Keep your hands to yourself" rather than "Don't hit others"). Affleck et al. (1980) add that rules should be simple, clearly stated, and directly enforceable by the teacher. Classroom rules should be explained to students and reviewed frequently.

Structure can also help the academic performance of students. When consistent classroom routines are established, students are aware of what they should do, where they should be, and how they should act. For example, the teacher may establish a specific time and place in the classroom for turning in assignments. Some teachers provide each student with a daily assignment card that spells out each of the activities that must be completed. Secondary teachers can establish a routine pattern of assignments (e.g., quiz on Wednesdays, essay due on Fridays) and provide students with a weekly assignment sheet (Raison, 1979). It is also possible to use student work folders that contain the schedule for the day, assignments to be completed, answer keys, and check-off sheets to record finished tasks (Eaton & Hansen, 1978).

Another way to provide structure is through the use of prompts and models. Somewhere in most elementary classrooms is a model of the alphabet for students to consult if they have difficulty remembering how to form letters. This technique can be used in most other subjects. For example, procedures for division, alphabetizing, or constructing a paragraph can be written on the board. These prompts help students to function independently.

FIGURE 7-7   Daily Assignment Sheet

Work for   Monday
   Name   George

MATH   Do page 68,   I did it _____   My score
            numbers 1   I scored it _____   was _____
            through 12.   I corrected it _____   right.

SPELLING   Do page 42,   I did it _____   My score
            numbers 4, 6, 8,   I scored it _____   was _____
            9, 10, 11, and 15.   I corrected it _____   right.

READING   Read pages 6   I did it _____   My score
            and 7. Do   I scored it _____   was _____
            worksheet 17A.   I corrected it _____   right.

Use Systematic Record-Keeping Procedures

A great many sources of data are available to the teacher in the general education classroom, and it is easy to become overwhelmed by masses of information. However, by using systematic record-keeping procedures, the teacher can collect sufficient information to make informed instructional decisions.

Teachers generally collect and record two types of data: activities completed (e.g., math workbook, pages 32–34) and actual measures of student performance on tests, quizzes, and other achievement indices (e.g., science test, 75%). Keeping detailed records of every activity completed by every student is probably not necessary. However, student performance should be measured in each major subject area at least once per week and more often if students are encountering difficulty.

One way to make data collection simpler is to enlist the aid of students. After correcting their academic work, they can record their scores or the number of correct responses. For example, Figure 7-7 shows George's daily assignment sheet for Monday. After completing an activity, he checks his answers with the key provided, records his score, and then corrects his mistakes. George can also learn to graph his scores so that he and his teacher can easily see his progress from day to day.

Smith et al. (1978) recommend that the following information be collected and recorded for each instructional objective: the date instruction began, the date the objective was achieved, and the student's performance level at completion. For groups of students working on the same skill, the teacher can simply record the starting and ending dates of instruction and the individual scores of each student.

Systematic record keeping requires consistency. Teachers should decide what data will be collected, how frequently, and what methods will be used for recording. It is best to begin gradually, perhaps with one or two subjects per week. The record-keeping system should be one with which the teacher is comfortable. Some teachers use computer programs such as grade books. Others favor loose-leaf notebooks divided into sections by academic subjects, a file folder for each instructional group, or a 5- × 8-inch index card for each student. The most important factors are that data are collected regularly, recorded in a systematic fashion, and then utilized to determine whether instructional modifications should be made.

USING EDUCATIONAL TECHNOLOGIES

In a broad sense, the technology of education includes all types of instructional strategies and approaches; thus, systematic instruction and behavior management techniques could be considered educational technologies. More common, however, is to use the term **educational technology** to refer to equipment and media with potential for contributing to the instructional process: computers, television and radio, audio- and videotapes, and so on. As Norris (1977) commented almost three decades ago, technologies such as these have the capability to "revolutionize the quality, productivity, and availability of education" (p. 451).

In the general education classroom, both modern and traditional technologies can aid the teacher in providing individualized instruction and enhancing the standard curriculum. Several breakthroughs in the development of **assistive technology** make this particularly true for students with disabilities. For example, assistive technologies allow students who cannot see to hear the words that appear on a computer screen. Other students, unable to type on a computer keyboard, can write by speaking into a microphone. Special educational applications of technology are described throughout the rest of this book in sections entitled "Spotlight on Technology." The "Spotlight" in this chapter focuses on a very common technology, the tape recorder, and how this device can be used to enhance instruction for students with special needs and their peers.

Spotlight on Technology

Tape Recorders

Audiotape recorders and players are one of the most common technologies available today. Tape players, particularly personal stereos, are popular with students of all ages. According to Mercer and Mercer (2005), these devices have several advantages for classroom use. They are inexpensive, easy to operate, small in size, and portable. When used with headphones, they are quiet. Only the student wearing the headphones hears the tape so that others in the classroom are not distracted.

Teachers can use tape recorders as part of instruction in several ways. Mercer and Mercer (2005) provide several suggestions:

1. A tape can be made of reading material (e.g., literature, stories, and magazines). The student can read along with the tape to practice reading. Thus, the tape can provide feedback, increase speed, and help the student identify and practice difficult words.
2. In a language activity, the student can use a tape recorder to make a tape of a story. Later, the student can write the story from the tape with a peer, aide, or teacher.
3. Oral directions can be put on tape to accompany seatwork activities. The student who has difficulty with oral directions can play the tape until the directions are understood.
4. Spelling tapes are useful for practice and taking tests. One commonly used format gives the spelling word; the word used in a sentence; and a pause, a beep, and the word spelled correctly. The pause can be eliminated by having

the student stop the tape recorder to write the word and then start it to check the spelling.
5. Stories, facts, or a report of an event can be recorded. News programs, commercials, telephone messages, weather reports, and teacher-made content can be used. The student listens and then responds to comprehension questions. For example, a weather report is taped and the student is required to answer the following questions: High temperature? Low temperature? Any rain? Forecast for tomorrow? What season is it?
6. One-minute samples of instrumental music can be taped for students to use in conducting timings. These tapes usually begin with the word "start" and end with the word "stop." The teacher may prefer to use only the words and omit the music. In place of a kitchen timer, tapes of different time spans can be used to mark the end of any timed activity.
7. Correction tapes can be used to provide feedback to students who have completed math seatwork.
8. Music can be recorded on tapes for students to listen to when they have completed an assignment. Also, pleasant background music can be played while students are engaged in activities such as cleaning up, settling down after recess, free-choice, seatwork, or art.
9. At the secondary level, class lectures and discussions can be taped. These tapes can be used to help the students review or understand the material.

Note. From *Teaching Students with Learning Problems*, 7th ed., by Cecil D. Mercer and Ann R. Mercer (p. 79). Copyright © 2005 by Pearson Education, Inc. Reprinted with permission.

Be Aware of Available Technologies

To use technology wisely, teachers must be aware of the resources available in their school and community and must keep informed about new developments. A vast array of technologies is currently available, and many are valuable tools for the presentation and practice of skills and information.

One way of classifying educational technologies is by their communication mode: visual, auditory, or multisensory. Visual media and equipment include photographs and cameras, slides and slide projectors, filmstrips and filmstrip projectors, and transparencies and overhead projectors. Visual technologies are often used with students with hearing losses. For example, with captioned films and television programs, the audio portion of the show is presented on the screen in text; the student reads the print captions, just as an English speaker would read the subtitles in a foreign film.

Records and record players, audiotapes and tape recorders, audio compact discs (CDs) and CD players, and radios are auditory technologies. They can be used by an entire class or selected individuals who listen through headphones. Students with vision losses benefit from auditory devices such as the talking calculator.

Multisensory technologies are common; these include language masters, films, videotapes, television, computers, and DVD (digital video disc) technology. The language master, an adaptation of the tape recorder, uses a card with an audiotape affixed to the bottom. As the card with its printed message moves through the machine, the audiotape plays.

An important trend is the increased use of computers for classroom instruction and other educational purposes. **Computer-assisted instruction,** or the direct delivery of instruction to learners via computers, has proved effective with several types of learners, including students with disabilities. In addition, computers are useful tools for students and for

FIGURE 7-9   Checklist for Evaluating Instructional Materials

Instruction
1. Are instruction procedures for each lesson clearly specified?
2. Does the material provide a maximum amount of direct teacher instruction on the skills/concepts presented?
3. Does the direct teacher instruction provide for active student involvement and responses?
4. Are the direct instructional lessons adaptable to small-group/individual instruction?
5. Is a variety of cueing and prompting techniques used to elicit correct child responses?
6. When using verbal instruction, does the instruction proceed in a clear, logical fashion?
7. Does the teacher use modeling and demonstration when appropriate to the skills being taught?
8. Does the material specify correction and feedback procedures for use during instruction?

Practice
1. Does the material contain appropriate practice activities that contribute to mastery of the skills/concepts?
2. Are the practice activities directly related to the desired outcome behaviors?
3. Does the material provide enough practice for the . . . learner [with special needs]?
4. Does the material provide for feedback on responses during practice?
5. Can the learner complete practice activities independently?
6. Does the material reduce the probability of error in independent practice activities?

Sequence of Instruction
1. Are the scope and sequence of the material clearly specified?
2. Are facts/concepts/skills ordered in a logical manner from simple to complex?
3. Does the sequence proceed in small steps, easily attainable by the . . . learner [with special needs]?

Content
1. Does the selection of the concepts and skills adequately represent the content area?
2. Is the content consistent with the stated objectives?
3. Is the information presented in the material accurate?
4. Is the information presented in the material current?
5. Are various points of view concerning treatment of minorities and . . . people [with disabilities], ideologies, social values, sex roles, socioeconomic class, etc., objectively represented?
6. Are the content and topic of the material relevant to the needs of . . . students [with special needs] as well as to the other students in the regular classroom?

Behavioral Objectives
1. Are objectives clearly stated for the material?
2. Are the objectives consistent with the goals for the classroom?
3. Are the objectives stated in behavioral terms including the desired child behavior, the criteria for measurement of the behavior, and the desired standard of performance?

Entry Behaviors
1. Does the material specify the prerequisite student skills needed to work with ease in the material?
2. Are the prerequisite student skills compatible with the objectives of the material?

Initial Assessment/Placement
1. Does the material provide a method to determine initial placement into the material?
2. Does the initial placement tool contain enough items to accurately place the learner into the material?

Ongoing Assessment/Evaluation
1. Does the material provide evaluation procedures for measuring progress and mastery of objectives?
2. Are there sufficient evaluative items to accurately measure learner progress?
3. Are procedures and/or materials for ongoing record keeping provided?

Review/Maintenance
1. Are practice and review of content material provided?
2. Are review and maintenance activities systematically and appropriately spaced?
3. Are adequate review and maintenance activities provided for the . . . learner [with special needs]?

Motivation/Interest
1. Are reinforcement procedures built in or suggested for use in the program?
2. Are procedures specified for providing feedback to the student on his/her progress?
3. Has the program been designed to motivate and appeal to students?

Adaptability to Individual Differences
1. Can the pace be adapted to variations in learner rate of mastery?
2. Can the method of response be adapted to the individual needs of the learner?
3. Can the method of instruction be adapted to the individual needs of the learner?
4. Can the child advance to subsequent tasks when he has demonstrated proficiency?
5. Can the learner be placed in the material at his own level?
6. Does the material offer alternative teaching strategies for students who are failing to master an objective?

Physical Characteristics of the Material
1. Is the format uncluttered?
2. Is the format grammatically correct and free of typographical errors?
3. Are photographs and illustrations clear, attractive, and consistent with the content?
4. Are the type size and style appropriate to the students?
5. Are auditory components of adequate clarity and amplification?
6. Are the materials durable?
7. Can the materials be easily stored and organized for classroom use?

Teacher Considerations
1. Is a teacher's manual or set of teacher guidelines provided?
2. Are teacher instructions clear, complete, and unambiguous?
3. Does the material specify the skills and abilities needed by the instructor to work effectively with the material?

Note: Adapted with permission of Merrill, an imprint of Macmillan Publishing Company, from *Teaching the Mildly Handicapped in the Regular Classroom* (2nd ed., pp. 125–127) by J. Affleck, S. Lowenbraun, and A. Archer. Copyright © 1980 Merrill Publishing Company, Columbus, Ohio.

Teachers often design their own teaching materials if commercial ones are unavailable or too costly. When time and effort are devoted to the production of new instructional tools, the teacher should be sure to make materials that will last. Cohen and Hart-Hester (1978) say, "Never make a material twice; make it durable from the start" (p. 57). For example, elementary grade teachers can laminate supplementary math problem worksheets; secondary grade teachers may wish to keep a file, notebook, or computer disk with class handouts or directions for homework assignments. In addition, teacher-designed materials should be saved for several years. A worksheet or activity from last year, although not useful this year, may be just the thing that is needed next year.

Commercial materials as well as those made by teachers should be stored within the classroom so that they can be easily located and retrieved by students and teachers alike. Mercer and Mercer (2005) recommend the use of a filing system for organization; materials are organized by subject area (e.g., reading) and then by skill (e.g., comprehension). Another possibility is a skill file system designed for student use, with practice materials sequenced according to the skills and skill tests included (Stowitschek et al., 1980). In addition, the books *Stephanie Winston's Best Organizing Tips* (Winston, 1995) and *Taming the Paper Tiger* (Hemphill, 1997), although not written specifically for educators, give several suggestions that can be used in establishing a management system for classroom materials.

Recruit, Train, and Supervise Instructional Personnel

In many cases, teachers do not have instructional aides, and they may view themselves as the only human instructional resource in their classrooms. However, two excellent sources of assistance are available to every teacher: peer tutors and adult volunteers.

Inclusion Tips for the Teacher

Peer Tutors and Adult Volunteers

Peer tutors and adult volunteers are valuable instructional resources. They assist the teacher by taking responsibility for some of the more routine duties in the classroom. One of the first steps in beginning a peer tutoring or adult volunteer program is specification of the duties that these assistants will assume. Remember when choosing tasks that it will be necessary to train tutors and volunteers to perform them.

Student tutors can be trained to

- provide students with feedback about response accuracy,
- correct written assignments,
- deliver reinforcers such as verbal praise and points in a token economy,
- teach specific skills to individuals or small groups of students,
- supervise independent activities such as learning centers, and
- administer simple assessments.

Adult volunteers can be trained to perform any of the duties suggested for student tutors. They can also learn to

- supervise small groups of students in the classroom, at lunch, during assemblies, and so on;

- collect and record data on student performance;
- assist in the preparation of instructional materials;
- perform routine clerical duties; and
- help with classroom housekeeping chores.

When selecting duties for peer tutors, keep in mind that they are students. Choose tasks that relate directly to school learning; save clerical and housekeeping chores for adult volunteers.

Another important consideration is the system that the teacher will use to communicate with tutors and volunteers after these classroom assistants are trained. Hammill and Bartel (1986) suggest using a notebook that contains three different forms:

- *Tutor's lesson plan*—a description of the instructional activities, procedures, and amount of time to be spent on each;
- *Tutor's log sheet*—a reporting form for the tutor to record student performance data and any observations about the tutoring session; and
- *Teacher's note*—a page for the teacher to give feedback to the tutor, praise good performance, and suggest ideas for changes.

Peer tutors are students who assist by teaching other students. They can come from the same class or can be older, more advanced students (usually called cross-age tutors). One approach with good research support is class-wide peer tutoring (Maheady, Harper, & Mallette, 2003). In this arrangement, students within a general education class provide tutoring support to each other. Maheady et al. describe class-wide peer tutoring as "a form of intra-class, reciprocal peer tutoring in which pupils alternated tutor and tutee roles during each session" (p. 1).

Students can learn to perform many instructional duties: They can be scoring monitors and check others' assignments; teach specific skills to individuals in need of extra help; or deliver reinforcers such as points, verbal praise, and feedback (Jenkins & Jenkins, 1985; Stowitschek et al., 1980). Ehly and Larsen (1980) and Utley, Mortweet, and Greenwood (1997) conclude from reviews of research that peer tutoring produces learning gains not only for the learner but also for the tutor. Thus, although tutoring is generally used to provide extra assistance to low-functioning students, such students also can improve their skills by becoming tutors. For instance, a sixth grader with special needs might be assigned as a cross-age tutor in a second-grade classroom. This experience could provide motivation and recognition to the older student while benefiting both individuals academically. Krouse, Gerber, and Kauffman (1981) caution that tutoring programs should ensure that the student who is tutored is not stigmatized.

Adult **volunteers** can also provide instructional assistance. Platt and Platt (1980) describe a program that recruited parents and retired persons to help in the schools. Each volunteer was asked to specify areas of interest; choices included working with students on a one-to-one basis, working with small groups, performing clerical duties, and supervising activities outside the classroom.

Training must be provided for instructional personnel, whether they are adults or students (Carroll, 2001). In one program (Heron, Heward, & Cooke, 1980; Parson & Heward, 1979), tutors were taught four skills: preparing learning materials, prompting student responses, praising correct answers, and plotting the results of the tutoring session. Teachers must also supervise and monitor the performance of tutors and volunteers. They can meet with their assistants before instruction or provide written directions. Each assistant should be observed frequently, and further training should be provided as needed. Consult the "Inclusion Tips for the Teacher" box for additional information about peer tutors and adult volunteers.

This chapter has presented several principles for the arrangement, management, and coordination of the classroom learning environment. The next chapter describes techniques for the effective use of one important type of instructional resource: computers and other technologies. Before going on, check "Things to Remember" to review coordination skills.

Things to Remember

- Teachers arrange, manage, and coordinate the learning environment.
- The physical environment of the classroom affects students' attitudes and social behavior; it should be safe, barrier free, comfortable, and attractive.
- Arranging classroom space by functions helps structure the environment for students with special needs and other class members.
- The instructional environment of the classroom affects both achievement and nonacademic performance.
- Large-group instruction is an effective use of time; homogeneous skill-specific groups are optimal for individualized instruction.
- Self-instructional learning materials are used to monitor the independent practice of students.

- Educational technologies can present new material, provide practice opportunities, serve as rewards, promote socialization, and help students with special needs bypass disabilities.
- Time, educational materials and equipment, and instructional personnel are essential learning resources that are managed by the teacher.
- Daily schedules assist in time management; time should be scheduled to maximize student involvement in important learning tasks.
- Peer tutors and adult volunteers can be effective classroom assistants.

ACTIVITIES

1. Several educational journals offer suggestions to teachers about coordination of the classroom learning environment. Examples are *Teaching Exceptional Children, Focus on Exceptional Children,* and *Intervention in School and Clinic.* Find an article that interests you and summarize its recommendations.

2. Visit a school, university, shopping mall, or library to check its accessibility. Are there architectural barriers that would deny access to some individuals with dis-

abilities? Watch for curbs, stairs, and steep inclines. If ramps are provided for wheelchairs, try traveling by this route. Is it less direct? Are information signs (e.g., signs on restrooms, elevators, telephones) provided in raised print and Braille?

3. Check the library, educational materials center, and catalogues from school supply houses for self-correcting materials. You might also want to consult the book *Self-Correcting Learning Materials for the Classroom* by Mercer, Mercer, and Bott (1984). Are such materials available for subjects you teach? Are they more or less expensive than other materials? In your opinion, could students use them independently? What self-correcting materials could you design and make yourself?

4. Talk with teachers who have used peer tutors or adult volunteers in their classrooms. How were the classroom assistants selected or recruited? Were they provided with a training program? How did the teacher communicate with these helpers? Ask the teachers to discuss the advantages of tutors and volunteers. Are there any disadvantages?

5. One of the most exciting areas in education today is technology. Try to discover some of the latest

CD-ROM Activities

Visit the sixth grade social studies classroom shown in the second video case study to see how this experienced teacher organizes the classroom learning environment.

- *What does the physical setup of the classroom look like?*

- *Where does the teacher position herself in the classroom?*

- *How do you know that there are guidelines in place for student behavior?*

technological innovations designed for use in education. You might contact a local school district, browse through a recent professional journal, or consult the website of an educational magazine such as *Technology & Learning* or *Instructor* (see the "Window on the Web" feature). Consider how the technologies you find described could be used to improve instruction for students with special needs.

Window on the Web

Online Magazines for Teachers

Technology & Learning

http://www.techlearning.com/content/about/tl current.html

Technology & Learning and *Instructor* are magazines for teachers that are published in two formats: a standard print version and a more abbreviated online version. For example, the website for *Technology & Learning* reprints some of the articles in the current issue of the magazine as well as recent columns from departments such as Editor's Desk, Trend Watch, Web Sightings, and What's New. Also available are searchable databases on technology products, grants related to technology, and technology conferences and events.

Instructor

http://teacher.scholastic.com/products/instructor.htm

Similarly, the *Instructor* website contains current articles and also features such as technology activities for the classroom, "CyberHunts," and "Web Sitings." The site also offers several searchable libraries including one for *Instructor* feature articles and another for electronic learning tools (e.g., "Search Tools That Do the Trick," "Choosing a Digital Camera for Your Classroom").

For more information, go to the Web Links module in Chapter 7 of the Companion Website.

Note: Courtesy of Technology & Learning.

Note: Courtesy of Scholastic.

Teaching with Classroom Technologies

CHAPTER

8

STUDENTS' STORIES

- David, a sixth-grade student, likes creative writing but dreads trying to find and fix all of the spelling errors he makes. For him, a word processor is almost a necessity.
- Although he has poor vision, Carlos is able to surf the Net; his computer has a large-screen display with magnification.
- Julie wears her technology to school every day: her hearing aids.
- Jimmy plays math games on the computer to practice his multiplication facts.

- Because Gariella's speech is difficult to understand, she "talks" in class with the help of her electronic communication device.
- Phuoc drives his power chair by manipulating a joystick, and he "types" by talking to his computer.

LOOKING AHEAD

In this chapter, you'll learn about strategies for using technology to enhance the general education experience for students with special needs. As you read, think about these questions:

- Each of the students described here uses some type of technology. From what you know now, do you believe these technologies help students bypass or compensate for a disability or special need?
- Computers are likely the most common technology found in schools today. What barriers might standard computers present to students like Carlos who have vision problems? To students like Phuoc who have physical limitations?
- Assistive technologies are specifically designed for persons with disabilities. Some of the students described here are using assistive devices, and some are not. In your judgment, which students are using off-the-shelf rather than assistive technologies? What are some of the advantages (and disadvantages) of off-the-shelf devices?

To answer these questions online, go to the Students' Stories Module in Chapter 8 of the Companion Website.

Today, technology is a common feature of schools and classrooms in the United States. In the 1980s, however, less than 40% of school districts owned computers (Quality Education Data, Inc., 1985). By the 1990s, more than 2.5 million computers were being used for public school instruction, with a national average of one computer for every 19 students (Market Data Retrieval, as cited in Kinnaman, 1992). Numbers have increased dramatically and, in Fall 2002, the ratio of students to instructional computers in U.S. public schools was 4.8 to 1 (DeBell & Chapman, 2003b). Access to the Internet has also increased dramatically, with 99% of public schools having access in 2002 (DeBell & Chapman, 2003b).

According to a recent report published by the U.S. Department of Education (DeBell & Chapman, 2003a), "Computers and the Internet recently passed a milestone: both are now used by a majority of Americans" (p.1). To learn more about how school-aged individuals use these technologies, check out the "For Your Information" section.

TYPES OF TECHNOLOGY

Technology has great potential for assisting teachers in the educational process, particularly for students with special needs (Edyburn, 2000; Lewis, 2000b). Although technology is not a panacea for the ills of education, when used appropriately, it can help teachers differentiate instruction in the general education classroom. Among the technologies now available for classroom use are computers, the Internet and World Wide Web, CD-ROMs and DVDs, more traditional educational technologies such as audio- and videotape players and recorders, and assistive technologies such as electronic communication aids and talking calculators designed specifically for people with disabilities.

One way to think about technology is to consider the ways in which it can be used. In this schema, three major types of technology are typically found in schools today:

- *Instructional technology.* Any type of device with the capacity to support the teaching–learning process; examples are classroom computers, VCRs and video disc players, and educational television;
- *Technology tools.* Hardware devices and/or software programs that help students to accomplish educational tasks; examples are word processing programs and hand-held electronic spellcheckers; and
- *Assistive technology.* Technology specially designed to aid individuals with disabilities; examples are alternative computer keyboards for students with physical needs and talking wristwatches for students who are blind.

For Your Information

How Today's Students Use Technology

Here are highlights from a recent report from the National Center for Education Statistics of the U.S. Department of Education (DeBell & Chapman, 2003a) on how U.S. children and adolescents use technology.

- *Most children and adolescents use ... technologies.* About 90% of children and adolescents ages 4–17 (47 million people) use computers, and about 59% (31 million persons) use the Internet.
- *Use begins at an early age.* About three-quarters of 5-year-olds use computers, and over 90% of teens (ages 13–17) do so. . . .
- *There is a "digital divide."* Computer and Internet use are divided along demographic and socioeconomic lines. . . .
- *Disability, urbanicity, and household type are factors in the digital divide. . . .* 5- through 17-year-olds without a disability are more likely to use computers and the Internet than their disabled peers, and children and adolescents living outside of central cities are more likely to use computers than those living in central cities. . . .
- *There are no differences between the sexes in overall computer or Internet use rates. . . .*
- *More children and adolescents use computers at school (81 percent) than at home (65 percent). . . .*
- *Use of home computers for playing games and for work on school assignments are common activities. . . .*
- *Home is the most common location for Internet access, followed by school. . . .*
- *Many disadvantaged children and adolescents use the Internet only at school. . . .*
- *Considering all locations, use of the Internet for work on school assignments, e-mail, and games are common activities.* (pp. iv–vii)

Note: From *Computer and Internet Use by Children and Adolescents in 2001: Statistical Analysis Report* (pp. iv–vii) by M. DeBell & C. Chapman (2003a). U.S. Department of Education, National Center for Education Statistics: Washington, DC. Retrieved August 17, 2004, from *http://nces.ed.gov/pubsearch/pubsinfo.asp?pubid= 2004014.* This material is not copyrighted.

Federal laws for students with disabilities require that schools consider the possible need for **assistive technology** devices and services when developing IEPs. An assistive technology device, according to federal law, is defined as

> any item, piece of equipment, or product system, whether acquired commercially off the shelf, modified, or customized, that is used to increase, maintain, or improve the functional capabilities of a child with a disability. [PL 108-446, Section 602 (1)].

In contrast, an assistive technology service is "any service that directly assists a child with a disability in the selection, acquisition, or use of an assistive technology device" [PL 108-446, Section 602 (2)].

Advantages and Disadvantages of Technology

Computers and other technologies are versatile tools that can be used for a variety of educational purposes. They offer several potential advantages including these four:

- *Technology allows individualization of instruction.* A case in point is the computer. Computers are also called personal computers (PCs) because they are intended for use by one person; they are a technology for individuals. If there were 30 students in a classroom, each sitting at a computer, these students could be engaged in activities in 30 different content areas. Or they could all be working on the same content, but each at the skill level appropriate for his or her level of learning. In addition, most computer programs allow learners to proceed at their own pace.
- *Technology motivates students.* Novelty is an important factor in motivation, and technology is still a new enough instructional medium to excite students' interest. In addition, students often perceive technology-based learning activities as more like play than work. Another motivating feature, particularly for students with learning needs, is that many software programs provide feedback to the learner in a nonjudgmental manner. If the student makes an error, the program simply says, "Not quite, Olivia. Try again."
- *Technology allows new types of learning and new ways of accomplishing old tasks.* With computers, teachers can provide students with a variety of learning experiences not usually possible in a traditional classroom setting. For example, using computer programs called simulations, students might learn to manage a small business, command troops in a Civil War battle, conduct a series of chemistry experiments, or travel to Jupiter. By interacting with the **World Wide Web,** students can move beyond classroom walls to visit the White House, see NASA's latest expedition, learn about current exhibits at the Smithsonian, check the status of the stock market, and interact with students in classrooms throughout the world.

Computers also provide new ways of doing old tasks. With word processing programs, for example, writing becomes a somewhat different process. As soon as the writer has entered text into the program, that text can be modified and manipulated quickly and easily. The writer can add or delete words or phrases, change the order of sentences or paragraphs, format the text in many different ways, and even add graphics. This flexibility makes writing an easier task for students because errors are less difficult to correct.

- *Technology helps students with special needs bypass or compensate for disabilities.* Computers and other technologies permit many students with special needs to bypass physical or sensory limitations so that they can take part in general education classroom activities. For example, a student who is paralyzed and able only to nod his head can "type" on a computer by using a special switch mounted on the headrest of his wheelchair. Or a student who is blind can use a computer to translate her Braille essay into regular print that her teacher can read. Computers can also help students compensate for their difficulties in basic academic skills. Students who spell poorly, for example, can write with a word processor, then use a spelling checker program to help locate and correct misspelled words.

There are also potential disadvantages to classroom technology use. Computers are only as good as the software programs they run or the websites to which they connect. Selection of appropriate instructional activities is critical. Not all technology-based learning tasks use sound principles of instruction. Although a wide selection of educational software is now available and the Internet offers a vast supply of potential resources, it may not be possible to find a program or website that fits the content, level, and interest needs of a particular student. In addition, although research shows that technology such as computers can improve student performance (Sivin-Kachala & Bialo, 1996), most applications do not provide field-test data to support their effectiveness.

Another potential area of difficulty is access to computer equipment and other technologies. A school may have a limited supply of state-of-the-art computers; and, if computers aren't available in the classroom, teachers may need to schedule their students in a central computer lab or media center for a limited time each week. In addition, technology quickly becomes outdated as new versions are introduced, and software designed to run on newer computer systems may not work on older ones. Another major consideration is cost. Technology is not an inexpensive addition to the teacher's instructional arsenal.

Universal Design and Accessibility for All

The principle of **universal design,** although often discussed in relation to technology, is relevant to all aspects of education

(Cawley, Foley, & Miller, 2003; Edyburn, 2004). Most simply, universal design is "an approach to the design of all products and environments to be usable by everyone, to the greatest extent possible, regardless of age, ability, or situation" (Center for Universal Design, 2004). An early example familiar to everyone is the curb cut. Although curb cuts make it easier for individuals who travel by wheelchair to negotiate curbs and cross the street, they also assist many others such as persons pushing baby strollers, toddlers learning to climb up and down steps, students pulling backpacks on wheels, and people who walk with a cane or crutches.

When students with special needs are members of general education classrooms, it is often necessary to adapt curriculum, modify instructional procedures, or change the ways in which students demonstrate how much they've learned. As chapter 4 discussed, teachers individualize instruction, differentiate to meet various students' needs, and make accommodations in how information is presented and the ways in which students respond. When the principles of universal design are applied to education, that flexibility is built in. Accessibility to all is considered when curriculum is developed, not later when it becomes more difficult to make changes. CAST, the Center for Applied Technology (2003), describes this approach:

> The central practical premise of UDL [Universal Design for Learning] is that a curriculum should include alternatives to make it accessible and appropriate for individuals with different backgrounds, learning styles, abilities, and disabilities in widely varied learning contexts. The "universal" in universal design does not imply one optimal solution for every-

one. Rather, it reflects an awareness of the unique nature of each learner and the need to accommodate differences, creating learning experiences that suit the learner and maximize his or her ability to progress.

Introducing universal design features in the development of a technology, a learning material, or a curriculum increases accessibility for all and reduces the need for after-the-fact adaptations.

One technology example is the Macintosh computer, which incorporates a range of universal access features. Among the built-in preferences for the Macintosh operating system are adaptations for persons who have difficulties seeing, hearing, using the keyboard, and using the mouse. For example, persons with low vision can activate the zoom feature to enlarge whatever is on the screen. Individuals who encounter problems using the mouse can activate Mouse Keys and move the pointer around the screen by pressing on the numeric keypad.

USING COMPUTERS FOR INSTRUCTION

Computer-assisted instruction takes place when computers are used as tutors to deliver instruction or aid in practice activities. In this application, computers serve as a type of instructional technology. Several types of computers are found in schools today, ranging from the most modern high-end machines to less powerful older models. However, all computer systems share the same five basic components.

The first basic component is the input device, or the method used to send information to the computer. The most common input devices are the computer keyboard and the mouse. Output devices such as the computer monitor and speakers are the second component type. They convey information from the computer to the user. Assistive technologies for students with disabilities often involve modifications to computer input and output modes.

The central processing unit (CPU), the third component, is the brain of the computer. It directs information flow and controls all operations. The fourth component, memory, is where information is stored within the computer. Computers are described by the amount of memory they contain and by the speed of their central processor; the more memory and speed, the better.

The fifth component is storage. In the early years of school computing, computer disks (sometimes called *diskettes*) were used to store information for later use. Zip disks are still used for this purpose, although the trend is toward the use of media such as CDs and DVDs with much larger capacities. One CD or compact disc can store a tremendous amount of information: approximately 250,000 pages of text, 15 hours of recorded audio, or 15,000 color photos (Holzberg, 1991; Oehring, 1992; Salpeter, 1988). DVDs or digitial video discs are characterized by "huge capacity, backward compatibility with CD technology, the potential for video quality that surpasses that of laserdisc, multichannel sound quality far better than that of audio CD, and great interactive-multimedia capabilities" (Shatz-Akin, 1997, p. 74).

Multimedia is one of the hallmarks of modern educational computing. Today's computers and software programs typically present information to users via a combination of several different media: text, graphics, animation, video, audio, and high-quality photos and artwork. In addition, modern multimedia programs are often **hypermedia** rather than traditional, linear software. In traditional software, the program controls the sequence of events and the way in which the user moves from one activity to another. In most cases, the progression is linear: activity 1, activity 2, and so on. Hypermedia applications are quite different. The user is presented with choices so that he or she can take greater control over the flow of interactions with the program. It is possible to choose all or none of the options available, and it is up to the user to determine in which order the selections are made.

One good example of hypermedia is how users interact with websites on the World Wide Web. Most web pages contain links that allow users to make choices about moving to different parts of the website or to different sites. For instance, at the website for the San Diego Zoological Society, students can move from the introductory page to pages that feature natural habitats at the zoo such as the Gorilla Tropics and Polar Bear Plunge, videos of the animals plus live feeds from video cameras such as the Panda Cam, or an interactive map and other information for visitors.

Instructional Software

Educational software was once a scarce commodity, but that is certainly not the case today. Thousands of instructional software programs are now available. Most current programs are technically excellent, many are educationally sound, and the number and variety of instructional programs continue to increase.

Instructional programs are available for most areas of the school curriculum, including basic skills subjects such as reading, spelling, writing, and mathematics as well as content-area subjects such as science, social studies, and history. There is instructional software for preschool children, programs to teach computer literacy and programming skills, and programs that address the development of prevocational and vocational skills.

Software can also be classified by the type of instructional mode used to present the content. Among the most common types are tutorials, drill-and-practice programs, and simulations. Descriptions of these and other types of instructional programs appear in Table 8-1.

TABLE 8-1	Types of Instructional Software	
SOFTWARE TYPE	**DESCRIPTION**	**EXAMPLE**
Tutorials	Tutorials present content that is new to the learner. They introduce and explain new skills or information and then supervise the student's first attempts to practice and apply this new material.	*Typing Tutor*
Drill-and-practice programs	Drill-and-practice programs review material introduced previously, giving practice so that performance can improve. Most such programs provide immediate feedback on the accuracy of responses; many impose speed demands. A variation is the *arcade-type* drill, which uses game features to motivate learners.	*Math Blaster*
Simulations	Simulation programs provide experience in situations difficult or impossible to duplicate in the classroom. For instance, students might travel to Mars or manage a presidential campaign. These programs provide students with information about situations they will encounter and then ask them to make decisions.	*Oregon Trail*
Problem-solving programs	Not tied to any one curriculum area, these programs present problems for students to solve. Students can practice critical thinking and acquire skills in problem analysis and solution.	*Thinking Things*
Discovery programs	In this type of software, students are encouraged to explore a rich learning environment. There is no attempt to teach specific content and no right or wrong answers.	*Living Books Library* (e.g., *Arthur's Birthday Party*)
Educational games	This type of software includes computer-based versions of traditional board, card, and paper-and-pencil games as well as other possibilities such as adventure games and quiz-show-type programs.	*Scrabble, Chessmaster*

Inclusion Tips for the Teacher

Principles for Evaluating Instructional Software

Try Before You Buy

There is no substitute for sitting down at the computer with a program and trying it out. Many software companies offer trial or demonstration versions of their programs for teachers to download from their websites and try out. When previewing a program is simply not possible, software reviews can provide critical information about a program's value.

Evaluate with Particular Students in Mind

A program may be appropriate for one group of learners but not for another; for example, it may meet the needs of kindergarten students but be much too juvenile for third graders. Take into account not only students' current grade in school but also their skill levels (which may differ from school placement) and any special needs they may have.

Look Carefully at the Program's Content and Mode of Instruction

Teachers should first consider what the software publisher says about the general purpose of the program, then review the program to form their own opinions. The fact that a program is labeled as reading software does not necessarily mean that it teaches reading skills; it could ask students to spell words, not read them. The mode of instruction is also a concern. Many programs advertised as tutorials are, in reality, drill programs.

Determine Whether the Program Makes Use of the Computer's Capabilities

The hallmark of the computer as an instructional device is its ability to interact with the learner. Programs that appear to be electronic textbooks (or, as some call them, electronic page turners) do not capitalize on the computer's capabilities. Programs should be more than software translations of instructional materials that exist (or should exist) in print form.

Consider the Demands Placed on the Student

The demands that software places on students, over and above those of the instructional content, can prevent students from being successful. There are five areas of concern:

1. *Computer use demands.* Before using any type of software, students must learn to operate the computer. More complicated programs may pose problems for young or inexperienced computer users.
2. *Academic demands.* One academic skill may be needed to profit from a program, even if the program addresses a different skill. For example, math, science, and social studies programs often require students to read text or to type in correctly spelled words. Demands such as these

may be a major barrier for students with academic learning problems.

3. *Physical demands.* Students respond in most programs by typing on the keyboard or moving the mouse. Keyboarding responses range from pressing any key (a response mode used in discovery programs for preschoolers) to typing words or connected text. However, some students with physical impairments may require assistive devices to enter information without using either the keyboard or mouse.
4. *Speed demands.* Some programs present information quickly and students cannot regulate the speed with which information appears on the screen; other programs require students to respond within a time limit. When programs are under user control, the student controls the pace and spends as much time as needed on any one part of the program.
5. *Accuracy demands.* Programs differ in how they handle errors. In some, students can type responses, then make corrections before signaling that they have finished; in others, the first response typed is considered the final response. Also, some programs provide prompts when responses are close to correct ("Did you mean to type *yes* instead of *yse?*").

Check the Adequacy of Instructional Procedures

There are several factors to evaluate in relation to instruction: the directions given to students, the accuracy of the program's content and how clearly it is presented, how feedback is presented to students, how the program reacts when students make errors, and what techniques are used to reinforce students for correct responses.

Evaluate the Program's Motivational Value

One way to determine a program's motivational value is to try it out with students to see how they like it. However, students may like a program at first but quickly tire of it. Programs that include game features may motivate reluctant learners. Also important is the interest level of the program. Programs with nursery rhyme characters will be insulting to middle school students, even if content and skill levels are appropriate.

Look for Program Flexibility

Flexible programs allow users to make choices. For example, students may be able to select from a range of different activities, determine the number of questions they will attempt, and choose the difficulty level of those questions. Teachers may be able to turn the program sound on or off, set the number of questions to be presented, and control important instructional variables, such as the amount of time allowed for responding. Some programs also record data on student performance and allow teachers to customize by adding new content.

See Whether the Documentation Is Clear and Complete

Print, on-screen, or web-based documentation should provide a full, clear explanation of the purpose of the software and its method of operation. Any available field-test data should be reviewed to see whether they support the program's effectiveness. Sometimes documentation suggests classroom learning activities to supplement or extend the program's content.

Making a Decision

All of these factors must be considered in deciding whether a particular software program should be incorporated as one of the classroom's instructional resources. Advantages and disadvantages must be weighed against each other to make the final determination.

Inclusion Tips for the Teacher

Ten Reasons for Automatically Rejecting a Program

Although Lathrop (1982) wrote these guidelines more than two decades ago, her words continue to ring true.

A few short years ago, we were generally pleased if a program would run. Today we demand much more from the courseware that we purchase. My "Terrible Ten" may differ from yours. Each of us applies our own criteria to the evaluation process. Yet I urge you to reject programs with any of the negative factors outlined here and to communicate to the publisher your reasons for the rejection. Our refusal to purchase courseware that is merely "adequate" can help to upgrade the overall quality of the instructional software market.

1. *Audible response to student errors.* Drill and practice programs are the worst offenders. They are most frequently used by the less able students, and NO student should be forced to advertise to the entire class that s/he has just made another mistake.
2. *Rewarding failure.* Hangman programs are classic examples of making it more fun to fail, by use of clever graphics, than to succeed.
3. *Any sound that cannot be controlled.* Sound can be effective as motivation or reward, but it is often distracting in the classroom or library media center. Constant repetition of the same sound also becomes annoying.
4. *Technical problems.* Programs marketed today MUST run smoothly without errors.
5. *Uncontrolled screen advance.* It is frustrating to have the screen advance while you are still reading it, and it is boring to wait for long seconds after finishing it. It is unnecessary to guess how long a screen should be displayed; let the user control the speed.
6. *Inadequate instructions.* We are no longer willing to guess how to operate a program.
7. *Errors of any kind.* Mistakes in factual content, spelling, grammar, etc., are totally unacceptable.
8. *Insults, sarcasm and derogatory remarks.* Students MUST NOT be attacked or belittled by the program.
9. *Poor documentation.* Instructional objectives, suggested student activities, instructions for teacher modification of the program and other classroom-related information should be standard with good courseware.
10. *Denial of a back-up copy.* If publishers insist on copy-locking their software, they should provide one free back-up copy. We are responsible for showing our good faith by refusing to make or to accept illegal copies of software for classroom use and by using our back-up copy for archival purposes only.

Note: From "The Terrible Ten in Educational Programming (My Top Ten Reasons for Automatically Rejecting a Program)" by A. Lathrop, 1982, *Educational Computer*, 2(5), p. 34. Copyright 1982 by *Educational Computer*.

One of the most important decisions educators face in the use of computers is the selection of appropriate software (Forgan & Weber, 2001). Good-quality software is the key to effective classroom computer use. Software is what brings the computer to life, what transforms the potential instructional value of this technology into a classroom reality. For assistance in making decisions about which instructional software programs best fit student needs, consult the "Inclusion Tips for the Teacher" section for principles for evaluating software.

After all of the evaluation factors have been considered, it is up to the teacher to decide whether the instructional program is worth adding to the classroom software collection. No piece of software will be perfect in every respect. Instead, it is necessary to weigh the advantages and disadvantages to determine whether a program will be a useful addition to the instructional resources already available within the classroom. However, certain characteristics immediately signal an unsatisfactory program. One expert's 10 reasons for automatically rejecting a program appear in the "Inclusion Tips for the Teacher" box.

TECHNOLOGY TOOLS FOR STUDENTS AND TEACHERS

Word processing programs are the software tools most widely used in school programs not only by students but also by teachers. Word processors present the user with the computer equivalent of a blank sheet of paper—an empty screen—and then provide a system for entering text onto that screen. Their main value, however, is the ease with which that text can be changed and manipulated. The writer can correct errors quickly and easily, alter the sequence and format of the text, and then store what has been written for later use.

Today's word processors routinely offer such features as spelling checkers, thesauruses, and the ability to import photos and other graphics, video, and Internet links. Programs specially designed for younger children may provide simpler operation and large-sized text. Others have the capacity to talk so that students can hear the text they have written read aloud.

Another variety of software tool often used in education is the **idea processor** or, as some call it, the concept mapping program (Puckett, 2004). This type of software helps students and teachers generate, manipulate, and organize their thoughts and ideas, usually in a visual format. Perhaps the best known examples are the *Inspiration* program and the version for younger students, *Kidspiration*.

Database management programs are popular with teachers, and students use them in some content-area subjects. Database programs assist in the organization and management of large bodies of information; in effect, they create a computer-based filing system. The user determines the type of information to be stored and the exact data to be included in each record. The major value of such a record-keeping system is that, once the information has been stored, it can be sorted and retrieved quickly and easily.

Integrated productivity programs may offer both a word processor and database management system (as well as other features such as **spreadsheets** for manipulating numerical information). The best known integrated productivity package is Microsoft Office. School versions of this package typically include a word processor, spreadsheet, an e-mail program, and a presentation tool. The **information presentation tool,** PowerPoint, assists students and teachers to organize and display many types of information (text, still and animated graphics, video, and sound) as computer- or web-based presentations.

Creativity tools aid in the design, development, and presentation of many different creative products including graphics and other types of visual arts, music, photographs, and movies. Also available are creativity tools for the development of web pages, websites, and web-based learning activities.

Among the software tools designed specially for teachers are those that help manage information about students. Examples are gradebook programs, software for managing and evaluating student portfolios, and programs to help in the development of IEPs for students with disabilities. Also available are tools for preparing instructional materials such as programs to generate crossword puzzles and word finds, special word processing fonts for creating handwriting practice activities, and programs that generate math fact worksheets.

Some of the most useful tools for educators and students are handheld devices, rather than computer applications. One example is the handheld spelling checker used in many classrooms. With the Franklin Spelling Ace®, for instance, students type in their best guess of a word's spelling and the aid provides them with a list of possible alternatives. Similar devices include electronic dictionaries, thesauruses, and foreign language aids. Also of interest are **personal digital assistants** (PDAs), handheld devices that offer a range of capabilities including scheduling, notetaking, storage of information such as e-books, and wireless transmission of information. In some schools, teachers use PDA technology to record information on student progress and performance. For more information on educational applications of PDAs, visit the K12 Handhelds website (http://www.k12handhelds.com).

THE INTERNET AS AN INSTRUCTIONAL TOOL

Perhaps the biggest change in educational technology in the past 10 years is the entry of the Internet into the classroom. As a recent National Center for Education Statistics study (DeBell & Chapman, 2003b) reports, in 2002 virtually every public school in the United States had Internet access, and that access was by broadband connection. Most schools (86%) had a presence on the web with their own web page or website. Also, 99% of the schools with Internet access were concerned enough about safeguarding students from inappropriate content that access was controlled in some way.

The Internet is a worldwide computer network. Begun in the 1970s as a U.S. military research project (Posth, 1997), it has evolved into a communication system that today reaches literally millions of people across the globe. The World Wide Web (WWW) is not quite the same as the Internet. According to the online encyclopedia Webopedia (2004), the web is "an information-sharing model that is built on top of the Internet." Sites on the web are multimedia; they often include not only text but also graphics, photos, music, voice, sound effects, video, and even live camera feeds.

The range of information available on the web is truly astounding. Information can be found on almost any subject, and it is possible to use the web for a variety of purposes including online shopping; "visiting" another state, another country, or even another planet; communication with family, friends, and professional colleagues; and getting up-to-the-minute news and weather, to name but a few possibilities. Among this vast array of options are valuable instructional resources for general education teachers who serve students with disabilities and other special needs.

Browsing the Web

Website addresses are everywhere. Turn on the TV, read a newspaper or magazine, pick up a catalog, or listen to the radio and you'll find something like

http://www.anyschool.edu

This address of a site on the World Wide Web is called a URL (pronounced "U-R-L") or Uniform Resource Locator. The first part of the address is a command. The letters *http* stand for HyperText Transfer Protocol. The letters *www* stand for the World Wide Web, and the middle portion of the address (*anyschool* in the example above) is a short name for the website. The last three letters indicate the type of site. For example, education sites are designated *edu,* government sites *gov,* sites of organizations *org,* and commercial sites *com.* When a URL is read aloud, a period in the address is read as "dot."

Sometimes a URL will be longer. That indicates that it is the address of a specific portion of a website. For example, in the website for an educational publisher, there may be a separate section for instructional software. To reach that section, the URL might be

http://www.anypublisher.com/software/index.html

The last letters of the address, *html* (or sometimes *htm*)stand for HyperText Markup Language, a computer language used to create web documents.

When the URL for a website is known, it is easy to access that site. The user logs onto the web, starts up a web browser software program (e.g., Internet Explorer), and opens a website. Usually that involves typing the URL in its entirety.

It is often possible to determine the URL of a company or organization by making an educated guess. For example, the URL for the software publisher Broderbund is http://www.broderbund.com. However, sometimes the guessing strategy does not work. For example, the web address for the Council for Exceptional Children is not http://www.cec.org, as would be predicted. Instead, it is http://www.cec.sped.org. When a URL is not available or predictable, it is necessary to search the web, a procedure that will be explained in a later section.

Navigation Techniques

When a user first starts up a web browser software program, that program goes directly to a home page. A home page can be any website. When purchased, programs are typically set to the website of their publisher. This can be changed to any other site. For example, a teacher might want the school's website to be his or her home page.

Most web pages contain links that allow movement to other locations, either within the same website or to other sites. When text is underlined, that signals that it is linked to something else. Consider this excerpt from a student's webpage:

I like all kinds of animals but especially <u>cats</u>. I used to live in <u>Chicago</u> but now I live in <u>San Diego</u>.

Three links are available: cats, Chicago, and San Diego. Clicking on the word <u>cats</u> could move the user to a photo of the student's cats (within the same page) or to an article on cats in an online encyclopedia (in a different website). Clicking on a city name might bring up the website sponsored by that city's tourist bureau.

Links are also found in graphics. In many websites, the first page contains a graphical menu that allows users to go to the section of the site in which they're interested. That graphical menu could be a menu bar with words describing the parts of the website, a drawing depicting the site, or a series of photos. In most cases where there are graphical links, text links are also provided, although these may be in very small print.

In a typical session on the web, a user begins with one website, selects links within that site, and then moves to another site either by selecting a link in the first site or by typing in another URL. This process is usually repeated several times. For example,

Exemplary Art Museum (first website)

Modern Art (part of first site)

Impressionism (part of first site)

Renoir (part of first site)

France (second website)

Paris (part of second site)

At some point in the session, the user may want to return to one of the pages visited previously. To return to the last page visited, the Back command is used. In the preceding example, if the user is on the Paris page, using the Back command would move him or her to the France page. The Forward command moves the user forward. Choosing forward from the France page would move the user to the Paris page. Another method is to use the special history menu in the web browser program (e.g., the Go menu in Internet Explorer). That menu lists the sites visited in the session and any one can be selected. It also lists Home as an option, if the user wants to return to the home page.

Bookmarks are another important feature of most web browsers. A bookmark records the URL of a website so that it can easily be accessed in the future. Whenever users find an interesting website, they can go to the Bookmark menu and choose the command to add a bookmark. The name of the website will then be listed on the Bookmark menu, and selecting that name will move the user to the website. The bookmark file can be edited, and it can be saved so that it can be shared with others.

Search Strategies

One of the most powerful features of the World Wide Web is the ability to search all of its websites. With just a few keystrokes, teachers and students have the ability to shift through literally millions of web pages to locate information on a specific topic. That topic can be very broad (e.g., educational reform) or quite narrow (e.g., hearing ear dogs for people with hearing impairments). It can be professional in nature or relate to more personal concerns (e.g., Hawaiian vacations, clogged toilets, the care and feeding of gerbils).

To search the web, the user goes to one of the many sites that provide search services. According to the Search Engine Watch website (Sullivan, 2004), the three top choices for search services are google.com, yahoo.com, and askjeeves.com. Also mentioned as good to consider were the search services alltheweb.com, aolsearch.aol.com, and hotbot.com.

The basic procedure for searches is quite simple. The user types in a descriptor (e.g., disability), clicks on "search," and the search service generates a list of "hits," that is, websites that match the descriptor. That list contains links to each of the matching sites and usually brief descriptions of them. In most cases, the most relevant sites (the ones with the closest match to the descriptor) appear first in the list.

The search engine in each service works a bit differently, and this results in varying numbers of hits from one service to another. For example, on a recent search for *disability*, Google and Yahoo reported more than 13 million hits, HotBot almost 3 million hits, and AOL Search around one-half million hits. Search services typically provide information on the way in which they go about searching the web so that users can make informed choices about which service to select for a specific purpose.

One of the problems that often occurs is that a search produces too many hits. Search services offer different ways of handling this problem, but most allow users to modify their search terms to narrow the scope of their search. For example, with Google's Advanced Search feature, it is possible to search for web pages that include *all* of the terms in the search query (e.g., searching for pages that include these terms in any order: "baseball," "girls," and "home runs"). Other possibilities are searching for exact phrases, searching for pages that include at least one of several search terms, and searching for pages that do *not* include specific terms.

The web is a rich source of valuable resources for teachers and students alike. To locate these resources, it would be possible to search the web using a descriptor such as "websites for teachers." A recent Google search with these search terms resulted in more than 3 million hits. This number could be reduced by adding additional descriptors such as age or grade levels or specific school subjects (e.g., reading, math, history, music). For information on a handful of useful sites, consult the "Window on the Web" feature.

Evaluating Websites

One of the primary advantages of the web, the vast number and variety of the resources it offers, is also its major disadvantage. It is quite easy for students and their teachers, overwhelmed with the quantity of Internet resources, to fail to pay sufficient attention to a much more important concern: the quality of web-based information. Because anyone can publish a website and there are no referees to determine if the information presented is even true, the World Wide Web is truly a "buyer beware" information marketplace.

Several excellent guides are available for use by teachers and other professionals in evaluating the quality of web-based resources. The Cornell University Library presents a number of evaluation resources on its website:

http://www.library.cornell.edu/olinuris/ref/research/webeval.html

One example is the set of five criteria that Kapoun (1998) suggests for evaluating websites. These criteria are

- accuracy,
- authority,
- currency,
- objectivity, and
- coverage.

In Kapoun's discussion of these criteria, he urges users to examine web pages with an attitude of skepticism. In Kapoun's words, "View any Web page as you would an infommercial on television. Ask yourself why was this written and for whom?"

Like their teachers, students also need to develop skill in evaluating web content. Schrock (2004) has developed a set of tools for students to use as they begin to learn how to critically evaluate websites. Guides are available for elementary grade, middle school level, and secondary school level students as well as Spanish language versions of all three guides. Another resource is the Web Site Evaluation Form designed in 2001 by Ron Goral and Joanne Lenburg of the Madison Metropolitan School District in Madison, Wisconsin. That form appears in the "Inclusion Tips for the Teacher" section.

E-Mail and Other Resources

E-mail, or electronic mail, is a quick, easy way to communicate with others who have access to the Internet. E-mail is provided as part of most educational and commercial Internet services. E-mail addresses take this format:

username@anyschool.edu

The first part of the address specifies the person. This person can be found at (signified by the symbol @) a particular

Window on the Web

Websites for Teachers

Federal Resources for Educational Excellence (FREE)

http://www.ed.gov/free/index.html

This site provides access to thousands of teaching and learning resources compiled by 35 different federal organizations including the Library of Congress, NASA, Smithsonian Institution, and the National Gallery of Art. New resources are added daily. Resources can be accessed by subject (e.g., arts, language arts, mathematics) or by searching the entire collection.

PBS TeacherSource

http://www.pbs.org/teachersource/

Sponsored by the Public Broadcasting System (PBS), this site contains more than 4,500 lesson plans and activities, some with connections to PBS videos. The site can be searched by keyword or the teacher can choose a subject (e.g., arts and literature, social studies), a grade range, and a topic. For instance, if a teacher selected "health and fitness," "grades 3–5," and "safety," some of the resources that might be identified are "Because Accidents Happen: Fire," "Challenging TV Violence," and "Building a Classroom Community and Bully-Free Zone."

Kathy Schrock's Guide for Educators

http://school.discovery.com/schrockguide/

Part of the website of the Discovery Channel, this site describes itself as a frequently updated "categorized list of sites useful for enhancing curriculum and professional growth." Teachers can access information by selecting from more than 20 different subjects (from Agricultural Education to World Languages/Regions) and by choosing one of the many "Teacher Helpers" (e.g., Assessment & Rubrics). Other features include "Site of the Day," search tools, and links to Discovery School activities such as Brain Boosters, Clip Art Gallery, Puzzlemaker, and Science Fair Central.

Education World

http://www.education-world.com/

Education World is a commercial site full of useful tools and information for teachers and administrators. The site menu includes six areas: Lesson Planning, Administrator's Desk, School Issues, Professional Development, Technology Integration, and More Resources. New resources are added frequently. For example, on one visit to the site, among the new additions were a "show-biz" science lesson, a geography worksheet, and a number cross puzzle.

Teacher Planet

http://www.teacherplanet.com

Another commercial site, Teacher Planet contains collections of lesson plans for teachers, theme units, worksheets, teacher tools, rubrics, and much more. The site's home page features a calendar with the current month's holidays and special events noted, and instructional resources are linked to each special date.

For more information, go to the Web Links module in Chapter 8 of the Companion Website.

---

school or district, and this location is an educational institution. Thus, a teacher's address might be

pqsmith@longhornelem.edu

Like URLs, e-mail addresses from businesses or commercial Internet providers end in *com* (e.g., mrchips@aol.com). E-mail addresses from other countries end in a country code such as *ca* for Canada, *jp* for Japan, *se* for Sweden, and *uk* for the United Kingdom.

Sending e-mail is quite simple. Using an e-mail program such as Outlook or Eudora (or the e-mail section of a commercial Internet provider), the user chooses "New Message."

Inclusion Tips for the Teacher

Helping Students Evaluate Websites

Web Site Evaluation Form

Site Name: _____

Site Address/URL: http:// _____

(Respond to all questions below. Leave blank any question that does not apply.)

Consider WHO is responsible for the web site:

- Does the publisher appear to be knowledgeable about the content?   ____ YES   ____ NO
- Does the publisher qualify as an authority or expert on the topic?   ____ YES   ____ NO
- Can you contact the publisher from the site?   ____ YES   ____ NO
- Is the site's sponsor identified?   ____ YES   ____ NO

Consider WHAT is the content/subject matter of the web site:

- Does the content appear to be accurate? Error free?   ____ YES   ____ NO
- Is the information presented in an objective manner, with a minimum of bias?   ____ YES   ____ NO
- Is there real depth-of-content (vs. information that is limited and superficial)?   ____ YES   ____ NO
- Are links from the site appropriate and/or supportive of the content?   ____ YES   ____ NO
- Does the content have educational or informational value?   ____ YES   ____ NO

Consider WHERE the web site resides:

- What type of domain is this site?   ____.gov   ____.com   ____.edu   ____.org   ____.net   ____.biz   Other _____
- Is this a personal page with a "~" or ".name" in the URL?   ____ YES   ____ NO

Consider WHEN the web site was last updated:

- Is the information current?   ____ YES   ____ NO
- Does the site provide information on when it was last updated?   ____ YES   ____ NO
- Does a current date matter?   ____ YES   ____ NO

Consider HOW the main page looks and functions:

- Is the page easy to understand and use?   ____ YES   ____ NO
- Is the page well organized?   ____ YES   ____ NO
- Does the page load in a reasonable amount of time?   ____ YES   ____ NO
- Do all of the links work?   ____ YES   ____ NO
- Is the page free from (excessive amounts of) advertising?   ____ YES   ____ NO

Consider WHY the web site exists:

- Is the site trying to
  - sell something?   ____ YES   ____ NO
  - inform?   ____ YES   ____ NO
  - persuade?   ____ YES   ____ NO
- Is the web site appropriate for your target audience?   ____ YES   ____ NO
- Is the Internet the best place to find this information (vs. books, journals, etc.)?   ____ YES   ____ NO

Comments:

Name/School: _____

Date: _____

Note: Website Evaluation Form developed by Ron Goral and Joanne Lenburg, 2001. Copyright 2001–2003 Madison Metropolitan School District, Madison, Wisconsin. Retrieved November 6, 2004, from http://www.madison.k12.wi.us/ tnl/detectives/eval form.htm

In most e-mail systems, the user will be asked to provide three types of information: the e-mail address of the person to whom the message should be sent, the subject of the message, and the message itself. A teacher might see something like this:

To:

From: myname@myschool.edu

Subject:

Message:

After "To" the teacher types in the e-mail address of the recipient. It is usually possible to type more than one address here so that the same message can be sent to several recipients. This is a very useful feature when it is necessary to share information across a group of individuals. The "From" space is often filled in automatically by the e-mail program. "Subject" typically is a brief description of the content of the message, and the "Message" area is where the electronic communication is typed. In many e-mail systems, it is also possible to attach computer files to e-mail messages. All sorts of files can be attached, including word processing documents and photos. For example, at many universities, students turn in their written assignments via e-mail.

When users open their e-mail program, they learn whether or not they have received any mail. Usually this information is provided in a list or table that indicates who sent the message, when the message was sent, and the subject. This allows users to scan their incoming mail and decide whether or not to read it. Once a message has been opened and read, the user typically has several options: replying to the message, sending a copy of the message to someone else, printing a copy of the message, and saving or discarding the message. In addition, most e-mail systems provide an electronic address book where users can record the e-mail addresses of persons with whom they correspond.

Newsgroups are electronic bulletin boards where individuals can post messages and read and respond to the messages that others leave. There are separate newsgroups for a very wide variety of topics including educational research, chinchillas, Elvis, genealogy, and movies. The names of newsgroups begin with an abbreviation that indicates their type. For example, those beginning with *alt* are alternative groups, those beginning with *comp* relate to computers, and those beginning with *k12* are designed for educators. Newsgroups related to disabilities include k12.ed.special and alt.disability. The Google website provides assistance in searching for newsgroups. The URL for this service is http://groups.google.com/

Real-time conferencing with other Internet users is also possible. For example, service providers such as America Online offer conference or chat rooms organized by topic. Users "enter" the chat room, then listen and perhaps contribute to the discussion. Electronic discussion groups may also be set up for specific purposes. For instance, a network news site on the web may offer the opportunity for persons to chat with an important news figure. Or, a university professor might set up an online discussion between his or her students and a prominent expert in the field.

Blogs, or web logs, are a more recent addition to the web. According to marketingterms.com, a blog is "a frequent, chronological publication of personal thoughts and Web links." Blogs are made up of journal entries arranged in chronological order, with the most recent appearing first. In many cases, the creator of the blog will include references to other websites and, in some, readers are able to respond to the blogger's message with their own comments. A good source of information about currently available blogs is http://www.blogwise.com. This site allows users to search for blogs by keyword and by country. A recent search located a number of blogs identified by keywords such as "teachers," "education," and "schools."

Newsgroups, online discussions, and blogs can be considered *pull* technologies (Fonner & Zabala, 1997). That is, the user must go to the information source and pull relevant material from it. Browsing the web and using search services would also be examples of pull technologies. In contrast, *push* technologies push relevant information directly to the user. The user specifies the types of information desired and that information is automatically forwarded to him or her.

Listservs are one type of push technology. A listserv is an e-mail mailing list to which a user subscribes. Like other resources on the Internet, listservs are available for a wide variety of topics including education. In fact, most professional organizations offer listservs as a service to their members to keep them updated about what the group is doing. Services such as Federal Resources for Educational Excellence (FREE) may also provide periodic updates to individuals who choose to subscribe.

To subscribe, the user sends an e-mail message to the listserv. The "Subject" portion of the e-mail is left blank. In the message area are three entries: the word SUBSCRIBE, the name of the listserv, and the user's first and last names. For instance, to sign up for the FREE electronic newsletter, a teacher would send an e-mail to listserv@listserv.ed.gov with this information as the message:

SUBSCRIBE EDINFO YOURFIRSTNAME YOURLASTNAME

The first message to be delivered by the listserv will be a notification that the subscription has been received. Then, messages will flow to the user as they are posted to the listserv.

Some listservs do not accept messages from individuals, but many do. It is important to remember when posting a message that it will likely reach everyone who subscribes to that listserv. In some cases, that means hundreds or even thousands of persons. Some listservs are moderated, and the moderator deletes inappropriate messages before they are transmitted to the entire readership. It is easy to be removed from a listserv. The procedure for subscribing is followed except that the message reads UNSUBSCRIBE or UNSUB followed by the name of the listserv.

Another web resource available to teachers is distance learning. As Witherspoon (1996) comments, virtual universities are now a reality. Individuals can enroll in online courses, communicate with instructors and classmates via e-mail, and participate in teleconferences and online discussions. Of course, learning is not limited to formal university education, even on the web. Organizations and agencies also sponsor learning opportunities. For example, the Council for Exceptional Children (CEC) features online workshops and courses as well as live web seminars on various topics.

ASSISTIVE TECHNOLOGIES FOR STUDENTS WITH DISABILITIES

If all of the learning materials, activities, and technologies within the general education classroom had been developed using the principles of universal design, it would not be necessary to discuss computer adaptations and other assistive technologies for students with special learning needs. However, this is not the case, so assistive technology has an important role to play in today's classroom where students with and without disabilities are working side by side. As discussed earlier in this chapter, assistive technology or AT is any type of technology designed specifically for use by persons with disabilities. Although *AT* is a commonly accepted term, Edyburn (2003) argues that "technology-enhanced performance" (p. 20) would be a better way to describe the process by which technology assists persons to bypass or compensate for disabilities.

Computer Adaptations

Some students, such as those with severe physical impairments or those who are blind, cannot interact with a standard computer system unless special adaptations have been made. Assistive technologies allow such students and others with less serious disabilities to use computers for learning. The two major types of adaptations are alternative input devices (i.e., alternatives to or enhancements of the standard computer keyboard) and alternative output devices (i.e., alternatives to or enhancements of the standard computer monitor). In addition, several other types of assistive devices are designed to

meet the instructional needs of learners with physical, sensory, and communication impairments.

Alternatives to the Computer Keyboard.   Special input devices can be used to enhance or bypass the keyboard for students who are not able to enter information into the computer by typing. These devices are most often used with young children, particularly preschoolers, and persons with physical impairments that affect control of hand and finger movement.

Sometimes all that is necessary is a simple adaptation to the standard keyboard or an alternative way of typing on that keyboard. For example, a student who is partially paralyzed but has good control of head and neck muscles might be able to type using a headpointer, a device like a hat or headband with a stick attached. The student positions the pointer on the key to be typed and then depresses that key. A keyguard can be used with a student with tremor. Keyguards are covers that fit over the standard keyboard with holes cut out so that a student can reach down and press one key without touching the keys around it.

Alternate keyboards attach to the computer and bypass the standard keyboard. They may be larger or smaller than the regular keyboard; typically less pressure is required to activate their "keys." Most alternative keyboards are one flat, touch-sensitive surface. Instead of having separate keys, the surface is divided into "key" areas. These areas may be larger than the keys on a standard keyboard, and/or there may be space between them so that the "keys" are easier to locate.

The "key" areas on alternate keyboards are arranged in different ways. Keys may be in the traditional configuration used on typewriters, they may be in alphabetical order for young children, or the keyboard may feature pictures or words rather than individual letters and numbers. One of the most common alternate keyboards, IntelliKeys, is described in a later chapter in one of the "Spotlight on Technology" sections throughout this book. See the "Spotlight" on page 196 to learn more about the types of technologies that will be featured.

Other devices bypass the keyboard by allowing students to respond via the screen of the computer monitor. For example, with a touch screen, the student simply touches the area of the screen where the chosen response is shown. Devices such as these are usually limited to software designed specifically to accept touch input.

Students with severe physical limitations can use switches to interact with computers. Figure 8-1 shows an example of an alternate input mode. A young child interacts with a computer by using a switch. Switch input is possible if the student is able to make some type of consistent movement: a movement of the head from side to side, movement

FIGURE 8-1 — Alternatives to the Standard Computer Keyboard

Note: Photo courtesy of Don Johnston.

of a hand or elbow back and forth, movement of a foot up and down, or even a wrinkling of the eyebrow or a sucking motion. Switches come in many forms to accommodate students' movement repertoires. Examples are plate, leaf, brow wrinkle, and "suck-and-puff" switches. Switches work only with specially designed software unless a special device is added to the computer. These devices make switch input possible with any program by placing an array of letters and numbers somewhere on the screen display. The letters and numbers are scanned (e.g., first the letter A is highlighted, then the letter B, and so on), and the student selects one by pressing the switch.

Scanning through a series of letters or other possible responses is a laborious process. A more efficient (but more expensive) mode of interacting with the computer is speech recognition. With a speech recognition device, the student simply speaks into a microphone to enter information. With some systems, however, the student must first "train" the device to recognize his or her voice; the student's vocabulary is then stored for use with any software.

Alternatives to the Computer Monitor. Alternative output devices bypass or enhance the visual display on the screen of the computer's monitor. One modification often used with students with visual problems is enlargement of the screen display. The regular monitor is replaced with a large-screen monitor, or a magnification device is used to increase the size of the screen display.

Speech can be added to the computer's output for young nonreaders, older students with reading difficulties, and students who are blind. One common way of adding speech is a device called a speech synthesizer; many of the

newer computers come equipped with synthesizers. Speech synthesizers use voice chips that store phonemic rules; words are built or synthesized from phonemes as letters are typed in, and mispronunciations can occur when words do not follow phonemic rules. Synthesized speech typically sounds somewhat robotic, although it is usually clear enough to be intelligible to students. Synthesizers work with programs written to take advantage of their speech capabilities; they do not work with all software. Many of the newer multimedia programs use digitized (rather than synthesized) speech. This higher quality, more natural-sounding speech is produced by recording actual speech and storing it as part of the program.

Software Designed for Students with Special Needs. Some software has been specially designed to accommodate the needs of students with disabilities. For example, talking word processing programs have been developed for students who are blind; when the student types in a letter, a speech synthesizer says the name of that letter as it appears on the screen. The student can also direct the synthesizer to read the program's menus and other on-screen directions and to review what has been written, either letter by letter or as words and sentences. Some beginning reading programs also talk, as do programs designed for students with delayed oral language. In addition, software has been developed to teach everyday living and vocational skills to students with mild cognitive disabilities.

However, most students with special needs can benefit from the software intended for average learners, if that software is well designed (Eiser, 1986; Shepard, 1986). In fact, special educators report that the software they use most often with students with mild disabilities is general education software (Lewis, 1997; Lewis & Harrison, 1988). Although teachers of general education classrooms may need to take extra care in the selection of instructional programs, the range of software available today offers many options appropriate for students with mild learning needs.

Assistive Technologies for Students with Physical Impairments

Mobility is a major need of some students with physical impairments. Some students use standard wheelchairs, that is, chairs they propel with their hands and arms. Others, with limited strength or movement in their upper bodies, use power chairs (or scooters) equipped with motors and batteries. Power chairs are usually controlled by a joystick that the student operates by moving his or her hand, arm, foot, head, or chin.

Spotlight on Technology

Technologies Featured in This Book

Throughout this book, the *Spotlight on Technology* sections highlight applications of technology with special relevance for students with special needs and their teachers. Sometimes, as in chapter 7, the technologies are familiar instructional tools like tape recorders. In other cases, the technologies are less well known but equally useful. In all cases, these sections focus on practical suggestions for the use of technology to improve the inclusion experience.

The table that follows provides a chapter-by-chapter list of the *Spotlight* technologies to be discussed in this book.

Chapter	Chapter Topic	Featured Technology
9	Students with Learning Disabilities and Attention Deficit Hyperactivity Disorders	• Writing Tools for Writers with Special Needs
10	Students with Mild Retardation and Severe Disabilities	• Developing Basic Reading Skills
11	Students with Behavioral Disorders	• Developing Basic Math Skills
		• Improving Reading Comprehension: *Start-to-Finish Books*
12	Students with Communication Disorders	• Augmentative Communication
13	Students with Autism Spectrum Disorder	• Photographic Activity Schedules
		• Using Pictures in an Augmentative Communication System
14	Students with Physical and Health Impairments	• Switch Access
		• The IntelliKeys Keyboard
15	Students with Visual and Hearing Impairments	• Braille Personal Notetakers
		• Classroom Amplification Devices
16	Students Who Are Gifted and Talented	• Webquests and Web Inquiry Projects
17	Culturally and Linguistically Diverse Students	• Software to Assist Language Learners
18	Students at Risk for School Failure	• The Neo Keyboard

Braces and prosthetic devices such as artificial limbs are aids that strengthen or replace portions of the body. In recent years, the design of these devices has improved, and lighter and stronger materials have been used in their construction. These changes have made braces and prosthetic devices more comfortable and better looking, which increases the likelihood that their owners will wear them. Now under development are prostheses that use microprocessors (such as those found in computers) to improve mobility and motor control.

In the classroom, students who have difficulty writing often use computers and calculators with print output. Audiotapes serve several purposes: recording class lectures, "reading" taped texts, and taping assignments or exams so they don't have to be written. Manual or electronic page turners assist students by holding a book in an open position for reading; to turn the page, the student activates the device with a chin or mouth movement.

Communication Aids

Some students are unable to speak, or their speech is very difficult to understand. To bypass this problem, communication aids are used. Communication aids allow students to "talk" by simply pointing or pressing a button. For example, a simple communication board may be a piece of cardboard with pictures, letters, or words on it; a student could point to a picture of a glass to indicate thirst or use an alphabet to spell out greetings or requests.

Electronic communication aids are more sophisticated because they "talk." One type of electronic communication device uses prerecorded speech. Spoken messages are recorded by a family member, teacher, or peer; to "speak," the student simply selects one of the available messages (see Figure 8-2). Other communication devices contain speech synthesizers. The student may spell out words by typing on the device's keyboard or messages may be preprogrammed

Note: Photo courtesy of Attainment Company.

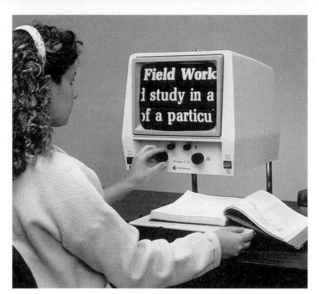

Note: Photo courtesy of Telesensory Company.

so that they can be activated by pressing a single key or a switch. When a word or phrase has been entered, the synthesizer pronounces it.

Assistive Technologies for Students with Visual Impairments

Audio aids help students with visual impairments learn by listening. For example, students can gain access to printed information by listening to tapes of books, magazines, and textbooks. Sometimes tapes use compressed speech; in this mode, the spoken word is speeded up so that large amounts of information can be reviewed in less time. Tape recorders can also be used to tape lectures or class notes so that information is available for later access. A talking calculator resembles a regular pocket calculator, but it provides both a visual and an audible display. When a key is pressed or a calculation completed, the calculator speaks.

Magnification devices enlarge visual images for students able to use their residual vision. Devices called low-vision aids resemble small telescopes or magnifying glasses; they are used to read print and look at visuals such as drawings and maps. Closed-circuit television systems are used to enlarge reading materials; the book or paper is placed on a platform and a video camera projects its image to a monitor that looks like a television screen (see Figure 8-3). Print is greatly enlarged, and the student can control the size and brightness of the display and whether the image is black on a white background or white on a dark background.

Devices that translate print to some other communication mode are designed for students unable to use sight for reading. Most devices convert printed material to synthesized speech. However, some convert print to a tactile image. For example, the Power Braille displays from Freedom Scientific convert information on the computer screen into a tactile Braille display.

Assistive Technologies for Students with Hearing Impairments

Several technologies assist students with hearing impairments to communicate with each other and persons in the hearing world. Hearing aids have become smaller and more versatile as a result of transistors and printed circuits. The four basic types of hearing aids are (1) the body aid (approximately the size of a portable calculator, it is strapped to the body or carried in the pocket and connected by a wire to an earpiece), (2) the behind-the-ear aid that hangs over the ear, (3) the eyeglass aid, and (4) the all-in-the-ear aid. All aids use an ear mold, a plastic earpiece customized to fit the individual. The all-in-the-ear aid contains all electronic components within the earpiece; in other types of aids, the ear mold serves to direct the amplified sound into the ear.

Cochlear implants are becoming more common for some individuals with serious hearing losses. The implants consist of a tiny external microphone, signal processor, and transmitter that are attached to a receiver implanted in the mastoid bone behind the ear, just under the skin. Electrical signals are

Window on the Web

Assistive Technology Resources

Closing the Gap

http://www.closingthegap.com

The Closing the Gap organization offers publications and a yearly conference on applications of technology for persons with disabilities. Its newspaper, *Closing the Gap*, is published six times yearly. The annual print *Resource Directory* is a comprehensive guide to hardware, software, publishers, and organizations related to special education technology. The website provides discussion forums, recent articles and columns from the newspaper, and a demonstration version of Solutions, a new subscription service. Solutions provides access to both current and archived newspaper articles and an online version of the *Resource Directory* with search capabilities.

CAST (Center for Applied Special Technology)

http://www.cast.org

This not-for-profit organization is well known for *Bobby*, a program designed to evaluate websites for their accessibility for persons with disabilities. CAST also has developed software programs such as the *WiggleWorks* reading series and *CAST eReader*, an access tool for electronic text. At present, CAST's focus is on universal design for learning (UDL), and the CAST website is a treasure trove of information on universal design. Among the available resources are Teaching Every Student, web-based learning activities for teachers and other professionals, and online versions of publications such as *Teaching Every Student in the Digital Age* (Rose & Meyer, 2002).

Alliance for Technology Access (ATA)

http://www.ataccess.org

The Alliance for Technology Access is a nationwide network of resource centers, developers, vendors, and others interested in the use of technology by individuals with disabilities. Its website includes a number of useful features such as an online version of the third edition of the ATA resource book, *Computer and Web Resources for People with Disabilities*. (A print version of the updated fourth edition can be ordered on the website.) In the Family Place in Cyberspace on the ATA website are several resources for families. Examples are We Can Play/¡Podemos jugar!, ideas for play activities in English and in Spanish; Access Transition, suggestions for students transitioning from public school to adulthood; and AT in K12, information about integrating technology into educational programs.

For more information, go to the Web Links module in Chapter 8 of the Companion Website.

---

transmitted from the receiver to the intact auditory nerve in the inner ear, bypassing the damaged cochlea or sensory organ. This system converts sounds to electrical signals that are transmitted to the brain for interpretation (Lowenbraun & Thompson, 1986). Although this option is not appropriate for all individuals, it does provide an option to many persons with profound hearing losses, particularly adults who have lost their hearing within the past 2 or 3 years. However, the use of cochlear implants has not been without controversy (D'Antonio, 1993). Representatives of the Deaf community have objected to the use of implants as a method to "fix" deafness, especially for children who are not yet old enough to de-

cide for themselves if they wish to belong to the deaf culture or the hearing culture.

Telecommunication Devices for the Deaf (TDDs) allow persons who are deaf or others who are nonverbal to communicate on the telephone. These devices resemble a portable typewriter or computer; the individual types a message on the keyboard and looks at a visual display for the response. Some TDDs also have printers so that a record of the telephone conversation can be made. The Americans with Disabilities Act requires that all companies providing phone services also provide relay services to allow TDD users and hearing persons to communicate; in effect, the relay operator acts as a translator. When the hearing person speaks, the operator types the message for the TDD user; when the TDD user types a response, the operator reads it aloud. Devices for individuals who are hard of hearing amplify telephone conversations through the handset of the telephone.

Closed captioning allows students with hearing impairments to enjoy regularly scheduled television programs. Written captions transmitted along with the television signal are decoded by a special device and projected onto the screen. The Americans with Disabilities Act requires that all televisions sold in the United States contain built-in decoding devices. Open captioned films and television programs provide captions visible to all viewers and do not require a special decoder. Amplification devices using infrared transmission facilitate television use for viewers who are hard of hearing.

Other types of assistive devices include these:

- Visual alerting systems for the telephone, doorbell, alarm clock, fire alarm, and smoke detector (these use bright strobe lights to attract attention);
- Amplification systems in classrooms, cinemas, theaters, auditoriums, and other public facilities, for use with or without hearing aids; and
- Tactile or vibrating devices for speech therapy, alarm clock systems, and paging systems.

Clearly, classroom computers represent only one of the technologies that can facilitate inclusion of students with disabilities in school and in the community. Assistive technologies such as the ones described in the preceding paragraphs also help students to bypass or compensate for disabilities that could interfere with their ability to succeed in the general education classroom. In addition, new technologies continue to emerge. For more information about resources on special education technologies, see the "Window on the Web" feature.

Web Accessibility

Web accessibility is just as important to students with disabilities as accessibility to other types of learning tools and materials. Because the web is a somewhat new instructional medium, it's important to think about the types of accessibility problems that people might encounter when navigating the web. The Alliance for Technology Access (ATA) describes several types of barriers that might hinder access:

- *Vision barriers.* Information on the web usually requires reading text on the screen. This can be a barrier for people with low vision, for whom the text is too small, and for people who cannot see the text at all.
- *Hearing barriers.* Some websites contain audio clips or QuickTime movies, which include an audio compo-

nent. These can produce a barrier for people who have hearing impairments.
- *Learning or cognitive barriers.* In some cases, the content itself is a barrier. Some people with disabilities have difficulty reading or understanding print material that appears on web pages. Others have difficulty understanding the message portrayed by the graphics.
- *Physical barriers.* The web uses a graphical user interface (GUI), which essentially means that the user points and clicks in order to navigate a web page, using Windows or a Mac. This, with most browser software, requires the use of a mouse, but some people with disabilities find the mouse to be a barrier.
- *Economic barriers.* Understanding the technological capabilities of the visitor to your site can help in designing accessible sites. (Alliance for Technology Access, n.d.)

The Alliance for Technology Access also recommends strategies for overcoming each of these barriers. Visit the ATA site at http://www.ataccess.org and look for the feature on Web Accessibility in the Related Resources portion of the site.

TEACHING WITH TECHNOLOGY

Bringing computers, software, assistive technology, and the World Wide Web into the classroom is only the first step in effective technology use. What must also occur is an integration process, in which technology is "fully included" into the instructional activities of the classroom. Technology is an instructional tool like textbooks and chalkboards. If it is to be used effectively, the teacher must consider it as one of the many resources available to assist in the teaching–learning process. The "Inclusion Tips for the Teacher" box presents the basic principles to consider when integrating computers and other technologies into the general education classroom. These principles underscore the need to consider technology as a tool for accomplishing important educational tasks, not as an end in itself.

This chapter has focused on strategies for the effective use of technology in the general education classroom. The next chapters describe specific techniques for teaching different types of students with special needs. Before turning to chapter 9 and considering students with learning disabilities, consult "Things to Remember" to review the primary concerns in classroom technology use.

Inclusion Tips for the Teacher

Principles for Integrating Technology

1. Start with the curriculum, not the technology. The needs of individual students and the curriculum designed to meet those needs should drive the selection of technologies and the ways in which they are used.

2. Take advantage of the motivational value of technology, but don't limit its use to that of a reward or a leisure time activity. Technology has too much value as a teaching tool to ignore its use in instruction.

3. Use technology to reinforce skills taught by the teacher. Technology can present guided practice activities, monitor students' responses, and provide students with immediate feedback.

4. Select technology activities that match the goals of instruction and the skill levels of individual students. No matter how dazzling the technology or how superb the instructional strategy, teaching an irrelevant skill is a waste of time.

5. Take advantage of the customization options that some technologies offer. Features such as the ability to control content and instructional parameters make it easier to adapt learning activities to students' needs.

6. Monitor students' work at the computer or with other technologies with the same diligence used to monitor other types of classroom work. If performance data are collected by the technology, use that information in making instructional decisions.

7. Use technology to present new information to students. Although technology is certainly not the only instructional strategy available for this purpose, it does provide teachers with an additional resource for introducing new material.

8. Enrich and extend the curriculum through technology. Technology opens doors to experiences that students can't access in other ways, and these experiences can expand both the depth and breadth of the standard curriculum.

9. Teach students to use technologies as tools, then provide opportunities and encouragement for practice. Technology can help students bypass or compensate for disabilities, empowering them to achieve greater levels of independence.

10. Extend the benefits of technology to teachers. Technology is truly mainstreamed when it becomes an important tool not only for students but also for teachers.

Note: From *Special Education Technology: Classroom Applications* by R. B. Lewis. Copyright © 1993 by Brooks/Cole Publishing Company, Pacific Grove, CA. Reprinted by permission of Wadsworth Publishing Co., a division of Thomson Learning: www.thomsonrights.com. Fax 800 730-2215

Things to Remember

- Technology, including both computers and the Internet, is a common feature of U.S. schools and classrooms.
- Three types of technology support education: instructional technology, technology tools, and assistive technology.
- Assistive technology is technology that is specially designed for persons with disabilities.
- Advantages of technology include its capacity for individualizing instruction, motivating students, and allowing new types of learning; technology can also help bypass or compensate for disabilities.
- The principle of universal design suggests that all types of learning activities should be developed with sufficient flexibility so that they are accessible to all learners.
- Computer systems are made up of five parts: input, output, central processing unit, memory, and storage; the most common input and output devices are the keyboard and the computer monitor.
- There are many types of educational programs and, when evaluating educational software, teachers should try a pro-

gram before buying it and evaluate the program's instructional features with particular students in mind.
- Technology tools include word processing and idea processing programs, information presentation tools, and creativity tools, among others.
- The Internet and World Wide Web offer many learning opportunities to students including a wealth of information resources and the ability to communicate with others throughout the world.
- Computer adaptations for students with special needs include modifications of or alternatives to standard input and output modes and the use of special software.
- Assistive devices help students with physical, sensory, and communication impairments.
- Web accessibility is just as important as the accessibility of any other learning tool.
- Technology does not reach its potential until it is fully integrated into the instructional life of the classroom.

ACTIVITIES

1. Visit a school and observe how teachers use technology in instruction. Find out where computers are located (in classrooms, a central computer lab, the library or media center, or a combination of these arrangements), what types of software are available, and what learning activities students accomplish with computers. How

do students interact with the web? What types of assistive technologies are being used in classrooms?

2. Observe a classroom or lab in which students are using technology. Are students actively involved in the learning task or does their attention wander? Do they appear excited about learning? Watch the interactions among students. Is any cooperative learning taking place?

CD-ROM Activities

Technology serves many purposes for students with special needs in inclusive classrooms. View the video clips identified below to identify two (or more) different purposes. Can you think of others?

- *In the case about assessing the middle school student, view the "Concerns" video clip to see how technology was used at home.*

- *In the high school classroom case study, view the clip entitled "Multiple Goals" to hear the teacher's explanation of the assignment.*

3. Use the information presented in this chapter to find out more about assistive technologies that might be useful for persons with different types of special needs. Be sure to consult one or more of the assistive technology resources described in the chapter's "Window on the Web" feature on AT.

4. Several professional organizations are concerned with technology in education, but one that focuses on individuals with disabilities is the Technology and Media (TAM) Division of The Council for Exceptional Children. Visit TAM's website (http://www.tamcec.org) to find out about the services it provides.

PART III

Methods for Teaching Students with Disabilities

Teaching Students with Learning Disabilities and Attention Deficit Hyperactivity Disorders

CHAPTER 9

Jane

Jane is a seventh grader with a learning disability; she has great difficulty remembering what she has learned, particularly in the area of written language. It took Jane several years to acquire basic reading and spelling skills; now, she can read fourth-grade material with adequate word recognition and good comprehension, and in spelling she performs at the third-grade level. This year in seventh grade, Jane attends general education classes for all subjects except English; during that period, she visits the special education resource teacher for reading and spelling instruction. With the help of her seventh-grade teacher, Mr. Henry, Jane is earning passing grades in math, science, and social studies. Classroom adaptations for Jane include taped textbooks and modified exams and assignments.

Danny

Danny is a student with learning disabilities who is 8 years old and in second grade. Although Danny can read and spell quite well for his age, he has difficulty with handwriting and math. His printing is large and uncoordinated, and he has trouble staying within the lines. Several of his letters and numbers are written incorrectly; for example, he confuses *b* and *d, n* and *u,* and 6 and 9. In math, Danny has learned some of the basic addition facts but has not yet begun subtraction. His math papers are messy and difficult to read; the margins are irregular and the columns of numbers poorly aligned. Danny visits the resource teacher for an hour each day for special help in math and handwriting. During the rest of the day, Danny participates in the activities of his second-grade classroom. Mrs. Rose, Danny's second-grade teacher, provides him with extra practice in math facts to help him progress more quickly. Handwriting assignments are also modified so that Danny can complete them successfully.

LOOKING AHEAD

We will learn more about assessments for Jane and Danny later in this chapter and we'll have a look at Jane's IEP. The majority of the chapter, however, provides suggestions for adapting and improving academic instruction for students such as these. As you read, keep these questions in mind:

- From what you know right now, what are Jane's areas of strength? Areas of need?
- Although Jane is in seventh grade, she reads at the fourth-grade level. What types of adaptations might be needed for her to take part in seventh-grade science and social studies instruction?
- If you were Danny's second-grade teacher, what types of modifications might you use for his handwriting assignments?
- Does Danny's poor handwriting interfere with his ability to do math? How could you separate out those two skill areas?

To answer these questions online, go to the Students' Stories module in Chapter 9 of the Companion Website.

A learning disability is a perplexing condition. Students with learning disabilities are of average intelligence and learn some things quickly and easily. However, because of deficits in attention, perception, and memory, they acquire other skills only with extreme difficulty. Students with learning disabilities may read well yet spell poorly. Or they may fail a written test but be able to answer every question correctly on an oral exam. These students with special needs are often members of general education classes; they can participate successfully if instructional modifications are made.

Students with learning disabilities have special needs in academic, classroom behavioral, physical, and social performance. However, the most common area requiring adaptation of classroom procedures is academic instruction. Students like Danny need extra help in acquiring basic skills; reading, handwriting, spelling, written expression, or math can be trouble areas. Older students, such as Jane, benefit from assistance in content-area subjects. Class requirements may need to be modified in science, social studies, and English courses to help students compensate for poor basic skills.

This chapter explores the characteristics of students with learning disabilities and provides methods for the general education teacher to use in gathering data, teaching basic skills, and modifying content-area instruction. In addition, the last section of this chapter suggests strategies for instructional modifications for another group of learners who often experience academic difficulties: students with attention deficit hyperactivity disorder (ADHD).

INDICATORS OF LEARNING DISABILITIES

For students with learning disabilities, the general education teacher is a vital member of the inclusion team. Classroom teachers are usually the first to notice signs of learning disabilities and refer students for special education assessment. In addition, general educators assist in gathering assessment information and in coordinating special services.

The legal definitions of learning disabilities and other disabilities were discussed in chapter 3. However, a learning disability is one of the most difficult disabilities to define. Debate over definitional issues has continued since the passage of PL 94–142, and new definitions of learning disabilities have been proposed.

One example is the definition of the National Joint Committee on Learning Disabilities (1994), a coalition of organizations concerned with this disability:

> *Learning disabilities* is a general term that refers to a heterogeneous group of disorders manifested by significant difficulties in the acquisition and use of listening, speaking, reading, writing, reasoning, or mathematical abilities. These disorders are intrinsic to the individual and presumed to be due to central nervous system dysfunction . . . .Even though a learning disability may occur concomitantly with other handicapping conditions . . . or environmental influences . . . it is not the direct result of those conditions or influences.

A more recent definition is that of the National Center for Learning Disabilities (2001):

A learning disability (LD) is a neurological disorder that affects the brain's ability to receive, process, store and respond to information. The term learning disability is used to describe the seeming unexplained difficulty a person of at least average intelligence has in acquiring basic academic skills. These skills are essential for success at school and work, and for coping with life in general. LD is not a single disorder. It is a term that refers to a group of disorders.

Common to both of these definitions of learning disabilities and to most others is an extreme difficulty in the acquisition of basic school skills despite adequate intellectual ability.

Students may be identified as having a learning disability at any age, but most are noticed during the early elementary grades. There are two major indicators of learning disabilities. First, students appear capable but experience extreme difficulty in some area(s) of learning. This is a discrepancy between expected and actual achievement. For example, a young child might be verbal and appear bright but be very slow to learn the alphabet, write his or her name, and count to 20. The second indicator is variation in performance; that is, there is a discrepancy among different areas of achievement. A fourth grader might perform well in math but read and spell poorly. Or a 10th grader might be a good science student except when required to express ideas in writing. In addition to these two main indicators of learning disabilities, teachers should watch for several other signs which are listed in the "Inclusion Tips for the Teacher" box. Although it is unlikely that any student would display all of the characteristics presented at his or her age level, most students with learning disabilities exhibit at least one or two.

Poor **learning strategies** may also be a sign of learning disabilities (Clark, 2000; Lerner, 2003; Mercer & Pullen, 2005; Reid, Hresko, & Swanson, 1996). Learning strategies are the methods students use to plan, begin, and complete learning tasks; students with learning disabilities tend to use less effective strategies than average achievers. For example, with memory tasks, average achievers rehearse the information they are trying to commit to memory, whereas students with learning disabilities do not. This difference in performance has led Torgesen (1977) to call students with learning disabilities *inactive learners* because they fail to become actively involved in the learning task. In contrast, Swanson (1989) suggests that these students are not passive but "*actively inefficient learners*" (p. 10).

Many school districts have developed checklists to help general education teachers identify students with learning disabilities, and several commercial measures such as the *Learning Disability Evaluation Scale* (McCarney, 1996) are also available. A teacher can use this rating scale to screen students for learning disabilities in academic areas (e.g., listening, thinking, speaking, reading, writing, spelling, mathematical calculations) and in areas such as attention, auditory discrimination, visual perception, fine-motor skills, and memory. A

newer measure, the *Learning Disabilities Diagnostic Inventory* (Hammill & Bryant, 1998), asks teachers to rate student performance in six areas: listening, speaking, reading, writing, mathematics, and reasoning.

ASSESSMENT PROCEDURES

When learning disabilities are suspected, the general education teacher refers students for special education assessment. Parents are notified of the reasons for referral and are presented with an assessment plan prepared by the multidisciplinary team. If consent is given for special education evaluation, the team begins to collect information about the student.

Assessment is an information-gathering process that includes both formal testing and informal procedures such as observation, inventories, and work sample analyses. In the assessment of learning disabilities, information is collected about the student's current intellectual functioning, academic achievement, and performance in areas related to the disability: information processing and strategies for learning. Figure 9-1 presents a portion of the special education assessment report for Jane, one of the students introduced at the beginning of this chapter.

Intellectual functioning is assessed by intelligence tests such as the *Wechsler Intelligence Scale for Children–Fourth Edition* (*WISC-IV*) (Wechsler, 2003). This is an individual test, appropriate for students age 6 to 17, that is administered by the school psychologist. Several intelligence quotient (or IQ) scores are obtained. The test average (or mean) is 100; scores between IQ 85 and 115 are considered to be within the average range of performance, and those between IQ 70 and 85 are considered low average (McLoughlin & Lewis, 2005). In this interpretation system, approximately 68% of the population falls within the average range of performance, 14% show low average performance, and 2% show below average performance. *WISC-IV* results include a total test score called the Full Scale IQ, and four composite scores. These are Verbal Comprehension, Perceptual Reasoning, Working Memory, and Processing Speed. As the report in Figure 9-1 indicates, Jane scored within the average range in most areas, although her performance fell in the low average range in Working Memory.

Most states require students to achieve an IQ score in the low average range or above to qualify for special education services for learning disabilities. This criterion is based on the assumption that students with learning disabilities show a discrepancy between average intellectual performance and poor academic skills. This discrepancy notion has been challenged in the past few years (Vaughn & Fuchs, 2003). Recommended instead is the use of failure to learn as the defining characteristic of learning disabilities. In this approach, sometimes called the response-to-instruction model, learning disabilities would

Inclusion Tips for the Teacher

Signs of Learning Disabilities

The signs of learning disabilities that follow are written for parents but are equally useful for teachers and other professionals. The signs appear on the Focus on Learning website (http://www.focusonlearning.org), a project of the Coordinated Campaign for Learning Disabilities.

Pre-School

Have You Noticed That Your Child Has:

- pronunciation problems?
- difficulty finding the right word?
- difficulty making rhymes?
- trouble learning numbers, alphabet, days of the week, colors and shapes?
- trouble concentrating?
- trouble interacting with peers?
- difficulty following directions or learning routines?
- difficulty controlling pencil, crayons, scissors?
- difficulty with buttoning, zipping, typing skills?

It is never too early to seek help for your child, but waiting too long could be very harmful.

Grades K–4

Does Your Child . . .

- have trouble learning the connection between letters and sounds?
- confuse basic words? (*run, eat, want*)
- make consistent reading and spelling errors?
- experience difficulty learning basic math concepts?
- have trouble learning about time?
- take a long time to learn new skills?
- have trouble remembering facts?

It is never too early to seek help for your child, but waiting too long could be very harmful.

Grades 5–8

Is Your Child Having Difficulty:

- with reading comprehension or math skills?
- with letter sequences? (*soiled* for *solid, left* for *felt*)
- with prefixes, suffixes, root words, and other spelling strategies?
- organizing his/her bedroom, notebook, papers, and desk? time management?
- keeping up with papers or assignments?
- with handwriting?
- understanding oral discussions and expressing thoughts aloud?

It is never too early to seek help for your child, but waiting too long could be very harmful.

High School and Adults

Is Your Child Having Difficulty:

- spelling the same word differently in a single document.
- taking on reading or writing tasks.
- with open-ended questions on tests.
- with memory skills.
- adapting skills from one setting to another.
- with a slow work pace.
- grasping abstract concepts.
- focusing on details.
- misreading information

It is never too early to seek help for your child, but waiting too long could be very harmful.

Note: Reprinted with permission from the Focus on Learning website, a project of the Coordinated Campaign for Learning Disabilities. Retrieved from http://www.focusonlearning.org/startingout2.htm

be indicated if students failed to progress when provided with instructional programs judged effective (Fuchs, Mock, Morgan, & Young, 2003; McNamara & Hollinger, 2003; Vaughn & Fuchs, 2003; Vaughn, Linan-Thompson, & Hickman, 2003).

This recommendation is gaining support. In fact, the current federal law, IDEA 2004, specifically states that schools are not required to document a discrepancy. However, schools "may use a process that determines if the child responds to a scientific, research-based intervention" (P.L. 108–446, Section 614 (b) (6) (B)).

After general ability level has been determined, academic achievement is assessed. One commonly used measure is the *Peabody Individual Achievement Test–Revised/Normative Update*

(PIAT-R/NU) (Markwardt, 1998). It is administered individually by the school psychologist or the special education resource teacher and is appropriate for students in kindergarten through grade 12. The *PIAT-R/NU* assesses several areas of school achievement, and results include grade scores, age scores, percentile ranks, and standard scores. *PIAT-R/NU* standard scores, like the IQ scores on the *WISC-IV,* have a mean of 100; the range of average performance extends from standard score 85 to 115.

Jane's *PIAT-R/NU* results also appear in Figure 9-1, and variation is seen among the different academic areas: Jane's achievement is average in math, reading comprehension, and general information but low average in reading recognition and spelling.

FIGURE 9-1	Special Education Assessment Results

Student: Jane   **Age:** 13 years, 2 months   **Grade:** 7

Intellectual Performance

The *Wechsler Intelligence Scale for Children–Fourth Edition (WISC-IV)* was administered to Jane by Ms. Ducharme, the school psychologist. Jane performed within average range on all scales of the *WISC-IV* except the Working Memory scale where her score fell in the low average range of performance. These results indicate that, overall, Jane shows average capabilities for academic learning. However, short-term memory may be a weak area for Jane.

Verbal Comprehension	108
Perceptual Reasoning	98
Working Memory	75
Processing Speed	95
Full Scale	94

Academic Performance

Mr. Ross, the resource teacher, administered the *Peabody Individual Achievement Test–Revised/Normative Update*. On that measure, Jane showed average performance in Mathematics, Reading Comprehension, and General Information (a measure of content-area knowledge). However, her performance fell within the low average range in Reading Recognition and Spelling. She earned these standard scores:

General Information	98
Reading Recognition	82
Reading Comprehension	88
Mathematics	101
Spelling	72
TOTAL TEST	84

Jane scored at the fourth-grade level in decoding, as measured by the Reading Recognition subtest. Spelling, at grade 3, was her weakest area. These results are consistent with the observations of Mr. Henry, Jane's seventh-grade teacher. Despite average intellectual performance, Jane continues to experience difficulty in some academic tasks.

Learning Abilities and Strategies

To find out more about Jane's memory skills, Ms. Ducharme administered portions of the *Woodcock-Johnson III Tests of Cognitive Abilities*. Jane's performance was within the low average range on tests of Long-Term Retrieval and tests of Short-Term Memory. Mr. Henry notes that Jane appears to comprehend grade 7 material but has great difficulty committing facts to memory. Mr. Ross, Jane's resource teacher, reports that Jane is beginning to learn strategies for memorizing information but is not yet able to use these strategies consistently. These teacher observations and test results point to a learning disability in the area of memory and the need for continued instruction in strategies for learning and recalling academic information.

The third area of assessment is information processing. Several newer measures are available such as the *Developmental Test of Visual Perception* (2nd ed.) (Hammill, Pearson, & Voress, 1993), *Motor-Free Visual Perception Test* (3rd ed.) (Colarusso & Hammill, 2003), *Developmental Test of Visual-Motor Integration* (4th ed.) (Beery, 1997), and *Test of Memory and Learning* (Reynolds & Bigler, 1994). More comprehensive measures such as the *Woodcock-Johnson III* (Woodcock, McGrew, & Mather, 2001) and the *Detroit Tests of Learning Aptitude* (4th ed.) (Hammill, 1998) provide information about students' functioning in areas such as memory, processing speed, auditory and visual processing, and attention. Tests are often supplemented with results of informal assessments such as observations of the student's strategies for learning. In

Jane's case, a memory problem is indicated by test results and her teachers' observations.

Once it has been established that a student is eligible for special education services, the team begins to gather information about educational needs. The general education teacher can provide valuable assistance at this point in the assessment process. For example, for Danny (the second grader described at the beginning of this chapter), specific data about math and handwriting performance must be collected. Formal tests are available, but more specific information is obtained from informal measures.

The general education teacher might decide to devise an informal procedure for a particular student. As shown in Figure 9-2, Danny's teacher prepared a criterion-referenced

FIGURE 9-2   Informal Assessment

Student: Danny   **Age:**   8 years, 4 months   **Grade:**   2

Criterion-Referenced Test of Basic Addition Facts

Objective: When presented with any 20 one-digit plus one-digit basic addition facts problems (e.g., 1 + 1, 4 + 3, 8 + 5), the student will write the correct answer to at least 18 problems within 2 minutes.

Test and Student's Responses:

1 +4 **5**	5 +2 **7**	3 +3 **6**	9 +4 **(14)**	0 +7 **7**	2 +7 **(8)**	4 +5 **9**
8 +1 **(10)**	5 +6 **11**	3 +5 **8**	7 +0 **7**	3 +8 **(12)**	4 +2 **6**	9 +7 **16**
6 +3 **9**	8 +9 **(16)**	1 +1 **2**	6 +8 **(15)**	2 +8 **10**	7 +9 **(14)**	

Criterion for Acceptance Performance: 18 correct responses in 2 minutes

Student's Score: 13 correct responses in 2 minutes

test of addition facts to assess current math skills; results indicate that Danny has not yet mastered the basic facts of addition. The teacher might also wish to obtain a sample of Danny's handwriting and analyze it to locate typical error patterns.

Other assessment procedures available to the classroom teacher are informal inventories, curriculum-based measurement, direct observation, and classroom tests. Also useful are the results from recently administered group achievement measures and placement tests for educational materials and programs. One area of special need for many students with learning disabilities is reading. The "Inclusion Tips for the Teacher" box suggests several ways to assess reading in the classroom. These include methods to determine students' reading levels and to measure the readability of textbooks and other instructional materials.

Inclusion Tips for the Teacher

Determining Reading Levels

To ensure effective instruction, the teacher must match reading materials to the skills of special students. There are several ways to accomplish this.

Oral Reading Sample

To check oral reading skills, the teacher can simply have the student read a portion of a textbook or other reading material aloud. If the student can read at least 95% of the words and successfully answer at least 75% of the comprehension questions the teacher asks, it is likely that the text is appropriate for the student (Kirk, Kliebhan, & Lerner, 1978). Oral reading samples should be collected in a private setting so that students are not embarrassed by the errors they make.

Cloze Procedure

With the cloze procedure, students can read silently or orally. This procedure is a valuable (and quick) way to determine whether class textbooks in subjects such as science, history, or shop are written at an appropriate level for students. The student reads a short passage in which every fifth (or seventh or nth word) has been replaced with a blank. The student must insert appropriate words in the blanks. If at least 44% to 57% of the missing words are correctly supplied, the passage is at the student's instructional level (Bormuth, 1968; Burron & Claybaugh, 1977).

Informal Reading Inventories

Another approach is to first determine the instructional reading level of the student and then select materials written at this level. Informal reading inventories (IRIs) are useful for this purpose. These measures contain several reading passages and comprehension questions for each passage. The student reads (usually aloud) and answers the questions; results are used to determine three reading level scores: Independent, Instructional, and Frustration.

According to McLoughlin and Lewis (2005), materials at the student's Independent Level can be read easily without assistance from the teacher, those at the Instructional Level are more difficult but appropriate for classroom reading instruction, and those at the Frustration Level are too difficult for the student. Students are expected to show 90% to 100% accuracy in comprehension at the Independent Level, 75% to 90% accuracy at the Instructional Level, and less than 75% accuracy at the Frustration Level (Kirk et al., 1978).

Three popular IRIs that are available commercially are the *Analytical Reading Inventory* (7th ed.) (Woods & Moe, 2003), *Classroom Reading Inventory* (10th ed.) (Silvaroli & Wheelock, 2003), and *Ekwall/Shanker Reading Inventory* (4th ed.) (Shanker & Ekwall, 2000); all are appropriate for students reading between the primer and grade 8 or 9 reading levels. It is important to remember that published IRIs may focus on

a different set of reading skills than those emphasized by the classroom reading series or other instructional materials.

If a student achieves an instructional reading level of grade 6 on an IRI, then books at that reading level will generally be appropriate for instruction. However, that student may not be able to read a sixth-grade science text. Grade levels of content-area texts refer to subject matter, not reading level, and such texts often require above-grade-level reading ability. For example, a fourth-grade social studies book can have a reading level of fifth, sixth, or even seventh grade.

Readability Measures

To select instructional materials that are appropriate for students with special needs, the teacher must match the reading levels of students with those of texts and other materials. A readability formula or graph can be used to discover the reading level of the books in a classroom. There are many readability measures that teachers can use to determine the reading level of materials such as textbooks (e.g., Dale & Chall, 1948; Flesch, 1951; Spache, 1953).

One relatively quick and easy method is that suggested by Fry (1968). It is appropriate for use with materials that range from first grade to college levels; extended versions are available for preprimer and primer materials (Maginnis, 1969) and reading matter at college and graduate school levels (Fry, 1977). Use the Fry readability graph and the directions on pages 211 and 212 to discover the approximate reading levels of texts, supplementary reading materials, newspapers and magazines, and any other type of reading matter you might use in your classroom. Once potentially appropriate materials have been identified by readability analyses, their suitability for particular students can be determined by oral reading samples or the cloze procedure.

DIRECTIONS: Randomly select 3 one hundred word passages from a book or an article. Plot average number of syllables and average number of sentences per 100 words on graph to determine the grade level of the material. Choose more passages per book if great variability is observed and conclude that the book has uneven readability. Few books will fall in [the] blue area but when they do grade level scores are invalid.

Count proper nouns, numerals and initializations as words. Count a syllable for each symbol. For example, "1945" is 1 word and 4 syllables and "IRA" is 1 word and 3 syllables.

EXAMPLE:	Syllables	Sentences
1st Hundred Words	124	6.6
2nd Hundred Words	141	5.5
3rd Hundred Words	<u>158</u>	<u>6.8</u>
AVERAGE	141	6.3

READABILITY 7th GRADE (see dot plotted on graph)

continued

continued

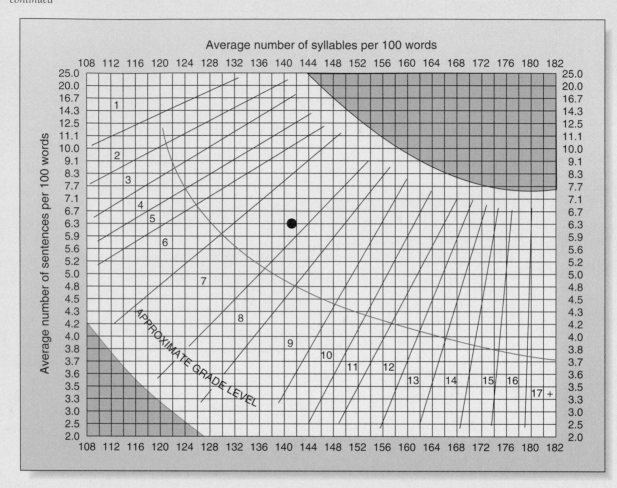

EXPANDED DIRECTIONS FOR WORKING READABILITY GRAPH

1. Randomly select three (3) sample passages and count out exactly 100 words beginning with the beginning of a sentence. Do count proper nouns, initializations, and numerals.
2. Count the number of sentences in the hundred words estimating length of the fraction of the last sentence to the nearest 1/10th.
3. Count the total number of syllables in the 100-word passage. If you don't have a hand counter available, an easy way is to simply put a mark above every syllable over one in each word, then when you get to the end of the passage, count the number of marks and add 100. Small calculators can also be used as counters by pushing numeral "1", then pushing the "+" sign for each word or syllable when counting.

4. Enter graph with average sentence length and average number of syllables; plot dot where the two lines intersect. Area where dot is plotted will give you the approximate grade level.
5. If a great deal of variability is found in syllable count or sentence count, putting more samples in the average is desirable.
6. A word is defined as a group of symbols with a space on either side; thus, "Joe," "IRA," "1945," and "&" are each one word.
7. A syllable is defined as a phonetic syllable. Generally, there are as many syllables as vowel sounds. For example, "stopped" is one syllable and "wanted" is two syllables. When counting syllables for numerals and initializations, count one syllable for each symbol. For example, "1945" is 4 syllables and "IRA" is 3 syllables, and "&" is 1 syllable.

Note: From "Fry's Readability Graph: Clarifications, Validity, and Extension to Level 17" by E. Fry, 1977, *Journal of Reading, 21,* 242–252. Reproduction permitted. No copyright.

FIGURE 9-3   IEP Goals and Services for Jane

Annual Goals

1. By the end of the school year, Jane will read sixth grade material with adequate word recognition skills and comprehension.
   Person responsible: Resource teacher
2. By the end of the school year, Jane will correctly spell all words on a high-frequency word list such as the Dolch list.
   Person responsible: Resource teacher
3. By the end of the school year, Jane will correct her spelling errors by using the dictionary or a word processing program with a spelling checker.
   Person responsible: Resource teacher
4. Jane will successfully complete all requirements for seventh grade math, science, and social studies.
   Person responsible: Seventh grade teacher

Amount of Participation in General Education
Jane will attend all seventh grade classes in general education with the exception of English.

Special Education and Related Services

1. Jane will receive special education services from the resource teacher (annual goals 1, 2, and 3) for one period daily.
2. The resource teacher will provide consultation to Jane's seventh grade teacher as needed (annual goal 4).

SPECIAL SERVICES

When assessment is complete, the team meets to plan the student's IEP. Figure 9-3 presents portions of the IEP for Jane. Like most students with learning disabilities, she is a general education student who leaves her classroom for only a short time each day for special education services.

Although the resource room is the most typical placement for students with learning disabilities, some districts provide self-contained special classes for those with comprehensive learning needs. In addition to part- or full-day special education, many students with learning disabilities receive assistance in oral language development from speech-language clinicians. Some receive counseling from the school psychologist, social worker, or counselor; those with motor problems may attend special physical education classes. For the general education teacher, consultant services are available to assist in including students with learning disabilities. To learn more about this group of students, consult the "For Your Information" feature.

CLASSROOM ADAPTATIONS

Academic instruction is the primary area in which adaptations are made for students with learning disabilities in the general education classroom, the rest of this chapter focuses on methods for meeting academic needs. Some students with learning disabilities also require assistance in classroom behavior; methods for teaching study skills and controlling disruptive behavior can be found in chapter 11. For students

who have difficulty relating to classmates, chapter 6 presents ways to increase social acceptance.

Two approaches are available for the instruction of students with learning disabilities. In the **remediation** approach (sometimes called the *remedial* approach), the teacher instructs the student in skills that are areas of need. For example, extra assistance in spelling might be provided to a fourth grader who spells at the second-grade level. **Compensation**, however, attempts to bypass the student's weaknesses. For instance, to compensate for the reading and writing problems of a high school student, the teacher might administer class tests orally. Remediation techniques are used to teach basic skills and are most appropriate for elementary-aged students. Compensation techniques bypass deficiencies in basic skills in order to teach content-area subjects; they are used most commonly in the late elementary grades, middle school, and high school.

The following sections of this chapter present several remediation techniques and compensatory strategies. Methods of teaching basic skills to younger students and methods for adapting content-area instruction are included. In the latter section, secondary teachers can find ideas for modifying assignments and exams, using taped texts, and compensating in other ways for the academic difficulties of students with special needs.

TEACHING BASIC SKILLS

Reading, handwriting, spelling, written expression, and math are often called basic skills; these "tool" subjects, once acquired, are used in the acquisition of new information and

For Your Information

Students with Learning Disabilities

- Students with learning disabilities make up about 5.5% of the school-aged population (U.S. Department of Education, 2002).
- Learning disabilities are the most common disability; in 2000–2001, 50% of the students served in special education were identified as having learning disabilities (U.S. Department of Education, 2002).
- Four times as many boys are identified as having learning disabilities as girls (Lerner, 2003).
- Reading is one of the academic skills in which students with learning disabilities experience difficulty most frequently. Other common problem areas are math, spelling, handwriting, and written expression.
- Current findings in brain research suggest that reading disabilities have a neurological basis (Lerner, 2003; Shaywitz, 2003).
- Among the most typical behavioral characteristics of students with learning disabilities are hyperactivity, impulsivity, and disorders of attention (Tarver & Hallahan, 1976).

- Terms such as *dyslexia* (a difficulty in reading) and *dyscalculia* (a computational difficulty) are sometimes used in reference to learning disabilities. Medical terms such as these do little to describe the learning problem. Instead of calling a student dyslexic, it is better to say he or she has a learning disability in the area of reading.
- Most students with learning disabilities are in general education classrooms for the majority of the school day and receive part-time special education services in areas of need. For example, in 1999–2000, approximately 83% of the students identified as having learning disabilities in the United States were served in regular classrooms (U.S. Department of Education, 2002).
- Among the famous people in history believed to have learning disabilities are Winston Churchill, Thomas Edison, Albert Einstein, Nelson Rockefeller, Leonardo da Vinci, and Woodrow Wilson. Famous people today include Tom Cruise, Jay Leno, and Whoopi Goldberg (Gorman, 2003).

concepts. Although most students learn the rudiments of basic skills in the early elementary grades, students with special needs may not. They may require additional instruction in order to progress. In general, basic skills instruction is provided to students with special needs by the general education teacher if it is a part of the classroom curriculum. Some students may receive tutoring in some skills as part of their special education program, but most will take part in at least some of the basic skills instruction in the regular classroom. The general education teacher can enhance the learning of special students by modifying the techniques used to teach basic skills. Three adaptations are recommended: providing prompts, giving additional instruction, and allowing extra guided practice.

Prompts are features added to learning tasks; they are particularly helpful for students with learning disabilities and others who have difficulty focusing attention on relevant instructional cues. Prompts also structure the task and help the student know exactly what to do. Danny could use the prompts in Figure 9-4 on page 216 to help improve his printing.

Providing additional direct instruction and allowing extra guided practice are adaptations that aid students with poor recall. To ensure successful learning, the teacher should break down the subject matter into small steps and present it as slowly as necessary. Several practice opportunities should be available; the teacher can monitor performance during practice, enlist the aid of a peer tutor or adult volunteer, or use self-correcting materials. The basic math self-instructional materials in Figure 9-5 on page 217 can help Danny learn addition facts.

Reading

Word recognition and comprehension are two very important subskills of reading. Word recognition is the ability to decode printed symbols; decoding is accomplished by sight if the word is familiar or by analysis of the word's phonetic components or its structure (roots, prefixes, suffixes, etc.). Reading comprehension—the ability to understand what is read—involves knowing the meanings of individual words, following the sequence of events in a passage, detecting the main ideas, drawing conclusions, and making inferences.

Two major approaches are used to teach reading skills: the code-emphasis approach and the meaning-emphasis approach. According to Mercer and Mercer (2005), code-emphasis programs teach decoding first, then comprehension; instruction in decoding stresses the regular relationships between letters and sounds. In contrast, meaning-based programs emphasize comprehension from the start; students practice decoding by reading common words.

The whole-language approach to reading instruction is an example of a meaning-emphasis program. In this approach, reading is not broken down into separate skill areas; thus, skills such as decoding are not taught separately. Instead, reading is integrated with the other language arts of listening, speaking, and writing (Lapp & Flood, 1992). According to McLoughlin and Lewis (2005), in whole-language classrooms students read whole texts (not fragments) from authentic literature, and instruction emphasizes meaningful interaction with those

Teaching Special Students in General Education Classrooms

215

Window on the Web

LD OnLine and Other LD Web Resources

LD OnLine

http://www.ldonline.org

LD OnLine is a community service of WETA, a public broadcasting system in Washington, DC. LD OnLine is one of the most complete sources of information about learning disabilities, and it also provides coverage of attention deficit hy-

Note: Courtesy of LD OnLine.

peractivity disorders. The site offers basic information about these disabilities in the ABCs of LD/ADHD section, more extensive coverage in LD in Depth, advice from well-known professionals in the Experts section, a Resources page with several sets of helpful links, and a Yellow Pages directory for help in finding schools, products, and professionals. First Person Essays feature accounts of "first-hand experiences with the challenges of learning disabilities." There are special sections of the site devoted to different audiences. For example, the KidZone publishes students' art and writing as well as books, activities, and articles for kids with learning disabilities. The Forums portion of the site provides online bulletin boards for parents, teachers, and individuals with learning disabilities on topics such as parenting, homeschooling, social skills, and postsecondary education. Visitors to LD OnLine can sign up to receive a free e-mail newsletter.

Other Web-Based Resources

A number of other resources on learning disabilities can be found on the web, including these:

- *LD Resources*   (http://www.ldresources.com), a helpful site hosted by Richard Wanderman, a nationally known expert on learning disabilities who calls himself a "successful dyslexic adult."
- *National Center for Learning Disabilities*   (http://www.ld.org), sponsor of the Get Ready to Read! Program.
- *Focus on Learning*   (http://www.focusonlearning.org), a site for parents hosted by the Coordinated Campaign for Learning Disabilities.
- *Teaching LD*   (http://www.teachingld.org), a site for teachers sponsored by the Division for Learning Disabilities of the Council for Exceptional Children.
- *Learning Disabilities Association of American*   (http://www.ldanatl.org), the website of LDA, the first parents' organization in the field of learning disabilities.
- *National Association for the Education of African American Children with Learning Disabilities*   (http://www.aacld.org), the website of a new organization for parents of African American students with LD.
- *Schwab Learning*   (http://www.schwablearning.org), described as "A Parent's Guide to Helping Kids with Learning Difficulties."

For more information, go to the Web Links module in Chapter 9 of the Companion Website.

---

texts, not development of isolated skills. Table 9-1 on page 217 compares whole-language and other implicit (i.e., meaning-emphasis) approaches to reading instruction to explicit (i.e., code-emphasis) and interactive approaches.

An extensive body of research now exists to guide how teachers go about delivering instruction in reading. First of all, research results clearly suggest that explicit code-emphasis programs are more effective than implicit meaning-emphasis programs, particularly for students with special needs and those at risk for learning problems (Chall, 1967, 1977, 1983, 1989, 2000; Rankin-Erickson & Pressley, 2000; Snow, Burns, & Griffin, 1998; Spear-Swerling & Sternberg, 2001;

Stahl & Miller, 1989; Vaughn, Gersten, & Chard, 2000). Two additional evidence-based recommendations for reading instruction concern the development of phonological awareness and reading fluency. **Phonological awareness,** a readiness skill for younger children, has been defined as "the ability to recognize that the words we hear are composed of individual sounds within the word" (Lerner, 2003, p. 257). **Reading fluency,** a skill area more pertinent to older readers, is the ability to read text both quickly and accurately.

In the general education classroom, code-emphasis programs provide beginning readers with a systematic method of decoding unfamiliar words. Students learn decoding strategies

FIGURE 9-4   Prompts for Basic Skills Instruction

Faded visual prompts in the instruction of manuscript letter formation

Additional visual cueing devices used in the instruction of handwriting

Directional arrows

Colored start and stop points for each stroke:

o Red
x Green

Color-coded baseline and top line:

Red

Green

Heavy-lined baseline:

Pale vertical lines (or sheet with vertical lines placed under handwriting sheet):

Note: Reprinted with permission of Merrill/Prentice Hall, an imprint of Macmillan Publishing Company, from *Teaching the Mildly Handicapped in the Regular Classroom* (2nd ed., p. 108) by J. Affleck, S. Lowenbraun, and A. Archer. Copyright © 1980 Merrill Publishing Company, Columbus, Ohio.

FIGURE 9-5   Materials for Independent Practice

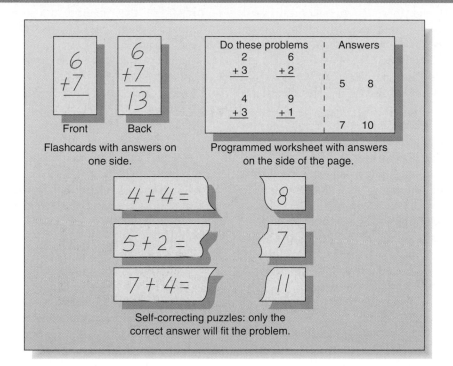

Flashcards with answers on one side.

Front   Back

Programmed worksheet with answers on the side of the page.

Self-correcting puzzles: only the correct answer will fit the problem.

TABLE 9-1   Approaches to Reading Instruction

EXPLICIT	INTERACTIVE	IMPLICIT
Reading Concepts		
Bottom-up reading (code emphasis)	Combination	Top-down reading (meaning emphasis)
Part-to-whole learning	Combination	Whole-to-part learning
Teacher-directed instruction	Combination	Student-directed instruction
Skill emphasis	Combination	Immersion emphasis
Reading viewed as a learned behavior that requires much teacher assistance		Reading acquired naturally through exposure to text
Reading Approaches and Programs		
Literature-Based Approach with systematic phonics	*Success for All*	Literature-Based Approach with little or no phonics
Phonics Approach	*Reading Recovery*	Whole-Language Approach
Phonological Awareness Training	Repeated Readings	Language Experience Approach
Reading Mastery and *Corrective Reading*	Peer-Assisted	Neurological Impress Method
Linguistic Approach	Reading method	High Interest–Low Vocabulary Method
Multisensory Reading Method (Fernald; Gillingham; Word Imprinting)	*B.A.L.A.N.C.E.*	
	Reciprocal Teaching	
	Learning Strategies	

Note: Reprinted with the permission of Merrill/Prentice Hall from *Teaching Students with Learning Problems* (7th ed.) by C. D. Mercer and A. R. Mercer (p. 319). Copyright © 2005 by Prentice-Hall, Inc.

and then practice with words that can be read using these strategies. Code-based reading materials feature a controlled vocabulary, that is, one limited to words that can be read by students who have mastered the strategies taught in the program.

Materials based on the **phonics** method represent the code-based approach to reading. Students first learn the sound for each letter (phoneme–grapheme combinations) and practice reading phonetically regular words; later, other types of words are introduced. Linguistic methods are an adaptation of the phonics approach; reading instruction begins with phonetically regular word families such as *at, bat, cat, rat,* and *sat.*

Reading programs that begin with a controlled vocabulary help students acquire skills quickly and gain confidence in their ability to decode print; however, students eventually must make the transition to a more conventional vocabulary selection. One way to accomplish this is to teach students to read common words that appear with high frequency in the English language. Because many of these words are irregular and therefore not readily decodable with phonics strategies, they are often taught as sight vocabulary. The *Dolch Basic Sight Word List* (Dolch, 1953) is one example of a high-frequency word list; an updated version of the Dolch list (Johnson, 1971) is shown in Table 9-2. Simms and Falcon (1987) suggest dividing this word list into categories for instruction. Categories might include self words (e.g., *I, me*), moving words (*come, play*), size words (*big, little*), and question words (*who, when*).

Reading is a problem area for many students with special needs, not only those with learning disabilities. Some have difficulty learning (or applying) word recognition skills; others fail to understand what they have read despite adequate decoding skills. Still others require assistance in both word recognition and comprehension. The following suggestions for modifying reading instruction for students with special needs include examples of prompts and ways to enhance the practice of reading skills:

- Add cues to help students decode troublesome words; for example, mark long vowels (sēēd), cross out silent letters (mākè), and divide words into syllables (dis-crim-i-nātè).
- Provide markers for students who lose their place while reading. They can move their finger along under the line of print or use an index card with an arrow for a guideline; cards with windows can be placed on the page to expose only a few words at a time.

- To enhance reading comprehension, tell students the purposes for reading and what to look for in the passage. For example, they might read a story to discover the main characters and the sequence of events, or a textbook chapter to learn important facts and main ideas. **Advanced organizers** that provide an overview of the passage to prepare students for what they will be reading are an effective strategy for increasing comprehension (Graham & Johnson, 1989). Mercer and Mercer (1993) suggest giving students a list of questions to guide their reading and the page numbers of the text on which answers can be found.
- Use peer tutors and volunteers for sight word drill.
- Provide high interest–low vocabulary reading materials to aid in the practice of silent reading. These materials appeal to students who read at a lower grade level than expected for their age; examples appear in Table 9-3. Other good resources are *Easy Reading: Book Series and Periodicals for Less Able Readers* (2nd ed.) (Ryder, Graves, & Graves, 1989) and *High Interest Easy Reading: An Annotated Booklist for Middle School and Senior High School* (7th ed.) (Phelan, 1996).
- Tape texts or stories; students can read the passage while listening to correct word pronunciation and phrasing of sentences.
- Use computer software to help teach basic reading skills. Many multimedia programs talk, allowing students to develop sight vocabulary as they read and listen to stories, poems, and other texts. (See the "Spotlight on Technology" feature in chapter 10 for more information about reading software.)
- Provide practice in reading comprehension with materials such as the *Specific Skill Series* (Boning, 1998). This program includes activities for skills such as using context clues, locating answers, following directions, identifying main ideas, and drawing conclusions. A source of ideas for other activities for comprehension practice is *Locating and Correcting Reading Difficulties* (8th ed.) (Shanker & Ekwall, 2002).
- To increase reading fluency, have students reread a passage several times. **Repeated readings** increase both speed and accuracy, which helps students master a selection before attempting more difficult selections. In addition to improving fluency, repeated readings also increase comprehension (Therrien, 2004). Sindelar (1987) says that "mastery is seldom achieved with a single reading, especially for students experiencing difficulty in learning to read" (p. 59).
- Teach students strategies for approaching comprehension tasks. In one study (Jenkins, Heliotis, Stein, & Haynes, 1987), students improved their comprehension of stories by learning to name the most important person (*Who?*) and the major event (*What's happening?*) in each paragraph.

TABLE 9-2	High-Frequency Word List

PREPRIMER	PRIMER	FIRST	SECOND	THIRD
1. the	45. when	89. many	133. know	177. don't
2. of	46. who	90. before	134. while	178. does
3. and	47. will	91. must	135. last	179. got
4. to	48. more	92. through	136. might	180. united
5. a	49. no	93. back	137. us	181. left
6. in	50. if	94. years	138. great	182. number
7. that	51. out	95. where	139. old	183. course
8. is	52. so	96. much	140. year	184. war
9. was	53. said	97. your	141. off	185. until
10. he	54. what	98. may	142. come	186. always
11. for	55. up	99. well	143. since	187. away
12. it	56. its	100. down	144. against	188. something
13. with	57. about	101. should	145. go	189. fact
14. as	58. into	102. because	146. came	190. through
15. his	59. than	103. each	147. right	191. water
16. on	60. them	104. just	148. used	192. less
17. be	61. can	105. those	149. take	193. public
18. at	62. only	106. people	150. three	194. put
19. by	63. other	107. Mr.	151. states	195. thing
20. I	64. new	108. how	152. himself	196. almost
21. this	65. some	109. too	153. few	197. hand
22. had	66. could	110. little	154. house	198. enough
23. not	67. time	111. state	155. use	199. far
24. are	68. these	112. good	156. during	200. took
25. but	69. two	113. very	157. without	201. head
26. from	70. may	114. make	158. again	202. yet
27. or	71. then	115. would	159. place	203. government
28. have	72. do	116. still	160. American	204. system
29. an	73. first	117. own	161. around	205. better
30. they	74. any	118. see	162. however	206. set
31. which	75. my	119. men	163. home	207. told
32. one	76. now	120. work	164. small	208. nothing
33. you	77. such	121. long	165. found	209. night
34. were	78. like	122. get	166. Mrs.	210. end
35. her	79. our	123. here	167. thought	211. why
36. all	80. over	124. between	168. went	212. called
37. she	81. man	125. both	169. say	213. didn't
38. there	82. me	126. life	170. part	214. eyes
39. would	83. even	127. being	171. once	215. find
40. their	84. most	128. under	172. general	216. going
41. we	85. made	129. never	173. high	217. look
42. him	86. after	130. day	174. upon	218. asked
43. been	87. also	131. same	175. school	219. later
44. has	88. did	132. another	176. every	220. knew

Note: From "The Dolch List Reexamined" by D. D. Johnson, 1971, *The Reading Teacher*, 24, pp. 455–456. Copyright 1971 by the International Reading Association. Reprinted by permission of D. D. Johnson and the International Reading Association.

TABLE 9-3	High Interest–Low Vocabulary Reading Materials		

TITLE	PUBLISHER	READING GRADE LEVEL	INTEREST GRADE LEVEL
American Adventure Series	Harper & Row	3–6	4–8
Basic Vocabulary Books	Garrard	2	1–6
Bestsellers	Globe Fearon	2–4	6–12
Breakthrough Series	Allyn & Bacon	2–6	6–12
Checkered Flag Series	Field Educational Publications	2–4	7–12
Childhood of Famous Americans Series	Bobbs-Merrill	4–5	7–9
Cowboy Sam Series	Benefic Press	PP–3	1–6
Dan Frontier Series	Benefic Press	PP–4	1–7
Deep Sea Adventures	Field Educational Publications	2–5	3–11
Everyreader Series	McGraw-Hill	6–8	5–12
Fastback Collection	Globe Fearon	4–5	6–12
First Reading Books	Garrard	1	1–4
Focus on Reading	SRA	1–6	3–12
Folklore of the World Books	Garrard	2	2–8
Interesting Reading Series	Follett	2–3	7–12
Jim Forest Readers	Field Educational Publications	1–3	1–7
Junior Science Books	Garrard	4–5	6–9
Morgan Bay Mysteries	Field Educational Publications	2–4	4–11
Morrow's High Interest/Easy Reading Books	William Morrow	1–8	4–10
Mystery, Adventure, and Science Fiction Collections	Steck-Vaughn	2–4	5–12
Mystery Adventure Series	Benefic Press	2–6	4–9
Pacemaker Classics	Globe/Fearon	3–4	5–12
Pacemaker Story Books	Xerox Education Publications	2	7–12
Pal Paperback Kits	Xerox Education Publications	1–5	5–12
Perspectives Set	High Noon Books	3–4	6–12
Phoenix Everyreaders	Phoenix Learning Resources	4	4–12
Pleasure Reading Books	Garrard	4	3–7
Power Up! Series	Steck-Vaughn	2–5	6–8
Racing Wheels Series	Benefic Press	2–4	4–9
Reading For Concepts Series	McGraw-Hill	3–8	5–12
Reading Reinforcement Skilltext Series	SRA	1–5	1–8
Reading Skill Builders	Reader's Digest Services	1–4	2–5
Sailor Jack Series	Benefic Press	PP–3	1–6
Scoreboard Series	High Noon Books	2	6–1
Space Science Fiction Series	Benefic Press	2–6	4–9
Sports Mystery Stories	Benefic Press	2–4	4–9
Spotlight on Literature	SRA	3–6	6–12
Sprint Libraries	Scholastic	1–3	3–6
Super Kits	Warner Educational Services	2–5	4–12
Teen-Age Tales	D. C. Heath	4–6	6–11
Tom & Ricky Mystery Series	High Noon Books	1	4–9
Top Picks	Reader's Digest Services	5–7	5–12
Trailblazers Series	High Noon Books	2	4–9
True Tales	Steck-Vaughn	3	4–12
Turning Point	Phoenix Learning Resources	1–4	7–12
What Is It Series	Benefic Press	1–4	1–8

- Another strategy, the SQ3R method (Robinson, 1961), can help students improve their comprehension of expository reading materials such as content-area textbooks. (*SQ3R* stands for *Survey, Question, Read, Recite,* and *Review.*) Expository text is usually more difficult to understand than narrative text (i.e., stories). In the SQ3R method, students begin by surveying the passage to get a general idea of its contents. Students ask questions about the text, then read to find the answers. The answers are recited without reference to the text, and then the entire passage is reviewed.
- **Reciprocal teaching** is an instructional approach developed by Palinscar and Brown (1988) that involves four interrelated strategies. Teachers help students develop comprehension skills and the ability to monitor their own comprehension by involving students in dialogues about texts. Lerner (2003) describes the four strategies. "*summarizing* the content of a passage, *asking questions* about a central point, *clarifying* the difficult parts of the material, and *predicting* what would happen next" (p. 140).
- The book *Strategies That Work: Teaching Comprehension to Enhance Understanding* (Harvey & Goudvis, 2000) suggests teaching young readers six strategies to enhance comprehension skills. These strategies are
  - Making connections between the text and the reader, the text and the world, and the text and other texts;
  - Asking questions about the text;
  - Visualizing what is happening in the text;
  - Making inferences from the text;
  - Determining importance in text; and
  - Synthesizing information.

Handwriting, Spelling, and Written Expression

Writing skills are built on reading skills, and many special students need extra assistance in this area (Saddler, 2004). One important subskill is handwriting, the mechanical process of forming letters and words. The goal in handwriting instruction is for students to write legibly and with sufficient speed. Usually students learn manuscript writing (printing) first, then they are introduced to cursive writing in the middle elementary grades. For students with difficulty in letter formation and spacing, cursive writing may be less demanding. For example, in printing, the letters *b* and *d* require a similar motor pattern and are easily confused; in cursive, they are written quite differently.

Students who fail to make a complete transition from printing to cursive writing often continue forming capital letters in manuscript while writing the rest of the word in cursive. If legibility and speed are not affected, this style is acceptable. In fact, many of the special cursive alphabets developed for students with handwriting problems contain print-style capitals; in addition, letters and words are written almost vertically with little slant. One example is the D'Nealian handwriting system (Thurber, 2001). In the modified alphabet proposed by Spalding and Spalding (1986), after students learn to form manuscript letters and five connecting strokes, the transition to cursive can be made with ease.

Spelling is the arrangement of letters to form words. Because English is not a completely phonetic language, many words cannot be spelled the way they sound. Although consonants have fairly reliable phoneme–grapheme correspondence, vowel letters take on several different sounds; for example, the letter *a* produces distinct sounds in *at, ate, all,* and *father*. For this reason, teaching spelling solely by phonics is probably not the best practice, particularly for students who learn words slowly. Although phonics skills should be a part of the spelling curriculum, words that appear frequently in written language should also be stressed; see, for example, the high-frequency word list in Table 9-2 earlier in this chapter. Combining basic instruction in phonics (with emphasis on consonant sounds) and instruction in spelling common words as well as words selected by the student is a practice that produces an excellent individualized spelling program.

When a formal classroom spelling program is used, lessons can be modified for special students as necessary; for instance, the number of words to be learned each week can be reduced. Teachers should carefully monitor the words included in each lesson. For example, if lists include similar words, such as *receive* and *piece,* students may become confused and, as a result, acquire few new spelling words.

Written expression is the process of putting one's thoughts down on paper. Several skills are needed: the mechanics of writing, such as handwriting, spelling, punctuation, and capitalization; language skills such as knowledge of word meanings and syntax (grammar); and thinking skills such as organization, sequence, and logic. Although written expression used to be "the neglected basic skill" (Freedman, 1982, p. 34), it is now considered an important part of the language arts curriculum. However, it is important to remember that, for many students with special needs, written language skills—like their counterparts in reading—must be taught directly.

Several ideas for teaching spelling, handwriting, and composition in the general education classroom are listed here, along with examples of prompts and suggestions for practice activities. Also, see the "Spotlight on Technology" feature for information about using computers to teach writing skills.

- Help students who are poor spellers begin to use the dictionary as an aid; provide them with a minidictionary or "My Words" booklet that contains high-frequency words and words that they often misspell.
- Use the test–study–test method for spelling instruction (Graham & Miller, 1979). Begin with a pretest to identify words students have already mastered, then focus study

Spotlight on Technology

Writing Tools for Writers with Special Needs

Writing has been described as a schizophrenic activity because the writer must assume two roles, that of an author and that of a secretary (Smith, 1982). Students with learning disabilities have particular difficulties with the secretarial aspects of writing: handwriting, spelling, capitalization and punctuation, usage, and grammar. Another problem area for students with learning disabilities is the planning stage of writing, which requires generating and organizing ideas.

Word processing programs and other writing tools may help alleviate some of these problems (Lewis, 1993, 1998, 2000). One of the major advantages of word processors is that writers can easily manipulate the text to organize, revise, and improve it. Spelling checkers, present in most word processors, help in the correction of spelling errors. Another advantage is that the writer's final product is printed; it is neater and easier to read than a handwritten paper. This is very important for students with learning disabilities and others with poor handwriting. As one teacher commented about a student who had learned to use a word processor, "Now, even with hunt and peck, his written assignments are done willingly, on time, and *I can read them!!!*" (Lewis, Dell, Lynch, Harrison, & Saba, 1987, p. 61).

Draft:Builder

The *Draft:Builder* program supports three stages of the writing process: generating and organizing ideas, adding notes, and preparing the first draft. The examples illustrate these stages. The first step in writing a report about *Frankenstein* is to list and organize the main ideas. As the tab at the top of the screen indicates, this stage is called Outline. The student adds ideas to the outline on the left, and a visual map appears on the right.

It is easy to move information around and to add and delete. Also, speech is available throughout *Draft:Builder*; to hear text read aloud, the student clicks on the Speak button.

In the second stage, Notes, the student begins to add information to the outline. In the example, the student is adding two notes to expand the information about the doctor as inventor.

Note: Courtesy of Don Johnston Incorporated.

In the third stage, Draft, the student is able to move notes from the outline into the first draft of a story or essay. The student can make changes to the draft here, then move the text to a word processing program for editing and preparation of the final draft.

Note: Courtesy of Don Johnston Incorporated.

Note: Courtesy of Don Johnston Incorporated.

Write:OutLoud

Write:OutLoud is one of the many word processing programs designed for classroom use. It has three major advantages for students with special needs. It's easy to learn and easy to operate. It talks; that is, it has the ability to read aloud whatever the student has written. And, third, it contains a spelling checker that also talks.

In *Write:OutLoud,* students can easily change the size and color of the letters and the color of the background. It is also possible to add graphics as the sample report on Rosa Parks, the freedom fighter, illustrates.

Note: Courtesy of Don Johnston Incorporated.

One of the most powerful features of this program is its ability to read text aloud. *Write:OutLoud* can be set to speak text automatically as it is entered. Choices include hearing each letter name, each word, each sentence, and/or each paragraph. Students also have the option of hearing any portion of the text read aloud after they've finished writing. To do that, they simply select the text they want to hear and click on the button with the speaker. It is important to note that it is also possible for speech to be turned off.

The spelling checker in *Write:OutLoud* works like a typical spelling checker. When the student chooses Spell Check, the program scans the text to locate spelling errors. When a misspelling is identified, the students see the misspelled word in a sentence (which can be read aloud) and several possible alternatives. Each alternative can be read aloud, a useful feature for students who may have problems reading.

Co:Writer

Co:Writer is a word prediction program. It works with other programs, such as word processors, to reduce the amount of typing students must do. Word prediction programs were originally developed for individuals with physical impairments to reduce the motor demands of the writing task. However, these programs have also been found useful with students with learning disabilities and others who have difficulty spelling (Lewis, Ashton, & Kieley, 1996).

When students are writing with a word processor, they activate *Co:Writer* by pressing the "+" key. A window pops up (see the example) and the student begins writing. When the first letter of a word is typed, *Co:Writer* attempts to predict the word the student wants to enter in the document.

Note: Courtesy of Don Johnston Incorporated.

Here, the student is writing about the stars and wants to use the word *constellation*. When the writer typed a somewhat phonetic version of the word (*kstl*), the program predicted *castle, constellation, kettle,* and *quite*. The student can hear any of these words read aloud and, if one is correct, select it by clicking on it or typing its number. If the list of suggested words does not contain the word the student wants, he or she types another letter and another set of words is predicted.

Draft:Builder, Write:OutLoud, and *Co:Writer* were developed by the Don Johnston company (http://www.donjohnston. com). Versions of *Write:OutLoud* and *Co:Writer* are also available for use with the portable keyboards developed by AlphaSmart (http://www.alphasmart.com).

activities on the words they need to learn. Students also should correct their own spelling tests under the teacher's direction. In a review of research on strategies for teaching spelling skills, Graham and Miller say that this approach is "the single most important factor in learning to spell" (p. 10).

- Provide handwriting prompts such as those shown earlier in this chapter in Figure 9-4. Fade the prompts as quickly as possible.
- Review rules for capitalization and punctuation before students begin writing; post rules on the bulletin board.
- Use instructional tapes for the practice of high-frequency and phonetically irregular spelling words. Students listen to the word, attempt to write it, and listen again to hear the correct spelling.
- For students who form letters slowly and laboriously, use newsprint and felt-tip pens for handwriting practice. When students write slowly on newsprint, the ink spreads, making individual letters indecipherable. Students must increase speed in order for their handwriting to be legible.
- Provide many different opportunities to practice written expression. Have students keep a daily journal, write three-sentence stories, compose a note to a friend each day, or describe an event or person. At first, keep writing activities brief; encourage clarity and accuracy.

- Teach writing as a multistage process. Isaacson (1987) describes three stages: prewriting (or planning), writing, and rewriting (or revising). Mercer and Pullen (2005) identify five: prewriting, drafting, revising (making changes in content), editing (correction of errors), and publishing. Whatever process model is used, provide guided practice at each stage. At the prewriting stage, for instance, students can engage in a variety of activities to generate ideas and gather information for writing. Students can think about the topic, read, or research ideas; they can observe or interview others or listen to speakers, watch demonstrations, or take part in field trips (Tompkins & Friend, 1986; Whitt, Paul, & Reynolds, 1988).
- Give students a format for writing compositions or essays. For example, have them list the main ideas they wish to present and formulate a title. The main ideas are then converted to topic sentences for paragraphs, and supporting sentences are added.
- **Mapping** is another strategy to help students organize their ideas for writing. Students list the key words and ideas they have identified for the topic they will write about, then draw a map showing the relationship between the main topic and key words (Tompkins &

FIGURE 9-6   Organizational Map for an Essay on Scorpions

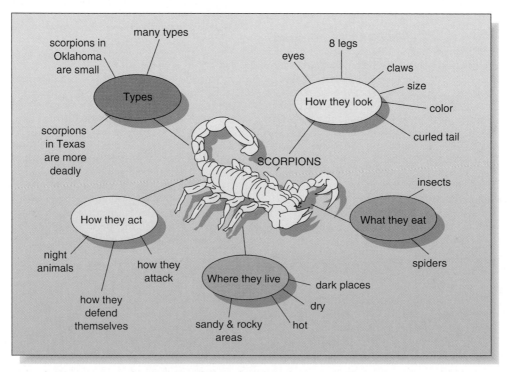

Note: From "On Your Mark, Get Set, Write" by G. E. Tompkins and M. Friend, 1986, *Teaching Exceptional Children, 18*(2), p. 86. Copyright 1985 by The Council for Exceptional Children Reprinted by permission.

Friend, 1986). Figure 9-6 shows a map developed by a group of students for a report on scorpions.

- Teach students specific strategies for planning the content of their writing. For narratives, Graham and Harris (1989) suggest the CSPACE strategy:

  C   character

  S   setting

  P   problem or purpose

  A   action

  C   conclusion

  E   emotion

The TREE strategy (Graham & Harris, 1989) is used when planning opinion essays:

  T   topic

  R   reasons

  E   examples

  E   ending

- Include structured activities for the revising stage of writing. One possibility is the formation of writing groups in the classroom. Each student reads his or her composition aloud to the group, and peers comment on specific strengths in the writing; the writer then asks for help (e.g., "Did the ending make sense?") (Tompkins & Friend, 1986). Students can also evaluate their own work using guides like the self-edit think sheet described by Englert and Raphael (1988). With this guide, students

  first look back at their papers, star the parts they like best, and anticipate readers' questions by putting question marks next to the unclear parts. Next, they rate the extent (e.g., "yes," "sort of," "no") to which they answered the text structure questions (e.g., Did I . . . "Tell what was being explained?" "Tell what materials you need?" "Make the steps clear?" etc.). (p. 518)

- Also teach strategies for locating and correcting writing errors. Schumaker, Nolan, and Deshler (1985) recommend the COPS strategy:

  C   capitalization

  O   overall appearance

  P   punctuation

  S   spelling

- Teach students to use word processors for writing. See the "Spotlight on Technology" earlier in this chapter for word processing tools that assist students in the drafting, revising, and editing stages of writing.

- Teach students what to do when spelling checkers in word processing programs detect a misspelling but cannot suggest the correct alternative. Spelling checkers are able to supply the correct word for spelling errors only about 50% of the time for students with learning disabil-

ities (MacArthur, Graham, Haynes, & DeLaPaz, 1996). One reason for this is that students' spellings are often far from accurate and the program is unable to "guess" the word the student is attempting to write. Ashton (1997) suggests the CHECK strategy. This strategy helps students make systematic changes in their word (altering the beginning letter, consonants, and vowels), attend to the words suggested by the program, and remain persistent.

  C   Check the beginning sound

  H   Hunt for the correct consonants

  E   Examine the vowels

  C   Changes in word lists may give hints

  K   Keeping repeating steps 1 through 4

Math

Many students with special needs require extra assistance in math (Geary, 2004). Within the area of math are two important subskills: computation and reasoning. Computation is based on the prerequisite skills of number concepts, reading and writing numerals, and counting. It includes mastery of number facts in the basic operations (addition, subtraction, multiplication, and division) and knowledge of **algorithms,** the procedures for performing operations. For example, in the algorithm for adding 2 two-digit numbers such as 25 and 48, it is necessary to begin with the right-hand or ones column (5 + 8 = 13); if the sum of the ones column is more than 9 (in this case 13), then the ones portion (3) is written in the ones column, and the tens portion (1) is carried over to the tens column.

In math reasoning, computation skills are used to solve problems. A typical classroom example is the word or story problem in which students are presented with a situation and asked to find a solution. Some students find these difficult because poor reading skills interfere with their understanding of the problem; others have trouble separating essential from superfluous information, determining the appropriate algorithm, and computing the answer.

In recent years, problem solving has become a more important part of the math curriculum due to reform efforts led by the National Council of Teachers of Mathematics (NCTM) (Woodward, 2004). For example, the NCTM (1989, 2000) recommends that students be actively engaged in authentic problem-solving tasks beginning in the early grades. Students who perform poorly in math reasoning tasks should receive extra instruction and practice in this area.

Ways of modifying math instruction in the general education classroom are presented here. Prompts to aid students in computation and reasoning and suggestions for classroom practice activities are included.

- Add visual prompts to help students solve computation problems; see the examples presented in Figure 4-11 in chapter 4.
- For students who have trouble spacing math problems and writing numbers, use paper that has been marked off in squares, or add guidelines so that students write within boundaries.
- Include only a few problems per page if students appear confused by several problems or if they have difficulty finishing their work.
- Use self-instructional materials for drill in number facts; see Figure 9-5 for ideas for materials that can be made by teachers. Or select one of the many software programs for math drill and practice. (Example programs are described in the "Spotlight on Technology" feature in chapter 11.)
- Work toward automatic recall of number facts. Facts are automatic when students no longer need to rely on counting strategies; their responses are quick, accurate, and consistent. To develop **automaticity** (also called *fluency*), Hasselbring, Goin, and Bransford (1987) suggest introducing no more than two or three facts and their reciprocals at a time. Timed drills are used for practice, with the goal being a 1-second response time.
- Manipulative objects help some students learn basic number concepts and relationships; for example, use beans, blocks, or poker chips to teach counting, the relationship of multiplication to addition, and so on.
- Provide verbal prompts to assist in the application of algorithms; for instance, Affleck, Lowenbraun, and Archer (1980) recommend the following for two-digit multiplication: "Multiply by the one's column first. Remember to line up the numbers carefully. Remember to cross multiply" (p. 109).
- Use real situations for word problems. For example, the students' own performance data or the number of points earned for appropriate behavior provide material for practice problems.
- Help students begin to analyze story problems by identifying the key words that often (but not always) signal the different operations. Mercer and Mercer (1989) call these "clue words" and give these examples:

  Addition: Altogether, sum, and, plus, finds
  Subtraction: Left, lost, spent, remains
  Multiplication: Rows, groups, altogether
  Division: Share, each, cost per month (p. 254)
- Set up a class store, bank, or stock exchange, and devise different activities for practice in math reasoning.
- Landi (2001) suggests using a four-part problem-solving strategy based on the work of Montague (1992). In this strategy, students learn to (1) paraphrase the problem, (2) visualize the problem (e.g., by making a diagram), (3) hypothesize about the procedures needed to solve the problem, and (4) estimate the answer to the problem. In

contrast, Montague, Warger, and Morgan (2000) present a more elaborate strategy, Solve It!:
- Read (for understanding)
- Paraphrase (your own words)
- Visualize (a picture or a diagram)
- Hypothesize (a plan to solve the problem)
- Estimate (predict the answer)
- Compute (do the arithmetic)
- Check (make sure everything is right) (p. 111)

MODIFYING CONTENT-AREA INSTRUCTION

In the late elementary grades, the curriculum shifts in emphasis from the acquisition of basic skills to the use of these tool subjects to gain other types of information. Content areas such as English, science, health, history, and social studies begin to dominate the curriculum. In high school, most courses are content subjects, and great variety is seen—foreign language, art, music, business, automotive technology, home economics, physical education and sports, agriculture, driver education, and so on.

Content-area instruction assumes that students have mastered the basic skills of reading, writing, and math. For many special students, this is simply not the case. For these students to benefit from instruction, modifications must be made. Two types of changes are recommended: changing the criteria for task performance and altering the characteristics of content-area tasks. Task criteria include speed and accuracy demands and the amount of work required. Task characteristics, in contrast, refer to the basic skills necessary for performance.

Compensatory strategies are used with older special students to enhance their chances of success. The most common strategy is the replacement of written language requirements with oral language requirements. Instead of reading and writing, students listen and speak; they use areas of strength to compensate for poor basic skills.

The following paragraphs describe several of the task demands that cause difficulty for special students in content-area instruction; suggestions for modifications are also presented.

Reading Assignments

Students whose reading level is less than expected for their grades often find content subjects unmanageable. They may be unable to read textbook assignments, or they may be able to read only slowly and with great effort. To help such students acquire the information presented in assigned readings, teachers can try the following modifications:

- Reduce the amount of reading required. Permit students to read only part of the assignment or to concentrate on the most important elements, such as headings, italicized words, and chapter previews and summaries.

Inclusion Tips for the Teacher

Taped Textbooks

With today's technology, texts and other books are available in a number of alternative formats including books on tape and digital texts (also called e-texts) available for downloading from the World Wide Web. These options are described later in this book in the chapter on visual and hearing impairments. Here the discussion centers on tapes prepared by teachers to meet the specific needs of students in their classrooms.

Deshler and Graham (1980) present guidelines for the use of tape-recorded materials with secondary students with special needs:

1. Teachers should decide what material is to be taped; it is probably necessary to record only key sections of reading assignments, rather than entire texts or chapters.

2. Tapes can be used not only to present content-area information but also to provide instruction in study skills. As Deshler and Graham note,

   While taping a reading assignment, a teacher has an excellent opportunity to demonstrate how to differentiate between main and supportive material within a chapter; how to use illustrations, graphs, charts, etc., to aid comprehension; how to use questions at the end of a section or chapter to determine major points; and how to use chapter titles, section headings, etc, to skim a reading section for main ideas. (p. 53)

3. To facilitate the acquisition of study skills, the teacher can mark the text to indicate important information, less crucial content that will be paraphrased, the point at which to stop the tape to complete activities, and so on.

4. Tapes should be of sufficient quality to ensure comprehension.

5. Principles of learning should guide tape preparation. Deshler and Graham list several important characteristics of an instructional tape:
   - Is well organized
   - Provides a variety of activities
   - Highlights or cues important points
   - Contains a variety of questions designed to facilitate recall and critical analyses
   - Repeats key concepts or ideas
   - Accommodates the assimilation and/or practice of new concepts or ideas
   - Provides immediate and delayed feedback. (p. 54)

6. Edwards (1980) adds that it is necessary to determine whether students learn best with or without the text in front of them while listening to the tape. She suggests conducting a quick, informal assessment of all students to see whether they should listen and read simultaneously or simply listen.

- Substitute materials written on a lower reading level. For example, use a sixth-grade history text for tenth graders. Many remedial reading versions of content subject texts are available from commercial publishers.
- Present the information through another medium. Possible methods are lecture; class discussion; visual aids such as photos, maps, slides, and filmstrips; audiovisual aids such as movies, videotapes, and television; resource people who can be interviewed; peer tutors and volunteers who act as readers; and audiotapes of reading material. One of the most typical adaptations is the use of taped texts. For more information about preparing and using these aids, see the accompanying "Inclusion Tips for the Teacher."

Written Assignments and Exams

Because they may be unable to read directions and questions, students with reading problems find written assignments and exams troublesome. For these students, the adaptations previously suggested can be used. For students who perform poorly in writing despite adequate reading skills, try the following modifications:

- For students who work slowly, reduce the length of the written task or extend the time limits.
- Allow students with poor handwriting to print or write with a word processor.
- Provide poor spellers with a dictionary or a list of commonly misspelled words.
- Consider a dictionary designed for poor spellers, available in most bookstores. In this dictionary, students look up words by their phonetic spellings to find the correct version. The Franklin Spelling Ace® is an electronic version of a poor speller's dictionary. It is a small, portable device; the student types in a phonetic spelling (e.g., *reseve* for *receive*), and a list of possible options is generated: *resolve, receive, reserve,* and so on.
- Permit students to write using a word processor with a spelling checker program to help identify and correct spelling errors.

- Design assignments and exams so that writing requirements are minimized. For example, use multiple-choice and completion formats rather than essays.
- Have students who are unable to compose and write at the same time compose on a tape recorder and then transcribe what they have dictated.
- Have students respond through a medium other than writing. Two possible methods are telling answers to peer tutors or volunteers who write them for the student and giving oral responses to the teacher.

Math Skills

Content-area subjects often require that students have rudimentary math skills. Basic facts and algorithms are necessary for success in algebra, geometry, trigonometry, home economics, and automotive technology. In some areas, such as higher math and vocational classes, computation skills are essential. Classes like English, history, and social studies can demand quantitative reasoning; for instance, graphs and charts are often used to convey important information.

The most common adaptation for students with poor math skills is the use of aids. Students can rely on facts tables for basic computation or use calculators for problems requiring more complex operations. This compensatory strategy is a useful one, and many adults also rely on electronic aids. However, simply providing students with calculators will probably not result in successful performance. Students need to learn how to operate calculators, estimate what the answer should be, and check their results.

By providing students with special needs with compensatory strategies for reading assignments, written work and exams, and math skills, the general education teacher helps bypass basic skills deficits in order to facilitate content-area instruction. Many students with special needs rely on compensatory procedures for their entire lives. Consider the words of Nelson Rockefeller, a former governor of New York and later vice president of the United States, who had a learning disability:

If it helps a dyslexic child to know that I went through the same thing . . .
  But can conduct press conferences today in three languages . . .
  And can read a speech on television . . .
  (Though I may have to rehearse it six times . . .
  (With my script in large type . . .
  (And my sentences broken into segments like these . . .
  (And long words broken into syllables) . . .
  And learned to read and communicate well enough to be elected Governor of New York four times. . . . (Rockefeller, 1976, p. 14)

ADAPTING INSTRUCTION FOR STUDENTS WITH ATTENTION DEFICIT HYPERACTIVITY DISORDERS

Students with attention deficit hyperactivity disorder have many of the same needs as students with learning disabilities and others with academic learning problems. However, unlike students with learning disabilities, students with ADHD may experience difficulty in most, if not all, school subjects. Problems with inattention, distractibility, impulsiveness, and hyperactivity affect all areas of learning. For some students with ADHD, these problems cause serious delays in academic achievement; for others, the effects are less severe.

Students with ADHD are identified by the behaviors they display. The definition currently accepted by most professionals is that of the American Psychiatric Association (1994). Figure 9-7 presents the major elements of the definition included in the fourth edition of that organization's *Diagnostic and Statistical Manual of Mental Disorders* (often called the *DSM-IV*). See the "Inclusion Tips for the Teacher" box to learn more about attention deficit hyperactivity disorders.

As chapter 3 discussed, federal special education law recognizes ADHD as a disability under the "other health impairment" category. Students with ADHD who do not meet criteria for special education may be eligible for services under Section 504 of the Rehabilitation Act of 1973. Such services typically include adaptations in general education programs. The U.S. Department of Education (1991) gives these examples of possible classroom modifications:

providing a structured learning environment; repeating and simplifying instructions about in-class and homework

FIGURE 9-7 Definition of ADHD

The American Psychiatric Association (1994) identifies several characteristics that may indicate attention deficit hyperactivity disorder. These characteristics must appear before age seven, persist for at least six months, be present in more than one environment (e.g., home, school, work), and cause "clinically significant distress or impairment in social, academic, or occupational functioning" (p. 84).

The first set of characteristics relates to inattention and the second to hyperactivity-impulsivity. Three classifications are possible: predominantly inattentive, predominantly hyperactive, or combined. For example, a student who shows six or more of the inattention characteristics but fewer than six of the hyperactivity-impulsivity characteristics would be identified as having ADHD, Predominantly Inattentive Type. The two sets of characteristics follow.

Inattention

Six (or more) of the following symptoms of **inattention** have persisted for at least 6 months to a degree that is maladaptive and inconsistent with developmental level:

Inattention

(a) often fails to give close attention to details or makes careless mistakes in schoolwork, work, or other activities

(b) often has difficulty sustaining attention in tasks or play activities

(c) often does not seem to listen when spoken to directly

(d) often does not follow through on instructions and fails to finish schoolwork, chores, or duties in the workplace (not due to oppositional behavior or failure to understand instructions)

(e) often has difficulties organizing tasks and activities

(f) often avoids, dislikes or is reluctant to engage in tasks that require sustained mental effort (such as schoolwork or homework)

(g) often loses things necessary for tasks or activities (e.g., toys, school assignments, pencils, books, or tools)

(h) is often easily distracted by extraneous stimuli

(i) is often forgetful in daily activities

Hyperactivity-Impulsivity

Six (or more) of the following symptoms of **hyperactivity-impulsivity** have persisted for at least 6 months to a degree that is maladaptive and inconsistent with developmental level:

Hyperactivity

(a) often fidgets with hands or feet or squirms in seat

(b) often leaves seat in classroom or in other situations in which remaining seated is expected

(c) often runs about or climbs excessively in situations in which it is inappropriate (in adolescents or adults, may be limited to subjective feelings of restlessness)

(d) often has difficulty playing or engaging in leisure activities quietly

(e) is often "on the go" or often acts as if "driven by a motor"

(f) often talks excessively

Impulsivity

(g) often blurts out answers before questions have been completed

(h) often has difficulty waiting in turn

(i) often interrupts or intrudes on others (e.g., butts into conversations or games) (pp. 83–84).

Note: Reprinted with permission from the *Diagnostic and Statistical Manual of Mental Disorders,* Fourth Edition, text revision. Copyright © 2000 by American Psychiatric Association.

assignments; supplementing verbal instructions with visual instructions; using behavioral management techniques; adjusting class schedules; modifying test delivery; using tape recorders, computer-aided instruction, and other audiovisual equipment; selecting modified textbooks or workbooks; and tailoring homework assignments. (p. 7)

Interventions for students with ADHD are often multimodal (Lerner & Lowenthal, 1993; Lerner, Lowenthal, & Lerner, 1995; Reeve, 1990). That is, they include not only instructional adaptations but also behavior management programs and medical treatment. Strategies for modifying instruction are discussed here; chapter 11 describes behavioral and medical interventions.

The major approach to adapting instruction for students with ADHD is to increase the structure of the classroom learning environment. In addition, the teacher attempts to

Inclusion Tips for the Teacher

Myths About ADHD

Read the myths below, then check the facts. Note that ADD, as used here, is synonymous with ADHD.

MYTH: Attention Deficit Disorder (ADD) does not really exist. It is simply the latest excuse for parents who do not discipline their children.

FACT: Scientific research tells us ADD is a biologically-based disorder that includes distractibility, impulsiveness, and sometimes hyperactivity. While the causes of ADD are not fully understood, recent research suggests that ADD can be inherited and may be due to an imbalance of neurotransmitters—chemicals used by the brain to control behavior—or abnormal glucose metabolism in the central nervous system. Before a student is labeled ADD, other possible causes of his or her behavior are ruled out.

MYTH: Children with ADD are no different from their peers; all children have a hard time sitting still and paying attention.

FACT: Before children are considered to have ADD, they must show symptoms that demonstrate behavior greatly different from what is expected for children of their age and background. They start to show the behaviors characteristic of ADD between ages three and seven. . . . These behaviors are persistent and occur in many different settings and situations. Furthermore, the behavior must be causing significant social, academic, or occupational impairment for the child to be diagnosed educationally as having ADD.

MYTH: Only a few people really have ADD.

FACT: Estimates of who has ADD range from 3 to 5 percent of the school-age population (between 1.46 and 2.44 million children). While boys outnumber girls by 4:1 to 9:1, experts believe that many girls with ADD are never diagnosed.

MYTH: Medication can cure students with ADD.

FACT: Medicine cannot cure ADD but can sometimes temporarily moderate its effects. Stimulant medication such as Ritalin, Cylert, and Dexedrine is effective in 70 percent of the children who take it. In these cases, medication causes children to exhibit a clear and immediate short-term increase in attention, control, concentration, and goal-directed effort. Medication also reduces disruptive behaviors, aggression, and hyperactivity.

However, there are side effects and no evidence for long-term effectiveness of medication. For example, recent stud-

ies show that medication has only limited short-term benefits on social adjustment and academic achievement. While medication can be incorporated into other treatment strategies, parents and teachers should not use medication as the sole method of helping the child.

MYTH: The longer you wait to deal with ADD in students, the better the chances are that they will outgrow it.

FACT: ADD symptoms continue into adolescence for 50–80 percent of the children with ADD. Many of them, between 30–50 percent, still will have ADD as adults. These adolescents and adults frequently show poor academic performance, poor self-image, and problems with peer relationships.

MYTH: There is little parents and teachers can do to control the behavior of children with ADD.

FACT: Teachers and parents have successfully used positive reinforcement procedures to increase desirable behaviors. A behavioral modification plan can give the child more privileges and independence as the child's behavior improves. Parents or teachers can give tokens or points to a child exhibiting desired behavior—such as remaining seated or being quiet—and can further reward children for good school performance and for finishing homework. Mild, short, immediate reprimands can counter and decrease negative and undesirable behaviors. Students with ADD can learn to follow classroom rules when there are pre-established consequences for misbehavior, rules are enforced consistently and immediately, and encouragement is given at home and in school.

MYTH: Students with ADD cannot learn in the regular classroom.

FACT: More than half of the children with ADD succeed in the mainstream classroom when teachers make appropriate adjustments. Most others require just a part-time program that gives them additional help in a resource room. Teachers can help students learn by providing increased variety. Often, altering features of instructional activities or materials, such as paper color, presentation rate, and response activities, helps teachers hold the attention of students with ADD. Active learning and motor activities also help. ADD students learn best when classroom organization is structured and predictable.

Note: From *Attention Deficit Disorder: Beyond the Myths* developed by the Chesapeake Institute, Washington, D.C., as part of a contract from the Office of Special Education Programs, U.S. Department of Education. No copyright.

decrease the sources of distraction within the classroom and, at the same time, make learning materials and activities more powerful so they will attract and sustain students' attention. Lerner and Lowenthal (1993) provide several specific suggestions drawn from the work of Abramowitz and O'Leary (1991) and Ysseldyke, Algozzine, and Thurlow (1992):

- Place the youngster in the least distracting location in the class. This may be in front of the class, away from doors, windows, air conditioners, heaters, and high-traffic areas. It may be necessary for the child to face a blank wall or be in a study carrel to enable the child to focus attention.

- Surround the student with good role models, preferably peers that the child views as significant others. Encourage peer tutoring and cooperative learning.
- Maintain a low pupil–teacher ratio whenever possible through the use of aides and volunteers.
- Avoid unnecessary changes in schedules and monitor transitions, because the child with ADD often has difficulty coping with changes. When unavoidable disruptions do occur, prepare the student as much as possible by explaining the situation and what behaviors are appropriate.
- Maintain eye contact with the student when giving verbal instructions. Make directions clear, concise, and simple. Repeat instructions as needed in a calm voice.
- Combine visual and tactile cues with verbal instructions since, generally, multiple modalities of instruction will be more effective in maintaining attention and in increasing learning.
- Make lists that will help the student organize tasks. Have the student check them off when they are finished. Students should complete study guides when listening to presentations.
- Adapt worksheets so that there is less material on each page.
- Break assignments into small chunks. Provide immediate feedback on each assignment. Allow extra time if needed for the student to finish the assignment.
- Ensure that the student has recorded homework assignments each day before leaving school. If necessary, set up a home-school program in which the parents help the child organize and complete the homework.
- If the child has difficulty staying in one place at school, alternate sitting with standing and activities which require moving around during the day.
- Provide activities that require active participation such as talking through problems or acting out the steps.
- Use learning aides such as computers, calculators, tape recorders, and programmed learning materials. They help to structure learning and maintain interest and motivation.
- Provide the student opportunities to demonstrate strengths at school. Set up times in which the student can assist peers. (pp. 4–5)

Reeve (1990) adds these recommendations:

- Help the child get started with individual seat work. Have the child verbalize to you what the task is and how he or she is to approach it. Check back periodically to see if the child is still on track.
- Make frequent contact with the child by touching or speaking the child's name. Be sure that you have his or her attention before speaking. . . .

- Give the child extra time to work on assignments or exams, without criticism or fanfare. . . .
- If note taking is a problem, arrange to have a more attentive classmate share notes by photocopying or using carbon paper; or give the child your notes.
- Use multiple choice or one-to-one oral tests to assess the child's mastery of content.
- Give regular feedback and praise successes. (p. 75)

Finally, Bender and Mathes (1995) present these suggestions for organizing the classroom:

- Use a physically structured classroom rather than an "open" classroom. Having walls and a door will block out distractions in the hallway.
- Seat students away from noise. Be cognizant of auditory as well as visual distractions. Seat students away from the door and from auditory distractions.
- Place desks away from each other. Space desks one arm or leg length apart. . . .
- Provide two desks for each student with ADHD. Students with ADHD may stand up and leave their desk without realizing why. Provide a second desk for them to go to when this happens, and acknowledge to the class that the student has a right to change desks when he or she wishes.
- Alternate activities to eliminate desk fatigue. Provide activities that encourage active responding, such as working at the board, "Simon Says," or standing or sitting to indicate a "yes" or "no" answer. (p. 229)

For additional ideas, see Carbone (2001) or Brown, Ilderton, and Taylor (2001). For tips for parents, consult *Identifying and Treating Attention Deficit Hyperactivity Disorder: A Resource for School and Home* (U.S. Department of Education, 2003), a pamphlet available for downloading from the Department of Education's website (http://www.ed.gov/about/reports/annual/osep/index.html). The "Window on the Web" feature describes the website of CHADD, an organization for parents and families of individuals with ADHD. This site is a rich source of ideas for classroom adaptations.

In this chapter, you have learned about ways to adapt classroom instruction for students with learning disabilities and those with ADHD. In the next chapter, you will meet another group of students who are often members of general education classes, students with mental retardation. Methods for teaching functional academics and improving general work habits will be presented. But first, check "Things to Remember" to review ways to meet the needs of students with learning disabilities and others with academic learning problems.

Window on the Web

CHADD

http://www.chadd.org

This website is sponsored by CHADD (Children and Adults with Attention-Deficit/ Hyperactivity Disorder), a national non-profit organization providing education, advocacy and support for individuals with AD/HD. The CHADD website offers information and resources to adults with AD/DH, parents, educators and health and medical professionals including education and employment rights of students, a professional directory, monthly "Ask the Experts" chats and discussion boards, and a listing of current research studies on AD/HD. Visitors to the website can sign up for a free electronic newsletter.

Note: Courtesy of CHADD.

www.help4adhd.org

The National Resource Center on AD/HD (NRC) a program of CHADD that is supported by funding from the U.S. Centers for Disease Control and Prevention, provides a website with resources in English and in Spanish. Designed for children and adults with AD/HD, the website includes topics such as diagnosis and treatment, dealing with the legal system, educational issues and how to live with AD/HD, a feature specifically targeted to adults with the disorder. Visitors to the website can view a list of frequently asked questions, as well as submit questions directly to NRC health information specialists.

Note: Courtesy of CHADD.

For more information, go to the Web Links module in Chapter 9 of the Companion Website.

Things to Remember

- The most common area in which adaptations are made for general education students with learning disabilities is academic instruction; these students may require assistance in acquiring basic skills and/or learning content-area information.
- Major indicators of learning disabilities are a discrepancy between expected and actual achievement and variation in performance.
- In assessment of learning disabilities, information is gathered about intellectual performance, academic achievement, information processing abilities, and strategies for learning; the general education teacher assists by collecting classroom performance data.

- Two approaches to the instruction of students with learning disabilities are remediation and compensation. The goal of remediation is the improvement of weaknesses; compensatory strategies, on the other hand, bypass or make up for weaknesses by using the strengths of the student.
- Remediation is used to teach younger students the basic skills of reading, handwriting, spelling, written expression, and math.
- In basic skills instruction, three adaptations are recommended: prompts, extra instruction, and additional guided practice.
- With older students, compensatory strategies are used to bypass basic skill deficiencies in order to teach content-area subjects.

- In content-area instruction, reading assignments, written work and exams, and math demands are modified by changing task criteria and characteristics.
- The most common compensatory strategy is the substitution of oral language tasks for reading and writing tasks.
- Inattention, distractibility, impulsiveness, and hyperactivity are indicators of ADHD.

- Instruction is modified for students with ADHD by increasing the structure of the learning environment and by eliminating distractions that compete with academic tasks for students' attention.

ACTIVITIES

1. Visit a special education resource room that serves students with learning disabilities. Observe the students and talk with the teacher. In what school subjects do students experience the most difficulty? What subjects are taught by the special education teacher? In what instructional activities do these students participate in the general education classroom?

2. Select one of the special education journals that focuses on learning disabilities. Choose from the *Journal of Learning Disabilities, Learning Disabilities Research & Practice,* and *Learning Disabilities: A Multidisciplinary Journal.* Look through recent issues for articles that present inclusion suggestions. Collect ideas for making instructional adaptations in the general education classroom.

3. Among the websites described in this chapter's "Window on the Web" features are those of two large parent organizations, the Learning Disabilities Association (LDA) and CHADD (Children and Adults with Attention-Deficit/Hyperactivity Disorder). Visit these sites, then compare them with that of the Division for Learning Disabilities (DLD), a professional organization that is part of the Council for Exceptional Children. Which sites have information for parents? Teachers? Both?

4. Pretend that you are a student with learning disabilities enrolled in a college course. You are doing quite well but anticipate that you will have trouble on the final exam. You fear that you won't be able to finish in the allotted 2 hours. How would you explain this to your instructor? What alternatives or instructional modifications could you suggest?

5. If possible, review one of the word processing programs described in "Spotlight on Technology" feature in this chapter. What are the program's major advantages for students with learning disabilities? Do you see any drawbacks? Would the program be equally effective for elementary and secondary students? If these programs are not available, try using your own word processor to check the spelling of the following sentences written by a sixth grader with learning disabilities.

The student wrote:

> once a upon a time ther was some gis and women in the woods. thes man and women are like cavmen.

The student read:

> Once upon a time there was some girls and women in the woods. These men and women are like cavemen.

Did your spelling checker find all of the errors? Was it able to suggest the correct spelling?

CD-ROM Activities

The case study showing the work of the middle school assessment team provides information about a young man who is not working up to his potential in school. Review the video clips entitled "Identify Strengths," "Identify Concerns," and "Academic Inroads" (and any others you need to) in order to respond to these questions:

- *What school subjects are strength areas for Tommy? Which subjects pose the most challenge?*

- *Describe Tommy's skills in reading and in writing. Is one skill area more difficult for him?*

- *What types of problems does Tommy have in focusing his attention? In organizing his time and belongings? What ideas does the team suggest to help Tommy improve in these areas?*

Teaching Students with Mild Retardation and Severe Disabilities

CHAPTER

10

Judy

Judy is a fourth-grade student with mild mental retardation. In most areas of academic and social development, 10-year-old Judy performs like a student who is 7 or 8. Her reading and math computation skills are at the second-grade level, and her spelling skills are at the first-grade level. At home, most of Judy's playmates are younger than she is; she enjoys interacting with first and second graders but doesn't appear interested in the more advanced games and activities of her age-mates. At school, Judy spends most of her day in a regular fourth-grade classroom and she has made friends with several of her classmates. In the morning, the special education resource teacher comes to Judy's classroom to teach reading to Judy and four other students. In the afternoon, Judy visits the resource room for instruction in spelling, handwriting, and written expression. Judy receives instruction from Mrs. Thomas, her fourth-grade teacher, in math, art, music, and physical education. To help Judy succeed in fourth-grade math, Mrs. Thomas modifies assignments and exams and provides Judy with extra practice in computational skills. Also, Judy's math program includes practice in the application of basic skills to daily life problems. For instance, she is learning to add and subtract money and to make change.

Joe

Joe is a high school student with mild retardation who is 15 years old and in the ninth grade. Joe wants to learn a marketable skill in high school so that he can get a job when he graduates. Because his basic academic skills are at approximately the fifth-grade level, Joe attends special education classes in Basic English and Basic Math. He is also enrolled in

LOOKING AHEAD

Later in this chapter you will see portions of Judy's special education assessment results as well as her IEP. You will also learn strategies for helping students like Judy and Joe to learn important academic skills and work habits—and to apply those skills and habits to real life problems. As you're reading this chapter, think about how you might answer these questions:

- What are Judy's areas of strengths at school and at home? How would you describe her social development in relation to other 10-year-olds?
- Judy will be entering middle school quite soon. In what areas would you anticipate she'd need the most support in making the transition?
- Joe wants to get a job when he graduates from high school. What academic skills will he need to successfully pursue his vocational plans? What general work habits will be the most important for him to learn?

To answer these questions online, go to the Students' Stories module in Chapter 10 of the Companion Website.

Career Exploration, a special education course that surveys several job options and provides instruction in general vocational skills, such as punctuality, job-related social skills, work completion, and filling out job applications. Joe attends two general education classes—Automotive Technology I and Physical Education. With the assistance of his general and special education teachers, Joe is earning passing grades in auto tech. Ms. Frye, Joe's reading teacher, provides tapes of textbooks so that Joe can keep up with reading assignments. Mr. Nash, the auto tech teacher, adapts the written assignments for Joe and allows him to take quizzes and exams orally. In addition, Joe's Career Exploration teacher works closely with Mr. Nash to ensure that Joe acquires the basic work skills important in auto shops. If Joe continues to succeed in his vocational education class, next year he will advance to Automotive Technology II.

Mental retardation is a comprehensive disability. It affects not only school learning but also the development of language, social, and vocational skills. Students with mental retardation are able to learn, but their learning proceeds more slowly than that of students with average ability. Consequently, students with retardation often perform at a level expected of younger students. At age 6, pupils with mild retardation may act like average 4-year-olds; at age 10, their school achievement may resemble that of second or third graders. Because it is difficult for these students to learn quickly, it is crucial that instruction focus on important areas that will help them become self-supporting adults. For most students with mild retardation, much of this instruction occurs in the general education classroom. With the aid and assistance of general and special educators, students with mild retardation can successfully participate in many classroom activities.

Students with mild retardation have special needs in academic, classroom behavioral, physical, and social performance and may require individualized assistance from special educators in several of these areas. In addition, when students with mild retardation are included in regular classes, the general education teacher must often modify classroom procedures for academic instruction. Younger students like Judy, who is described in the "Students' Stories" section, may need extra help in basic skills such as reading, math, and spelling; such students may also require help in learning to generalize skills from one situation to another. In middle school and high school, students like Joe often continue their study of basic skills and begin to acquire important career skills; when included in general education, they may participate in regular vocational education classes. Throughout the school years, instruction for youngsters with mild retardation focuses on the development of basic academic skills and the application of these and other skills to career preparation.

This chapter describes the characteristics of students with mild mental retardation. It also presents methods for the general education teacher to use in gathering data, teaching functional academic skills, and improving students' general work habits. Most students identified as mentally retarded have mild disabilities. Students are considered to have a severe disability when their retardation is moderate or severe, rather than mild. Students with severe disabilities are often members of special classes located within neighborhood schools; some are included in regular classrooms. The final section of this chapter addresses this group of learners and suggests ways to promote the inclusion of students with severe disabilities as members of the school community and to adapt classroom instruction to meet severe learning needs. To become more familiar with the disability of mental retardation, consult one of the resources described in the accompanying "Window on the Web" feature.

INDICATORS OF MENTAL RETARDATION

The general educator is an important member of the inclusion team for students with mild retardation. These students usually begin their education in the general education classroom and are referred for special education assessment when they are slow to acquire basic academic skills. The classroom teacher plays a role in not only instruction but also identification and referral; in addition, general education services are coordinated with the services of special educators such as the resource teacher.

Students are generally identified as having mild retardation during the first few years of school. There are two main indicators of mild mental retardation. First, although such students are able to learn, their rate of learning is slow. Because of this, their level of development resembles that of younger children. For example, a second-grade student may be just beginning to learn to say the alphabet, count, and write his or her name. The second indicator is that most areas of development are delayed. Unlike students with learning disabilities, individuals with mild retardation perform poorly on most tasks when compared to peers. Their disability is comprehensive; it impinges on performance at school, at home, in the neighborhood, and in the community. These students fail to meet age expectations in intellectual and language development, academic achievement, social competence, and prevocational skills.

Students with mild retardation, although characterized by slower learning rates, are able to profit from many of the instructional activities in the general education classroom.

Window on the Web

Websites About Mental Retardation

http://thearc.org

Founded in 1950, The Arc of the United States (formerly the Association for Retarded Citizens) is the largest national volunteer organization related to mental retardation. Its mission, stated on the website, is working "to include all children and adults with cognitive, intellectual, and developmental disabilities in every community." The Arc website offers resources such as information on topics in mental retardation and related areas, updates on legislation and other current events (see the Governmental Affairs section), and the organization's position statements on topics such as inclusion, human and civil rights, and self-determination. Visitors can also search the website for specific topics, visit the active Discussion Boards, or access links to other sites related to mental retardation.

Note: Courtesy of The ARC.

http://www.aamr.org

The American Association on Mental Retardation (AAMR), founded in 1876, is the nation's oldest organization for professionals and others interested in mental retardation. AAMR's website provides information for its members and others about the organization's policies and positions, journals, publications, and annual meeting. One interesting feature of the site is the AAMR Reading Room, a searchable database of on-line reference material about mental retardation and developmental disabilities. The material can also be accessed by topic areas such as aging, genetics, quality of life, and technology.

Note: Courtesy of AAMR.

For more information, go to the Web Links module in Chapter 10 of the Companion Website.

These individuals make up the great majority of all persons with retardation, and, according to the Association for Retarded Citizens (n.d.), "Their retardation is not usually apparent until they enter school. And then, as adults, they often lose their identity as retarded when they enter the job market and daily community life" (p. 5).

Students with mild retardation learn in the same ways that average students do. However, some types of learning cause them particular difficulty. For example, reading comprehension skills appear more difficult for students with mild retardation than reading recognition. Similarly, such students are less successful with math problem solving than math computation (Thomas & Patton, 1990). Evidence also suggests that students with mild retardation have memory and attention problems and difficulty applying learned skills to new situations (Drew, Logan, & Hardman, 1992; Forness & Kavale, 1993; Turnbull, Turnbull, Shank, & Smith, 2004).

These and other indicators of mild mental retardation can be noticed by the general education teacher. Students who learn slowly, perform at a level appropriate for younger individuals, and show consistent delays in several areas are prime candidates for referral for special education assessment. Consult the "For Your Information" material to learn more about students with mild retardation.

ASSESSMENT PROCEDURES

When mental retardation is suspected, the multidisciplinary team meets and prepares an assessment plan. According to McLoughlin and Lewis (2005), it is important to collect information about at least three areas of current performance: academic achievement, intellectual functioning, and adaptive behavior. However, there is some variation in the specific guidelines that states use to determine eligibility for public

For Your Information

Students with Mild Retardation

- Mental retardation is one of the most common disabilities; in 2000–2001, 10.6% of the students served in special education programs were identified as mentally retarded (U.S. Department of Education, 2002).
- There is still concern today about the overrepresentation of students from some racial/ethnic groups in special education programs for individuals with mild retardation (Artiles & Trent, 1994; Chinn & Hughes, 1987; Janesick, 1995). According to a study by Harry (cited in U.S. Department of Education, 1996), African American students made up 16% of the U.S. school population but 35% of students identified as mildly retarded.
- The President's Committee for People with Intellectual Disabilities (formerly the President's Committee on Mental Retardation) (2004) estimates that approximately 3% of the population is mentally retarded.
- Individuals with mild retardation account for approximately 87% of the persons identified as retarded (The Arc, 2002).

- For most persons with mild retardation, the cause of the disability is unknown (Hallahan & Kauffman, 1988; Morrison & Polloway, 1995; Smith, 2004).
- According to Kirk and Gallagher (1979), students with mild retardation are those who are able to profit from academic instruction; the IQ range associated with this group is 50 to 70 or 75, which is equivalent to that of adults with mental ages of 7.5 to 11 years (Becker, Engelmann, & Thomas, 1975).
- During their school years, students with mild retardation acquire basic academic skills up to approximately the sixth-grade level; as adults they can achieve the necessary social and vocational skills to become at least minimally self-supporting (President's Committee on Mental Retardation, 1975; The Arc, 2002).
- The most typical special education placement for students with mild retardation is part-time service in a resource room or special class. During the remainder of their school day, they are included with age peers in the general education classroom (Blake, 1981; Heward & Orlansky, 1992).

school services for students with retardation. States differ in the IQ scores used as cutoffs for determining retardation. Also, although impaired adaptive behavior is generally accepted as an important indicator of retardation, not all states include this area in their definition of mental retardation (Bruininks, Thurlow, & Gilman, 1987; Patrick & Reschly, 1982). Therefore, teachers must become aware of the specific guidelines in force in their states and school districts.

When individuals are referred for consideration for special education services for students with retardation, academic achievement is measured to determine whether there is an educational performance problem. The *Peabody Individual Achievement Test–Revised/Normative Update (PIAT-R/NU)* (Markwardt, 1998), which was described in chapter 9, can be administered, or the team can select another individual measure, such as the achievement portion of the *Woodcock-Johnson III (WJ III)* (Woodcock, McGrew, & Mather, 2001).

The *WJ III,* which is generally administered by the school psychologist or special educator, is appropriate for students from age 2 through adulthood. Its standard battery assesses reading, oral language, mathematics, written language, and academic knowledge. Grade and age scores, standard scores, and percentile rank scores are available for each subtest and each academic skill area. The mean (or average) standard score on the *WJ III* is 100, and scores between 85 and 115 are considered to be within the average range of performance. The assessment results in Figure 10-1 show that Judy, introduced at

the beginning of this chapter, is performing below grade-level expectations in all academic subjects assessed by the *WJ III.*

Another major step in assessment is the determination of the student's general ability level. This is particularly important if mild retardation is suspected because below average intellectual performance is one of the criteria for this disability. The *Wechsler Intelligence Scale for Children–Fourth Edition (WISC-IV)* (Wechsler, 2003), which was described in chapter 9, is usually used to assess global ability in school-aged children. Judy's assessment results in Figure 10-1 include *WISC-IV* scores; all IQs fall below 70, which indicates current functioning within the below average range.

Adaptive behavior is a third consideration in assessment when mental retardation is suspected. According to the American Association on Mental Retardation's (2002) definition of mental retardation, it is important to document not only below average intellectual performance but also impaired adaptive behavior. Measures such as the *AAMR Adaptive Behavior Scale—School* (2nd ed.) (Lambert, Nihira, & Leland, 1993) and the *Scales of Independent Behavior—Revised (SIB-R)* (Bruininks, Woodcock, Weatherman, & Hill, 1996) can be used to gather information about the student's social competence.

On the *AAMR* scale, teachers and others rate the student's performance in areas such as independent functioning, physical development, economic activity, language development, and numbers and time; the scale is appropriate for use with students ages 3 to 21. The *SIB-R,* designed for preschool through

FIGURE 10-1   Special Education Assessment Results

Student: Judy   **Age:** 10 years, 5 months   **Grade:** 4

Academic Performance

Judy was administered the standard achievement battery of the *Woodcock-Johnson III* by Mrs. Simeon, the resource teacher. These results were obtained:

Area	Grade Score	Standard Score	Percentile Rank
Broad Reading	1.8	68	2
Broad Mathematics	2.8	73	3
Broad Written Language	1.6	62	1

Judy's skills fall in the low average to below average range of performance in all areas, a result confirmed by her fourth grade teacher, Mrs. Thomas. Judy's grade scores indicate performance at the grade 1 to grade 2 level. In Broad Reading, she earned a percentile rank of 2, which indicates that her performance was equal to or better than that of only 2 percent of her age peers in the test's norm group. In Broad Written Language, she achieved a percentile rank of 1. Her performance was somewhat better in Math, where she earned a percentile rank of 3. These results indicate serious achievement problems in three basic skill areas, with the most severe problems occurring in reading and written language skills.

Intellectual Performance

The *Wechsler Intelligence Scale—Fourth Edition* was administered to Judy by Mr. Henry, the school psychologist. Judy's intelligence quotient (IQ) scores were as follows:

Verbal Comprehension	64
Perceptual Reasoning	61
Working Memory	58
Processing Speed	60
Full Scale	59

All IQ scores fall within the below average range. These results point to the possibility of mild mental retardation.

Adaptive Behavior

Mrs. Simeon interviewed Judy's parents to learn more about Judy's performance at home and in community situations. The *Scales of Independent Behavior—Revised* were used for this purpose, with the following results:

Area	Standard Score
Motor Skills	82
Social Interaction and Communication Skills	65
Personal Living Skills	68
Community Living Skills	72

Judy's adaptive behavior, as reported by her parents, fell in the below average range of performance in two areas, Social Interaction and Communication Skills and Personal Living Skills. This finding, along with the results of other measures and the information provided by Judy's classroom teacher, supports the conclusion of mild mental retardation. Intellectual performance is below average, adaptive behavior appears to be impaired, and academic achievement falls within the low average and below average ranges.

adulthood, uses interviews with parents, teachers, or others to gather information about current functioning levels. This measure assesses several different aspects of adaptive behavior: Motor Skills, Social Interaction and Communication Skills, Personal Living Skills, and Community Living Skills. Several types of scores are available, including standard scores and percentile ranks. The case of Judy in Figure 10-1 illustrates a student with low performance in two areas of adaptive behavior.

If a student is found to perform below age expectations in academic achievement, general intellectual ability, and adaptive behavior, the team may decide that the student is eligible for special education services for students with retardation. The next step is to determine the precise educational needs of the student. All members of the team, including the student's parents, have valuable information to contribute; however, the general education teacher is probably the person most knowledgeable about the student's current academic skill levels. Before an educational program for a student with mild retardation can be planned, information is needed about current school performance and the student's ability to use basic academic skills to solve daily life problems. Also, the prevocational and career skills of the student must be considered. Teachers can develop informal assessments for this purpose, or they can choose from commercially available measures, such as the criterion-referenced tests by Brigance.

BRIGANCE® inventories are available for preschool, elementary, and secondary students: the *Diagnostic Inventory of Early Development–Revised* (Brigance, 1991) for children from birth to developmental age 7, the *Diagnostic Comprehensive Inventory of Basic Skills–Revised* (Brigance, 1999) for grades prekindergarten through 9, and the *Diagnostic Inventory of Essential Skills* (Brigance, 1981) for assessment of grades 4 through 11 achievement. A special feature of the secondary *BRIGANCE®* instrument is its coverage of basic skills not only in isolation but also as applied to daily life and vocational areas. Table 10-1 presents a listing of functional skill subtests from which teachers can choose.

The *BRIGANCE®* inventories allow teachers to determine which skills have been mastered by the student and which must still be taught. Each criterion-referenced test includes simple directions for administration and scoring, plus a recommended instructional objective for the skill. For example, on the Warning/Safety Signs subtest the student is asked to read 40 signs, such as "Keep Out" and "High Voltage"; the objective recommended for this skill is

> By (*date*), when presented with a list of 40 words and
> phrases frequently seen on warning and safety signs,
> (*student's name*) will read (*number*) correctly.

These objectives, if appropriate for the student, can aid the team in preparation of the IEP.

SPECIAL SERVICES

Individualized education programs for students with mild retardation usually contain several annual goals. Typical areas of instruction are reading, math, oral language, written language, and vocational preparation and other types of transition services. Special education services can be provided by the resource teacher or, for students with severe delays, the teacher of a special class. Others such as the speech-language clinician and the adapted physical education teacher often provide support services for children and adolescents with mild retardation.

These special students are included in general education programs to the maximum extent appropriate. Some may participate in only nonacademic classroom activities such as art, music, and physical education; others, like Judy and Joe, are included in academic programming. A portion of Judy's IEP in Figure 10-2 on page 243 shows that, although Judy visits the resource room for an hour each afternoon, the majority of her instruction takes place in the fourth-grade classroom.

CLASSROOM ADAPTATIONS

Classroom instruction is the primary area in which adaptations are made for students with mild retardation in general education programs; this section focuses on methods for meeting the special academic needs of these students. Some individuals with mild retardation also require assistance in the area of classroom conduct; chapter 11 presents strategies for controlling disruptive behaviors. Chapter 6 contains suggestions for increasing the social acceptance of special students who have difficulty relating to classmates.

Habilitation is the major approach to the education of mainstreamed students with mild retardation. The goal is not to remediate or compensate for skill deficiencies; instead, instruction is directed toward the development of the crucial skills necessary for successful adulthood. Habilitation is the process of becoming capable or qualified; for students with mild retardation, this means the acquisition of skills that are important for daily life, citizenship, and a future career. Because these special students learn more slowly than their age peers, their educational program must concentrate on the most crucial and functional skills.

Transition and **career education** services are one way of conceptualizing the habilitation process for students with mild retardation. According to the Council for Exceptional Children (1993a), career education and transition are "the totality of experiences through which one learns to live a meaningful, satisfying work life." Brolin (1986) expands this definition:

> Career education is not simply preparation for a job. It is also preparation for other productive work roles that comprise one's total career functioning. This includes the work of a homemaker and family member, the participation as a citizen and volunteer, and the engagement in productive leisure and recreational pursuits that are of benefit to oneself and others. (p. vii)

TABLE 10-1	Functional Skills Assessed by the *BRIGANCE® Diagnostic Inventory of Essential Skills*

AREA	SUBTESTS
Functional Word Recognition	Basic Sight Vocabulary
	Direction Words
	Abbreviations
	Warning/Safety Signs
	Reads Number Words
Schedules and Graphs	Reads Class Schedule
	Reads Television Schedule
	Identifies and Interprets Graphs
Forms	School Information Form
	Computer Base Form
Measurement	Equivalent Values of Coins and the Dollar Bill
	Total Values of Collections of Coins and Bills
	Conversion of Coins
	Time
	Equivalent Units of Time
	Conversion of Units of Time
	Equivalent Calendar Units
	Conversion of Calendar Units
	Calendar
	Dates
	Ruler
	Equivalent Units of Measurement
	Conversion of Units of Measurement
	Meters and Gauges
	Concepts of Fahrenheit Temperature
Health and Safety	Medical Vocabulary
	Medical Labels
	Health Evaluation Form
	Health Practices and Attitude Rating Scale
	Self-Concept Rating Scale
	Warning Labels
Vocational	Attitude Rating Scale
	Personality Rating Scale
	Responsibility and Self-Discipline Rating Scale
	Job Interests and Aptitudes
	Health and Physical Problems/Handicaps
	Application for a Social Security Number
	Choosing a Career
	Employment Signs
	Employment Vocabulary
	Employment Abbreviations
	"Help Wanted" Advertisements
	Simple Application for Employment
	Complex Application for Employment
	Job Interview Questions
	Job Interview Preparation Rating Scale
	Job Interview Rating Scale

continued

TABLE 10-1   continued

AREA	SUBTESTS
Vocational *(continued)*	W-4 Form
	Future Time on Clock
	Past Time on Clock
	Time Duration on Clock
	Payroll Deductions
	Federal Income Tax Return—Form 1040A
	Unemployment Compensation Form
Money and Finance	Price Signs
	Computes Totals for Amounts of Money
	Making Change
	Comprehends and Computes Purchase Savings
	Computes Expenses Using Charts and Tables
	Banking and Credit Vocabulary
	Manages a Checking Account
	Computes Interest on Loans
	Reads and Comprehends a Credit Agreement
	Application for a Credit Card
	Reads and Comprehends Monthly Credit Statement
Travel and Transportation	Traffic Signs
	Traffic Symbols
	Car Parts Vocabulary
	Identifies Car Parts
	Application for Driver's Instruction Permit
	Auto Safety Rating Scale
	Gas Mileage and Cost
	Mileage Table
	Bus Schedule and Map of Route
	Road Map
Food and Clothing	Food Vocabulary
	Food Preparation Vocabulary
	Basic Recipe Directions
	Food Labels
	Conversion of Recipes to Different Servings
	Foods for a Daily Balanced Diet
	Computes Cost of Purchasing Different Quantities
	Food Quantity at Best Price
	Personal Sizes of Clothing
	Clothing Labels
Oral Communication and Telephone Skills	Speaking Skills
	Speaking Skills Rating Scale
	Listening Skills
	Listening Skills Rating Scale
	Telephone
	Telephone Book
	Telephone Yellow Pages

Note: From the *BRIGANCE® Diagnostic Inventory of Essential Skills.* Copyright 1981 by Curriculum Associates. Reproduced by permission of the publisher.

FIGURE 10-2 IEP Goals and Services for Judy

Annual Goals
1. By the end of the school year, Judy will read grade 2 material with adequate word recognition and comprehension.
   Person responsible: Resource teacher
2. By the end of the school year, Judy will correctly spell a minimum of 100 high-frequency words.
   Person responsible: Resource teacher
3. By the end of the school year, Judy will legibly print all lower- and uppercase manuscript letters.
   Person responsible: Resource teacher
4. By the end of the school year, Judy will write simple sentences and personal information, such as her name, address, and telephone number.
   Person responsible: Resource teacher
5. By the end of the school year, Judy will perform math computation problems at grade 3.5 level.
   Person responsible: Fourth grade teacher
6. By the end of the school year, Judy will achieve minimum competencies in math application skills such as time, money, and measurement.
   Person responsible: Fourth grade teacher
7. Judy will successfully complete minimum requirements for fourth grade art, music, and physical education.
   Person responsible: Fourth grade teacher

Amount of Participation in General Education
Judy will receive instruction in the regular fourth grade class for the entire day except for 1 hour in the afternoon.

Special Education and Related Services
1. The resource teacher will provide special education services to Judy for 1 hour each morning in the fourth grade classroom (goal 1) and for 1 hour each afternoon in the resource room (goals 2, 3, and 4).
2. The resource teacher will provide consultation for Judy's fourth grade teacher as needed.

Kokaska and Brolin (1985) identify three major curriculum areas important in preparing for adulthood: daily living skills, personal-social skills, and occupational skills; specific competency areas are listed in Figure 10-3. In the system described by Cronin and Patton (1993), life skills are organized into six major domains: employment-education, home and family, leisure pursuits, personal responsibility and relationships, emotional-physical health, and community involvement.

One important factor to consider in a transition and career education program is the sequence in which competencies are presented. Kokaska (1980) recommends the following progression for special students:

- career awareness (kindergarten onward)
- career exploration (Grade 6 onward)
- career preparation (Grade 6–7 onward)
- career placement, follow-up, and continuing education (Grade 10 onward). (p. 38)

In the last two stages, career preparation and career placement, students may have the opportunity to participate in supervised job placements on the school campus and in the community. Community-based training is an important component of career preparation for students with mild retardation because it promotes the generalization of work skills to actual work environments.

Transition and career education training can be infused into the general education classroom curriculum in several ways. First, by providing academic skill instruction, the general education teacher emphasizes one important component of career preparation: literacy, which is essential for most work and many life tasks. Second, the classroom teacher can help students by providing instruction and practice in the application of basic school and work skills to life problems. Such assistance is particularly important for students with mild retardation, who often have difficulty generalizing skills and information from one situation to another. Third, a portion of the general education curriculum can be devoted to career awareness and exploration. At the secondary level, much of the curriculum is already career oriented; students learn specific job skills in vocational classes, and in college preparatory courses students acquire skills and information necessary for further training.

The following sections present methods for teaching students with mild retardation in the general education classroom.

FIGURE 10-3   Important Competencies for Adulthood

Daily Living Skills
Managing family finances
Selecting, managing, and maintaining a home
Caring for personal needs
Raising children—family living
Buying and preparing food
Buying and caring for clothing
Engaging in civic activities
Utilizing recreation and leisure
Getting around the community (mobility)

Personal-Social Skills
Achieving self-awareness
Acquiring self-confidence
Achieving socially responsible behavior
Maintaining good interpersonal skills
Achieving independence
Achieving problem-solving skills
Communicating adequately with others

Occupational Skills
Knowing and exploring occupational possibilities
Selecting and planning occupational choices
Exhibiting appropriate work habits and behaviors
Exhibiting sufficient physical-manual skills
Obtaining a specific occupational skill
Seeking, securing, and maintaining employment

Note: Reprinted with permission of Merrill, an imprint of Macmillan Publishing Company, from *Career Education for Handicapped Individuals* (2nd ed., pp. 46–47) by C. J. Kokaska and D. E. Brolin, Copyright © 1985 Merrill Publishing Company, Columbus, Ohio.

Included are ways to teach functional academic skills and techniques for improving students' general work habits.

TEACHING FUNCTIONAL ACADEMICS

Students with mild retardation need special help to acquire the basic skills of reading, handwriting, spelling, written expression, and math. Typically, they receive instruction in these areas from the special education teacher; many students also participate in instructional activities in the general education classroom. In teaching basic skills to persons with mild retardation, the classroom teacher will find the techniques recommended for students with learning disabilities useful. As described in chapter 9, academic instruction is adapted to

special needs by providing prompts, giving additional instruction, and allowing extra guided practice. Several strategies for adapting basic skills instruction were suggested in chapter 9. For students who learn slowly and require much repetition and practice, computers can be a useful tool for learning academic skills. See the accompanying "Spotlight on Technology" material (pages 246–247) for information about software programs that help develop basic reading skills.

The need to provide instruction and practice in skill generalization is a major consideration when teaching students with mild retardation. These students have difficulty applying skills and information learned in one situation to a new but similar problem or situation. For example, a student might add and subtract whole numbers easily when given a worksheet of computation problems but be unable to apply this skill to adding and subtracting coins. For this reason, educational programs for students with retardation focus on **functional skills,** that is, skills required for the satisfactory performance of everyday life tasks. Basic skills instruction must go beyond textbooks and workbook pages; it must extend into the real world if special students are to use tool subjects to solve the problems of everyday life.

Two major strategies are used for teaching functional academic skills. In one, the **unit approach,** instruction in several basic skill areas is integrated around a central theme of interest and value to the students; this approach is probably best used with younger students. In the other approach, reading, writing, and math are taught as separate subjects, but functional practice activities are designed to promote generalization of skills to life problems.

The Unit Approach

Instructional units allow the teacher to present functional academics in a meaningful context. First, an important life theme is selected; then, basic skills are presented, and practice opportunities related to the theme are provided. Meyen (1981) provides two examples. The first unit, "Time," is intended for intermediate grade students. Basic skills instruction and practice are included within subtopics such as recreation, seasons, measurement, money, and holidays. The second unit, "Home Safety and Maintenance," is also for intermediate grade students. It features subtopics such as basic first aid, emergencies, and drugs and poisonous substances.

Many unit themes would be appropriate for special students and other members of general education classrooms. For example, "Becoming a Consumer" is a topic that could be adapted to varying skill, age, and interest levels. For younger students, this unit could be used to teach basic money skills, such as identifying coins and bills, adding and subtracting amounts of money, and making change. For older (or more capable) students, appropriate consumer skills are reading advertisements, comparison shopping, and installment buying. Other flexible unit themes are transportation (e.g., riding the school bus, using public transportation, driving a car), getting a job (e.g., chores at home, the want ads, job applications and interviews), and money management (e.g., budgeting your allowance, using the automatic teller machine and bank, handling paychecks and taxes).

Functional Practice Activities

The classroom teacher can design practice activities in any basic skill area so that they relate to daily life problems. One source of ideas for functional activities is a transition and career education curriculum, such as the one outlined earlier in Figure 10-3. The key factor to be kept in mind when developing practice tasks is their relevance to life and work activities. Of course, the teacher must also consider the students' skill levels and the amount of supervision required during student practice.

Reading is an excellent skill to practice with everyday materials. Activities can focus on reading for information or reading as a leisure pastime. Some examples of reading materials appropriate for functional activities are listed here:

- Signs commonly found in buildings and in the community (e.g., *Women, Men, Stop, Do Not Enter*);
- Community and student newspapers and magazines;
- Menus for fast-food and regular restaurants;
- Schedules for classes, television, movies, buses, and trains;

- The phone book;
- Advertisements for consumer goods and jobs;
- Directions for building models, assembling toys, or completing forms; and
- Labels on foods, medicines, and clothing.

Figure 10-4 on page 248 lists important career and vocational words suggested by Schilit and Caldwell (1980); practice of words such as these is appropriate for secondary students.

Many daily life activities can be used to practice handwriting, spelling, and written expression. The tasks that follow emphasize writing as a means of communication:

- making a shopping list or a things-to-do list,
- leaving a note for a friend or family member,
- writing an e-mail message,
- writing a postcard, invitation, or friendly letter,
- completing a job application,
- ordering something by mail by filling in an order blank,
- writing a business letter,
- applying for a Social Security number or a driver's permit, and
- writing down a telephone message for someone.

The skill area of math also offers numerous opportunities for functional practice. Computation ability is often required in everyday life, particularly in tasks involving time, money, and measurement. Examples are

- making a purchase;
- budgeting an allowance or paycheck;
- comparison shopping;

Spotlight on Technology

Developing Basic Reading Skills

Computers can be used to develop reading skills in children just beginning to learn to read and in older students with difficulties in reading. For this to occur, it is necessary to use software that talks. The programs described here all offer high-quality digitized (prerecorded) speech.

Phonics Instruction with *Simon S. I. O.*

Simon S. I. O. ("Sounds it Out") from Don Johnston Inc. (http://www.donjohnston.com) is designed to help students learn the sounds that correspond to letters. This sequential program contains more than 50 levels, and levels are based on word families. For example, in Stage 1 of *Simon S. I. O.*, the first level is based on the *at* word family and introduces the sounds of *b* and *r*. Level 20 of Stage 1 is based on the *eed* word family and it introduces the sounds *w* and *sp*.

Among the activities on *Simon S. I. O.* are identifying the first sound of words, the last sound, and both sounds; spelling words; reading words aloud and recording them; and finding a word when it is pronounced. As these examples show, the screen display is consistent from activity to activity.

Note: Courtesy of Don Johnston Incorporated.

Simon, the tutor, appears in the upper left-hand corner. He gives instructions and provides feedback on the student's responses. The "pronouncer" (a small speaker beneath Simon) reads the words and sounds aloud. Help is always available, and the student can move from one activity to another using the activity bar at the top of the screen.

Developing Phonics and Spelling Skills with *WordMaker*

WordMaker (http://www.donjohnston.com) is an interesting program that provides students with opportunities to practice phonemic awareness, manipulate letters, spell words, sort words by rhyme, and see what they have learned as a word wall. In the sample screen, the student hears a word, in this case *sun,* and must drag letters to the blanks to spell the word. To find out whether the word is spelled correctly, the student clicks on the check mark in the upper right-hand corner.

Note: Courtesy of Don Johnston Incorporated.

Note: Courtesy of Don Johnston Incorporated.

In later activities, the screen shows a similar task without picture cues. For example, the student might be asked to select from several available letters to spell the word *glow*. *WordMaker* keeps a record of student progress, and the words the student learns are presented on a word wall (which can be printed).

Note: Courtesy of Don Johnston Incorporated.

Learning Sight Words with the *Edmark Reading* Program

Originally designed as a print program, *Edmark Reading* is now available as a software program (http://www.riverdeep.net/edmark/). The program focuses on teaching beginning reading skills, with emphasis on words from the high-frequency Dolch list. Level 1 of the program teaches 150 words and Level 2 teaches 200 additional words. The instructional sequence is very systematic, with numerous opportunities for learners to practice skills. Among the lesson formats are Pre-Reading (i.e., matching), Word Recognition, Word Practice, and Stories.

Increasing Reading Fluency with *Read Naturally*

Read Naturally is a program designed to increase students' reading fluency and comprehension. Available in both print and software editions (http://www.readnaturally.com), *Read Naturally* encourages faster, more accurate reading via three strategies: modeling, repeated reading, and progress monitoring. To begin, the student reads a brief nonfiction passage on the screen and clicks on difficult words. In the software version the program determines the number of words read correctly (i.e., those not marked as difficult) within a 1-minute time period. This is called a "cold" timing. The student reads along as the passage is read aloud by a narrator, and finally practices the passage without the narrator's assistance (see the sample screen). Before the student can "pass" a passage he or she must reach goal, have 3 or fewer errors, read with good expression, and answer all questions correctly.

Note: Courtesy of Read Naturally.

FIGURE 10-4	**Important Career and Vocational Words**		
1. rules	26. supervisor	51. entrance	76. withholding
2. boss	27. vacation	52. responsibility	77. vote
3. emergency	28. apply	53. hospital	78. break
4. danger	29. fulltime	54. hourly rate	79. cooperation
5. job	30. income	55. schedule	80. dependable
6. social security	31. quit	56. instructions	81. money
7. first-aid	32. check	57. save	82. physical
8. help-wanted	33. careful	58. union	83. hazardous
9. safety	34. dangerous	59. credit	84. net income
10. warning	35. employee	60. elevator	85. strike
11. signature	36. layoff	61. punctuality	86. owner
12. time	37. take-home-pay	62. rights	87. repair
13. attendance	38. unemployed	63. hours	88. alarm
14. absent	39. cost	64. payroll	89. gross income
15. telephone	40. deduction	65. attitude	90. manager
16. bill	41. fired	66. reliable	91. reference
17. hired	42. closed	67. work	92. uniform
18. overtime	43. parttime	68. caution	93. hard-hat
19. punch in	44. correct	69. license	94. authority
20. directions	45. foreman	70. poison	95. training
21. paycheck	46. time-and-a-half	71. office	96. holiday
22. wages	47. worker	72. power	97. late
23. appointment	48. buy	73. qualifications	98. personal
24. income tax	49. raise	74. earn	99. tools
25. interview	50. on-the-job	75. transportation	100. areas

Note: From "A Word List of Essential Career/Vocational Words for Mentally Retarded Students" by J. Schilit and M. L. Caldwell, 1980, *Education and Training of the Mentally Retarded, 15,* p. 115. Copyright 1980 by The Council for Exceptional Children. Reprinted with permission.

- using a checking or savings account;
- using a credit card;
- applying for a loan;
- selecting and preparing food;
- using measurement, as in reading a thermometer, determining a person's weight and height, and measuring the length and width of a room; and
- using time, as in telling time, using a calendar, and computing time (e.g., "If it takes 20 minutes to walk to school, at what time must you leave home to arrive at school at 8:00 A.M.?")

Functional tasks often require more than one basic skill. For instance, in planning and cooking a meal, several skills are needed: reading (ads, labels, cooking and preparation directions), writing (shopping list), and math (buying foods, measuring ingredients, computing cooking times). When tasks such as these are used with special students, the teacher should be sure that the students are proficient in all necessary skills; that is, a math practice activity should be designed so that low reading skills are not an obstacle.

When students with mild retardation are included in general education for basic skills instruction, the assignment of grades is often difficult. Students can be working hard and making progress, but their performance may remain at a lower level than that expected for their grade placement. Alternatives for grading students with special needs are suggested in the "Inclusion Tips for the Teacher" box. See the article by Salend and Duhaney (2002) for more information.

IMPROVING GENERAL WORK HABITS

Work habits can be viewed as the behaviors a person exhibits when presented with a task to perform. Many work behaviors apply to all types of tasks. For example, no matter what type of work is involved, it is necessary to begin work promptly,

Inclusion Tips for the Teacher

Differential Grading

Report cards are a major way for teachers to inform parents of their children's progress in school. However, with students with special needs, grading performance in general education classes is often difficult. How should the teacher grade Judy, who is included in the fourth-grade class but is successfully completing math assignments at the third-grade level? Here are some alternatives:

1. State the student's current grade level in the academic subject, and grade the student's performance at that grade level.

   Judy, Grade 4

   Math grade level _3_

   Math performance at Grade 3 level _B_

2. State the student's current grade level in the academic subject, and grade the student's work behaviors rather than skill performance.

   Judy, Grade 4

   Math grade level _3_

   Works independently _B_

   Completes assignments _B+_

   Neatness _B_

3. State the student's IEP goals and objectives in the academic subject, and indicate which have been met and which still require work.

   Judy, Grade 4

   Goal: By the end of the school year, Judy will perform math computation problems at the 3.5 grade level. _in progress_

   Objectives:
   a. Judy will add and subtract two-digit numbers with regrouping with 90% accuracy. _achieved_
   b. Judy will write multiplication facts with 90% accuracy. _achieved_
   c. Judy will multiply two-digit numbers with regrouping with 90% accuracy. _in progress_
   d. Judy will write division facts with 90% accuracy. _in progress_

   Other options include replacing traditional letter grades with simplified grading systems such as pass/fail or satisfactory/needs improvement (McLoughlin & Lewis, 2005). Teachers also can assign multiple grades in a subject area; for example, the student might earn one grade for reading achievement and another for effort in reading activities (Banbury, 1987).

---

stay on task, and complete the task. Important not only on the job but also in school and daily life, work habits are a necessary part of the curriculum for children and youth with mild retardation. Kokaska and Brolin (1985) identify these important work behaviors:

- following directions
- working with others
- working at a satisfactory rate
- accepting supervision
- recognizing the importance of attendance and punctuality
- meeting demands for quality work
- demonstrating occupational safety skills. (pp. 157–160)

Several of these skills are just as important for classroom success as they are for vocational endeavors.

General education teachers can help students develop and improve their general work habits in three ways. First, the acquisition of work habits must be accepted as a valuable educational goal. Second, students must receive instruction and practice in specific work behaviors. Third, good work performance must be reinforced. The following paragraphs suggest ways to promote three general work habits.

Attendance and Punctuality

These work habits are key ingredients in successful school and job performance. Students with poor attendance and those who are frequently tardy may fall behind their classmates in important school skills. Adults whose work records show frequent absences and late arrivals may find themselves unemployed. Attendance and punctuality are typically expected by teachers but are not addressed directly in instruction. For many special students, these work habits must become part of the curriculum so that students are taught the behaviors, provided with practice opportunities, and rewarded for successful performance. To teach these work habits, the teacher first communicates to students that attendance and punctuality are important. One way to do this is to incorporate these behaviors into the class rules. For example, the rule for punctuality might be "When the bell rings, be in your seat." It is also necessary to explain why attendance and punctuality are important for students (and for employees). To do this, the teacher might lead the class in a discussion of the disadvantages of being tardy for school (or work).

When students are aware of the teacher's expectations, then appropriate work behaviors can be rewarded. There are several ways to reinforce students for attending class and arriving on time:

- Keep a record of attendance and punctuality. At the end of each week, allow students with good records to participate in a special free-time activity.
- Have students keep a log of their own attendance and punctuality. This can be done in the form of a journal or graph or even with a time clock.
- Present a certificate or award to students with good attendance. Begin gradually by rewarding students who come to school each day for 1 week.
- Encourage punctuality by scheduling a favorite activity at the beginning of the class period.
- Use individual contracts for students who are chronically absent or habitually late. Negotiate the terms of the contract so that acceptable performance is followed by a privilege, activity, or reward that the student values.

Work Completion

A second important work behavior critical for school and job success is task completion. Students and employees are expected to complete their work assignments. In school, the teacher must be sure that learning tasks are appropriate for the skill levels of the student. Kolstoe (1976) offers the following suggestions for teachers of students with retardation:

- The tasks should be uncomplicated. . . .
- The tasks should be brief. . . .
- The tasks should be sequentially presented. . . .
- Each learning task should be the kind in which success is possible. . . .
- Learning tasks should be applied to objects, problems, and situations in the learner's life environment. (p. 27)

When tasks are at an appropriate level for the learner, the teacher can concentrate on building work completion skills. Students should first be told that they are expected to finish their work. Then, task completion should be reinforced by the teacher. Ways to encourage and reward work completion are identified here:

- Make free-time activities contingent on work completion. For example, tell students, "If you finish your work, then you may listen to a CD or read a magazine."
- Have students record the number of tasks they complete each day. They can then graph the data and see how they progress from day to day.
- For students who are overwhelmed by lengthy assignments, break the work into several short tasks. Reward these students after the completion of each short task.

- Begin gradually with students who rarely complete tasks. First, expect and reward one task per day, then two tasks, and so on.

Working with Others

In many situations at school and on the job, people must work closely with one another. This interaction necessitates communication, cooperation, and civility. Job-related social skills are particularly important for youngsters with mild retardation because, as Kokaska and Brolin (1985) note, one of the most common reasons for job failure is the inability to get along with coworkers and supervisors.

Practice in working with others can begin at any age. In most general education classrooms, students have many opportunities to work with peers. Besides the most typical examples of group instruction and class discussions, the teacher can design special projects to be completed by teams of students: for example, preparing group science reports, writing a class newspaper, putting up a bulletin board, or planning a class field trip.

When students work in groups, the teacher must often provide instruction and guidance in important interpersonal skills. Students need to learn to share work materials, work quietly with others, be polite to coworkers, and complete tasks by working cooperatively. These skills can be practiced in any classroom and, once acquired, are among the most valuable of all general work habits for student and adult workers alike.

By helping students with special needs learn functional academic skills and work habits, the teacher is providing them with important tools that they will use for the rest of their lives. Consider the story of Bill Yore, as told by Kokaska and Brolin (1985). Bill, a young man who was in special education programs all his life, graduated from high school at age 19, and was selected by his classmates as one of the commencement speakers. In his speech, Bill said:

> It isn't easy competing with other kids, even when you are normal much less handicapped. But, the love and the patience were there for 19 long years. And, tonight I am proud to stand here and say that I am that boy—almost condemned to an institution. True, I am not an A student. But neither am I a dropout. I may never go to college but I won't be on the welfare rolls either. I may never be a great man in this world, but I will be a man in whatever way I am able to do it. (p. 386)

STRATEGIES FOR WORKING WITH STUDENTS WITH SEVERE DISABILITIES

The educational needs of students with severe disabilities are more complex than those of students with mild retardation.

There is a greater degree of retardation, and poor intellectual performance may be accompanied by physical impairments, sensory impairments, or even emotional disturbance. According to Pumpian (1988), "individuals are typically identified as severely [disabled]. . . when the severity and/or multiplicity of their [disabilities]. . . pose major challenges to them, their families, and society in general in nearly all aspects of growth, development, and functioning" (p. 181).

Until quite recently, such students were educated almost exclusively in special schools and residential facilities; prior to the passage of PL 94–142, many were denied the opportunity to participate in public education in any form. However, within the past decade, advances in research and changes in educational philosophy have led to increased participation of students with severe disabilities in public school life. In the 1999–2000 school year, for example, approximately 94% of the students identified as mentally retarded in the United States attended regular schools in which special education services were delivered in a general education classroom, resource room, or special class (U.S. Department of Education, 2002). Although many of these students were mildly retarded, a significant number had been identified as having severe disabilities.

Although many students with severe disabilities now attend regular schools, physical proximity is not sufficient to guarantee their successful integration into the school community. Falvey, Grenot-Scheyer, and Bishop (1989) identify several other factors that must be considered. In an optimal program, students with severe disabilities would attend neighborhood schools with same-age peers; however, no school would enroll a disproportionate number of students with severe (or other) disabilities. Special educators and support staff would be available to provide students with an appropriate instructional program. And the school would be both physically and socially accessible to students with severe disabilities.

Social accessibility refers to the availability of opportunities for interaction between students with and without disabilities. When students with severe disabilities are members of a special class within a regular school, they should have the same access to school functions and activities as others within the school community. For example, they should arrive at and depart from school at the same times and places as other students, they should attend school assemblies and social events, they should eat lunch at one of the regular lunchtimes, and their recess or physical education activities should be scheduled similarly to those of other classes.

Research supports the benefits of integration, not only for students with severe disabilities but also for their peers without disabilities. Positive interactions occur between these groups of students, and typical students begin to develop more positive attitudes toward individuals with disabilities (Brinker, 1985). Parents of students with severe disabilities also report satisfaction (McDonnell, 1987). Few reported that their children were mistreated or isolated; most said that their children had made or will make friends at school with peers without disabilities.

In addition to providing opportunities for interaction, it is also possible to set up structured programs that facilitate the building of relationships between students with and without disabilities. One approach is a peer tutoring program in which general education students are trained as tutors for students with severe disabilities (e.g., Kohl, Moses, & Stettner-Eaton, 1983). Special class students benefit from positive peer models and the additional instructional resources, while typical peers develop an understanding of and appreciation for individual differences. Tutors may also gain social status among their general education classmates (Sasso & Rude, 1988). A more innovative approach is the "Special Friends" program of Voeltz (1980, 1982). In this program, the relationship between peers with and without disabilities is social rather than pedagogical; the outcome is the building of new friendships and a positive change in the attitudes of general education students.

Full Inclusion

In the past several years, advocates for students with severe disabilities have taken the position that all students should be members of general education classrooms (Kennedy & Horn, 2004; Stainback & Stainback, 1988, 1990b, 1992; Stainback, Stainback, & Forest, 1989; Thousand & Villa, 1990). Called full inclusion, this movement encourages full-time general education placement for students with severe disabilities and others with identified special education needs. The general education teacher becomes responsible for the education of all students, although special educators and other staff are available to support students and teachers as needed. When a student with severe disabilities is fully included, general and special educators collaborate to ensure that the following occur:

a. The student's natural participation as a regular member of the class
b. The systematic instruction of the student's IEP objectives.
c. The adaptation of the core curriculum and/or materials to facilitate student participation and learning. (Neary, Halvorsen, & Smithey, 1991, p. 1)

According to Voltz, Brazil, and Ford (2001), "the concept of inclusion implies a sense of belonging and acceptance" (p. 24).

One of the major goals of full inclusion is the development of friendships between students with and without disabilities. Opportunities for social interactions increase when students with severe disabilities are full-time members of general education classrooms. Also, students without disabilities can be directly involved in the full inclusion effort. For example, Forest and Lusthaus (1989) recommend two strategies, circles of friends and MAPS. A circle of friends is a network of students who volunteer to offer friendship to a student with disabilities; see the "Inclusion Tips for the Teacher" box to see how a circle works.

MAPS stands for Making Action Plans (York, Doyle, & Kronberg, 1992); it was originally called the McGill Action Planning System (Lusthaus & Forest, 1987; Vandercook,

Inclusion Tips for the Teacher

Circles of Friends

Forest and Lusthaus (1989) provide this example to describe the establishment of a circle of friends for May, a student with disabilities who is going to join a seventh grade general education class.

In September, a few days before May Russell would be attending her new seventh grade classroom, an integration consultant visited the class to speak with the students. She asked them the following series of questions. The students' actual responses are included here, too.

Consultant (C)

C—"Hi, I've come to talk to you about May who is coming to your class next week. You met her last week when she visited with her mother. For years May has gone to a segregated school or been in a self-contained life skills class. What does that mean?"

Students (S)

S—"Places for retarded people"

"Schools for kids who are really bad"

"Like the one near my house where all the wheelchairs go"

C—"Well, May is coming here and I'll tell you a secret. Everyone is really scared. Her mother and father are scared. Mr. Gorman [teacher] is scared. Mr. Cullen

[principal] is scared. I'm scared. Why do you think all of us are so scared?"

S—"You all think we'll be mean to her."

"You think we'll tease her and be mean to her."

"You think she'll be left out."

C—"There are some things we don't want you to do when she arrives. What do you think these are?"

S—"Don't treat her like a baby."

"Don't pity her."

"Don't ignore her."

"Don't feel sorry for her."

C—"Why are we doing this? Why is May coming to this class?"

S—"Why not? She's our age, she should be here."

"How would you feel if you were 12 and never were with kids your own age?"

"It's dumb for her not to be here."

"She needs friends."

"She needs a boy friend."

C—"What do you think we want you to do?"

S—"Treat her like one of us."

Teaching Special Students in General Education Classrooms   253

"Make her feel welcome."

"Help her make friends."

"Help her with her work."

"Call her and invite her to our parties."

C—"I want to switch gears for a few minutes and ask you to all do an exercise with me called 'circle of friends.' I do this very same thing with teachers and parents and I think you are all grown up enough to handle it."

(The consultant handed out a sheet with four concentric circles on it. After the first circle, each circle was a little larger and farther away from the center of the page where a stick person was drawn.)

C—"There are four circles. On each circle you are to list people you know. I want you to think about whom you would put in your first circle. These are the people closest to you, people you really love. You can do this privately or in pairs, and you can tell us or keep it private."

(The consultant filled in her own circles on the chalkboard while the students did theirs at their seats. When finished, the facilitator shared her circles and then asked for volunteers to share theirs.)

S—"OK. In my first circle I put in my mom, my dad, Matt who is my best friend, and Stacey—that's my Mom's best friend and she often helps me when I have a problem."

C—"Why did you put those people in your first circle?"

S—"They are people I feel close to. I love them."

C—"What do you do with the people in circle one?"

S—"I share my secrets, I can be myself, I go to them when I'm hurt, I trust them, I love them."

C—"Now let's do circle two—these are people you really like but not enough to put in circle one."

S—"I put in my dog and my two best friends Tim and Todd, and my teacher Mr. Gorman. I put them in because I can do everything with them and we have fun together and we visit a lot."

C—"The third circle is groups of people you like or people you do things with, like Scouts, swimming, hockey, etc."

S—"I have lots—I'm in Boy Scouts, my church, my Sunday school, this class, my street hockey group, and my family is like a group."

C—"The last circle is for people you pay to be in your lives, like your doctor, dentist, and so on."

S—"I put in my doctor and my eye glass doctor, that's all."

C—"Now I want you to think about a person's circle. Here's a fantasy person named Sebastian. He's your age (12) and his circle looks like this. He only has his Mom in circle one and the rest of his circles are empty except for circle four, which is filled with doctors, social workers, therapists, etc. Think hard for a few minutes because this is real serious. How would you feel if your life looked like Sebastian's?"

(This is a list of responses from the seventh grade students in the brainstorming session.)

S—"Lonely, depressed, unwanted, terrible, disgusted, like what's the use of living, I'd want to commit suicide, like dying, awful, crazy, hurt, nobody cares, angry, furious, mad."

C—"How do you think you'd act?"

S—(Again, a list of responses from the brainstorming.) "I'd hide and keep my head down all day, I'd hit people, I'd cry all day, I'd hate everyone, I'd kill myself, I'd want to kill others, I'd steal, I'd curse and spit, I'd fight."

C—"OK, I want to wind this up for today and I'll be back in a few weeks to see what's happening. Remember, I came and we started talking about May who will be in your class soon. Well, right now her life looks a bit like Sebastian's imaginary circle. So why did I do all this?"

S—"To help us understand about all the new kids who are coming into our classes—about how they must feel."

C—"What I'd like is for a group of you to act as a welcome committee and another group to act as a telephone crew. I want a phone caller for each day of the week. Do you think that's a good idea?"

S—"Wow, yeah—what a neat idea!"

C—"Remember, friends don't develop overnight. This is just the start. Not all of you will be May's friends—though all of you can be 'friendly.' My dream and hope is that out of this great class May will have at least six friends who will do things with her in school and most of all after school and on weekends. This won't happen fast, but I bet it will happen. Who wants to help?"

Note: From "Promoting Educational Equity for All Students" by M. Forest and E. Lusthaus in *Educating All Students in the Mainstream of Regular Education* (pp. 47–49) by S. Stainback, W. Stainback, and M. Forest (Eds.), 1989. Copyright 1989 by Paul H. Brookes, P.O. Box 10624, Baltimore, MD 21285-0624. Reprinted with permission from Dr. Marsha Forest, Inclusion Press, 416-658-5363 or fax 416-658-5067, Web page http://inclusion.com.

York, & Forest, 1989). It is a team approach to planning the inclusion process. Members of the team include the student, parents (and perhaps other family members), professionals, and the student's circle of friends. In the MAPS process, the team addresses seven major questions:

1. What is the individual's history?
2. What is your dream for the individual?
3. What is your nightmare?
4. Who is the individual?
5. What are the individual's strengths, gifts, and abilities?
6. What are the individual's needs?
7. What would the individual's ideal day at school look like and what must be done to make it happen? (Vandercook et al., 1989, pp. 207–208)

When students with severe disabilities are included in general education classrooms, it is often necessary to adapt instructional procedures. One concern is the curriculum. (Wolfe & Hall, 2003) Giangreco, Cloninger, and Iverson (1990) present four alternatives. First, the student with severe disabilities can participate in the same learning activities with the same goals as other students in the class. Second, in a multilevel curriculum, the student can work in the same curriculum area as classmates but at a different level. For example, while peers work on algebraic problems, a student with severe disabilities might practice addition and subtraction skills (York et al., 1992). Or, while classmates read a book and write a book report, a student with severe disabilities might listen to a story on tape, tape-record reactions to the story, and draw a picture illustrating the story (Wehman, 1997).

Third, in curriculum overlapping, all students participate in the same learning activities but pursue goals in different subject areas. Giangreco and colleagues (1990) provide this example:

> Suppose students are in science lab learning about properties of electricity. A student with special needs may be involved in these activities for the primary purpose of pursuing objectives from other curriculum areas (e.g., communication, socialization) such as following directions, accepting assistance from others, or engaging in a school job with a nonhandicapped peer. (as cited in Thousand & Villa, 1990, p. 15)

The fourth option is an alternative curriculum. This is recommended for use only when it is impossible to address a student's educational goals within the general education classroom setting.

Vandercook and York (1990) have developed the Regular Classroom Integration Checklist to help teachers assess progress toward full inclusion of students with severe disabilities. As can be seen in Figure 10-5, that checklist is divided into four sections. The first, "Go with the Flow," is used to determine whether all students follow the same classroom routines. "Acting Cool" is concerned with participation in class activities, "Talking Straight" with communication, and "Looking Good" with personal appearance. Items receiving a "no" response should be addressed by the team when it meets to discuss ways to improve the inclusion process.

Research is beginning to emerge about the effect of full inclusion on students with severe disabilities, their families, their peers, and their teachers. In a review of inclusion research, Hunt and Goetz (1997) summarized their conclusions in these six guidelines:

1. Parental involvement is an essential component of effective inclusive schooling. . . .
2. Students with severe disabilities can achieve positive academic and learning outcomes in academic settings. . . .
3. Students with severe disabilities realize acceptance, interactions, and friendships in inclusive settings. . . .
4. Students without disabilities experience positive outcomes when students with severe disabilities are their classmates. . . .
5. Collaborative efforts among school personnel are essential to achieving successful inclusive schools. . . .
6. Curricular adaptations are a vital component in effective inclusion efforts. . . . (pp. 25–26)

However, in one study, less than half of parents of students with severe disabilities said they believed that full inclusion would be a good idea for their child (Palmer, Fuller, Arora, & Nelson, 2001). In addition, it is important to note that very little research has focused on the academic achievement of fully included students with severe disabilities or the ways in which the general education curriculum should be adapted for these students (Hunt & Goetz, 1997; Nietupski, Hamre-Nietupski, Curtin, & Shrikanth, 1997). Despite this, Werts, Wolery, Snyder, and Caldwell (1996) report that special and general educators are in full agreement about the types of supports general education teachers need to make full inclusion programs successful. Three supports were identified as most critical: sufficient training, support from a team of professionals, and additional personnel to provide assistance in the general education classroom.

In this chapter you have learned ways to adapt classroom instruction to help students with mild retardation learn functional academic skills and basic work habits. You have also learned more about students with severe disabilities and strategies for increasing their participation as members of the school community. In the next chapter, you will meet students with behavioral disorders. Methods for teaching study skills and handling disruptive behavior will be presented. First, however, consult "Things to Remember" to review ways to help students with retardation succeed in the general education classroom.

FIGURE 10-5   Inclusion Checklist

Directions: Record a "y" for yes and an "n" for no on the blank preceding each item. If the answer to any of the items is "no" your team may wish to consider whether any changes should be made and what those changes might be.

Go with the Flow:

_____ Does the student enter the classroom at the same time as classmates? _____

_____ Is the student positioned so that she or he can see and participate in what is going on? _____

_____ Is the student positioned so that classmates and teachers may easily interact with him or her (e.g., without teacher between the student and his or her classmates, not isolated from classmates)? _____

_____ Does the student engage in classroom activities at the same time as classmates? _____

_____ Does the student make transitions in the classroom at the same time as classmates? _____

_____ Is the student involved in the same activities as his or her classmates? _____

_____ Does the student exit the classroom at the same time as classmates? _____

Acting Cool:

_____ Is the student actively involved in class activities (e.g., asks or responds to questions, plays a role in group activities)? _____

_____ Is the student encouraged to follow the same classroom and social rules as classmates (e.g., hugs others only when appropriate, stays in seat during instruction)? _____

_____ Is the student given assistance only as necessary (assistance should be faded as soon as possible)? _____

_____ Is assistance provided for the student by classmates (e.g., transitions to other classrooms, within the classroom)? _____

_____ Are classmates encouraged to provide assistance to the student? _____

_____ Are classmates encouraged to ask for assistance from the student? _____

_____ Is assistance provided for the student by classroom teachers? _____

_____ Does the student use the same or similar materials during classroom activities as his or her classmates (e.g., Tom Cruise notebooks, school mascot folders)? _____

Talking Straight:

_____ Does the student have a way to communicate with classmates? _____

_____ Do classmates know how to communicate with the student? _____

continued

FIGURE 10-5   continued

_____ Does the student greet others in a manner similar to that of his or her classmates? _____

_____ Does the student socialize with classmates? _____

_____ Is this facilitated? _____

_____ Does the student interact with teachers? _____

_____ Is this facilitated? _____

_____ Do teachers (e.g., classroom teachers, special education support staff) provide the same type of feedback (e.g., praise, discipline) for the student as for his or her classmates? _____

_____ If the student uses an alternative communication system do classmates know how to use it? _____

_____ If the student uses an alternative communication system do teachers know how to use it? _____

_____ Is the system always available to the student? _____

Looking Good:

_____ Is the student given the opportunity to attend to his or her appearance as classmates do (e.g., check appearance in mirror between classes)? _____

_____ Does the student have accessories which are similar to his or her classmates (e.g., oversize tote bags, friendship bracelets, hair jewelry)? _____

_____ Is the student dressed similarly to classmates? _____

_____ Is clothing that's needed for activities age appropriate (e.g., napkins instead of bibs, "cool" paint shirts)? _____

_____ Are personal supplies or belongings carried or transported discreetly? _____

_____ Is the student's equipment (e.g., wheelchair) kept clean? _____

   Given the opportunity (and assistance as needed):

_____ Is the student's hair combed?

_____ Are the student's hands clean and dry?

_____ Does the student change clothing to maintain a neat appearance?

_____ Does the student use chewing gum, breath mints, breath spray?

Note: From "A Team Approach to Program Development and Support" by T. Vandercook and J. York in _Support Network for Inclusive Schooling_ (pp. 117–118) by W. Stainback and S. Stainback (Eds.), 1990. Copyright 1990 by Paul H. Brookes, P.O. Box 10624, Baltimore, MD 21285-0624. Reprinted with permission.

Things to Remember

- Academic instruction is the most common area in which adaptations must be made in the general education classroom for students with mild retardation. They require assistance in acquisition of basic skills and work habits and in the application of these skills to daily life and career situations.
- Major indicators of mild retardation are a slow rate of learning and consistent delays in most areas of development.
- In assessment of mild retardation, information is gathered about academic achievement, intellectual performance, and adaptive behavior. The general education teacher assists by collecting classroom performance data.
- The major approach to the education of students with mild retardation is habilitation; instruction is directed toward development of the critical skills necessary for successful adulthood.
- Transition and career education services are one way to view habilitation of students with mild retardation; in this approach, students are prepared for adult life by instruction in functional academic, daily living, personal-social, and vocational skills.

- When students with mild retardation participate in general education classes for basic skills instruction or vocational education, the teacher assists by teaching functional academic skills and improving the general work habits of the students.
- Two approaches to teaching functional academics are instructional units and functional practice activities; both help students generalize learned skills to daily life and vocational situations.
- General work habits important for school and later employment include attendance and punctuality, work completion, and working with others. The general education teacher promotes the development of these skills in students with mild retardation with instruction, guided practice, and reinforcement of appropriate performance.
- Students with severe disabilities may attend special classes within regular schools or be fully included in general education classrooms. Both options offer opportunities for interactions between peers with and without disabilities and participation in age-appropriate school activities.

ACTIVITIES

1. Visit a special education classroom, either a resource room or a special class, that serves students with mild retardation. Observe the students and talk with the teacher. In what school subjects do students experience the most difficulty? What subjects are taught by the special education teacher? Are transition and career education services part of the curriculum? Find out how many of the students are included in general education for at least part of the school day. Do they participate in academic instruction in the regular classroom? In nonacademic subjects such as music and art? In social activities?

2. Select one of the special education journals that focuses on mental retardation. Choose from the *American Journal on Mental Retardation, Education and Training in Mental Retardation and Developmental Disabilities,* and *Mental Retardation.* Look through recent issues for articles with suggestions that classroom teachers can use. Collect ideas for teaching

functional academics and for incorporating transition and career education skills into the general education curriculum.

3. Make a list of the questions you have about mental retardation and the inclusion of students with retardation in general education classrooms. Visit at least five websites to find answers to your questions. Start with the sites described in this chapter's "Window on the Web" and use the links they provide to locate other resources. In your opinion, which sites are most valuable for teachers?

4. Imagine that you are a general education teacher with several students with mild retardation in your class. Design an instructional program to improve the general work habits of all your students. What work habits will you include in your program? How will you explain the program to the class? How will you implement the program? Outline a method for evaluating your program.

CD-ROM Activities

The high school case study portrays a physics class made up of students with a wide range of skills and talents. It is quite likely that one or more of these students has been identified as having a cognitive deficit such as retardation. Look at the video clips listed below, then describe some of the strategies in place in this inclusive classroom that make it a welcoming environment for all of the students.

- *The video clip entitled "Peer Supports," in which three students with quite different skill levels all contribute to the solution of a problem;*

- *The video clip entitled "Empower Students," in which the teacher tells one of his students to "Give it your best shot"; and*

- *One other video clip of your choosing.*

5. Contact local school districts to find out how students with severe disabilities are served. Do students attend special classes located in regular neighborhood schools? Are students fully included in general education classes? Visit an integrated site and observe how students with severe disabilities participate in school life. If the school has a full inclusion program, use the checklist in Figure 10-5 to guide your observation.

r
s

w
ir
c
(A
n
ir
tr
w
g
al
re
d
le

m
uc
st
pi
R:

For Your Information

Students with Behavioral Disorders

- Research literature suggests that 3% to 6% of school-aged students have behavioral disorders, although current programs for students with behavioral disorders serve slightly under 1% of the school-age population (Kauffman, 2001).
- Students identified as having behavior disorders make up about 8% of the total of all students receiving special education services (U.S. Department of Education, 2002).
- Students with behavioral disorders are found in both elementary and secondary schools; at least 50% of the public school programs for students with behavioral disorders are at the secondary level (Grosenick & Huntze, 1980).
- Nelson (1993) states that "although studies do not consistently find more boys than girls with behavior problems, boys tend to be overrepresented in programs for behaviorally disordered children as much as ten to one" (p. 542).

- The majority of students with behavioral disorders spend most of their school day in the general education classroom.
- Many children in need of mental health services do not receive appropriate care until their problems have become so extreme that they require residential treatment (Knitzer, 1989).
- Most students with behavioral disorders encounter problems in the general education classroom because they lack appropriate social and study skills. Instruction in these areas will lead to skill improvement that will enhance their chances for success when they are included in the general education program (Sugai & Lewis, 1996).
- The intelligence level of students with behavioral disorders does not vary significantly from that of the general school population. However, these students fall behind their peers in academic achievement, and the gap seems to widen as the students progress through school, unless they receive high-quality academic instruction.

problem only when it interferes with a student's academic performance, relationships with teachers or peers, or the operation of the instructional program. Second, the behaviors of concern should occur consistently over an extended period of time. In most cases, one instance of an unacceptable behavior is not sufficient to warrant the attention of the teacher. However, if the behavior in question is extreme (e.g., one that could lead to the injury of another student), then just one occurrence may be justification for a referral.

Another guideline suggests that the nature of the inappropriate behavior be considered. The actions of students with behavioral disorders will differ from what teachers expect of typical students. The difference can lie in the frequency of the inappropriate behavior; such students may talk out in class not once or twice a period but once or twice a minute. They may have more intense reactions; a student may become extremely upset over an incident that most students would treat lightly. Or behaviors may be of longer duration; instead of quickly calming down after a disagreement, a student may remain upset throughout the school day.

Several other indicators of behavioral disorders appear regularly in the professional literature. These include descriptors such as *disobedient, defiant, attention seeking, irritable, anxious, timid, preoccupied,* and *passive*. Although these terms suggest student behaviors that may concern teachers, they have limited value because they are subjective and can be interpreted differently. Before clear communication can occur, a careful definition of terms is needed; what one teacher considers "hyper" or attention seeking may be perfectly acceptable to another. It is also important to look at the reasons for

student behaviors that suggest such labels: A student who is passive may be tired, and one who is anxious and irritable may be concerned about the illness of a family member.

Different professionals hold varying views on what constitutes typical and disordered behavior. Such behavioral expectations influence teachers' decisions about which students should be referred for consideration for special services. If a teacher prefers a quiet and orderly classroom in which students remain seated at their desks, an active student may be perceived as a problem. However, this student may fit quite well in a classroom in which student activity, movement, and interaction are encouraged by the teacher. Prior to initiating a referral, the teacher should attempt all possible interventions in the general education class. Often this is accomplished with the assistance of a special education consultant.

The problems of substance abuse and suicide are gaining increasing attention from educators. **Substance abuse** is the voluntary intake of chemicals with adverse social and physical consequences. Alcohol and various other drugs (e.g., narcotics, depressants, marijuana, cocaine) can cause side effects that have a detrimental impact on the student's ability to perform appropriately in the school environment. For example, teachers may observe changes in the student's ability to attend to instruction; temperament; work quality; attitudes toward school, parents, or peers; or self-concept (Coleman, 1986; Kerr & Nelson, 2002). In addition, many children who were born to mothers who were addicted to alcohol or drugs enter school with behavioral disorders "that include an inability to control anger and other impulses" (Guetzloe, 1996, p. 4). Suicide is one of the leading causes of death in adolescents; it occurs more frequently in males, although females have a much higher rate of suicide attempts (Kauffman, 2001). It is often associated with feelings of depression and hopelessness and is more likely to occur among active drug and alcohol abusers. Educators should not attempt to deal with such students without outside assistance. However, teachers should be alert to the problem and aware of resources within the school and community for suicide prevention and crisis intervention. Additional information on these and other related topics is provided in chapter 18.

Students with severe behavioral disorders are less likely to be found in general education classroom programs. Disabilities such as **autism spectrum disorder** (a developmental disorder with poorly developed communication and social skills) and psychiatric disorders such as **psychosis** (lack of contact with reality) are typically identified in the preschool years or early grades. School districts generally provide special programs in which these students spend the majority of their time in special classes or special schools. If students with severe behavioral disorders are returned to the general education program, they and their teachers receive a great deal of support from special educators. Chapter 13 presents more information about educational programs for students with autism spectrum disorder

ASSESSMENT PROCEDURES

When behavioral disorders are suspected, and the behavior problems exhibited by a student do not respond to the interventions available in the general education classroom, the student is referred to the assessment team to determine eligibility and need for special education services. Parents are notified of the referral and the team's plans for special education assessment. When parents grant permission, the team can begin to collect formal assessment information.

As with students with learning disabilities and mild retardation, several major areas are addressed in the special education assessment of students with behavioral disorders. Academic performance is one; measures such as the *Peabody Individual Achievement Test–Revised/Normative Update* (Markwardt, 1998) and the *Woodcock-Johnson III* (Woodcock, McGrew, & Mother, 2001) help determine whether reading, spelling, and math are areas of need. Intellectual ability is another area of concern; tests such as the *Wechsler Intelligence Scale for Children–Fourth Edition* (Wechsler, 2003) provide information about intellectual functioning. In many states, students must perform within an average IQ range to be considered for programs for individuals with behavioral disorders.

A third major concern is classroom behavior. Information about the student's typical patterns of behavior is gathered from teachers and parents. Interviews can be conducted, or the team can consider results from behavior checklists and rating scales. The *Behavior Rating Profile* (2nd ed.) (Brown & Hammill, 1990) uses the input of teachers, parents, peers, and students themselves to determine whether students have

significant difficulty in home behavior, school conduct, or relationships with peers. With the *Behavior Evaluation Scale–2* (McCarney & Leigh, 1990), teachers rate the frequency of five types of behaviors: Learning Problems, Interpersonal Difficulties, Inappropriate Behavior, Unhappiness/Depression, and Physical Symptoms/Fears. Other measures such as projective tests are sometimes used; however, the information they provide is of little use to the teacher and the prereferral or IEP teams in planning an appropriate intervention plan. On projective tests, students are asked to describe ambiguous stimuli such as inkblots, and the students' personality traits are inferred from their responses.

Direct observation, as described in chapters 5 and 6, is the best source of data for planning behavioral change programs. Observation gives the teacher specific information about the current behavior of the student and later serves as a basis for evaluation of student progress. Because a variety of measurement systems are available, the teacher can select or design one to generate the type of data needed to plan appropriate interventions for any particular student.

Assessment of student behavior is most effective when specific behaviors are pinpointed and accurate information is collected about the occurrence of these behaviors. In the case of Jake, the eighth grader described at the beginning of this chapter, Mr. Johnson, Jake's English teacher, was particularly concerned about two of Jake's problem behaviors: tardiness and failure to complete assignments on time. To gather more data on these behaviors, Mr. Johnson set up the observation system shown in Figure 11-1. Each day Mr. Johnson noted the number of minutes that Jake was late to class (duration recording), the number of assignments that were due, and the number of assignments that Jake completed on time (event recording). The results of this observation were then used as a basis for developing and evaluating the intervention plan for Jake.

If Jake's behavior were more severe (e.g., aggressive behaviors), it would also be important to conduct a functional analysis to collect information on (1) the elements in the setting that influence the behavior (e.g., the presence of particular students; recess versus classroom; individual versus group interactions) and (2) specific events that occur before and after the behavior (i.e., antecedents and consequences). This information on factors that contribute to the occurrence of the behavior would be essential in designing an appropriate intervention.

In some cases, it is not necessary to collect new assessment information. For example, Tina's first-grade teacher was also concerned about specific behaviors. The teacher considered gathering data on the frequency of Tina's interactions with other students and her participation in class discussions. However, an observation period was not really necessary because Tina never exhibited these behaviors. Instead, the teacher decided to begin the intervention program at once.

Mike's case was reviewed by the prereferral team and his interactions at home, in the classroom, and on the playground

FIGURE 11-1   Observational Data

Student:	Jake
Behaviors Observed:	Number of minutes late to class
	Number of assignments completed on time/number of assignments due
Setting:	English 8, Period 3

Day	Number of Minutes Late	Assignments Completed/ Assignments Due	Percentage of Assignments Completed
1	10	0/5	0
2	5	1/4	25
3	2	1/2	50
4	7	0/3	0
5	11	0/4	0
6	4	2/6	33
7	4	1/4	25
8	6	0/2	0
9	3	0/2	0
10	8	0/3	0

were carefully examined to determine the factors that were influencing his behavioral problems. Observations by the school psychologist and the special education teacher determined that interactions between Mike and adults, both in school and at home, tended to be quite negative. Moreover, as Mike's resistance to adult direction and the level of his acting-out behavior increased, the adults interacting with him tended to become even more coercive.

The initial interventions with Mike involved improving the ways in which the adults in Mike's life interacted with him: increasing the preciseness of the directions given to Mike, avoiding angry interchanges with him, and increasing positive feedback to Mike for those appropriate behaviors that he did exhibit. In addition, the prereferral team worked with his teacher to implement social skills instruction that focused on improving Mike's skills in (1) avoiding situations in which he typically became angry and (2) learning adaptive strategies for coping with these situations.

SPECIAL SERVICES

If assessment results indicate that an individual is eligible for services for students with behavioral disorders, the team

meets to design the IEP. Most students identified as having behavioral disorders remain in the general education classroom for at least a portion of the school day. As shown in Figure 11-2, Jake will participate in four general education classes and receive special education services from the resource teacher for two periods each day. In addition, consultation services are available to Jake's general education teachers.

Other professionals can also provide support to students with behavioral disorders. In addition to the special instruction provided for the student by the resource teacher, the resource teacher or another consultant may be available to assist the student's general education classroom teacher. Students can also visit the school psychologist, school counselor, or school social worker for regular counseling sessions. Some students and their families can be referred to community agencies that offer family counseling or other appropriate services.

Although most students with behavioral disorders are educated in the general education class, those with severe disabilities may attend special classes or special schools. In extreme cases, residential or hospital settings may be the most appropriate placement.

FIGURE 11-2   IEP Goals and Services for Jake

Annual Goals

1. By the end of the school year, Jake will complete and return to the teacher all assignments at the time they are due.
   Persons responsible: Resource teacher, eighth-grade teachers
2. By the end of the school year, Jake will arrive on time to classes at least 4 out of 5 days per week.
   Persons responsible: Resource teacher, eighth-grade teachers
3. By the end of the school year, Jake will remain in his seat during class time unless he is given permission to leave.
   Persons responsible: Resource teacher, eighth-grade teachers
4. By the end of the school year, Jake will reduce the number of his arguments with teachers and other students to less than two per week.
   Persons responsible: Resource teacher, eighth-grade teachers
5. Jake will continue to perform at the eighth-grade level or above in reading and math.
   Person responsible: Resource teacher

Amount of Participation in General Education

Jake will attend the general education eighth-grade social studies, English, physical education, and shop classes.

Special Education and Related Services

1. Jake will receive special education services from the resource teacher (annual goals 1, 2, 3, 4, and 5) for two periods daily.
2. The resource teacher will provide consultation to Jake's eighth-grade teachers as needed to accomplish annual goals 1, 2, 3, and 4.

CLASSROOM ADAPTATIONS

When students with behavioral disorders are included in the general education program, the classroom teacher may find it necessary to make program adaptations in three areas: classroom behavior, social skills, and academic instruction. Suggestions for classroom modifications to meet academic needs were presented in the previous two chapters; the techniques and strategies described for students with learning disabilities and mild retardation are also applicable to students with behavioral disorders. See the "Spotlight on Technology" feature for additional ideas for teaching math skills, an area in which students with behavioral disorders often experience difficulty.

Techniques for social skills training were discussed in chapter 6. This chapter provides additional suggestions for improving social skills as well as methods for improving classroom conduct and teaching study skills. Although these strategies are suggested for students with behavioral disorders, they can be used with equal success with any student, special or typical, who disrupts classroom activities or has not yet acquired effective study skills.

Several approaches have been advocated for use with students with behavioral disorders. Some of these strategies assume that it is necessary to determine what is wrong with the student and study the student's past for possible causes; for example, the history of the student's family and his or her early childhood experiences might be investigated. This approach offers little aid to the classroom teacher in dealing with problem behaviors encountered daily in the classroom. As chapter 5 explained, the teacher is most effective in controlling behavior problems if the emphasis is on the current status of the student and if information is gathered about the status of the student's observable behaviors and the factors that influence these behaviors. This chapter adopts the same viewpoint.

In systematic management of behavior, the teacher first identifies the behavior(s) of interest, collects data on their current status, examines the factors that may contribute to the occurrence of the behaviors, designs and institutes an intervention program, and then collects additional data to evaluate the effectiveness of the intervention and determine whether it should be continued, modified, or abandoned. There are three possible instructional goals:

- increase the occurrence of an appropriate behavior,
- decrease the occurrence of an inappropriate behavior, or
- teach a new behavior that is presently absent from a student's repertoire.

Examples of these goals are increasing the number of times Johnny comes to class on time, decreasing the number of times Harvey leaves his seat during class, and teaching Esther a new study strategy, such as skimming a chapter for major ideas before reading it.

Teachers must assume that students with behavioral disorders can learn the appropriate behaviors expected of all students in the general education classroom. The teachers who

Spotlight on Technology

Developing Basic Math Skills

Math software is plentiful. In fact, it is likely that more programs are available for math than for any other academic subject. It is important to note that these programs tend to focus on the practice of basic math skills, rather than the development of more advanced skills such the solution of quantitative problems. For students who require assistance in developing basic math skills, however, drill programs are often appropriate.

Practicing Math Facts: *Turbo Math* and *Math Blaster* Programs

The *Turbo Math* series (http://www.nordicsoftware.com) includes *Turbo Math Facts* for grades K–6 and *Turbo Math Maniac* for grades 2–12. Both offer practice in addition, subtraction, multiplication, and division. Also, both offer incentives for successful performance: Students earn money or points so that they can take part in a race (with race cars in *Facts* and motorcycles in *Maniacs*). These programs track student performance so that teachers can monitor how well students are progressing.

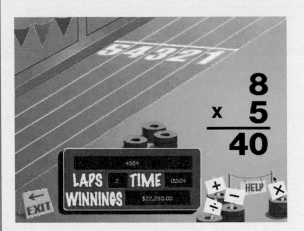

Multiplication Activity from *Turbo Math Facts*

Note: Courtesy of Nordic Software.

The *Math Blaster* series (http://www.greatsource.com) includes a number of programs, all featuring an arcade-game format as an incentive. This series also offers teachers the ability to select the types of activities students will engage in, and data are collected to allow assessment of students' progress. Among the *Math Blaster* programs are:

- *Math Blaster Ages 4–6:* number sentences, counting, addition and subtraction
- *Math Blaster Ages 5–7 (Grades K–2):* counting, telling time, money, measurement

- *Math Blaster Ages 6–8 (Grades 1–3):* addition, subtraction, simple fractions, charts and graphs
- *Math Blaster Ages 7–9 (Grades 2–4):* addition, subtraction, multiplication, and division; fractions, decimals, and percent; basic geometry
- *Math Blaster Ages 9–12 (Grades 4–6):* equations, estimation, and fractions

Math Blaster

Note: Courtesy of Knowledge Adventure.

Increasing Math Fluency: *FASTT Math*

FASTT Math (http://www.tomsnyder.com) is designed to help students develop fluency in basic math facts. Appropriate for grades 2 and up, this program focuses on addition, subtraction, multiplication, and division facts as well as multidigit problems.

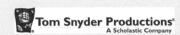

Algebra and Beyond

Software is also available to help students with the more advanced math skills that are part of the high school curriculum. Among the choices are *Math Blaster Pre-Algebra* and *Math Blaster Algebra; Cosmic Geometry* from the Mighty Math series (http://www.broderbund.com); and *Algebra World, Geometry World,* and *The Trigonometry Explorer* (http://www.mathrealm.com).

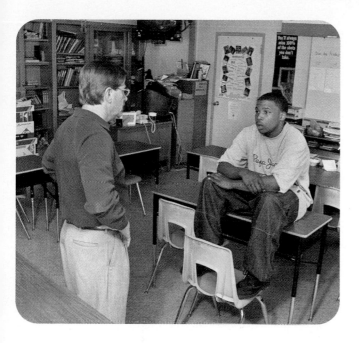

2. Can the intervention be implemented consistently? If it cannot, another strategy should be selected.

3. How will data be collected to assess student progress? Can this be done consistently?

4. Do students have the prerequisite skills necessary to learn the appropriate behavior? If not, what skills must be taught?

5. Are dangerous behaviors involved that require immediate elimination or remediation? If not, which intervention being considered is the most positive and the least intrusive?

6. How can students be involved in the intervention? Can they record their own performance data? Help to develop contingency contracts? Serve as models or recorders for other students?

7. What reinforcers are meaningful to the student(s) for whom the program is designed? Is it possible to use these reinforcers with the program?

8. What resources are needed? Does the intervention require teacher time? Aide time? Reinforcers? Are these available?

9. What other factors must be considered? For example, must the physical arrangement of the classroom be changed? Must peer tutors be recruited and trained?

10. What criteria and evidence will be used to determine the success or failure of the program? What alternative interventions can be used if the original program fails?

Specific strategies are available for effectively improving the behaviors of students with emotional and behavioral disorders. Remember, however, that in order for programs to be effective with these students, the implementation of these strategies (e.g., data-based interventions, continuous assessment and monitoring of progress) requires a high level of precision, duration, and intensity (Kauffman, Lloyd, Baker, & Riedel, 1995).

CONTROLLING DISRUPTIVE BEHAVIORS

One of the most common concerns of classroom teachers is the student who disrupts the instructional process. Whether typical or special, students with conduct problems call attention to themselves by arriving late, talking out in class, moving about the classroom, and interacting poorly with others. These inappropriate behaviors indicate poor social skills or poor general work habits. Whereas chapters 6 and 10 have discussed methods for developing good social and work skills, the following sections concentrate on what to do with students who have acquired inappropriate work habits or social skills that interrupt classroom activities.

Tardiness

Students who arrive late begin the school day or class period at a disadvantage. Tardiness affects the performance of these

work directly with students with special needs hold the primary responsibility for planning and carrying out interventions to change problem behaviors. Although others, such as the psychologist or counselor, can provide some assistance, the general education teacher spends the majority of the school day with the student and is therefore responsible for bringing about improvement in classroom behavior.

Many students who exhibit behavioral disorders at school may also display some of these behaviors at home. It can be very helpful to involve parents by informing them of the interventions that are being implemented at school and to consider providing them with suggestions regarding activities they may use at home. Concerned parents are generally open to suggestions regarding dealing with difficult behaviors. These recommendations can be communicated at conferences, through written suggestions, at specific training meetings, or through suggested readings.

The remainder of this chapter presents several ways to handle disruptive behavior in the classroom and help students acquire effective study skills. Before selecting one of these interventions (or designing an alternative), the teacher should carefully consider each of the following questions:

1. Can the intervention be carried out in the classroom? That is, is it feasible? Consider the type of problem (e.g., tardiness versus drug abuse), the age of the students involved, the resources within the classroom (e.g., availability of an aide, the experience and training of the teacher), the factors that contribute to the occurrence or maintenance of the behavior (e.g., attention of the teacher or peers, instructional situation versus recess), and the structure of the classroom.

students and interrupts and distracts the teacher and other students. Most students are late occasionally; however, frequent tardiness is an inappropriate behavior that must be resolved so that the student can become an active classroom participant. Suggestions for decreasing tardiness are presented next. Before implementing one of these plans, though, the teacher must be sure to collect data on current performance.

- Reward students for arriving on time. For example, students who arrive before the late bell rings can be given tickets for a raffle or have the opportunity to copy answers from the board for a couple of quiz questions. More structured programs may provide points or tokens redeemable for reinforcers. Criteria can be set up to encourage improvement in arrival time. For example, students can earn 5 points if they arrive on time and 2 points if they arrive less than 5 minutes late. Gradually reduce the number of minutes students are allowed to arrive late until it is possible to earn points only by being on time.
- Help students analyze the skills or steps required to arrive on time. For example, determine the times they should leave home, arrive at school, and be in the area of the classroom. Use this task analysis to establish a program to help students gradually master the skills needed for punctuality.
- Place a sign-in sheet at the door so students can record their name and time of arrival. Students who are late can leave tardy slips or excuses in an envelope attached to the sign-in sheet. The teacher can review these at a time that does not disrupt other classroom activities (Emmer, Evertson, Sanford, Clements, & Worsham, 1989).
- Schedule activities that students enjoy at the start of the class period. Allow only those students who are on time to class to participate.
- Set up contracts with students to specify the consequences of tardiness and punctuality. Be sure to identify clearly the criteria for success, who will keep the records, and the reinforcers that the students can earn. Students can record their own data if teachers periodically verify their accuracy.
- Discuss student tardiness with parents. Alert them to the extent of the problem, and encourage them to support the school's rules and to require, and reinforce, punctuality at home.
- Encourage parents to give their children watches so that students can keep track of time. If this is not possible, help students locate public clocks that they can consult.
- Arrange with parents to provide rewards at home. When students meet the prespecified punctuality criteria, they receive the rewards.
- Set up a system in which tardy students lose an equal number of minutes in a favorite activity.
- Group students into teams, and provide special reinforcers each week for the team with the best punctuality record.

- Assign peer tutors to help students get from class to class or from playground to classroom on time. As students develop appropriate skills, reduce the amount of assistance.
- Provide additional grade points for on-time arrival. For example, a student might earn 5 bonus points on an assignment if the assignment is started at the beginning of class.
- When students arrive on time, allow them to choose where they will sit. That is, use classroom seating preferences as reinforcers.

When any one of these interventions is implemented in the classroom, the teacher must continue to collect data on student performance to ensure that the program is effective. An alternative should be selected only after the intervention has been consistently implemented over a period of time, modifications have been made, and collected data have proved that the intervention is not working.

Verbal Outbursts

When students talk out in class, they disrupt the orderly flow of classroom activities. The teacher is distracted, and the work of other students is interrupted. Examples of verbal outbursts considered inappropriate by most teachers are answering out of turn, making irrelevant comments, arguing with the teacher or peers, and chatting with classmates during instruction. The following strategies are used to decrease the occurrence of this problem behavior:

- Establish clearly stated classroom rules regarding student verbal interactions. State the specific circumstances under which students are permitted to talk (e.g., when asked a question by the teacher, when asking the teacher a question after being called on, during assigned group work), and model the acceptable and unacceptable voice levels for each occasion. Teach these rules and provide students with opportunities to practice with teacher supervision and to obtain feedback that provides recognition for appropriate interactions and correction of inappropriate behaviors.
- Reinforce students who are good behavioral models for others, that is, those who speak out in class only at appropriate times or when teacher permission has been granted. Make the reinforcers strong enough so that students with problem behaviors will consider changing their ways. Teachers might try reinforcers such as early departure for recess or lunch, first place in line, or a certain number of minutes in a special activity.
- Recognize and reinforce problem students when they exhibit an appropriate behavior that is incompatible with the inappropriate verbal behavior, such as raising their hands and gaining recognition before answering ques-

tions in class. Clearly identify why the reinforcer is provided. For example, the teacher might say, "I like the way you raised your hand before you talked. You may take this book to the office for me." A statement such as this identifies the appropriate behavior and provides both a social reward and an activity reinforcer. Often these students are used to gaining recognition only when they exhibit inappropriate behaviors.

- Set up a system in which a loss of points results if students talk out. List the cost of talking out on the reinforcement menu or the student contract.
- Have students record the number of times they talk out in class each day. They can graph the data each day for a week and then compute the weekly total. Their goal for the next week is to decrease the number of times they talk out. Provide reinforcers if they meet their targets.
- Set up time periods in which students receive reinforcers for not talking out. Start with short time segments and gradually increase these to longer periods. The teacher might begin with 5-minute periods, then 10-minute periods, and so on until students are able to refrain from making verbal outbursts for an entire class period or activity.
- If classroom noise (caused by several loud students) becomes a problem, use an obvious signal such as "Stop talking!" or briefly turning off the classroom lights to alert students to be quiet.

Excess Activity: Moving About the Classroom

A familiar conduct problem is the active student who moves about the classroom at inappropriate times. Such students leave their seats during instruction and interrupt the teacher's attempt to present information. They also move about when they have been assigned independent work tasks at their desks, interfering with their own academic progress and also disturbing the work of others. Some students remain at their desks but are constantly in motion; they wiggle and squirm in their seats, bounce up and down, tap their desks with their fingers, and kneel on their chairs.

Active behaviors such as these are described by some as hyperactivity. However, this label does not specify an observable behavior that can be counted or measured in any way. "Hyper" behaviors can be improved, but first they must be pinpointed and described in appropriate, observable terms. Consult the suggestions here for ways to decrease the occurrence of inappropriate activity in the classroom:

- Find out whether students fully understand the class rules about when they should remain in their seats and when they can move about the room. Demonstrate appropriate in-seat and transition behaviors, and clarify any misinterpretations the students may have. Reteach and provide

practice for any rules the students do not remember. Briefly remind students of the rules before a transition time. As needed, provide reinforcement and correction.

- Provide frequent reinforcers for appropriate behavior; for example, students might receive rewards for remaining in their seats during instruction. If students are permitted to share reinforcers with other students seated nearby, these peers will often encourage the target students to behave appropriately.
- Record the amount of time the student is out of his or her seat; reduce time in a favorite activity by an equal amount or provide for a loss of points for each minute away from the desk.
- Allow opportunities for movement. Set up a system in which students can earn the chance to move about the room or travel to other parts of the school. For example, running errands to the office can serve as a reinforcer.
- Use extinction to reduce the occurrence of inappropriate movement. That is, provide no attention or reinforcement for inappropriate behaviors, but reward appropriate ones.
- Anticipate student movement and arrange to be near students when they are most likely to leave their seats. Often the proximity of the teacher, or a reminder provided by the teacher, will prevent inappropriate movement.
- Have students record their own in-seat behavior. They can begin with 5- or 10-minute intervals and note whether they remain seated during this time; if they leave their seats during the interval, they do not receive a check mark for that time period. At first, students can be reinforced for each successful interval. Then requirements are gradually increased so that students must perform successfully in 8 out of 10 intervals to earn reinforcers. The requirements are increased until expectations are consistent with those for all students in the class.
- Use a timing device to check student behavior. This can be a timer or a tape recording with preset random signals. When the signal is heard, reinforce students only if they are exhibiting appropriate behavior. Be sure to vary the number of minutes between signals so that students are not aware of when their behavior will be observed.

Social Relationships

Many students have difficulty getting along with others. This type of classroom conduct problem can be characterized by either aggressive behaviors or withdrawal; in either case, students do not establish and maintain satisfactory social relationships with teachers and peers. Examples of aggressive behaviors are fighting, swearing, arguing, refusing to follow directions, and antagonizing others. Withdrawn students, in contrast, may have limited interactions with teachers and peers and may avoid both physical proximity and verbal communication.

Many of the programs mentioned in chapter 6 provide specific problem-solving strategies and lessons for teaching the behaviors associated with appropriate social skills. The following suggestions can also help improve the social behaviors of students in the classroom:

- Provide students with examples of nonaggressive behaviors that can be used in situations that might lead to aggression. One way to do this is with good models; these can be adults, peers such as classmates or peer tutors, or films and videotapes.
- Use role playing to help students practice nonaggressive responses. Simulations provide students with an opportunity to learn appropriate behaviors before encountering difficult situations in daily life.
- Teach students acceptable responses to verbal or physical attacks. Options include calling for assistance, leaving the area, or saying something nonaggressive, such as "You played well in the softball game yesterday" or "I like the car I saw you driving after school." If students have not learned options such as these, they may react by fighting back or verbally attacking the aggressor. They need to learn a range of alternative responses and know which are appropriate for use in which situation.
- Incorporate strategies for reducing **bullying** in the classroom and other parts of the school environment. The "Inclusion Tips for the Teacher" section provides suggestions.
- Reinforce students who substitute appropriate, nonaggressive responses for the aggressive behaviors they previously exhibited. For example, provide a special reinforcer when students spend the lunch period or recess playing a game rather than arguing, fighting, or name calling.

- Use extinction for inappropriate verbal behaviors such as swearing, arguing, and teasing. Supply reinforcers for other students in the classroom to encourage them to ignore this type of problem behavior.
- Provide a penalty or punisher when a student exhibits an inappropriate behavior. This action might be removing the student to a setting without reinforcement (time-out), taking away activity time or other reinforcers earned (response cost), or introducing an aversive such as scolding or notification of parents. This type of intervention should be used sparingly, but it is sometimes necessary to stop a problem behavior quickly. Punishment, when used, should be administered immediately each time the inappropriate behavior occurs. Punishment is most effective when used in conjunction with positive reinforcement of appropriate behaviors. In fact, Walker (1995) indicates that the combination of teacher praise, token reinforcement, and response cost "represents the most powerful and potentially effective intervention for changing the behavior of acting-out children" (p. 197).
- Carefully review the social skills of withdrawn students, and determine their specific strengths and weaknesses. Provide instruction in important areas of need, such as how to greet others or what to do to start and participate in a conversation with others.
- Encourage the social interaction of withdrawn students with reinforcement techniques. Reinforcers can be used with the withdrawn student to encourage interaction, but, especially at first, it may be better to reinforce the student's peers. Focusing a great deal of attention on the withdrawn student at the start of the intervention may cause further withdrawal and avoidance of interactions.
- Include the withdrawn student in a classroom group assigned to complete a project or activity. Furnish specific activities that lead to interactions. For example, in completing worksheets, each student can be given a different portion of the materials needed to answer the questions. Provide reinforcers to the entire group when the target student is an active participant.
- Pair a withdrawn student with a peer tutor, cross-age tutor, or adult volunteer. The tutor or volunteer should model appropriate social interactions and reinforce the target student for like behaviors.

It is important to note that students with more severe antisocial, violent, or acting-out behavioral problems (e.g., hostility or aggression toward others, a willingness to commit rule infractions or to violate social norms, defiance of adult authority) may require more intensive interventions to deal with their problem behaviors. Typically, special education programs have specialists or consultants available to assist general education teachers in designing and implementing these interventions. In addition, there are many resources that provide detailed de-

Inclusion Tips for the Teacher

How to Reduce Classroom Bullying

Migliore (2003) presents these strategies for reducing classroom bullying:

1. Lead a class discussion on bullying.
2. Write a specific no-bullying policy into your classroom rules.
3. Teach social skills routinely through specific lessons and in conjunction with other activities throughout the day.
4. Teach students how to avoid being a victim and what to do if they are victimized.
5. Support students who speak out about bullying or who seek extra adult help.
6. Use extra effort to include all students in class activities.
7. Reinforce responsible, positive behaviors whenever possible.
8. Use a confidential "message box" for student suggestions or comments on classroom concerns.
9. Always model respectful behavior toward students.
10. Make sure that situations that have the potential of becoming aggressive are closely supervised.
11. Intervene immediately with an approach that matches the incident if bullying occurs.
12. Insist that the bully make amends if the incident involves a specific targeted victim.
13. Arrange your class schedule to minimize chaos.
14. Provide many ways to gain recognition in your classroom.
15. Have a clear process to report bullying.
16. Enlist students in no-bullying activities.
17. Encourage administrators and faculty members to write a no-bullying policy into the school handbook.
18. Plan an in-service meeting for all staff members to address bullying.
19. Involve parents with your no-bullying efforts.
20. Use the PTA to publicize the school's no-bullying policy. (pp. 172–176)

Note: From "Eliminating Bullying in Your Classroom," by F. T. Migliore, *Intervention in School and Clinic, 38* (3) 172–176. Reprinted with permission.

scriptions of strategies and interventions to deal with more severe challenging behaviors. For ideas about one important area of concern, see the "Inclusion Tips for the Teacher" section on page 274 on preventing violence in the schools.

TEACHING STUDY SKILLS

Students with poor study habits are at a distinct disadvantage in the general education classroom (Archer & Gleason, 1995; Heron & Harris, 2001). They may have difficulty maintaining attention in class, staying on task, organizing their work, or producing accurate responses. These problems have grave effects on academic performance and hinder a teacher's instructional effort. With students who fail to complete assignments, assessing current skill levels and progress is difficult because few work samples are available. As these students fall further and further behind their classmates, teachers become frustrated, and the probability increases that classroom conduct problems will occur.

Teachers have not typically taught study skills in a systematic fashion. However, programs such as *Skills for School Success* (Archer & Gleason, 1994) for grades 3 to 6 or *Advanced Skills for School Success* (Archer, 1992) for grades 7 to 12 provide teachers with a method, and the materials, to teach students a wide range of school and study skills such as organizing a notebook, keeping a calendar, writing neat papers, and completing assignments. Skills such as these should be included as part of the school curriculum; they should be taught directly with opportunities for guided and independent practice. The sections that follow discuss strategies to promote several important study skills; included are ideas to help students increase their ability to maintain attention, organize their work, and respond accurately. Another way to improve study skills is to increase reading comprehension. See the "Spotlight on Technology" feature for more information.

Maintaining Attention

Students with classroom behavior problems often spend a great deal of instructional time engaging in off-task behavior; their attention is not directed toward the appropriate classroom activity. They may stare into space, watch other students, doodle on their papers, or attend to stimuli that are irrelevant to the instructional task. Such students do not make effective use of independent study time. Instead of maintaining attention on the specific task, they attend to other features of the environment. Or their attention span is brief, and they shift attention from the instructional task to some other aspect of the classroom. Some engage in disruptive behaviors and interrupt the concentration of others. One

Inclusion Tips for the Teacher

Preventing School Violence

According to the findings from a recent government study of violence in U.S. schools (Miller & Chandler, 2003), "in 1999–2000, 71% of public elementary and secondary schools experienced at least one violent incident" (p. 6). It is interesting to note that the most common incident was physical attacks or fights without a weapon (64% of all schools) followed by threats of attacks without a weapon (52%). Serious violent incidents were less common, ranging from 11% of schools reporting at least one threat of a physical assault with a weapon to 1% or less of schools reporting robberies with a weapon or rape.

Two recent government publications are designed to help teachers, parents, and the entire school community reduce the number of violent incidents in schools. The first, *Early Warning, Timely Response: A Guide to Safe Schools* (Dwyer, Osher, & Warger, 1998), identifies these characteristics of a school that is safe and responsive to all children:

- Focus on academic achievement
- Involve families in meaningful ways
- Develop links to the community
- Emphasize positive relationships among students and staff
- Discuss safety issues openly
- Treat students with equal respect

- Create ways for students to share their concerns
- Help children feel safe expressing their feelings
- Have in place a system for referring children who are suspected of being abused or neglected
- Offer extended day programs for children
- Promote good citizenship and character
- Identify problems and assess progress toward solutions
- Support students in making the transition to adult life and the workplace. (pp. 3–5)

Copies of this guide can be downloaded from the website of the National Association of School Psychologists (http://www.nasponline.org/NEAT/crisisresponse resources.html).

The second publication is called *Safeguarding Our Children: An Action Guide* (Dwyer & Osher, 2000). It describes a comprehensive three-level approach to preventing school violence: building a schoolwide foundation, responding to warning signs with early intervention, and providing intensive interventions to troubled children. Copies of this guide in both English and Spanish can be downloaded from the website of the Center for Effective Collaboration and Practice (http://cecp.air.org/guide/actionguide.htm).

of the following strategies might help students improve their on-task behavior:

- Before presenting important verbal information to students, use a cue to alert them, such as "Listen," "Ready?" or "It's time to begin the lesson!" Establish a standard way of beginning lessons, and use the signal word or phrase only at times when you wish to obtain everyone's attention.
- Make teacher attention or other reinforcers contingent on attending behavior. Students with severe attention problems will need strong reinforcers provided immediately. This approach is much more effective than scolding students for not attending.
- When presenting information to students, seat them in a semicircle or U-shaped formation to ensure that all students can maintain visual contact with the teacher.
- Provide clear directions. Students with attention problems may be unable to follow long sets of directions with several steps. Simplify the directions and provide reinforcement when students complete each step. Avoid directions such as "Everyone return to your seat, get out your science book, turn to page 28, and answer the first five questions." Instead, start with the first step ("Every-

one return to your seat") and provide reinforcement when students comply.
- Present lessons at a brisk pace. Time spent on unimportant points or skills already mastered by the group can contribute to student inattention.
- Continually monitor whether students are attending to the lesson. Be prepared to modify your instructional approach if students seem confused or inattentive or if the material is too difficult.
- Use physical proximity to encourage attention. When students start to shift attention from the task, move closer to them.
- Reduce the predictability of your actions by varying the presentation of lessons. Ask different kinds of questions, vary the intonation of your voice, and let students know that they may be asked questions at any time.
- Provide students with individual work areas in which there are few distractions. These can be cubicles, carrels, or study booths. Be sure to consider both visual and auditory distractions when selecting an appropriate place for student offices.
- Hold students accountable for attending to the lesson and learning the material presented. Periodic teacher checks

Spotlight on Technology

Improving Reading Comprehension: *Start-to-Finish Books*

Start-to-Finish Books is a large collection of accessible books for students who struggle with reading. The Gold Library of *Start-to-Finish* features "considerate text" written at the grade 2/3 level. Vocabulary has been simplified to increase comprehension and sentences are shorter and less complex. Each book comes in three formats: a paperback book, an audiotape, and a computer version. The computer version provides support by reading text aloud with word-by-word highlighting. The screen below from *Liddy and the Volcanoes* shows a short text, a graphic, and commands such as the Speak button.

Chapter 7: Mount Vesuvius

When Liddy was in the tenth grade, she decided to be in the school science fair. Her trip to the Cascade Range made her want to learn more about volcanoes, and the science fair gave her a chance to do it.

Liddy's father told her about a famous volcano in Italy named Mount Vesuvius. "Mount Vesuvius completely buried two cities," he told her.

"You could make a model of Vesuvius," her father said. "I can get some chemicals to make a real eruption!"

Contents
1
2

1 OF 10

Note: Courtesy of Don Johnston Incorporated.

The Gold Library contains more than 50 individual titles. They are grouped into series such as Classic Adventures (e.g., *Treasure Island*), Classic Literature (e.g., *Romeo and Juliet*), A Step into History (e.g., *Rosa Parks: Freedom Fighter),* Natural Disasters (e.g., *Liddy and the Volcanoes*), Sherlock Holmes Mysteries, Ancient History, and Overcoming the Odds: Sports Biographies. Each book contains 10 to 12 chapters with approximately 100 to 150 words per page. At the end of each chapter, students take a comprehension quiz. Results are stored so that teachers can see records of student progress.

The Blue Library of the *Start-to-Finish Book* collection features longer books with more difficult text (grade 4/5) for more mature readers. More text appears on the screen and fewer graphics are used. Several titles are available including those from the series Myths and Legends (e.g., *Greek Myths*), Classic Adventure (e.g., *Call of the Wild*), and The World Around Us (e.g., *Jane Goodall and the Chimpanzees of Gombe*).

The newest component of *Start-to-Finish Books* is a series called *Literacy Starters*. Designed for readers with limited skills, each *Literacy Starter Set* contains three brief books, one with emergent-level text, one with transitional text, and one with conventional text. Among the *Set* series available are *Sports—Safety & Success, Plants—Science & Surroundings*, and *Early Settlers—Changes & Challenges.*

of students' understanding with techniques such as random questioning can increase student involvement.

- Simplify instructional materials so that only relevant information remains. For example, pictures or drawings can be distracting in reading materials.

Organizational Skills

Some students lack the ability to plan ahead. They are unorganized and use class time poorly. Such students can miss the important parts of task directions; fail to ask appropriate questions about assignments; and neglect to bring pens, pencils, and other necessary equipment to class. At test time, they are not prepared and have difficulty using the time allotted for the test effectively. The following suggestions may help students learn to plan ahead and become more organized:

- To help students budget their time, develop a schedule that divides the class period into short segments, each a few minutes in length. Make a list of activities to be finished during each time period, and reinforce students when these tasks are completed. Gradually allow students to help in devising the daily schedule until this is an independent activity. As students learn to complete their work, make the reinforcers more difficult to earn. For example, reinforcement might be delivered only after the satisfactory completion of work for two intervals rather than one.

- State directions for assignments and classroom work clearly and concisely; include only essential information. Alert students well ahead of time to work that is due and provide older pupils with a weekly schedule of assignments.

- Assist students in organizing their materials. This may involve teaching them how to organize their desks or how

FIGURE 11-3   Study Techniques for Secondary Students

1. The student should first obtain an overview of the assignment. He should begin by writing exactly the assignment task the teacher has given—is he to read? to answer questions? to outline?
2. With a definitive purpose in mind, the student can more efficiently address the task. He should write what he hopes to gain as a result of his effort so that he has a clear and concrete goal to serve as a guide.
3. The student should use the aids provided through the structure of the text. Chapter titles, subheadings, and summaries are valuable to the student taking notes of "important" information. Further they provide "cues" to the student of the information that is important.
4. The next step is actually outlining or noting information in an organized manner. The teacher can assist here by asking the student to write only the information he feels is the most important and using this as a basis for comparing with the teacher's notes. (A tendency of many students is to copy verbatim or to take excessive notes without really assimilating the information.)
5. The student should attempt to summarize the material in the assignment (with the goal he has established for the reading in mind). He should ask himself the following questions: have I the necessary information to meet the goal? am I able to discuss the main points in my own words? what does this material really mean?

Note: From *Mainstreaming the Learning Disabled Adolescent* (p. 33) by D. M. Woodward, 1981, Austin, TX: PRO-ED. Copyright 1981 by PRO-ED, Inc.

to set up a notebook. Student notebooks should contain a calendar, a place for recording assignments due, and sections for notes and assignments for each subject or class; they can also hold materials such as paper, pencils, pens, and rulers. The teacher should check notebooks periodically and reinforce or reinstruct students as necessary. Parents should be informed of the notebook requirements and encouraged to compliment students for organizing their work.

- Present directions for assignments and classwork both verbally and in writing. Students can practice by first listening to directions and taking notes and later checking their accuracy with written directions.
- Begin with work directions that have only a few steps. Reinforce students for following each step. Gradually increase the standards for success; the time period allowed for task completion can be shortened, or the accuracy criterion raised. When students are able to follow simple directions, then introduce ones that are more complex.
- Teach students to ask appropriate questions about directions and assignments by providing a model. The model can be a demonstration by the teacher or a written set of questions to ask when a task is unclear. Allow students to practice asking questions about hypothetical assignments.
- Group students together for completing individual assignments. Reinforce the group if all members finish their work and meet the criterion for accuracy.
- Make a list of materials needed to complete an assignment, and have students assemble these before beginning work. Later, require that students prepare such a list before they start an assignment. Grade both the list and the assignment itself.

- Encourage parents to set aside quiet time—with no television, radio, or telephone—each evening for their children to study and complete assignments.
- Work with parents in setting up a home program to reinforce studying. Parents can talk with the teacher each week or sign a checksheet to report whether the student has spent the appropriate time studying at home.

Other sources of information about teaching organizational skills to special students, particularly those in middle school and high school, are *Teaching Adolescents with Mild Disabilities* by Platt and Olson (1997), *Teaching Students with Learning and Behavior Problems* (3rd ed.) by Rivera and Smith (1997), and *Teaching Students with Mild and High Incidence Disabilities at the Secondary Level* (2nd ed.) by Sabornie and deBettencourt (2003). Woodward (1981) also presents many useful ideas; Figure 11-3 lists Woodward's suggestions for helping secondary students learn study techniques.

Increasing Accuracy

Inaccurate responses occur for many reasons. For students with behavioral disorders, a rapid response rate is one common cause. In this instance, students work quickly, without taking time to think about their answers or check them for accuracy. In class discussions, these students may blurt out a response before carefully considering the question. Such students are characterized by the speed with which they work and the resulting high number of incorrect responses; a term used to describe this behavior is *impulsivity*. To help hasty students increase the accuracy of their work, teachers can try one of the strategies described here:

FIGURE 11-4   How to Be a Better Test-Taker

To the Student:

If you have ever studied for a test only to find your efforts didn't pay off in a good grade because you didn't study efficiently, this packet can help. Follow the suggestions in the order presented. Read each item carefully. Review wherever you feel necessary. Begin!

1. When taking a test, don't panic! Be prepared with a pencil (with eraser), pen, and paper.
2. Carefully examine the entire test before starting to answer any questions. It is very important that you understand what you are to do in response to the test. Knowing whether the teacher wants one word answers or discussion responses, for example, makes a difference in the correctness of your response.
3. After you have looked at the number of questions and the type of response required, estimate how much time you are going to devote to each question or area. Pay particular attention to the weight each question carries. An essay question worth 25 points out of a 100 possible points must be given more time than two multiple-choice questions of 2 points each.
4. Answer first those questions you feel most confident of the answers.
5. When you are responding to an essay question, it is a good idea to write down the key ideas or main points in brief form. This will help you include everything you feel is of importance in your answer.
6. It is a good idea to try to answer all the questions in a test (unless you're told that you could be penalized for wrong answers). If you are really stumped on a question, go on to another. Sometimes another question will help you to remember the answer to the question you have been struggling with.
7. Write clearly. You are likely to lose points if the teacher has great difficulty reading your writing.
8. Leave time to reread your paper before you hand it in. Pay attention to punctuation and spelling. Most importantly, ask yourself if you wrote what you intended.
9. In objective tests, don't waste time on questions that are confusing to you.
10. Once you have made a guess to a question you are unsure of, you should not change it; first guesses are usually best.

Note: From *Mainstreaming the Learning Disabled Adolescent* (p. 35) by D. M. Woodward, 1981, Austin, TX: PRO-ED. Copyright 1981 by PRO-ED, Inc.

- When giving assignments, remind students that part of the task is checking for accuracy, and reinforce students for completing this step. Teachers can observe students to see whether they are checking their work, or reinforcement can be contingent on a continual decrease in the number of errors.
- Provide reinforcement for accurate responses. For example, students might earn tokens for each correct response.
- Model appropriate proofreading procedures. Show the class examples of work containing errors, and review how to make corrections. Students may be taught to use a proofreading strategy such as COPS, in which students check Capitalization, Overall appearance, Punctuation, and Spelling (Schumaker, Nolan, & Deshler, 1985).
- Carefully design instructional materials to achieve high rates of student success, which is associated with higher levels of student learning. Poorly designed instruction leads to student frustration and poor levels of performance.
- Teach students strategies for taking tests and examinations An example of a program to improve test-taking skills appears in Figure 11-4; teachers might also be in-

terested in the article "Improving Test-Taking Skills of LD Adolescents" by Markel (1981).
- Encourage students to think before they speak. For example, after asking a question, require students to observe a short 5- to 10-second "thinking time" before responding. As students learn to deliberate before answering, gradually reduce the structure of this requirement.
- Use a cognitive training technique to help students learn to direct their own problem solving. Consult the accompanying "Inclusion Tips for the Teacher" for information about the self-instructional training program described by Finch and Spirito (1980).
- Kauffman (2001) suggests that careless student errors can be reduced through the use of response cost procedures. That is, when errors are made, students lose something, such as part of their recess time. The procedure can be made more effective by adding a provision that students must complete an additional question or problem correctly for each error made.
- Use peer tutors to help students correct work or practice correct responses. For instance, the teacher might provide tutors with questions likely to be asked in class, and the tutor and student can then practice those questions.

Inclusion Tips for the Teacher

Self-Instructional Training

According to Finch and Spirito (1980), self-instructional training is a procedure in which students learn a step-by-step system for attacking a problem by means of specific verbalizations. That is, students learn specific strategies to talk themselves through problem situations; they themselves give the instructions.

Finch and Spirito (1980) describe the four general types of verbal messages used in the program:

1. Problem definition ("What is it I should do in this situation?")

2. Focusing of attention ("I have to concentrate and do what I'm supposed to do.")

3. Coping statements ("Even though I made a mistake, I can continue more slowly.")

4. Self-reinforcement ("Great! I did it! That was good.")

Students learn this strategy by observing the teacher, who models completion of a task using the verbalization procedures. Then the students perform the task and begin by instructing themselves out loud. Next, they perform the task using only whispered instructions. Eventually, the instructions are internalized, and students are able to direct their own problem-solving behavior.

Tutors should be reminded to encourage students to think before they respond.

In this chapter, you have learned ways to handle disruptive behavior in the general education classroom and improve the study skills of students with behavioral disorders and others with similar needs. Techniques for teaching students with communication disorders in the general education classroom will be described in the next chapter. Before proceeding, check "Things to Remember" to review strategies used to meet the needs of students identified as having behavioral disorders.

Things to Remember

- The most common areas in which adaptations must be made for students with behavioral disorders are social skills and classroom behavior. Although these students usually require assistance in academic instruction, the most urgent needs are generally control of disruptive behaviors and acquisition of appropriate social and study skills.
- The major indicators of behavioral disorders are actions that deviate significantly in frequency, intensity, and duration from those expected of the student's typical peers of the same age and gender.
- Many students with behavioral disorders have academic needs that closely resemble those of students with learning disabilities and require the use of similar instructional interventions.

- Assessment of behavioral disorders is most useful when data are gathered about the current status of students' problem behaviors.
- Typical disruptive behaviors of students include tardiness, verbal outbursts and other acting-out behaviors, inappropriate physical activity, and poor social relationships.
- In the area of study skills, students with behavioral disorders experience difficulty maintaining attention, organizing work, and responding with accuracy.
- Students with behavioral disorders are capable of learning to act appropriately; their school conduct and work habits can be improved with proper instructional and behavioral management techniques.

ACTIVITIES

1. Observe a student who has been identified as having behavioral disorders in a general education classroom. Describe how this student's behavior differs from that of typical class peers. How does the teacher treat this student? How do classmates react? For this student and one or two "normal" students, try to get a count of the number of positive and negative interactions with the teacher and with other students; compare your data. Look back through this chapter for intervention ideas that might be appropriate for the student. Select one and defend your choice.

2. Interview a special educator who works with students with behavioral disorders. Ask that teacher for recommendations of appropriate techniques to use in the general education classroom. In the teacher's view, what are the important differences between students with behavioral disorders who succeed in the general education program and those who require a special class? Write a summary of your interview, and discuss any of the teacher's points with which you disagree.

3. Read two articles that discuss techniques for working with students with behavioral disorders. *Behavioral Disorders, Journal of Applied Behavior Analysis, Teaching Exceptional Children*, and *Education and Treatment of Children* are journals in which such articles often appear. Carefully consider the articles you have read, and describe how these techniques could be used in a general education class.

4. Survey your local community for agencies that provide services to students with behavioral disorders. These agencies may deal with acting-out or withdrawn students, drug abuse, or suicide prevention. Local school districts or mental health organizations may be able to provide the names of some appropriate agencies. Contact two agencies and find out what types of services they offer. How do these programs differ from school programs? Are services offered to parents? In your view, how useful are these programs?

5. Assume that you have been selected to explain behavioral disorders to another teacher. Prepare an outline of your presentation, including the benefits of these students being included in the general education program. Formulate four questions that you anticipate the teacher is likely to ask, and prepare answers for these questions.

6. Watch a movie that includes information about individuals who have unusual or disordered behavior (such as *To Sir with Love, Rain Man,* or *Blackboard Jungle*). Describe their behaviors in terms that would be meaningful in planning for their educational needs. Explain how a general education teacher could accommodate a school-aged individual with similar needs in his or her classroom. What type(s) of special support or services might be needed by the student? By the teacher? Discuss any questions you would have about the feasibility and appropriateness of the placement.

CD-ROM Activities

Review the case study featuring the preschool classroom and look for examples of students' behaviors that have potential for disrupting classroom learning. Then, view the video clip entitled "Keystone Behaviors" to answer these questions:

- *Observe the young boy and identify the behaviors that appear to be interfering with his attention to the task at hand. Describe each behavior (be sure to use observable terms), then count the frequency of occurrence or time the duration.*

- *What strategies does the teacher employ to bring the student back to the task? Could you suggest other possible strategies?*

Teaching Students with Communication Disorders

CHAPTER

12

Elaine, Jeff, and Rocky

There are three children with communication problems in Ms. Ranson's first-grade class. Despite their speech and language difficulties, these students participate in all general education class activities. Each also receives individual help twice each week from the speech-language pathologist. We will look more closely at the special education needs of two of these children—Elaine and Rocky—later in the chapter.

Elaine speaks clearly and distinctly but has difficulty producing the *r* sound. Because of this articulation problem, she calls her teacher Ms. Wanson.

Jeff's speech is like that of a much younger child. He mispronounces sounds, omits some, and speaks hurriedly and indistinctly. Jeff's teacher and classmates often find it difficult to understand what he is saying.

Rocky speaks intelligibly but makes many grammatical errors. He uses incomplete sentences and may mix plural nouns with singular verbs ("boys runs"). In addition, his speaking vocabulary is limited, and his knowledge of word meanings is poor for his age.

Willy

Willy stutters. He is in 10th grade and is a good student. On written reports, assignments, and exams, Willy excels. However, because of his dysfluency in speech, he is reluctant to answer questions in class, participate in discussions, or give oral reports. Willy has several close friends around whom he is comfortable speaking, but he is hesitant to talk with people he does not know well. Although attending general education classes for all his academic work, Willy receives special education services from the speech-language pathologist. This specialist is working with Willy to reduce his dysfluency and to overcome his embarrassment in speaking. She also consults with Willy's general education teachers to help them provide a nonthreatening classroom environment in which Willy will feel comfortable and will practice speaking in front of others.

LOOKING AHEAD

There are many different types of communication disorders, and the adaptations required in general education classrooms vary from student to student. As you will learn in this chapter, the two major strategies involve encouraging oral communication and teaching new language skills. Think about these questions as you read:

- Compare the communication problems of the three first graders, Elaine, Jeff, and Rocky. Which are speech problems? Language problems? What dimensions of language are involved?
- From what you know about Willy the 10th grader, what are his strengths? Also, what challenges does he face because of his communication problems?
- What strategies could you use to create a classroom environment where students like Elaine, Jeff, Rocky, and Willy would feel comfortable practicing their communication skills?

To answer these questions online, go to the Students' Stories Module in Chapter 12 of the Companion Website.

When children enter school, they are expected to be able to communicate. This expectation may not be realized in students with speech and language impairments. Communication disorders, one of the most common of all disabilities, affect a student's ability to interact with teachers and classmates. Students with speech problems may mispronounce words or sounds, speak with dysfluency, or have an unusual voice quality; as a result, their speech is difficult for the listener to understand. Students with language problems may fail to understand the speech of others and may have trouble expressing their own thoughts in words. Although communication disorders can accompany other disabilities such as learning disabilities, mental retardation, and hearing impairment, most students with speech and language impairments remain in the general education classroom. Special services are provided to them on a part-time basis by professionals such as speech-language pathologists.

The special needs of students with communication problems fall in the areas of academic and social performance. In instruction, the general education teacher may need to make minor adaptations in order to stress language, listening, and speaking skills for such students. Creating an accepting classroom environment is also important. Students with communication impairments are more likely to practice verbal interactions with others if their classmates and teacher are tolerant, accepting, and supportive.

This chapter describes the characteristics of students with communication disorders and suggests methods for the general education teacher to use in gathering data, teaching listening and speaking skills, and creating an accepting classroom environment. To become more familiar with speech and language impairments and their impact on communication, try one of the simulations described in Table 12-1.

INDICATORS OF COMMUNICATION DISORDERS

Because students with communication disorders typically remain members of general education classrooms for their entire educational careers, the general education teacher is an important professional on the inclusion team. It is the general education teacher who notes signs of communication difficulties, refers individual students for special education assessment, helps gather assessment information, and later coordinates students' classroom instruction with special speech and language services.

Communication disorders are of two types: those that affect language and those that affect speech. **Language** is the ability to communicate using symbols; it includes both oral and written communication and requires both expression and reception of ideas. **Speech** is one aspect of oral language; it is the vehicle by which thoughts are expressed in oral communication.

According to the American Speech-Language-Hearing Association (ASHA) (n.d.), language and speech disorders can be differentiated as follows:

A *language disorder* is characterized by an inability to use the symbols of language through (a) proper use of words and their meanings, (b) appropriate grammatical patterns, and (c) proper use of speech sounds.

A *speech disorder* is characterized by difficulty in (a) producing speech sounds (articulation), (b) maintaining speech rhythm (fluent speech), and (c) controlling vocal production (voice). (p. 1, italics added)

The National Information Center for Children and Youth with Disabilities (1997b) includes as characteristics of language disorders "improper use of words and their meanings, inability to express ideas, inappropriate grammatical pat-

TABLE 12-1	Simulations of Speech and Language Impairments	
COMMUNICATION SITUATION	**TYPE OF DISORDER**	**SUGGESTED SIMULATION**
You are speaking to a group of teachers and parents. Describe the instructional program in your classroom.	Delayed speech	Deliver your speech without talking. You may gesture.
You have just met your new principal. Introduce yourself and welcome him or her to your school.	Articulation	Introduce yourself after you have placed one or two saltine crackers in your mouth. Don't chew.
You are reporting to the school board about the new parent involvement program at your school.	Poor voice quality	Tape record your speech and then play it back at the wrong speed.
You are chatting with the parents of several of your students about the upcoming school play.	Dysfluency or stuttering	S-say th-the f-first s-sound o-of e-each w-word, th-then th-the w-word i-itself.

American Speech-Language-Hearing Association

http://www.asha.org

The American Speech-Language-Hearing Association (ASHA) is the major professional organization in the field of communication disorders. As such, it serves speech-language pathologists, audiologists, and others interested in speech, language, and hearing development and disorders in children and in adults. The ASHA website offers features for three categories of visitors: ASHA members, students (and prospective students), and the public. The public section of the website provides online information on topics such as

Note: Courtesy of American Speech-Language-Hearing Association.

"Hearing Screening and Assessment" and "Speech and Language Disorders," as well as directions for obtaining information packets and brochures on a range of topics (e.g., stuttering, swallowing problems, child language). Several of these print resources are available in both English and Spanish versions. The student segment of this site focuses on information about careers, graduate programs, and certification. Although one segment of the site is open only to ASHA members, the "About ASHA" portion provides information about ASHA publications, news releases, and legislation and lobbying efforts.

For more information, go to the Web Links module in Chapter 12 of the Companion Website.

terns, reduced vocabulary, and inability to follow directions" (p 1). Thus, students with language disorders experience difficulty understanding or expressing ideas appropriate to their age. Those with speech impairments show poor speech sound production, fluency, or voice quality for their age.

Most speech problems are detected at an early age; articulation disorders are most commonly found among children in the first few grades of school. Language disorders are also identified in young children but can persist throughout the elementary and secondary years. Speech disorders are usually obvious to the listener. In fact, Van Riper (1978) maintains that one criterion for identifying a communication disorder is speech unusual enough to bring attention to itself. *Unusual,* however, is not a very precise description of a possible problem. The questions in the "Inclusion Tips for the Teacher" box can assist in obtaining more specific information.

ASSESSMENT PROCEDURES

When communication disorders are suspected, the assessment team meets to prepare an assessment plan. One important consideration is the student's hearing; the school nurse is consulted to determine whether a hearing loss is contributing to poor speech or language performance. If the problem appears to be a minor speech disorder, the speech-language pathologist takes primary responsibility for assessment. If more serious difficulties are suspected, several specialists participate in gathering assessment information. Formal assessment begins when the parents of the referred student have given written consent.

In evaluating a student's speech, the speech-language pathologist can administer a standardized measure such as the *Goldman-Fristoe Test of Articulation–2* (Goldman & Fristoe, 2000). The specialist also talks with the student in an informal setting in order to evaluate speech fluency and voice quality. The classroom teacher may be asked to contribute observations concerning the usual speech patterns of the student.

Figure 12-1 presents a checklist that the teacher can use to evaluate the speech of young elementary children. Voice quality, speech fluency, and sound production are included. The checklist also provides the ages at which students are expected to produce the various speech sounds; these are general guidelines and should be used with caution when evaluating the performance of an individual child.

Most children have mastered the sounds of the English language by the age of 8. Some, however, progress more slowly. Consider Elaine the first grader introduced at the beginning of this chapter who has yet to master the *r* sound. Her articulation error is one of substitution; she replaces the *r* sound with the *w* sound. Other types of articulation errors are omissions, distortions, and additions of sounds.

Inclusion Tips for the Teacher

Recognizing Speech Problems

Perhaps the best way to determine whether a person has a speech problem is to ask yourself the following questions:

1. *Can I understand this person?*   This is the simplest judgment you will have to make. If you cannot understand or can understand only with difficulty what a person is saying, she has a communication disorder.

2. *Does this person sound strange?*   If you can understand someone, but he doesn't sound like you expect him to, he has a problem. An adult who sounds like Elmer Fudd, a 200-pound adult male who sounds like a nine-year-old girl, and a person who has a flat, expressionless manner of speaking all have communication problems.

3. *Does this person have any peculiar physical characteristics when speaking?*   A person who has distracting mannerisms that interfere with his message has a problem. These mannerisms might include unnecessary or unexpected movements of the lips, tongue, nostrils, arms, legs, or posture.

4. *Is the communication in a style inappropriate to the situation?*   We do not expect the president of the United States to greet Congress before his annual State of the Union address by saying, "Hey, baby, what's happenin'? It's cool at my pad, what's goin' down here?". . . . Our point is that we normally shift our style of communication to fit a given situation. A speaker unable to do this may have a problem.

5. *Do I enjoy listening to this speaker?*   This is a judgment we all feel comfortable making. If the reason we don't enjoy a speaker is that we don't like her message, the speaker doesn't have a problem. If, on the other hand, we don't enjoy a speaker for one of the reasons mentioned here, she probably does have a problem. . . . Speakers who can alienate people merely by introducing themselves need help.

6. *Is the speaker damaging his communication mechanisms?*   Like most other parts of the body, the organs used in communication can be misused. Although diagnoses of physiological abuse can only be made by specialists, listeners can often detect signs of strain in a speaker. Teachers should always refer to professionals children they think may be injuring their voices. An unnecessary referral hurts no one, but overlooking a symptom can have disastrous consequences.

7. *Does the speaker suffer when attempting to communicate?*   This is difficult to judge, because a listener cannot usually determine how a person feels about her efforts to communicate. Many people considered normal communicators by their peers suffer emotionally as a result of shortcomings they imagine. Communication problems such as these that do not have obvious symptoms are among the most difficult to treat.

Note: From *An Introduction to Special Education* (2nd ed.) by William H. Berdine and Edward Blackhurst. Published by Allyn & Bacon. Copyright © 1985 Pearson Education. Reprinted by permission of the publisher.

The assessment of language disorders requires the expertise of several disciplines. In addition to the general education teacher and the speech-language pathologist, the assessment team may include the school nurse, an audiologist or other specialist in the detection of hearing losses, the school psychologist, and the special education teacher. The student is evaluated in many areas: hearing, intellectual performance, academic achievement, and language skills.

Language assessment typically focuses on both reception and expression. The student's ability to receive and understand information from language is evaluated; likewise, the student's skill in using the symbols of language to express thoughts is assessed. One standardized measure that looks at both of these dimensions is the *Test of Language Development—Primary* (3rd ed.) (Newcomer & Hammill, 1997), an individual test appropriate for students aged 4 to 9. This test assesses three important features of language: **semantics**, the meaningful aspects of language; **syntax**, the grammatical aspects of language; and **phonology**, the sound system of language.

Figure 12-2 presents a portion of the assessment report for Rocky, the first grader with grammar and vocabulary problems who was described at the beginning of this chapter. The results of the *Test of Language Development–Primary* show that Rocky understands language well but has difficulty in expression, particularly in semantics and syntax.

Many other measures are available to the speech-language pathologist or special education teacher responsible for language assessment. Examples include the *Test of Language Development–Intermediate* (3rd ed.) (Hammill & Newcomer, 1997) for students aged 8 to 13, the *Clinical Evaluation of Language Fundamentals–4* (Semel, Wiig, & Secord, 2003) for students aged 5 to 21, and the *Test of Adolescent and Adult Language* (3rd ed.) (Hammill, Brown, Larsen, & Wiederholt, 1994) for individuals aged 12 to 25. These measures concentrate on semantics, syntax, and phonology.

To assess the fourth dimension of language, pragmatics, professionals often rely on informal procedures. **Pragmatics** is the use of language; that is, how language functions in the various

FIGURE 12-1   Speech Checklist

Student _____ Age _____ Grade _____
Teacher _____ Date of Evaluation _____

1. **Voice Quality** (check all that are appropriate)
   The student's *usual* voice quality is
____ pleasant to listen to	____ monotone
____ unpleasant to listen to	____ very high-pitched
____ hoarse or husky	____ very low-pitched
____ like a whisper	____ very loud
____ nasal	____ very soft

2. **Speech Fluency** (check one)
   The student's *usual* speech is
   ____ very fluent
   ____ generally fluent with occasional hesitations, repetitions, and/or prolongations of sounds and syllables
   ____ frequently dysfluent and characterized by hesitations, repetitions, and/or prolongations of sounds and syllables

3. **Sound Production** (check each sound that the student *usually* produces clearly and correctly)*
   Sounds expected by age 5†
____ /p/ as in *pal*	____ /g/ as in *goat*	____ /n/ as in *not*	____ /t/ as in *tap*
____ /m/ as in *map*	____ /d/ as in *dog*	____ /b/ as in *ball*	____ /ng/ as in *ring*
____ /f/ as in *fat*	____ /h/ as in *hit*	____ /k/ as in *kill*	____ /y/ as in *year*

   Sounds expected by age 6†
   ____ /r/ as in *rag*   ____ /l/ as in *lad*

   Sounds expected by age 7†
   ____ /ch/ as in *church*   ____ /sh/ as in *ship*   ____ /j/ as in *junk*
   ____ /th/ (voiceless) as in *thank*

   Sounds expected by age 8†
   ____ /s/ as in *son*   ____ /z/ as in *zoo*   ____ /v/ as in *very*
   ____ /th/ (voiced) as in *this*

   Sounds expected after age 8†
   ____ /zh/ as in *azure* or *pleasure*

*Only consonant sounds are listed because most children are able to produce vowel and diphthong sounds upon entry to school.
†Age norms derived from Sander (1972).

situations in which communication occurs. Clearly, language use varies according to the purpose of communication, audience, and setting. For example, when the message to be communicated is that today's homework has not been completed, the language a student uses to communicate that message to the teacher is likely to differ from that used with a classmate.

In addition, a student's parents and general education teacher are valuable sources of information about language performance. These team members have observed the student over long time periods and can comment on the student's usual facility with language tasks. By observing typical classroom activities, the teacher can gather data about the student's performance of language skills such as

- understanding oral directions,
- speaking in complete sentences,
- using age-appropriate vocabulary in oral communication, and
- using correct grammar in speech.

SPECIAL SERVICES

As with all individuals with disabilities, the special services provided to students with communication disorders depend on the severity and extent of the students' educational needs. For many students with speech problems, only minor educational adaptations are necessary. Such students are members of general education classrooms and fully capable of participation in instructional activities. They leave the classroom only for short periods of time to receive special services from the speech-language pathologist on a daily or weekly basis.

FIGURE 12-2   Special Education Assessment Results

Student: Rocky   **Age:** 6 years, 2 months   **Grade:** 1

Classroom Performance

Ms. Ranson, Rocky's first-grade teacher, reported that Rocky is experiencing difficulty in classroom language tasks. According to Ms. Ranson's observations, Rocky appears to be a bright child but one who has not yet learned the grammatical rules and vocabulary expected of a first-grade student. Rocky's progress in math is adequate, but he makes mistakes in oral reading that reflect his problems with grammar. Also, he has difficulty expressing his thoughts when speaking in class and in play situations with the other children.

Hearing

Results of a routine hearing screening at the beginning of the school year indicated that Rocky's hearing is adequate.

Intellectual Performance

Mr. Scott, the school psychologist, administered the *Wechsler Intelligence Scale for Children—Fourth Edition* to Rocky. All subtest and IQ scores were within the average range, which indicates adequate intellectual performance.

Oral Language Skills

To learn more about Rocky's oral language skills, Mrs. Putnam, the speech-language pathologist, administered the *Test of Language Development—Primary* to Rocky. This test includes measures of both receptive and expressive language. On the receptive language tests, Rocky scored within the average range; he shows adequate skills in understanding the semantic, syntactical, and phonological aspects of language.

Expressive language tasks were more difficult for Rocky, as the following results indicate. (Average performance is indicated by standard scores of 85 to 115.)

Language Area	Subtest	Standard Score
Expressive Semantics	Oral Vocabulary	78
Expressive Syntax	Sentence Imitation	80
Expressive Syntax	Grammatic Completion	76
Expressive Phonology	Word Articulation	95

Expressive phonology, assessed by the Word Articulation subtest, was within the average range. However, other expressive skills fell within the low average range of performance. Rocky's major areas of need are expressive semantics and syntax. Rocky's oral vocabulary is more typical of a 4- or 5-year-old child than a first grader, and his command of grammatical structures is limited for his age.

Elaine, the first grader introduced earlier, is an example of a student with a speech disorder who is successfully included in general education. Elaine's problem was identified early in her school career, and she is receiving the special help she needs to overcome her problem.

Other types of communication disorders may require more extensive special programming. Rocky, the first grader with difficulty in expressive language, requires special help to learn better language skills. Figure 12-3 shows that his IEP goals focus on improvement of expressive vocabulary and grammar. However, Rocky remains with his first-grade class for instruction in all academic subjects.

Some students with communication disorders also have social needs. Because of their speech or language problems, they have difficulty interacting with others and may feel iso-

lated or disliked. Willy, the 10th-grade student described at the beginning of this chapter, is keenly aware of his dysfluent speech and, as a result, remains silent throughout most of the school day. The IEP for Willy stresses not only more fluent speech but also an increased number of interactions with teachers and classmates.

The general education classroom is the most typical placement for students with speech and language impairments. If communication problems are related to other disabilities such as learning disabilities, resource services may be provided. If more severe disabilities such as mental retardation or a hearing impairment are present, the intensive services available in a special class setting may be needed. Most students, however, remain in the general education classroom and receive special services only on a part-time basis. The general education

FIGURE 12-3	IEP Goals and Services for Rocky

Annual Goals

1. By the end of the school year, Rocky will speak in grammatically correct sentences with agreement in number between subjects and verbs.
   Person responsible: Speech-language pathologist
2. By the end of the school year, Rocky will increase his speaking vocabulary by at least 100 words.
   Person responsible: Speech-language pathologist
3. Rocky will successfully complete all requirements for first-grade reading, language arts, math, and other academic subjects.
   Person responsible: First-grade teacher

Amount of Participation in General Education

Rocky will attend the general education first-grade class for all academic instruction.

Special Education and Related Services

1. Rocky will receive special education services from the speech-language pathologist (annual goals 1 and 2) for 30 minutes daily.
2. The speech-language pathologist will provide consultation to Rocky's first-grade teacher as necessary.

teacher provides all academic instruction and receives consultant help from the speech-language pathologist as necessary. To learn more about individuals with communication disorders, consult the accompanying "For Your Information" material.

CLASSROOM ADAPTATIONS

The general education teacher usually does not have to make major classroom adaptations in order to meet the special needs of students with communication disorders. Even though characterized by speech or language problems, these students are generally able to participate in all aspects of the general education curriculum. Special attention is needed in only two areas: speech and language skills and social acceptance.

Students with speech impairments may need to improve articulation, voice quality, or fluency. To meet these needs, an individualized special education program is provided by the speech-language pathologist. The major goal in the general education classroom becomes practice of oral communication. Students require a nonthreatening environment in which to try out the new speech skills they are learning in their special education program. By collaborating with the speech-language pathologist, the general education teacher can target these skills for reinforcement in the general education classroom. The classroom teacher assists by encouraging the students' participation and ensuring that their attempts at oral communication are accepted with tolerance and support by classmates.

Students with language impairments experience difficulty in the reception and expression of oral communication. Again, although the speech-language pathologist takes primary responsibility for instruction in the areas of educational need, students should have opportunities within the general education classroom to practice the new language skills they are learning. The general education teacher also assists by modeling appropriate grammar, stressing vocabulary development in all curriculum areas, and modifying the language aspects of classroom activities and assignments.

The following sections include methods for teaching students with communication disorders, ways to encourage practice of oral communication by students with speech disorders, and suggestions for teaching language skills to students with grammar and vocabulary needs.

ENCOURAGING ORAL COMMUNICATION

For students with speech impairments, the general education classroom should be a place where they can hear correct speech and feel comfortable enough to practice their newly learned communication skills. To accomplish this, the general education teacher must provide good speech models, an accepting environment, and opportunities for practicing oral communication skills.

Students with special needs require good models of oral communication. The teacher is the primary model and should be careful to speak clearly, fluently, and with appropriate articulation. Sunderland (2004) also suggests that teachers monitor the rate of their speech, the length and complexity of their sentences, and the number of directions given at any one time. Classmates are also able to help. By demonstrating appropriate speech, they, too, serve as important models for special students.

How the teacher and classroom peers react to speech errors made by students with special needs is a major factor in encouraging oral communication. It is crucial that the

For Your Information

Students with Communication Disorders

- Students with communication disorders are estimated to make up about 2% of the school-aged population. Communication disorders are the second most prevalent disability, accounting for approximately one-fifth of the students served by special education (U.S. Department of Education, 2002).
- The most typical types of communication disorders in school-aged children are articulation problems and language impairments (Heward, 2003; Smith, 2004).
- Speech and language problems are most often found in young children. The prime time for identification of communication disorders is the first and second grades.
- Expectations for communication skills are related to the age of the child. For example, young preschool children are expected to pass through a developmental stage in which dysfluencies are common (American Speech-Language-Hearing Association, 1997; Swift, 1988).

- The great majority of school-aged children with communication disorders remain in general education, and only a very few receive special services in a special class or school; in 1999–2000, almost 95% of students with speech or language impairments were educated in the general education classroom for the majority of the school day (U.S. Department of Education, 2002).
- Every child and adult who speaks makes articulation errors, and everyone's speech at one time or another is marked by dysfluencies. Deviations in speech are considered communication disorders only when they become frequent and severe enough to interfere with the ability to communicate.
- Speech characterized by an accent or dialect is different but is not considered disordered.

communication attempts of students with speech disorders be treated with respect and tolerance. If the teacher and peers are accepting listeners, then special students will feel comfortable enough to practice oral communication. Guidelines for establishing a tolerant classroom climate are identified here:

- When students with speech problems speak, the teacher should listen with full attention and ensure that other students listen.
- Speech errors should not be criticized by the teacher or classmates. However, the teacher may wish to demon-

strate correct speech for the student by repeating what was said. For example, if the student says, "The story was about a wittle wabbit," the teacher might say, "Right! The story was about a little rabbit."

- The teacher should not call attention to speech errors. If the teacher accepts misarticulations and dysfluencies and attends to the content of what the student is saying, peers are more likely to do the same. This approach is particularly important with dysfluency problems that may become much more serious if attention is called to them.
- Peers should not be allowed to ridicule or make fun of speech errors. The teacher should make it clear that this is not appropriate behavior. One way to help peers understand the problems of special students is by using simulations. Table 12-1 earlier in this chapter presented ways to experience simulated oral communication problems.
- The teacher should take care when placing students with speech problems in situations in which their communication difficulties might interfere. For example, if class members are reading tongue twisters aloud, "six silly snakes" should be reserved for the student who can articulate the s sound. In other words, the teacher should carefully consider which oral classroom activities are appropriate to assign to students who are unsure of their communication abilities or embarrassed by speaking.
- Changing the nature of the communication situation can sometimes improve stuttering problems. Shames and Ramig (1994) report that dysfluencies often decrease (or, in some cases, disappear) when students sing, read aloud in unison with another person, whisper, speak in a mon-

otone, speak in a higher or lower pitch than usual, or speak in time to a metronome.

- For some students with communication problems, speech is slow and labored. A stutterer may take a long time to produce a single sentence, a student with cerebral palsy may make facial grimaces as he or she struggles to articulate each word, and a person who communicates by means of a communication board or an electronic communication aid may require several seconds to select the message he or she wants to convey to the listener. Such students require patient listeners. Attempts to hurry them will likely result in slower, not faster, communication; finishing their sentences for them will discourage and frustrate them further.

The teacher should model appropriate listening skills for the class and also attempt to sensitize students to the need to wait quietly and listen while others speak. In some situations, the teacher may want to speed communication by phrasing questions to students with speech problems so that only short responses are required. In other situations, these students should be encouraged to express their thoughts and opinions more fully. The "Spotlight on Technology" feature provides additional information on alternative methods of communication such as communication boards and electronic communication devices.

In addition to providing good speech models and an accepting environment, the classroom teacher should ensure that students with speech impairments have frequent opportunities to practice their communication skills. McCormick (1986) recommends that practice take place in a variety of contexts throughout the school day. Oral communication can be incorporated into most areas of the curriculum. Whether the subject is reading, math, or social studies, students can practice speaking with the teacher, in small work groups, and during class discussions. Lunchtime, work breaks, and recess create natural opportunities for socialization and talking with others, as do many free-time activities in the classroom. Culatta and Culatta (1993) provide these suggestions for creating communication opportunities:

- *Do not anticipate needs.* A child who is given paper without crayons or who is provided with only a small amount of juice at a time is encountering the need to communicate.
- *Arrange for unusual or novel events to occur.* A child who sees a box of cereal taped to the wall is likely to want to share that event and seek information about it. Language can also be evoked by engaging in such actions as "inadvertently" throwing away toys, wearing clothes that are too big, and trying to eat soup with a fork.
- *Arrange for the child to convey information to others.* In the cafeteria the child may be asked to direct others to their seats, describe the menu, convey the location of utensils, and report the acceptability of the food to the cook. Many opportunities to convey experiences to others can be created throughout the day.

- *Provide the child with choices.* During a snack activity, the child can decide what to drink, where to sit, whether to use a napkin or a paper plate, and who should be responsible for cleaning up. Each decision requires communication. (pp. 251–252)

An important goal of any inclusion program is the participation of students with special needs in as many classroom activities as possible. For students with speech problems, both social and academic activities should be considered. One way to promote acceptance while maximizing communication opportunities is to seat the student with special needs in the midst of several typical peers. In traditional classrooms, students with special needs are usually seated near the teacher in an arrangement that does not encourage student interaction (see Figure 12-4 on page 292). Instead, the classroom environment should be modified so that the student is surrounded by good speech models and has natural opportunities for communication.

TEACHING LANGUAGE SKILLS

Students with language impairments receive individualized help from the speech-language pathologist. They may require assistance in the development of receptive language skills and/or expressive language skills; instruction focuses on the area of need, whether it is grammatical construction (syntax) or vocabulary development (semantics). The general education teacher can help students with language problems by modeling appropriate grammar, by helping expand their listening and speaking vocabularies, and by modifying classroom activities and assignments that require language skills.

For students with difficulty in the area of syntax, the classroom teacher must provide a consistent model of grammatically correct speech. The teacher should correct students' grammatical errors by demonstrating the proper construction. If, for instance, a student comments, "It's funner to swim than to water ski," the teacher can respond, "It's more fun to swim? Why?" With this approach, the student hears the grammatically correct version of the statement without being criticized for poor language.

Some students with language disorders need help in vocabulary development. They may not be familiar with the words their classmates and teachers use; they may fail to express themselves in the vocabulary expected of their age level. The classroom teacher can help these special students increase their receptive and expressive vocabularies by following these suggestions:

- Encourage students to ask about the meanings of words they do not understand.
- Use demonstration to teach the meanings of some words. Because prepositions and action verbs are often hard to explain in words, *show* students their meanings.

Spotlight on Technology

Augmentative Communication

When students do not talk or their speech is not intelligible, an **augmentative communication** system may be used to increase their ability to communicate. There are many types of augmentative communication systems. For example, if you have a cold and find it difficult to talk, you might augment your usual means of communication by using more gestures or even writing notes rather than speaking. In classrooms, two types of systems are used most often with students with communication disorders: communication boards and electronic communication devices.

Communication Boards

Communication boards are considered a "low" technology. According to Lewis (1993),

> A communication board can be as simple as a piece of paper or cardboard with two photographs pasted on it, or as elaborate as a notebook filled with pages of messages for a variety of different communication situations. The essential elements are the "board" itself, which may be composed of paper or a sturdier material, and the choices depicted on the board by photos, drawings, or some kind of symbol system. (p. 383)

To use a communication board, the student simply points to one of the choices. For some students, all choices are depicted by photos or drawings. Other students are able to use communication boards with letters, words, and phrases.

Computers can be used to make communication boards with programs such as *Boardmaker* from Mayer-Johnson Company (http://www.mayer-johnson.com). This program contains more than 3,000 picture symbols from the Mayer-Johnson Picture Communication Symbol collection (Johnson, 1981, 1985, 1992). *Boardmaker* is easy to use. The teacher has full control over the choice of symbols included on the board and the number, size, and spacing of the symbols. Boards can be printed in black and white or color, and the print labels accompanying each symbol are available in more than 10 languages.

Note: The Picture Communication Symbols™ © 1981-2004 by Mayer-Johnson LLC. All rights reserved worldwide. Used with permission.

News-2-You is a weekly newspaper for students with special needs. As this sample page from the color edition illustrates, it provides information about current events via both words and symbols.

Note: Courtesy of News-2-You.

Several different editions of the paper are available: regular in black and white and regular in color, simplified, and higher. The regular editions are 16 to 22 pages long with news, a joke, activities, and a recipe. Two editions have the capacity to talk: the regular edition in color and the simplified edition. To subscribe—and then download issues weekly—visit the website at http://www.news-2-you.com. Subscribers have access to all editions, communication boards for each issue, and pictures to use with the *Boardmaker* program. Access to Joey's Locker, a collection of weekly add-on activities, can be purchased for an additional fee.

Electronic Communication Devices

Electronic communication devices "talk." Because of this capability, they are sometimes called *voice output communication aids,* or VOCAs. Some electronic devices use prerecorded speech, others contain speech synthesizers, and still others use both technologies.

The Go Talk VOCA from Attainment Company (http://www.attainmentcompany.com), shown on the next page, is an example of a relatively inexpensive VOCA. On its surface are nine touch-sensitive "keys"; the student presses a key to play back a prerecorded message. Four levels are available so that a total of 36 messages can be recorded. The key area is covered by an overlay with photos, drawings, words, or phrases that illustrate the messages. The Go Talk unit can store up to 6 minutes of prerecorded speech (8 to 15 seconds per message). Thus, this VOCA can be set up so that, as students move from one activity to another during the school day, messages are available for each class or school activity.

Note: Courtesy of Attainment Company.

Devices such as the Go Talk VOCA, although inexpensive, may not be appropriate for a more advanced student because they can store only a limited number of messages. More sophisticated (and more expensive) devices may be required. Examples are the MightyMo and MiniMo from DynaVox Technologies (http://www.dynavoxtech.com). These augmentative communication devices offer high-quality digitized (recorded) speech; choices include an adult male voice, adult female voice, and a gender-neutral child's voice. Screen displays are in color, and users touch the screen to make selections; the choices shown can be customized to fit individual needs. The display is dynamic; once one choice is made, the screen changes and other choices appear. They are, in effect, computers that can store thousands of messages, which makes them very versatile communication devices.

Note: Courtesy of DynaVox Systems LLC, Pittsburgh, PA (866-DYNAVOX).

- Use definitions, explanations, and examples to teach other words. For example, define *container* as something that holds something else; then give examples of objects that are containers and objects that are not.
- Provide multiple examples of word meanings. For example, if students are learning the word *break,* they might "break cookies and crackers, encounter objects that keep falling apart, break spaghetti in order to glue the pieces on a picture, and break carrot sticks for lunch" (Culatta & Culatta, 1993, p. 252).
- Include vocabulary instruction in all curriculum areas. Teach the meanings of new reading words, math terms, and new vocabulary in science, social studies, and art.
- Teach students to use regular or picture dictionaries to discover the meanings of unfamiliar words.
- Give students opportunities throughout the school day to practice the new vocabulary they are learning.

- Sunderland (2004) adds: "Encourage the child to elaborate (e.g., 'That's very interesting! Tell me more!')" (p. 212).

In addition to helping students with language impairments acquire correct grammar and new word meanings, the general education teacher may need to make adaptations in classroom activities and assignments. With students who have difficulty listening with understanding, directions for school tasks should be brief, to the point, and in simple language. With students who find it hard to express themselves, questions that require a yes or no response are easier to answer than open-ended questions. For example, "Is the platypus a mammal?" may be an easier question for a student with language disorders than "What type of animal is the platypus?"

Some students may require direct instruction in listening skills. Bauwens and Hourcade (1989) suggest teaching the LISTEN strategy to improve students' ability to attend and listen to

FIGURE 12-4   Traditional and Modified Classroom Environments

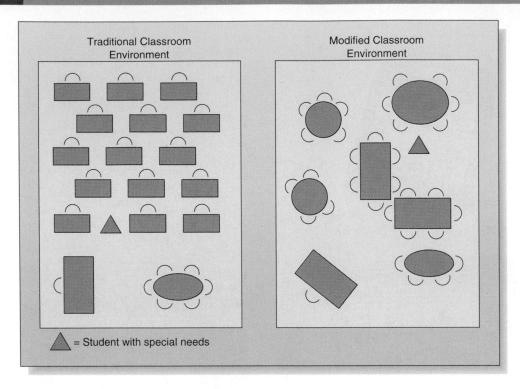

Note: Adapted with permission of Merrill, an imprint of Macmillan Publishing Company, from *Language Arts for the Mildly Handicapped* (pp. 201, 203) by S. B. Cohen and S. P. Plaskon. Copyright © 1980 Merrill Publishing Company, Columbus, Ohio.

oral directions. LISTEN is an acronym for a six-step procedure: "Look, Idle your motor, Sit up straight, Turn to me, Engage your brain, Now . . ." (p. 61). The teacher models this strategy, and students practice it to mastery. The goal is for students to internalize the strategy so that they follow each step automatically whenever the teacher says, "Listen."

Older students may benefit from instruction in the skills needed for listening to lectures in content-area classes. One activity for developing these skills uses tape recordings of news broadcasts (Forster & Doyle, 1989). The teacher prepares an outline of the news items, including major points but leaving space for students to add supporting details; the outline also lists background concepts and vocabulary with which students may be unfamiliar. Students begin the activity by reviewing the outline, and the teacher explains any terms or concepts that students do not recognize or understand. As students listen to the tape, they underline key points on the outline and add details. Students have the opportunity to ask questions before taking a quiz on the information presented in the news broadcast.

The general education teacher plays an important role in the education of students with communication disorders. When these students are provided with a classroom environment that encourages the learning and practice of speech and language skills, their chances for successful performance in school (and in life) increase. Many speech and language problems are developmental in nature; they appear in young children and, with maturation and appropriate treatment, may disappear. The special education program is only part of the appropriate treatment for students with communication disorders. Another important component is the instruction and support received from the teacher in the general education classroom.

Students who leave the classroom to visit the speech-language pathologist or resource teacher may return to discover that the class has moved on to a different activity. To help these students feel more a part of their classroom, see the "Inclusion Tips for the Teacher."

In this chapter, you have learned ways to teach language skills to students with communication disorders. You have also learned methods for creating a classroom climate that encourages the practice of speaking skills. In chapter 13, you will meet students with autism spectrum disorder. Before going on, check "Things to Remember" to review ways to help students with speech and language disorders succeed in general education.

Inclusion Tips for the Teacher

When Students Leave the Classroom for Special Services

Many students with special needs leave the general education classroom for a short time each day to visit a special education teacher. While they are gone, the activities of the classroom continue. When they return, they may feel lost, confused, and unsure of what they should be doing. To help students reenter the classroom and regain their bearings quickly and easily, try these suggestions:

1. Work with the special education teacher to arrange the best time for each student to leave the classroom. Usually, it is better for students to receive special education services when their class is working on
   - independent practice rather than direct instruction,
   - the student's best rather than worst subject, or
   - the student's least liked rather than favorite activity.

2. Maintain a regular daily schedule so that you and the student know what will be missed each day.

3. Help the student take responsibility for leaving the classroom for special education services at the appropriate time. One method is to provide the student with a drawing of a clock showing the time to leave.

4. Arrange a communication system so that when the student returns, he or she knows how to find out what to do. The student might
   - go directly to the teacher for instructions,
   - look for a note on the board,
   - check in the work folder on his or her desk, or
   - consult a classmate who has been assigned as a buddy.

5. Do not penalize the student for leaving the class for special education help. Avoid scheduling treats and special activities during the time the student is out of the room. Do not double the workload by requiring the student to keep up with the current class activity as well as make up what was missed during his or her absence.

Things to Remember

- The primary areas of need for students with communication disorders are speech and language; because of their communication difficulties these students may also require assistance in social interactions.
- Major indicators of speech impairments are misarticulations of speech sounds, dysfluent speech, and unusual voice quality.
- Major indicators of language impairments are problems in reception or expression of grammatical constructions and vocabulary.
- In assessment of communication disorders, information is gathered about a possible hearing loss, current performance in speech and language, and, for serious problems, general intellectual performance.
- Students with communication disorders receive individualized special education from the speech-language pathologist.

  These students remain in the general education class and take part in special services for only short periods each day or several times each week.
- Major instructional adaptations are usually not necessary to accommodate the needs of students with communication disorders in the general education classroom.
- For students with speech impairments, the general education teacher provides an accepting classroom environment in which students can feel comfortable practicing newly acquired communication skills.
- For students with language impairments, the general education teacher assists their acquisition of language skills by modeling appropriate grammar and helping them expand their listening and speaking vocabularies. Classroom activities and assignments that require language skills may need to be modified.

ACTIVITIES

1. Interview a speech-language pathologist to find out more about students with communication disorders. Ask this professional to describe his or her caseload. How many students does he or she serve? What are their ages and typical problems? Do most students participate in general education classes for the majority of the day? If so, what effects do their speech and language disorders have on their performance in the general education classroom?

2. Locate one of the journals that deals primarily with communication disorders. You might select the *American Journal of Speech-Language Pathology; Jour-* *nal of Speech, Language, and Hearing Research;* or *Language, Speech, and Hearing Services in the Schools.* Look through recent issues for articles that present suggestions for encouraging oral communication and teaching language skills. Do you find any ideas that could be used by general education teachers?

3. The major professional organization in the field of communication disorders is the American Speech-Language-Hearing Association (ASHA). Its national headquarters is located at 10801 Rockville Pike, Rockville, MD 20852. Write to ASHA or visit its website (http://www.asha.org) to find out more about this organization. Or talk with a speech-language pathologist or audiologist who is an ASHA member.

4. Communication disorders can be found in people of any age. Survey your community to locate agencies that provide services to adults with speech and language problems. What services are available? How do these differ from the services offered by the public schools to children and adolescents?

5. In a group, try one or more of the communication disorder simulations described in Table 12-1. Afterward, discuss your reactions to the following questions: What were the feelings of the person with the simulated speech or language disorder? Did he or she feel frustrated? Anxious? Angry? How did the listeners feel? Were they sympathetic? Impatient? Embarrassed? What recommendations can the group make to teachers of students with communication disorders?

CD-ROM Activities

Choose two of the three classroom case studies to view. Focus on the teacher and how he or she uses language in the classroom. Use your observations to respond to these questions:

- *Are the teachers good speech models? Why do you think so?*

- *What strategies do the teachers use to help students develop their listening and speaking skills?*

- *In your view, would students with speech or language problems be comfortable practicing their communication skills in these classrooms?*

Teaching Students with Autism Spectrum Disorder

Laura J. Hall
San Diego State University

CHAPTER

13

Dan

Dan is currently included in a K-1 class where he excels in his reading abilities. He has a large receptive vocabulary and will speak, particularly with adults, and specifically about Spiderman. He recalls and imitates the part of Spiderman from the movies and will be found reciting lines to himself during play activities. He enjoys drawing and has difficulty with transitions especially when he is leaving preferred activities such as art.

Mario

Mario is in a middle school classroom. He has a classroom aide to assist him with academic skills. Math is an area of strength. Mario has limited oral communication skills and uses visual aides such as photographs and picture symbols as augmentative devices. He has been interested in cars since he was very young and he would like to work on a race track in the future.

LOOKING AHEAD

Throughout this chapter, you will see examples of strategies used in the general education classroom to more fully include students like Dan and Mario. As you learn more about teaching students with autism spectrum disorder, keep these questions in mind:

- What are Dan's and Mario's areas of strength? How could their teachers make use of those strengths in the instructional program?
- Would you expect Dan to have special needs in the area of classroom behavior? Social acceptance?
- What about Mario? In what areas do you think he will need the most support in the general education classroom?

To answer these questions online, go to the Students' Stories module in Chapter 13 of the Companion Website.

Autism became a distinct category within special education in 1990 with the passage of PL 101-476, part of the amendments to the original Education for All Handicapped Children Act. Autism is a developmental disability described as significantly affecting verbal communication, nonverbal communication, and social interaction, thereby influencing the child's educational performance. Other characteristics that are often associated with autism are resistance to change in environment or routine, unusual responses to sensory experiences, and engagement in repetitive activities and stereotyped movements (Knoblauch & Sorenson, 1998).

Students classified with **autism spectrum disorder** (ASD) can exhibit a range of skills from severe delays to giftedness. In fact, the same student may have some skills that are delayed, such as social or language skills, and others, such as math, that are well advanced for his or her age. Even in those areas that are, by definition, impaired for students with this disorder (communication, social interaction, behavior), the severity of this impairment varies by individual. For this reason the classification is referred to as a *spectrum disorder* because of the range and variation in the skills and impairments presented.

Although this variation of skills presents an added challenge for the classroom teacher, there are some strategies that work well for most individuals on the spectrum. These strategies will be featured in this chapter. Consultation with specialists is frequently recommended depending on the area and severity of delay. Consultation with parents is highly recommended because consistency across environments is especially important for students with this disorder. Although the characteristics of one child with autism spectrum disorder may be different from the characteristics of another, some preferences and behaviors occur frequently for these students, and the students described in *Students' Stories* represent two common profiles.

INDICATORS OF AUTISM SPECTRUM DISORDER

Autism spectrum disorder or autistic disorder is one of the classifications within the category of Pervasive Developmental Disorders (PDD) according to the fourth edition text revision of the *Diagnostic and Statistical Manual of Mental Disorders* (*DSM-IV-TR*) (American Psychiatric Association [APA], 2000), the manual commonly used to diagnose and describe neurological and psychological disorders. Qualitative impairments are evident for individuals with autism in three areas:

1. social interaction (nonverbal behavior, peer relationships, socioemotional reciprocity);
2. communication (delays in spoken language, inability to initiate or sustain a conversation, repetitive use of language, and lack of make-believe or imaginative play); and
3. restrictive, repetitive, and stereotyped patterns of behavior (preoccupation with an interest, compulsive adherence to routine, motor mannerisms and occupations with parts of objects).

Consult the "For Your Information" feature for descriptions of the common characteristics of autism.

If the student has impairments in social interaction and restrictive, repetitive, and stereotyped patterns of behavior—and not in the area of communication and language—then the student is diagnosed with **Asperger's syndrome** (Atwood, 1998). These students typically have age-appropriate communication and language skills, but have difficulties with social relationships and are usually focused on one topic or activity at a time. Students diagnosed with Asperger's syndrome do not have significant delays in cognitive development compared with students with autism who also may have mental retardation (Scheuermann & Webber, 2002).

For Your Information

Common Characteristics of Autism

- "Autism is a complex developmental disability that typically appears during the first three years of life" (Autism Society of America, 2004).
- The prevalence of autism spectrum disorder is estimated to be 2 to 6 per 1,000 births, and race, ethnicity, or socioeconomic status do not affect prevalence (Yeargin-Allsopp et al., 2003).
- There is a higher rate of autism within families, indicating a genetic influence (Cook, 1998).

- Autism occurs four times more often in boys than girls (Cowley, 2003).
- Delays in *language* may include lack of speech, lack of the first initiation of conversations, and repetitive use of language.
- Delays in *social skills* may include failure to develop peer relationships, lack of social or emotional reciprocity, and lack of eye-to-eye gaze, facial expressions, and body postures.
- Delays in *symbolic or imaginative play* often occur (APA, 2000).

In 1993 Catherine Maurice published a book about her struggle to obtain a diagnosis and find effective treatment for her two children with autism. Her book, *Let Me Hear Your Voice,* was influential in encouraging parents to search for educators with knowledge and skills in applied behavior analysis. Books and articles written by other parents (e.g., Seroussi, 2000) and by adults with autism (e.g., Grandin, 1995) have provided important perspectives that are relevant for educators working with students with autism spectrum disorders and their families. Working in collaboration with families results in many benefits for the student (Turnbull & Turnbull, 2001). To learn more about an important organization for families and others interested in autism, review the "Window on the Web" material.

ASSESSMENT PROCEDURES

Delays in at least one of the three focal areas for students with autism occurs prior to age 3. Diagnosis is typically made by a physician or other professional experienced in the use of diagnostic instruments or by those trained to use diagnostic tools created specifically for autism spectrum disorder such as the *Autism Diagnostic Observation Schedule (ADOS)* (Lord, Rutter, DiLavore & Risi, 2001) and *Autism Diagnostic Interview Revised* (Rutter, LeCouteur, & Lord, 2003).

Consistent with good assessment practices, multiple measures for determining a diagnosis are recommended and may include one or more instruments. Several rating scales are available that are frequently used as one of the diagnostic tools, and teachers who suspect that a student may have autism spectrum disorder (ASD) may be asked to complete one of these scales. The *Childhood Autism Rating Scale (CARS)* (Schopler, Reichler, & Renner, 1988) is a 15-item behavior scale that was one of the first developed to screen for ASD. Figure 13-1 depicts a portion of the *CARS* Rating Sheet and provides two examples of items and how each should be rated on a scale of 1 (within normal limits for age) to 4 (severely abnormal for that age).

Teachers also may be asked to complete the *Autism Screening Instrument for Educational Planning* (Krug, Arick, & Almond, 1980), which contains five subtests that include an interaction assessment, educational or functional skills assessment, vocal sample, learning rate indicator, and a behavior checklist. The *Gilliam Autism Rating Scale* (Gilliam, 1995) includes 56 items that closely match the *DSM-IV* diagnostic categories; items are rated from 0 (never observed) to 3 (frequently observed). This scale can be completed by anyone who has direct and sustained contact with the individual.

The *Psychoeducational Profile Revised (PEP-R)* (Schopler, Reichler, Bashford, Lansing, & Marcus, 1990) is an instrument designed to be used for educational planning for individuals with autism spectrum disorder. Through a series of interactive activities, the assessor identifies the strengths, weaknesses, and learning style of the student. The results of the assessment are provided in developmental age equivalents for the areas of imitation, perception, fine- and gross-motor skills, eye-hand integration, cognitive performance, cognitive verbal, and overall

Window on the Web

Autism Society of America

http://www.autism-society.org

The Autism Society of America, founded in 1965 by parents of children with autism, currently has chapters in many states throughout the United States. Information on definition, characteristics, and conference events focused on individuals with autism spectrum disorder and their families can be found at this website. Information on autism is available in English ("All about Autism") and in Spanish ("Informacion general sobre el autismo"). This website lists resources for parents and professionals and "Action Alerts" that provide information about new and relevant legislation and research activities pertaining to autism.

Note: Courtesy of Autism Society of America.

For more information, go to the Web Links module in Chapter 13 of the Companion Website.

FIGURE 13-1   Sample Items from the *Childhood Autism Rating Scale*

• CARS Rating Sheet •

Directions: For each category, use the space provided below each scale for taking notes concerning the behaviors relevant to each scale. After you have finished observing the child, rate the behaviors relevant to each item of the scale. For each item, circle the number which corresponds to the statement that best describes the child. You may indicate the child is between two descriptions by using ratings of 1.5, 2.5, or 3.5. Abbreviated rating criteria are presented for each scale. See chapter 2 of the Manual for detailed rating criteria.

	I. RELATING TO PEOPLE		III. EMOTIONAL RESPONSE
1	**No evidence of difficulty or abnormality in relating to people** • The child's behavior is appropriate for his or her age. Some shyness, fussiness, or annoyance at being told what to do may be observed, but not to an atypical degree.	1	**Age-appropriate and situation-appropriate emotional responses** • The child shows the appropriate type and degree of emotional response as indicated by a change in facial expression, posture, and manner.
1.5		1.5	
2	**Mildly abnormal relationships** • The child may avoid looking the adult in the eye, avoid the adult or become fussy if interaction is forced, be excessively shy, not be as responsive to the adult as is typical, or cling to parents somewhat more than most children of the same age.	2	**Mildly abnormal emotional responses** • The child occasionally displays a somewhat inappropriate type or degree of emotional reactions. Reactions are sometimes unrelated to the objects or events surrounding them.
2.5	**Moderately abnormal relationships** • The child shows aloofness (seems unaware of adult) at times. Persistent and forceful attempts are necessary to get the child's attention at times. Minimal contact is initiated by the child.	2.5	
3		3	**Moderately abnormal emotional responses** • The child shows definite signs of inappropriate type and/or degree of emotional response. Reactions may be quite inhibited or excessive and unrelated to the situation; may grimace, laugh, or become rigid even though no apparent emotion-producing objects or events are present.
3.5	**Severely abnormal relationships** • The child is consistently aloof or unaware of what the adult is doing. He or she almost never responds or initiates contact with the adult. Only the most persistent attempts to get the child's attention have any effect.	3.5	**Severely abnormal emotional responses** • Responses are seldom appropriate to the situation; once the child gets in a certain mood, it is very difficult to change the mood. Conversely, the child may show wildly different emotions when nothing has changed.
4		4	
	Observations:		**Observations:**

Note: Sample items from *The Childhood Autism Rating Scale* by E. Schopler, R. J. Reichler, and B. R. Renner. Copyright 1988 by Western Psychological Services. Reprinted by permission of WPS, 12031 Wilshire Boulevard, Los Angeles, CA 90025 (www.wpspublish.com). All rights reserved.

development. The manual describes the materials, administration, and scoring criteria (passing, emerging, and failing) for each item. Figure 13-2 presents a portion of the assessment results for Dan, including a report of the results from the *PEP-R*.

Incorporating student preferences and developing a system that supports student motivation are key to creating a successful educational experience for a student with autism spectrum disorder (Dyer, 1989). Establishing student preferences for activities, topics, academic subjects, and form and intensity of sensory stimulation may be obtained by asking parents, caregivers, and previous teachers. For some students a more formal preference assessment may need to be conducted.

Mason, McGee, Farmer-Dougan, and Risley (1989) adapted a reinforcer assessment for nonverbal students with autism. They presented an array of objects (edibles, vibrating toys, music boxes) and activities (hugs, spinning in the air, clapping hands) and assessed preferences for pairs of items by noting which item was reached for within 5 seconds of presentation. Following the identification of a group of preferred items, students choose several items from this group each day to use as rewards for com-

pleting educational activities. Incorporating these preferred items increased attention to task and decreased problem behaviors. DeLeon and Iwata (1996) found that presenting an array of seven items and having the student choose one item at a time was an effective method of determining preferences. In this method the item chosen by the student is not replaced and the remaining items of the array are rearranged. Researchers have confirmed that this method is effective for determining the preferences of students with autism (Carr, Nicholson, & Higbee, 2000). To learn more about incorporating rewards into the instructional program for students with autism spectrum disorder, consult the "Inclusion Tips for the Teacher" box on page 302.

SPECIAL SERVICES

It is highly likely that the general education teacher will be working with a special educator who can help modify curriculum to meet the learning needs of the individual with autism spectrum disorder. Special education teachers can also help design a motivational system for the included student if

FIGURE 13-2   Assessment Results for Dan

Student: Dan   **Age:** 5 years, 8 months   **Grade:** K-1

Classroom Performance

Dan participates well in those activities that he enjoys such as art and reading readiness. He has a very long attention span for these tasks. He is able to communicate well about topics of interest, although his speech can be difficult to understand at times due to its speed and lack of articulation for some sounds. It is clear that Dan does not prefer large group activities such as circle time, especially during music activities. He is able to transition from activities and stay with circle time with the use of an individualized token system. Skills in math and social interaction with peers are priority areas for Dan.

Measures of Characteristics Related to Autism

Several measures were used to determine if there was a match between Dan's performance and the characteristics typically found in students with autism spectrum disorder.

Childhood Autism Rating Scale (CARS)
Total score = 36, mild to moderately autistic

Gilliam Autism Rating Scale (GARS)

Subtests	Standard Score
Stereotyped Behaviors	6
Communication	8
Social Interaction	30
Developmental Disturbance	11
AUTISM QUOTIENT	95 (average probability of autism)

Psychoeducational Profile Revised (PEP-R)

Developmental Area	Age Equivalent
Imitation	36–42 months
Perception	28–38 months
Fine Motor	60–72 months
Gross Motor	52–70 months
Eye–Hand Integration	46–49 months
Cognitive Performance	40–42 months
Cognitive Verbal	36–38 months

Results indicate a high probability of mild to moderate autism. Results of the *PEP-R* indicate that fine- and gross-motor skills are areas of strength for Dan. He enjoys drawing and putting items together and can engage in these activities for long periods of time. He prefers to be left alone during these activities and, when asked to imitate the drawings of others or build a structure like a model, he frequently walks away from the task. Dan received passing scores on each of the gross-motor items. He displays right hand and foot dominance. He can unscrew lids and drink from a cup appropriately. He uses the handrail when walking down the steps and is able to carry, push, and throw a ball. When Dan was asked to play an interactive game with the ball, he participated briefly and then said, "He is done with playing ball."

one is necessary and assist in setting up the physical arrangement of the classroom environment to help facilitate social interaction, maximize student participation in activities, and decrease the likelihood of problem behavior.

Special educators assist in adapting curriculum. For example, Mario is motivated to read text on the topics of automobiles and racing. He is also motivated to acquire those vocational skills that are helpful in preparing him for posi-

tions on the race track. Spiderman is a winning context for Dan. It is important not to overuse this topic so it does not lose the power to facilitate engagement. It is also important to aim to expand his areas of interest.

Federal (National Research Council, 2001) and state (New York State Department of Health Early Intervention Program, 1999) task forces commissioned to determine effective approaches for the instruction of children with autism

Inclusion Tips for the Teacher

Incorporating a Motivational System

- Identify preferred activities/items through formal or informal assessments.
- Arrange the student's schedule so that preferred activities/items follow less preferred activities (Sulzer-Azaroff & Mayer, 1991).
- Clearly state these contingencies with the student: "First *X*, then *Y*" (Schopler et al., 1995).
- Use identified preferred activities as part of a formal behavior management plan.

- Students who can read may have a written contract that describes the rewards to be given contingent on appropriate behavior for a select period of time.
- Embed preferred topics, items, and materials into educational activities.
- A formal token system can be included and tokens traded for preferred activities once the required number of tokens have been obtained by the student (Alberto & Troutman, 2003).

spectrum disorder have recommended that strategies based on **applied behavior analysis** be included in any program. To provide additional assistance to general education teachers, school districts may employ an autism specialist who knows how to use effective teaching strategies based on the principles of applied behavior analysis, such as discrete trial teaching (Anderson, Taras, & Cannon; 1996) or incidental teaching approaches (Fenske, Krantz, & McClannahan, 2001). Information about applied behavior analysis and strategies used for individuals with autism can be found at http://www.behavior.org under the autism section.

Because many students with ASD have some form of communication impairment, the services of specialists in speech and language are commonly sought. Speech-language pathologists may provide educators with strategies to assist with the articulation of words or the formation of complete sentences. These specialists also would know about activities that can strengthen the oral-motor muscles that support spoken language. Speech-language pathologists, along with assistive technology specialists, can design augmentative or alternative communication systems and provide training for staff in the use of such systems. Collaboration with the speech-language pathologist is vital because any communication system only works if it is used consistently throughout the day.

It is not uncommon for an occupational therapist to be part of the IEP team with a focus on the sensory challenges that can be presented for individuals with autism. Sensory-stimulating activities such as spinning objects and playing with light by flicking fingers in front of the eyes can be part of the behaviors seen in individuals diagnosed with autism spectrum disorder. Sensory-avoidance activities such as toe walking, tantrums at bath time, or covering the ears during music activities also may be qualities of the student with ASD. The sensory systems are considered the domain of the occupational therapist and, following consultation with this specialist, activities or a "sensory diet" may be recommended. Although occupational therapists are well established in

school systems and their suggested activities are widely used, it is important to note that there is little research supporting the use of sensory activities to address the atypical behaviors of individuals with autism (Dawson & Watling, 2000).

Figure 13-3 identifies some of the goals selected for Dan by the IEP team, which includes his parents, special education consultant, speech-language pathologist, occupational therapist, and the general education, or classroom, teacher.

CLASSROOM ADAPTATIONS

Some form of classroom adaptations is likely to be needed to make the educational experience for the student with ASD successful. Almost all students with autism spectrum disorder benefit from a schedule of daily activities (Schopler, Mesibov, & Heorsey, 1995). The schedule may take the form of a visual sequence of photographs or picture symbols placed on the student's desk, near the coat closet, or in some central location of the classroom to be evident during transitions (Hodgdon, 1998). It may be a written list of activities or the commonly used daily planner for those students who can read. Knowing what will come next and when transitions are likely to occur increases the student's understanding of the environment and decreases the likelihood of stress and challenging behavior during uncertain transition periods. In the chapter entitled *Tools to Give Information,* Linda Hodgdon (1995) lists several suggestions for how teachers can use visual materials to create schedules. Figure 13-4 provides an example of how schedules can be used to assist with transitions.

Generally speaking, students with autism spectrum disorder like to follow a routine and like to know what is happening next. For this reason, it is often a good idea to prepare students with ASD for transitions by informing them prior to their occurrence. Some teachers have found that using a visual timer such as a kitchen timer to indicate when an activity will end has been helpful.

FIGURE 13-3 IEP Goals and Services for Dan

Annual Goals

1. By the end of the school year, Dan will demonstrate the math skills of one-to-one correspondence for 10 small objects by counting each object out loud correctly for four out of five math sessions.
   Person responsible: Special education teacher, grade K-1 teacher

2. By the end of the school year, with the inclusion of a token system, Dan will participate in circle time activities for 10 minutes by staying in his chair and attending to the teacher for four out of five circle time activities.
   Person responsible: Special education teacher, grade K-1 teacher

3. By the end of the school year, Dan will initiate a greeting to at least one peer per day for 8 out of 10 days by looking at the peer and saying "Hi, *peer's name*" so that he can be understood by others.
   Person responsible: Speech-language pathologist

Amount of Participation in General Education

Dan will attend the general education K-1 grade class for all instruction.

Special Education and Related Services

1. The special education teacher will consult with the classroom teacher on a weekly basis to address curriculum design, evaluate the effectiveness of the token system, and assist with classroom adaptations to increase social interaction with peers.

2. Dan will receive two weekly one-to-one sessions with the speech-language pathologist to address his language and social skills.

Organizing schedules is a key component of the *structured teaching* approach that has been used with students with autism spectrum and other communication disorders for more than 20 years (Schopler et al., 1995). To facilitate increased flexibility for students, teachers could add a question mark or a choice of activities in the schedule. Photographs of preferred items or activities can be placed on a choice board for selection by the student (McClannahan & Krantz, 1999).

If the student with ASD likes videos and movies, like Dan, then the use of video-priming may be a strategy that can be helpful for those activities that are particularly difficult for the student. Let's take going to the mall as an example. The process includes taking a video of someone walking from the car, into the mall entrance, walking to one or two stores, and then returning to the car. The entire video should be about 1 to 4 minutes. The student would then watch this tape prior to going to the mall and it would show what will happen and when the activity will be over. Video-priming has been demonstrated as helpful for some students with autism spectrum disorder (Schreibman, Whalen, & Stahmer, 2000). See "Inclusion Tips for the Teacher" for ideas on helping students make smooth transitions.

Both Dan and Mario have classroom adaptations to facilitate smooth transitions. Mario carries a daily planner that has a plastic sleeve insert where small pictures of his daily schedule are placed and reviewed by the teacher each morning. When he was younger, he had a posted schedule with photographs depicting his daily routine. These were then reduced in size and then drawings were used. He now can follow a schedule with small drawings or pictures placed in his notebook planner.

Dan would often tantrum when it was time to finish preferred activities such as drawing or time in the book corner. A token system (Sulzer-Azaroff & Mayer, 1991) was developed and reviewed with Dan. Each time he moved from one activity to another appropriately he received a token, or one part of a puzzle, that when complete was the face of Spiderman. When he had a complete Spiderman face, he could trade this in for 10 minutes of watching his favorite part of the Spiderman movie on the VCR. This system has been working very well, and the IEP team has been discussing the benefits of changing the token system to pennies so that Dan can learn about the value of money.

Authors have found that time and place to work independently is something that is preferred by students with autism (Schopler et al., 1995). In fact, group work where interactions with peers are required will be more of a challenge for these students. It is a good idea to include both forms of activities throughout the day so that students are not overwhelmed by group work but at the same time are challenged to work on the areas that are most difficult such as social interaction skills.

Attention to irrelevant stimuli or overattention to parts of objects is one of the diagnostic characteristics of this disorder (APA, 2000). For example, during a calendar activity Dan may be focusing on the shape of a cloud used on the weather board instead of on the day of the week or the current weather conditions. During a lesson about the main characters in a story, Mario may be focusing on a small but irrelevant car in the background of an illustration. It is important for general educators to be aware that students with autism spectrum disorder can be distracted by the items hanging on the walls and bulletin boards of the classroom. Students also may attend to the

FIGURE 13-4   Sample Visual Schedules

PROBLEM: Sarah has difficulty doing the same activities as the rest of the class. When it is time for one activity to stop and another one to start, she is apt to resist the change. Instead of staying with the group during an activity, she wanders around the room or runs to the play area to pull out toys.

SOLUTION: Use the schedule to engage Sarah in establishing a routine for changing activities. When it is time to change, go to the schedule to remove the last activity and identify what comes next. Use the schedule to redirect Sarah back to the current activity if she leaves it. Show her and tell her, "the schedule says "_____.""

Note: From *Visual Strategies for Improving Communication, Volume 1: Practical Supports for School and Home* by L. A. Hodgdon. Copyright 1995 by QuirkRoberts Publishing. www.UseVisualStrategies.com Reprinted with permission.

Inclusion Tips for the Teacher

Facilitating Smooth Transitions

- Incorporate a transition warning system such as a re-minder, timer, or cleanup or transition song.
- Use visual strategies, such as items from the next activity or photos of the area for the next activity, to give to the student just prior to the transition (Hodgdon, 1998).
- Identify an area where transitional objects or photographs should be placed. Possibilities are an envelope or a box (Schopler et al., 1995).
- Promote independence by asking students to "Check your schedule" to determine the next activity.

- Review the schedule for the day at a specified period each day.
- Use video-priming for especially difficult periods in the day (Schreibman et al., 2000).
- Consider designing a Social Story (see "Window on the Web" feature later in this chapter) to address appropriate behavior for waiting in line or going to an assembly (Gray & Garand, 1993).

irrelevant details of the educational materials presented for instruction. This may mean that a decision is made to have one part of the room free from materials on the wall near the desk of the student with ASD. In addition, educational materials may need to be adapted so that they are clear of distracting information when a concept is first introduced.

Some students with autism spectrum disorder do not respond well to oral instructions by teachers. Some students with ASD do not attend to the words spoken or have difficulty determining the meaning of the instruction. Importantly, some students develop a dependency on prompts from adults. Students may learn that they do not have to attend to and comprehend what the teacher is saying because someone will repeat the instruction for them or provide some other cue. An effective strategy used to avoid such prompt dependency (MacDuff, Krantz & McClannahan, 2001) is the incorporation of photographic activity schedules (McClannahan & Krantz, 1999). The researcher-practitioners who developed this strategy have found that even young children can be taught to independently follow picture cues in a book format. Schedules can be made for older students to facilitate completion of vocational activities. For more information about photographic activity schedules see the "Spotlight on Technology" feature.

TEACHING COMMUNICATION AND LANGUAGE

How a communication system will be adapted for use throughout the day is a key consideration when selecting the form and type of communication system for a student (Rowland

Spotlight on Technology

Photographic Activity Schedules

In their book, *Activity Schedules for Children with Autism*, McClannahan and Krantz (1999) describe how they teach students with autism spectrum disorder to first obtain picture/object correspondence and then to follow photographic cues. They teach the students to turn the pages of a book, point to the photograph, and then complete the activity represented in the photograph. Students need to be able to complete all the activities depicted before those activities are included in the schedule. An important aspect of the activity schedules is the method used to teach the students. Most-to-least prompts (e.g., hand-over hand) are administered from behind the student so that the student does not learn to wait for an adult cue, but rather follows what is in the photographic schedule independently. Text is added to the activity schedules and eventually the photographs are faded, resulting in the student following a schedule in text as would a typical student. Here are some examples of photographs with text that can be used for a choice board or in an activity schedule.

Note: Photograph from p. 84 of Activity Schedules for Children with Autism by L. E. McClannahan and P. J. Krantz. Copyright 1999 by Lynn E. McClannahan and Patricia J. Krantz.

Spotlight on Technology

Using Pictures in an Augmentative Communication System

Students with ASD may need to be taught the value of a communication system in order to meet their wants and needs. Students may have a history of crying or screaming to get what they want or taking the hand of an adult and moving that person toward the object or activity that they prefer. Frost and Bondy (1998) have put together a method to teach children with developmental disabilities to begin the communicative act through the exchange of a picture or photograph of the preferred item. Many programs are designed using picture symbols from the Mayer-Johnson Company (http://www.mayer-johnson.com). This company offers a wide range of picture communication symbols (PCS) (Johnson, 1995).

The Picture Exchange Communication System (PECS) (Frost & Bondy, 1998) has been widely adopted for students without oral communication skills (http://www.pecs.com). In the early phases of this program, students learn about the communication act of approaching an adult and exchanging a picture/photograph for what they want. Later phases include teaching discrimination of items to select preferred ones, requesting in sentence form, and then commenting on what the student observes in the environment. Research is currently under way to determine the characteristics of the students who benefit from this system as well as the frequency and timing for

Note: Photograph from p. 97 of *A Picture's Worth: PECS and Other Visual Communication Strategies in Autism* by A. Bondy and L. Frost. Copyright 2002 by Woodbine House.

the development of oral language. The accompanying photograph (Bondy & Frost, 2002) provides an example of the materials used by a student who is using PECS in a sentence form with adjectives to describe what he or she wants.

& Schweigert, 2000). A communication system is only valuable if it can be used frequently and easily by the student. Augmentative communication systems were discussed in the previous chapter on students with communication disorders. When a student has an augmentative or alternative system, it is imperative that the system be adapted for use throughout daily activities (Prizant, Wetherby, & Rydell, 2000). If the student is using a voice output device, then it must be made portable. No system should be designed to be used only during one or two activities. To learn about a communication system that uses pictures, consult the "Spotlight on Technology" material.

If the student with ASD uses an augmentative system, then the teacher will focus on using this system while also providing opportunities for oral communication. This is likely to mean arranging the environment so that the student is motivated to communicate. For example, Mario has several racing magazines that he reads following his adapted reading lesson of the grade-level curriculum. These magazines can be placed on a high shelf so that Mario needs to ask for assistance to get them. He then could be asked to describe the cover of the magazine he wants or to tell the teacher what articles are included in the magazine he would prefer. If the student is us-

ing the picture exchange communication system (Frost & Bondy, 1998); then access to the picture book and facilitation of its use throughout the classroom must be provided.

The teacher will also need to include extra time for the student to initiate and respond to others. Because oral communication may be difficult, students may need more time than their typical peers to answer any questions or to formulate their own comment or question. Allowing time for delayed responses has been a successful strategy to promote independence in student initiations (Taylor, 2001). One form of the time-delay procedure involves using a prompt to help students respond to a social cue. Initially, the prompt is paired with the cue but gradually the time intervening between the cue and the prompt is increased. The goal is for the student to respond to the social cue without needing the prompt (Charlop & Walsh, 1986). For example, if someone asks Mario, "What is your name?" the teacher may model, "My name is Mario" immediately, and fade the time before this prompt is given until Mario responds on his own.

Students with autism spectrum disorder also may need to learn the nonverbal aspects of communication. They may need to learn to raise their hands if they have a question or in response to the teacher's comment. They are less likely to learn by imitating others. Therefore, if these skills are lacking, then they need to be directly taught. Taking turns (Koegel, Koegel, & Carter, 1999), reading facial expressions of emotion (Taylor & McDonough, 1996), attending to instructions given to an entire group, using gestures when communicating (Buffington, Kranz, McClannahan, & Poulson, 1998), and understanding the content behind voice tone (Lamers & Hall, 2003) are some of the skills that are likely to be weak or lacking for students with autism spectrum disorder.

Even if the student can speak clearly and has a good vocabulary, it is likely that he or she will need practice initiating conversations, speaking in sentences, staying on the topic, and ending social interactions appropriately. One of the defining characteristics of ASD is that the student is not motivated by social contexts or is not interested in interacting with others, especially peers (APA, 2000). Improving impairments in social interaction skills are key objectives to be addressed by most of the students on the autism spectrum including those with Asperger's syndrome.

PROMOTING SOCIAL SKILLS

Socioemotional development is delayed for students identified with autism spectrum disorder (APA, 2000). One of the early diagnostic indicators of ASD is a lack of joint attention at an early age. In other words, there is no interest in sharing an experience or object with another person. Development of joint attention typically occurs by 6 to 18 months (Adamson & Chance, 1998). However, lack of this behavior begins the pattern of not relating to others that leaves the child with autism without many of the benefits gained from social interaction. This results in impairments in the ability to learn new skills through modeling or imitation and in the ability to interact socially with siblings, peers, and adults. Social skills are

important for successful functioning at home and at school (Scheuermann & Webber, 2002). Gutstein and Sheely (2002) have developed a curriculum for addressing the social deficits for individuals with ASD with an initial focus on attending, referencing, and regulating social interaction. Through a series of play and social activities, the authors aim to increase socioemotional skills sufficiently so that playmate and friendship relationships can be formed.

One of the advantages of including students with autism spectrum disorder in a class with typical peers is that many opportunities are available for addressing impairments in social skills. Merely placing a student with ASD in a classroom with peers, however, is not going to make a difference (Taylor, 2001). If no structures or strategies are put into place to promote peer interaction, then it is likely that the student will choose either to stay alone or interact only with adults (Gena & Kymissis, 2001). Sometimes adults such as teachers or aides are surprised when they become aware that a student with ASD who has good conversational skills when interacting with them does not interact with peers unless necessary.

Due to the avoidance of peer interactions, it is a good idea to place the student with ASD in a central location in the classroom where the student can be near peers for any small group activities and to receive social bids or initiations from peers. If the student is placed in the back of the classroom, especially if he or she is assigned a classroom aide, this may isolate the student and deter peer interaction (Hall & McGregor, 2000).

Strategies that have resulted in increased peer interactions have included the use of peer tutors or enlisting the assistance of a peer to facilitate the practice of skills such as greetings, play initiation, and following instructions. Taylor and Jasper (2001) have outlined programs that can be used to increase social interaction with peers that include beginning skills (eye contact, greetings, requests items), intermediate skills (follows directions, pretends, offers information), and advanced skills (comments about play, expresses empathy, responds to changes in conversational topic).

Laushey and Heflin (2000) evaluated a peer-mediated strategy of a buddy system in which peers in a kindergarten class were taught to stay, play, and talk to their buddy. Compared with proximity to peers alone, this strategy increased the social skills of the students with autism such as asking for an object, getting the attention of a peer, waiting for a turn, and looking at the direction of the speaker. The use of peers who volunteer to be part of a Friends Club or are selected by the student with autism to be part of the Lunch Bunch also has been effective in increasing the social skills of students with autism spectrum disorder in elementary classes (Wagner, 1999). Identifying the preferred peer of the student with autism spectrum disorder and including that peer in social activities may increase the generalization of social interaction across settings (Hall & Smith, 1996).

Window on the Web

The Social Stories™ Website

http://www.thegraycenter.org/Social_Stories.htm

Among the resources on the website of the Gray Center for Social Learning and Understanding is the "Official Social Stories™" website. The guidelines for writing a Social Story and some sample Social Stories including some for adolescents are found at this web address. Included in these guidelines is the importance of having a high proportion of descriptive sentences in each story. Carol Gray's books and materials can be purchased at this site along with other books focused on individuals with ASD. Information about the journal titled *Social Stories™ Quarterly* also can be found at this address.

Note: Courtesy of the Gray Center for Social Learning and Understanding.

Companion Website

For more information, go to the Web Links module in Chapter 13 of the Companion Website

The use of scripts has helped students with autism increase the quantity and quality of interactions with peers. Typically developing students learn social "scripts" by watching others in a social context. They learn when to say hello and good-bye and when and how to conduct, enter, and exit conversations. Students with ASD can capitalize on any visual strengths by looking at a written script and practicing the social situation until it becomes fluent (Krantz & McClannahan, 1993). Once students memorize the basic script of a social interaction for a given context, they often add and change the script to make it more individualized and more like their own voice. Just like when adults first learn the steps of a line dance, we look stiff and robotic until we are comfortable with the steps and can relax and dance them fluently, students with autism spectrum disorder learning a new social script may appear stiff until they are comfortable with what to say given the social context.

Carol Gray has found the use of Social Stories to be an effective method of facilitating appropriate peer interaction (Gray & Garand, 1993). Individualized stories are written to describe the situation and ideal behavior of the main character (the student with ASD) in the story. Gray has found that stories written for students with autism need to have flexibility written into the descriptive statements and any directive comments used. Dan's teacher might write a social story entitled "Who Does Spiderman Play With?" This story might describe the *usual* time of day when children play together and the kinds of activities that Spiderman likes to do with other children. The story may include a line such as "I will try to ask someone to play tag with me on the playground." Social stories are read to the students prior to the setting or activity described in the story. See the "Window on the Web" feature to learn more about social stories.

Students who prefer a visual means of communication may benefit from the use of videotapes of social interactions that the student can imitate. Video-modeling has been used successfully to teach students with autism to share toys and to make comments during play (Taylor, Levin, & Jasper, 1999). Video-modeling also has been used to teach conversational skills (Charlop & Milstein, 1989). As with other instructional strategies, watching these tapes alone may not be sufficient to result in imitation; some additional structure may need to be included as part of video-modeling.

Once a student has obtained a social skill, or any skill, it is important to facilitate the generalization of that skill with multiple social partners. Students with autism spectrum disorder have difficulty generalizing new skills to new contexts (Scheuermann & Webber, 2002). It is not unusual for a student with ASD to learn to respond to a question or to follow the oral instructions of one adult very well, but not answer when asked the same exact question by a peer or a stranger. Consequently, it is important to plan for generalization at the beginning of developing any curriculum objectives (Sulzer-Azaroff & Mayer, 1991). For social situations, this means including multiple social partners while the student is learning a new skill. It is especially important for a student with autism spectrum disorder not to interact exclusively with an assigned classroom aide because it is likely that any skills will be demonstrated for that person alone.

In this chapter, you have learned about the educational needs of students with autism spectrum disorder. Methods for making classrooms adaptations, teaching communication and language development, and promoting social skills have been presented. In the next chapter, you will meet students with physical and health impairments. Before turning to chapter 14, however, check "Things to Remember."

Things to Remember

- Capitalize on the strengths of students with autism spectrum disorder.
- Develop important skills. Even when students are at a young age, choose skills that will assist in finding future employment.
- Embed frequent communication opportunities throughout the day so that communication is practiced until it is fluent.
- Socioemotional development is an area of weakness for students with autism spectrum disorder. Mediating the emotional context in a situation by describing the critical features

of facial expressions, labeling emotions, and explaining why situations are funny is helpful for these students.
- Arrange the environment to facilitate peer interaction. Establish that classmates who help others are highly regarded in your classroom.
- Students with autism spectrum disorder have difficulty with generalization so it is very important to plan the use of multiple materials, in multiple contexts, and with multiple people.

ACTIVITIES

1. Arrange to observe at least one student with autism spectrum disorder during two educational sessions. What form of communication is the student using? Does the student have any of the typical behaviors associated with this disorder? What strategies does the educator use to increase the communication or social skills of this student?

2. Interview a teacher who has been including a student with autism spectrum disorder in the general education classroom for at least 6 months. What surprises did he or she discover? What are the student's strengths?

3. Read an article on autism that appeared in the popular press. Examples can be found in these magazines:

The New Yorker (Sheehan, 2003; December 2003), Newsweek (Cowley, 2003; September 2003), Times (Nash, 2002), or Parents (Seroussi, 2000). Describe the perspective of parents on diagnosing and finding services for their child with autism spectrum disorder. Would a parent have a similar experience in your school district?

4. Find a journal in the library that has a focus on ASD such as the Journal of Autism and Developmental Disabilities or Focus on Autism. Read two or three articles from a recent issue to find out about some of the key issues in the field. If your library does not have these journals, try the special issue devoted to ASD in the Journal of the Association for Persons with Severe Handicaps (Volume 24, 1999) or the journal Research in Developmental Disabilities.

5. Go to the website for the Autism Society of America (http://www.autism-society.org) and read some of the current issues under the "Advocacy" section. What actions are parents requesting to improve policies for individuals with autism? What new research is currently under way to benefit those with autism spectrum disorder?

6. Identify the services for individuals with autism spectrum disorder in your community by contacting educational and recreational agencies. Is there a local parent support group or a local chapter of the Autism Society of America? Are there private agencies that can be hired by parents to provide in-home educational programs?

CD-ROM Activities

Look again at the preschool case study and the one featuring the sixth grade classroom. In each, the teacher takes special care to help students make smooth transitions from one activity to another. View the video clips described below, then describe the strategies used by these teachers. Are their approaches similar in any way?

- In the case study of the preschool classroom, view the video clip entitled "Structure Routines."

- In the case study of the sixth grade classroom, view the video clips entitled "Increasing Interest" and "Clear Expectations."

Teaching Students with Physical and Health Impairments

CHAPTER 14

Tim

Tim is a 16-year-old high school sophomore with spastic cerebral palsy. He is quite mobile with the aid of his braces and crutches; he is able to move from class to class, use the restroom, and eat in the lunchroom without assistance. Tim attends all general education classes during the day (except for adapted physical education) and is maintaining a B average this semester. He does not receive resource services, but the special education teacher is available to assist Tim's teachers when necessary. In class, Tim uses a laptop computer and word processing program because his handwriting is poor; however, he is expected to complete assignments and exams within the usual time limits. Tim has been in general education classes since the first grade and has several friends at his high school. This semester he is taking the driver's education course, and he's very excited about getting his driver's license.

Maxine

Maxine is 10 years old and in the fourth grade. She enjoys school and has many friends both at school and in her neighborhood. Every day Maxine must take the medication that has helped to control her epileptic seizures for the past 3 years. Despite this medication, she has generalized tonic-clonic seizures (formerly called grand mal seizures) at school about once a month. Mrs. Emerick, Maxine's teacher, knows what to do when a seizure occurs, and she and the school nurse have explained the nature of Maxine's condition to the other students in the class. Although her classmates are quite understanding, Maxine worries about what they think when seizures occur. In the past year she has become more concerned about this problem, and she visits the school counselor once a week to talk about her feelings. In all other respects, Maxine is typical. She is a good student. She

LOOKING AHEAD

Later in this chapter, we will take a look at part of Hank's IEP to see the types of special services he might require to support his success in the general education program. Among the topics discussed in this chapter are strategies for meeting the physical and health needs of students like Hank, Tim, and Maxine; ways to modify the physical environment; and how to adapt instructional materials. As you read, keep these questions in mind:

- Although all are identified as having some type of physical or health problem, Tim, Maxine, and Hank pose quite different challenges to their teachers. Compare and contrast the major strengths of these students.
- If you were Tim's teacher, how might you adapt classroom learning activities so that he could participate?
- If you were Hank's teacher, how might you adapt the physical environment of the classroom?
- What types of modifications would be needed if Maxine was a student in your classroom?

To answer these questions online, go to the Students' Stories Module in Chapter 14 of the Companion Website.

performs well in all school subjects and is particularly interested in science and math.

Hank

Hank is 13 years old and attends Madison Middle School. When he was in the first grade, he suffered a spinal injury in a bike accident and now travels by wheelchair. He is able to get to all of his classes because some of the school's architectural barriers have been removed; for instance, a ramp has been built so that he can bypass the three steps up to the door of his English classroom. Hank missed a lot of school during his elementary years and had difficulty acquiring reading skills. At present, he attends general education classes for the majority of the school day but continues to visit the special education teacher for assistance in reading. Hank is a sports enthusiast who keeps up with all the high school and professional teams. He attends an adapted physical education class but is often frustrated because he is not able to participate in many of the athletic activities in which he is interested. Hank has a small circle of close friends, and he is well liked by his teachers. He's an active participant in class discussions and usually maintains at least a C average. This semester he has had several medical appointments that have caused him to miss school at least one day each week; his grades have not yet suffered, but he is beginning to fall behind in some of his classes.

Students with physical and health impairments are an extremely heterogeneous group with a wide variety of conditions and diseases; **cerebral palsy,** paralysis, **epilepsy,** clubfoot, asthma, polio, **diabetes,** and allergies are just a few. Some physical and health impairments are **congenital,** that is, present at birth; others are acquired after birth through disease or injury. Physical and health problems can have grave, little, or no effect on school performance. Some students with physical and health impairments require no special adaptations; others need only modification of the physical environment. For others, it is necessary to adapt instructional activities in the general education classroom or to provide special instruction in areas of need, such as mobility, communication, and basic skills. A few of these students may have multiple disabilities with various medically related needs that require extensive services from the school nurse or other trained individuals. Students with similar impairments may have very different special needs; one student with lower limb paralysis may be active and outgoing, whereas another may be withdrawn and unwilling to interact with others.

Teachers often believe that they should create a protective environment for students with physical and health impairments. However, such an environment discourages the development of skills necessary for independence. Dependency is one of the greatest problems of these students, and teachers must take care not to add to this difficulty. Expectations for students with physical and health impairments should be realistic and geared toward the actual capabilities of individual students. The goal is the same as that for any other students: the development of skills that lead to independence.

This chapter describes the characteristics of students with physical and health impairments who are included in the general education program and presents methods for the general education teacher to use in gathering assessment data and modifying classroom procedures and activities to meet special needs. Consult the "For Your Information" box to learn more about physical and health impairments.

INDICATORS OF PHYSICAL AND HEALTH IMPAIRMENTS

General education teachers are important members of the teams that assist in planning for students with physical and health impairments. Depending on the nature of the student's problem, the general education teacher may be involved in a variety of activities. He or she can help identify a physical or health impairment, provide the prereferral or assessment team with information about the student's current classroom performance, or take primary responsibility for the education and management of the student. In the general education classroom, a range of possible adaptations may be necessary; these include additional instruction for students with frequent absences, modification of the physical environment to allow mobility, and adaptations of instructional materials and activities.

Some students with physical and health impairments begin their school careers with an identified disability. With others, the problem is first noted after they enter school, or it may result from an accident or disease that occurs during the school years. Because students in this group may have many different physical disabilities and health problems that can serve as impairments, it is not possible to make a single list of signs or symptoms that identify this group. The glossary of terms provided in the "For Your Information" box on page 314 describes several of the most common physical and health impairments.

Knowledge about a student's physical or health problem does not provide educators with much information about instructional programming. As Reynolds and Birch (1988) point out:

 a. The names of the medical conditions give few clues to individual special education needs;

For Your Information

Students with Physical and Health Impairments

- The U.S. Department of Education (2002) reports that 73,057 students (aged 6 to 21) with orthopedic impairments and 291,850 with other health impairments received special education services in the 2000–2001 school year. The number of students with orthopedic impairments served increased by 42% from 1991–1992 to 2000–2001. The number of students with other health impairments represented a 397% increase from 1991 to 1992.

- It is estimated that students with physical and health impairments make up approximately 0.7% of the school-aged population; they account for only about 6.3% of the students with disabilities who receive special education services (U.S. Department of Education, 2002).

- The presence of a medical condition does not automatically signal the need for special education services. As Reynolds and Birch (1982) suggest, "for every 20 children with medically significant conditions, perhaps 4 or 5 of them will be in need of special educational programming" (p. 301).

- Heward (2003) reports that 1 out of 500 students of school age is hospitalized each year because of a traumatic head injury. In addition, "traumatic brain injury is the leading cause of death in children and the most common acquired disability in childhood" (p. 478).

- According to the U.S. Department of Education (2002), the number of students with traumatic brain injury (aged 6 to 21) receiving special education services increased from 245 in the 1991–1992 school year to 14,844 in 2000–2001, an increase of almost 6,000%.

- Cerebral palsy is one of the most complex of all physical impairments; because it results from damage to the brain, other areas of functioning including speech, vision, hearing, and intelligence can also be affected. However, there is no relationship between the extent of physical impairment and intellectual performance; individuals with severe motor involvement may be intellectually gifted (Bowe, 2000).

- At the end of 2000, more than 8,908 children under the age of 13 and 4,061 in the age range of 13 to 19 had been diagnosed as having acquired immunodeficiency syndrome (AIDS) in the United States (Centers for Disease Control and Prevention 2001). Byrom and Katz (1991) report that about 80% of these children were infected by their mothers during pregnancy and about 19% received contaminated blood products during transfusions. The rights of students with HIV/AIDS to an appropriate education have been protected by the provisions of federal special education laws and by the courts (Zirkel, 1989).

- Different, and relatively new, diseases such as Lyme disease, Tourette's syndrome, or Reyes syndrome appear periodically (Sklaire, 1989). Lyme disease, which results from the bite of a deer tick, was first noticed in the 1970s. It starts with a rash and can lead to swollen joints and stiffness; complications can affect the heart and nervous system. Tourette's syndrome is a rare neurobiological disorder that typically affects children between the ages of 2 and 15. While its cause is not known, it appears to be related to a chemical imbalance; Prestia (2003) explains that "tics are the defining feature of the disorder" (p. 67); tics are involuntary movements that can be motor or vocal in nature. Reyes syndrome can result from administering aspirin to children and youth with flu or chicken pox, and it can be fatal. Education regarding the use of alternates to aspirin has led to a reduction in the number of cases of Reyes syndrome.

- Most students with physical and health impairments spend the majority of the school day in the general education classroom; many of these students also receive special education services from a resource teacher or other specialist(s), such as a physical therapist, occupational therapist, or adapted physical education teacher.

- Many famous people have had physical and health impairments, including several presidents of the United States: Theodore Roosevelt (asthma), Franklin Delano Roosevelt (polio), and John F. Kennedy (back problems).

b. only a minority of children with these conditions have any special education needs at all; and

c. there is no educational justification for grouping these children in school by their medical diagnoses. (p. 269)

As with other students with special needs, it is necessary to go beyond the label and consider the individual needs of the student.

The special needs of students with physical and health impairments are almost as diverse as their physical disabilities. Some require no special assistance in school, others need minor modifications, and a few benefit from extensive special ed-

ucation services. One frequent area of need for students with physical impairments is mobility; for many, the major school adaptation necessary is proper arrangement of the physical environment. Some students also receive services from occupational therapists (e.g., to assist in the development of independent physical daily living skills) or physical therapists (e.g., ambulation training, assistance with mobility, positioning and transfer skills) (Neal, Bigby, & Nicholson, 2004).

Other students may experience difficulty in learning academic skills, because of excessive absences, fatigue attributable to a medical condition or medication, or learning problems similar to those of pupils with learning disabilities,

For Your Information

Glossary of Medical Terms

Reynolds and Birch (1988) discuss several of the physical impairments and health problems that can be found in general education classrooms. Following is a list of the medical terms for these disabilities and a brief description of each.

Allergies

Adverse sensitivities or low tolerances to specific substances that are not problems to people in general. Reactions may take many forms; the most common are watering eyes, sneezing, nasal discharge, itching, or rash.

Arthritis

Inflammation of a joint, making motion difficult, painful, and limited.

Asthma

Repeated occurrence of wheezing coughs, difficult breathing, and feeling of constriction because of bronchial contractions.

Cerebral palsy

Several forms of paralysis due to damage to the brain. The most common forms are ataxia, shown by marked inability to coordinate bodily movements; athetosis, appearing as slow, repeated movements of the limbs; and spasticity, characterized by abrupt contractions of muscles or muscle groups, producing interference with and distortion of movement. All forms involve involuntary movements, and they appear in various combinations in different body locations depending on the nature and sites of the brain damage.

Congenital anomaly

Any body organ or part existing in an abnormal form from the time of birth. It can include, for example, the whole body, as in dwarfism (unusually small size) or albinism (absence of pigmentation); can be limited to one part (absence of an arm or a leg); can be clefts (cleft lip or palate); or can affect internal parts like the spine or spinal cord (spina bifida) or the heart.

Diabetes

Disorder of metabolism of carbohydrates that is indicated by excessive amounts of glucose in the blood or urine.

Epilepsy

Disorder of the brain sometimes resulting in convulsive movements and periods of unconsciousness lasting several minutes and sometimes in brief lapses of consciousness (up to 10 seconds) or feelings of unreality, dizziness, or semiconsciousness.

Hemophilia

A condition in which the normal blood clotting procedure is defective, with consequent difficulty in stopping bleeding when it occurs for any reason on the surface or within the body.

Leukemia

A form of cancer affecting the balance of cells in the blood and, therefore, the normal functioning of the blood.

Muscular dystrophy

A group of chronic inherited disorders characterized by progressive weakening and wasting of voluntary skeletal muscles.

Poliomyelitis

A viral infection that can result in the paralysis of body parts or systems, depending on the parts of the nervous system attacked.

Rheumatic fever

A disease that is characterized by fever, inflammation, and pain around the joints and inflammation of the muscle and valves of the heart.

Spina bifida

An anomaly characterized by a defect in the bone that encases the spinal cord.

Traumatic injuries

Impairments that result from accidents. They include a great variety of conditions ranging through amputations, paralyses, and limitations of body functions.

Note: Excerpted from *Adaptive Mainstreaming: A Primer for Teachers and Principals*, 3/e, by Maynard C. Reynolds and Jack W. Birch. Published by Allyn and Bacon, Boston, MA. Copyright © 1988 by Pearson Education. Reprinted by permission of the publisher.

---

behavioral disorders, and mild retardation. Social skill development is often impeded by restricted opportunities to interact with others. Another possible area of need is social acceptance; teachers and peers may be hesitant to interact with a student whose disability is immediately obvious or with one whose condition seems strange and somewhat frightening. For example, the student with convulsive disorders who experiences epileptic seizures may be alarming to the observer unless this condition is understood. Figure 14-1 presents information on the different types of seizures and the characteristics of each.

The general education teacher may be the first professional to identify the possible physical and health problems of students included in the general education program. Teachers should be aware of the general health status of their students and take note of any changes, whether sudden or gradual. With many physical and medical problems, it is possible to look for specific signs and symptoms. As Figure 14-2 illustrates, several student behaviors can be indicative of the conditions of diabetes and epilepsy. If a physical or health impairment is suspected, the teacher should contact the school nurse or physician for further information.

An increasing number of children with extensive health management or medical needs are entering the educational system because medical technology has allowed them to survive early medical crises and to be capable of attending school. Many of these students are considered to be

medically fragile and their participation in a school setting requires the use of technology (e.g., heart monitors, oxygen tanks, or suctioning units), medical support (e.g., consultation or special emergency strategies), and other related services to survive and/or participate in the educational program (Pendergast, 1995; Rapport, 1996).

With the movement toward including a greater number of students with more severe special needs or multiple disabilities in general education, an increasing number of students who are medically fragile are likely to be placed in the general education classroom. Teachers in these general education classrooms should participate in the IEP meetings for the student and have a clear understanding of their specific responsibilities when the student is placed in their classroom. In addition, they should be provided information on the full range of related services required to meet the student's educational and medical needs and be aware of the other professionals and support personnel who are assigned the responsibility for implementing this part of the IEP. Another important consideration is the use of **universal precautions** when handling blood or other bodily fluids in the classroom. See the "Inclusion Tips for the Teacher" box for more information.

ASSESSMENT PROCEDURES

Because of the diverse nature of the problems exhibited by students with physical and health impairments, the teams considering these students must take care to select appropriate assessment devices to gather information about educational needs. The procedures used differ from student to

---

FIGURE 14-1	Epileptic Seizures

The word *epilepsy* comes from the Greek word for "seizures." Seizures of one kind or another are the main symptoms of all forms of epilepsy. Seizures occur when there are excessive electrical discharges in some nerve cells of the brain. When this happens, the brain loses conscious control over certain body functions and consciousness may be lost or altered. Loss of control is temporary and the brain functions normally between seizures.

Generalized tonic-clonic (grand mal) seizures are the most potentially disruptive in the classroom. The child becomes stiff and slumps to the floor unconscious. Rigid muscles give way to jerking, breathing is suspended and saliva may escape from the lips. The seizure may last for several minutes, and the child will regain consciousness in a confused or drowsy state, but otherwise unaffected.

Generalized absence (petit mal) seizures, most common in children, usually last only for 5 to 20 seconds. They may be accompanied by staring or twitching of the eyelids and are frequently mistaken for "daydreaming." The child is seldom aware he has had a seizure, although he may be aware that his "mind had gone blank" for a few seconds.

Complex partial (psychomotor or temporal lobe) seizures have the most complex behavior pattern. They may include constant chewing or lip smacking, purposeless walking or repetitive hand and arm movements, confusion and dizziness. The seizure may last from a minute to several hours.

Note: From *Epilepsy School Alert* by the Epilepsy Foundation of America, 1974, Washington, DC: Author. Copyright 1974 by the Epilepsy Foundation of America. Reprinted by permission.

FIGURE 14-2   Classroom Signs of Diabetes and Epilepsy

Diabetes

The American Diabetes Association (n.d.) provides these guidelines for identifying possible signs of diabetes in school-aged individuals:

Often diabetes goes undiagnosed because many of its symptoms seem so harmless. Recent studies indicate that the early detection of diabetes symptoms and treatment can decrease the chance of developing the complications of diabetes.
Some diabetes symptoms include:

- Frequent urination
- Excessive thirst
- Extreme hunger
- Unusual weight loss
- Increased fatigue
- Irritability
- Blurry vision

If you have one or more of these diabetes symptoms, see your doctor right away.

Epilepsy

In 2000, the Epilepsy Foundation of America issued a press release urging parents and other caregivers to be aware of the hidden signs of epilepsy:

Seizures are the most common neurological disorder of childhood. But not all seizures are convulsions, and symptoms can be difficult to recognize. Many of the "hidden" signs mimic normal behavior. Recognition of these signs is important in the early diagnosis and treatment to avoid learning disabilities, social problems and safety risks associated with epilepsy in young children. Early diagnosis offers the child with epilepsy a better chance of treatment success and a future free of seizures. . . .
The "hidden signs" of seizures in children include:

- Short attention blackouts that look like daydreaming.
- Sudden falls for no reason.
- Lack of response for brief periods.
- Dazed behavior.
- Unusual sleepiness and irritability when wakened from sleep.
- Head nodding.
- Rapid blinking.
- Frequent complaints from the child that things look, sound, taste, smell or feel "funny."
- Clusters of "jackknife" movements by babies who are sitting down.
- Clusters of grabbing movements with both arms in babies lying on their backs.
- Sudden stomach pain followed by confusion and sleepiness.
- Repeated movements that look out of place or unnatural.
- Frequent stumbling or unusual clumsiness.
- Sudden repeated episodes of fear for no apparent reason.

Note: From "Diabetes Symptoms" on the website of the National Diabetes Association (n.d.) and from "The Epilepsy Foundation Urges Caregivers, Parents of Young Children to Know the Hidden Signs of Epilepsy" on the website of the Epilepsy Foundation of America (2000). Copyright © 2004 American Diabetes Association. Reprinted with permission from the American Diabetes Association.

student, and in many cases health professionals and other specialists must be included as part of the assessment team. For example, physical therapists, occupational therapists, adapted physical education teachers, and school nurses and physicians may provide important information about the effects of a disability on school performance. Other team members who play critical roles in assessment are the general education teacher, special educators, speech-language pathologist, and school psychologist.

Students with physical and health impairments often require classroom adaptations to help them function successfully in general education settings. To obtain the information needed to design and implement these adaptations, the assessment team collects assessment data about current levels

Inclusion Tips for the Teacher

Universal Precautions to Prevent Infection in the Classroom

Heward (2003) advises that "all teachers and school personnel must be trained in *universal precautions* for dealing with blood and bodily fluids from any child (e.g., how to safely administer first aid for a cut or tend to a child's nose bleed)" (p. 454). In their article on preventing infection in the classroom, Edens, Murdick, and Gartin (2003) identify several essential skills for teachers:

> At minimum, teachers must know the proper method of gloving, clean-up procedures for potential biohazard areas that might occur in the classroom, and proper hand-washing techniques. (p. 62)

Edens et al. (2003) suggest that teachers carry with them vinyl gloves; latex gloves are not recommended because of the possibility of latex allergy. Before putting on gloves, teachers should remove any jewelry that might cause a puncture. When removing gloves, it is necessary to avoid touching the outside surfaces with unprotected hands. Contaminated gloves should be discarded.

The next step is washing the hands. Edens et al. (2003) provide detailed procedures:

1. Roll out two paper towel sections. One is to dry your hands and the other is to turn off the faucet.
2. Turn on the faucet.
3. Wet hands under water (warm or hot).
4. Apply liquid soap to the hands. A generous amount should be used to work up a good lather.
5. Rub hands in a circular motion, covering the front and back of the hands as well as between the fingers. If needed, a brush may be used to scrub under the fingernails.
6. Each area is to be rubbed with soap ten times or for 10–30 seconds with 30 seconds suggested for health care workers.
7. Rinse hands thoroughly.
8. Dry hands thoroughly on the paper towel rolled out in the beginning of the hand washing process.
9. Discard in a receptacle.
10. Turn off the faucet using the dry paper towel (a dry paper towel spreads germs less than a moist paper towel).
11. Use this dry paper towel to open the door to exit.
12. If only hot air dryers are available, use a tissue, a newspaper or magazine page, or even clothing to turn off the faucet and then open the door. (p. 63)

School or district policies should be followed when cleaning up potential biohazard areas in the classroom. For more information, contact your school principal or nurse.

---

of performance in important skills. Sirvis (1988) suggests that assessment should focus on the following areas:

- *Activities of daily living.* Assessment of current and potential skills in self-help and daily living (e.g., eating, toileting, personal hygiene, cooking, travel on public transportation).
- *Mobility.* Current ability and potential to move from place to place and to become independent. Special equipment or assistive devices such as special wheelchairs or support devices may be required to facilitate mobility.
- *Physical abilities and limitations.* Identification of the effect of physical factors on the student's present and future plans for schooling, employment, recreation, and independent functioning.
- *Psychosocial development.* Study of factors that interfere with social and emotional development and with the student's ability and opportunities to interact with others.
- *Communication.* Evaluation of the student's ability to understand and express language. May lead to the use of various communication devices such as computers, communication boards, augmentative communication devices, or other aids.
- *Academic potential.* While the academic assessment may be similar to that used with other students, it is es-

sential that the students are not penalized because of their physical limitations. This may require adaptations such as modifications in the physical setup, elimination of timed tasks, or alternative response modes such as verbal rather than written responses.
- *Adaptations for learning.* Enhancement of the potential for independence by identifying needed classroom academic and physical adaptations for the student.
- *Transition skills.* Identification of the factors necessary for a successful transition from school to living and working in the community. This is not limited to assessing job skills but should include other factors that will affect post-school performance.

Sirvis (1988) warns that standardized tests should be used cautiously with students with physical impairments. Communication problems or poor motor coordination can affect a student's ability to respond within the test's time limits or to provide adequate verbal responses. Sirvis also contends that students with physical impairments can be at a disadvantage when responding to norm-referenced tests because their physical problems may restrict their ability to explore the world around them.

Criterion-referenced tests that compare a student's performance to the goals of the curriculum rather than to the performance of others are especially useful with this group of

Window on the Web

Websites About Physical and Health Conditions

A number of websites provide information about physical and health impairments. Several of these sites focus on one condition (e.g., epilepsy), while others are more general in nature.

Websites Focusing on Specific Conditions

- AIDSinfo (www.hivatis.org)
- American Cancer Society (www.cancer.org)
- American Diabetes Association (www.diabetes.org)
- Brain Injury Association, Inc. (www.biausa.org)
- Epilepsy Foundation of America (www.efa.org
- Leukemia & Lymphoma Society (www.leukemia.org)
- Muscular Dystrophy Association (www.mdausa.org)
- National Institute of Diabetes & Digestive & Kidney Diseases (www.niddk.nih.gov)
- National Resource Center for Traumatic Brain Injury (www.neuro.pmr.vcu.edu)
- Spina Bifida Association of America (www.sbaa.org)
- United Cerebral Palsy Association (www.ucpa.org)

More General Websites

- American Academy of Pediatrics (www.aap.org)
- Centers for Disease Control and Prevention (www.cdc.gov)
- Easter Seals (www.easter-seals.org)
- Internet Resources for Special Children (www.irsc.org)
- National Rehabilitation Information Center (www.naric.com)

For more information, go to the Web Links module in Chapter 14 of the Companion Website.

students with special needs. Criterion-referenced measures provide a way to evaluate a student's current level of performance and progress without the limitation of standardized tests. They also supply the teacher with information that is helpful in the design of instructional/management programs.

Direct observation is another useful technique. The teacher can collect data on a variety of student behaviors, such as academic performance, the frequency of seizures, the time taken to complete assignments, the types of interactions with others, and the frequency of inappropriate classroom behaviors. Classroom observation data provide the teams serving students with special needs with important information about current school performance of a student and can also be useful to medical personnel responsible for management of physical or health problems.

The general education teacher should review the assessment results of other professionals who aid in the evaluation of a student with physical or health impairments. The information gathered in assessment can be extremely useful for the teacher working with the student in the general education classroom. If portions of the assessment reports are unclear, the teacher should seek assistance from the school nurse, special educator,

physician, other appropriate professionals, or the student's parents. For a classroom program that develops the independence as well as the academic and behavioral skills of students, a clear picture of their capabilities and limitations is imperative.

SPECIAL SERVICES

When assessment is complete, an IEP is developed by the IEP team for each student found eligible for special education services. For students with physical or health impairments, IEP goals may address several areas and involve services from a wide variety of professionals—for example, general education teachers, special education teachers, physical or occupational therapists, school nurses, social workers, counselors, speech and language specialists, adapted physical education teachers, and vocational counselors. Figure 14-3 shows portions of the IEP for Hank, the middle school student introduced at the beginning of this chapter. Although Hank is included in the general education program for the majority of the school day, he receives help in reading from the resource teacher, and he is learning leisure time skills in adapted physical education.

Most students with physical and health impairments spend the majority of their day in the general education classroom and only attend a resource room for academic assistance or visit a specialist for some other type of necessary service. Special classes and schools are available for students with severe or multiple disabilities; these placements are usually reserved for individuals with complex physical needs accompanied by severe learning problems. As noted earlier in this chapter, increased attention has been aimed at including students who are medically fragile and those with more severe disabilities in the general education program whenever it is appropriate to meet their special educational needs. When students cannot attend school because of prolonged illness or the need for extensive medical services, home and hospital

FIGURE 14-3   IEP Goals and Services for Hank

Annual Goals

1. By the end of the school year, Hank will demonstrate the basic skills necessary to participate in two group-oriented recreational activities.
   Person responsible: Adapted physical education teacher
2. By the end of the school year, Hank will participate in 4 hours of self-directed recreational activity each week.
   Person responsible: Adapted physical education teacher
3. By the end of the school year, Hank will read materials at the sixth-grade level with adequate word recognition and comprehension.
   Person responsible: Resource teacher
4. Hank will successfully complete eighth-grade math, English, social studies, and science.
   Persons responsible: Eighth-grade teachers

Amount of Participation in General Education

Hank will attend eighth-grade general education classes in math, English, social studies, and science.

Special Education and Related Services

1. Hank will receive special education services from the adapted physical education teacher (annual goals 1 and 2) for one period per day.
2. Hank will receive special education services from the resource teacher (annual goal 3) for one period per day.
3. The resource teacher, adapted physical education teacher, and school nurse will provide consultation to Hank's eighth-grade teachers as needed.

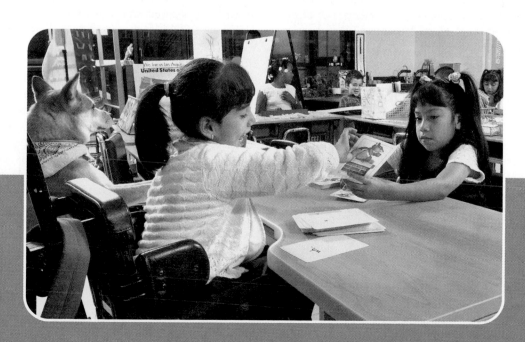

services can be provided. Consultant services are also available to the general education teacher from a variety of specialists who attempt to assist the teacher in making classroom adaptations to facilitate the successful inclusion of students with health and physical impairments.

CLASSROOM ADAPTATIONS

When students with physical and health impairments enter the general education classroom, one of the teacher's first tasks is to learn about their disabilities. Other students must also become aware of the problems of these students with special needs and learn about possible ways of helping them function as independently as possible. In addition, it may be necessary to adapt portions of the general education program to allow full participation of students with physical and health impairments. The areas in which modifications are usually required are the arrangement of the physical environment and the format and structure of instructional activities and assignments.

The following sections of this chapter describe methods for meeting physical and health needs in the general education classroom, modifying the physical environment, and adapting instructional activities. For students with specific needs in academic instruction, the teacher should refer to the methods suggested for students with learning disabilities (chapter 9) and mild retardation (chapter 10). If classroom behavior is a concern, the suggestions provided for students with behavioral disorders (chapter 11) might prove helpful.

Reynolds and Birch (1988) point out that students with physical and health impairments "seldom need to be taught material that is outside the curriculum for all other pupils" (p. 281). That is, the general education curriculum with its emphasis on academic skills is appropriate. However, several additional curriculum areas may benefit students with physical and health impairments. Mobility training (instruction in planning travel within the school building) may help some students conserve their limited energy. For secondary students, continued instruction in writing skills (handwriting, typing, or using computers and word processors) may be necessary. Other possible areas of benefit are driver's training, recreation and use of leisure time, and sex education. In many cases, these additions to the general education curriculum are offered as part of the student's special education program.

MEETING PHYSICAL AND HEALTH NEEDS

Students' physical and health needs are an important area of concern to any teacher. Students with identified physical and health impairments often require special diets, have restrictions placed on their physical activities, take medication during the school day, or require other health-related services (e.g., seizure, nutrition, or glucose monitoring; transfer and lifting) that are provided by the school nurse or other quali-fied person (Bigby, 2004; Mukherjee, Lightfoot, & Sloper, 2000). Often misconceptions arise about the needs of students with disabilities; an example of these is provided in the accompanying "Inclusion Tips for the Teacher" material.

The teacher's first step in meeting special physical and health needs is to learn as much as possible about each student's limitations and capabilities. One source of information is the assessment data collected by the assessment team. Recent evaluations will describe the current functioning levels of the student in important areas such as mobility, communication, academic achievement, classroom behavior, and social skills. Cross (1993) suggests that teachers contact the student's parents and the professionals who have worked with that student in the past to determine the best ways to meet physical and health needs. Figure 14-4 lists questions that teachers can ask to find out more about a student's specific requirements.

Medical personnel such as the school nurse and the student's physician are another excellent source of information (Bigby, 2004). Typically the school nurse helps the assessment and IEP teams interpret medical reports and translate medical findings into educationally relevant information. The nurse might explain why certain students have activity restrictions, how different medications affect students' classroom behavior, and what the reasons are for medical treatments and procedures. The nurse can also help teachers learn to deal with unusual medical situations, such as epileptic seizures in the classroom. If teachers are aware of the proper procedures to follow should a seizure occur, they will face the situation more calmly and be of more assistance to the student and the student's peers. To learn about what to do in case of a seizure, see the "Inclusion Tips for the Teacher" box on page 323.

When teachers are fully aware of the needs of students with physical and health impairments, the next step is consideration of what information to provide to other students in the class. This issue should be discussed with the prereferral and IEP teams, including the student's parents and, if appropriate, the student. In some cases, parents and students may be reluctant to have teachers inform students in the general education class about the specific nature of the problem. However, with disabilities and conditions that are obvious to a student's peers, the general education teacher or the school nurse should prepare the class by explaining the impairment and the ways in which it will affect the student's participation in class activities. Older students with special needs may want to give this explanation themselves. This approach should be encouraged because these students, as adults, will often have occasion to explain their disabilities to friends, acquaintances, and potential employers.

Information about physical and health needs of students should be presented factually, with emphasis not only on the student's problems but also the student's abilities. Any questions peers might have should be answered openly and accurately. This sharing of information is particularly important with young students, who may wonder whether

Inclusion Tips for the Teacher

Misconceptions About Students with Diabetes

Although everyone has heard of juvenile diabetes, and many think they understand the disease, there are still many classic misconceptions regarding the manifestations of the symptoms and the effect on learning and classroom behavior. The following is a list of classic myths.

Misconception 1:
The student will tell you when he or she is either high or low. This is not always true. Some students do not know when they are high or low. Even when they do know, students want to be the same as everyone else and do not want to draw attention to their condition. They are sometimes embarrassed to say that they are having a diabetic reaction. They would rather just ask quietly to go to the nurse. Also, students may not realize that the particular set of symptoms they are feeling is related to the diabetes.

Misconception 2:
Diabetes is affected only by food intake, and if a student eats properly, the diabetes will be under control. This is definitely not true. The level of the student's blood sugar is always a balancing act between the amount of activity, such as a basketball game or dancing, and food intake. In some students, activity can make their blood sugar level lower for up to 12 hours, whereas in others the sugar levels may get higher. In other words, one day the student may have close to normal sugar levels, yet even within the same day, the sugar level may change by 300 points due to a bad food choice or a strenuous activity.

Misconception 3:
Bathroom and nurse privileges can wait a few minutes. This is an emphatic, NO, they cannot wait! By the time a student is aware that he or she is low, the minutes of waiting may be crucial, and the student may soon go into a diabetic coma. As long as a student is astute enough to know the feelings of being low, then that is the time to go to check and take care of their needs. Conversely, the symptoms of high blood sugar are just as important to eradicate. Little learning can take place while that dry mouth is present, or while a student has to go to the bathroom.

Note: From *Misconceptions about Students with Diabetes* by the Juvenile Diabetes Research Foundation, n.d., New York: Author.

needing to ride in a wheelchair is contagious or whether being naughty causes seizures. The teacher should anticipate such concerns and attempt to quell apprehensions with a matter-of-fact explanation.

One subject that many teachers find difficult to discuss with their students is death. If there is a child or adolescent in the class with a terminal illness, this discussion may become necessary. Some thoughts on helping students deal with the death of a classmate are presented in Figure 14-5. Other resources that may be of interest are "Death in My Classroom?" by Postel (1986); another resource is the article on students with cancer by Spinelli (2004).

To accommodate the physical and health needs of students with special needs who are included in the general education classroom, alterations in some classroom routines and procedures may be necessary. These students should not be automatically excused from classroom activities simply because they have a disability. However, if they do have medical restrictions that prevent participation or if their disabilities truly impose limits, then classroom standards should be changed. Examples of appropriate modifications appear here:

- If students in wheelchairs or those with mobility problems travel slowly, they can be dismissed a few minutes early from class so that they can arrive at their next class or activity on time.
- Students should be allowed to take breaks during the day if these are necessary for rest, a visit to the bathroom, medication, or a special diet.
- Classroom procedures should be put in place for emergency situations. For example, in the case of a fire drill, someone should be assigned the responsibility of making certain that students with mobility problems are assisted in leaving the classroom quickly.
- For some students, it is hard to follow dietary or activity restrictions. The student who is on a low-carbohydrate diet may want to eat candy; one who is restricted to short exercise periods may want to join the others playing football at recess. These students should be provided with attractive alternatives to help them adhere to their medical regimens. For instance, instead of snacks for classroom rewards, activities can be used as reinforcers; or if students are unable to play sports, they can be appointed coaching assistants to the teacher.

Students with physical and health impairments may require some assistance, but it is equally important that these students be offered opportunities to learn to function independently. Often it is quicker and easier for the teacher or peers

FIGURE 14-4   Questions to Ask About Physical and Health Needs

Medical Concerns
- In addition to the child's primary disorder, does the child have additional problems such as seizures or diabetes? Does the child have any sensory disorders?
- Does the child take medication? How frequently, and in what amounts?
- If medication is taken, is the school authorized to administer the medication during school hours?
- What are the expected side effects of the medication? What are the other possible side effects?
- What procedures should be followed in the event of a seizure, insulin shock, diabetic coma, or other problem, with regard to contacting the child's parents or medical personnel?
- Should the child's activities be restricted in any way?

Travel
- How will the child be transported to school?
- Will the child arrive at the usual time?
- Will someone need to meet the child at the entrance to the school to provide assistance in getting the child on and off the vehicle?
- Will the child need special accommodations to travel within the school building or the classroom?

Transfer and Lifting
- What methods are used to get the child on and off the school bus?
- What is the preferred way to lift and transfer the child out of a wheelchair and onto a chair or to the floor?
- What cautions or limitations are there regarding transfer and lifting?
- How much help does the child really need with movement and transfer?

Communication
- If the child does not communicate verbally, what particular or unique means of communication does the child use?
- Does the child have a speech or language problem?
- Does the child use gestures? If so, what are they? Is a pointer used? Does the child use the same signal consistently for *yes, no,* or other common words?
- Can the child write? Type? How?
- Is an electronic communication aid used? If so, are there any special instructions necessary for the child to use it or for the teacher to understand and maintain it? Are fresh batteries or a charger needed?
- Can the child make his or her needs known to the teacher? How?

Self-Care
- What types of help does the child need with self-care activities such as feeding, dressing, toileting, and so forth?
- What equipment, such as a special feeding tray, does the child need?

Positioning
- What positioning aids or devices (braces, pillows, wedges, etc.) does the child use?
- What particular positions are the most useful for specific academic activities? What positions for resting?
- What positions are best for toileting, feeding, dressing, and other activities?
- Are there any other special aids or devices that I should know about?

Educational Needs
- What is the child's current level of achievement and of developmental and vocational functioning?
- What are the child's strengths and weaknesses?
- To what extent is achievement in school affected by physical disabilities?
- What medical considerations must be taken into account (that is, to what extent is the child able to participate in classroom activities)?
- What physical modifications to the classroom need to be made?
- What special equipment must be acquired?
- What related services will be needed?

Inclusion Tips for the Teacher

What to Do for Seizures

When tonic-clonic (also known as grand mal) seizures occur in the classroom, the teacher should remain calm, assist the child with the seizure, and assure the other students that their classmate is not in pain and that the seizure will last only a few minutes.

The Epilepsy Foundation of America (2001) suggests that the teacher take the following steps to safeguard the student having a tonic-clonic seizure:

First aid for a convulsive seizure protects the child from injury while the seizure runs its course. The seizure itself triggers mechanisms in the brain to bring it safely to an end. There are no other first aid steps that can hasten that process.

When this type of seizure happens, the teacher should:

- Keep calm. Reassure the other children that the child will be fine in a minute.
- Ease the child gently to the floor and clear the area around him of anything that could hurt him.
- Put something flat and soft (like a folded jacket) under his head so it will not bang against the floor as his body jerks.
- Turn him gently onto his side. This keeps his airway clear and allows any fluid in his mouth to drain harmlessly away.

DON'T try to force his mouth open.
DON'T try to hold on to his tongue.
DON'T put anything in his mouth.
DON'T restrain his movements.
- When the jerking movements stop, let the child rest until full consciousness returns.
- Breathing may have been shallow during the seizure, and may even have stopped briefly. This can give the child's lips or skin a bluish tinge, which corrects naturally as the seizure ends. In the unlikely event that breathing does not begin again, check the child's airway for any obstruction. It is rarely necessary to give artificial respiration.

Some students recover quickly after this type of seizure; others need more time. A short period of rest is usually advised. If the student is able to remain in the classroom afterwards, however, he or she should be encouraged to do so. Staying in the classroom (or returning to it as soon as possible) allows for continued participation in classroom activity and is psychologically less difficult for the student. If a student has frequent seizures, handling them can become routine once the teacher and classmates learn what to expect.

---

to do things for these students rather than allow them to do things for themselves. For example, a student may take 5 minutes to put on a jacket, whereas, with assistance, only a few seconds are required. However, such skills are acquired only with practice, and another's help may actually hinder learning.

MODIFYING THE PHYSICAL ENVIRONMENT

One major consideration in the education of students with physical and health impairments is the physical environment of the classroom and school. For some students with mobility problems, this may be the prime area in which modifications must be made. The following guidelines should help ensure that the physical environment is suitably arranged to accommodate students with disabilities:

- Evaluate the school and classroom for accessibility. Architectural barriers that restrict the travel of students in wheelchairs or students with physical limitations may prevent their full participation in the educational program. The most brilliant student cannot benefit from the best of programs if stairs are the only route to the classroom and the student uses a wheelchair. Use the check-

list in the accompanying "Inclusion Tips for the Teacher" box to evaluate the accessibility of your school building. If problems are evident, bring these to the attention of the school principal and the teams working with students with special needs.
- Arrange the classroom to facilitate mobility. Be sure sufficient room is allowed for students in wheelchairs or those who use crutches to travel from one work area to another.
- Make all areas and activities within the general education classroom accessible to students with mobility problems. This includes chalkboards, bookcases, storage cupboards, coatracks, art supplies, bulletin boards, display cases, computers, audiovisual equipment, activity centers, and so on.
- Consider the seating arrangements for students with special needs. Students in wheelchairs may need a special table or lapboard on which to write. Others may require special chairs that provide extra support; for instance, arm- or footrests can help students maintain an upright position for reading and writing activities. Check with the school nurse, special education teacher, or physical therapist for specific information about the positioning needs of each student.

| FIGURE 14-5 | When a Classmate Dies |

The Compassionate Friends is a nonprofit organization dedicated to providing support to those who have lost a child. The website of The Compassionate Friends offers these suggestions to teachers of children who have lost a brother, sister, or classmate:

When a student or a brother or sister of a student dies, teachers should examine their own feelings about death and grief. Share your feelings with the children within your class. Know that it's okay to cry, be sad or angry, and even smile. Children cannot be shielded from death and grief, and a thoughtful approach taken in the classroom can help them in the future.

If a student seeks you out to talk, be available and really listen. Hear with your ears, your eyes, and your heart. A warm hug says, "I know what happened and I care. I am here if you need me."

Be open and honest with your feelings. Create an atmosphere of open acceptance that invites questions and fosters confidence that you are concerned.

Encourage children to express their grief openly, but in ways that are not disruptive to the class or damaging to other students. Acknowledge the reality that grief hurts, but do not attempt to rescue the child (or the class, or yourself) from that pain. Be supportive and available to classmates who may want to know how they can help.

Provide a quiet, private place where a student may go whenever he or she feels a need to be alone. Almost anything that happens in the classroom may trigger tears. Respect the need that students have to grieve while helping classmates realize that grief is a natural and normal reaction to loss.

Help students to recognize that death is a natural part of life. Use such opportunities as a fallen leaf, a wilted flower, and the death of an insect, bird, or class pet to discuss death as a part of the life cycle. Explore feelings about death, loss, and grief through books while fostering discussions as a classroom family.

From *Suggestions for Teachers and School Counselors* by The Compassionate Friends. Copyright by The Compassionate Friends, USA. Retrieved November 22, 2004 from http://compassionatefriends.org/Brochures/teachers.htm

- Provide storage space for students' aids and equipment. For example, crutches should be within their owner's easy reach without presenting a hazard to others moving about the classroom. One method is to use crutch holders on the back or sides of a student's chair.
- Be sure that special equipment is kept in good working order. For example, check wheelchairs periodically for proper fit, comfort, and good repair. If there is need for modification or repair, notify the student's parents or the special educator who works with the student.
- For students with crutches, Glazzard (1982) suggests chairs with wheels to facilitate movement about the classroom; an office chair on rollers is appropriate. In rooms without carpets, crutches can slip when students use them to help themselves up from a sitting position. If assistance is needed, show their peers in the general education class how to use one of their feet as a brace to prevent the crutch from slipping.
- Students with limited strength or poor coordination may need easy access to work equipment. Desks with open storage space are preferable to those with a lid that must be raised. Pencil grooves on the desk top or a small box to hold pencils, pens, and erasers can help keep work materials close at hand.

ADAPTING INSTRUCTIONAL ACTIVITIES

In addition to meeting the physical and health needs and modifying the classroom environment, it may also be necessary to adapt instructional activities and procedures. Glazzard (1982) suggests several ideas for assisting students with poor coordination or inadequate muscle control:

- Tape the student's paper to the desk with a piece of masking tape applied to the top and bottom of the paper.
- Attach one end of a string to a pencil and the other end to the desk with a thumbtack or masking tape so that a student can easily retrieve a dropped pencil.
- Appoint a student to bring teacher handouts to the student's desk.
- Allow students to answer questions orally, or have them record answers for later evaluation. It is often laborious for some . . . students [with disabilities] to write their answers. If they have poor muscle control in their hands they must exert much more energy than the . . . [typical] students to write their answers.
- Make a copy of your lecture notes for the child with disabilities who writes slowly or with difficulty. It would also be simple for a classmate to insert a sheet of

Inclusion Tips for the Teacher

Checking Your School for Accessibility

Sidewalks

Are there curb cuts which provide access?
Is there a width of at least 48"?
Are they level, without irregular surfaces?
Is there a level area 5' by 5' if the door swings in?

Ramps

Are handrails present (32" high)?
Is the grade of the ramp less than a 1" rise in every 12" length?
Does it have a nonslip surface in all types of weather?

Doors (including elevator)

Is there an opening of at least 32" when door is open?
Are floors level for 5' in both directions of the door?
Are the thresholds navigable (1/2")?

Floor

Do hallways, stairs, and class areas have carpeting or some other non-slip surface?

Toilets

Is one stall 3' wide by 4'8" deep with handrails 33" high?
Is the toilet seat 20" high and urinals 19" from floor?
Are sinks, towel dispensers, mirrors, etc. 36–40" from floor?

Water fountains

Are the controls hand operated?
Is the spout in the front of the unit?
Are they mounted 26—30" from the floor?

Note: From "Environmental Alternatives for the Physically Handicapped" by B. B. Greer, J. Allsop, and J. G. Greer in *Implementing Learning in the Least Restrictive Environment* (pp. 128–129) by J. W. Schifani, R. M. Anderson, and S. J. Odle (Eds.), 1980, Austin, TX: PRO-ED. Copyright 1980 by PRO-ED. Reprinted by permission.

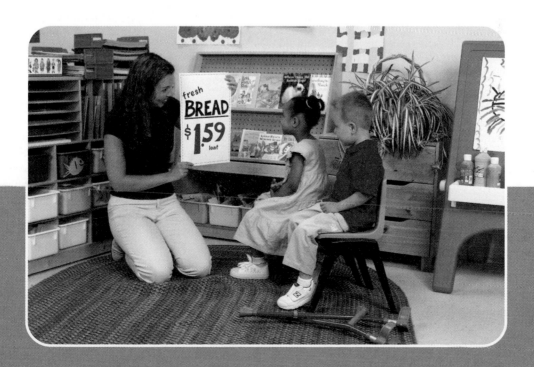

Spotlight on Technology

The IntelliKeys Keyboard

IntelliKeys is a versatile and easy-to-use alternative keyboard. The newest version, IntelliKeys USB, works with both Windows and Macintosh computers by plugging into the USB port. When IntelliKeys is installed, the standard keyboard and mouse remain operational.

Note: Used with permission of IntelliTools, Inc.

Note: Used with permission of IntelliTools, Inc.

IntelliKeys is called "the keyboard with the changing face." IntelliKeys comes with several standard "smart" overlays that fit on its surface. To use an overlay, the teacher simply places it on the keyboard; a bar code on the back of the overlay tells IntelliKeys which standard overlay is in place. Among the standard overlays included with the keyboard are an ABC overlay with the letters in alphabetical order, a QWERTY overlay with the letters arranged in standard keyboard format, a numbers overlay, one to manipulate the mouse, and one for web access.

The Set-Up overlay is used to configure IntelliKeys for students with special physical needs. Several adjustments are possible, including changing the response rate and repeat rate of keys. Also, keys such as Shift can be set so that the student presses them in sequence, not simultaneously (e.g., press Shift, then press the key of the letter to be capitalized). This helps students who have difficulty pressing two keys on the keyboard at the same time.

If the standard overlays do not meet the needs of a particular student, the teacher can easily create a new overlay and reprogram the IntelliKeys keyboard. The *Overlay Maker* program is used for this purpose. A talking word processor, *IntelliTalk*, is designed for use with IntelliKeys but works equally well with standard keyboards for students able to access them. Also available is *IntelliPics Studio*, a multimedia authoring tool. For more information, go to the IntelliTools website (http://www.intellitools.com).

---

carbon paper under his or her paper so that a duplicate set of notes can be supplied to the . . . student [with disabilities].

- Provide . . . students [with disabilities] with plastic or wooden rulers to use as bookmarks. They are easier to manipulate than paper markers.
- A . . . child [with disabilities] may use a shoulder bag to carry books and supplies from class to class. The book bag leaves arms free to handle crutches. (pp. 7–8)

Be creative, but remember that simple modifications are sometimes all that's necessary. Don't use clamps and tape if a paperweight will work just as well.

Many of the technological aids available to assist students with physical and health impairments in the general education program have been described in chapter 8. These devices help students compensate for the effects of their disabilities on mobility, communication, and academic learning. See the "Spotlight on Technology" feature for more information about switches and how these simple devices can provide access to a wide variety of activities in the classroom, at home, and in the community.

Some students with physical and health impairments may require further adaptations in instruction in order to keep pace in the general education classroom. When students miss school because of illness or medical treatment ex-

Spotlight on Technology

Switch Access

Because of physical impairments, some students cannot grip a pencil or pen, hold a book or turn its pages, or play with toys designed for typical children. However, students can access these activities if they have voluntary control over at least one type of motor movement. That movement can involve any part of the body: lifting a finger, raising an eyebrow, moving a hand outward from the body, pressing downward with a foot, or blowing through a tube. Movements such as these allow students to operate a switch, and switches can control a number of different devices.

Many types of switches are available, but each requires only a single action. With some switches, the student pushes or pulls; with others, he or she pinches or squeezes, sucks or blows, changes the position of a body part, or makes a small muscle movement such as flexing the muscles in a hand. Switches requiring a pushing motion are most common; see the photo for examples of push switches.

Note: Photo courtesy of AbleNet Inc.

Students who are switch users can control toys, appliances, and even the lights in their home or classroom. Here are some examples:

- *Battery-operated devices* can be converted for switch use by adding a device called a battery adapter. One source of battery adapters and similar assistive devices is AbleNet Inc. (http://www.ablenetinc.com).
- Some battery-operated devices already *adapted for switch use* are also available. Companies such as Enabling Devices/Toys for Special Children (http://www.enablingdevices.com) offer toys for switch users, while AbleNet Inc. offers battery-operated scissors, digital cameras, and clip-on fans.
- *Electrical appliances* can be accessed by switch with a device such as the AbleNet PowerLink®3 control unit. The appliance and the switch are plugged into the control unit and it in turn is plugged into a wall socket. With this configuration, a student could press the switch to turn on a television, blender, hair dryer, or fan.
- *Automatic pageturners* hold a book or magazine, then turn its pages when the user presses a switch.
- Some *environmental control devices* can be operated by switch. Options these devices offer include turning on lights and appliances, automatically dialing the telephone, and automatically releasing a door lock.
- Some *electronic communication devices* accept switch input. To select a message, the student presses a switch rather than a key on the device's keyboard.
- *Computers* can also be adapted for switch use.

---

tra instruction should be provided so that they do not fall far behind. For those who work slowly, the teacher can alter requirements for assignments and exams; more time can be allowed, or the amount of work can be reduced. If students have difficulty speaking or writing, other response modes can be substituted. For example, instead of writing, a student might type, tape-record, or dictate a response to a peer. By adapting instruction in these ways, the general education teacher creates a learning environment in which students with special needs have every chance for success. For more information about adaptations for one group of students with physical and health impairments, those with traumatic brain injuries, see the "Inclusion Tips for the Teacher" box

When a child or adolescent receives a head injury, the first interventions will be medical. It is likely that the student will be hospitalized for some period of time, then continue rehabilitation on an outpatient basis with professionals such as occupational and physical therapists. Depending on the length of hospitalization, the student may attend hospital school; once back at home, he or she may receive educational services from a teacher who visits several times a week. Planning the student's return to school requires a team approach; Mira and Tyler (1991) recommend collaboration between hospital staff, school personnel, and the student and his or her family. Consider, for example, the reentry plan developed for Barbara, a

Inclusion Tips for the Teacher

Working with Students with Traumatic Brain Injury

Students with traumatic brain injury (TBI) may have special needs in a variety of areas including physical, academic, socioemotional, and behavioral performance. Although teachers expect students who have received serious head injuries to experience difficulty with learning tasks (and, depending on the injury, with tasks requiring physical skills), they often do not anticipate the socioemotional consequences that can accompany this disability. Tucker and Colson (1992) describe the types of behaviors that some students with TBI may show:

- *Overestimates abilities*—Student brags to friends that he or she is still the fastest runner or will win the spelling bee.
- *Lowered social inhibition and judgment*—Student tries to touch and hug everyone.
- *Lowered impulse control*—Student interrupts teachers and peers at inappropriate times.
- *Faulty reasoning*—Student confronts peers and teachers with unfair accusations.
- *Lowered initiative*—Student will not begin a task without a reminder or assistance.
- *Depression*—Student appears uninterested and passive, even in activities once considered highly enjoyable. The emotional stress of the injury may be prolonged and can be overwhelming.
- *Fatigue*—This can be a result of both the injury and medication. Sleep disorders are common.
- *Acting-outbehaviour*—Student may yell or curse about being asked to do a task he or she doesn't want to do. He or she may walk out of class or knock over a desk.
- *Impulsivity*—Student may be unable to wait his or her turn at a drinking fountain or in the cafeteria. He or she may talk out during a test or speak before being called on.
- *Rigidity*—Student may be unable to adapt to changes in schedule or routine. Student may be unwilling to go to an assembly if it is scheduled during the regular math period.
- *Flat affect*—Student seems to have no voice inflections. Face seems expressionless, eyes seem vacant, he or she doesn't laugh or smile appropriately.
- *Low motivation*—What appears as low motivation may be confusion and inability to conceptualize and plan how to do the task.

- *Agitation and irritability*—Varying degrees of agitation and irritability may manifest themselves, such as becoming annoyed over picky things to becoming aggressive toward self or teachers.

The following recommendations should be considered when dealing with the student with traumatic brain injury in the school setting (National Information Center for Children and Youth with Disabilities, 1997a):

It will be important to determine whether the child needs to relearn material previously known. Supervision may be needed (i.e., between the classroom and restroom) as the child may have difficulty with orientation. Teachers should also be aware that, because the child's short-term memory may be impaired, what appears to have been learned may be forgotten later in the day. To work constructively with students with TBI, educators may need to:

- Provide repetition and consistency;
- Demonstrate new tasks, state instructions, and provide examples to illustrate ideas and concepts;
- Avoid figurative language;
- Reinforce lengthening periods of attention to appropriate tasks;
- Probe skill acquisition frequently and provide repeated practice;
- Teach compensatory strategies for increasing memory;
- Be prepared for students' reduced stamina and increased fatigue and provide rest breaks as needed; and
- Keep the environment as distraction-free as possible.

Initially, it may be important for teachers to gauge whether the child can follow one-step instructions well before challenging the child with a sequence of two or more directions. Often attention is focused on the child's disabilities after the injury, which reduces self-esteem; therefore, it is important to build opportunities for success and to maximize the child's strength.

Note: From "Traumatic Brain Injury: An Overview of School Re-Entry" by B. F. Tucker and S. E. Colson, 1992, *Intervention in School and Clinic*, 27, p. 201. Copyright 1992 by PRO-ED, Inc. Adapted with permission. Also from *Traumatic Brain Injury*, p. 2, National Information Center for Children and Youth with Disabilities, 1997a, Washington, DC. Not copyrighted.

16-year-old who sustained a severe head injury in an auto accident:

1. *Reduce course load:* Barbara enrolled in a limited number of academic courses with the understanding that others could be added
2. *Special scheduling:* Barbara took her most taxing courses early in the day, when she was most alert.

3. *Resource room:* Barbara would begin and end the day in the resource room with an aide present to provide assistance.
4. *Rest breaks:* Barbara was allowed to rest in the nurse's office when she became fatigued.
5. *Adaptive physical education:* Barbara would receive adaptive PE with an aide present to assist her at all times, because of the danger of her falling.

6. *Student aide:* One of her friends would assist her in moving from one class to the next.
7. *Extra set of books:* Barbara was given an extra set of books to keep at home, to avoid having to carry them back and forth.
8. *Lunch room provisions:* Because Barbara was still physically unsteady, someone would carry her lunch tray and have her seated before the lunchroom crowds arrived.
9. *Counseling:* Meetings were scheduled with the school counselor, and she was given the option for other meetings as needed.
10. *Other modifications:* Barbara would be allowed to have someone take notes for her in her class and tape her lectures, and she would be able to take her exams in a setting other than the regular classroom, with extra time allowed. She also would have use of a computer to complete assignments. (p. 7)

In this chapter, you have learned about the special needs of students with physical and health impairments. Methods for accommodating their disabilities within the general education classroom, modifying the physical environment, and adapting instructional activities have been suggested. The next chapter describes ways to make accommodations for the educational needs of students with sensory disabilities—those with visual and hearing impairments.

Things to Remember

- The special needs of students with physical and health impairments are diverse and vary with each individual. Some students require no educational adaptations, some require modification of the physical environment because they have limited energy or mobility, and others require modification of instructional activities. Medically fragile students may have special health management needs. However, the major goal for all of these students is circumvention of the restrictions imposed by their physical or health impairments.
- There are a great many conditions that can produce special physical and health needs. Among the most common are traumatic brain injuries, epilepsy, cerebral palsy, diabetes, and asthma.
- Some physical and health impairments are congenital, whereas others occur after birth and are due to injury, accident, or disease.

- The primary purpose of assessing physical and health impairments is to gather information about the impact of the disabilities on educational performance and participation in instructional activities. It is also important to consider the effect of the disabilities on the development of social, vocational, and leisure skills. Medical information is useful only when it is interpreted in relation to classroom functioning and special health needs.
- One primary need of students with physical and health impairments is the opportunity to develop independence. Students should be encouraged to learn the skills necessary to assume responsibility for their own needs.
- In the general education classroom, the teacher provides for physical and health needs, ensures an accessible environment, and accommodates learning difficulties by adapting instruction.

ACTIVITIES

1. Use the checklist provided in "Inclusion Tips for the Teacher: Checking Your School for Accessibility" to check the accessibility of one of your local public schools. Also consider whether instructional activities within the classroom are accessible. Can a student in a wheelchair write on the chalkboard? Remove a book from the bookcase? Hang up a coat? Use the classroom computer? If possible, borrow a wheelchair and travel through the school and several classrooms to gain a better understanding of what environmental features can act as barriers.

2. Visit a school with a special education program for students with physical and health impairments. Talk with the teacher and find out what types of disorders the students have. Are most of the students included in the general education program? How are these students accepted by their peers? What adaptations are necessary in the general education classroom?

3. Interview a young person or adult with a physical or health impairment. What impact does this condition have on daily life? That is, how does it affect routine tasks such as eating, dressing, shopping, traveling, and working? How do others react to the disability, and how does the person with disabilities deal with these reactions?

4. Identify a school setting that has a medically fragile student included in the general education program. Visit the school and observe the student's educational program, talk with the teachers involved, and review any concerns that may arise in implementing the program. Prepare a short report on your findings related to the appropriateness of the program and its success.

5. Learn more about agencies that provide services to those with physical and health impairments by visiting the websites of the United Cerebral Palsy Association, Epilepsy Foundation, of-America, Brain Injury Association, American Diabetes Association, or others mentioned in this chapter's "Window on the Web" feature. Several of these organizations provide information on branches in your community and can help you locate their local office. Determine what services these agencies provide and the information they provide for parents, teachers, and individuals with physical or health impairments. How does one go about obtaining additional information or services?

6. Locate journal articles that present suggestions for including students with physical and health impairments in the general education program. Good places to look include special education journals such as *Teaching Exceptional Children* or *Intervention in School and Clinic*.

CD-ROM Activities

From the information provided on the CD-ROM, the three classrooms featured in the video case studies do not appear to include any students with physical or health impairments. Think about what changes might be necessary in the sixth grade social studies class if such students were to be included, then respond to these questions:

- *What modifications might be needed in the classroom learning environment if a student who travels by wheelchair were to become a member of this social studies class?*

- *What might the teacher do to accommodate a student who has little stamina and tires easily? What about a student who has recently been diagnosed as diabetic?*

Teaching Students with Visual and Hearing Impairments

Kristina M. English
University of Pittsburgh

CHAPTER

15

Marco

Marco is an 11-year-old fifth grader who lost his right eye at the age of 3 from a tumor on the retina (retinoblastoma). He has a prosthetic for that eye, and subsequent cheomotherapy caused significant damage to his left eye. With correction, his left eye has a visual acuity of 20/120, which means he cannot read the writing on the classroom blackboard from the first row. His teacher therefore uses the board only minimally, and when she does, she reads everything aloud and also has the classroom aide enter the information into a computer to develop printouts in large type. Worksheets are also designed with large type, as are labels identifying the activities and equipment in the room. Marco uses a desk level magnifier to read material in smaller print. His reading skills are at grade level but he is 2 years behind in math skills. His handwriting is fairly illegible, so he is learning keyboarding skills with a "talking" computer program. He is a sociable child and liked by his peers, but recently he has been withdrawing from playground activity; because of his monocular vision, he is becoming wary of the increasingly unpredictable actions of unstructured play.

Beverly

Beverly is a 17-year-old junior in high school who has been blind since birth. She has attended general education classes since the first grade. She also has been active in choir, plays the guitar, and is in the drama club. This year, she attends general education classes for all of her academic subjects. In the regular physical education class, she excels in swimming and gymnastics. Beverly uses an electronic device to take class notes in Braille, transfers those notes to her computer, and completes her assignments with a talking word processor. In math, she uses a talking calculator and, when materials for her classes are not available in tape-recorded or Braille formats, two of her fellow

LOOKING AHEAD

You'll see portions of the IEPs for two of these students, Marco and Ahmeer, later in this chapter. Consider the questions that follow and look for possible answers as you read about strategies for arranging the learning environment and modifying instructional procedures for students with visual and hearing impairments.

- Identify the educational strengths of each of these students.
- If you were Marco's teacher, what strategies would you use to encourage his participation in playground games?
- Identify the types of support that Beverly uses to be a successful high school junior. What do you think her needs will be when she enters college?
- One of Ahmeer's educational needs is language development. What activities would you recommend to help this kindergartener practice classroom listening and speaking skills?
- Carly, like Beverly, is a junior this year. What supports is she using now? Would you predict that she'd need the same types of assistance in college?

 To answer these questions online, go to the Students' Stories module in Chapter 15 of the Companion Website.

students act as readers so that she can keep up with her reading assignments. Beverly receives special services from a mobility instructor who is helping her develop the skills needed to use public transportation to travel around town. An itinerant teacher of students with visual impairments provides assistance and special instructional materials to Beverly and also to her teachers when needed.

Ahmeer

Ahmeer is a 5-year-old boy with a moderate hearing loss in both ears, acquired at the age of 6 months from bacterial meningitis. He wears hearing aids on both ears and with them he can hear most speech sounds, if the environment is quiet. However, even low levels of noise will interfere with his ability to hear and concentrate. His language development is about a year behind his peers. A psychological assessment indicated his nonverbal intelligence to be within normal range. His speech is 50% intelligible to his teachers and 30% intelligible to unfamiliar listeners. His social skills are immature but are improving. He is not yet informing adults when the bat-

teries in his hearing aids are dead; instead, adults first observe inattentive behaviors and then check and replace the batteries.

Carly

Carly is a high school junior who has a congenital profound hearing loss in both ears. She has worn hearing aids since her loss was diagnosed at the age of 2; even though these are "power aids," she can only hear very loud sounds with them. People's voices are almost imperceptible to her, and she cannot understand anyone without using speechreading. She is mainstreamed in a small rural school, and has a full-time interpreter who uses the Signed Exact English (SEE) method. She is a strong student in many subjects, but does not enjoy math. She is an effective speechreader, and her speech is fairly intelligible, although soft and nasal. She has several close friends, all of whom learned to sign to communicate with her. At the age of 16, she obtained a cochlear implant for her right ear and is receiving auditory training to learn how to interpret auditory information. Carly plans to attend college on a softball scholarship.

Each of the students introduced in the "Students' Stories" has a specific and different hearing or visual impairment. They all, however, share a sensory loss. Such students can exhibit a wide range of abilities and can experience a variety of problems in school. Their visual and hearing impairments can be mild, moderate, or severe. Although their performance in most areas falls within a range similar to that of typical students, their school achievement is generally poorer than that expected for their age and grade. Students with visual impairments have difficulty with mobility and with reading print or other visual materials (Hazekamp & Huebner, 1989); those with hearing impairments experience problems in language development and oral communication (Luetke-Stahlman & Luckner, 1991). Many students with visual and hearing disabilities are also in need of social skills training (Eaton & Wall, 1999; Loeding & Greenan, 1999; Luckner & Carter, 2001; McGaha & Farran, 2001; Webster & Roe, 1998) and have other disabilities (e.g., learning disabilities) that often go undiagnosed (Easterbrooks, 1999; Layton & Lock, 2001). Both the degree of the disability and the specific characteristics of the student influence the nature and extent of the impairment.

Special education for students with sensory impairments may be provided in a special class or resource room; in many cases, students remain in the general education class and receive special instruction, materials, or equipment to supplement or enrich their educational program. The goal of special education for students with visual and hearing impairments is the same as it is for other students with disabilities—facilitation of learning. This may require teaching students to

make use of remaining sensory abilities or helping them learn to use other abilities to compensate for their disabilities.

Students with visual impairments are taught to rely on unaffected senses, such as hearing and touch. For example, they may learn to read **Braille,** to develop their listening skills, and to travel using **orientation** and **mobility** skills. For students with visual impairments with some usable vision, the educational program may include instruction in the use of **low-vision aids,** such as magnification devices, large-print reading materials, and new technological devices (Hasselbring & Glaser, 2000). Students with hearing impairments may require instruction in speech and language, training in other communication systems such as **speechreading** and **sign language,** or assistance in learning to use and care for **amplification devices** such as hearing aids and cochlear implants. It is generally necessary to provide **auditory training** to students with hearing impairments in order for them to develop listening skills by learning to use their residual hearing. In addition to the specific sensory needs of these students, adaptations in the general education classroom may be needed to give them the opportunity to participate in instructional activities and social interactions.

The characteristics of students with visual and hearing impairments, methods for adapting the classroom environment, and instructional procedures for the general education teacher are described in this chapter. The "For Your Information" feature provides readers with background information on individuals with sensory impairments and helps to familiarize teachers with the problems these students may encounter.

For Your Information

Students with Sensory Impairments

- In the 2000–2001 school year, special education services were provided to 25,975 students with visual impairments and 70,767 with hearing impairments. Compared with 1991–1992, this represented a 8% increase in the number of students with visual impairments and a 16% increase in the number of students with hearing impairments (U.S. Department of Education, 2002).

- About 1 student in 1,000 has a highly significant, noncorrectable visual impairment (Bowe, 2000), but only about 3 out of 10 of these students are considered blind for educational purposes (Reynolds & Birch, 1988).

- The loss of vision can slow the pace of intellectual and social development because it limits access to the normal range and variety of experiences (Caton, 1993).

- Students with visual impairments may be somewhat below grade level in school because of factors such as school absences for medical reasons and the difficulty of acquiring adequate instructional materials in Braille or large print (Caton, 1993).

- About 8 out of every 100 children in the United States have what is termed an educationally significant hearing loss (U.S. Public Health Service, 1990).

- Hearing losses are measured in decibels (dB) and can be categorized by severity; individuals with losses in the speech range may have a mild (20–40 dB), moderate (40–60 dB), severe (60–80 dB), or profound (80 dB or greater) hearing impairment.

- Amplification of unintelligible sounds may do nothing for the person with a hearing impairment except make the unintelligible sound louder.

- American Sign Language (called Ameslan or ASL) is the fourth most used language in the United States (after English, Spanish, and Italian). It employs both fingerspelling and signs, with its own system and rules for formation of signs; it is not merely a manual form of English (Cartwright, Cartwright, & Ward, 1995).

- Speechreading (or lipreading) is a system of interpreting a speaker's words and message without hearing the speaker's voice. The speechreader watches the lips, mouth, tongue, gestures, and facial movements of the speaker in order to decode the message. This approach is difficult because many words are identical in appearance. For example, the words *pie* and *buy* appear the same on the lips. According to Green and Fischgrund (1993), "only 30% to 40% of the sounds in our language are produced with visible lip movements, so the speechreader has many gaps to fill in" (p. 293).

- Approximately 55% of the students with visual and hearing impairments spend most of their school day in the general education classroom; about 13% of the students in these categories are school dropouts (U.S. Department of Education, 2002).

- It is not accurate to presume that persons with sensory losses develop extraordinary perceptions with unimpaired senses. That is the "myth of sensory compensation."

INDICATORS OF VISUAL AND HEARING IMPAIRMENTS

The general education teacher plays an important role on the various teams assigned to assist students with visual and hearing impairments. Many of these students are initially identified and referred for consideration for special education services by the general education classroom teacher. In addition, general education teachers assist in collecting information about their students' classroom performance and in coordinating the services provided by various specialists.

Visual and hearing impairments can be congenital or **adventitious.** An adventitious impairment is one that is acquired as a result of illness or accident. Students with severe impairments are generally identified by parents or a physician prior to entrance into school; those with impairments that are milder or that result from illness or accident may be identified during the school years. Students who acquire impairments after they have experienced normal vision or hearing (with normal development of speech and language) are usually affected less adversely than those whose impairments are present at birth.

The extent of a vision or hearing loss is determined only after all possible corrections have been made. If a sensory impairment can be corrected so that the student has adequate vision or hearing, then the student is not considered to have a disability and be in need of special education. If impairments remain after corrections have been made (e.g., eyeglasses, hearing aids, and all possible medical treatments, including surgery), then the student is considered to have a disability.

Students with visual impairments may be **blind** or **partially sighted.** These designations are based on measures of visual acuity (the ability to resolve very fine detail) and may have little educational relevance, just as an IQ score is not always an accurate predictor of academic achievement. Students who are blind are defined legally as (1) those whose visual acuity is 20/200 or less in the better eye with the best possible correction or (2) those whose field of vision is restricted to an arc of 20 degrees or less at its widest point (National Information

Center for Children and Youth with Disabilities, 2001b). A larger group is made up of students who are partially sighted, whose vision in the best eye is between 20/70 and 20/200 after correction. The designation of 20/200 roughly indicates that the individual can see at 20 feet what a person with normal vision can see at 200 feet. Grayson (n.d.) indicates that "the American Foundation for the Blind prefers that the term blindness be reserved for a complete loss which can accurately be determined by ophthalmic measurements" (p. 1).

Legal terminology to describe visual impairments often lacks meaning for the educator. Instead, teachers are primarily concerned with a child's functional use of residual vision and how it is used when light, locations, and contrasts change. Teachers need to know whether the student's remaining vision will allow learning with visually presented material, whether learning must be through other senses, or what combination of these approaches will be most beneficial (Corn & Webne, 2001). Many students who are legally blind are not considered **educationally blind.** Some are able to read regular print; others can read print that is enlarged typographically or viewed through a magnifying device. Because of the limited educational relevance of the legal terms and acuity scores, teachers should be aware that it is important to acquire information on the visual functioning of students included in the general education program; assumptions regarding their ability to use their vision should not be based on a label or acuity score.

Students with visual impairments who have not been identified before entering school are often located as a result of the periodic vision screening conducted for all students in a school. The general education teacher can play an important role by carefully observing students in the classroom. The signs and symptoms of vision problems listed in Figure 15-1 can alert the teacher to students in need of further investigation.

Students with hearing impairments may be **deaf** or **hard of hearing.** Students who are deaf (about 10% of those with hearing loss) are not able to use their hearing to understand speech, even with a hearing aid. Students who are hard of hearing (90% of those with hearing loss) have a significant hearing loss in one or both ears that requires some special adaptations; they are able to use hearing to understand speech, often through the use of hearing aids (Heward, 2003).

Conductive hearing losses are caused by interference with the transmission of sound from the outer ear to the inner ear; this interference can occur in either the outer or the middle ear. Individuals with this type of loss are usually treated by medication or surgery, but occasionally hearing aids are prescribed. An impairment to the auditory nerve or inner ear results in a sensorineural hearing loss. Surgery and medication are generally less effective in treating this type of loss; most individuals with a **sensorineural hearing loss** will benefit from the use of hearing aids. A mixed hearing loss involves both conductive and sensorineural impairments. Functional hearing losses have no known organic origin, can be due to emotional factors, and are generally not improved by sound amplification (National Information Center for Children and Youth with Disabilities, 2001a).

The types of hearing losses described above usually occur in both ears; however, some children have a **unilateral hearing loss,** with normal hearing in one ear and a hearing loss in the other. For years, conventional wisdom assumed that "one good ear was enough"; however, research has shown that children with unilateral hearing loss are 10 times more likely to fail a grade

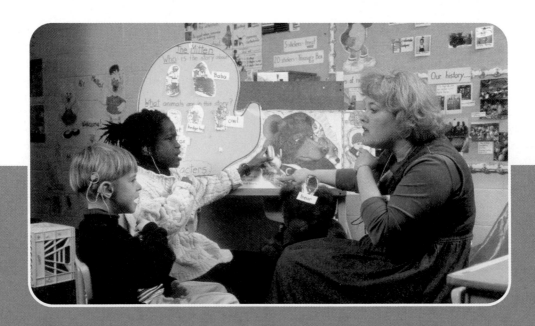

FIGURE 15-1	Signs of Possible Vision Problems

Prevent Blindness America (2001) urges teachers and parents to watch for these signs that a child might be experiencing vision problems.

Behavior

- Rubs eyes excessively.
- Squints, shuts, or covers one eye.
- Tilts or thrusts head forward, or holds head in unusual angles while reading.
- Has difficulty with reading or other close-up work.
- Holds objects close to eyes.
- Blinks more than usual or is irritable when doing close-up work.
- Moves head rather than eyes while reading.
- Is unable to see distant things clearly.
- Demonstrates aversion to glare or bright light.
- Has difficulty copying from blackboard and books.

Appearance

- Crossed or maligned eyes
- Red-rimmed, encrusted, or swollen eyelids
- Inflamed or watery eyes
- Recurring styes (infections) on eyelids
- Color photos of eyes show white reflection instead of typical red or no reflection
- Uncontrolled eye movements or drooping eyelids

Complaints

- Eyes itch, burn, or feel scratchy
- Cannot see well
- Dizziness, headaches, nausea following close-up work
- Blurred or double vision

If students exhibit any of these problems for a period of time, they should be referred to the school nurse or appropriate special education personnel. Regular eye exams are important because some eye problems have no signs or symptoms.

FIGURE 15-2	Signs of Hearing Problems

The American Academy of Otolaryngology (1995) provides these indicators of possible hearing problems.

Behavior

- Does not accurately turn in the direction of a soft voice on the first call.
- Is not alert to environmental sounds.
- Does not respond to sound or does not locate where sound is coming from.
- Does not sound like or use speech like other children of similar age.
- Does not show consistent growth in the understanding and the use of words to communicate.
- Seems consistently inattentive; says "what?" or "huh?" more than other children.
- Misunderstands verbal directions.

Appearance

- Drainage or blood from ears
- Continual tugging of ears
- Mouth breathing

Complaints

- Cannot hear well
- Tired

Hearing loss is frequently called an "invisible disability" because the usual site of damage is beyond the eardrum, and indicators are more behavioral than physical. As with suspicions about visual impairment, refer children exhibiting these symptoms to the school nurse or appropriate special education personnel. Regularly scheduled hearing screenings are usually required by state law because hearing loss can be difficult to detect.

by age 10 than children without hearing loss (Bess, Dodd-Murphy, & Parker, 1998); therefore, it is now considered best practice to keep these children on a watch list in order to identify problems as soon as they develop (English & Church, 1999).

Frequency and intensity are two of the physical characteristics of sound used in measuring hearing loss. Frequency, or pitch, is expressed in a unit called hertz (Hz). An example of pitch is the musical scale; as the voice ascends the scale, pitch or frequency increases. Intensity, or loudness, is measured in decibels (dB). These symbols often appear on reports of students' hearing losses, with a loss indicated in decibels at each hertz

level. It is important for the educator to consider a hearing loss in relation to speech sounds. Most speech is between 500 and 2,000 Hz in frequency and between 40 and 65 dB in intensity (Green & Fischgrund, 1993). A student with a 75- to 80-dB loss in the 1,000- to 4,000-Hz range would have a severe loss that would affect his or her ability to understand speech.

In most parts of the United States, congenital hearing losses are detected via newborn screening procedures. Acquired hearing loss and hearing loss not identified at birth are usually diagnosed during the preschool years by parents or physicians. Finally, hearing losses are often detected during annual school hearing screenings. By carefully observing the behaviors of students, the classroom teacher can be alert to signs and symptoms that indicate possible hearing impairments. Warning signals to watch for are listed in Figure 15-2;

these and other indicators of visual or hearing impairments may be noticed by the teacher. Students who do not respond normally to visual or auditory stimuli are potential candidates for special education assessment.

ASSESSMENT PROCEDURES

When students are suspected of having visual or hearing impairments, they are referred to the prereferral team to determine if appropriate interventions can be implemented in the general education classroom. If this team determines that a more extensive review is needed, a referral is made to the special education assessment team. An assessment plan is then developed and presented to the parents, who must grant permission before it is implemented. This assessment should determine the student's intellectual functioning, academic achievement, and communicative status. It must be conducted in an appropriate mode of communication (e.g., Braille or sign language when appropriate) and must assess all areas that relate to the suspected sensory impairment. The assessment should determine the student's capabilities and identify factors that are interfering with school performance.

Assessments of students with visual and hearing impairments can be conducted by a variety of professionals. Several—such as special education teachers of students with visual or hearing impairments, ophthalmologists, and audiologists—may assess only this type of special student. Many instruments commonly used to evaluate the ability or achievement of other students with disabilities may be inappropriate for students with sensory impairments. To obtain accurate and reliable information about these individuals, measures must be selected carefully and, if necessary, adapted to allow students to circumvent their disabilities.

The intellectual functioning of pupils with visual and hearing impairments can be assessed with adapted, modified, or specially designed measures. Verbal portions of the *Wechsler Intelligence Scale for Children* have been used to assess students with visual impairments. In addition, some measures have been specifically designed to provide an indication of the capability of students with visual or hearing impairments. For example, the *Perkins-Binet Intelligence Scale* (Davis, 1980) is designed for students with visual impairments who are ages 2 to 22. This adaptation of the *Stanford-Binet Intelligence Scale* has two forms, one for those with nonusable vision and another for those with usable vision. Approximately 25% to 30% of the items are performance based, and the test yields both mental age and intelligence quotients. The *Hiskey-Nebraska Test of Learning Aptitude* (Hiskey, 1966) is a measure of the learning aptitude of individuals between the ages of 3 and 16 who are deaf.

Many academic assessment instruments for sighted or hearing students can be administered with little or no modification to individuals who are partially sighted or hard of hearing.

Students with more severe impairments may require adaptations, such as communicating in sign language or transcribing portions of the test into Braille. In addition, students can be allowed extra time to finish portions of a test if this is necessary to reflect their skill levels adequately. However, if modifications have been made in the administration procedures of standardized tests, they must be noted in the assessment report.

Vision and hearing assessments are normally conducted by specially trained individuals. These assessments can be useful in indicating the extent of an impairment and determining possible remedies (e.g., glasses, low-vision aids, hearing aids) that can reduce the impact of the impairment on the student's educational performance. Students who are partially sighted should be encouraged to have their vision rechecked frequently because their visual efficiency may improve and adjustments may be needed in their optical aids or the type size used for their materials (Harley & Lawrence, 1984). Ophthalmologists are medical doctors who specialize in the diagnosis and treatment of defects and diseases of the eye. An optometrist is a nonmedical practitioner licensed to measure refractive errors and eye muscle disturbances. Both of these professionals measure vision and prescribe corrective lenses, but only the ophthalmologist may perform surgery, prescribe medication, and administer other medical treatments. Medical doctors concerned with hearing impairments are the otolaryngologist (who diagnoses and treats ear, nose, and throat disorders) and the otologist (who specializes in the treatment of ear diseases and disorders).

The **Snellen chart** is commonly used for vision screening of students; its purpose is to identify students with possible visual acuity problems who are in need of a more thorough evaluation by a vision specialist. The chart is composed of rows of letters of various sizes, which students must identify from a preset distance. For young children, the Snellen chart contains only the letter E in various sizes and orientations; this allows the child to point in the direction the E is facing rather than name various letters. Hearing is assessed with a device called an **audiometer.** The student listens to tones or speech delivered via air or bone conduction at a variety of frequencies and intensities.

A mobility specialist may meet with students with visual impairments to assess their orientation and mobility skills and to determine their need for training in these areas. Other specialists may evaluate students' ability to use low-vision aids or read printed material. For students with hearing impairments, the speech-language pathologist is the professional who determines current functioning in oral communication and language development. The educational audiologist is responsible for ensuring that hearing aids and other amplification systems are functioning properly.

Direct observation and informal assessment by the teacher can provide a great deal of information for the prereferral and assessment teams. Much of the data needed to determine a student's requirements for special services and to prepare the goals for the IEP can most effectively be gathered by the teacher or specialists while the student is performing under typical conditions in the general education classroom.

SPECIAL SERVICES

Information gathered through the assessment process is used by the IEP team to develop a student's IEP. The IEPs of students with visual and hearing impairments usually contain several goals. Students with visual impairments often have goals in the use of vision aids, improvement of listening skills, development of Braille reading and writing ability, notetaking, mobility, and academic skill areas. Figure 15-3 shows portions of an IEP for Marco, one of the students introduced at the beginning of this chapter. Marco is a fifth grader who is partially sighted.

Students with hearing impairments may have goals in speechreading, speech and language, auditory training, sign language, and the use of amplification devices. Ahmeer, the kindergarten student described at the start of this chapter, has a moderate bilateral hearing loss that resulted from a disease in early childhood. A portion of Ahmeer's IEP appears in Figure 15-4.

The majority of students with sensory impairments spend some portion of their school day included in the general education program. Many receive services from an itinerant special education teacher to supplement the activities provided in the general education class. For those spending the entire day in the general education classroom, teacher consultants may work with the general education teacher to help design needed classroom adaptations and provide special materials or equipment.

FIGURE 15-3 IEP Goals and Services for Marco

Annual Goals

1. By the end of the year, Marco will achieve 90% accuracy levels in keyboarding skills, in order to take notes throughout the day with a laptop computer.
   Person responsible: Resource teacher

2. By the end of the year, Marco will decrease his math errors by correcting his work with a talking calculator.
   Person responsible: Resource teacher

3. By the end of the year, Marco will increase his participation in physical education within the context of a predictable team-sport activity.
   Person responsible: Adaptive physical education teacher

4. By the end of the year, Marco will successfully complete all requirements for fifth grade.
   Persons responsible: General education teacher, resource teacher

Amount of Participation in General Education
Marco will attend the entire day in the fifth grade with the exception of one hour per day in the special education program.

Special Education and Related Services

1. Marco will receive special education services from the resource teacher (annual goals 1, 2, and 4) for one hour daily.

2. Marco will receive special education services from the adaptive physical education teacher (annual goal 3) during regularly scheduled PE classes.

FIGURE 15-4   IEP Goals and Services for Ahmeer

Annual Goals

1. By the end of the year, Ahmeer will demonstrate language skills appropriate for his age.
   Persons responsible: General education teacher, speech-language pathologist, and itinerant teacher for children who are deaf and hard of hearing.

2. By the end of the year, Ahmeer will use speech with 80% intelligibility as rated by familiar listeners.
   Person responsible: Speech-language pathologist.

3. By the end of the year, Ahmeer will assume responsibility for the maintenance of his hearing aids and his classroom FM system, including checking batteries and replacing dead batteries (a fundamental self-advocacy skill).
   Persons responsible: General education teacher, speech-language pathologist, educational audiologist.

4. By the end of the year, Ahmeer will successfully complete all kindergarten requirements.
   Persons responsible: General education teacher, speech-language pathologist, itinerant teacher.

Amount of Participation in General Education

Ahmeer will spend the entire day in the kindergarten classroom with the exception of one hour a day in special education and related services.

Special Education and Related Services

1. Ahmeer will receive special education services from the speech-language pathologist (annual goals 1–4) for one hour, 3 days a week.

2. Ahmeer will receive special education services from the itinerant teacher (goals 1 and 4) for one hour, 2 days a week.

3. The educational audiologist will provide inservicing and equipment maintenance for all amplification devices across the school year, and will teach Ahmeer how to manage these systems (annual goal 3).

Other students may attend a resource room. Very young students or those with multiple or more severe disabilities may spend the majority of their school day in a special class and participate in general education classroom activities when there is some assurance that they can have successful involvement and progress in the general curriculum. Students with sensory impairments receive services from a variety of specialists, such as speech-language pathologists, adapted physical education teachers, and vocational rehabilitation counselors. The school system or outside agencies may offer these students special programs, such as instruction in daily living skills or recreational activities. The special services required for different students with similar impairments may vary considerably. For information on internet resources about students with sensory impairments, see the "Window on the Web".

In making decisions about including students with disabilities in the general education program, the views of parents and those of students themselves must be considered. In the past few years, for example, many members of the Deaf community have become advocates for special schools for students who are deaf. This position reflects a growing awareness of Deaf culture and the Deaf community's pride in that culture. For example, in 1988, students at Gallaudet University, a university for students who are deaf, staged a protest until trustees named a person who was deaf as president. Another example is the testimony given by Jesse Thomas, a 15-year-old who is deaf, before the National Council on Disabilities:

> I think I have to explain that I am not disabled, I'm just deaf. Deaf persons are a minority group. They use American Sign Language (ASL) and are part of the Deaf Culture. One of the main reasons that mainstreaming is not good is because mainstreaming lacks Deaf Culture and ASL. I can't really explain Deaf Culture. I do know that Deaf Culture makes me proud of who I am—DEAF. (as cited in Heward, 2000, p. 396)

CLASSROOM ADAPTATIONS

Students with visual or hearing impairments who are in the general education program frequently require adaptations in the arrangement of the learning environment and in the structure of instructional procedures. Extensive curricular adaptations are typically not needed. Although additional hands-on experiences may be beneficial for students with sensory impairments, other adjustments correspond to those generally provided for typical students.

The idea of adapting instruction for students with visual and hearing impairments is not new. In 1900, for example, Helen Keller wrote specifications for her own classroom adaptations. Much has been written about the obviously gifted Helen Keller, who had severe impairments in both hearing and vision. Her familiar story and struggle to adapt to a world she could neither see nor hear is captured in the letter she wrote to the chairman of the academic board at Radcliffe College. In this letter, she asks for adaptations to the regular, not special, college classroom.

> Dear Sir:
>
> As an aid to me in determining my plans for study the coming year, I apply to you for information as to the possibility of my taking the regular courses in Radcliffe College.
>
> Since receiving my certificate of admission to Radcliffe last July, I have been studying with a private tutor, Horace, Aeschylus, French, German, Rhetoric, English History, English Literature and Criticism, and English Composition.
>
> In college I should wish to continue most, if not all, of these subjects. The conditions under which I work require the presence of Miss Sullivan, who has been my teacher and

Window on the Web

Websites About Sensory Impairments

Websites About Visual Impairments

- American Council of the Blind (www.acb.org)
- American Foundation for the Blind (www.afb.org)
- American Printing House for the Blind, Inc. (www.aph.org)
- Blindness Resource Center (www.nyise.org/blind.htm)
- National Association for Visually Handicapped (www.navh.org)
- National Eye Institute (www.nei.nih.gov)
- National Federation of the Blind (www.nfb.org)
- National Library Service for the Blind and Physically Handicapped (NLS), The Library of Congress (www.loc.gov/nls)

Websites About Hearing Impairments

- Alexander Graham Bell Association for the Deaf and Hard of Hearing (www.agbell.org)
- American Society for Deaf Children (www.deafchildren.org)
- Beginnings for Parents of Children who are Deaf or Hard of Hearing (http://www.beginningssvcs.com)
- Educational Audiology Association (www.edaud.org)
- Laurent Clerc National Deaf Education Center and Clearinghouse (clerccenter.gallaudet.edu)
- National Association of the Deaf (www.nad.org)
- National Institute on Deafness and Other Communication Disorders (www.nidcd.nih.gov)
- Self Help for Hard of Hearing People (www.shhh.org)

For more information, go to the Web Links module in Chapter 15 of the Companion Website.

companion for thirteen years, as an interpreter of oral speech and as a reader of examination papers. In college, she, or possibly in some subjects someone else, would of necessity be with me in the lecture room and at recitations. I should do all my written work on a typewriter, and if a Professor could not understand my speech, I could write out my answers to his questions and hand them to him after the recitation.

Is it possible for the College to accommodate itself to these unprecedented conditions, so as to enable me to pursue my studies at Radcliffe? I realize that the obstacles in the way of my receiving a college education are very great—to others they may seem insurmountable; but, dear Sir, a true soldier does not acknowledge defeat before the battle. (Keller, 1965, p. 151)

The classroom adaptations described in chapter 14 are similar to those required for students with visual and hearing impairments. The teacher should be sure to explain the special student's impairment(s) to the other students in the general education class. A careful explanation facilitates the acceptance of students with disabilities by their peers. However, teachers and students should be careful not to become overprotective of students with disabilities; they must be encouraged to develop independence.

ARRANGING THE LEARNING ENVIRONMENT

Students with sensory impairments may require adaptations in the arrangement of the classroom, seating patterns, and other factors related to lighting, sound transmission, and proximity to activities. The following are suggestions for general education classroom teachers working with students with visual impairments:

- Use a clock orientation to help students become familiar with the room and to clarify locations: for example, the teacher's desk is at 12 o'clock, the bookshelves are at 3 o'clock, computers are at 6 o'clock, the door is at 11 o'clock (Smith, Polloway, Patton, & Dowdy, 1998)
- Be sure students' tables or desktops are large enough for Braillewriters and other equipment (Maron & Martinez, 1980).
- Copyholders, easels, and adjustable tops on desks help students to maintain good posture for close-eye activities (Harley & Lawrence, 1984).
- Provide an accessible storage area with adequate space for large pieces of equipment such as optical devices or reading stands and Braille or large-print books (Torres & Corn, 1990).
- Do not place students who are partially sighted where they must face the glare of a primary source of light, such as a window (Pasanella & Volkmor, 1981). However, lighting should be adequate; some students may need additional light from a source such as a desk lamp or a window.
- Seat students so that they are able to participate in activities with other class members. A flexible seating arrangement will allow students to be close to different classroom activities or to adjust the amount of light available as needed. For example, a student might relocate to obtain a better view of the teacher, the chalkboard, or the projection screen, or to obtain a greater amount of light for a particular activity.
- Use copy machines to enlarge print materials for students with visual impairments (Torres & Corn, 1990).
- Allow students to become oriented to the classroom; permit them to explore (Maron & Martinez, 1980).
- Attend to the auditory environment. Children with visual impairment depend on what they hear to compensate for what they do not see, so reduce or eliminate auditory distractions (squeaks from a hamster wheel, buzzing from a loose fluorescent light bulb, etc.). Wait until classroom noise subsides before giving oral instructions. Identify fixed noise sources (for example, the ticking of a clock) to help the child's orientation to the physical space (Webster & Roe, 1998).
- Prepare and rehearse procedures for emergency situations (fire drill evacuations, etc.).
- Ask the child what assistance or help is needed.

Other suggestions for developing the mobility skills of students with visual impairments are listed in the "Inclusion Tips for the Teacher" section.

Students with hearing impairments require other types of adaptations to facilitate their successful inclusion in the general education program:

- The student's seat should be away from noise and close to the area where instruction takes place.
- Seating arrangements should permit the student to face the teacher and other students. Teachers should take care not to turn their back to students with hearing impairments while speaking. During a class discussion, it may be necessary to allow the student to move around the room to be able to see those who are speaking (Reynolds & Birch, 1988).
- If an interpreter is provided, that individual should be seated near the student. The student and the interpreter should have some flexibility in where they choose to sit.
- Speakers should avoid standing with a direct light behind them; if the teacher stands in front of a window, it may not be possible to see what he or she is saying (English, 1995).
- Keep classroom and background noise to a minimum; when students wear hearing aids, all sounds are amplified (Reynolds & Birch, 1988).
- Verify that fire alarm/emergency signals have a visual component (for example, strobe light) in addition to the customary auditory component.
- Label items in the classroom to help in the development of vocabulary for the young student. This practice can also help other students in learning to read (Glazzard, 1980).

For many students with sensory impairments, special assistive aids and equipment (such as those described in chapter 8) are helpful, and students should be encouraged to use the special devices that have been provided. Become acquainted with one type of device designed to help students with visual impairments communicate with others by consulting the "Spotlight on Technology" feature.

Other adaptations are often required to meet the individual needs of students. Special educators, the students' parents, and often the students themselves can give suggestions for such adaptations. Careful observation of students in a classroom setting provides information on how the educational environment can best be modified.

MODIFYING INSTRUCTIONAL PROCEDURES

When students with visual or hearing impairments are present in the general education classroom, it may be necessary for the teacher to modify instructional procedures. These adaptations depend on the individual needs and capabilities of the students with special needs and vary from minimal to extensive. Spe-

Inclusion Tips for the Teacher

Mobility Skills for Students with Visual Impairments

For students who are blind, or those with limited vision, the orientation and mobility specialist provides instruction in how to travel from one place to another. According to Mandell and Fiscus (1981), "*Orientation* refers to the ability to understand the relationship between self and environment through intact sensory input. *Mobility* refers to one's ability to travel safely and independently through the physical environment" (p. 209, emphasis added). Independent travel is an important skill for individuals who are blind, and several types of travel aids are available: a long cane, a guide dog (for older students and adults), and electronic devices that signal the presence of obstacles in the path of travel. The general education teacher can support and supplement the training provided by the mobility specialist, as Craig and Howard (1981) suggest:

- Eliminate unnecessary obstacles; inform students of changes in room arrangement or of any temporary obstacles, such as a portable movie screen.
- Keep doors completely closed or completely open to eliminate the possibility of the student running into a partially open door.
- Initially, allow the student to travel with a companion to frequently used rooms, such as the library, restroom, and auditorium. Discuss the route, pointing out right and left turns and any distinguishing landmarks.
- Allow the student to move about freely until he has familiarized himself with the room or route.
- Discourage reliance upon sighted guides once the student has demonstrated the ability to travel independently.

- If necessary, make provisions for a sighted guide for fire drills, field trips, assemblies, and seating in rooms that ordinarily have unassigned seating. (p. 191)

Recommendations for persons who will act as sighted guides are provided by the Arkansas Enterprises for the Blind (n.d.):

- When offering assistance to a . . . person [who is blind], be direct. Speak in a normal tone. Simply ask: "May I be of help?" Address him directly; this helps him locate you.
- Never "grab" . . . [the] arm [of a person who is blind]; he can't anticipate your movements if you do. Permit him to take your arm and say: "Here's my left arm" or the right, as the case may be. He knows, then, how to take your arm and he will respond to your motion much as a dancer follows a partner.
- In walking with a . . . person [who is blind] proceed at a normal pace; hesitate slightly before stepping up or down; don't drag him over the curb. After crossing a street, see that he is started in the direction he wants to take, and caution him of any unusual obstructions ahead.
- In showing a . . . person [who is blind] to a chair, place his hand upon the back of it; don't try to push him into it. His touch will tell him the type, width and height of the chair. (p. 2)

cialists are generally available to assist the teacher in developing and implementing modified instructional strategies.

Students with visual impairments who are included in the general education program may require instruction from a specialist to acquire the skills needed to use low-vision aids or to read and write Braille. In addition, some students need special materials or equipment; others use only those materials available in the classroom. Suggestions for teachers working with students with visual impairments in a general education setting are listed here:

- Change instructional procedures only when absolutely necessary. Curricular goals should remain the same for typical and special students (Blankenship & Lilly, 1981).
- Many of the print materials used in the general education classroom may be available in other formats. Work with the student's special education teacher to locate large-print, Braille, or tape-recorded texts. Text in electronic text, often called **e-text,** may also be available for downloading from the Internet (Edyburn, 2003). Start looking well ahead of the time when materials are needed to en-

sure their availability. For information about sources of materials for students with visual (and hearing) impairments, see Figure 15-5.

- When descriptive language is used to interpret events that involve facial expressions or gestures, students are less likely to be off task (Spenciner, 1992).
- Allow adequate time for students with visual impairments to complete reading assignments; some students may need extra time to locate their materials, find the starting place, and complete the task (Spenciner, 1992). Some teachers report needing to provide 50% to 100% more time to complete some assignments (Mastropieri & Scruggs, 2004).
- Encourage students to use a word processor or to type communications that must be read by sighted individuals; examples include written reports, homework assignments, and personal correspondence. The special education teacher may provide word processing and typing instruction; the general education teacher can help by allowing students access to a computer or a typewriter in the classroom (Hasselbring & Glaser, 2000).

Spotlight on Technology

Braille Personal Notetakers

Braille personal notetakers are portable electronic devices that allow students who are blind to take notes in class, complete written assignments, and write answers to exam questions. One example is the Braille Lite M20 from Freedom Scientific (www.freedomscientific.com). It is lightweight (approximately 2 pounds), quite small (8.25 by 5 by 1.5 inches), and is powered by a battery or household current. Its eight-key keyboard is designed for typing Braille, not standard text. Two keys are used for word processing. The other six correspond to the six dots found in Braille; the student presses one, two, three, or more keys depending on the Braille character he or she wants to type.

Braille Lite contains a built-in speech synthesizer so that it can read the student's text aloud. It also converts Braille to standard text that can be edited with the full range of standard word processing features (including spellcheck) provided by the Braille Lite. This notetaker also has a built-in modem and supports standard e-mail services, can file share with a personal computer, and allows the use of removable compact flash storage cards. In addition, the student can use the built-in talking clock, calendar, scientific calculator, stop watch, and telephone directory.

Another feature of the Braille Lite is its dynamic Braille display. This is a tactile display; small pins corresponding to the dots in the Braille cell are raised electronically to form Braille characters. Twenty Braille cells are displayed at a time on the Braille Lite. This type of Braille is called paperless or refreshable Braille. It does not need to be printed on paper, and it can be reused (or refreshed) by lowering the pins and then arranging them to form a different set of Braille characters. Another model, the Braille Lite M40, provides a 40-cell Braille display. This larger display allows the student to review more material at one time and improves the review of computer screen layouts.

Braille 'N Speak, another device from Freedom Scientific, is used by many students. Although it is smaller and less expensive than the Braille Lite, Braille 'N Speak contains many of the same word processing and notetaking features but provides only speech output; no refreshable Braille display is available.

When the students are ready to print their work, they can connect the personal notetaker to a Braille printer, a standard printer, or a printer that produces pages with text in both Braille and print formats. Printers with both Braille and print output are very useful in general education settings because a student who is blind and a teacher who is sighted can both read from the same copy. It is also possible to connect personal notetakers to computers. This allows the student to use the notetaker as a Braille keyboard to edit and spell check the text he or she has produced using a talking screen reader designed for writers with visual impairments. These screen readers like Jaws® "speak" everything on the screen (including instructions and menu choices), not just the text the student has written.

With assistive devices such as personal notetakers, students who are blind can participate in general education classroom activities without having to rely on others for notetaking or the production of written assignments. For example, when writing a paper, a student might draft the outline on the personal notetaker, print it in Braille to review it, use the notetaker's talking screen reader program to expand the outline into a draft of the paper, then transfer the draft to a computer for a spelling check before printing the final version for his or her classmates or teacher.

Note: Courtesy of Freedom Scientific.

- Say aloud material that is being written on the chalkboard or on the overhead projector (Spenciner, 1992). Abstract concepts such as time, distance, quantity, or estimation may require experiential components (Webster & Roe, 1998).
- Avoid using glossy paper or white boards if possible, because these produce glare.
- Provide students with instruction and experiences that develop critical listening skills; individuals with visual impairments do not automatically have better listening skills (Blankenship & Lilly, 1981).

- Occasionally provide tape-recorded materials to students who read Braille or large print in order to vary the presentation of reading material (Spenciner, 1992).
- Vigorous physical exercise helps students with visual impairments in the development of balance, spatial orientation, and eye–hand coordination. Encourage them to compete with sighted peers whenever possible (Reynolds & Birch, 1988).
- Become familiar with the various types of special equipment used by the students with visual impairments in

FIGURE 15-5	Sources of Materials for Students with Sensory Impairments

Large-Print Materials:
- American Printing House for the Blind, Inc., 1839 Frankfort Ave., P.O. Box 6085, Louisville, KY 40206; (800) 223-1839; (502) 895-2405
  Web address: www.aph.org
- National Association for Visually Handicapped, 22 West 21st Street, NY, NY 10010; (212) 889-3141; San Francisco: (415) 221-3201
  Web address: www.navh.org

Braille Materials:
- American Printing House for the Blind (address above)
- Library of Congress National Library Service for the Blind and Physically Handicapped, 1291 Taylor Street, NW, Washington, DC 20542; (202) 707-5100; (800) 424-8567
  Web address: www.loc.gov/nls

Tape-Recorded Materials:
- American Printing House for the Blind, Inc. (address above)
- Library of Congress National Library Service for the Blind and Physically Handicapped (address above)
- Recording for the Blind and Dyslexic, 20 Roszel Road, Princeton, NJ 08540; (800) 221-4792
  Web address: www.rfbd.org
- Descriptive Video Service, the CPB/WGBH National Center for Accessible Media, 125 Western Ave, Boston, MA 02134; (617) 300-3400; TTY: (617) 300-2489
  Web address: http://main.wgbh.org/wgbh/pages/mag/

E-Text (Electronic Text):
- Electronic Text Center
  Web address: http://etext.lib.virginia.edu/
- Project Gutenberg
  Web address: www.promo.net/pg/
- Worditude.com
  Web address: www.worditude.com/ebook/index.html

Captioned Films and Videos:
- Captioned Media Program, National Association of the Deaf, 1447 E. Main Street, Spartanburg, SC 29307; (800) 237-6213; TTY: (800) 237-6819
  Web address: www.cfv.org
- The Caption Center, the CPB/WGBH National Center for Accessible Media (address above)
- National Captioning Institute, 1900 Gallows Road, Suite 3000, Vienna, VA 22182; Voice/TTY: 703-917-7600
  Web address: www.ncicap.org

your class. Let the special education teacher know immediately of any necessary replacement or repairs. Perkins **Braillewriters** are small machines that are often used to write (type) material in Braille; the **slate and stylus** is a small handheld device also used to write Braille. Devices such as an abacus, Braille ruler, or raised relief map are also useful for students. To learn more about the Braille system, consult Figure 15-6.

In addition to the special equipment available for students with visual impairments, the teacher can use general education classroom materials more effectively by adapting them. Glazzard (1980) suggests several ideas for the modification of materials:

- Use a heavy black marking pen on dittoed worksheets. It makes them easier to see.

FIGURE 15-6   Braille: Tactile Communication for Individuals Who Are Blind

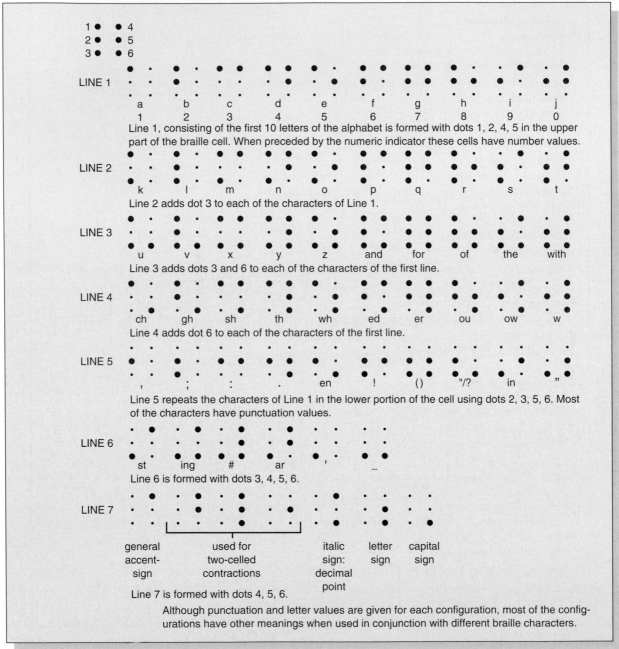

Note: From *Understanding Braille* by the American Foundation for the Blind, 1969, New York: Author. Reprinted by permission.

- Use a marking pen to delineate lines on writing paper or purchase heavy-lined paper.
- Write chalkboard directions on a separate piece of paper for the child with poor vision. Keep copying work for the . . . student to a minimum.

- Ask parents or other students to read reference material or lengthy reading assignments to the . . . student [with visual impairments].
- Record reading material or other assignments for the . . . child [with visual impairments]. Aides, parents, volun-

teers, or other students are possible sources of help for recording assignments.

- A magnifying glass may be helpful for enlarging the print of regular class materials. It is less tiring for some . . . students [with visual impairments] to use such an aid. (pp. 27–28)

Pasanella and Volkmor (1981) provide additional suggestions that general education teachers might find helpful in communicating with students with visual impairments:

- Use a vocabulary that is related to sight, such as the words see and look. . . . [P]ersons [with visual impairments] use those words, too.
- Call the student by name when you are speaking to him.
- Talk directly to the student. Look him in the face and remind classmates to do the same.
- Some . . . students [with visual impairments] develop unusual mannerisms. Gently remind them about more appropriate behaviors.
- Tell the student who you are when you approach him or her and tell him when you leave.
- Encourage the student to use any adaptive aids s/he needs and to explain their use to other classmates. (pp. 186–187)

Students with hearing impairments may also require adaptations in the general education classroom. Specialists provide many of these students with instruction in speechreading, fingerspelling, and sign language. Educators of students with hearing impairments do not agree on the most appropriate communication method for this group, but many professionals advocate **total communication.** This approach combines the oral/aural method of communication (speech, speechreading, and audition) with the manual method (fingerspelling and sign language). The manual alphabet, shown in Figure 15-7, allows students to fingerspell names and technical terms that are not available in sign language. The following suggestions can help the teacher work with students with hearing impairments who are included in the general education program:

- Teachers and students should speak naturally, use natural gestures, and maintain face-to-face contact when speaking with a student with a hearing impairment (Reynolds & Birch, 1988).
- Encourage students with hearing impairments to use their hearing aids and/or cochlear implant at all times.
- Find out the best seating position for the student to speechread the teacher's verbal presentations to the class by discussing this with the student (Rees, 1992).
- An overhead projector permits a teacher to write material that can be seen by all students while the teacher continues to face the class (English, 1995). However, the projector must have a quiet fan. Also remember that when the projector is being used, the room is typically dark, which

means the student who depends on speechreading will not be able to see the teacher's face. Work with the student to determine the most helpful strategy.

- Provide copies of the teacher's notes or those of two other students when material is presented in lecture format; it is not possible to speechread and take notes simultaneously. Write assignments, outlines of lectures, and public address announcements on the board (Reynolds & Birch, 1988).
- Use **captioned films** whenever possible. Many films and videotapes used in the classroom are available in a captioned version. (See Figure 15-5 for information about sources for captioned films and videos.)
- Maximize the use of other visual teaching strategies such as using bulletin boards and materials that include pictures, illustrations, artifacts, slides, and computer graphics (Luckner, Bowen, & Carter, 2001).
- Hearing aids should be checked daily. Consult with a speech-language pathologist or educational audiologist to determine who will assume this responsibility. The "Spotlight on Technology" feature describes the use of hearing aids and classroom amplification devices with students with hearing impairments.
- Question students with hearing impairments to determine whether they understand information presented in class. Do not assume that students understand the material.
- Clearly explain concepts being taught. Use visual examples whenever possible, and keep terminology consistent.
- Do not talk when distributing handouts because the student with a hearing impairment cannot look for papers and watch the teacher at the same time (Rees, 1992).
- Talk in full sentences. Avoid the use of single words, and rephrase the entire sentence if it was not understood; content and meaning are easier to grasp in context (Reynolds & Birch, 1988).
- Provide assignments both orally and in writing to avoid confusion (Rees, 1992).
- Speechreading and attending to auditory stimuli with deficient hearing can be tiring tasks; watch for student fatigue.
- Start lectures with an outline of material to be presented and end the lecture with a summary of the key points (Rees, 1992).
- During class discussions, allow only one person to speak at a time and signal who is talking so the student with hearing impairment knows where to look (Rees, 1992).
- The academic problems of many students are related to their language impairments, not to a lack of intelligence. Closely monitor their achievement (Blankenship & Lilly, 1981).
- Classmates of a student with a hearing impairment may wish to learn sign language. Arrange for instruction in this area if it is appropriate (Blankenship & Lilly, 1981).
- Encourage independence in students with hearing impairments and help them develop skills to act as their

FIGURE 15-7 The Manual Alphabet

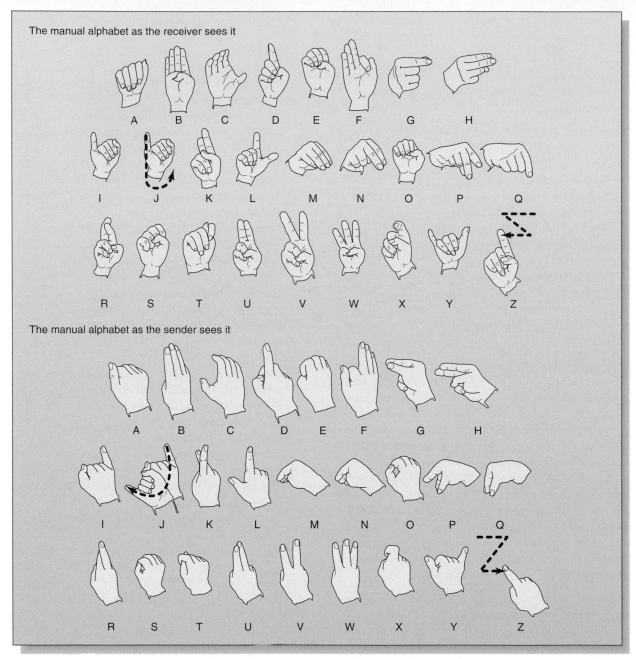

The manual alphabet as the receiver sees it

The manual alphabet as the sender sees it

Note: From the National Association of the Deaf, n.d. Copyright by the National Association of the Deaf. Reprinted by permission.

Spotlight on Technology

Classroom Amplification Devices

Students with hearing impairments benefit from technological devices that amplify sounds in order to optimize residual hearing. Some amplification systems also overcome the problem of listening in noisy situations.

Hearing Aids

Hearing aids differ in shape and style (see chapter 8), but all operate on the same principles. Sound is picked up by a microphone, amplified, and delivered to a receiver in the canal of the ear. Unfortunately, all sounds are amplified, making it difficult for the user to discriminate between conversation and all other noises in the background. In the classroom, a student with a hearing impairment will likely find it difficult to follow a teacher's instructions in the presence of competing noise (rustling paper, shuffling feet, pencil sharpeners, aquarium motors, heating systems, etc.).

The hearing aid user is also affected by two other factors: distance and direction. As distance between the speaker and the hearing aid user increases, the intensity of the speaker's voice decreases. To a person with a hearing impairment, this decrease has a significantly negative impact on speech perception. As a speaker turns away from a hearing aid user, the speech signal again becomes weaker and sometimes distorted. To overcome these limitations of a hearing aid, a teacher would need to directly face the student with a hearing impairment at all times, and speak at a distance of approximately 12 inches from the hearing aid microphone. Obviously, this strategy is not a practical recommendation.

FM Technology

Fortunately, technology is available to address these hearing aid limitations. FM technology is used in an instrument specially designed to address the problems of noise, distance, and direction (Flexer, Wray, & Ireland, 1989; Maxon, Brackett, & van den Berg, 1991). To use an FM system (previously called an auditory trainer), the classroom teacher wears a wireless microphone, and the student wears a wireless receiver. Some

receivers look and operate like personal stereos. Recently, receivers have also been designed to be worn as behind-the-ear hearing aids. This new type of receiver is a preferred choice among students if cosmetic concerns become an issue.

The FM system has three advantages: (1) The teacher's voice is amplified 12 to 15 decibels above the classroom noise; (2) the teacher's voice is transmitted at an even intensity across a distance of up to 100 feet; and (3) the teacher's voice is not affected by direction. This threefold "FM advantage" has helped make the FM system standard equipment in special classrooms for students with hearing impairments for many years. Because the FM system is easy to use, it has been introduced into general education settings with much success. However, because there is a real risk of overamplification, FM systems must be fitted and monitored by an audiologist.

Another amplification system used in classrooms is called sound field amplification. FM technology is used to transmit the teacher's voice by a microphone to one or more speakers placed around the classroom. The teacher's voice is slightly amplified and conveyed to the whole room (that is, the sound field); students in the back of class hear the teacher's voice as loudly as the students in front. If there is a student in the classroom with a hearing impairment, he or she may wear either an FM receiver or his or her personal hearing aids, depending on the audiologist's recommendation. Research indicates that all members in the class can benefit from sound field amplification; for example, students have demonstrated significant academic gains and an increase in on-task behavior. Teachers also report a noticeable reduction in vocal fatigue (Berg, 1987; Sarff, 1981; Zabel & Tabor, 1993).

Cochlear Implants

Finally, another type of amplification showing up in increasing numbers in the general classroom is called a **cochlear implant.** Part of this device is surgically implanted in the child's inner ear to bypass the sensory organ and to stimulate the auditory nerve directly. Another component of the device is a hearing-aid-looking component that rests on the outer

continued

continued

ear. Its microphone picks up sound; a small processor converts the sound to electrical energy, and then a magnet carries that energy through the skull to the implant. Like hearing aids, implants do not "cure" hearing loss; users still have to contend with the adverse effects of background noise and will typically need therapy to learn how to interpret the auditory input. To help with localization, some children use a hearing aid on the nonimplanted side. If a student has a cochlear implant, the teacher will want to meet with the educational audiologist or the implant center's audiologist for information and support. For more information, visit this website: www.utdallas.edu/~loizou/cimplants/tutorial.

own advocates. English (1997) and Marttila and Mills (1995) have designed self-advocacy curriculums for students with hearing losses.

- Work closely with specialists to ensure that students with hearing impairments are provided with appropriate experiences in the general education classroom.

Specific suggestions for working with students who are hard of hearing are presented in the "Inclusion Tips for the Teacher" box. In addition, Harrington (1976) makes the following recommendations about communicating with a student with a hearing impairment:

(a) If you have difficulty understanding the child, ask him to repeat; (b) Do not call attention to the child's speech errors in the classroom. Record and share them with the speech clinician; (c) Realize that the child may have limited vocabulary and syntax, both receptively and expressively. His/her failure to understand may be related to this language deficit as well as the inability to hear normally. (p. 25)

General education teachers ordinarily are not required to become proficient in specialized techniques, such as Braille or sign language. However, they must be aware of students' needs and be familiar with the specialists who provide assistance in adapting instructional procedures for students with sensory impairments. Teachers must also appreciate how visual and hearing impairments increase the demands on students' ability to concentrate and process information. With both kinds of sensory impairments, students must work harder to keep pace with their peers. The effort involved in expending this extra energy has been called **vigilance,** akin to functioning at 110% capacity for long periods of time. This heightened state of attention obviously will be fatiguing, so students often "recharge their batteries" by withdrawing their attention from instruction or conversation—younger children even take short naps. This is a legitimate coping strategy called **respite,** an understandable mental health choice (Gottlieb, 1997). However, these behaviors can be misinterpreted to imply rudeness or lack of interest, and children are frequently scolded for conserving or restoring their energy in this way. Teachers can help students understand how they expend and conserve cognitive and physical energy by discussing different respite strategies and how to use them effectively.

This chapter has presented information on adapting the classroom environment and instructional procedures for students with visual and hearing impairments. Many such students are fully capable of spending the majority of the school day in the general education classroom when appropriate adaptations are introduced. In the next chapter, you will meet students who are gifted and talented and will learn methods for promoting the achievement of these individuals.

Inclusion Tips for the Teacher

Students Who Are Hard of Hearing

Hearing Aid Basics

- Do not expect a hearing aid to "correct" hearing impairments like glasses correct visual impairments. The instrument will make sounds louder but not necessarily clearer. In addition, a conventional hearing aid amplifies all sounds; it cannot sort out the teacher's instruction from the general background noise. Recent advances in electronics allow some hearing aids to be "programmed" to reduce speech-in-noise problems; however, these are relatively expensive and not often recommended for children's use.

- If the aid "whistles" or produces feedback while in the child's ear, check the earpiece (or earmold) to see whether it has been inserted properly. Feedback will naturally occur if the aid is covered with a hand or a hat, or if the student leans close to a wall or turns the volume too high. However, if the earmold is fully in the ear, if the aid is not covered, and if the volume is at the appropriate setting, and feedback still occurs, the earmold may be too small and need to be replaced. Inform the parent of the situation. Reducing the volume is only a temporary solution.

- Obtain a battery tester and a hearing aid stethoscope from the school audiologist and request training in conducting a hearing aid check. Hearing aids must be checked every day.

- Ask parents to provide spare batteries to keep at school, and let them know when dead batteries are replaced.

- Encourage the student to develop self-management skills for hearing aid care. Students should be able to check their own hearing aid batteries by third grade. If a battery dies during the school day, students should advise their teachers immediately; reinforce these self-advocacy skills.

Classroom Acoustic Considerations

Noise has a detrimental effect on the listening abilities of all students, but particularly students with hearing impairments (American Speech-Language-Hearing Association, 1995). New standards in classroom acoustics have been developed by the Acoustical Society of America, providing easy directions about how to evaluate and improve a classroom's auditory environment (http://asa.aip.org/classroom/booklet.html).

A classroom's acoustical environment can be immediately improved by reducing or eliminating noise sources. A careful "listening inspection" of the classroom will help the teacher identify noise sources that most adults have learned to ignore but most children find distracting; examples are fish tank filters, computers, printers, and fans from overhead projectors. If noise sources cannot be eliminated or reduced, the student with a hearing impairment should work away from noise as much as possible.

In addition to conducting a "listening inspection," teachers can request the following environmental modifications to significantly reduce noise and reverberation problems:

- Carpeting, acoustic ceiling tile, and walls covered with bulletin board or similar materials, which absorb rather than reflect noise.

- Acoustic treatments for noise sources such as rumbling plumbing, rattling window blinds, and buzzing fluores-

cent lights. Noise from heating, ventilation, and air conditioning systems can be reduced with inexpensive baffles.

- Acoustic modifications to a classroom can generally be accomplished by the site custodial staff at little cost and will result in an environment conducive for learning for students with normal hearing as well as those with hearing impairments.

Strategies to Optimize Visual Information

Students with hearing impairments need as much visual cueing as possible. Comprehension increases significantly when a student can watch the teacher's face in order to lipread or, more accurately, speechread. Here are some suggestions to improve speechreading conditions:

- Speak in a normal fashion, without exaggeration or an increase in volume. Speak in phrases, at a normal pace. If there is a misunderstanding, rephrase rather than repeat.

- As often as possible, the teacher should directly face a student with a hearing impairment, at eye level. Proximity is also very important; it is too difficult to speechread beyond 10 feet.

- When the room is darkened for films or slides, the student will not be able to speechread the teacher. Ask another student to take notes.

- Be aware that some people are naturally better speechreaders than others and that, even for the best speechreaders, only one-third of English speech sounds are visible. Speechreading becomes more difficult when the speaker has a foreign accent or a mustache that covers the mouth.

Other Teaching Strategies

- Students with hearing impairments often have some language deficits as a result of inconsistent auditory input. Pre-tutoring helps a student develop familiarity with new vocabulary and concepts before they are presented in class. Have the student read ahead on a subject to allow for extra time to consider new material. This can be accomplished as a homework assignment or with a resource teacher.

- As often as possible, write page numbers, homework assignments, public address announcements, key vocabulary, and so forth, on the chalkboard.

- Routinely check comprehension with questions that require more than yes or no answers. When simply asked, "Do you understand?" a student with a hearing impairment may prefer to nod his or her head rather than volunteer that he or she does not fully understand.

- For older students, it is helpful to have another student act as a notetaker. If the notes are made on NCR (no carbon required) paper, a copy can also be provided for a notebook available to any class member who may have missed information during class lectures. A student with a hearing impairment will then have a copy without conspicuously requiring special assistance.

Things to Remember

- Students with visual or hearing impairments commonly require modification of the learning environment and adaptation of instructional procedures to facilitate their performance in the general education classroom.

- Students with severe visual and hearing impairments are typically identified before they enter school. Milder impairments may be identified as a result of school screening programs or teacher observation and referral.

- Sensory impairments may be congenital, or they may occur as a result of illness or accident.

- Legal definitions of visual impairment have little educational relevance. Educators need to know whether students can use their remaining vision to learn or whether they must rely on other senses.

- An educator needs to know the effects of a hearing loss on a student's ability to use and understand speech. Speech and language are the most significant areas in which hearing impairments affect students educationally.

- Students with visual or hearing impairments can learn to use other senses to compensate for their disabilities. Individuals who are blind can develop tactile reading skills and improve their listening skills; persons with hearing impairments can learn to speechread and to communicate manually. Students with visual impairments may also need orientation and mobility training to facilitate independent travel in the school and community.

- Many technological developments have improved the opportunities for students with sensory impairments to communicate with others; examples include FM classroom amplification systems for students with hearing impairments and Braille notetakers and computer programs that provide speech or tactile output for students who are blind.

- Special educators are generally available to assist general education teachers in making classroom adaptations and obtaining appropriate materials for students with sensory impairments who are included in the general education classroom.

ACTIVITIES

1. Observe the classroom behavior of a student with a visual or hearing impairment. Keep a record of the adaptations made by the student and by others. What problems, if any, are encountered? Can the student adjust as unexpected events occur? What reactions do you observe from other students? From teachers? Write a brief summary of your observations.

2. Interview the parents of a student with a sensory impairment. When were they first aware of the disability? How did they react? Does the student encounter any difficulties at home or in the neighborhood? Has inclusion in the general education program been a positive experience for the student? Are the parents apprehensive about the student's eventual adulthood? How do they encourage their child to become independent? Describe your impressions of the interview.

3. Read two articles about students with sensory impairments, one about visual impairments and one about hearing losses. The *Journal of Visual Impairment and Blindness* and the *Sight-Saving Review* provide ar-

ticles related to visual impairments; *American Annals of the Deaf, Volta Review,* and *Language, Speech, and Hearing Services in Schools* discuss hearing impairments. Summarize each article's relevance for the general education teacher.

4. Contact a large and a small school district to determine what services they offer to students with visual and hearing impairments. Are all the services needed by these students provided within the district, or must services be contracted from another district? What personnel are employed to provide instruction for these students? Is the percentage of students with sensory impairments about the same in both districts? What services are provided for general education teachers?

5. Write a short report describing one of the new electronic devices being used by persons who are blind or deaf. You can find information about assistive technology by visiting the sites highlighted in this chapter's "Window on the Web" feature. Choose a device, explain how it works, its advantages and disadvantages,

CD-ROM Activities

The three classrooms that are featured in the video case studies on the CD-ROM do not appear to include students with visual impairments or students who are deaf or hard of hearing. However, such students could join these classrooms at any time. Think about what changes might be needed if one or more students with sensory impairments became a member of the high school physics class, then answer these questions:

- *What types of adaptations would be needed to allow a student with low vision to use the classroom computers to do research for the class project?*

- *If a deaf student were to become a member of the class, what accommodations might be necessary so that he or she could benefit from the teacher's lectures and the discussions among students?*

cost, and special benefits to the user. If possible, interview an individual who actually uses the device. Find out how this person evaluated the device and include this information in your report. Determine whether the device is available for students in a local school district.

6. Two new technologies have recently become available for students with hearing impairments. One, called the AudiSee, uses a tiny head-mounted camera aimed at the teacher's face (www.sforh.com/communication/audisee.html). The image of the face is transmitted to a laptop computer so that the student can easily speechread the teacher from any seat in the classroom. Another electronic device is the iCommunicator (www.myicommunicator.com). It uses a head-mounted microphone to pick up the teacher's voice and transmit it to a laptop computer, then converts speech into text and also sign language. The text can be saved as lecture notes. Visit the websites, then prepare a brief report explaining how each device works. Include a discussion of the potential advantages of these technologies for students included in the general education classroom.

PART IV

Methods for Teaching Students with Other Needs in General Education

Teaching Students Who Are Gifted and Talented

Margie K. Kitano
San Diego State University

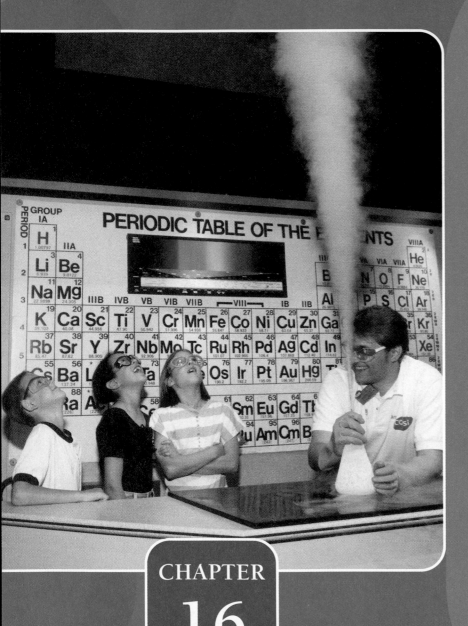

CHAPTER

16

Kay

Kay is a high school junior who was identified in the second grade as gifted. Since that time, special adaptations have been provided in much of her education, especially in the area of mathematics. Her current program allows her to complete a 3-year high school curriculum in 2 years, and she plans to enroll as a full-time college student at age 16. At present, she is taking courses in calculus and computer programming at the local junior college, in addition to her regular high school program. In her after-school hours, she plays on the school golf team, serves as president of the math club, and has helped with set designs for several of the drama club's plays.

Luis

Luis is a 6-year-old first grader who has recently been identified as gifted. He was able to read when he entered kindergarten and

now is in an advanced reading group in the school's resource program for students who are gifted. The resource teacher assists the general education teacher by providing Luis with individualized assignments in most academic areas; Luis has already mastered much of the material appropriate for his classmates. Math is an exception; Luis's performance in this area is only average. Although assessment results indicate that Luis is quite capable, his interest in math is low. His teacher hopes to engage his interest in mathematics by helping him explore relationships between math and music. Luis possesses a passion for music and has learned to play both the piano and the guitar; he takes music lessons twice a week at the local recreation center.

Johnny

Johnny is a sixth grader with special talent in writing. Although he did not learn to read until he entered school, he

LOOKING AHEAD

Later in this chapter we will take a look at the goals and services from Luis's individualized education program. This chapter suggests strategies for providing educational options to gifted and talented students, developing creativity and problem-solving skills, and assisting students who are underachieving. As you read, think about these questions:

- Kay, Luis, and Johnny present quite different pictures of extraordinary ability. Compare and contrast their strengths.
- If you were Kay's high school English teacher, what types of activities could you introduce to challenge her higher level thinking skills?
- Luis excels in some but not all school subjects. Would you consider Luis an underachiever? What strategies (besides making connections with music) could the first-grade teacher use to pique Luis's interest and improve his performance in math?
- What advice would you offer Johnny's sixth grade teacher for nurturing his writing ability?

To answer these questions online, go to the Students' Stories module in Chapter 16 of the Companion Website.

began to write short stories and poems in first grade. Several of his pieces have been published in children's magazines. Although his spelling is not always the best, his vocabulary and ability to use words are far beyond those expected of a 12-year-old student. Johnny's school has no special programs for students who are talented, and he does not qualify for the gifted program because his achievement is average in all areas except writing. Despite the lack of special services, Johnny's teacher is interested in helping him progress and maintain his interest in writing. She allows him to select his own topics for classroom writing assignments, reads and critiques any poems or stories he brings to her, and is investigating ways to help Johnny enroll in the creative writing course offered at the high school in the summer.

Students who are gifted and talented exist at all ages and grade levels within the school system. They are distinguished by their exceptional ability and come from both sexes and all economic, ethnic, cultural, and language backgrounds. Students can have both disabilities and gifts and talents, making them "twice exceptional." Gifted and talented individuals are among the most neglected of all groups of special students. Most "spend their school days without attention paid to their special learning needs" (U.S. Department of Education, 1993, p. 2) because these needs are not universally recognized. Potentially gifted children who live in poverty are especially underserved, as are English learners and children from African American, Latino, Native American, and some Asian groups.

Many teachers and parents do not clearly understand the needs of students who are gifted and talented. Some educators continue to believe that these students, because of their exceptional abilities, are capable of realizing their maximum potential without the benefit of specially designed educational adaptations or programs. Colangelo and Davis (2003) explain:

> One common argument against special educational programs for the gifted is the belief that these students "will make it on their own." A corollary is "Give the help to students who really need it." However, many students labeled *gifted* do *not* make it on their own. Inadequate curriculum, unsupportive educators, social and emotional difficulties, peer pressures, and inadequate parenting all can extinguish the potentially high accomplishment of gifted children and adolescents. (p. 5)

Students who are gifted and talented have special learning needs that are not fully met by the general education program. Such students should be identified in order to adapt the general education program or provide special educational services. In this way, it is possible to help them achieve at a level commensurate with their potential (Clark, 2002; Culross, 1997; Parker, 1989).

This chapter examines the characteristics of students with special gifts and talents who are included in the general education program and also describes methods for the general education teacher to use in gathering data and designing and implementing program adaptations.

DEFINITIONS

A 1972 report to Congress on the education of the gifted and talented, now called the Marland Report for then U.S. Commissioner of Education Sydney Marland, brought national recognition to the plight of gifted and talented students. The report (U.S. Department of Health, Education, and Welfare, 1972) indicated that 3% to 5% of the nation's students could be considered gifted and that schools were not meeting most of their needs. The report provided a federal definition for gifted and talented that was used with modification in subsequent federal legislation (PL 95-561, The Gifted and Talented Children's Act of 1978; PL 100-297, The Jacob K. Javits Gifted and Talented Students Education Act of 1988).

A 1993 report by the U.S. Department of Education, titled *National Excellence: A Case for Developing America's Talent*, reiterated concern that the nation was "squandering" its precious resource of talented students by not challenging them to excel. The report also emphasized the needs of gifted students from economically and culturally diverse backgrounds: "This problem is especially severe among economically disadvantaged and minority students, who have access to fewer advanced educational opportunities and whose talents often go unnoticed" (p. 1). This report reaffirmed and updated the Marland definition of the gifted and talented, emphasizing "talent" to connote a developing ability:

> Children and youth with outstanding talent perform or show the potential for performing at remarkably high levels of accomplishment when compared with others of their age, experience, or environment.
>
> These children and youth exhibit high performance capability in intellectual, creative, and/or artistic areas, possess an unusual leadership capacity, or excel in specific academic fields. They require services or activities not ordinarily provided by the schools.

Outstanding talents are present in children and youth from all cultural groups, across all economic strata, and in all areas of human endeavor. (p. 26)

Experts have offered other definitions and conceptualizations of the terms **giftedness** and **talented**. For example, based on studies of eminent individuals, Renzulli (1978) derived a three-ring definition requiring above-average ability, high creativity, and strong task commitment. Recent theories of intelligence, most notably Gardner's multiple intelligences and Sternberg's triarchic conceptions, have broadened our notions beyond a single dimension and suggest that intelligence can be enhanced. Gardner has proposed nine categories of intelligence: linguistic, logical-mathematical, musical, spatial, bodily-kinesthetic, interpersonal, intrapersonal, naturalist, and existential (Von Károlyi, Ramos-Ford, & Gardner, 2003). Sternberg's (2003) theory of successful intelligence includes three main types of abilities: analytic, synthetic, and practical.

Although universal agreement has not been reached concerning a definition of this group of students, some form of the federal definition is often cited, and a majority of states continue to use the term *gifted and talented* (Stephens & Karnes, 2000).

A major purpose of the Marland and *National Excellence* definitions was to expand the concept of giftedness beyond IQ. By specifying a range of domains as well as both performance and potential, an expected outcome would be greater inclusion. Yet in practice, IQ tests, teacher recommendations, grades, and standardized achievement tests are most frequently used to identify students as gifted. Such measures screen out many gifted students who have the highest needs for special services: those who are culturally and linguistically diverse, twice exceptional, economically disadvantaged, or highly creative (Richert, 2003).

As a result, students in these categories continue to be underrepresented in programs for the gifted relative to their proportions in the total school population. Table 16-1 shows national projections for general enrollments and enrollments in gifted and talented programs by ethnic, English learner, and disability groups for the year 2000 (Office of Civil Rights, 2004). These data indicate, for example, that while Latino students constitute 16.13% of the general enrollment, they comprise only 9.54% of enrollment in programs for the gifted. The term "Asian or Pacific Islander" includes a large number of diverse ethnic, cultural, and language groups, some of whom also are underrepresented in programs for the gifted and talented (Kitano & DiJiosia, 2002).

The decades-long underrepresentation of some students of color in programs for the gifted has resulted in a movement to increase inclusion by retaining gifted students in general education settings rather than grouping them together for in-

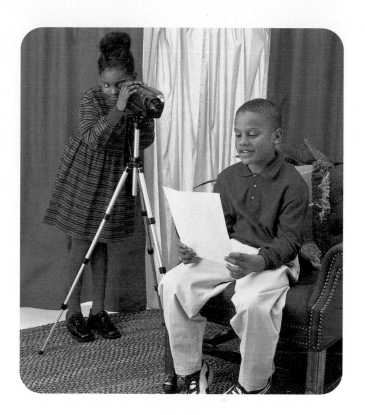

structional purposes. Ironically, the research on gifted students indicates that grouping them together for appropriately challenging work better meets their academic needs (Kulik, 2003).

INDICATORS OF TALENT AND GIFTEDNESS

Some students who are gifted and talented have highly unusual abilities that are identified early in life by their parents. For most students, however, it is the classroom teacher who first notices their special abilities. Students who are gifted and talented can be identified at any time during their school careers, but they are most likely to come to their teachers' attention during the elementary school years.

Giftedness and talent have several indicators that teachers might look for. However, Heward (2000) cautions that general descriptions of group characteristics are not always effective in the identification of individuals; students may be gifted or talented and display several or none of the specific characteristics included on a list. As with all special individuals, the student's unique needs must be considered.

The accompanying "Inclusion Tips for the Teacher" material summarizes some of the major indicators of giftedness and talent that can be observed in the general education classroom. Although these special students do not generally display all these signs, the presence of one or two of them is cause for a

TABLE 16-1 National Projections for Enrollment in Gifted/Talented Programs by Race/Ethnicity, English Learner Status, and Disability

	AMERICAN INDIAN OR ALASKAN NATIVE (%)	ASIAN OR PACIFIC ISLANDER (%)	HISPANIC (%)	BLACK, NOT HISPANIC (%)	WHITE, NOT HISPANIC (%)	ENGLISH LEARNERS (%)	STUDENTS WITH DISABILITIES (%)
ENROLLMENT IN SCHOOL	1.16	4.14	16.13	16.99	61.58	7.57	12.49
IN GIFTED/ TALENTED PROGRAMS	0.91	7.08	9.54	8.23	74.24	1.57	1.68
MATHEMATICS ADVANCED PLACEMENT	0.48	12.93	8.73	6.98	70.88	1.44	0.87
SCIENCE ADVANCED PLACEMENT	0.63	13.38	9.13	7.16	69.70	1.21	1.02

Note: From *Office of Civil Rights Elementary and Secondary School Survey* (2000), retrieved from http://205.207.175.84/ocr2000r/wdsdata.html

Inclusion Tips for the Teacher

Signs of Giftedness and Talent

There are numerous lists of characteristics or distinguishing features and attributes of gifted and talented children. Teachers and parents should interpret any single list, including this one, as only an example of possible traits.

Few gifted children will display all of the characteristics in a given list; however, when clusters of these characteristics are present, they do serve as fairly reliable indicators. Giftedness may exist in only one area of academic learning, such as mathematics, or may be quite general across the school curriculum. . . . These characteristics are signals to indicate that a particular child might warrant closer observation and could require specialized educational attention, pending a more comprehensive assessment.

General Behavioral Characteristics

- Many typically learn to read earlier with a better comprehension of the nuances of the language. As many as half of the gifted and talented population have learned to read before entering school. They often read widely, quickly, and intensely and have large vocabularies.
- They commonly learn basic skills better, more quickly, and with less practice.
- They are frequently able to pick up and interpret nonverbal cues and can draw inferences which other children have to have spelled out for them.
- They take less for granted, seeking the "hows" and "whys."
- They display a better ability to work independently at an earlier age and for longer periods of time than other children.
- They can sustain longer periods of concentration and attention
- Their interests are often both widely eclectic and intensely focused.
- They frequently have seemingly boundless energy, which sometimes leads to a misdiagnosis of "hyperactive."
- They are usually able to respond and relate well to parents, teachers, and other adults. They may prefer the company of older children and adults to that of their peers.
- They are willing to examine the unusual and are highly inquisitive.
- Their behavior is often well organized, goal directed, and efficient with respect to tasks and problems.
- They exhibit an intrinsic motivation to learn, find out, or explore and are often very persistent. "I'd rather do it myself" is a common attitude.
- They enjoy learning new things and new ways of doing things.
- They have a longer attention and concentration span than their peers.

Learning Characteristics

- They may show keen powers of observation, exhibit a sense of the significant, and have an eye for important details.

- They may read a great deal on their own, preferring books and magazines written for youngsters older than themselves.
- They often take great pleasure in intellectual activity.
- They have well developed powers of abstraction, conceptualization, and synthesizing abilities.
- They generally have rapid insight into cause–effect relationships.
- They often display a questioning attitude and seek information for the sake of having it as much as for its instrumental value.
- They are often skeptical, critical, and evaluative. They are quick to spot inconsistencies.
- They often have a large storehouse of information regarding a variety of topics which they can recall quickly.
- They show a ready grasp of underlying principles and can often make valid generalizations about events, people, and objects.
- They readily perceive similarities, differences, and anomalies.
- They often attack complicated material by separating it into its components and analyzing it systematically.

Creative Characteristics

- They are fluent thinkers, able to produce a large quantity of possibilities, consequences, or related ideas.
- They are flexible thinkers able to use many different alternatives and approaches to problem solving.
- They are original thinkers, seeking new, unusual, or unconventional associations and combinations among items of information. They also have an ability to see relationships among seemingly unrelated objects, ideas, or facts.
- They are elaborative thinkers, producing new steps, ideas, responses, or other embellishments to a basic idea, situation, or problem.
- They show a willingness to entertain complexity and seem to thrive in problem situations.
- They are good guessers and can construct hypotheses or "what if" questions readily.
- They often are aware of their own impulsiveness and the irrationality within themselves and show emotional sensitivity.
- They have a high level of curiosity about objects, ideas, situations, or events.
- They often display intellectual playfulness, fantasize, and imagine readily.
- They can be less intellectually inhibited than their peers in expressing opinions and ideas and often exhibit spirited disagreement.
- They have a sensitivity to beauty and are attracted to aesthetic dimensions.

Note: From "Characteristics of Intellectually Gifted Children" (Digest 344) by J. R. Whitmore, 1985, *Digests on the Gifted* (Reston, VA: The Council for Exceptional Children), pp. 1–2. Material is in the public domain.

FIGURE 16-1   Two Sides of Gifted Behavior

List A: Positive Aspects
1. Expresses ideas and feelings well
2. Can move at a rapid pace
3. Works conscientiously
4. Wants to learn, explore, and seek more information
5. Develops broad knowledge and an extensive store of vicarious experiences
6. Is sensitive to the feelings and rights of others
7. Makes steady progress
8. Makes original and stimulating contributions to discussions
9. Sees relationships easily
10. Learns material quickly
11. Is able to use reading skills to obtain new information
12. Contributes to enjoyment of life for self and others
13. Completes assigned tasks
14. Requires little drill for learning

List B: Not-So-Positive Aspects
1. May be glib, making fluent statements based on little or no knowledge or understanding
2. May dominate discussions
3. May be impatient to proceed to the next level or task
4. May be considered nosey
5. May choose reading at the expense of active participation in social, creative, or physical activities
6. May struggle against rules, regulations, and standardized procedures
7. May lead discussions "off the track"
8. May be frustrated by the apparent absence of logic in activities and daily events
9. May become bored by repetitions
10. May use humor to manipulate
11. May resist a schedule based on time rather than task
12. May lose interest quickly

Note: Reprinted with the permission of Prentice-Hall, Inc., from *Exceptional Children,* 6th ed., by William L. Heward, Copyright © 2000 by Merrill/Prentice-Hall, Inc.

teacher to consider further assessment. Heward (2000) points out that even though descriptions of students who are gifted usually emphasize only positive characteristics, these students can also display less attractive behaviors. Figure 16-1 presents both sides of the giftedness coin.

Several techniques are used to identify students who are gifted and talented. These include referrals from teachers, parents, peers, or students themselves; group measures of achievement or intellectual performance; and observation of special academic or creative achievements. Screening every student for potential gifts and talents—for example, through a culture-fair group measure—may be one strategy for decreasing the number of potentially gifted students who are overlooked through referral. Although teachers are the most common source of referrals, their accuracy as identifiers is questionable, especially with younger children (Smutny, 2000) and in classes with many students from diverse ethnic, cultural, or linguistic groups (Baldwin, 1991; Kitano, 1989; Piirto, 1999). Even with training, teachers tend to look for the stereotypical student who is gifted—one who is highly motivated and adjusted to school—and often overlook the unique student with a set of unusual skills and abilities. The "Inclusion Tips for the Teacher" box provides information on some popular myths about gifted students and some truths found by professionals working with gifted students.

Behavior checklists or rating scales can prove helpful to the teacher. For example, the *Scales for Rating the Behavior Characteristics of Superior Students* (Renzulli, Smith, White, Callahan,

& Hartman, 2001) is used by a teacher to rate a student's performance in the areas of learning, motivation, and creativity. This type of scale provides information on a student's strengths and is useful for both identification and educational planning.

Kitano (1989) provides several suggestions to teachers to assist them in improving their accuracy in identifying gifted children:

- Consider all children as potential candidates for giftedness. For example, a hyperactive, disruptive, or unkempt child may also be gifted.
- Recognize that "negative" traits [e.g., List B in Figure 16-1]. . . do not disqualify a child from consideration as gifted. Although gifted and average children may display negative behaviors, gifted children will also demonstrate their strengths when provided with opportunities to do so.
- Look for and analyze the strengths exhibited by all children, including those who do not display stereotypical achieving, cooperating, and conforming behaviors. For example, the child who touches expensive equipment after being admonished not to touch may be exhibiting extreme curiosity rather than defiance.
- Provide opportunities for and encourage children to express their abilities. For example, the teacher can informally assess reading and writing skills by inviting children individually to read to them at the book center and encouraging volunteer efforts to write their names and other words.

Inclusion Tips for the Teacher

Common Myths and Truths About Gifted Students

Myths About Gifted Students

- Gifted students do not need help. If they are really gifted, they can manage on their own.
- Gifted students have fewer problems than others because their intelligence and abilities somehow exempt them from the hassles of daily life.
- The future of a gifted student is assured: a world of opportunities lies before the student.
- Gifted students are self-directed; they know where they are heading.
- The social and emotional development of the gifted student is at the same level as his or her intellectual development.
- Gifted students are nerds and social isolates.
- The primary value of the gifted student lies in his or her brain power.
- The gifted student's family always prizes his or her abilities.
- Gifted students need to serve as examples to others and they should always assume extra responsibility.
- Gifted students make everyone else smarter.
- Gifted students can accomplish anything they put their minds to. All they have to do is apply themselves.
- Gifted students are naturally creative and do not need encouragement.
- Gifted children are easy to raise and a welcome addition to any classroom.

Truths About Gifted Students

- Gifted students are often perfectionistic and idealistic. They may equate achievement and grades with self-esteem

and self-worth, which sometimes leads to fear of failure and interferes with achievement.
- Gifted students may experience heightened sensitivity to their own expectations and those of others, resulting in guilt over achievements or grades perceived to be low.
- Gifted students are asynchronous. Their chronological age, social, physical, emotional, and intellectual development may all be at different levels. For example, a 5-year-old may be able to read and comprehend a third grade book but may not be able to write legibly.
- Some gifted children are "mappers" (sequential learners), while others are "leapers" (spatial learners). Leapers may not know how they got a "right answer." Mappers may get lost in the steps leading to the right answer.
- Gifted students may be so far ahead of their chronological age mates that they know more than half the curriculum before the school year begins! Their boredom can result in low achievement and grades.
- Gifted children are problem solvers. They benefit from working on open-ended, interdisciplinary problems; for example, how to solve a shortage of community resources. Gifted students often refuse to work for grades alone.
- Gifted students often think abstractly and with such complexity that they may need help with concrete study- and test-taking skills. They may not be able to select one answer in a multiple choice question because they see how all the answers might be correct.
- Gifted students who do well in school may define success as getting an "A" and failure as any grade less than an "A." By early adolescence they may be unwilling to try anything where they are not certain of guaranteed success.

Note: ERIC Clearinghouse on Disabilities and Gifted Education (2000). *Common Myths about Gifted Students* and "College Planning for Gifted Students" by Sandra Berger, 1998, published by the Council for Exceptional Children.

- Use parents as informants. Parents serve as effective identifiers of gifted children. . . . Moreover, they can provide accurate observations about what their children can and cannot do (p. 60).

Special attention should be paid to the inclusion of qualified students from diverse ethnic, cultural, or linguistic groups and those with disabilities in programs for students who are gifted and talented (Castellano, 2003; Cline & Schwartz, 1999; Karnes & Johnson, 1991; Klein, 1989). See the "Inclusion Tips for the Teacher" box for characteristics that may assist in identifying gifted students from low-income backgrounds.

Although there has been an increasing awareness of the needs of gifted students who also have other exceptionalities such as ADHD (e.g., Flint, 2001; Zentall, Hall, & Grskovic,

2001), learning disabilities (e.g., Fetzer, 2000; Shaywitz et al., 2001), behavioral disorders (e.g., Morrison & Omdal, 2000), or physical or sensory impairments (e.g., Cline & Schwartz, 1999), many students with these disabilities have been precluded from being identified as gifted because of the difficulties involved in correctly identifying their abilities and educational needs. Total reliance on standardized tests should be avoided; norm-referenced measures can lead to the exclusion of many such students who are excellent candidates for programs for students who are gifted and talented. Educators should use several different measures, rather than only one or two (Feldhusen, 2001; Masse, 2001) and stress procedures that reduce the potential bias that may interfere with identifying students from these populations (Clark, 2002; Cline & Schwartz, 1999; Piirto, 1999). To learn more about students with special gifts and talents, consult the "For Your Information" material.

Inclusion Tips for the Teacher

Characteristics of Gifted Students from Low-Income Backgrounds

- Has high mathematical abilities
- Is curious; varied interests
- Is independent
- Has good imagination
- Is fluent in nonverbal communication
- Improvises when solving problems
- Learns quickly through experience
- Retains and uses information well

- Shows a desire to learn in daily work
- Is original and creative
- Uses language rich in imagery
- Responds well to visual media; concrete activities
- Shows leadership among peers; is responsible
- Shows relationships among unrelated ideas
- Is entrepreneurial
- Has a keen sense of humor

Note: From Johnsen, S. K. (2004a, p 18). Definitions, models, and characteristics of gifted students. In S. K. Johnsen (Ed.), *Identifying gifted students: A practical guide* (pp. 1–21). Waco, TX: Prufrock Press. Reprinted with permission.

For Your Information

Students Who Are Gifted and Talented

- Although the earliest federal program on gifted education was created in 1931, it was the post–World War II threat of communism that stimulated major federal interest in the gifted. The successful launching of the Sputnik satellite in 1957 spurred development of programs, especially in science and mathematics (Wickstrom, 2004).
- As of 2001, only 27 states mandated gifted education and only 9 required an individualized education program for gifted students (Shaunessy, 2003).
- A nationwide poll (Rose, Gallup, & Elam, 1997) indicates that "a small majority (52%) of the public supports the placement of gifted and talented students in separate classes. This response takes added significance from the fact that 66% of poll respondents also said they believe that grouping students according to ability will improve student achievement a great deal or quite a lot" (p. 53).
- Many students who are gifted may have high levels of activity in the classroom because of boredom or intense interest in an activity and may be considered to be hyperactive (e.g., have ADHD) and in need of special education services. This possibility should be carefully evaluated before decisions are made regarding changes in their programs (Webb & Latimer, 1993).
- Highly effective teachers of the gifted and talented prefer abstract themes and concepts, are open and flexible, and value logical analysis and objectivity. They display enthusiasm,

self-confidence, high energy, and an achievement orientation. Additionally, at the secondary level, they tend to possess a strong background in an academic discipline and passion for their subject matter (Mills, 2003).
- Males and females do not differ in intellectual ability, but there have traditionally been significant differences in their achievement (Cline & Schwartz, 1999). Girls tend to achieve better than boys until puberty, when boys begin to excel, especially in math and science. In the adult years, the expectations of society continue to have a negative effect on the achievement of many women (Kerr, 1997; Pendarvis, 1993). Females are frequently found to disguise their abilities and limit their achievement to "socially acceptable" levels (Parke, 1989).
- Gifted males tend to experience heightened emotional sensitivity and empathy for others. If peers, teachers, and family members disparage their sensitivity, gifted males may stifle their feelings and withdraw emotionally. Gifted males benefit from teachers who validate and help them express their feelings (Hébert, 2002).
- Professionals and parents interested in gifted education are concerned that the school reform movement designed to increase the inclusion of students with disabilities in general education programs will also lead to a reduction in the opportunities to provide specialized programs for students who are gifted and talented (Culross, 1997).

ASSESSMENT PROCEDURES

When a student is identified as a potential candidate for special education services for students who are gifted and talented, the next step is a comprehensive assessment. The purpose is to gather information about the learning needs and abilities of the student in order to assist in planning appropriate educational modifications. Both formal and informal measures are used; examples of possible informal procedures are direct observation, inventories, checklists, and analysis of various types of work samples. In some states, there are specific guidelines for determining eligibility for special education programs for gifted and talented pupils; in others, this decision is left to the discretion of the local school district (Dettmer, 1994; Stephens, 2000). Care should be taken to gather only information that will be used in the actual identification process. It is inappropriate to collect a variety of data and then determine eligibility solely on the basis of an intelligence test score (Reis & Renzulli, 1985; Sternberg, 1991; Sternberg & Grigorenko, 2000).

In the past, many programs for students who are gifted relied almost exclusively on norm-referenced tests of intelligence for assessment. Measures such as the *Wechsler Intelligence Scale for Children–Fourth Edition (WISC-IV)* (Wechsler, 2003) and the *Stanford-Binet Intelligence Scales, Fifth Edition* (Roid, 2003) remain in use today, particularly for identification of students who are academically talented. Practices vary widely regarding minimum scores for eligibility for services for students who are gifted; a *WISC-IV* score of IQ 115 may qualify a student in one state or school district, whereas a score of 130 or 135 may be necessary in another.

Although individual IQ tests such as the *WISC* and the *Stanford-Binet* are considered the single most reliable indicator of intellectual giftedness, they have many drawbacks. They are expensive to use and can be administered only by special personnel. They are biased in favor of middle- and upper-class students and discriminate against those students who have disabilities or come from diverse ethnic, cultural, or linguistic groups. Nonverbal ability measures, such as the *Naglieri Nonverbal Ability Test,* the *Universal Nonverbal Ability Test,* and *Raven Progressive Matrices* demonstrate reduced bias and increased inclusion of culturally and linguistically diverse students and students from low-income backgrounds. The *DISCOVER* system (Maker, 2001), based on problem solving and multiple intelligences, demonstrates effectiveness in identifying giftedness among culturally and linguistically diverse elementary through high school students.

Intelligence tests, including those that are less culturally biased, fail to assess such important abilities as creativity, leadership, and specific talents. Measures such as the *Torrance*

Tests of Creative Thinking (Torrance, 1966) can be used to assess creativity. Such tests help identify divergent thinkers who may be overlooked on intelligence tests. In describing these instruments, Gay (1981) noted that

> one such test asks the individual to list as many uses as he or she can think of for an ordinary brick. Think about it and list a few. If you listed uses such as build a school, build a house, build a library, etc., then you are not very creative; all of those uses are really the same, namely, you can use a brick to build something. Now, if you are creative, you listed different uses such as break a window, drown a rat, and hit a robber on the head. (p. 128)

Creativity test results should be supplemented with information from other sources, such as analysis of students' creative products and performances and direct observation of student behavior.

Observation techniques help to objectively assess and describe a student's academic and social performance in the classroom. For example, a teacher can observe the amount and reading levels of material the student reads each week, the number of social interactions per class period, or the time taken to complete an assignment. Information such as this not only helps to determine the student's current performance levels but also assists in the development of program modifications.

Analysis of work samples is conducted somewhat differently with students who are gifted and talented. Instead of searching for error patterns, the purpose is to discover a student's strengths and potential for further achievement. In the area of academics, a teacher looks for advanced school skills or competence in a subject matter not normally taught in the general education curriculum.

Examples include the precocious kindergartner who reads and understands fourth-grade material and the second grader who has special knowledge in botany and zoology. For information about specific talents, the teacher should consider a wide variety of student products, such as writings, artwork, musical compositions, and inventions; other possibilities are dramatic or musical performances. A teacher can analyze these work samples or ask for assistance from others. Subject matter experts and practicing artists, musicians, or writers may be better able to judge whether students' work is exceptional and whether students have the potential to benefit from advanced study in the area.

In addition to the strengths of students who are gifted and talented, areas of relative weakness should also be considered. This is particularly important for students with major discrepancies between ability and achievement and those who excel in one or two areas but not in others. The assessment procedures suggested for students with learning disabilities and behavioral disorders are appropriate for gathering information about academic achievement and school conduct. The procedures suggested in chapter 6 can be helpful if social acceptance problems are suspected. Typically, Individualized Education Programs (IEPs) are not required for students who are gifted and talented. However, it is good practice to develop a written educational plan. Figure 16-2 presents portions of the IE plan for Luis, the first grader introduced at the beginning of this chapter.

Johnsen (2004b) suggests that identification procedures for students with gifts and talents should ensure that instruments match student characteristics and program services. To ensure an effective identification process, she recommends the following questions be used as guidelines:

1. Is the procedure based on best research and recommendations?
2. Does it match the district's definition and program options?
3. Do all students have an equal opportunity to be nominated?
4. Are special populations considered in the nomination process?
5. Are all students able to demonstrate their strengths?
6. Are assessments fair to student cultures?
7. Are all students able to demonstrate their abilities in classroom activities?
8. Are multiple sources of information used?
9. Are all data considered during the selection phase?
10. Are the students' data evaluated objectively?
11. Are all students who need a differentiated education being identified?
12. Do identified students perform well in the program that matches their gifts and talents? (pp. 114–115)

FIGURE 16-2 Individualized Education Goals and Services for Luis

Annual Goals

1. By the end of the school year, Luis will read fifth-grade material on a topic of his choice, demonstrating depth of comprehension through oral, written, or visual extensions or syntheses to be shared with his classmates (e.g., retelling from a different perspective, a song, storyboard, brochure, or diorama).
Person responsible: Resource teacher

2. By the end of the school year, Luis will write short reports on topics of his choice. The written products will demonstrate correct spelling and sentence structure and higher level thinking, for example, detailed descriptions, comparisons, diverse points of view, original ideas.
Persons responsible: First-grade teacher, resource teacher

3. By the end of the school year, Luis will successfully complete all requirements for first-grade math.
Person responsible: First-grade teacher

4. By the end of the school year, Luis will successfully play a series of songs on both the guitar and the piano.
Person responsible: Parent

Amount of Participation in General Education

Luis will attend the regular first-grade class for all subjects except reading.

Special Education and Related Services

1. Luis will receive special education services from the resource teacher for students who are gifted (annual goals 1 and 2) for 1 hour daily.

2. The resource teacher will provide consultation to Luis's first-grade teacher as needed.

CLASSROOM ADAPTATIONS

Given their higher intelligence and more rapid learning rate, gifted students require services different from those offered by the regular program. **Differentiation** of the curriculum and instruction can occur in the general classroom or in special settings. Undifferentiated, the regular school curriculum does not provide the challenge needed by gifted students. Many gifted children have already mastered up to one-half of the standard elementary curriculum, and teachers typically do not make accommodations for their learning needs (U.S. Department of Education, 1993).

Classrooms adaptations must be made in curriculum and instruction for students who are gifted and talented. The following sections of this chapter address ways in which the general education teacher can select appropriate educational options, promote the development of creativity and problem solving, and assist underachieving students in better realizing their capabilities.

EDUCATIONAL OPTIONS FOR STUDENTS WHO ARE GIFTED AND TALENTED

Individualized programs can be delivered in several ways to students who are gifted and talented. In many of these options, the student remains in the general education classroom with age peers. Special instruction can be provided within this class by the general education teacher, on a part-time basis by a special teacher in a special class or resource room, or in a setting outside the school when school is not in session.

The selection of an appropriate method for providing service depends on many factors. One important consideration is the relationship between student needs and program goals. According to Pendarvis (1993), educational modifications for students who are gifted and talented can be designed to accomplish the following things:

- Quicken the pace of learning by moving the student through activities faster than would be appropriate for children of average ability.
- Broaden the range of experiences and knowledge of gifted children by teaching subjects not offered in the general education curriculum at the children's grade level.
- Develop skills of analysis and expression in academic or artistic disciplines.
- Provide opportunity for concentrated, in-depth study of areas in which the students are especially interested or able. (p. 587)

General education teachers can accommodate the needs of gifted learners in their classrooms through implementation of differentiated program, instructional, and curriculum models.

Differentiated Program Models

Three program adaptations are recommended for gifted and talented learners either alone or in combination: acceleration, enrichment, and grouping. While we can distinguish these three options conceptually, they overlap in practice.

Acceleration refers to changing the pace of instruction, moving faster through the regular education curriculum. Students may be admitted to school at a younger than usual age or be allowed to skip one or more grades. Another way to accelerate is the telescoping of grades; for instance, the course of study for two grades might be compressed into one school year. Accelerating high school students through the use of advanced placement into selected college coursework provides

these students with an opportunity for accelerated learning regarding advanced concepts (Van Tassel-Baska, 2001).

Enrichment typically means providing richer and more varied educational experiences through increased depth and breath in content, instructional strategies requiring higher level thinking skills, and instructional resources that go beyond the typical curriculum (Davis & Rimm, 2004). Enrichment activities may address such goals as increasing creativity or critical thinking, encouraging students to pursue their own interests, engaging students in research, and involving them in independent or small group projects. To learn more about the available educational options for providing enrichment and acceleration, consult the list of programs described in Figure 16-3.

Grouping brings gifted students together for part or all of the day. Grouping is a structural accommodation that typically involves acceleration or enrichment. By grouping students who are gifted in mathematics, for example, teachers can offer the math curriculum at a more rapid pace. Within the general education classroom, teachers "cluster" gifted (and high-achieving) students together to engage them in more challenging activities.

Findings across multiple studies indicate that grouping of gifted students for advanced or accelerated instruction is more effective than grouping without acceleration. Students who are grouped for acceleration outperform their nonaccelerated peers by about one year. Students grouped together for enrichment outperform regular mixed-ability groups by the equivalent of 4 months (Kulik, 2003).

Differentiating Instructional Models

Among the most commonly recommended models for accommodating gifted and talented learners in the general education classroom are curriculum compacting, tiered assignments, and problem-based learning.

Feldhusen, Van Winkle, and Ehle (1996) stress the importance of determining what knowledge and skills have already been mastered by students to determine the level at which instruction will begin. The goal of **curriculum compacting** is to expand the amount of time academically capable students have to work on more challenging material by "either eliminating work that has been mastered previously or streamlining work that may be mastered at a pace commensurate with the student's ability" (Feldhusen et al., 1996, p. 50). This permits the student to replace unnecessary repetition of the basics with enriched and accelerated learning activities (Kennedy, 1995). The curriculum compacting technique also ensures that the gifted students cover the essential elements of the general education curriculum and it "is a powerful technique for adapting and developing curriculum for talented students in the regular classroom" (Howard, 2000, p. 560).

FIGURE 16-3   Options for Providing Enrichment and Acceleration

Acceleration
- Subject matter acceleration—remaining at grade level while advancing in specific subject areas (e.g., advanced placement classes).
- Telescoping—covering more than a full year's work in a given year (e.g., multiage grouping).
- Grade skipping—bypassing at least one year of instruction (e.g., early graduation).
- Early entrance—entering school at least one year younger than the norm (e.g., early admission to kindergarten or college).

Enrichment in the Regular Classroom
- Individualized programming
- Independent study
- Ability grouping
- Cluster grouping—all students who are gifted at a grade level are placed with one teacher to facilitate differentiated instruction.
- Flexible scheduling—students attend class less often than peers, perhaps for only 4 days each week.
- Use of faster paced, higher level materials
- Field trips
- Use of community resource persons at school

Special Classes
- Honors classes and seminars
- Advanced Placement
- Extra coursework
- Special course offerings (e.g., Junior Great Books)
- Use of a resource room or itinerant teacher on a weekly basis
- Segregated "pull-out" program for part of the day or week
- Full-time placement in a special class
- Special study centers
- Magnet schools—one may specialize in science, another in language arts. Students choose to enroll in a school that will serve them best.
- School within a school—a portion of the school is reserved for specialized classes for students who are gifted.
- Specialized school for students who are gifted (e.g., Bronx High School of Science)
- International Baccaulaureate

Flexible Scheduling (i.e., Offerings Outside the School Day)
- Extracurricular clubs
- Early-bird classes—special classes held before school
- Extended day
- Extended school year
- Saturday or after-school workshops, classes, excursions
- Summer courses
- Evening courses
- Online courses

Off-Campus Options
- Mentorships
- Individual study with a community member
- Internships—working in the field with a specialist
- Outreach activities—programs developed for students who are gifted at local museums, colleges, businesses, etc.
- Residential summer institutes
- Community-based career education
- Student exchange programs
- Credit for educational experiences outside school (e.g., travel)

Note: From "Gifted and Talented" by L. K. Silverman in *Exceptional Children and Youth* (3rd ed., pp. 281–283) by E. L. Meyer and T. M. Skritic (Eds.), 1988, Denver: Love. Copyright 1988 by Love. Adapted by permission.

Winebrenner (2001) has identified five steps to successful compacting:

1. Identify the learning objectives or standards all students must learn.
2. Offer a pretest opportunity to volunteers who think they may have already mastered the content, OR plan an alternate path through the content for those students who can learn the required material in less time than their age peers.
3. Plan and offer curriculum extensions for kids who are successful with the compacting opportunities.
4. Eliminate all drill, practice, review, or preparation for state or standardized tests for students who have already mastered such things.
5. Keep accurate records of students' compacting activities. (p. 32)

Research on gifted learners in general elementary classrooms indicates that curriculum compacting enables teacher to eliminate between 40% and 50% of the curriculum across content areas without negatively affecting students' achievement test scores. Students maintain their achievement scores even when the replacement activities are not in the same content area (Reis, Westberg, Kulikowich, & Purcell 1998). These findings suggest that curriculum compacting permits gifted students to pursue their special interests beyond the regular curriculum without decreasing their subject matter knowledge.

Tiering assignments refers to the practice of differentiating tasks within a classroom based on student readiness levels. Typically, all students receive assignments that address the same content objective or topic (e.g., understanding a sonnet) with specific activities varying in degree of difficulty. This method is especially useful in the general education classroom, where current performance levels vary from below grade level to well above grade level, as is the case for many gifted students. "This instructional strategy allows a teacher to accomplish two critical things at once. First, tiering allows the teacher to keep all students focused on the same essential learning goals. Second tiering enables the teacher to develop student tasks and products that are at appropriate levels of complexity for the varied learners in the classroom" (Tomlinson, 2001, p. 37). Consider an example provided by Heacox (2002) in which the goal for all students in the classroom is to acquire knowledge about rain forests through the development of a brochure. Depending on readiness level, students create a brochure on rain forests to (a) inform audiences about an environmental issue, (b) describe different points of view on an environmental issue, or (c) present a convincing argument after determining their own position on an issue related to rain forests. The three tasks require different levels of complexity from factual to analytic to persuasive. Depending on unit goals and learner needs, the teacher can tier by challenge level, complexity, resources, outcome, process, or product (Heacox, 2002).

Problem-based learning is a strategy that simulates real-world problem finding and problem solving by engaging students as stakeholders in situations with undefined problems and incomplete information. Students define issues, create hypotheses, conduct investigations, evaluate earlier hypotheses, develop and justify solutions, and consider ethical implications. As in the real world, they move forward, hit dead ends, revisit data, revise their thinking, choose new paths, and move on (Stepien & Pyke, 1997). The teacher develops the engagement scenario to ensure students cover preidentified knowledge and concepts, identifies resources, monitors student progress, provides supporting lessons as needed, and debriefs. General education teachers can implement problem-based learning for the whole classroom, with modifications for the gifted that include advanced content, complexity, interdisciplinary connections, higher order thinking skills, and ethical dilemmas (Gallagher, 2001). This strategy can also be used with a gifted student cluster. Problem-based learning is well matched to gifted learners' greater adeptness at problem finding and conceptual reasoning (Gallagher, 2001). The "Inclusion Tips for the Teacher" presents a sample lesson that includes a problem-based learning activity used to extend the curriculum for gifted students whose social studies curriculum has been compacted.

Differentiated Curriculum Models

General education teachers can select from an array of curriculum models developed for gifted students (Davis & Rimm, 2004; Van Tassel-Baska, 2001). Earlier emphasis on differentiation through higher order thinking skills in isolation has shifted to emphasis on content and depth of disciplinary knowledge while integrating thinking skills. One goal of gifted education is to enable gifted students to become "experts" as opposed to "novices" in the disciplines. Experts display a depth of content knowledge, skill in applying the methods of the discipline, ability to perceive meaningful patterns, rapid speed and accuracy in problem solving within the discipline, and automaticity of mental processing (Gallagher, 2003).

Van Tassel-Baska's (2003) Integrated Curriculum Model (ICM) combines advanced content, high-level thinking processes, and core themes and ideas in teaching a discipline (e.g., language arts, science, social studies). Research supports the effectiveness of ICM units with gifted students in a variety of educational settings. For example, gifted students from both economically disadvantaged and advantaged backgrounds showed significant gains in literary analysis and persuasive writing skills using the ICM language arts units.

Sternberg's (2003) theory of successful intelligence serves as the basis for curriculum development that involves teaching for analytical, creative, and practical thinking as well as for traditional memory learning. For example (Sternberg,

Inclusion Tips for the Teacher

A Sample Lesson for Gifted Learners

This sample lesson (adapted from Kitano & Pedersen, 2002) illustrates how curriculum compacting, problem-based learning, and a multicultural curriculum can be integrated for gifted learners.

Fifth-grade teacher Candace Perkins used curriculum compacting and problem-based learning to enrich the social studies curriculum of gifted students in her general education classroom. She created the problem-based learning scenario to encourage students to investigate diverse perspectives. She began by giving all students as a pretest the end-of-unit test on the American Revolution. Students who achieved 98% on the pretest had already mastered the core content. These students were given the opportunity to engage in a problem-based learning activity (Stepien & Pyke, 1997) on the same subject. Ms. Perkins presented the following engagement scenario:

The year is 1775. Sentiment among the colonists is hostile toward the King of England. Many patriots are in favor of becoming independent of British rule. As trusted advisors, you are asked to gather information to help assess whether independence would be a realistic goal. Your reports will be presented at the Second Continental Congress.

Participating students assumed the roles of experts (e.g., domestic advisor, international advisor, sociologist) preparing reports to be presented at the Continental Congress (to be held in class). They conducted their research in small groups using multiple sources (encyclopedias, textbooks, videos, Internet) while Ms. Perkins led the rest of the class through the core unit on the American Revolution.

Some of the students working on the scenario required no support from the teacher. A few experienced difficulty organizing their research. Ms. Perkins provided these students with a matrix graphic that helped the students to summarize material from several sources addressing the same issue and to synthesize their findings.

A gifted African American girl shared her enthusiasm: "I'm working on slavery and blacks during the American Revolution. I think this is the best thing I've done so far in school for social studies. I've put a lot of effort into it and take my time at home instead of playing. Like I ask my Grandma questions about what she knows. I love to study. I love to study what happens to slaves and blacks and what our history was. My questions are did the slaves fight in the Revolutionary War? What side were they on? What happened to them after the war?"

Another student investigated women's roles in the Revolutionary War. The students' collective presentations to the Second Continental Congress (i.e., the class) enriched all students' knowledge of the historical events of the period and enabled them to grasp a broader truth.

Note: Adapted from "Multicultural Content Integration in Gifted Education: Lesson from the Field," by M. K. Kitano and K. S. Pedersen (2002), *Journal for the Education of the Gifted, 25*(3), 269–289. Reprinted with permission.

1997), in art, students might compare and contrast how Rembrandt and Dali used light in their paintings (analytical), draw a beam of light (creative), and determine how the lighting in a given painting could be recreated in the classroom (practical). Research suggests that students taught for successful intelligence outperform students taught in traditional ways (Sternberg & Grigorenko, 2000, 2002).

The Parallel Curriculum Model (Tomlinson et al., 2002) constitutes an emerging practice. It synthesizes several approaches to curriculum for the gifted by proposing that teachers help gifted learners explore a discipline in four ways. The first is through the core curriculum—the framework of knowledge and skills defining a discipline. The Curriculum of Connections expands the core by enabling students to make connections within or across disciplines, times, cultures, and places. The Curriculum of Practice guides students in functioning like an expert in the discipline would function by applying concepts, skills, and methods of the discipline. The Curriculum of Identity helps students understand their own skills, interests, and values with respect to the discipline.

Integration of multicultural content and high-level thinking has been recommended as a strategy for engaging diverse and mainstream gifted learners. Ford and Harris's (1999) framework for multicultural gifted curriculum integrates increasingly transformative multicultural goals with higher level cognitive strategies. They view multicultural gifted curriculum as a promising strategy for engaging gifted students of color and providing needed opportunities to identify and connect with the curriculum. Kitano and Pedersen (2002) argue that all gifted students irrespective of background benefit from a challenging multicultural curriculum that integrates multicultural content, strategies appropriate for gifted students (e.g., problem-based learning), and culturally consonant instruction (accommodations for differences in approaches to communication and learning). The sample lesson presented earlier in the "Inclusion Tips for the Teacher" section provides an example of this integration.

An easy way to summarize accommodations for gifted students is to think of four types of differentiation: content, process, product, and environment (Maker & Nielson, 1996;

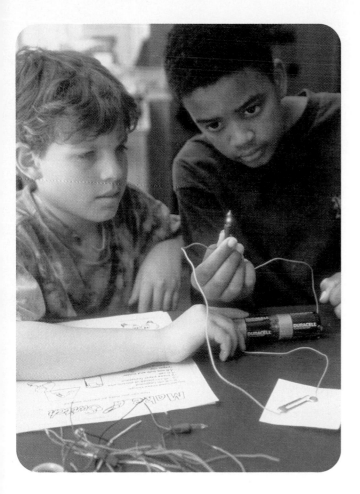

1. Teach pupils to be efficient and effective at independent study, instilling and polishing the skills called for in self-directed learning and in analyzing and solving problems on one's own.

2. Help pupils to invoke and apply complex cognitive processes such as creative thinking, critiques, and pro and con analyses.

3. Encourage pupils to press discussions of questions or issues all the way to the culminating activity of decision making and to clear communication to others of plans, status reports, or solutions based on the decisions.

4. Establish the human interaction skills necessary to work smoothly with groups of all ages and of all levels of cognitive development.

5. Aid pupils in acquiring respect for all other humans whatever their gifts or talents and in understanding themselves in relation to all others.

6. Build pupils' positive expectations about careers and about lives as adults that optimize their talents and gifts. (p. 185)

Creativity and problem solving are two important areas in which students who are gifted and talented may require special attention and instruction. No single accepted definition of **creativity** exists (Coleman & Cross, 2001). Cropley and Urban (2000) suggest that novelty serves as the common element and offers the following definition: "the production of relevant and effective novel ideas" (p. 486) promoting the common good. They argue that a combination of intelligence and creativity defines giftedness, because research suggests that productively gifted adults evidence both. Additionally, there is increasing evidence that creativity may be domain specific (Coleman & Cross, 2001), such that creativity in music, for example, is different from creativity in physics.

According to Davis (2003), creative adults show both creative abilities (e.g., fluency, flexibility, originality, elaboration, sensitivity to missing information, critical and analogical thinking) and creative personality traits. Personality traits related to creativity in adults include:

- original, imaginative, and unconventional;
- aware of own creative ability;
- independent, self-confident, unconcerned about impressing others;
- risk taking; not afraid to try something new;
- motivated, adventurous, spontaneous;
- curious, inquisitive, questioning;
- playful, sense of humor;
- likes complexity, novelty, ambiguity, incongruity;
- artistic;
- open-minded, receptive to new ideas, experiences, and viewpoints;
- reflective and introspective, needing time alone; and
- intuitive, perceptive.

Winebrenner, 2001). Gifted students require more advanced and complex content and materials that offer greater depth. Process differentiation can occur through instruction that is more open ended and appropriately paced and encourages higher level thinking, creativity, and pursuit of interests. Products enable students to demonstrate their understanding and can range from written reports to exhibitions, performances, or poems developed for real audiences. Environmental differentiation can include changes in the physical setting (library, lab), atmosphere (learner centered), or schedule. Time limits can be flexible to permit pursuit of in-depth research.

PROMOTING CREATIVITY AND PROBLEM SOLVING

When students who are gifted and talented are included in the general education classroom, their teacher is responsible for making program adaptations that facilitate maximum growth and development. Reynolds and Birch (1982) present six principles to help teachers provide appropriate educational experiences for this group of special students:

Teachers can enhance creativity in children. Goals for creativity training should focus on fostering creative consciousness and attitudes, improving understanding of creativity, exercising creative abilities, teaching creative thinking techniques, and involving students in creative activities (Davis, 2003). Teachers need to create a psychologically safe classroom environment; help students become aware of their creativity; encourage fantasy and imagination; give positive, constructive evaluations; help students resist peer pressure to conform; encourage questions, humor, risk taking, and original responses; and be aware that difficult behavior can be a manifestation of creativity (p. 320).

One component of creativity is divergent thinking. In divergent thinking, several solutions to one problem are suggested. Four factors are important:

- *Fluency*—the ability to generate many responses.
- *Flexibility*—the ability to change the form, modify information, or shift perspectives.
- *Originality*—the ability to generate novel responses.
- *Elaboration*—the ability to embellish an idea with details (Silverman, 1988, p. 276)

For ideas about ways to encourage creative thinking in gifted and talented students, consider the following suggestions:

- Provide regular opportunities for creative thinking. Creativity can be incorporated into most school subjects as soon as basic skills are acquired. Do not, however, ac-

cept novelty when accuracy is the goal. For example, spelling is one of the areas in which creativity should not be encouraged.

- Develop fluency with brainstorming sessions. Present a problem and see how many possible solutions can be suggested within a certain period of time. While students are brainstorming, do not evaluate the proposed solutions; instead, encourage a high rate of response. Younger students can practice with problems such as how to finance a trip to the toy store; older students may wish to suggest solutions for societal problems, such as how to provide proper health care for senior citizens or funding for public education. As for all the strategies, fluency should be integrated with curriculum content, for example, asking students to think of many ways to produce the number 32. In this example, solutions require evaluation.
- Encourage flexibility by considering various perspectives on an event. For example, in studying rain forests, have students imagine, and then confirm through research, the perspectives of all stakeholder groups, including the animals. Have students list solutions to a school problem from their own point of view. In literature, students can rewrite or visually depict the story from a different character's perspective.
- Develop original thinking by providing opportunities for its occurrence. Suggest problems or needs and direct students to come up with novel solutions. For example, in physical education, students might consider developing

a new game or adapting a traditional one to equitably include peers with various disabilities.

- In elaboration, ideas are expanded and made more detailed. Give students practice in elaborative thinking by presenting simple statements that they must expand. Use quotations or sayings, such as "All's well that ends well" and "All people are created equal." Or consider one of the novel responses produced in an original thinking exercise; have students expand the idea to include directions for implementation, ways of evaluating effectiveness, potential advantages, and possible disadvantages.

The "Spotlight on Technology" feature describes two web-based strategies for promoting higher level thinking skills, creativity, and problem solving. These strategies are WebQuests and Web Inquiry projects.

Problem solving is an extension of divergent thinking. It is important for students to become sensitive to the fact that problems exist and that they possess the skills required to develop appropriate solutions for these problems (Feldhusen, 1989). In his structure of intellect model, Guilford (1967) describes five types of mental operations: cognition, memory, divergent production, convergent production, and evaluation. Cognition and memory relate to the gathering of information about a specific problem. In divergent thinking,

several solutions are proposed; in convergent thinking, one "best" solution is selected. The final step is evaluation, in which the success of the selected solution is assessed; if the result is unsatisfactory, another solution can be chosen.

These different types of mental operations relate closely to the problem-solving model suggested by Gordon (1974). In this approach, conflicts are resolved by means of a six-step process:

1. defining the problem
2. generating possible solutions
3. evaluating the solutions
4. deciding which solution is best
5. deciding how to implement the solution
6. assessing how well the solution solved the problem. (p. 228)

In the second step, all possible solutions are specified (divergent production). Then the solutions are considered, and one is selected (convergent production). The process ends with implementation and evaluation of the chosen alternative.

The Gordon model is one that can be taught to students included in the general education program and then used for the solution of classroom problems. It is also useful as a general strategy for attacking any problem situation. To students who are gifted and talented, it represents a powerful tool to guide analysis, synthesis, and evaluation activities.

Spotlight on Technology

WebQuests and Web Inquiry Projects

WebQuests and Web Inquiry Projects (WIPs) are strategies designed to enable teachers to effectively use Internet resources in the classroom to support student learning of subject matter and skills in virtually any discipline (Molebash, Dodge, Bell, Mason, & Irving, 2004). Together, they offer inquiry opportunities appropriate for gifted students that range from structured (WebQuests) to open (WIPs).

WebQuests, created by Bernie Dodge and Tom March, typically engage students in a problem scenario, assign roles as stakeholders in the scenario, and provide links to Internet sources giving information critical to problem solution. Dodge (1995) lists as critical attributes a stage-setting introduction, an interesting task, a set of information sources embedded in the WebQuest as links, steps for accomplishing the task, guidance on organizing the information, and a conclu-

sion. WebQuests are considered structured inquiry in that the teacher presents the problem and prescribes procedures students will use for investigating. WebQuests can serve as scaffolding to more open-ended WIPs.

Web Inquiry Projects provide students with a snippet of information called a "hook," intended to arouse student interest and curiosity. Students are encouraged to ask questions, determine the types of data needed to answer their questions, identify procedures for collecting data, locate and analyze the data, and report their findings, which often lead to new questions. Thus, WIPs involve students in more open inquiry in which they formulate questions and determine procedures for investigation. Examples of both WebQuests and WIPs can be accessed at http://edweb.sdsu.edu/wip/

ASSISTING STUDENTS WHO ARE UNDERACHIEVING

Underachieving students who are gifted and talented are one of the great tragedies of education. Because their potential for achievement is so high, their failure to thrive in school represents a double loss. The reasons for underachievement are many and complex and include factors related to the school, home, student, and peers (Peters, Grager-Loidl, & Supplee, 2000).

Some, particularly students from diverse ethnic, cultural, or linguistic groups and those with disabilities, may simply be overlooked. Hallahan and Kauffman (1988) address this issue and others in their recommendations to general education teachers:

1. The teacher should periodically review the characteristics of all the pupils in the class in order not to overlook any child who may be gifted. Which students in the class show particular ability, creativity, and task commitment? Are there pupils in the class, especially pupils who are economically disadvantaged or. . . [from a diverse ethnic, cultural, or linguistic] group, whose abilities may be less obvious according to white middle-class standards or who may be masking their abilities because of peer pressure for conformity?

2. The teacher must analyze and adjust his or her educational requirements for gifted pupils. Is the gifted child turned off to education because the work is not challenging or is not suitable for his superior intellectual powers? Is the gifted child underachieving simply because he is not being given appropriate work? Especially with the disadvantaged or culturally different gifted, it is important to present specific educational tasks in a structured environment with the firm and consistent expectation that they will be completed. . . .

3. The teacher must seek out and employ the resources of the school and community that can be used to the advantage of gifted children. Are there other teachers or older students with knowledge of the problems and methods of inquiry in a field of special interest who can help the child in independent study or small-group activities? Are there residents of other communities with special expertise who are willing to tutor the child or use him as an assistant?

4. The teacher should support whatever movement there may be in the school system toward establishing special programs for the gifted. Are there parents of gifted children whose pleas for special programs should be encouraged? Are there workshops for teachers? Does the school system employ resource teachers or specialists who will help. . . [general education] teachers find methods, materials, community resources? (pp. 453–454)

Olenchak and Reis's (2002) recommendations for gifted students with learning disabilities include several that can be implemented by the general education teacher:

- focusing on strengths as opposed to deficits, acceleration in areas of academic strength;
- an IEP that addresses both strengths and needs;
- interest-based independent studies; and
- advanced-level courses (online or in person) in areas of strength for gifted students with learning disabilities in middle and high schools.

Pendarvis (1993) adds several ideas gleaned from various sources for removing the barriers to achievement:

- Don't give the students lectures or "pep talks" to get them to try harder. This has been shown to have detrimental effects on achievement.
- Show support and respect for the students' efforts.
- Establish appropriate standards and provide the instruction, guidance, and support to help students meet them.
- Encourage cooperation, rather than competition, in the classroom.
- Reward small gains in achievement, and don't expect quick success. (p. 583)

Coleman and Cross (2001) describe underachievement among gifted students as "likely to be one means of camouflaging competence" (p. 217). They note that, without early identification and guidance, a supportive teacher or counselor, and remedial-skills training in a sympathetic atmosphere, "underachievement is resistant to intervention" (p. 217). Recent research suggests that underachieving gifted students are not a homogeneous group, and interventions must be tailored to the individual student. McCoach and Siegle (2003) found that many underachieving gifted students see no benefits to schools. These authors recommend that interventions include creating classrooms and assignments that are more enjoyable and intrinsically motivating as well as activities that encourage students to value learning tasks or the outcome of those tasks for their future. Several suggestions for whetting students' appetites for learning appear in the following "Inclusion Tips for the Teacher" material. Additional resources are Winebrenner's (2001) *Teaching Gifted Kids in the Regular Classroom*, Karnes and Bean's (2001) *Methods and Materials for Teaching the Gifted*, and Gross, Sleap, and Pretorius's (1999) *Gifted Students in Secondary Schools: Differentiating the Curriculum*. The "Window on the Web" provides websites for organizations, resources, and special programs that offer more information about giftedness and talent.

In this chapter, you have learned about some of the characteristics of students who are unusually bright and those with special gifts and talents. Methods for identifying appropriate educational options, promoting creativity and problem solving, and assisting underachievers have been suggested. In the next chapter, you will meet another group of students with special needs—those from culturally and linguistically diverse backgrounds.

Inclusion Tips for the Teacher

Promoting Appropriate Instruction for Gifted Students

Kennedy (1995) provides several suggestions for general education teachers to consider when reviewing their classroom practices with gifted students:

1. *Resist policies requiring more work of those who finish assignments quickly and easily.* Instead, explore ways to assign different work which may be more complex, more abstract, and both deeper and wider. Find curriculum compacting strategies that work, and use them regularly.

2. *Seek out supplemental materials and ideas which extend, not merely reinforce, the curriculum.* Develop interdisciplinary units and learning centers that call for higher level thinking. Don't dwell on comprehension-level questions and tasks for those who have no problems with comprehension. Encourage activities that call for analysis, synthesis, and critical thinking, and push beyond superficial responses.

3. *De-emphasize grades and other extrinsic rewards.* Encourage learning for its own sake, and help perfectionists establish realistic goals and priorities. Try to ensure that the self-esteem of talented learners does not rest solely on their products and achievements.

4. *Encourage intellectual and academic risk-taking.* The flawless completion of a simple worksheet by an academically talented student calls for little or no reward, but struggling with a complex, open-ended issue should earn praise. Provide frequent opportunities to stretch mental muscles.

5. *Help all children develop social skills to relate well to one another.* For gifted children this may require special efforts to see things from other viewpoints. Training in how to "read" others and how to send accurate verbal and nonverbal messages may also be helpful. Tolerate neither elitist attitudes nor anti-gifted discrimination.

6. *Take time to listen to responses that may at first appear to be off-target.* Gifted children often are divergent thinkers who get more out of a story or remark and have creative approaches to problems. Hear them out, and help them elaborate on their ideas.

7. *Provide opportunities for independent investigations in areas of interest.* Gifted children are often intensely, even passionately, curious about certain topics. Facilitate their in-depth explorations by teaching research skills as needed, redirecting them to good resources, and providing support as they plan and complete appropriate products.

8. *Be aware of the special needs of gifted girls.* Encourage them to establish realistically high-level educational and career goals, and give them additional encouragement to succeed in math and science (pp. 233–234).

Window on the Web

Websites About Giftedness and Talent

Organizations Related to Gifted and Talented Education

- GT World (http://www.gtworld.org)
- National Association for Gifted Children (NAGC) (http://www.nagc.org)
- National Foundation for Gifted and Creative Children (http://www.nfgcc.org)
- The Association for the Gifted (http://www.cectag.org)
- World Council for Gifted and Talented Children (http://www.worldgifted.org)
- Supporting the Emotional Needs of the Gifted, Inc. (http://www.SENGifted.org)

Web Resources

- Hoagies' Gifted Education Page (http://www.hoagiesgifted.org)
- Odyssey of the Mind (http://www.odysseyofthemind.com)

continued

continued

Special Programs and Research Centers

- Connie Belin and Jacqueline N. Blank International Center for Talented & Gifted Education, University of Iowa (http://www.uiowa.edu/~belinctr)
- Northwestern University Center for Talent Development (http://www.ctd.northwestern.edu)
- Duke University Talent Identification Program (TIP) (http://www.tip.duke.edu)
- Education Program for Gifted Youth at Stanford University (http://www.epgy.stanford.edu/epgy)
- Jacob K. Javits Gifted and Talented Students Education Program (http://www.ed.gov/programs/javits/index.html)
- National Consortium for Specialized Secondary Schools of Mathematics, Science, and Technology (http://www.ncsssmst.org)
- National Research Center on Gifted and Talented at the University of Connecticut (http://www.ucc.uconn.edu:80/~wwwgt/nrcgt.html)
- The Center for Talented Youth at the Johns Hopkins University (http://www.jhu.edu/~gifted)
- College of William and Mary Center for Gifted Education (cfge.wm.edu)

For more information, go to the Web Links module in Chapter 16 of the Companion Website.

Things to Remember

- For achievement to be commensurate with potential, students who are gifted and talented require special educational adaptations in the general education class or in separate programs.
- Students who are gifted and talented are characterized by their above-average ability. Their gift or talent can be in intellectual performance, creativity, academic achievement, leadership potential, or special areas of endeavor such as art or music.
- This group of special students is composed of both males and females and individuals representing all socioeconomic strata and cultures. As a group, students who are gifted and talented are more verbal, learn more rapidly, and are better adjusted than their typical class peers.
- The major educational adaptations for students who are gifted and talented are acceleration, enrichment, and grouping for challenging instruction. General education teachers can use curriculum compacting to reduce the coverage of material already mastered. Tiered assignments and problem-based learning also can be used in the general education classroom to differentiate instruction for gifted students.

- One important goal in the education of this group of special students is to provide opportunities to develop disciplinary and interdisciplinary expertise through a challenging curriculum.
- Teachers can support gifted students' development of creativity and problem-solving skills by engaging them in divergent thinking and convergence and evaluation as they encounter unanswered questions, problems, and issues in their studies.
- Students who are gifted and talented do not all excel in school; some, considered underachievers, remain unidentified or lack sufficient motivation to perform near their potential.
- Most students who are gifted and talented remain in the general education program for the majority of their school careers. To meet their special learning needs, educators must adapt the instructional procedures in the general education classroom.
- It is not necessary to be gifted or talented to be an effective teacher of such students. It is more important to be passionate about knowledge acquisition, self-confident, open, and an adept facilitator of learning.

ACTIVITIES

1. Observe a general education classroom in which one or more students have been identified as gifted or talented. Are these pupils involved in any special programs outside the classroom or school? What special provisions are made in the general education classroom? Are techniques such as curriculum compacting used to eliminate the need for students to work on material they have already mastered or to streamline the pace at which they master other materials? Do the behaviors of these students differ in any way from those of their peers? Are they well accepted by their classmates and teacher?

2. Interview children or young adults who have been identified as gifted or talented. What are their current interests? What do they like and dislike about school? Ask them to suggest ways in which the school experience could be made more valuable to them.

3. Locate articles that discuss education of pupils who are gifted and talented. *G/T/C (Gifted/Talented/Creative), Gifted and Talented International, Roeper Review, Journal of Creative Behavior, Journal for the Education of the Gifted, Gifted Child Today, Journal of Secondary Gifted Education,* and *The Gifted Child Quarterly* are possible sources. Can you find suggestions for general education class adaptations? For assisting underachievers? For students from diverse ethnic, cultural, or linguistic groups?

4. Contact local schools to find out what services are available for youngsters who are gifted and talented. What procedures are used to identify students? Are there special classes? Early admission? Resource services? Enrichment programs to augment the general education classroom? What assistance is available to the general education teacher? Are students with disabilities enrolled in the program?

5. Ask several members of your community to define the terms *gifted* and *talented.* You might select teachers, students, school administrators, parents of school-aged children, and others with no current connection with the public school system. Compare their definitions to see whether there is any consensus. Use the information you have collected to prepare a set of local definitions meaningful to the persons in your community. Be clear and concise, and use language understandable to both educators and the general public.

CD-ROM Activities

View the video case study featuring the high school physics class and look for the young woman student who would likely be identified as gifted. Think about her special needs as you answer these questions:

- *How could the classroom bridge project be adapted to challenge this student's higher level thinking skills?*

- *What research tools and information sources are available to students in this classroom? What others could be provided to enrich the experience even more for very capable learners?*

Teaching Culturally and Linguistically Diverse Students

CHAPTER

17

Juanito

Let's begin with the case of Juanito, or Pablo, or Pedro, who is attending school for the first time. He comes to school with a language that has served him quite well for his first five years and with possibly some knowledge of English. He has grown up in a Mexican American family with traditional values unique to his culture and has been socialized in this culture. He goes to a school which reflects the values of the dominant society. This child comes in having a different language and a different culture from that of the school. He finds himself in a strange and threatening situation, not only with the need to master a new language, but to make immediate use of it in order to function as a student. Moreover, many of the social relationships and cultural attitudes on which the total school program is based are completely outside his experience. (Sierra, 1973, p. 43).

Chau

Chau became an honor student this year. Seventeen years old and a tenth grader, she is enrolled in a college prep curriculum with plans for becoming a counseling psychologist. . . . Born to a privileged Vietnamese family, Chau was six years old when the North Vietnamese entered Saigon as victors. She remembers hiding for hours with relatives in a cellar until the shooting stopped and then walking home over, and on, the bodies of those massacred. She remembers the government troops replacing a picture of her grandparents with one of Ho Chi Minh and then removing all furniture, clothes, and other belongings from her home. . . . And she remembers her first attempt to flee Vietnam with two brothers. Discovered by roving government troops, one brother escaped, one was killed, and Chau was shot and left for dead. (Cegelka, 1988, p. 547)

LOOKING AHEAD

This chapter is about students like Juanito, Chau, and others who might be considered to add diversity to the general education classroom. As you read, think about these questions:

- Why is it important to be familiar with the cultures of the students in your classroom?
- If you were Juanito's teacher, what steps could you take to make him and his family feel welcome in your classroom?
- How might life experiences like those of Chau influence a student's view on the value of schooling?
- What types of classroom adaptations would you recommend to assist students who are English learners?

To answer these questions online, go to the Students' Stories module in Chapter 17 of the Companion Website.

The United States is a nation rich in diversity, and the composition of many general education classrooms reflects this richness. Students may differ from one another and from their teachers in many ways, including in culture and in language. Because of this, such students may be considered culturally and/or linguistically diverse. When such diversity is encouraged and fostered by society, the approach is known as *cultural pluralism* (Rueda & Prieto, 1979).

Although every person is an individual with distinct characteristics, each is influenced by the culture in which he or she is reared and in which he or she lives. Andersen and Taylor (2002) define **culture** as

> the complex system of meaning and behavior that defines the way of life for a given group or society. It includes beliefs, habits, language, and dress, among other things. (p. 60)

Aragon (1973) adds that those who are members of a cultural group "must subscribe to a common set of values and beliefs or have a common set of ethics" (p. 26).

Students in schools in the United States represent many different cultures. The dominant culture, sometimes called the *macroculture,* has its roots in western European traditions. According to Gollnick and Chinn (1990), "the major cultural influence on the United States, particularly on its institutions, has been white, Anglo-Saxon, and Protestant" (p. 12). Persons living in the United States are influenced by the macroculture whether or not they choose to adopt all of its values and belief systems.

Each individual is also influenced by his or her membership in several microcultures. A *microculture* is a group of individuals who share some, but not all, of the cultural patterns of the macroculture and a common set of cultural patterns distinct from those of the macroculture (Gollnick & Chinn, 1998). Microcultures may be based on factors such as ethnicity or national origin, socioeconomic class, religion, gender, age, disability, or the area of the country in which a person lives (Gollnick & Chinn, 1998). Consider, for example, the differences between the customs and mores of New England and those of the Deep South or the differences in cultural patterns among Irish Americans, Mexican Americans, and Chinese Americans.

The term *minority* is used to describe groups with fewer members than the "majority" group. In the past, U.S. census data and other sources of demographic information often defined the following populations as minorities: black; Hispanic; Asian and Pacific Islander; and American Indian, Eskimo, and Aleut. However, a change occurred with the 2000 census. When citizens were asked to indicate their group membership, they could choose between "one race" or "two or more races." Also, individuals of all races were asked to indicate whether or not they considered themselves Hispanic or Latino. These category changes resulted in a more complex picture of the diversity within the United States, as Table 17-1 shows. It is also important to recognize that each of these groups is itself heterogeneous. For example, among people with Asian roots are those who identify themselves as

For Your Information

Cultural and Linguistic Diversity in the United States

- Gollnick and Chinn (1998) report that "the United States is comprised of at least 276 ethnic groups, including 170 Native American groups" (p. 78).
- Asian Americans include (but are not limited to) Japanese, Chinese, Filipino, Korean, Vietnamese, Cambodian, Laotian, Guamanian, Indian, Pakistani, Burmese, Thai, Marshallese, Saipanese, Ponapean, and Yapese individuals (Cheng, 1991; Decano, 1979; Garcia, 1978). Asian Americans are the fastest growing "minority" group, now numbering more than 10 million (Chan, 1998; U.S. Census Bureau, 2000a).
- Native Americans number more than 2 million and show great diversity in culture and language, as evidenced by the more than 500 different tribal groups and the more than 200 different Native American languages in use today (Garcia, 1978; Joe & Malach, 1998; McDonald, 1989; Pepper, 1976).

- The largest bilingual group is Hispanics (sometimes called Latinos). Hispanics can be any race. According to the latest census, they number more than 35 million persons (U.S. Census Bureau, 2000a).
- African Americans are the largest "minority"; the more than 34 million African Americans make up 12% of the U.S. population (U.S. Census Bureau, 2000a; Willis, 1998).
- More than 44 million people in the United States—or almost 18% of the population ages 5 and above—speak languages other than English (U.S. Census Bureau, 2000b). The most common language is Spanish, spoken by more than 26 million persons.
- Students who are English learners numbered 4.5 million in 2000–2001. They made up 11.7% of elementary school enrollment and 6.9% of the secondary school enrollment (Kindler, 2002a).

Chinese, Vietnamese, Laotian, Hmong, Cambodian, Filipino, Korean, Japanese, and Asian Indian (Cheng, 1991; U.S. Census Bureau, 2000b). Also, the Native American population is made up of more than 500 tribes with more than 200 different languages (McDonald, 1989).

Table 17-1 also presents recent information about the composition of U.S. public schools. Although school data are not collected in precisely the same way as census data, the table shows that school populations contain larger proportion of persons of color than the population at large. For example, while black or African Americans make up 12.3% of the U.S. population, students who are black and non-Hispanic make up 17.2% of the elementary and secondary school population. This trend is present in all student groups except students considered white and non-Hispanic.

Minority is considered to be a pejorative term. In addition, in many parts of the country, it is inaccurate. Consider these statistics about the changing nature of the U.S. population:

- America's racial profile is rapidly changing. Between 1980 and 1990, the rate of increase in the population for white Americans was 6 percent, while the rate of increase for racial and ethnic minorities was much higher: 53 percent for Hispanics, 13.2 percent for African-Americans, and 107.8 percent for Asians. . . .
- Taken together as a group, it is a more frequent phenomenon for minorities to comprise the majority of public school students. Large city school populations are overwhelmingly minority, for example: for fall 1993, the figure for Miami was 84 percent; Chicago, 89 percent; Philadelphia, 78 percent; Baltimore, 84 percent;

Houston, 88 percent; and Los Angeles, 88 percent. [PL 105–17, Individuals with Disabilities Education Act Amendments of 1997, Sec. 601(c)(7)]
- The limited English proficient population is the fastest growing in our Nation, and the growth is occurring in many parts of our Nation. In the Nation's two largest school districts, limited-English students make up almost half of all students initially entering school at the kindergarten level. [PL 101–476, Individuals with Disabilities Education Act, 1990, Sec. 610 (j)(1)]

There have been many approaches to the education of students from culturally and linguistically diverse groups. Kitano (1991) describes two major philosophical positions underlying these approaches: assimilation and pluralism. In assimilation, the goal is to move students away from their original culture and teach them the skills needed to compete in the macroculture. In pluralism, students are encouraged to retain their original culture, and, to promote educational success, schools make accommodations based on students' experiential backgrounds.

Multicultural education is an instructional approach based on the pluralistic perspective. This approach is defined as "education which values cultural pluralism" (American Association of Colleges for Teacher Education, 1973, p. 264). Gollnick and Chinn (1998) identify six fundamental beliefs and assumptions underlying the concept of multicultural education:

- Cultural differences have strength and value.
- Schools should be models for the expression of human rights and respect for cultural differences.

TABLE 17-1 Diversity in the United States and in U.S. Public Schools

| | U.S. POPULATION | | U.S. SCHOOLS | |
CHARACTERISTIC	NUMBER	PERCENT	GROUP	PERCENT
One race				
White	211,460,626	75.1	White, non-Hispanic	60.3
Black or African American	34,658,190	12.3	Black, non-Hispanic	17.2
American Indian and Alaska Native	2,475,956	0.9	American Indian/Alaska Native	1.2
Asian	10,242,998	3.6	Asian/Pacific Islander	4.2
Native Hawaiian and other Pacific Islander	398,835	0.1		
Some other race	15,359,073	5.5		
Two or more races	6,826,228	2.4		
Hispanic or Latino (of any race)	35,305,818	12.5	Hispanic	17.1

Note: U.S. population data from U.S. Census Bureau. (2000). *Profile of General Demographic Characteristics: 2000.* Washington, DC: Author. Retrieved June 1, 2001, from the World Wide Web: http://factfinder.census.gov/servlet/BasicFactsServlet

U.S. school population data from U.S. Department of Education, National Center for Education Statistics. (2002). *Common Core of Data, State Nonfiscal Survey of Public Elementary/Secondary Education.* Retrieved October 15, 2004, from http://nces.ed.gov/quicktables/Detail.asp?Key=963

- Social justice and equality for all people should be of paramount importance in the design and delivery of curricula.
- Attitudes and values necessary for the continuation of a democratic society can be promoted in schools.
- Schooling can provide the knowledge, dispositions, and skills for the redistribution of power and income among cultural groups.
- Educators working with families and communities can create an environment that is supportive of multiculturalism. (p. 28)

Somewhat different terms are used today in education to describe teachers, classrooms, schools, and programs that welcome and nurture the diversity of students and their families. These terms include *cultural responsiveness* (Correa & Heward, 2003), *cross-cultural competence* (Lynch & Hanson, 2004), and *cultural synchronization* (Irvine, 1990, cited in Cooper, 2003; Monroe & Obidah, 2004).

Figure 17-1 presents a checklist developed by Ortiz (1988) for evaluating a school or district's educational environment and its effectiveness for culturally diverse learners. Among the factors to consider are the relevance of the cur-

| FIGURE 17-1 | Evaluating the Educational Context |

For each of the items below, circle "Yes" if the statement is characteristic of your school (or your district, if you prefer). Circle "No" if the statement is not characteristic of your school or district.

Yes	No	1.	My school/district supports cultural pluralism.
Yes	No	2.	The curriculum incorporates students' contemporary culture, not only history, customs and holidays.
Yes	No	3.	The curriculum helps students strike a balance between cultural pride and identity on one hand and appreciation of cultures different from their own on the other.
Yes	No	4.	The curriculum teaches certain humanistic values such as the negative effects of prejudice and discrimination.
Yes	No	5.	My school/district is integrated (or facilitates opportunities for cross-cultural interaction).
Yes	No	6.	Inservices routinely incorporate considerations in teaching linguistically/culturally diverse students.
Yes	No	7.	Children are encouraged to use their native language.
Yes	No	8.	The administration supports bilingual education.
Yes	No	9.	Minority parents are actively encouraged to participate in school activities.
Yes	No	10.	Training is provided to facilitate involvement of minority parents in their children's education.
Yes	No	11.	The regular classroom curriculum is appropriate for the diverse student populations served.
Yes	No	12.	Regular classroom (not only bilingual education or ESL) teachers understand how limited English proficient students acquire English competence and incorporate language development activities in subject matter instruction.
Yes	No	13.	Minority students do as well on achievement tests as do Anglo students.
Yes	No	14.	Poor students do as well as middle- and upper-income students on tests of academic achievement.
Yes	No	15.	As much emphasis is given to developing higher cognitive skills as is given to basic skill attainment.
Yes	No	16.	Teachers are facilitators of learning as opposed to transmitters of information and facts.
Yes	No	17.	Teachers adjust instructional approaches and activities to accommodate culturally-conditioned learning styles.
Yes	No	18.	Informal assessment is given as much emphasis as is formal assessment in psychoeducational evaluations of linguistically/culturally different students.
Yes	No	19.	Teachers are trained in informal assessment procedures.
Yes	No	20.	Reading and writing instruction is characterized by student control and an emphasis on meaningful communication and creativity.
Yes	No	21.	There is a well-articulated prereferral process in place to assure that students receive appropriate educational opportunities before they are referred to special education.
Yes	No	22.	The emphasis of assessment is on gleaning information to guide intervention.
Yes	No	23.	Students participate in school governance.
Yes	No	24.	Teachers are involved in planning and selecting inservice training topics and activities.
Yes	No	25.	My school/district would be described as a "happy" place by minority students and parents.

Note: This questionnaire was developed by Alba A. Ortiz, Department of Special Education, the University of Texas at Austin; it appeared in the *Bilingual Special Education Newsletter* (Vol. 7, Spring 1988) published by the University of Texas at Austin. The questionnaire may be reproduced without special permission when appropriate credit is given to the author.

riculum, parental participation, student involvement, and opportunities for teachers to continue to refine their skills.

DIVERSITY IN THE GENERAL EDUCATION CLASSROOM

Students are considered culturally diverse when their home culture is at variance with that of the school. According to Hodgkinson (1993):

> . . . the population of American schools today truly represents the world. Children come to school today with different diets, different religions (there were more Moslems than Episcopalians in the U.S. in 1991), different individual and group loyalties, different music, different languages. (p. 620)

Some culturally diverse students were born in the United States and have lived there all their lives; others are recent immigrants still experiencing the shock of adapting to an entirely new culture. Immigrants come from all parts of the world, but in recent years the majority have been Latin Americans and Asians (Hodgkinson, 1993; Kellogg, 1988). Some are refugees who were forced to flee their homelands. The article "Educating Refugees: Understanding the Basics" (1989) reports that "in many cases, refugees have had to abruptly leave their home culture, language, family and friends, and may never be able to return to their countries" (p. 1).

Some students differ from their peers in not only culture but also language. They may speak with an accent or in a dialect; some may know little English and may feel more comfortable speaking the language of their home. Correa and Heward (1996) estimate that more than 8 million U.S. students have limited proficiency in English. The population of a single district or school may reflect several of the more than 3,000 languages spoken in the world (Cheng, 1991; Winzer &

Mazurek, 1998). Smith (2001) reports that more than 100 languages are spoken in urban districts such as those of New York City, Chicago, Los Angeles, and Fairfax County, Virginia. Cegelka (1988) provides examples of individual schools in California that serve 25 to 38 different language groups.

Some culturally diverse students have special learning needs, and others do not. Some have disabilities, some are gifted, and others are average achievers. Like their peers, most are best served in the general education classroom. However, the general education teacher must recognize the impact of cultural and linguistic diversity on the performance of these students. Knowledge of and respect for differences among cultural groups will help the teacher provide a more successful educational experience for all students.

CULTURAL DIVERSITY

Culture influences behavior. Within each culture is a set of values and beliefs that guides the members of that culture in social interactions. However, what is accepted as desirable conduct in one culture may be considered inappropriate in another. The classroom teacher must be aware of such differences in order to understand the behavior of students from diverse groups.

Before proceeding, it is important to point out that descriptions of cultures are necessarily generalizations. As such, they provide some guidance in understanding the customs and beliefs of a group of persons but little information about specific individuals within that group. As Lynch (2004a) warns:

> Culture is only one of the characteristics that determine individuals' and families' attitudes, values, beliefs, and ways of behaving. . . . Assuming that cultural information . . . applies to all individuals from the cultural group is not only inaccurate but also dangerous; it can lead to stereotyping that diminishes rather than enhances cross-cultural competence. The goal of cultural learning is insight, not stereotype. When applying cultural information to an individual or family, it is wise to proceed with caution. (p. 58)

Also important to consider are these key points about culture (Lynch, 2004b):

1. *Culture is not static; it is dynamic and ever changing. . . .*
2. *Culture, language, ethnicity, and race are not the only determinants of one's values, beliefs, and behaviors. . . .*
3. *In describing any culture or cultural practice, within-group differences are as great as across-group differences—sometimes greater. . . .*
4. *Discussions of culture and ethnicity are typically framed in terms of differences in relation to another group. . . .*
5. *Everyone is the product of one or more cultures, and everyone has a culture. . . . (pp. 23–24)*

Window on the Web

Websites Related to Diversity

We Hold These Truths to Be Self-Evident

http://edweb.sdsu.edu/people/CMathison/truths/truths.html

This site is an online learning activity on democratic schooling designed for educators. Included are resources and information on students with disabilities, gender issues in education, and a number of cultures: Latino, gay and lesbian, African American, American Indian, and Asian American.

We Hold These Truths to be Self-Evident:
Evidence of Democratic Principles in Our Schools

Note: Courtesy of Carla Mathison.

National Clearinghouse for English Language Acquisition

http://www.ncela.gwu.edu/

The website of the National Clearinghouse for English Language Acquisition is operated by George Washington University and funded by the U.S. Department of Education's Office of English Language Acquisition, Language Enhancement and Academic Achievement for Limited English Proficient Students. It features resources on a number of topics (e.g., Language and Culture, Curriculum and Instruction), resources for specific audiences (e.g., Parents and Community, Teachers, Student Researchers), statistics related to English learners, a practice section containing research-based strategies for educating diverse learners (e.g., Toolkit for Effective Instruction for English Language Learners), information about policy, and an Ask an Expert section.

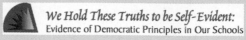

National Clearinghouse for English Language Acquisition &
Language Instruction Educational Programs

Note: Courtesy of NCELA.

Companion Website

For more information, go to the Web Links module in Chapter 17 of the Companion Website.

Keeping these points in mind, it is also important for teachers to gather information about the cultures of the students in their classrooms. The literature provides some assistance as do websites such as those described in the "Window on the Web" feature.

Pepper (1976) and Joe and Malach (2004) observe that there are many differences between the values of the dominant culture in the United States and those of the Native American culture. For example, whereas the macroculture emphasizes competition and individual achievement, Native American culture stresses cooperation, collaboration, and group achievement. Also, in contrast to the dominant culture, in which words are the primary mode of communication, Native American students are more likely to express themselves through actions. These cultural differences can affect a student's ability to conform to the expectations of the school. In discussing points of divergence between the two cultures, Walker (1988) notes:

- Family or cultural expectations for child behavior may differ from the expectations of the educational setting. For example, levels of independence in decision making might be greater for American Indian children.

- Identification of a child with his or her peer group may be more important than selection or recognition as an individual, thus inhibiting performance [by] noncompetitiveness.

- Cultural and family expectations for verbal interactions with adults may be contradictory to teacher expectations. (pp. 50–51)

Other cultures also have value systems that may be in conflict with the expectations of the dominant-culture school. Kitano (1973) describes several characteristics of Asian culture that may affect student behavior:

- The Asian doesn't do anything that would make him stand out from the group. . . .

- The Asian culture utilizes a much more indirect or subtle means of communication than we usually find here in this country. . . .

- The Asian family structure is based on the traditional agrarian family model; males are considered more desirable than females. . . .

- Very few Asians engage in free participation in group discussions. Generally, they feel that if they say something, it must be profound and important (p. 14).

Chan and Lee (2004) add that the traditional Asian culture is characterized by its roots in an agricultural civilization, polytheistic and spiritualistic religion, heart-oriented philosophy, collectivist (we) social orientation, family-centered home life, and indirect communication style. In contrast, the U.S. mainstream culture reflects an industrial civilization, monotheistic religion, mind-oriented philosophy, individual (I) social orientation, individual-centered home life, and direct communication style.

Several authors have addressed the effects of Latino culture on student behavior (Aragon & Marquez, 1973; Condon, Peters, & Sueiro-Ross, 1979; Rodriguez, Cole, Stile, & Gallegos, 1979; Sierra, 1973; Zuniga, 2004). Cultural characteristics frequently mentioned are the existence of close family ties and strong family loyalties, preference for cooperative rather than competitive activities, emphasis on interpersonal relationships rather than tasks, and a relaxed sense of time (in relation to that of the macroculture).

Likewise, values of the African American culture can influence students' classroom behavior. Willis (2004) observes that African Americans have a collective orientation and are more oriented to situation than time; the mainstream culture, in contrast, is characterized by orientations that are individual and favor time rather than situation. Teachers expect students to speak one at a time and to listen quietly while others are speaking. However, African American culture emphasizes general audience participation and spontaneity, not taking turns (Ratleff, 1989). Schools value verbal expression over other modes of communication. In contrast, African American culture encourages not only speech but other forms of expression as well, including body language, nonverbal communication, and visual and dramatic expression (Ratleff, 1989; Rivera & Rogers-Adkinson, 1997). Franklin (1992) adds that African American students prefer

student-centered classrooms with multiple opportunities for interpersonal interactions.

Although all persons are influenced by their cultures, they remain individuals; no group of people is homogeneous. However, it is worthwhile for teachers to attempt to gain insight into the cultural backgrounds of their students—and to identify their own values and belief systems. Lynch (2004b) identifies three components of cross-cultural competence for teachers and other professionals: awareness of one's own culture, awareness and understanding of students' cultures, and development of effective cross-cultural communication skills.

LINGUISTIC DIVERSITY

Language is another important consideration in the education of students from diverse backgrounds. Although some students are quite competent in English, others enter school speaking little or no English. The language of a student's family also concerns the teacher. Even if a child is fluent in English, the parents may not feel comfortable conversing in that language. For many (but certainly not all) culturally diverse students, the language spoken in the home is not English but the family's **heritage language.** Their parents and siblings may speak Spanish, one of many Asian languages, or one of many Native American tongues. Students who enter school with few English language skills are at a distinct disadvantage; as noted by Sierra (1973), the school expects these students not only to speak English but also to use that language to acquire other school skills.

According to the national Clearinghouse for English Language Acquisition (Kindler, 2002b), in 1999–2000, more than 400 languages were spoken by English learners in U.S. schools. Table 17-2 identifies the ten most common languages.

TABLE 17-2	Common Languages in U.S. Schools*		
LANGUAGE	**ESTIMATED NUMBER OF ENGLISH LEARNERS**	**ESTIMATED PERCENTAGE OF ENGLISH LEARNERS (%)**	**DIALECTS, VARIANTS, AND ALTERNATE NAMES**
Spanish	2,820,005	76.6	
Vietnamese	86,365	2.3	
Hmong	81,119	2.2	
Creole (Haitian)	39,867	1.1	Includes "French Creole"
Korean	38,984	1.1	
Cantonese	26,826	1.0	
Arabic	34,326	0.9	Regional Arabic dialects
Russian	34,083	0.9	
Navajo	33,936	0.9	Dine
Tagalog	30,303	0.8	Pilipino, Filipino

Note: From Kindler, A. L. (2002), *What Are the Most Common Language Groups for LEP students?* National Clearinghouse for English Language Acquisition. Retrieved October 16, 2004, from http://www.ncela.gwu.edu/expert/askncela/05toplangs.htm

Table 17-2 also illustrates that Spanish is the most common language group for students who are **English learners.** Much has been written regarding the overlap between language and culture and the difficulties this overlap presents in the education of students whose dominant language is Spanish. Condon et al. (1979) cite the examples of Lado (1968), which identify communication problems that can occur among speakers of Spanish and speakers of English:

- The use of the name "Jesús" for a boy is quite common in Hispanic society, but not in the Anglo-Saxon community, where it is regarded as inappropriate, if not sacrilegious.
- To be "informal" in Spanish is "to be neglectful," but to be so in English simply conveys the notion of "casual" behavior.
- "Compromiso" as it applies to negotiations carries a negative connotation in Hispanic culture which is not found in its English counterpart "compromise." (p. 82)

Evans and Guevara discuss other problems of communication that result from the interdependence of language and culture, and the examples that follow are drawn from their article (1974, p. 17). One major concern is that it is not always possible to translate a word from one language to another. A case in point is the English word *pet.* Because there is no equivalent in Spanish, it might be translated as *animal doméstico* (an animal that has been domesticated) or *animalito* (little animal). In addition, translations may be inaccurate.

The word *tool* in English refers to a category that contains many different exemplars. In Spanish, there is no general term for *tools.* Instead, native speakers talk about *fierros* (tools made of iron or steel), *equipo* (equipment), or *útiles* (utensils). Another example is the English word *hot;* in Spanish it can translate as *caliente* (hot in temperature) or *picante* (spicy hot).

When children learn English after their heritage language, their speech may sound somewhat different from that of students who are native speakers of English. A teacher may note that they speak with an accent. One reason for this is the nonequivalence of speech sounds between languages. Taylor (1986) points out that Spanish speech sounds can interfere with English pronunciation. For instance, a Spanish speaker may substitute *chair* for *share* and *watch* for *wash* in English.

Note that not all culturally diverse students speak more than one language; for many, English is the language of their home, and it is the only language that they know. However, they may speak a dialect of English rather than the standard English of the public school. One example is Black English, considered by many experts to be a dialect of standard English. Black English is also called Vernacular Black English or Ebonics (Gollnick & Chinn, 1998), and it is characterized by its own formal rules and structures. Among the examples Bryen (1974) gives of Black English (versus "standard" English) are *He goin* (versus *He is gone*), *John, he live in New York* (versus *John lives in New York*), and *He be here* (versus *He is here all the time*) (p. 593).

ASSESSMENT AND SPECIAL SERVICES

Although most culturally diverse students receive their education in the general education classroom, some may be referred for assessment if they appear to have special learning needs. If students are identified as gifted or talented or as having a disability they may be provided with appropriate special education services. Others may qualify for bilingual education or services for English learners, if either of these are available within the district. According to Gonzalez (1978), students are in need of bilingual instruction if (1) their primary or home language is other than English and (2) their school performance indicates academic underachievement.

Bilingual education is concerned with both language and culture, and programs take many forms depending on their goals. According to Baca (1998), *transitional* or "early-exit" bilingual education programs utilize the student's native language and culture to facilitate the acquisition of English. The goal is to integrate the student into the general education curriculum as quickly as possible. *Maintenance* or "late-exit" programs, in contrast, are designed to develop the student's native language skills and cultural competence as well as to teach English; the goal is to maintain the first language and augment (not replace) it with English. Gersten and Woodward (1994) prefer the term *native language emphasis* to describe programs with strong native language components. According to Gersten and Jiménez (1998), this model of bilingual education is the most common in use today.

Cummins (1989) maintains that educators should encourage students to develop proficiency in their first language (L1), even if bilingual education programs are not available. To do this, teachers should follow these suggestions:

- Encourage students to use their L1 around the school.
- Provide opportunities for students from the same ethnic group to communicate with one another in their L1 where possible (e.g., in cooperative learning groups on at least some occasions).
- Recruit people who can tutor students in their L1.
- Provide books written in the various languages in both classrooms and the school library.
- Incorporate greetings and information in the various languages in newsletters and other official school communications (Cummins, 1989, p. 113).

Another approach to the education of students who are English learners is instruction solely in English, with emphasis on the development of English language skills. According to Kindler (2002a), "English was the exclusive language of instruction" (p. 14) for 53.9% of U.S. students who were not proficient in English. This approach has been known by many names: sheltered English, structured immersion, English as a second language (ESL), and English for speakers of other languages (ESOL). Instruction takes place only in English, and no effort is made to maintain or develop proficiency in the student's first language. Schools often use this approach when there are insufficient numbers of non-English-speaking

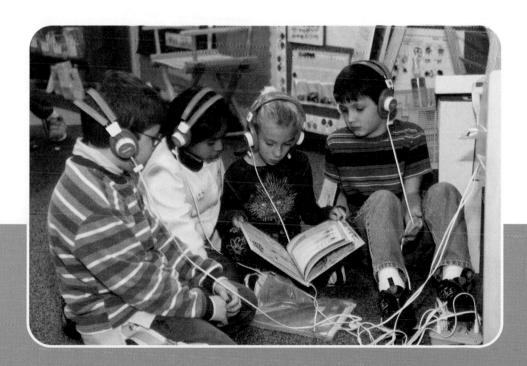

Spotlight on Technology

Software to Assist Language Learners

Are some of your students interested in learning Spanish? Would you like to brush up your Spanish (or French or Russian or . . .)? Several types of software programs are available to help.

One older program is *JumpStart Languages* from Knowledge Adventures (http://www.jumpstart.com). Designed for younger children, this program includes games, stories, and activities in four languages: Spanish, French, Japanese, and English. Students learn the sounds of the various languages as well as everyday vocabulary, color and number words, and conversational phrases.

Transparent Language (http://www.transparent.com) is a company that offers programs for a range of languages and ages. The series for younger students is called *KidSpeak* with versions in Spanish, French, and multiple languages. In the multiple language version, *KidSpeak 6-in-1 Languages,* stu-

Transparent.com
Revolutionary Language Products & More!

Note: Courtesy of Transparent.com.

dents learn 700 words and phrases in Spanish, French, German, Italian, Hebrew, and Japanese.

Older language students might enjoy one of the programs in Transparent Language's *LanguageNow!* series. Examples are *SpanishNow!, EnglishNow! for Spanish Speakers,* versions for other common languages (e.g., French, German, Italian, Russian), and versions for languages that are less often taught in K–12 schools (e.g., Polish, Arabic, Chinese, Japanese, Swedish). *WordAce!,* also from Transparent Language, is a talking foreign language dictionary program available in 12 languages.

---

students to form a bilingual education class, when students represent a number of different language groups, or when there is a shortage of teachers fluent in the language spoken by students. See the accompanying "Spotlight on Technology" feature for information about software programs for persons learning new language skills.

When students from culturally diverse backgrounds are evaluated either for special education or bilingual education services, it is necessary to ensure that assessment procedures are nonbiased. That is, measurement devices must not discriminate on the basis of race, culture, or language (McLoughlin & Lewis, 2005). The language of the student is an obvious consideration. If the student has limited proficiency in English, it is futile to use an English-language test to assess aptitude or school achievement. In fact, if the student's primary language is Spanish, Navajo, or Tagalog, the only justification for testing in English is to determine the student's facility in this second language.

The cultural background of the student is another important concern. If a measure has been designed for use with mainstream culture students, those who differ in experiential background are unjustly penalized. Consider the example of Williams that is cited by Alley and Foster (1978):

> "When is Washington's birthday?" If you are of the majority culture, you probably would answer "February 22." This response would be scored correct according to the Wechsler Adult Intelligence Scale scoring criteria. . . . If, however, you were to respond "April 5," your response would be scored as

incorrect, using that scoring criteria. The implication is that you must associate George rather than Booker T. with Washington. This item could be classified as culture-biased. (p. 1)

In the general education classroom, the teacher should also take care when assessing students from various cultural backgrounds. Many typical classroom measures are in opposition to the values held by some cultures. For instance, students who are not influenced by clock time may fare poorly on tests of speed or timed assignments. Those who prefer cooperation to competition may feel threatened by class contests. Individuals who are reluctant to stand out from the group may not respond to awards, prizes, and recognition as incentives.

CLASSROOM ADAPTATIONS

Most culturally and linguistically diverse students are full-time members of general education classes. Although some students with special needs may receive services from a special education resource teacher or from an expert in bilingual education, most of their school career is typically spent in general education settings. Therefore, the general education teacher must be aware of cultural and linguistic differences and their effects on performance in academics, classroom conduct, and social interactions.

Montgomery (2001) uses the term *culturally responsive classrooms* to describe classrooms that promote the success of diverse learners. In her view, such classrooms

> specifically acknowledge the presence of culturally diverse students and the need for these students to find relevant connections among themselves and with the subject matter and the tasks teachers ask them to perform. (p. 4)

This viewpoint can help guide the development of instructional programs that promote the acceptance of students who differ from their peers in culture and language as well as the academic success of diverse students. See Figure 17-2 for the key components of effective pedagogy identified by the Center for Research on Education, Diversity and Excellence (2002).

Teachers can use several strategies to adapt instruction to better meet the needs of students from diverse groups. One approach recommended by experts is **cooperative learning** (e.g., Baca & Almanza, 1991; Franklin, 1992; Padrón, Waxman, & Rivera, 2002; Ruiz, 1989). Many cultures value cooperation over competition and prefer interpersonal interactions to interactions with tasks. Cooperative learning, in which students work together to accomplish a common goal, is therefore more congruent with the values of these cultures than individualistic or competitive learning situations. See chapter 6 for descriptions of several types of cooperative learning strategies and the research supporting this approach.

Franklin (1992) discusses the major characteristics of culturally sensitive instruction for African American students. According to Franklin, these include:

- Presenting instruction at a faster pace, with greater verve and rhythm;
- Increasing the amount of stimulation in the classroom by combining media (e.g., speech, singing, music, print, movement, visuals) and by providing a variety of different types of activities;

FIGURE 17-2   Standards for Effective Pedagogy for Diverse Learners

Teachers and Students Working Together
Teach through instructional group activities in which students and teacher work together to create a product or an idea.

Developing Language Skills Across All Curriculum
Apply literacy strategies and develop language competence in all subject areas.

Connecting Lessons to Students' Lives
Contextualize teaching and curriculum in students' existing experiences in home, community, and school.

Engaging Students with Challenging Lessons
Maintain challenging standards for student performance; design activities to advance understanding to more complex levels.

Emphasizing Dialogue over Lecture
Instruct through teacher–student dialogue, especially academic, goal-directed small-group conversations, rather than lectures.

Note: From Center for Research on Education, Diversity and Excellence. (2002). *The Five Standards for Effective Pedagogy.* Retrieved October 16, 2004, from http://www.crede.ucsc.edu/standards/standards.html

- Using several types of verbal activities such as rap, choral reading, chants, and responsive reading;
- Encouraging divergent thinking;
- Considering students' individual experiential backgrounds when choosing instructional materials and activities;
- Incorporating real-life tasks into the curriculum;
- Increasing the "people focus" of instruction so there are many opportunities for person-to-person interactions; and
- Frequently using small groups for cooperative learning and peer tutoring.

Ruiz's (1989) work focuses on another group of students: those who enter school more proficient in Spanish than in English. Ruiz presents the following guidelines for planning instruction for English learners. Although these guidelines address the language arts curriculum in the elementary grades, many are also applicable to other subjects and other age groups.

- Take into account students' sociocultural backgrounds and their effects on oral language, reading and writing, and second-language learning. . . .
- Follow developmental processes in literacy acquisition.

Inclusion Tips for the Teacher

Teaching English Learners

Echevarria (1995) suggests that teachers follow six steps when presenting sheltered English instruction to English learners:

1. *Target vocabulary.* Select several terms or words critical to the lesson. Define those words at the outset of the lesson and keep them posted for visual reference for the students. The vocabulary then becomes part of a word bank to which words are continually added. As previous lessons are built upon, the word banks serve to orient students and create a context for greater understanding.

2. *Select a main concept.* Most chapters or lessons can be summarized by one or two key concepts. Focus on the main concept, with the lesson's goal being attainment of that concept. Chapter readings can be outlined or reduced to manageable parts, making the content more comprehensible. A unit of study is more valuable when students fully understand the main ideas and have developed the related academic vocabulary rather than covering every detail with only a cursory understanding.

3. *Create a context.* This is where the teacher's creativity is put to work. Anything and everything should be used to provide a context for the information to make it more understandable: visuals, sketches on an overhead, gestures, real objects (realia), facial expressions, props, manipulatives, bulletin boards, and the like. Demonstrate what the book is talking about; provide the students with the requisite experiences to add meaning to the topic. If they have difficulty understanding the story's reference to a phrase like "Her attitude was as sour as a lemon," give them the experience of tasting a lemon; if the lesson involves learning the name and function of the teeth, give each child a slice of apple to test out the function of each tooth (e.g., incisor cuts and bicuspid crushes).

4. *Make connections.* Provide the students with opportunities to relate their background experiences to the topic at hand. The teacher may need to facilitate this process by asking probing questions and then relating the students' comments to the topic. Being able to identify with the topic makes instruction more meaningful to students.

5. *Check for understanding.* Second-language learners require repetition, clarification, and elaboration. Check frequently for understanding by reviewing target vocabulary and concepts. Use different types of questions to elicit responses and assess understanding in a variety of ways. Above all, maintain a supportive atmosphere in which students are comfortable asking for clarification and participating in the lesson.

6. *Encourage Student-to-Student Interaction.* Because sheltered instruction is highly interactive in nature, it provides students with an optimum opportunity to practice the language they are acquiring. Planning needs to include cooperative activities and projects that group native speakers of English with non-native speakers. For example, partners might work together with a globe to locate specific areas. Cooperative groups might complete a worksheet together, or small groups might plan and execute role playing of the topic.

Note: From "Sheltered Instruction for Students with Learning Disabilities who have Limited English Proficiency" by J. Echevarria, 1995, *Intervention in School and Clinic, 30,* p. 303. Copyright 1995 by PRO-ED, Inc. Reprinted by permission.

- Locate curriculum in a meaningful context where the communicative purpose is clear and authentic.
- Connect curriculum with the students' personal experiences.
- Incorporate children's literature into reading, writing, and English-as-a-second language (ESL) lessons.
- Involve parents as active partners in the instruction of their children.
- Give students experience with whole texts in reading, writing, and ESL lessons.
- Incorporate collaborative learning whenever possible. (p. 134)

Language instruction for linguistically diverse students often focuses on the development of skill in English rather than in both English and the heritage language. In this approach, the goal is to teach English language skills at the same time that students are learning specific content-area knowledge (California Teachers of English to Speakers of Other Languages, 1992; Northcutt & Watson, 1986). To do this, the teacher analyzes the content of the lesson to identify key concepts and vocabulary. Then, he or she systematically teaches those concepts and vocabulary by using instructional techniques designed to maximize students' ability to comprehend English language input (Krashen, 1987). These techniques include linking new information to students' background knowledge; use of clear, consistent language with many repetitions; and incorporation of extralingual cues such as visual aids, media, props, realia (i.e., real objects), demonstrations, dramatizations, and so forth (Freeman & Freeman, 1988; Gersten & Jiménez, 1998; Ratleff, 1989; Towell & Wink, 1993). If the teacher or aide speaks the language of the student, key concepts can be pretaught in that language prior to the start of the lesson. See the "Inclusion Tips for the Teacher" box for

Echevarria's (1995) recommendations for incorporating English instruction into lessons.

PROMOTING ACCEPTANCE OF DIVERSITY

Peer acceptance is a special need for many diverse students. Students who appear different by virtue of language, dress, or customs may find interactions with classmates difficult. One way to overcome this problem is through instruction. When students learn about the language and culture of groups other than their own, differences become less frightening and easier to understand. When students learn more about each other, diversity is more likely to be treated not only with tolerance but also with respect. McCormick (1990) provides suggestions to assist the teacher of the general education classroom. Among these are:

- As you identify the different ethnic groups in your classroom, become informed about their characteristics and learning styles.
- Encourage and assist students in sharing their culture in the classroom; you can start the process by sharing your own cultural values and traditions.
- Know as much as possible about . . . students' home and community, interests, talents, skills, and potentials and develop an instructional program accordingly. (p. 75)

It is also important that the school curriculum and instructional materials such as textbooks reflect the contributions of all cultural groups. That has not always been the case, as these examples provided by the National Coalition of Advocates for Students (1985) show:

> Witnesses told us of Native American children sitting through lessons about "taming the frontier" and of Columbus "discovering America"; of world history texts which devote no more than a few paragraphs to Africa; of Asian history courses that treat "all Japanese, Chinese, and Filipino people, whose histories are all different and all need to be told" as if they were one; of schools in the Southwest which teach the history of their region with little more than a cursory look at its rich pre-Anglo culture. (p. 17)

Vaughn, Bos, and Schumm (2003) make several recommendations to help teachers include multicultural content in the classroom program:

- To teach cultural content you need knowledge of cultural groups. Read books that survey the histories of cultural groups in the United States. . . .
- Make sure that your room conveys positive images of various cultural groups (through bulletin boards, posters, literature, software, and so on).
- Plan time in which you and your students can learn about each other's cultural backgrounds. . . .

- Be culturally conscious in selecting teaching materials. If the materials you use include stereotypes or present only one perspective, point out the limitation to the students.
- Use trade books, films, videotapes, and recordings to supplement the textbook and to present more varied perspectives.
- Use literature to enrich students' understanding of cultural pluralism. . . .
- Make sure that not only classroom but also schoolwide activities (such as plays, sports, and clubs) are culturally integrated. (p. 281)

The suggestions that follow are designed to help refugee students adjust to their new culture and school environment ("Educating Refugees: Understanding the Basics," 1989). However, several of these strategies apply equally well to all diverse students:

Adjusting to a New Culture

- Enhance students' self-esteem by focusing on their positive qualities and the progress they have already made.
- Help students develop realistic expectations for adjustment to the United States.
- Help students develop coping skills such as not overreacting to stressful situations and making the best of difficult situations.

Culture and Family

- Learn about cultural differences and be sensitive to these differences when working with students.
- Provide opportunities for students to share information about their culture during social studies, geography, and other classes.
- Familiarize yourself with different cultural, medical, and religious practices, such as fasting or holiday celebrations, that might affect students' school attendance and participation.
- Learn to correctly pronounce students' names in the proper order and how to address students' parents. For example, the order of Vietnamese names is family name, middle name, and first name. Vietnamese people are usually addressed using their first name.

Educational Concerns

- When new students arrive, have students from the same linguistic and cultural background who have been at the school longer become "buddies" to help the new students become oriented.
- During class, pose questions related to the content of instruction to check if students have understood; do not assume they understand simply because they appear to have understood.
- Use nonverbal gestures to supplement your instruction.

- Make sure newly arrived students meet and interact with American students, especially in classes that do not require much English proficiency, such as art, physical education, and music.
- Write out class assignments and important instructions to reinforce your oral statements. (p. 1)

Another important consideration for the general education teacher is communication with parents and other family members of diverse students (Flett & Conderman, 2001; Kalyanpur & Harry, 1999; Parette & Petch-Hogan, 2000). Lynch (1981), in a study of parents' views of special education services, identified several barriers to parents' participation in the public school programs of their children. Two

major roadblocks were language and culture. Suggestions for overcoming these barriers are presented in the "Inclusion Tips for the Teacher" material.

In summary, multicultural education is an attempt to affirm the value and worth of cultural diversity. In many ways, the mainstreaming movement of the past and the inclusion movement of today echo this ideal: Mainstreaming and inclusion are attempts to integrate but not obliterate differences. This point is well made by McLaughlin-Williams (1971):

> Mainstreaming can become a force for the valuing of individual differences, a process to foster acceptance of varying physical, psychological, educational, and racial characteristics, and a futuristic model to celebrate variance as a desirable state. (as cited in Fuchigami, 1980, p. 640)

Inclusion Tips for the Teacher

Welcoming Diverse Families to the School

Language Considerations

- If you are not bilingual, have someone available who is when you talk to parents. Better yet, encourage them to bring a bilingual friend or relative. Make an attempt to learn words, phrases, and to say something positive about the child in the family's preferred language.
- Be sure that printed materials for parents are available in their preferred language.
- Provide a sign language interpreter for parents who are deaf or hard of hearing.

Cultural Considerations

- Learn as much as you can about the cultures that your students represent through talking with the parents and other staff, reading books, attending in-service sessions,

and viewing films. Family structures, values, and child-rearing practices vary greatly. You can then use the cultural differences as strengths rather than working at cross-purposes.
- Instead of lumping all groups together, recognize the many differences that exist within groups of Hispanics, Anglos, blacks, Pan-Asians. Each country, each region, and most important, each individual has unique ways of interpreting their cultural experience.
- Weed out the stereotypes and prejudices that have been acquired through your own cultural roots. Try to approach people individually and openly.
- Use cultural differences to bring schools and families together. Utilize celebrations and the special traditions that go with them as ways of learning and working together.
- Never feel that you have to apologize for your own culture or ethnicity. We all have something special to contribute.

Note: From *But I've Tried Everything! A Special Educator's Guide to Working with Parents* (pp. 37–39) by E. W. Lynch, 1981, San Diego, CA: San Diego State University. The development of this book was supported by the State of California, Department of Education, Project Number 37–3062–80–3293–7100. Reprinted by permission.

Things to Remember

- General education classrooms often reflect the cultural and linguistic diversity of the United States.
- Cultural pluralism is the belief that cultural and linguistic diversity is a strength, not a weakness.
- African Americans make up the largest "minority" group, whereas Hispanics represent the largest bilingual culture.
- A student's language and culture can affect school behavior and academic success; if the student's background is discrepant from the culture of the school, the student may fail to meet scholastic expectations.
- Students who enter school with few English language skills are at a distinct disadvantage; however, not all diverse students are English language learners.

- Most culturally and linguistically diverse students are educated in general education classes. Those with special learning needs may receive special education services, bilingual education services, or instruction only in English.
- Assessment of students from diverse groups must be nonbiased; measures must not discriminate on the basis of race, culture, or language.
- Students who learn about the language and culture of others are more likely to accept diversity.
- Inclusion and multicultural education share the same goal: to teach students to appreciate the value of individual differences.

ACTIVITIES

1. Write a short paper that describes your cultural background. Include your family's traditions for holidays, foods, ceremonies such as weddings, child-rearing practices, and so on. Exchange papers with one of your classmates. What similarities do you find? What differences?

CD-ROM Activities

The student under discussion in the video case study featuring the assessment team does not appear to be a member of a family that is linguistically or culturally diverse. If he were, it's likely that the deliberations of the assessment team would be somewhat different. Consider these possibilities:

- *If the student's family spoke a language other than English at home, what other factors might the assessment team wish to consider?*

- *Suppose the student was a recent immigrant from Russia, Thailand, or one of the countries in Africa. How would that fact affect the types of information that the assessment team might gather?*

2. Interview someone who learned English as a second or third language. Ask that person to describe some of the problems that occur in translating from one language to another. Are there some concepts that cannot be expressed in the English language?

3. Look through several of the textbooks used in elementary or secondary classrooms. Do these texts include information about the contributions of several cultures? Do the illustrations depict a pluralistic society?

4. Observe in a classroom that serves students who are diverse in language and culture. Can you identify any special needs? In what ways does the teacher adapt instruction to meet the needs of diverse students? How are social interactions among students encouraged?

5. It was noted that both inclusion and multicultural approaches to education are attempts to integrate but not obliterate differences. Discuss your reactions to this statement.

6. In a recent study, Pang and Park (2003) examined stereotypic thinking in university students by asking them to visualize, then describe a scene in which they are sitting in a park and an American walks by. How do you think the students described the American? Did they display any biases? Read the article to learn the results.

Teaching Students at Risk for School Failure

CHAPTER

18

On a typical day in the United States:

- 846 low-birthweight babies were born
- 76 infants (under age 1) died
- 33 children ages 1–14 died
- 18 teens died from accidents
- 5 teens died from homicide

- 4 teens committed suicide
- Almost 400 children were born to females ages 15–17
- 750 children were added to the poverty population
- 1,680 children were added to the count of families where no parent has full-time, year-round employment. (*KIDS COUNT Data Book*, 2004, p. 32)

LOOKING AHEAD

This chapter focuses on students who are at risk for school failure. As you read, consider these questions:

- What do you think the term *at risk* means?
- Do the statistics about a typical day in the United States reflect risk factors? Describe those factors and how they might influence school failure.
- What strategies could schools use to promote the school success of students at risk?

To answer these questions online go to the Students' Stories module in Chapter 18 of the Companion Website.

The kindergartner who comes to school hungry, the 15-year-old who is 2 months pregnant, the young boy who seeks solace from drugs when his stepfather beats him, the lonely adolescent who sees little reason for living—these are students at risk. The factors that place them at risk—substance abuse, delinquency, abusive caregivers, and so on—interfere with their ability to benefit from the school experience.

A Phi Delta Kappa study considered children at risk "if they are likely to fail—either in school or in life" (Frymier & Gansneder, 1989, p. 142). The inclusion of failure "in life" in the definition considers the individual's involvement in areas such as drug abuse, suicide, physical or sexual abuse, delinquency, or other factors that may contribute to future problems. Although these students usually have not been identified as individuals with disabilities (and may never be considered eligible for special education services), it is important that educators provide them with educational experiences appropriate to their special needs. Ogden and Germinario (1988) describe the problem as follows:

> All children are at times students-at-risk and there is a portion of every school population that consistently shows a lack of the necessary intellectual, emotional and/or social skills to take full advantage of the educational opportunities available to them. Often these students become disenchanted, and ultimately openly or passively reject school—they are then students-at-high-risk. (p. xvii)

McWhirter, McWhirter, McWhirter, and McWhirter (1998) add that "at-riskness must be viewed not as a discrete, unitary diagnostic category but as a series of steps along a continuum" (p. 7).

Although educators generally agree that many students are at risk, they do not necessarily agree on who these students are or how to deal with their problems. All 50 states have made some attempt to consider the question; only 25 states have formally defined the at-risk population. These definitions vary widely, from limiting the group to only dropouts to associating students at risk with a long list of adverse social and economic conditions (e.g., truancy, absenteeism, drug abuse, delinquency, teenage pregnancy, poverty). The states have taken a similar piecemeal approach to providing programs that attempt to remedy the problems of students at risk.

According to various sources, from 25% to 35% (Frymier & Gansneder, 1989; Hodgkinson, 1993) to as many as 35% to 40% (Siegel & Senna, 1994; "Technology," 1988) of the K–12 school population can be considered at risk. High numbers of students at risk can be found in schools in urban (Cuban, 1989), suburban, and rural (Helge, 1991) communities. The potential for being identified as at risk is higher for students raised in disadvantaged or impoverished home settings (Biddle, 1997). These students are often not able to meet the academic demands of the school because of their delayed physical and psychological development (Butler, 1989). The

longer students live under poverty conditions, the more likely they are to be underachievers in school (Manning & Baruth, 1995; Reeves, 1988) and to experience emotional or behavioral problems (Recer, 1989). Many other factors such as drug or alcohol abuse, child abuse or neglect, eating disorders, suicide, delinquency, single-parent homes, and teenage pregnancy are thought to be related to a student's potential inclusion in the at-risk population.

School personnel encounter challenges in providing educational programs for students at risk. First, this group is not protected by equal access laws such as those that protect the educational rights of students with disabilities. Second, if students at risk do not receive an adequate education, they may fail to become contributors to society and instead be forced to rely on society for support. Third, programs for at risk students may need to include life and social skills, skill areas once considered within the domain of the family. Finally, failure to meet the educational needs of students at risk may result in continued negative attitudes for the students at risk, negative consequences for their current school peers, and negative effects for their own children in the future (McWhirter et al., 1998; Ogden & Germinario, 1988; Reeves, 1988; Stevens & Price, 1992).

One group of individuals at risk warrants special mention: gay, lesbian, bisexual, and transgendered students. Salend (2005) explains that transgendered individuals "do not identify themselves as either of the two sexes" (p. 138). These students are likely to be disproportionately at risk in the areas considered in this chapter (McWhirter et al., 1998). McWhirter et al. provide this explanation in relation to gay and lesbian students:

> Most gay and lesbian youth experience stress in their lives because of their sexual orientation. On one hand, adverse responses of disapproval and rejection to an adolescent's homosexual orientation from family members, friends, and peers [are] common. On the other hand, inability or unwillingness to accept or acknowledge same-sex attraction leads to early feelings of confusion and alienation. These young people are vulnerable because of their fear of reaction from family and friends regarding their sexual orientation. However, not disclosing to family and friends may also be stressful, as it frequently entails living a lie, becoming emotionally isolated, and feeling terribly lonely.
>
> Although lesbian and gay young people receive services from multiple systems, including education, mental health, child welfare, juvenile justice, and health, these service providers rarely identify or address the special needs of this population. Lesbian and gay young people are particularly vulnerable to alcohol and other drug abuse as they cope with the isolation, rejection, and stressors they experience. Homosexuals are probably the most frequent victims of hate violence, and because educators do little to support gay and lesbian adolescents, they frequently leave school before graduation. Finally, the suicide rate of homosexual youths is considerably higher than that of heterosexual youths. (p. 15)

Inclusion Tips for the Teacher

Does Your Classroom Promote Equity for All?

You can evaluate how well your own classroom practices promote equity for *all students* by addressing the following questions:

- Do I avoid grouping students based on gender and race, such as by forming separate lines, separate teams, separate seating arrangements, and separate academic learning groups, and comparing students across gender and racial variables?
- Do I know about the beliefs, traditions, customs, and experiences of all students in my classroom?
- Do I assign students of both sexes and *all races* to class and school jobs on a rotating basis?
- Do I use textbooks and teaching materials that include the contributions of both sexes and *all races and groups*?
- Do I use gender/race-inclusive and gender-neutral language?
- Do I provide male and female students with same-sex and same-race models and mentors who represent a variety of perspectives and professions?
- Do I encourage *all students* to explore various careers, as well as academic, extracurricular, and recreational activities?
- Do I decorate the classroom with pictures of males and females from *all races, religions, sexual orientations, and economic backgrounds* and performing a variety of activities?

- Do I use cooperative learning groups and cross-sex and cross-race seating arrangements?
- Do I encourage and teach students to examine and discuss books, stories, movies, and other materials in terms of stereotypes and perspectives across race, religion, sexual orientation, socioeconomic status, and gender?
- Do I identify and eliminate gender, racial, and other forms of bias in my assessment strategies and my curriculum?
- Do I encourage female and male students of *all races* to take risks, make decisions, assume leadership positions, and seek challenges?
- Do I affirm efforts and attributes that contribute to success in *all students*?

How would you rate how well you create a classroom environment that promotes equity for *all your students*? ( ) Excellent ( ) Good ( ) Needs Improvement ( ) Needs Much Improvement

What are some goals and steps you could adopt to promote equity in your classroom?

Note: From *Creating Inclusive Classrooms* (5th ed., p. 139) by S. J. Salend, 2005. Copyright 2005 by Merrill/Prentice Hall. Reprinted with permission.

Consult the "Inclusion Tips for the Teacher" to learn how to evaluate whether your classroom promotes equity for all students, including those at risk.

Every school and district should consider the potential consequences of not providing assistance to students at risk. Failing to respond to the special needs of these students can increase not only the likelihood of school failure but also school dropout rates. Additional information can be found in the accompanying "For Your Information" feature.

Many of the classroom techniques and strategies discussed earlier in this text are appropriate for students at risk. These approaches include effective educational interventions as well as optimum behavior management and instruction in academics and social skills. If these components are provided, students are more likely to experience gains in achievement and develop an overall sense of confidence and personal worth. Technologies such as the Neo keyboard, which is described in the "Spotlight on Technology" feature, can also prove useful with this population of students.

It is important to note that teachers and other school personnel are not expected to become therapists. Their primary role is to work on the learning problems of the student as part

of their daily instructional responsibilities and, when appropriate, to help identify other more serious problems (e.g., addiction, suicide, child abuse) and refer these cases to experts (Manning & Baruth, 1995; McWhirter et al., 1998; Ogden & Germinario, 1988).

The remainder of the chapter will present information about the at-risk categories of dropouts, suicide, drug and alcohol abuse, teenage pregnancy and sexually transmitted diseases, child abuse and neglect, eating disorders, and delinquency. The extent of each problem, contributing factors, potential prevention and intervention techniques, and alternative services available outside the school setting will be discussed.

DROPOUTS

Bill's Story

By his sophomore year, Bill had become so disenchanted with his monotonous school program that he began cutting class regularly. He recalls that the year he dropped out he went to school no more than 60 days. Bill explains that since both his parents worked, "It was easy; I'd cut out and go home to watch TV, get high with friends, or sleep all day. Nobody did

For Your Information

Students at Risk

- In a recent national survey, the public identified lack of discipline, overcrowding, drugs, and violence as among the biggest problems facing public schools today (Rose & Gallup, 2003).
- In 2001, the high school dropout rate was 10.7% for youth ages 16 to 24 in the United States. The rate for males (12.2%) was higher than that for females (9.3%), and youth of Hispanic origin (27.0%) were more likely to drop out than their white (7.3%) and black (10.9%) counterparts (National Center for Education Statistics, 2003).
- According to the *KIDS COUNT Data Book* (2004), "despite the enormous wealth in the United States, our child poverty rate is among the highest in the developed world" (p. 42).
- Research suggests that retention of students in grade increases the odds of dropping out by 75% to 90% (Phi Delta Kappa, 2000). Gastright (1989) reports that "80% of the dropouts had been retained at least once" (p. 2).
- Children who are abused and neglected "are more likely to suffer from depression, alcoholism, drug abuse and severe obesity. They are also more likely to require special education in school and to become juvenile delinquents and adult criminals" (Prevent Child Abuse America, 2001, p. 1).
- Salend (2005) reports that "currently, fewer than 50% of the children in the United States live with both biological parents, and it is estimated that 59% of all children will live in a single-parent household before they reach the age of 18" (p. 142).
- The American Academy of Child and Adolescent Psychiatry (2004) reports that "each year in the U.S., thousands of teenagers commit suicide. Suicide is the third leading cause of death for 15-to-24-year-olds, and the sixth leading cause of death for 5-to-14-year-olds."
- Approximately 84% of the students enrolled in the ninth grade complete high school graduation requirements by the time they are 19 years old; 87% complete those requirements by the time they are 24 (National Center for Education Statistics, 2000).

Spotlight on Technology

The Neo Keyboard

Neo by AlphaSmart is a simple, portable, low cost "computer companion." Like its predecessor, the AlphaSmart, Neo is easy to use: students simply turn it on and type. Text is saved automatically and the device turns itself off automatically when not in use. The Neo is battery-powered; three standard AA alkaline batteries provide more than 700 hours of use.

Neo features a built-in word processor, AlphaWord Plus, with spell check, thesaurus, and other features. The size of text shown on the Neo's screen can be changed (from two to six lines of text visible at one time), and students can store more than 100 pages of text in the Neo's eight files. When it's time to print, students can easily transfer text to a computer for further editing or directly to the printer.

The major advantage of Neo for students and teachers is its ease of use. However, the major advantage for schools is its low cost. Each Neo ranges in cost from approximately $230 to $250 for the rechargeable model (October 2004 prices), and the price is reduced when several devices are purchased. Thus, for the price of one computer, a school could buy several Neos. This increases the number of students with access to word processing technology. For more information and ideas about classroom applications, visit the AlphaSmart website at http://www.alphasmart.com.

Note: Courtesy of AlphaSmart, Inc.

anything about it." Bill's family had moved six times since kindergarten, and he reported that he had not yet found a school he considered worth going to. The times he was in school were, in his opinion, "a waste of time." He often asked, "Why are we learning this?" He thought about going to see his counselor but decided, "Why bother?" In his two years of high school, Bill saw his counselor for one 10-minute interview, despite failing several classes each semester. "At the end they called twice to tell me to come in and sign out, but I didn't." No one tried to talk Bill out of dropping out. In fact, it was easy; he just never came back. (Grossnickle, 1986, p. 11)

Although educators and researchers agree that the number of students dropping out of school is a major problem, they do not agree on who should be considered dropouts. The U.S. Census Bureau provides the most concise definition; it considers a **dropout** to be anyone over the age of 18 who is no longer enrolled in and has not graduated from high school. The national dropout rate, using this definition, is reported to be 14.5% (National Center for Education Statistics, 2000). In addition, their figures indicate that the number of students completing high school credential requirements has not increased between 1991 and 1999. Dropout rates in inner-city schools are often cited as being more than 50% ("Technology," 1988) and sometimes as high as 80% (Bowen, 1988); rates may be as high as 40% to 50% in small or rural schools (Phelps & Prock, 1991).

Siegel and Senna (1994) report that the "rate of delinquency is significantly higher for those who drop out of school than among those who do not" (p. 356). It is estimated that the cost to the nation of welfare, crime prevention, unemployment, and lost tax revenues resulting from dropouts alone is at least $60 billion annually—possibly as high as $228 billion; this is at least $60,000 per dropout (McNergney & Haberman, 1988). These figures make the importance of providing for the educational needs of this group of at-risk students readily apparent.

Assumptions based solely on the data on current dropout rates may be somewhat misleading because, during the past 100 years or so, the dropout rate has actually decreased and the number of students completing high school has increased. In 1890, only 6.7% of 14- to 17-year-olds attended high school; 3.5% of 17-year-olds graduated. By the 1970s, this figure had increased to 76% and, by the mid-1990s, to 89%. However, because life today requires higher skill levels, current dropouts are less likely to become contributing members of society (Berliner & Biddle, 1995; Phi Delta Kappa, 1998).

Kunisawa (1988), in a discussion of a longitudinal study of high school students, portrayed school dropouts in this way:

> Dropouts are usually from low-income or poverty settings, often from a minority group background (although not often Asian-American), and have very low basic academic skills (especially in reading and math). Their parents are not high school graduates, are generally uninterested in their child's progress in school, and do not provide a support system for academic progress. English is often not spoken in the home, and many dropouts are children of single parents. Dropout rates are higher among males than females. Males are more likely to leave school to get a job (which usually turns out to be a failure), while females tend to drop out in order to have a child. Dropouts are generally bored in school; they perceive themselves accurately as failures in the school culture and are usually very alienated from school. (p. 62)

Reducing the dropout rate is a major challenge for educators. The call to raise the standards for student performance as part of the movement to reform educational programs has created additional problems for students at risk. The increase in standards has not been accompanied by an increase in assistance for the students who had difficulty meeting the old standards (Hill, 1989, Woodring, 1989). Although the dropout rate has decreased during the past 100 years, the ability of the dropout to assimilate into society has also decreased. The number of jobs available for workers lacking basic skills is much smaller (Slavin, 1989), and the dropouts can no longer "go West" or return to the farm as they did earlier in the century (Woodring, 1989).

The school can play an important role in helping reduce the number of dropouts. Information gathered from research can provide a general framework for a prevention program; however, educators must examine their own local setting to identify their specific needs (Gastright, 1989). A variety of recommendations are provided here for preventing students from dropping out of school:

- There is need for early prevention programs that provide services such as prenatal and postnatal care for young mothers, day care and preschool programs, and health care programs for students at risk. Such programs are the most promising and cost-effective interventions (Butler, 1989; Hill, 1989; Kunisawa, 1988).

- Teachers can play an important role by developing an interest in the progress of all students and establishing a level of personal interaction that communicates this interest to the students (Barone, 1989; Denti & Guerin, 1999).
- "Prevention and early intervention are much more promising than waiting for learning deficits to accumulate and only then providing remedial and special education services" (Slavin, Madden, & Karweit, 1989, p. 355).
- Although teachers and administrators seem to have a good basic knowledge of the characteristics and attributes of potential high school dropouts, they appear to have a negative outlook regarding their own ability to encourage a dropout to return to school (Soderberg, 1988).
- Teachers must communicate a feeling that the student is capable of achieving and be accountable for providing the type of instruction designed to ensure that achievement will occur (Gajar, Goodman, & McAfee, 1993; McWhirter et al., 1998).
- Quality instruction that improves students' skills increases the likelihood that they will achieve and benefit from their school experiences (Cuban, 1989; Slavin et al., 1989).
- Consistent attendance is critical if students are to benefit from the educational program. Students who miss a great deal of school are more likely to drop out. Strong attendance policies should be established and enforced. Teachers and staff should be involved in following up on student absences and should reinforce students for attendance (Gajar et al., 1993; Kerr & Nelson, 2002).
- Job training programs that develop specific job skills and work behaviors (e.g., reporting on time, following directions) are needed to support the employment of students at risk because they are likely to be a group with a high rate of unemployment (Denti & Guerin, 1999; "Project," 1988; Snider, 1988).

Many experts stress the importance of involving parents in their children's education. Parents should be informed of their child's progress and encouraged to support their child's education and attendance at school. School personnel may need to assist parents in obtaining services from social or health agencies in the community. It is critical that every available resource be directed at reducing the risk factors that potentially lead students to drop out of school. The school's efforts should focus on making the student a success in school and in life. For more information about potential drop outs and other students at risk, see the "Window on the Web."

SUICIDE

The Stories of Jimmy and Jeanine

To the casual observer, Jimmy was a fairly typical teenager—reticent, especially around adults, and a moderate achiever in school. He had few close friends, all of them quiet and unassuming around the tougher kids at school. According to his homeroom teacher, Jimmy kept mostly to himself. These traits are typical of adolescents and aren't necessarily reason for special concern or attention. That's why Jimmy's death was initially thought to be an accident. One dark weekday morning, while delivering papers on his bike, Jimmy suddenly swerved into the path of an oncoming truck and was killed instantly. At first police thought that the unsafe conditions—darkness and light drizzle that made the road slippery—caused Jimmy to lose control of his bike. That was until a note describing his feelings of hopelessness and rejection was found in his school locker. Part of his note read, "Why me, why always me? They make fun of everything I do, everything that I am. It's such a cruel punishment."

* * *

Jeanine was an ebullient 16-year-old. Her grades were good, and she was popular enough to be elected to homecoming court. She was regarded by the faculty as a model student and a fine representative of her school. Then, gradually, she became apathetic. Parents and teachers thought the change was only a temporary emotional "phase" that many young women go through. Her death by drug overdose shocked everyone. How could this lovely, popular young lady with a promising future do such a terrible thing? She left no note to explain the confusion. However, subsequent investigations uncovered the apparent cause: Jeanine had been rejected by three of her friends who became jealous of her success and popularity. They apparently started a rumor that Jeanine was promiscuous and had contracted a venereal disease. Feeling overwhelmed and isolated, Jeanine took what she thought was the only way out. (Kirk, 1993, p. 5)

Suicide is the third leading cause of death among adolescents (after unintentional injury and homicide). During the past 20 years, suicide rates for 15- to 19-year-olds have increased 6%; they have increased more than 100% for 10- to 14-year-olds (National Youth Violence Prevention Resource Center, 2001). Some experts would argue that it is the leading cause of death in the under-14 age range, but they contend that it is difficult to get an accurate count because the stigma placed on suicide often leads suicides to be labeled accidents (Kauffman, 2001).

A recent study of high-school-age students in the United States estimated that 19.3% of this group seriously considered suicide in 1999 and 8.3% attempted to take their own lives (Centers for Disease Control and Prevention, 2000). Among high school students, as many as 350 suicides are attempted for every 1 completed; in the 14-and-under group, each year "suicide attempts lead to the hospitalization of an estimated 12,000 youngsters" (Guetzloe, 1993, p. 34).

Males are four to five times as likely to complete the act of suicide, yet females are three to nine times more likely to attempt suicide (Kirk, 1993; Vannatta, 1997). Note that students with special needs, especially those with severe behavioral disorders, often have a disproportionately high representation in the group attempting suicide (Guetzloe, 1988, 1989).

Window on the Web

Websites About Risk Factors

At Risk

- Center for Research on the Education of Students Placed at Risk (CRESPAR) (http://www.csos.jhu.edu/crespar/)
- National Institute on the Education of At-Risk Students (http://www.ed.gov/offices/OERI/At-Risk)

Dropouts

- National Dropout Prevention Centers (http://www.dropoutprevention.org)
- U.S. Department of Education (http://www.ed.gov)

Suicide

- American Academy of Child and Adolescent Psychiatry (http://www.aacap.org)
- American Foundation for Suicide Prevention (http://www.afsp.org)
- SOS High School Suicide Prevention Program (http://www.mentalhealthscreening.org/sos_highschool)

Substance Abuse

- Center for Substance Abuse Prevention (CSAP) (http://prevention.samhsa.gov/About/)
- Center for Substance Abuse Treatment (CSAT) (http://csat.samhsa.gov/)
- National Institute on Alcohol Abuse and Alcoholism (NIAAA), National Institutes of Health (http://www.niaaa.nih.gov)
- National Institute on Drug Abuse, National Institutes of Health (http://www.nida.nih.gov)
- Prevention Online, PRELINE, National Clearinghouse for Alcohol and Drug Information (http://www.health.org)

Teenage Pregnancy and Sexually Transmitted Diseases

- American Foundation for AIDS Research (http://www.amfar.org)
- National Center for HIV, STD and TB Prevention (http://www.cdc.gov/std/ and http://www.cdc.gov/hiv/dhap.htm)
- National Institute of Allergy and Infectious Diseases (http://www.niaid.nih.gov/default.htm)

Child Abuse and Neglect

- American Academy of Child and Adolescent Psychiatry (http://www.aacap.org)
- Child Abuse Prevention Association (http://www.childabuseprevention.org)
- National Clearinghouse on Child Abuse and Neglect Information, sponsored by the U.S. Department of Health and Human Services (http://nccanch.acf.hhs.gov/)
- Prevent Child Abuse America (http://www.preventchildabuse.org)

Eating Disorders

- Alliance for Eating Disorders Awareness (http://www.eatingdisorderinfo.org)
- American Academy of Child and Adolescent Psychiatry (http://www.aacap.org)
- American Obesity Association (http://www.obesity.org)
- Harvard Eating Disorders Center (http://www.hedc.org)
- National Association of Anorexia Nervosa and Associated Disorders (http://www.anad.org)
- National Eating Disorders Screening Program (http://www.mentalhealthscreening.org/eat/eat-fact.htm)

Delinquency

- Children's Defense Fund (http://www.childrensdefense.org)
- National Criminal Justice Reference Service (http://www.ncjrs.org)
- National Citizens' Crime Prevention Campaign (http://www.weprevent.org)
- National Youth Violence Prevention Resource Center (http://www.safeyouth.org)
- Office of Juvenile Justice and Delinquency Prevention, U.S. Department of Justice (http://www.ojjdp.ncjrs.org)

For more information, go to the Web Links module in Chapter 18 of the Companion Website.

FIGURE 18-1   Suicide Warning Signs

At-Risk Adolescent Checklist

Listed below are several factors associated with at-risk adolescents. None of these factors alone is an indication of suicidal tendencies; but educators should be alert to clusters of these factors, which could indicate potential problems.

1. Inability to compete in school, failing grades.
2. Family instability (divorce, blended family, neglect, and abuse).
3. Death or chronic illness of a loved one or pet, or the anniversary of such an event.
4. Failure to communicate feelings of unhappiness.
5. Health problems.
6. Major disappointment or humiliation (real or imagined).
7. Economic insecurity.
8. Parental role failure.
9. Desire for revenge against a girlfriend, boyfriend, or significant other.
10. Sense of not belonging to anyone (family, community, school).
11. Family history of suicide or suicide attempts.

Symptoms of Suicidal Youth Checklist

1. Extreme mood swings (violent or rebellious behavior, sudden cheerfulness).
2. Difficulty concentrating.
3. Sudden lifestyle changes.
4. Withdrawal or isolation from peers, family, or school activities.
5. Neglect of personal appearance.
6. Previous suicide attempts.
7. Loss of friends (boyfriend, girlfriend, best friend).
8. Giving away possessions, putting affairs together, voluntarily cleaning room, or throwing things out.
9. Decline in school work, failing grades, cheating.
10. Noticeable change in sleeping habits and energy level.
11. Frequent suicidal talk (revealed through writing, drawings, or indirect verbal expression).
12. Drug use (half of suicidal youngsters are involved in substance abuse).
13. Many unexplained absences.

Note: From *Responding to Adolescent Suicide* (pp. 25–26) by B. D. Garfinkel, E. Crosby, M. R. Herbert, A. L. Matus, J. K. Pfeifer, and P. L. Sheras (The Phi Delta Kappa Task Force on Adolescent Suicide), 1988, Bloomington, IN: The Phi Delta Kappa Educational Foundation. Copyright 1988 by The Phi Delta Kappa Educational Foundation. Reprinted with permission.

Teachers can play an important role in identifying students who may be suicide candidates, although suicide attempts often occur without warning. As part of a prevention program, school staff should be trained to identify warning signs and follow appropriate procedures after these signs have been noted. Warning signs are provided in Figure 18-1.

Adolescent suicide is usually precipitated by a combination of factors. Depression, impulsivity, stress, physical or sexual abuse, or drug and alcohol abuse are frequently associated with suicide attempts.

Another factor that often contributes to suicide among students is the death of another adolescent from suicide or an accident (Dismuke, 1988; Garfinkel et al., 1988). Such events may cause a contagion effect that leads to cluster suicides (i.e., a series of suicide attempts by friends or acquaintances). Specific suggestions for dealing with suicide threats and with potential cluster suicides are found in the accompanying "Inclusion Tips for the Teacher" material.

Teachers and other school personnel can carry out a number of activities that have the potential to reduce the number of suicides. Social skills training programs (such as those mentioned in chapter 6) can help develop skills that permit students to establish a network of social relationships and reduce their vulnerability to social isolation and possible depression (Patros & Shamoo, 1989). Providing experiences that lead to the development and reinforcement of personal

Inclusion Tips for the Teacher

Dealing with Potential Suicides

Suicide Threat Checklist

Do these things:

1. Remain calm. Stay with the student. Remember, the student is overwhelmed, confused, as well as ambivalent.

2. Get vital information if possible (name, address, home phone number, parent's work number). Send another teacher or student to get help.

3. Clear other students from the scene. Direct them to return to class.

4. Assure the student that he or she has done the right thing by talking to you. Try to win the student's trust. Assure the student that emergency help is coming. Tell the student that there are options available.

5. Get the student to talk. Listen! Listen! Listen! Repeat back what you hear the student saying (help the student define the problem). Acknowledge the student's feelings ("You are really angry." "You must feel humiliated.").

6. Establish direct eye contact with the student. Speak in a calm, low voice. If student is about to commit suicide, buy time. Say, "Don't jump. Stand there. Talk with me. I'll listen." Show that you are not shocked by discussing suicide.

7. Try to get the student to agree to a verbal "no suicide" contract ("No matter what happens, I will not kill myself.").

8. Monitor the student's behavior constantly.

9. Make a mental note at the time of the incident of what the student says.

10. Ask the principal or another administrator to contact the parents with the message that their child is hurt and they will be called back immediately with the name of the hospital where they can join their child. Tell them to keep the telephone line clear.

Do not do these things:

1. Do not ignore your intuitions if suicide is suspected.

2. Do not minimize the student's threat. Take it seriously.

3. Do not be concerned about long periods of silence. Give the student time to think.

4. Do not leave the student. Do not let him or her go to the restroom.

5. Do not lose patience with the student.

6. Do not argue with the student about whether suicide is right or wrong.

7. Do not promise confidentiality. Instead promise help and promise privacy.

8. Do not discuss the incident in the teacher's lounge or with another student. (Garfinkel et al., 1988, p. 26)

Reducing the Effects of a Suicide

The following are recommendations to help communities prevent young people from killing themselves and, when a young person does commit suicide, to help communities handle the situation as well as possible.

1. Plan community action to deal with any event or situation that might cause a suicide cluster before trouble starts.

2. Appoint a committee of community representatives and a community agency to coordinate a response to suicide among the young.

3. Identify people and groups in the community who can help prevent suicide clusters or respond when one occurs.

4. Put the response plan into action when a suicide cluster occurs—or when one is suspected.

5. When such a situation arises, immediately prepare the groups that are key to the community response to take up their assigned responsibilities.

6. Avoid any action that could be interpreted as glorifying suicide, and minimize any sensational aspects of suicides or suicide attempts.

7. Identify people who may be especially likely to kill themselves and put them in touch with a counselor.

8. Arrange for a timely flow of accurate, appropriate information to the news media after a suicide.

9. Identify elements in the environment—school, home, and community—that might increase the likelihood of suicide. Change those elements—or get rid of them.

10. If a group of youngsters do kill themselves, find out whether their deaths are connected to any long-term issue—and, if so, deal with it. (Dismuke, 1988, p. 21)

Note: From *Responding to Adolescent Suicide* (p. 26) by B. D. Garfinkel, E. Crosby, M. R. Herbert, A. L. Matus, J. K. Pfeifer, and P. L. Sheras (The Phi Delta Kappa Task Force on Adolescent Suicide), 1988, Bloomington, IN: The Phi Delta Kappa Educational Foundation; and from "Reducing Suicides" by D. Dismuke, November 1988, *NEA Today* (Washington, DC: National Education Association), p. 21. Reprinted by permission.

self-worth is important in programs designed to prevent suicide (Guetzloe, 1989).

Schools serving adolescents should consider their legal responsibilities regarding the physical and psychological safety of students, develop a plan for dealing with suicide, and communicate this to all staff members. In addition, it is essential that mental health clinics, crisis centers, counseling agencies, suicide hotlines, and other community resources in the area of suicide prevention be identified and information provided to the entire staff describing how these services supplement those provided by the school. It is also important that the staff be aware of the referral process that must be used for each of these agencies; often there is not a great deal of time available to search for this information. School personnel should not assume responsibilities for follow-up or long-term counseling if they do not have the expertise or time available. The responsibility for this care should be delegated to the appropriate agency in the community (Capuzzi, 1988).

DRUG AND ALCOHOL ABUSE

Students' Stories from Phoenix House

They started young, usually with pot, and moved on to coke—sometimes snorted, sometimes injected, sometimes freebased. Now they're patients at Phoenix House, a residential treatment center in Orange County, Calif. "When I first smoked rock I fell in love," says Samantha. "I wanted to do more right away. I would lie, steal—anything for a hit off the pipe. It gets hold of you real fast." To Amy, "coke was the wonder drug, and freebasing was better than sex. I had no morals: I'd do anything with my body for coke." Dan, a bleached-blond 15-year-old from Orange County, stole from his parents, from his employer and from neighbors. "I used all the cash for drugs," he says. "I didn't care about food, I didn't care about a bed. It was scary on the street, but the cocaine made it all right." Dan says about half the kids at his old high school now use coke. (Morganthau, 1986, p. 63)

Students' use of drugs continues to be one of the top five problems of U.S. schools identified in the annual Gallup polls of the public's views on education (Rose & Gallup, 2001, 2003). According to the National Institute on Drug Abuse (2001), the most common drug use activities of high school seniors are drinking alcohol (80% have participated at least once) and smoking (61%), although nearly 54% try at least one illicit controlled substance or drug, with marijuana the most frequent (49%).

Alcohol and tobacco appear to be the most abused drugs because they are the most readily available and the most highly visible due to the amount of advertising they receive (Horton, 1985). Data reported from the 2001 Monitoring the Future National Survey (Johnston, O'Malley, & Bachman, 2001) indicate that, in the 12-month period prior to being polled, 41% of the students in the 12th-grade group had used an illicit

drug; 32% had been drunk in the past month; and 30% admitted to binge drinking (five or more drinks in a row) during the past 2 weeks. Marijuana had been used at some time by 49% of this group, and 22% currently used it. This study also determined that 7% of high school seniors had used cocaine at least once; 11% of the students had used LSD; and 17% of eighth graders had used inhalants (i.e., glues, aerosols, and solvents). An earlier report indicated that the average age at which students first used alcohol was 12.8 years (Needham, 1989).

The data on **drug and alcohol abuse** for students are not completely surprising when considered next to statistics on the adult population. For example, alcohol consumption is at its lowest level in 30 years, and still 56% of Americans drink alcoholic beverages ("Alcohol Use," 1989). Individuals who abuse drugs or alcohol are very much at risk for failure in school and in other aspects of their lives (Elmquist, 1991).

Factors such as having friends who provide drugs and encourage their use, low socioeconomic status, disturbed families, adult family members using drugs, poor school performance, stressful life events, deviant behaviors, depression, or anxiety can all contribute to the possibility that an individual will be at risk for use or abuse of alcohol and drugs. The greater the number of these factors influencing a specific student, the more likely that student is to abuse alcohol and other drugs (Newcomb & Bentler, 1989). Figure 18-2 lists a series of symptoms that can help educators to identify students involved in drug and alcohol abuse.

A variety of programs directed at preventing and/or treating drug and alcohol abuse have been developed, and many have had limited success. These programs have often attempted to reduce the use of milder drugs such as cigarettes, alcohol, and marijuana on the theory that their use will lead to the use of harder drugs. Prevention programs whose sole purpose is to provide information on drug and alcohol abuse have not been highly successful. Programs that involve improving peer interactions and enhancing social skills and assertiveness or refusal skills have been the most effective in reducing the use of drugs, but they have had less impact on individuals currently abusing drugs. Interventions that involve individuals in alternative activities, build their confidence, broaden their experiences, and improve social competence were the most successful in reducing the abuse of drugs (Kauffman, 2001; Newcomb & Bentler, 1989).

Studies on the effectiveness of various types of treatment programs are needed so that programs can become more accountable to the students they serve and their families. Problems have occurred when programs have placed individuals into the wrong type of program (sometimes because of an error and other times because of a need to fill that program's beds). For example, if parents agree to have a mildly involved adolescent (i.e., one who has used a drug infrequently as a result of normal experimentation or social pressure) "thrown in" with youth who are truly drug abusers, the adolescent

| FIGURE 18-2 | Signs of Alcohol and Other Drug Use |

Signs of alcohol and other drug use [AOD] vary, but there are some common indicators of AOD problems. Look for changes in performance, appearance, and behavior. These signs may indicate AOD use, but they may also reflect normal teenage growing pains. Therefore, look for a series of changes, not isolated single behaviors. Several changes together indicate a pattern associated with use.

Changes in Performance:
- Distinct downward turn in grades—not just from Cs to Fs, but from As to Bs and Cs
- Assignments not completed
- A loss of interest in school; in extracurricular activities
- Poor classroom behavior such as inattentiveness, sleeping in class, hostility
- Missing school for unknown reasons
- In trouble with school, at work, or with the police
- Increased discipline problems
- Memory loss

Changes in Behavior:
- Decrease in energy and endurance
- Changes in friends (secrecy about new friends, new friends with different lifestyles)
- Secrecy about activities (lies and avoids talking about activities)
- Borrows lots of money, or has too much cash
- Mood swings; excessive anger, irritability
- Preferred style of music changes (pop rock to heavy metal)
- Starts pulling away from the family, old friends, and school
- Hostile or argumentative attitude; extremely negative, unmotivated, defensive
- Refusal or hostility when asked to talk about possible alcohol or other drug use

Changes in Appearance and Physical Changes:
- Weight loss or gain
- Uncoordinated
- Poor physical appearance or unusually neat. A striking change in personal habits
- New interest in the drug culture (drug-related posters, clothes, magazines)
- Smells of alcohol, tobacco, marijuana
- Frequent use of eye drops and breath mints
- Bloodshot eyes
- Persistent cough or cold symptoms (e.g., runny nose)
- Always thirsty, increased or decreased appetite, rapid speech
- AOD paraphernalia (empty alcohol containers, cigarettes, pipes, rolling papers, baggies, paper packets, roach clips, razor blades, straws, glass or plastic vials, pill bottles, tablets and capsules, colored stoppers, syringes, spoons, matches or lighters, needles, medicine droppers, toy balloons, tin foil, cleaning rags, spray cans, glue containers, household products)

Note: From "School-Based Alcohol and Other Drug Prevention Programs: Guidelines for the Special Educator" by D. L. Elmquist, 1991, *Intervention in School and Clinic, 27*(1), p. 14. Copyright 1991 by PRO-ED, Inc. Reprinted with permission.

may be alienated from his or her family and exposed to an environment that may actually encourage further drug abuse (Newcomb & Bentler, 1989). Any recommended treatment must be matched to the individual needs of the student. Also, programs tend to be more effective if they involve other members of the family. In the accompanying "Inclusion Tips for the Teacher," Miksic (1987) has outlined the essential elements of a prevention program for drug abuse.

Many aspects of the treatment program for students who are drug or alcohol abusers will incorporate the services of public or private community agencies. Teachers should not expect to be counselors or investigators; their responsibility is to make appropriate referrals when they see signs of drug use or abuse. In addition, teachers may be called on to assist in managing suspected drug abuse episodes involving intoxication or withdrawal crises. At these times, they should remain

Inclusion Tips for the Teacher

Successful Drug Abuse Prevention Programs

Listed here are a series of elements that are considered essential in developing a school drug abuse prevention program:

1. Establish a clear, well-defined policy for teachers and students spelling out how teachers and administrators will deal with apparent or substantiated drug use or possession.
2. Encourage teachers to establish a basic drug education curriculum for their grade levels—keeping it simple, brief, and nonjudgmental and emphasizing the teachers' concern for the students' physical and psychological welfare.
3. Help teachers increase their awareness of local drug problems and use community service agencies.
4. Provide an atmosphere in which the teacher can develop the skills and sensitivity for resolving classroom and individual problems and for leading group discussions about topics such as adolescent development and drug use.
5. Develop an intervention program that involves families as well as students by offering both one-to-one and group counseling centers and drop-in centers within the school. (A drop-in center could be staffed by an education counselor with some training in drug abuse counseling.)

6. Try to get all teachers to review their role perceptions. If they feel their jobs are basically unfulfilling and that they are unable to empathize with students and deal with affective as well as cognitive training, this may lead to constructive career reorientation.
7. Develop peer-group approaches with positive role models for group or individual support. Different types of peer programs are discussed in the National Institute on Drug Abuse publication, "Adolescent Peer Pressure" (NIDA Publication No. ADM 83-1152).
8. Promote understanding of the emotional structure and perceptions that often accompany drug use. Many drug-using students feel they are incompetent and unreasonably rejected by adults and peers. They need an understanding approach rather than a disciplinary and judgmental attitude that confirms their belief that teachers and administrators are only concerned about keeping order, not about helping students.

Note: This list is reprinted with permission of Merrill, an imprint of Macmillan Publishing Company, from "Drug Abuse Management in Adolescent Special Education" by S. Miksic in *Helping Adolescents with Learning and Behavior Problems* (p. 245) by M. M. Kerr, C. M. Nelson, and D. L. Lambert, Copyright © 1987 Merrill Publishing Company, Columbus, Ohio.

calm and nonconfrontational because demonstrating control is not as important as ensuring safety (Kauffman, 2001).

The long-term effects of the use and abuse of drugs are not yet known. However, it is well documented that drug and alcohol abuse impairs the ability of students to function effectively in school and in their interactions with others. Educators can play an important role in decreasing the number of students who use and abuse alcohol and other drugs by including accurate information on drug and alcohol use in the school curriculum, being aware of the signs of potential problems, and helping to refer students to the appropriate professional resources.

TEENAGE PREGNANCY AND SEXUALLY TRANSMITTED DISEASES

The Stories of Barbara and Joshua

At age 15, Barbara quit school in the fourth month of her pregnancy. She was afraid that the baby might be "damaged" due to heavy drug use at the time of conception, but she has decided to keep the baby rather than have an abortion. Her boyfriend had denied that the baby is his. Barbara suspects it was her boyfriend who smashed the windshield of her mother's car as a threat to leave him out of this "mess." Barbara's mother is unemployed and on welfare. Their plan is to

have the mother babysit and Barbara will get a job to support the three of them. Barbara does not see returning to school as an option for her. She feels that her problems with school were mostly her fault and does not blame her teachers or the school. (Grossnickle, 1986, pp. 13–14)

* * *

Joshua is a 17-year-old teenager from a typical American family. He has been diagnosed with AIDS. He contracted the virus through sexual experimentation. He has been prevented from attending school. His mother and father cry and feel helpless in the battle to keep him alive. He now weighs 86 pounds. He is often too sick to go out of the house. He will die soon. He is very frightened. (Gray & House, 1989, p. 231)

Each year, about half of the 15- to 19-year-old girls in the United States are sexually active (Cartwright, Cartwright, & Ward, 1995) and approximately 1 million pregnancies occur each year in this group (Kann et al., 2000). Adolescents in the United States have pregnancy rates that are much higher than those of other Western industrialized countries (5.3% compared to 0.6% to 3.2% elsewhere). Of the teenage girls who become pregnant, (1) 50% never complete high school (Woodring, 1989), (2) 40% of the pregnancies end in abortion (Furstenberg, Brooks-Gunn, & Chase-Lansdale, 1989), and (3) 90% of the babies that are born are kept and raised by the teenage mothers (Mathes & Irby, 1993). Recent figures indicate that about 13% of all babies are born to teenagers (Mathes & Irby, 1993). Sixty percent of white males are sexually active by age 18, and 60% of African American males are sexually active by age 16.

While the teenage birthrate is declining, the current rates are still much higher than they were in the mid-1980s (Ventura & Curtin, 1999). Although the birthrates have steadily declined for both white and African American mothers, the rates for Hispanic mothers continue to be quite stable. Birth and infant mortality rates are somewhat lower for white teenagers than for both African American and Hispanic teenage mothers, yet all groups are likely to have low-birthweight infants and to lack timely prenatal care (Jacobson, 1996; National Center for Health Statistics, 1996).

When a teenage mother plans to raise her baby, a number of potential problems arise. She is generally unprepared for this role and is very likely to terminate her education by failing or dropping out of school. Many of the babies born to teenage mothers are likely to be premature and/or have medical problems and a higher than average risk of poor cognitive development. These difficulties may occur because many of the mothers do not have appropriate nutrition or health care during pregnancy, and it is not likely that they will be able to provide these essentials for their child. The teenager's child is apt to be at high risk for failure because of potential health, nutritional, and emotional problems, and it is probable that he or she will need special attention at school (Bonjean & Rittenmeyer, 1987; Cartwright et al., 1995; East, 1999; Mathes & Irby, 1993).

The high level of sexual activity reported in teenagers also increases the possibility of contracting **sexually transmitted diseases (STDs)** such as acquired immune deficiency syndrome (AIDS), genital warts, herpes, syphilis, or gonor-

rhea (Brooks-Gunn & Furstenberg, 1989). It is estimated that more than 3 million teenagers acquire an STD every year (Donovan, 1993; Kann et al., 2000). The most frequently diagnosed STD among adolescents is chlamydia, an infection of the vagina or urinary tract (McWhirter et al., 1998). Males (1993) estimates that the rate of STDs among teenage girls is 2.5 times higher than that of boys in the same age group. More than 50% of the teenagers who are known to have AIDS are from ethnic minority groups (Steel, 1995).

Many factors contribute to the level of teenage sexual activity and pregnancy. Social attitudes and the attitudes of peers often encourage sexual activity. Many teenagers have not been exposed to sex education or the use of contraceptives, and they lack knowledge about pregnancy prevention and the consequences of sexual behavior. Lack of close relationships with parents or friends may contribute to a need to participate in sexual activities in order to be "accepted" by others (Brooks-Gunn & Furstenberg, 1989; Cartwright et al., 1995; Trad, 1999).

The school must play several roles in dealing with this issue. First, educational programs must provide information on sex education and STDs to ensure that students are aware of the possible ramifications of sexual activity (Johns, Moncloa, & Gong, 2000; Kirby, 1999). Second, because Title IX of the Education Amendments of 1972 protects the teenage mother from discrimination, schools are obligated to continue to provide educational programs for these students (Bettinger, 1989). Finally, because children of teenage mothers are more likely to be at risk for potential failure, the school can improve the probability of their success by supporting the development of infant and preschool programs and attending to their risk status and their needs when they enter the general education program (Furstenberg et al., 1989).

Prevention programs introduced in schools typically provide general information on sexuality and contraception, attempt to modify attitudes in order to discourage early sexual activity, or provide specific information on family planning or contraception. These primary prevention programs have had limited success and "may promote healthier—but probably not less—childbearing by teenagers" (Males, 1993, p. 568). At present, many experts believe that actually providing family planning and contraception is most likely to reduce the early childbearing rate. A sex education curriculum should be carefully developed to provide information on the "social, health and economic risks related to sex and teen pregnancies" (Ogden & Germinario, 1988, p. 150).

In addition to informing students about all STDs, students should be specifically taught about how AIDS is transmitted (i.e., via sexual intercourse or exchange of blood) and the ways in which the transmission of this disease can be prevented (Schonfeld & Quackenbush, 2000; Yarber, 1987). After carefully reviewing many AIDS education programs, Popham (1993) indicates that in order for programs to teach students to "avoid behavior that places them at risk of HIV infection, students need to be knowledgeable about HIV and AIDS, skilled in avoiding behaviors that place them at risk of infection, and motivated to use their HIV-relevant skills and knowledge" (p. 561).

Students must be provided with the information they will need to make their own decisions regarding their sexual activity. In some communities, the school must approach this topic with a great deal of care. Teachers must take into account the values of parents, students, and the community, and they must carefully examine their own values when they provide instruction and guidance in this area. Cartwright and others (1989) provide teachers with an important reminder:

> A teacher may be the one person a girl who thinks or knows she is pregnant approaches for advice or for help. It is essential that teachers be aware of their own reactions to this situation and be able to control their own feelings in order to provide the assistance requested or to arrange for referrals to appropriate health-care agencies. (pp. 430–431)

CHILD ABUSE AND NEGLECT

Kara's Story

Kara, age 5, always presented a neat, well-ordered picture. Although not expensive, her clothes were well-chosen, clean, and pressed. Her long-sleeved blouses and colorful tights seemed a bit strange in warmer weather, but the teacher made no comments about them. The child was very affectionate, almost to the point of smothering; her endearing ways made her an easy candidate for teacher's pet. It was not until Kara unexplainably wet her pants and the teacher helped her remove her tights to clean up, that anything seemed amiss. Kara's small legs revealed numerous bruises in various stages of healing. An examination by the school nurse attested to the abuse Kara had suffered over her entire body. (Tower, 1987, p. 24)

Child abuse and neglect can occur in many forms. The National Clearinghouse on Child Abuse and Neglect (2001) provides information on the federal law related to these prob-

lems, the Child Abuse Prevention and Treatment Act (CAPTA). As amended and reauthorized in October 1996 (PL 104-235, Section 111; 42 U.S.C. 5106g), CAPTA defines child abuse and neglect as, at a minimum:

- Any recent act or failure to act on the part of a parent or caretaker which results in death, serious physical or emotional harm, sexual abuse or exploitation.
- An act or failure to act which presents an imminent risk of serious harm.

CAPTA defines sexual abuse as:

- The employment, use, persuasion, inducement, enticement, or coercion of any child to engage in, or assist any other person to engage in, any sexually explicit conduct or simulation of such conduct for the purpose of producing a visual depiction of such conduct
- The rape, and in cases of caretaker or inter-familial relationships, statutory rape, molestation, prostitution, or other form of sexual exploitation of children, or incest with children. . . .

Each State is responsible for providing its own definitions of child abuse and neglect within the civil and criminal context. Civil laws, or statutes, describe the circumstances and conditions that obligate mandated reporters to report known or suspected cases of abuse, and they provide definitions necessary for juvenile/family courts to take custody of a child alleged to have been maltreated. Criminal statutes specify the forms of maltreatment that are criminally punishable. (National Clearinghouse on Child Abuse and Neglect, 2001, p. 1)

Reports indicate more than 3 million cases of child abuse and neglect are reported annually (Goldson, 2001; National Committee to Prevent Child Abuse, 1997). Bauer and Shea (1989) indicate that abused and neglected children may not relate well with peers or adults and are likely to have "deficits in measured intelligence, academic performance, and readiness to learn" (p. 303).

No single set of characteristics can be associated with those who abuse children. Abusive behavior can occur because of various types of stress (e.g., marital stress), lack of basic knowledge of appropriate child-rearing practices, low tolerance for child behaviors such as crying or whining, or an inaccurate assessment of the motivation for the child's misbehavior (Emery, 1989). London and Stile (1982) indicate that the following characteristics are often found in child abusers:

- A history of being abused and/or neglected as a child.
- Uses physical punishment as the primary method of disciplining a child.
- Has unrealistic expectations that are inconsistent with the developmental age of the child.
- Has had no models of successful family relationships and, therefore, has little notion of parenting skills.

- Does not have friends or family to help with the heavy demands of caring for small children.
- Reports that there was not much love or emotional support from adults during his/her childhood.
- Has poor impulse control.
- Has an undue fear of "spoiling" the child by "giving in" to the child or allowing the child to "get away with" anything. (p. 11)

It is possible that abuse is more likely to occur with students with special needs than with their "typical" peers (Warger, Tewey, & Megivern, 1991). Some students with special needs are more difficult to control in the home, or they may exhibit high levels of inappropriate or irritating behaviors. Others may lack the skills required to respond as appropriately as the parent would like them to in social situations, or they are "easy marks" because they are incapable of defending themselves. The "Inclusion Tips for the Teacher" box provides information on identifying suspected child abuse.

The actual number of cases of child abuse and neglect is hard to determine because experts estimate that only 20% of

the cases are reported. It is difficult to obtain accurate statistics in this area because (1) definitions and reporting requirements vary across states and agencies, (2) people are not trained to recognize abuse, (3) individuals are unwilling to report cases because they do not want to get involved, and (4) agencies assigned to protect children have a difficult time obtaining evidence that maltreatment has occurred.

Educators have legal, ethical, and professional responsibilities to report cases of abuse and neglect and assist these children at school. It is their obligation to obtain the information necessary to report these cases accurately and provide for the needs of these students in the school setting (London & Stile, 1982). Educators are legally responsible for reporting child abuse, and "every state provides immunity by law from civil suit and criminal prosecution that might arise from the reporting of suspected child abuse or neglect" (Fischer & Sorenson, 1985, p. 188). Guidelines for a school's reporting policy and a set of suggested procedures for teachers to follow in preparing reports on child abuse and neglect are presented in Figure 18-3 on p. 411. It is important, however, that each teacher know the required

---

Inclusion Tips for the Teacher

Identifying Child Abuse

School personnel need assistance in determining if a situation they have observed is a case of child abuse that should be reported. The following list of descriptions of abuse, and the indicators for each, will be useful in helping educators recognize child abuse.

Physical Abuse

Physical abuse is characterized by inflicting physical injury by punching, beating, kicking, biting, burning, or otherwise harming a child. Although the injury is not an accident, the parent or caretaker may not have intended to hurt the child.

Physical Abuse—Physical Indicators

Child shows evidence of unexplained or repeated injury or injuries in the form of:

a. lacerations, punctures, or missing teeth
b. fractures, sprains, or dislocations
c. rope burns, immersion burns, or cigarette or cigar burns (especially on soles of feet, palms, back, or buttocks—these are seldom self-inflicted)
d. bruises or welts reflecting shape of object used to inflict the injury or injuries or several different surface areas
e. new injuries before old injuries have healed.

Physical Abuse—Behavioral Indicators

The child is or may be:

a. wary of adult contacts
b. consistently on the alert for danger
c. subject to frequent and severe mood changes
d. frightened of parents and avoids home (consistently arrives at school early or leaves late)
e. apprehensive when other children cry
f. demonstrating behavioral extremes (aggressive, disruptive, or destructive; or unusually shy, withdrawn, passive, or overly compliant).

Child Neglect

Child neglect is characterized by failure to provide for the child's basic needs. Neglect can be physical, educational, or emotional. Physical neglect includes refusal of or delay in seeking health care, abandonment, expulsion from home or not allowing a runaway to return home, and inadequate supervision. Educational neglect includes permission of chronic truancy, failure to enroll a child of mandatory school age, and inattention to a special educational need. Emotional neglect includes such actions as chronic or extreme spouse abuse in the child's presence, permission of drug or alcohol

continued

continued

use by the child, and refusal of or failure to provide needed psychological care.

Neglect—Physical Indicators

Child shows evidence of:

a. constant fatigue or listlessness
b. unattended physical problems or medical needs
c. consistent hunger (begs for food, undernourished)
d. poor hygiene, unbathed, filthy clothing, or inappropriate dress for the weather
e. abandonment.

Neglect—Behavioral Indicators

Child is or may be:

a. constantly hungry, begs for food
b. rejected by other children because of offensive body odor
c. constantly falling asleep in class
d. constantly arriving at school early and leaving late
e. left alone for substantial periods of time.

Sexual Abuse

Sexual abuse includes fondling a child's genitals, intercourse, incest, rape, sodomy, exhibitionism, and sexual exploitation. To be considered child abuse, these acts have to be committed by a parent [or other caregiver] responsible for the care of a child.

Sexual Abuse—Physical Indicators

Child shows evidence of:

a. difficulty in walking or sitting
b. torn, stained, or bloody underclothes
c. pain or itching in genital area
d. semen around the genitals or on clothing
e. lacerations, bruises, or bleeding in external genitalia, vaginal, or anal area
f. venereal disease (especially in young children)
g. pregnancy.

Sexual Abuse—Behavioral Indicators

Child shows evidence of:

a. bizarre, sophisticated, or unusual sexual behavior or knowledge
b. regression (Some sexually abused children, especially younger ones, will retreat into a fantasy world, or exhibit infantile behaviors, which may be interpreted as retardation.)
c. delinquency or aggression (The anger and hostility these children, particularly teenagers, feel toward the perpetrator may cause them to adopt aggressive behavior toward others.)
d. poor peer relationships (Because of guilt feelings the child cannot form relationships with peers.)
e. running away to escape from the home situation (Running away may be an indirect manner of asking for help in a situation in which they feel powerless.)
f. unwillingness to participate in physical activities (Young children who have been highly stimulated sexually or have had forced sexual intercourse may find it painful to sit during school or to play at active games.)
g. drug use/abuse (The use of alcohol and other drugs may be the child's method of handling his/her guilt and anxieties.)
h. indirect allusion (Sometimes sexually abused children confide in someone they feel may be helpful by using vague or indirect allusions to the home situation; e.g., "I'm afraid to go home tonight," "I'd like to come and live with you," or "I want to live in a foster home.")
i. seductive behavior (If a child views sexual contact as a positive source of attention, he/she may adopt seductive behaviors with peers or adults.).

Emotional Maltreatment

This form of child abuse and neglect includes acts or omissions by the parents that have caused, or could cause, serious behavioral, cognitive, emotional, or mental disorders. Examples include refusal to acknowledge the child's worth and needs, depriving them of normal social experiences, verbally terrorizing them and creating a climate of fear, ignoring them, or corrupting them through encouragement to engage in destructive behavior and reinforcing the deviance.

Emotional Maltreatment—Physical Indicators

Child shows evidence of:

a. habit disorders (sucking, biting, rocking)
b. conduct disorders (hyper- or hypo-activity, antisocial, destructive)
c. neurotic traits (sleep disorders, speech [disorders], enuresis, inhibition of play)
d. psychoneurotic reactions (hysteria, obsessions, depression, compulsion, phobias, hypochondria)
e. physical manifestations of nervous disorders (overweight, skin rashes).

Emotional Maltreatment—Behavioral Indicators

Child shows evidence of:

a. low self-esteem
b. behavior extremes (compliant and passive or aggressive, demanding, disruptive)
c. overly compliant behavior
d. developmental lags (physical, mental, and emotional)
e. seeking affection
f. attempting suicide
g. excessive temper tantrums.

Note: From *The School's Role in the Prevention of Child Abuse* (pp. 19–22) by S. B. London and S. W. Stile, 1982, Bloomington, IN: The Phi Delta Kappa Educational Foundation. Copyright 1982 by The Phi Delta Kappa Educational Foundation. Also from *Abuse and Neglect of Exceptional Children* (pp. 3–4) by C. L. Warger, S. Tewey, and M. Megivern, 1991, Reston, VA: The Council for Exceptional Children. Adapted by permission.

FIGURE 18-3   Reporting Child Abuse and Neglect

School Reporting Policy

Although educators are responsible for reporting child abuse and neglect, it is important that the school system has an established reporting procedure. Such a policy should include specific information such as:

1. At what point should the teacher report child abuse? Suspicion? Reasonable cause to believe? (This may be based not only on school policy but also on state law.)
2. Whom does the teacher notify? Nurse? Principal? School social worker?
3. What specific information does the teacher need to know to report?
4. What actions should the teacher have taken before reporting to validate suspicions?
5. What other school personnel should be involved?
6. Who makes the report to the appropriate authorities? How?
7. What information should be included in the report? (This may be dictated by state law or protective agency policy.)
8. What follow-up is expected on reported cases?
9. What role will the school play in possible community/child protection teams?
10. What commitment does the school have to inservice training or community programs?

Teacher's Checklist for Preparing to Report

Certainly reporting child abuse is neither easy or clear-cut. But the potential benefit for the abused child is worth every effort you are able to expend. Consider the following points when preparing to report:

1. Have you documented your data and written down the information to organize it in your own mind?
2. Have you analyzed your data? What causes you to suspect abuse/neglect? List the symptoms—physical or behavioral.
3. Have you been able to observe the parent/child interaction? Does the parent see the child as worthwhile or different and/or hard to handle?
4. Have you spoken with other professionals within the school? Do they have reason to suspect abuse/neglect? Why?
5. Do you know the reporting policy of your school? Do you know the answers to the questions listed above (i.e., in **School Reporting Policy**)? To whom do you report?
6. Do you have the necessary information required for a report? State law usually requires the following information:
   - names of the child and parents
   - address
   - age and sex of the child
   - type and extent of the child's injuries or complaints
   - evidence of prior injuries
   - explanation of the injuries given by the child
   - name and telephone number of the reporter
   - actions taken by the reporter (such as detaining the child, photographs)
   - other pertinent information
7. Do you (or does the school) have the exact telephone number and address of the agency to which you should report?
8. Have you talked with your administrator about the support you will receive once the report is made? What if the parents try to remove the child from your class? Will you have the support of the administration?
9. Does the school have on hand the necessary report forms?
10. Have you set up a support system for yourself with other teachers or administrators? (After the report is made, you may feel vulnerable and need to talk.)

Now you should be ready to report, knowing that you are providing a chance for both the child and the family to receive much-needed help.

Note: From *How Schools Can Help Combat Child Abuse and Neglect* (2nd ed., pp. 50–51, 53, 67–68) by C. C. Tower, 1987, Washington, DC: National Education Association. Copyright 1987 by National Education Association of the United States. Adapted by permission.

guidelines and timelines for reporting abuse in his or her own school assignment.

In the area of child abuse and neglect, the responsibilities of educators do not end with identifying and reporting suspected cases of abuse or neglect. Educators should also (1) model appropriate adult–pupil interactions; (2) support positive pupil–pupil interactions; (3) include opportunities for students to develop parenting skills as part of the school's curriculum; (4) support and participate in the development of prevention activities that involve parents; (5) encourage the development of programs that respond to the specific needs of students at risk; and (6) ensure that cases are monitored, reported, investigated, and that the school is informed of the disposition of the case (London & Stile, 1982).

Students need to be informed (1) that all individuals have basic human needs (i.e., for food, shelter, safety, and affection); (2) of acceptable ways that adults interact with children so that they would be able to tell whether they were being abused or exploited; (3) that an adult should be contacted if they are confused or concerned about something that is occurring in their life; (4) how they should deal with others to protect themselves from possible abuse; (5) of resources available to them in the community; and (6) who should be notified in the case of an emergency situation, such as someone approaching them on the street or attempting to enter their home when their parents are away (Tower, 1987). These topics should be covered at each appropriate grade level and may be included as part of the programs for sex education or the teaching of parenting skills.

EATING DISORDERS

Julie's Story
Julie is a pretty, intelligent 15-year-old who has been hospitalized twice for anorexia nervosa. She is the youngest of three children in an intact family. Her father is a professor at a prominent university and her mother is an artist with her studio in the home. The two older children are also bright and successful. The oldest, a son, has graduated from one of the Ivy League schools and is now in medical school. The older sister is currently attending a small, private, liberal arts school and earning almost straight As. She, too, expects to do graduate work. Julie has always been a good student and, according to her parents, after numerous food allergies as a baby, was the easiest to raise. Julie, however, thinks she is ugly, fat, not well-liked by her peers, and not as competent as her siblings. She also thinks her parents think the two older siblings are brighter and more productive. When she was 13 Julie started overeating and then gagging herself afterwards. This quickly led to strict dieting and strenuous exercise. Julie had a boyfriend, Nick, but shortly before the second hospitalization, they quit dating. There had been much conflict between them: Nick wanted more sexual in-

timacy than Julie. She finally acquiesced, but felt much ambivalence and guilt afterward. She feels Nick broke up with her because he thought she was promiscuous. (Epanchin, 1987, p. 175)

At least 25% of all adolescents exhibit symptoms of anorexia nervosa, bulimia, or obesity (Maloney & Klykylo, 1985; Torgan, 2002). Problems related to their condition can contribute to their risk for failure in school and in their interactions with others. Although these students may require services provided by professionals outside the school setting, it is important that educators be aware of the symptoms of these disorders and be able to identify and refer these students for the appropriate treatment.

Individuals with **anorexia nervosa** choose to restrict their intake of food to such an extent that they lose 20% to 25% of their appropriate body weight. Approximately 90% of the cases occur in young women who are overly concerned about being overweight and have a distorted idea of their body appearance (often thinking they are fat when they are actually underweight) (Crosscope-Happel, Hutchins, Getz, & Hayes, 2000). Anorexia is most likely to occur in 14- or 15-year-old girls and usually begins with dieting that turns into an obsession with weight loss. At one time, approximately 10% to 20% of anorexic individuals died from starvation or from complications arising from the disorder; this number has dropped sharply as awareness of the disorder has increased (Coleman, 1986).

Bulimia nervosa involves primarily young women who have recurrent episodes of binge eating that are followed by induced vomiting and the use of laxatives, fasting, or drugs to reduce weight. Bulimics tend to go on a food binge when they are under stress, angry, depressed, or lonely and then try to remove the food from their body before it can be digested. They are preoccupied with both eating and losing weight. Frequently these individuals hide their disorder from others (Levine, 1987).

Binge eating disorder is characterized by recurrent episodes of binge eating without the purging behavior of bulimia (National Eating Disorders Screening Program, 2001). According to the National Institute of Mental Health (2001) "binge-eating episodes are associated with at least three of the following: eating much more rapidly than normal; eating until feeling uncomfortably full; eating large amounts of food when not feeling physically hungry; eating alone because of being embarrassed by how much one is eating; feeling disgusted with oneself, depressed, or very guilty after overeating" (p. 6).

According to one definition, **obesity** occurs when body weight exceeds ideal weight by 20% or more. More modern definitions use body mass index (BMI) rather than actual weight. According to the American Obesity Association, in children and adolescents, *overweight* is defined as being at or above the 85th percentile in BMI, whereas *obesity* is defined as being at or above the 95th percentile in BMI. Torgan (2002) reports these facts about childhood obesity:

Obesity in kids is now epidemic in the United States. The number of children who are overweight has doubled in the last two to three decades; currently one child in five is overweight. The increase is in both children and adolescents, and in all age, race and gender groups. (p. 1)

There are many causes of obesity including genetics, inappropriate eating habits, family eating behaviors and attitudes, and lack of exercise (Maloney & Klykylo, 1985; Torgan, 2002). The American Obesity Association (2002) warns that obesity in children is associated with a number of health risks including diabetes, hypertension, and asthma.

The school's health curriculum should include information on eating disorders and provide a forum for developing knowledge and skills in (1) how to deal with stress, depression, and anxiety; (2) the role of society in setting specific expectations for physical appearance; (3) normal growth and development; and (4) appropriate nutrition. Educators who identify students who are at risk because of a potential eating disorder should consider contacting the school nurse or a counselor or referring the student to local mental health support services. Individuals with anorexia have responded well to behavioral interventions that provide positive reinforcement for weight gain, and bulimics often respond positively to treatment for depression or to participation in support groups with other bulimics (Coleman, 1986). Obesity can often be treated through behavioral approaches (e.g., self-monitoring and reinforcement) and the teaching of appropriate eating and exercise habits (Doleys & Bruno, 1982).

DELINQUENCY

The Story of "Scarface"

The child, nicknamed "Scarface" because of the cuts and scars on his face, was 10 years old, only 5 feet tall, and weighed just 90 pounds. His spindly legs barely touched the floor as he sat in detention, waiting for his court-appointed lawyer. He was accused of molesting a 10-year-old girl on the school grounds while one of his friends held her down. The judge released him into the custody of his parents. Over the next 10 weeks, he was arrested five more times—more times than any other juvenile in Washington, D.C., in that year, 1985. His other arrests were for holding up and robbing two men, threatening a woman with an iron pipe, participating in a brawl, illegally entering a car, and roughing up a woman and snatching her purse. (Kauffman, 2001, p. 406)

Of the 2.5 million juveniles arrested in 1999 (27% of all arrests involved a female), 487,600 were arrested for crimes such as vandalism, drug abuse, or running away; 484,400 were arrested for more serious crimes such as larceny-theft, robbery, aggravated assault, murder, or forcible rape. This represents a 25% drop from the beginning of the decade (Snyder, 2000). However, these figures may represent a very small percentage of the actual delinquent acts (Siegel & Senna, 1994), perhaps as few as 2% of the violations that are actually committed by delinquents (Patterson, DeBaryshe, & Ramsey, 1989).

Delinquents are much more likely to be boys. Those who show early signs of delinquent behavior and are arrested before they are 12 are more likely to continue their antisocial behavior as adults (Kauffman, 2001). Those arrested for the first time later in their teens are more likely to be one-time offenders. About 50% of the children who are antisocial become adolescent delinquents, and approximately 50% to 75% of the adolescent delinquents become adult offenders (Patterson et al., 1989). Each year, about 450,000 delinquents are placed in juvenile detention centers and state training schools, while 300,000 are sent to adult jails (Leone, Rutherford, & Nelson, 1991b).

Many factors have been noted as contributing to **delinquency.** Low intelligence, constitutional differences, location of the community (urban versus rural), cultural forces, community attitudes, failure in school, drug or alcohol abuse, poor self-concept, poor impulse control, and emotional problems have all been identified as contributing to the occurrence of delinquency (Cartwright et al., 1995). Patterson and others (1989) suggest that ineffective parenting (lack of appropriate discipline and monitoring) is a major contributor to the antisocial behavior of children. Antisocial behaviors eventually contribute to failure in academic areas and rejection by peers, and these failures can in turn lead to seeking acceptance in a deviant peer group and eventually to delinquency. The peer group is thought to provide the adolescent with antisocial attitudes and an opportunity to commit delinquent acts. Usually peers shape behavior by positively reinforcing deviant acts and punishing socially conforming behavior. Families with a history of antisocial behavior, low socioeconomic status, divorce, marital conflict, low educational level of the parent(s), unemployment, and the use of physical discipline have also been found to be related to the likelihood of delinquent behavior.

When interventions such as academic remediation, parent training, or social skills training have been attempted independently, they have at best had limited success that generally did not endure over time. The most receptive candidates for effective interventions are likely to be elementary students identified as lacking social and academic skills and exhibiting antisocial behaviors. Potential interventions that show the most promise combine specific training for the parents to improve their child management practices (e.g., effective, positive, and consistent discipline; appropriate supervision and monitoring) with training in social skills and academic remediation for the students (Kauffman, 2001; Patterson et al., 1989). Educators should be actively involved in developing programs that identify these students early in their school years, and they should work to coordinate the efforts and resources of the school and those of appropriate community agencies that can assist in working with the parents.

The information presented in this chapter should help you identify students at risk and understand the difficulties they experience that are likely to interfere with their success in school, at home, and in the community. Many of the specific educational techniques described in earlier chapters will prove helpful in working with students at risk because their skills and educational needs in some areas are often similar to those of other students with special needs. When educators work to provide educational experiences that are appropriate for these students, their opportunities for success increase and the likelihood that they will experience failure in school and life decreases.

Things to Remember

- The factors that place students at risk—substance abuse, delinquency, abusive caregivers, and so on—interfere with their ability to benefit from the school experience.
- Definitions of students at risk vary greatly from state to state and sometimes from district to district within the same state.
- Students at risk do not belong exclusively to any one group, community, or population, although poverty appears to increase risk levels.
- Educators can increase the probability that many students at risk will be contributors to society.
- The attitudes that students at risk take with them as they leave school will affect the attitudes of their younger siblings and, later, those of their own children.
- Students at risk benefit from effective educational interventions as well as optimum behavior management and instruction in academics and social skills.
- Teachers and other school personnel are not expected to become therapists for students at risk, but they can assist in referring them to appropriate services.
- A dropout is anyone over the age of 18 who is no longer enrolled in and has not graduated from high school.
- Suicide is the third leading cause of death among 15- to 24-year-olds.
- Teachers and other school personnel can carry out activities that have the potential ro reduce the number of suicides amoung students.

- Drug abuse is viewed by the general population as one of the top problems in our schools and the nation at large.
- Both the teenage mother and her children are at high risk for failure.
- The high level of sexual activity reported among teenagers increases the possibility that they will contract sexually transmitted diseases.
- No single set of characteristics is associated with those who abuse children.
- The actual number of cases of child abuse and neglect is difficult to determine because experts estimate that only 20% of the cases are reported.
- About one-fourth of adolescents show symptoms of eating disorders such as anorexia nervosa, bulimia, and obesity.
- The most promising interventions for delinquents combine specific training in child management practices for parents with training in social skills and academic remediation for students.
- Educators should be aware of the characteristics of students at risk so that they can identify and refer these students for the appropriate treatment.

ACTIVITIES

1. Write a short paper that establishes your position on providing mandatory educational programs tailored to meet the needs of students at risk. Tell how students would be identified, how eligibility for these services would be determined, and who would be responsible for providing the services.

2. Contact a local school district and determine the types of programs they offer for students at risk. Establish who supervises these programs (e.g., special education, remedial services), the specific programs offered, the type of training required for the personnel who deliver the services, and any agencies they work with in the community. From what you know about both the community and students at risk, does the program seem to be adequate? Be prepared to describe your findings and state what changes you would recommend.

3. Identify a student with whom you are familiar who would fit into one of the at-risk groups described in the chapter. Write a brief description of the student's background as well as his or her current progress (or lack of it) in school. Explain how you would use specific methods or techniques discussed in this chapter, or earlier in the book, to reduce the likelihood that the student would experience failure.

4. Locate community agencies that serve individuals who are at risk. Consider agencies such as telephone hotlines for suicide prevention, child abuse, or drug abuse. Determine the types of services they provide and whether their services are readily available to school-age students.

5. Obtain information that will help you to determine the policy and procedures for identifying and reporting child abuse and neglect in a local school or school district. If possible, also include specific information on the state laws and the penalties for not reporting cases of abuse or neglect in a timely fashion. Prepare a written description of these, with information on the agencies that work with the school to investigate the reports and enforce the laws related to abuse and neglect.

6. Write a letter to a legislator in which you describe what you consider to be the types of societal changes that would reduce the number of students at risk for failure in school, and tell how legislation could produce or influence those changes. Explain the types of losses that we currently experience (in both human and financial terms) as a result of the high number of students at risk.

CD-ROM Activities

Self-advocacy is one skill that is important for all students to learn, but particularly so for students who are at risk for school failure. View the video clip entitled "Self Advocacy" in the high school case study to respond to these questions:

- *What strategies does the teacher use to help students identify and explain their choices? Do you think that these types of interactions help students develop decision-making skills?*

- *How could these strategies be adapted for use with students who are members of one of the groups potentially at risk?*

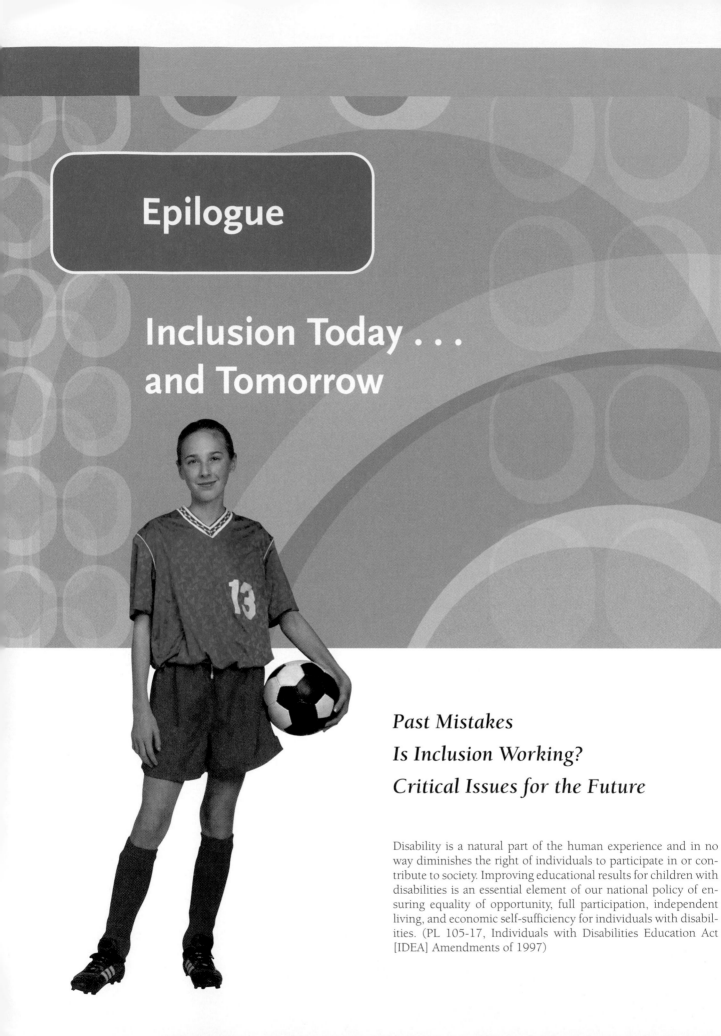

Epilogue

Inclusion Today . . .
and Tomorrow

Past Mistakes

Is Inclusion Working?

Critical Issues for the Future

Disability is a natural part of the human experience and in no way diminishes the right of individuals to participate in or contribute to society. Improving educational results for children with disabilities is an essential element of our national policy of ensuring equality of opportunity, full participation, independent living, and economic self-sufficiency for individuals with disabilities. (PL 105-17, Individuals with Disabilities Education Act [IDEA] Amendments of 1997)

Today, inclusion is part of the reality of public schooling in the United States. Although it is not possible to fix an exact date for the birth of this movement, the passage of the Education for All Handicapped Children Act in 1975 stands out as one of the critical starting points. With this law, students with disabilities were guaranteed the right to a free, appropriate public education. That education was to take place in the Least Restrictive Environment (LRE); to the maximum extent appropriate, youngsters with disabilities were to be educated alongside their peers without disabilities. To many educators, this exhortation for placement in the LRE became a mandate for mainstreaming in the 1970s and 1980s and for inclusion in the 1990s and into the next century.

What has happened as a result of the implementation of laws such as PL 94-142, IDEA, and their amendments? As countless teachers and administrators have asked, is inclusion working? What have we learned, what mistakes have we made, and, most important, how can we make it better? What can be done to improve the effectiveness of inclusion?

PAST MISTAKES

As mainstreaming became a common practice in public schools in the years following the passage of PL 94-142, mistakes were made, and the educational community learned from them. Perhaps the most critical error was the overenthusiastic endorsement of the general education classroom as the optimal placement for all children and youth with disabilities. The evils of special classes as segregated settings that perpetuate labeling and misclassification of culturally and linguistically diverse students were well publicized (e.g., Dunn, 1968). The alternative—placement in the mainstream with special education services as support—appeared a better approach. In a conscientious attempt to right past wrongs, educators in the late 1970s rushed to place a massive mainstreaming program into operation. However, along the way, several important mistakes were made.

- *Inadequate preparation of mainstreaming participants.* Many programs began without attempts to inform and prepare general education teachers, other school personnel, students without disabilities, and concerned parents of the changes that would occur in the general education classroom. Such preparation is vital not only to counteract negative attitudes toward individuals with disabilities (Alexander & Strain, 1978), but also to provide skills and information to the professionals responsible for the education of students with disabilities.
- *Misunderstanding of the principle of Least Restrictive Environment.* In many cases, the mandate for placement in the LRE was equated with full-time placement in general

education classes. The term *Least Restrictive Environment,* however, presupposes a continuum of service alternatives for students with disabilities; general education is only one option, albeit the one often deemed least restrictive. In the selection of placements, although the restrictiveness of the educational environment should be considered, the primary goals is an appropriate match between the services provided and the student's needs.

- *Inappropriate selection of students for full-time mainstreaming.* Full-time placement in the general education classroom simply is not appropriate for all students with disabilities. Some students require more intensive services, at least for part of the school day or for a portion of their school career. In the early days of mainstreaming, this reality was often overlooked in an overzealous attempt to serve students in a more normalized (and less expensive) educational setting.
- *Insufficient support to mainstreamed students.* Students with disabilities usually require support and assistance from special education professionals to perform adequately and independently in the general education environment. Early mainstreaming programs devoted little effort to this crucial component of the inclusion process.
- *Insufficient support for general education teachers.* General education teachers often require aid and assistance from special educators, particularly when mainstreaming is a new venture. This support has not always been available. Special educators, committed to a variety of other duties, have often lacked the time (and, in some cases, the expertise) to provide appropriate and ongoing consultation services.
- *Inadequate communication among team members.* One component of mainstreaming is the complex network of communication among team members: general education teachers talking with special education teachers, educators building communication links with the home, and older students with disabilities being allowed a voice in their own education. This team approach has not always proved successful. At worst, it has resulted in acrimony as professionals haggle over territorial rights and parents are relegated to the role of passive observers. At best, it has required enormous amounts of time and energy as professionals and parents have learned to work together.

The mistakes of early mainstreaming efforts should not be used as an indictment of the entire movement. Many of the errors made were developmental in nature, a result of hasty implementation in the light of unforeseen contingencies. Inclusion in general education remains one of the appropriate options for educating students with disabilities. Our past experiences serve best as a guide for the improvement of present programs and the launching of better efforts in the future.

IS INCLUSION WORKING?

Determining the effectiveness of inclusion is a complex task. Inclusion affects several constituent groups, and expected benefits vary from group to group. Some of the questions that arise in the evaluation of inclusion are identified here:

1. What effects does placement in the general classroom have on *students with disabilities?* Are such students accepted by peers and teachers? If not, what are the consequences in terms of lowered self-esteem? Is general education classroom instruction (even when augmented by part-time special services) sufficient to bring about the satisfactory progress of learners with disabilities in crucial academic, social, and vocational skill areas? What are the lifelong effects of inclusion? That is, does inclusion in the classroom result in inclusion in the community?

2. How does the inclusion of special students influence the educational experience of *students without disabilities?* What are the social and personal benefits that accrue from interactions with individuals with disabilities in the general education setting? How does instruction change when inclusion occurs? Does instructional quality decline when teachers are forced to divide attention between able students and those who are less able? Or does the overall quality of instruction improve as teachers learn new techniques for the solution of educational problems?

3. Is inclusion a positive experience for *general education teachers* or only another claim placed on the time and energy of overworked professionals? Do teachers become more tolerant of individual differences with the inclusion of students with disabilities? Are sufficient support services available, and do teachers know when and how to use these services? How does inclusion affect the teacher's ability to present instruction, provide practice, ensure mastery, and manage classroom behavior?

4. How has inclusion affected *special education teachers?* How have the roles of special educators changed as the duties of consultation and collaboration have been added to the central function of instruction? Have special education resource programs become tutorial services, acting only as an adjunct to the general education program? Is the consultant function one that most special educators perform effectively?

Is inclusion working? Although this is much too simplistic a question, it can be answered. The answer is yes; inclusion is working very well for some students and some teachers in some schools. The answer is also no; it is not working perfectly everywhere for everyone. The literature on inclusion (and its predecessor, mainstreaming) provides more specific answers to questions about effectiveness.

Early Research on Mainstreaming

Much of the research on the effectiveness of mainstreaming predates the federal mandate for service in the LRE. In large part this literature is composed of comparisons of general education class versus special class placement for students with mild retardation. (For reviews of this research, see MacMillan, 1982; Strain & Kerr, 1981; Zigler & Muenchow, 1979.) Studies of effects on the academic achievement of students with disabilities and their acceptance by peers do not consistently favor either placement. According to Zigler and Muenchow (1979), "The data on the merits of educating retarded children with their nonretarded peers are simply inconclusive" (p. 994).

More recent analyses shed some light on this issue. Using a technique called meta-analysis, Carlberg and Kavale (1980) synthesized the results of 50 studies of special versus general education class placement. These authors reported negative effects of special class placement on pupils with low IQs but more positive effects on students with learning disabilities and those with behavioral disorders. Forness, Kavale, Blum, and Lloyd (1997) contend that the overall results of the 1980 meta-analysis support the conclusion that special class placement is an intervention that does not work.

Leinhardt and Pallay (1982) reviewed the results of research on a range of educational environments, including special classes, resource programs, general education classes with support services, and general education classes with no support services. They concluded:

There were several examples of successful programs for mildly handicapped students that used isolated environments. Among the two isolated environments, resource rooms and self-contained classes, there is weak evidence that the less restrictive of the two, the resource room, may be superior. There are also examples of successful programs which help nonachieving students in the mainstream without removing them from the regular class. (p. 564)

Madden and Slavin (1983) present a somewhat different perspective. Their conclusions from a review of the literature are that "research favors placement in regular classes using individualized instruction or supplemented by well-designed resource programs for the achievement, behavior, and social emotional adjustment of academically handicapped students" (p. 519).

Differences in the interpretation of research results can be attributed to two major factors. First, there is no one optimal placement for all students with disabilities; the search for such a panacea in efficacy research is an impossible quest. For some students with disabilities, the general education class with resource support is most appropriate; for others, the more intensive intervention of a special class is necessary, at least at some point in their educational career. Second, studies of the relative effectiveness of a range of educational placements are asking the wrong question. As Forness and Kavale (1984) point out, "Where we teach may not be as important as what and how we teach" (p. 242). That is, it is not the location of the teaching act that is critical, but the quality of the curriculum taught and the instructional procedures used to teach it.

Leinhardt and Pallay (1982) share this view, identifying several curricular and instructional factors that promote the achievement of students with disabilities:

- Small class size,
- Consistency between curricular goals and instructional activities,
- Mastery learning and a formal management system,
- Increased time for cognitive activities, and
- Increased instructional time.

These factors are the same as those identified by teacher effectiveness research as important for the achievement of students without disabilities (Brophy & Good, 1986). Good teaching is good teaching, whatever the setting and whoever the audience.

Advocacy Efforts

Two advocacy efforts that marked the late 1980s and early 1990s influenced the direction of school programming for students with disabilities: the Regular Education Initiative (REI) and full inclusion. The REI movement advocated collaboration between special and general education, provision of special services within the general education classroom, and a commitment to serve all students with learning problems, not just those with identified disabilities. In the article considered the position statement for the REI, "Educating Children with Learning Problems: A Shared Responsibility," Will (1986b) called the current service delivery system a "flawed vision of education for our children" (p. 412). She pointed to the large number of students not eligible for special education who experience difficulty in school and exhorted special educators to "establish a partnership with regular education to cooperatively assess the educational needs of students with learning problems and to cooperatively develop effective educational strategies for meeting those needs" (p. 415).

While the REI focused primarily on students with mild disabilities, full inclusion was concerned with a broader population, including those with the most severe disabilities. The full inclusion movement began in the field of severe disabilities, and its proponents advocate full-time general education class placement for all students, regardless of the severity of their disability (Biklen, 1985; Lipsky & Gartner, 1989; Thousand & Villa, 1990; York & Vandercook, 1991). Full inclu-

sion is based on the premise that all students have the right to be members of the school community and that no student should be excluded. According to Stainback and Stainback (1990a), "An inclusive school is one that educates all students in the mainstream. . . . An inclusive school is a place where everybody belongs . . . " (p. 3).

In support of this position, Taylor (1988) points out that the concept of least restrictive environment may be a faulty one for students with severe disabilities. LRE legitimizes restrictive environments and confuses the intensity of service needed with the amount of segregation. Taylor contends that it is not necessary to segregate students with severe disabilities in order to meet their many educational needs. Brown and others (1991) offer a more moderate view. Although the "homeroom" of all students should be a general education classroom, students with severe disabilities should have the opportunity to spend time in other educational environments, depending on their individual needs.

The REI and full inclusion movements have caused much controversy within the field of special education. The major issue appears to be the need for a continuum of special education services, as required by federal laws. Proponents of REI and full inclusion endorsed full-time placement in general education; critics of these movements pointed to the need for a range of service options. As Braaten, Kauffman, Braaten, Polsgrove, and Nelson (1988) comment, "Research clearly does not support the assertion that all students can be managed and taught effectively in regular classrooms" (p. 23). Similar views have been expressed by several of the professional organizations concerned with the education of students with mild disabilities, including the Council for Learning Disabilities (1993), the National Joint Committee on Learning Disabilities (1993), and the Learning Disabilities Association of America (1993). These organizations argue that no one placement option is appropriate for all students.

One of the major fears of special educators who opposed the REI and full inclusion is that students with disabilities will be placed in general education classrooms on a full-time basis without adequate support. Although provision of special services within the general education class is a viable model for some students, others require more intensive intervention. Kauffman, Lloyd, Baker, and Riedel (1995) contend that general education is not the best placement for all students with emotional or behavioral disorders, students who according to these authors have problems that are "severe, pervasive, and chronic—not minor, situational, or transitory" (p. 542). In addition, Schumaker and Deshler (1988) point out that full-time inclusion faces many barriers at the secondary level. In middle school and high school, there are large gaps between the skills of students with mild disabilities and the demands of the instructional setting, and instruction tends to be teacher centered rather than student centered. Bringing about the systems changes needed to implement either the REI or full inclusion in secondary schools would be a difficult and lengthy process.

Another consideration is the already difficult task facing the general education teacher as he or she attempts to meet the needs of the diverse group of learners who make up a regular class. The general education classroom includes an increasing number of students at risk for school failure, as chapter 18 has described. It is the view of Kauffman, Gerber, and Semmel (1988) that "more variability than now exists in most regular classrooms is not a reasonable option without additional protected resources for the teacher" (p. 10). In a challenge to advocates of full inclusion, Fuchs and Fuchs (1994) ask, "Why do full inclusionists believe general education can respond appropriately to all students heretofore receiving special education (as well as Chapter 1 and English as a second language instruction)? How can the mainstream improve so dramatically to incorporate an increase in diversity when it has such obvious difficulty accommodating the student diversity it already has...?" (p. 302).

Compounding the increased variability in the general education classroom are trends in educational reform such as higher academic standards, increased graduation requirements, more rigorous evaluation of student achievement, and improved discipline (Braaten & Braaten, 1988; Timar & Kirp, 1989). Such reforms have direct implications for learners with disabilities and students at risk. Braaten and Braaten (1988) suggest that "the increased demand for greater skill development in mathematics, science, foreign language, and technology may benefit the general population but further burden students with special needs who are having difficulty coping with current requirements" (p. 46).

As in most debates, both advocates and critics of REI and full inclusion have made several valid points. More collaboration is needed between general and special education, and the general education classroom is an appropriate full-time placement for many students with disabilities as long as adequate support is provided to those students and their teachers. However, the general education classroom should remain one of a set of placement options for students with disabilities. As Will (1986a) describes it, the basic principle underlying the concept of least restrictive environment "is that placement decisions must be made on an individual basis and that various alternative placements must be available in order to ensure that each handicapped child receives an education which is appropriate to his or her individual needs" (p. 1).

Research on Full Inclusion

The research base for full inclusion is beginning to develop, although it is not yet substantial. In 1997, the *Journal of Special Education* published a special issue on research in severe disabilities. One highlight of this issue was a review by Hunt and Goetz (1997) of the research to date on inclusive programs for students with severe disabilities. Hunt and Goetz identified 19 studies that addressed five areas related to full inclusion: parents' perceptions of full inclusion, school and classroom practices, costs, achievement outcomes for students with severe disabilities, and social outcomes.

Researchers in severe disabilities were most concerned with the social effects of inclusion (Hunt & Goetz, 1997). Six studies were conducted on social relationships and friendships, and results suggest positive outcomes for students with severe disabilities. Only two studies addressed student achievement (Hunt, Staub, Alwell, & Goetz, 1994; Sharpe, York, & Knight, 1994, as cited in Hunt & Goetz, 1997). Both examined the effects of inclusion on the academic achievement of general education students without disabilities. One also investigated whether students with severe disabilities were able to acquire basic communication skills as part of their participation in cooperative learning experiences in math in general education classrooms (Hunt et al., 1994, as cited in Hunt & Goetz, 1997). Results indicate that the achievement of typical peers is not affected by inclusion and that students with severe disabilities can acquire communication skills in the general education setting. A more recent study (Logan & Keefe, 1997) found that students with severe disabilities included in general education classrooms received more academic instruction, more one-to-one instruction, and more teacher attention than similar students in self-contained special education classrooms.

In contrast, the research on full inclusion of students with mild disabilities tends to focus on academic, rather than social, outcomes. Zigmond and colleagues (1995) report on the results of three large-scale research projects at the University of Pittsburgh, University of Washington, and Vanderbilt University. Each developed a model inclusion program using research-based practices for students with learning disabilities and implemented that program in general education classrooms over a 3- or 4-year period. All projects "required large investments of time and resources for preparation, planning, training, technical assistance, and support. All three were able to win the cooperation of general education school personnel in a genuine restructuring effort" (p. 539).

Despite these efforts, the academic outcomes for students with learning disabilities were disappointing. Zigmond et al. (1995) report:

> . . . a majority of students with learning disabilities (63%) did not register average or better achievement gains. Even more disconcerting, we found that, for 40% of our LD sample, gains were less than half the size of the grade-level averages. In other words, 40% of students with learning disabilities who were being educated full-time or primarily in general education settings not only were failing to make average gains, but also were slipping behind at what many would consider a disturbing rate. (p. 539)

The authors concluded that "general education settings produce achievement outcomes for students with learning disabilities that are neither desirable nor acceptable" (p. 539).

In a recent study of current implementation efforts, McLeskey, Hoppey, Williamson, and Rentz (2004) shed doubt on the extent to which the full inclusion movement has become a reality for students with learning disabilities. These researchers report that in the 1990s only 15 states made progress toward educating students with LD in less restrictive settings. More alarming, however, are the results of a recent review of empirical research. In this 2003 study, Kavale and Mostert conclude that "full inclusion in practice is much more than a flawed concept played out in schools—it may well be that full inclusion is doing more harm than good" (p. 196).

This body of research places in stark relief the differences between professionals who advocate full inclusion for students with severe disabilities and those who are more skeptical about full-time general education placement for students with milder disabilities. Professionals concerned with severe disabilities focus on social outcomes and the ways in which inclusion can enhance the social acceptance and participation of students with disabilities. Those concerned with milder disabilities, particularly learning disabilities, are more interested in academic outcomes and whether general education programs can foster the development of reading, math, and written language skills for students with problems in these areas. Roberts and Mather (1995) summarize the position of professionals in learning disabilities in these words: "To be anti-full inclusion is not to be pro-exclusion (Lieberman, 1992), but instead to support appropriate, individualized educational programs" (p. 54). That is the position espoused in this book and our rationale for choosing the term *inclusion* (rather than *full inclusion*) to describe the participation of students with disabilities in general education.

CRITICAL ISSUES FOR THE FUTURE

Inclusion is basically an equity issue; it is an expression of the belief that all students, including those with disabilities, have an equal right to participate in the educational experience. Inclusion is also an integration issue, promoting the concept that students should not be excluded from the normal educational program solely on the basis of a physical, cognitive, or emotional disability. The inclusion movement has forced U.S. education to reconsider one of its basic issues: Is education designed to serve only those who learn quickly and easily when placed in the standard instructional environment, or is the goal to educate all students, even those who learn with difficulty?

One important result of inclusion has been to focus attention on students who, although not identified as having a disability, encounter failure in the educational system. As students with disabilities joined the ranks of the general education classroom, it soon became apparent that some of their peers without disabilities had similar needs and benefited from similar instructional modifications. As we move into the future, let us attempt to improve the quality of education for all students who are members of general education classrooms—students with disabilities and those without, students who represent the U.S. macroculture and those from diverse cultural and linguistic backgrounds, gifted students and students at risk for school failure. To this end, the following recommendations are offered:

- *Continue to evaluate the practice of inclusion and to identify effective approaches to educating students with disabilities in the general education classroom.* Research should continue to examine the effects of inclusion on all participants. In addition, it is necessary to document effective inclusion strategies and to seek or develop promising new approaches. Determining what has gone wrong can prevent the recurrence of past mistakes; identifying effective practices can increase the probability of future successes.

- *Increase the use of technology and nonprofessional personnel in the general education classroom.* The teacher need not be the only instructional resource in the general education classroom. With proper training, instructional aides, adult volunteers, and peers can substantially increase a given classroom's capability to provide students with opportunities to learn. For this to occur, educators must recognize that direct delivery of instruction is not the only valid role of the teacher. Management of instruction delivered by other is also appropriate and may be the more efficient method to guarantee appropriate educational experiences for all students included in the general education classroom setting. Also often overlooked as aids to the classroom teacher are computers and other technologies. When educators overcome their reluctance to deal with hardware, they discover the potential of such devices not only in the delivery of instruction but also in the management of classroom information.

- *Search out ways to predict the success of inclusion in the general education classroom.* One pressing need in inclusion is the development and refinement of a set of criteria or indicators to determine when inclusion in a particular classroom is likely to be successful for a particular student. However, such judgments cannot be based solely on the student's characteristics; the nature of the classroom environment in which the student is to function must also be considered (Dardig, 1981; Wood & Miederhoff, 1989). To determine the probability of successful inclusion, it is necessary to take into account the characteristics of the classroom, the instructional techniques in use, the capabilities of the general education teacher and his or her skills in adapting instruction to meet individual needs, and the kinds of special education services and personnel required to support the student's and teacher's efforts.

- *Develop strategies to assist students with disabilities in the generalization and maintenance of important functional skills.* Students with disabilities are often plagued by difficulty in transferring information learned in one setting to another situation or environment. This problem becomes critical when students acquire skills under the tutelage of the special education teacher in the resource room and then are expected to generalize and maintain those skills in the general education classroom setting. Steps toward a solution to this problem will benefit students with disabilities, particularly when emphasis is placed on functional skills that are both currently relevant and important to successful adulthood.

- *Increase efforts to ensure nonbiased assessment.* In an attempt to safeguard against the misidentification of students from diverse groups as disabled, PL 94-142 and IDEA mandate procedures for nondiscriminatory assessment. Evaluation measures are to be administered by trained personnel; validated for the purpose for which they are used; in the student's native language; and nondiscriminatory in terms of race, culture, and disability. Although the requirements of law are clear, they have been difficult to implement because of the lack of appropriate assessment tools (McLoughlin & Lewis, 2005). Many measures in widespread use lack adequate validation, appropriate instruments have not been developed for all purposes in all languages, and the problem of measuring skills and abilities without cultural bias has not been solved (de Valenzuela & Baca, 1998). Work must continue to ensure the fair and unbiased assessment of culturally and linguistically diverse students.

- *Examine current practices in the labeling and classification of students with disabilities.* One unfortunate result of the current system of labeling and classifying special students on the basis of disability has been the erroneous conclusion that students with different labels require totally different treatments (Lovitt, 1982). Although the curriculum concerns for various groups of students may differ, instructional techniques remain the same across different areas of exceptionality. That is, the skills appropriate for students with mild retardation may be different from those appropriate for students with learning disabilities, but the ways in which teachers go about skill instruction do not vary across groups (Hallahan & Kauffman, 1976). To put it simply, good teaching has the same characteristics whether it occurs in science instruction in the general education class, vocational training in the special class, or individualized reading instruction in the resource room. The ideal classification system for students with disabilities would reflect both the salient differences in curriculum and the universality of instructional techniques.

- *Increase the use of direct, explicit instruction and other educational approaches with empirical support.* Research on instructional factors affecting student achievement has produced important results, and the teacher's role is quite clear. Students learn when they spend time engaged in the learning process, when learning activities are related to the goals of instruction, and when they have ample opportunity to respond and receive feedback on their responses. Because it promotes these conditions, direct instruction has emerged as an effective strategy for teaching basic academic skills. Although research must continue, educators should begin to discard unsubstantiated teaching methodologies and employ in their stead those approaches with empirical support.

- *Increase the meaningful involvement of parents and students in the inclusion process.* The right to make educational decisions does not belong exclusively to educators. Parents and students are also concerned, and their interest is more immediate, more personal, and more enduring than that of professionals. Education will command higher regard from its constituents when it begins to welcome—not merely permit—the continuous participation of these involved individuals.

- *Transform inclusion from a school-based practice to a lifelong condition for individuals with disabilities.* The ultimate test of the inclusion movement is its effect on the adulthood of today's children and adolescents. If students with disabilities mature into competent adults who are included within the workplace and the social fabric of the community, then inclusion has been a success. Although the general education classroom is only the first step, it is a crucial one. If we are successful today, the next generation of teachers and students will regard inclusion of individuals with disabilities in general education as an expected, ordinary, and unexceptional occurrence.

Glossary

Academic problems. Difficulties encountered in the acquisition, maintenance, and generalization of basic school skills and content-area subjects.

Acceleration. Progress through the curriculum at an increased rate.

Access. Ease of entry to and travel from place to place within a building or location.

Acquisition. The initial learning of information or skills.

Adapted physical education teacher. A specialist who modifies physical education instruction to meet the needs of students with special needs.

Adaptive behavior. The individual's ability to change in order to cope with the demands of the environment; also called *social competence*.

Advanced organizers. Information presented to students prior to an instructional task as a preview or overview.

Adventitious. Acquired after birth, for example, as a result of illness or accident.

Algorithm. A procedure used to perform an operation in mathematics.

Amplification device. Anything that increases the volume of sound.

Anorexia nervosa. The disorder in which individuals (usually young women) choose to restrict their intake of food to such an extent that they lose 20% to 25% of their appropriate body weight.

Antecedent. The event or condition that occurs immediately before a behavior of interest. See also *Consequence*.

Applied behavior analysis. A system for the understanding and improvement of human behavior focusing on objectively defined and measurable behaviors of social significance.

Architectural barriers. Obstructions in the physical environment that prevent access.

Asperger's syndrome. A disorder characterized by qualitative impairments in social interaction and restrictive or repetitive patterns of behavior without significant delays in cognitive development or adaptive behavior other than social interaction.

Assessment. The process by which information is gathered about students in order to make educational decisions.

Assistive technology. Any technology designed specifically for individuals with disabilities; includes add-ons to computer systems and stand-alone devices.

Assistive technology specialist. Individual responsible for advising the team serving students with special needs regarding the selection, acquisition, or use of assistive technology devices that can increase, maintain, or improve the functional capabilities of students with a disability.

At risk. See *Students at risk for school failure*.

Attention deficit hyperactivity disorder (ADHD). A term used in psychiatric classification systems to describe individuals who show poor attention, impulsivity, and sometimes hyperactivity.

Audiologist. A specialist trained in the evaluation and remediation of hearing losses.

Audiometer. A device to assess hearing ability.

Auditory training. Instruction to improve listening skills by teaching individuals with hearing impairments to use as much of their residual hearing as possible.

Augmentative communication. Any system or device designed to enhance the communication abilities of individuals who are nonverbal or whose speech is difficult to understand.

Authoring program. A type of computer program designed to facilitate the teacher's authoring (i.e., writing) of computer-based lessons.

Autism. See *Autism spectrum disorder*.

Autism spectrum disorder. A pervasive developmental disorder with qualitative impairments in communication, social interaction, and restrictive or repetitive patterns of behavior that first occur prior to age 3.

Automaticity. In skill learning, the ability to perform a skill both accurately and quickly without thought.

Baseline data. Information collected about a behavior before an intervention is implemented.

Basic skills. The "tool" subjects of listening, speaking, reading, writing, spelling, and mathematics.

Behavioral disorder. A disability in which students are characterized by inappropriate school behavior.

Bilingual education. Programs emphasizing both the language of the home and English.

Binge eating disorder. A type of eating disorder in which the individual consumes large amounts of food. See also *Bulimia nervosa*.

Blind. A legal designation, often with little educational relevance, that indicates (1) visual acuity of 20/200 or less in the better eye with the best possible correction or (2) a field of vision restricted to an angle subtending an arc of 20 degrees or less.

Blindness. The condition in which so little information is received through the eye that other senses must be used for learning.

Blog. An online journal; also called a *web log*.

Braille. A system of raised dots that can be decoded by touch.

Braillewriter. A machine used to type material in Braille.

Bulimia nervosa. The disorder in which individuals (primarily young women) have recurrent episodes of binge eating that are followed by induced vomiting, use of laxatives, fasting, or taking drugs to reduce weight.

Bullying. Behavior in which one student threatens or attempts to intimidate another.

Captioned film. A film adapted for viewers who are deaf; dialogue appears in print superimposed on the screen.

Career education. Instruction in the application of basic skills and content-area information to problems of daily life, independent living, and vocational independence.

Cerebral palsy. A motor impairment due to damage to the brain, usually occurring before, during, or shortly following birth.

Child abuse and neglect. The physical or mental injury, sexual abuse or exploitation, negligent treatment, or maltreatment of a child under the age of 18 or the age specified by the child protection law of the state in question, by a person who is responsible for the child's welfare, under circumstances which indicate that the child's health or welfare is harmed or threatened.

Choral responding. An instructional technique in which groups of students answer the teacher's question in unison.

Classroom conduct problems. Inappropriate school behaviors that interfere with classroom instruction, impede social interaction with teachers and peers, or endanger others.

Clinical teaching. An instructional technique in which data are gathered both before and during the implementation of an intervention in order to evaluate the effectiveness of that intervention.

Cloze procedure. A method used to determine whether reading material is appropriate for a particular student.

Cochlear implant. An amplification device that uses electrodes surgically inserted in the inner ear, and other hearing-aid-type components that pick up and transmit sound to the electrodes.

Cognitive training. The behavior change method that attempts to teach students new thinking strategies for controlling their own behavior.

Compensation. The instructional technique in which a student's weaknesses are bypassed.

Computer-assisted instruction. The delivery of instruction to learners via computers.

Conductive hearing loss. A hearing loss caused by damage or disease in the outer or middle ear.

Congenital. Present at birth.

Consequence. The event or condition that occurs after a behavior of interest. See also *Antecedent*.

Content-area subjects. Bodies of knowledge in the academic curriculum; for example, English and other languages, the sciences, mathematics, and the social sciences.

Contingency contract. A written agreement between a student and a teacher that states what the student must do to earn a specific reward.

Contingent observation. A type of time-out procedure in which a student is removed from a reinforcing event and can watch but not participate.

Cooperative learning. The instructional model in which students work together as a team to complete activities or assignments (in contrast to competitive learning, in which each student works alone).

Creativity. The process of generating novel solutions or products.

Creativity tool. A type of computer program that aids in the design, development, and presentation of creative products including those in art, music, video, and website design.

Criterion-referenced test. An informal assessment device that measures whether students have mastered the educational goals stated in instructional objectives.

Culturally and linguistically diverse students. Students whose home cultures (and perhaps languages) differ from that of the school. Such students may require special assistance to succeed in general education.

Culture. A subgroup of the population that shares beliefs, values, practices, and language.

Curriculum compacting. Eliminating instruction on content or skills already mastered so that gifted students can move to more challenging material.

Curriculum-based assessment. The use of current classroom performance as the basis for determining students' educational needs.

Curriculum-based measurement. A type of curriculum-based assessment in which the teacher takes frequent, brief samples of student performance in important skill areas to evaluate progress toward curricular goals. See also *Curriculum-based assessment*.

Database management program. A type of computer program that facilitates the storage of information and its retrieval.

Deaf. See *Deafness*.

Deafness. The condition in which so little information is received through the sense of hearing that other senses must be used for learning.

Delinquency. Offenses against the legal and social standards of society. The term refers to unacceptable behavior on the part of young people, classified by law as underage, that causes them to be charged as lawbreakers.

Demonstration. The instructional procedure in which a new skill is modeled.

Desktop publishing program. A computer program that allows the user to manipulate both text and graphics.

Diabetes. A disorder of metabolism.

Differentiated instruction. Instruction within the general education setting that is varied to meet the needs of different learners.

Differentiation. Providing services different from those offered in the general program.

Direct teaching. The teacher's demonstration of appropriate strategies for the performance of a learning task, encouragement of maximal student response opportunities, and provision of frequent systematic feedback on task performance; also called *direct instruction* or *active teaching*.

Discovery learning. An instructional technique in which the teacher presents students with opportunities for learning; skills are not taught directly.

Distractibility. Difficulty in maintaining attention.

Divergent thinking. The production of several solutions to one problem.

Dropout. Any individual over the age of 18 who is no longer enrolled in and has not graduated from high school.

Drug and alcohol abuse. Use of alcohol or other drugs that cause negative reactions or other adverse consequences to the individual user, others, or property.

Duration recording. The system of recording observation data in which the length of time a behavior occurs is noted.

Dysfluency. Difficulty in the production of fluent, rhythmic speech; for example, stuttering.

Early interventionist. A specialist who provides educational services to infants, toddlers, and preschoolers with special needs and to the families of these children. These services may be provided in the home, school, or other settings.

Educational technology. Any technology used to support the teaching–learning process; also called *instructional technology*.

Educationally blind. Having vision impaired to the extent that tactile or auditory materials must be used for reading.

E-mail. Electronic mail; the type of mail sent over the Internet.

Engaged time. The actual time during which students are actively involved and participating in instruction.

English learner. An individual who is learning English as his or her second or subsequent language. Also called *English Language Learner*.

Enrichment. The instructional technique in which something is added to the regular school program in order to enrich it.

Epilepsy. A convulsive disorder of the central nervous system.

Error analysis. The technique in which student work samples are studied for patterns of errors.

E-text. Electronic text such as books downloadable from the Internet.

Etiology. Cause.

Event recording. The system of recording observation data in which the number of times a behavior occurs is noted.

Explicit instruction. Systematic and specific instruction in the knowledge or skill area the student is expected to acquire. See also *Direct teaching*.

Extinction. A procedure used to decrease the occurrence of a behavior by removing reinforcers that have previously followed the behavior.

Flexible grouping. A method of instructional grouping in which arrangements of students change frequently and placement decisions are based on a variety of criteria (e.g., skills, interests, proximity).

Fluency. The ability to perform a skill quickly and accurately.

Full inclusion. Full-time integration in general education classrooms of all students with special needs, regarding of the severity of their disabilities. See also *Inclusion*.

Functional assessment. A systematic process designed to collect data to help educators (1) understand a problem behavior and (2) develop effective methods for modifying the behavior. Also called *functional behavioral analysis*.

Functional skills. Important skills selected for instruction because of their usefulness in everyday life.

Generalization. The application or transfer of learned material to similar situations and problems.

Gifted and talented students. Students with exceptional potential or ability in intellectual, academic, leadership, creative, or artistic domains and who require specialized services to realize their potential.

Giftedness. Superior intellect; it can be accompanied by creative ability.

Group contingencies. Reinforcement provided to members of a group dependent on whether the entire group has reached a criterion level established by the teacher.

Grouping. Bringing gifted students together for instruction; can be within a general classroom or specialized setting.

Guided practice. The performance of a task under supervision; feedback, correction, and confirmation are immediate.

Habilitation. The instructional approach directed toward the development of the critical skills necessary for successful adulthood.

Hard of hearing. Characterized by a condition in which hearing, although impaired, can be used as one of the senses for learning.

Hearing impairment. A disability characterized by a decrease in the ability to hear. See also *Deafness* and *Hard of hearing*.

Heritage language. The language of the student's family and cultural group.

Heterogeneous grouping. A method of instructional grouping that places together students whose instructional needs are somehow dissimilar.

High interest–low vocabulary. Reading materials that appeal to students who read at a lower grade level than that expected for their age.

Hyperactivity. Excessive activity.

Hypermedia. A computer program in which the user, not the program, determines the sequence in which various media (text, voice, video, etc.) are accessed.

Idea processor. A type of computer program that assists in the generation and manipulation of ideas.

Impulsivity. Lack of reflectivity; activity without careful thought and reflection.

Inclusion. Meaningful participation of students with special needs in general education classrooms and programs.

Independent practice. The performance of a skill without supervision; feedback is delayed.

Individualized Education Program (IEP). A written educational plan that specifies a special student's current levels of educational performance, and annual goals; prepared by a team that includes the student's parent(s), teacher(s), and, if appropriate, the student.

Individualized instruction. Instruction designed to meet the needs of each student; it can be group instruction or tutorial as long as a high proportion of correct responses is maintained.

Informal assessment. The process of gathering information about students with measures and techniques such as inventories, criterion-referenced tests, and observation; teachers often design their own informal assessment strategies.

Informal reading inventory. An informal assessment device that aids in determining a student's instructional reading level.

Information presentation tool. A type of computer program that facilitates the presentation of text and/or graphics-based information.

Information processing. The method by which persons receive, store, and express information; also called *psychological processing*.

Instruction. The teaching process. See also *Direct teaching* and *Individualized instruction*.

Instructional environment. In the context of the classroom, the procedures, materials, and equipment used by the teacher to increase student performance.

Instructional technology. See *Educational technology*.

Instructional unit. See *Unit approach*.

Internet. A worldwide computer network that includes e-mail, the World Wide Web, and other resources.

Interval recording. The system of recording observation data in which the occurrence or nonoccurrence of a behavior within a specific time interval is noted.

Inventory. An informal assessment device that samples a variety of skills within a subject matter area; for example, an informal reading inventory.

Itinerant teacher. A professional who travels from school to school rather than providing instruction at one school site.

Knowledge of results. Information provided to students about the accuracy of their responses.

Language. The ability to communicate using symbols.

Learning center. An area of the classroom designed for use of self-instructional materials for independent practice.

Learning disability. A disorder in the ability to process information that can result in attention, perception, or memory deficits. Students with learning disabilities experience difficulty in school learning despite adequate hearing, vision, and intelligence.

Learning strategies. Methods students use to acquire, rehearse, organize, and recall information.

Least Restrictive Environment (LRE). The most appropriate educational placement that is closest to general education.

Listserv. An electronic mailing list to which a user subscribes to receive e-mail messages related to a specific topic.

Local education agency. Typically, a local school district that is governed by a public board of education to provide public elementary and/or secondary schools in a city, township, or county.

Low vision. The condition in which vision, although impaired, can be used as one of the senses for learning.

Low-vision aid. Any device that aids vision by magnification.

Mainstreaming. The inclusion of students with special needs in the general educational program for any part of the school day. See also *Inclusion*.

Maintenance. The recall of information previously learned.

Mapping. An instructional strategy to help students organize ideas for writing; students draw a map showing the relationship between the main topic and key words.

Mediated instruction. Any instructional procedure that includes the use of media.

Medically fragile. Students with a chronic medical condition that requires ongoing medical management and accommodation during the school day.

Mental retardation. A disability in which subaverage general intellectual functioning is associated with deficits in adaptive behavior.

Mobility. The ability to move from place to place.

Modeling. The reinforcement of another individual, the model, for exhibiting the desired behavior in the presence of the target student. When the target student imitates the desired behavior, he or she is then reinforced.

Multicultural education. The instructional approach that emphasizes the value of diverse cultures.

Multimedia. Computers and computer software that present information to the user through a variety of media such as photos, video, voice, and music.

Narrative recording. A system of observation in which the observer describes all behaviors that occur.

Negative attention. Use of a negative verbal or nonverbal response (e.g., "Stop" or a frown) that indicates disapproval of a student's behavior. The procedure attempts to reduce the behavior quickly without interfering with ongoing classroom activities.

Negative reinforcement. A procedure used to increase the occurrence of a behavior by following it with the removal of an aversive event or condition.

Newsgroup. An online discussion group where users can read and post messages related to a specific topic.

Norm-referenced test. A test designed to compare the performance of one student with that of students in the norm group of the same age or grade; used to determine whether students have significant problems in relation to peers.

Obesity. The condition in which the body weight of an individual exceeds the ideal weight by 20% or more.

Occupational therapist. A specialist who provides therapy and instruction to students with motor disabilities.

Operant behavior. A behavior that is learned and therefore under the voluntary control of the individual.

Orientation. The determination of one's position in space, especially in relation to objects or reference points in the environment.

Partially sighted. Having vision that is impaired but can be used as one of the senses for learning.

Peer tutor. A student who provides instruction to another student.

Permanent product recording. The system of recording observation data in which permanent products (such as written assignments, videotapes, and audiotapes) are evaluated.

Personal digital assistant. A small handheld device used to store, organize, and retrieve information electronically.

Phonics. The word recognition strategy in which print letters (graphemes) are converted to letter sounds (phonemes).

Phonological awareness. The ability to recognize individual sounds within words.

Phonology. The sound system of language.

Physical and health impairments. Physical disabilities and medical conditions that result in chronic health problems.

Physical environment. In the context of the school, the classroom and its furnishings.

Physical therapist. A specialist who provides treatment under the supervision of a physician to students with motor disabilities.

Portfolio assessment. The process of gathering information about students by assembling samples of their work over time.

Positive reinforcement. A procedure used to increase the occurrence of a behavior by following it with a pleasant or positive event.

Practice. The performance of a learned skill. See also *Guided practice* and *Independent practice*.

Pragmatics. The use of language; language within the context of communication.

Premack principle. The practice of providing a reinforcement after the completion of a less desired task; for example, if Joan takes out the garbage, then she may watch television.

Prereferral interventions. Modifications of the general education program designed to promote a student's success in the regular classroom and prevent referral for services such as special education.

Problem solving. The process of attempting to resolve a question or problem.

Problem-based learning. Instructional strategy engaging students in problem identification, inquiry/research, and problem solving based on a real or realistic scenario.

Program modification. One of the types of service available to students with IEPs; includes any change made in the general education program to support the successful progress of a student with disabilities.

Programmed instruction. A method of instruction in which learners progress at their own pace through small incremental steps that provide immediate feedback about response accuracy.

Prompt. Any feature added to learning tasks that assists students in task performance. Prompts can be verbal, visual, or physical.

Psychosis. A type of emotional disturbance characterized by lack of contact with reality.

Punishment. A procedure used to decrease the occurrence of a behavior by following it with the presentation of an aversive event.

Readability measure. A method of determining the reading level of a given material.

Reading fluency. The ability to read quickly and accurately.

Reciprocal teaching. An approach to teaching reading comprehension skills in which teachers engage students in dialogues about texts.

Referral. The process by which a student is identified for study; it can result in consideration for special education services.

Reinforcement. Anything that increases the probability of occurrence of a behavior. See also *Negative reinforcement* and *Positive reinforcement*.

Reinforcement menu. A listing of reinforcers and the number of points or tokens needed to purchase each; it is used in a token economy system.

Related services. Auxiliary services such as psychological services for assessment, transportation, or physical therapy that are available to help students with disabilities derive maximum benefit from special education.

Remediation. The instructional approach that focuses on correcting the weaknesses of the student.

Repeated readings. An instructional technique in which students read a passage several times to increase comprehension.

Resource room. A service arrangement in which special education is provided to students for a portion of the school day. Typically the student is placed in a general education classroom and visits the resource room only for short periods.

Respite. A coping strategy used by individuals with disabilities after they have exerted a great deal of energy and need to withdraw temporarily.

Response cost. A mild form of punishment in which an inappropriate behavior is followed by the loss or withdrawal of earned reinforcers or privileges.

Rubric. An assessment tool for evaluating curricular progress; provides brief descriptions of student performance at various levels.

Seizure. The loss or alteration of consciousness due to a convulsive disorder.

Self-correcting materials. Instructional materials that provide the student with the correct response so that answers can be checked for accuracy.

Self-instruction. A procedure in which students learn specific strategies to talk themselves through problem situations.

Self-instructional learning materials. Instructional materials that provide feedback to students and thus allow independent practice.

Self-monitoring. Observing, recording, and evaluating one's own behavior; for example, students might observe/record the number of times they leave their chairs, graph the data, and then review the graph daily to determine whether they are improving.

Semantics. The aspects of language related to meaning.

Sensorineural hearing loss. A hearing loss caused by impairment of the auditory nerve.

Sequence analysis. A system of observation in which the observer describes each behavior and attempts to identify its antecedent and consequence.

Sexually transmitted diseases (STDs). Diseases such as chlamydia, genital warts, gonorrhea, syphilis, herpes, and acquired immune deficiency syndrome (AIDS) that are transmitted most frequently through sexual contact with an individual who has the disease, although newborns may be infected *in utero* or during passage through the birth canal.

Shaping. The reinforcement of successive approximations or small progressive steps toward a desired behavior.

Sheltered English. A teaching technique for students learning English in which content-area lessons include systematic instruction in English language skills.

Sign language. The system of manual communication in which gestures express thoughts.

Skill-specific group. A homogeneous instructional group made up of students who require instruction in the same area.

Slate and stylus. A small handheld device used to write Braille.

Snellen chart. A measure used in screening for visual acuity problems.

Sociometric measure. An assessment device used to determine how students perceive their peers.

Special class. A service arrangement in which students with special needs are grouped together in a self-contained class; students may leave the special class for short periods to participate in general education activities.

Special education. Instruction that is specially designed to meet the unique educational needs of students with disabilities.

Special educator. A professional educator trained to meet the instructional needs of students with special needs; usually, an educator who serves students with disabilities or gifted and talented students.

Special students. Those students with special learning needs who require instructional adaptations in order to learn successfully; includes students with disabilities, gifted and talented students, culturally and linguistically diverse students, and students at risk for school failure.

Speech. The vehicle by which thoughts are expressed in oral communication.

Speech and language impairments. Disabilities characterized by deficits in speech, receptive language, and/or expressive language.

Speech-language pathologist. A specialist who serves students with speech and language impairments.

Speechreading. The process of decoding speech by watching the speaker's face.

Spreadsheet. A type of computer program used to manipulate and analyze numerical information.

Students at risk for school failure. General education students who show poor achievement and/or are likely to drop out of school.

Students with disabilities. Students with special learning needs due to physical, sensory, cognitive, or emotional impairments. Included are students with learning disabilities, mental retardation, behavioral disorders, speech and language impairments, physical and health impairments, vision impairments, hearing impairments, autism spectrum disorder, traumatic brain injury, and multiple disabilities.

Study skill problems. Inappropriate classroom behaviors that interfere with the student's own academic performance or with the teacher's ability to assess academic progress.

Substance abuse. The voluntary intake of chemicals (e.g., alcohol, narcotics) that can produce adverse social and physical consequences.

Supplementary aids and services. Supports provided to students with disabilities to enable them to participate in general education programs.

Support for school personnel. One of the types of service available to students with IEPs; refers to services provided to teachers and other school employees, rather than to students.

Syntax. The grammatical aspects of language.

Talented. Having a special ability in an area such as music or leadership.

Task analysis. The process of breaking down a task into smaller subtasks.

Team-based contingencies. Reinforcement provided to team members based on the performance of their team; teams can compete against each other or against a preset criterion level.

Technology. See *Assistive technology* and *Educational technology*.

Thematic unit. A method of organizing the curriculum by themes; also called *instructional unit* when those themes address important life skills.

Tiering assignments. Differentiation strategy that matches task to student readiness level while enabling all students to achieve the general content goal.

Time management. The organization and scheduling of time for its most effective use.

Time-out. A mild form of punishment in which either the individual is removed from an event that is reinforcing or reinforcement is withdrawn for a specified period of time.

Token economy. A behavior change system in which students are presented with tokens rather than reinforcers after the occurrence of a desired behavior; the tokens can be cashed in for reinforcers at a later time.

Total communication. A method of communication combining oral techniques (speech and speechreading) and manual techniques (fingerspelling and sign language).

Transition. Process of preparing students to meet the challenges of adulthood including those involved in postsecondary education, vocational pursuits, and home and community.

Traumatic brain injury. A disability caused by injury or accident involving damage to the brain.

Unilateral hearing loss. A condition involving only one ear, the other ear having no hearing loss.

Unit approach. A method of organizing the curriculum by important life themes.

Universal design. The principle by which all environments are designed for all users, including those with disabilities.

Universal precautions. Procedures recommended for use when handling blood or other bodily fluids to prevent spread of infection.

Vigilance. A coping strategy used by individuals with disabilities when they want to sustain a high level of energy for a long period of time.

Visual impairment. A limitation in the ability to see.

Vocational rehabilitation counselor. A specialist who assists individuals with disabilities in obtaining employment.

Volunteer. A classroom assistant from the community.

Word processing program. A type of computer program that facilitates written composition by making it easy to manipulate text.

World Wide Web (WWW). That portion of the Internet in which information is presented not only in text but also in graphics; audio, video, and other multimedia features are sometimes available.

References

Abramowitz, A. J., & O'Leary, S. G. (1991). Behavior interventions for the classroom: Implications for students with ADHD. *School Psychology Review, 20,* 221–235.

Adamson, L. B., & Chance, S. E. (1998). Coordinating attention to people, objects & language. In A. M. Wetherby, S. F. Warren, & J. Reichle, (Eds.), *Transitions in prelinguistic communication* (pp. 15–37). Baltimore: Brookes.

Adelson, R. (2004). Instruction versus exploration in science learning. *Monitor on Psychology, 35*(6), 34–36.

Affleck, J. Q., Lowenbraun, S., & Archer, A. L. (1980). *Teaching the mildly handicapped in the regular classroom* (2nd ed.). Columbus, OH: Merrill/Prentice Hall.

Aiello, B. (1979). Hey, what's it like to be handicapped? *Education Unlimited, 1*(2), 28–31.

Airasian, P. W. (1996). *Assessment in the classroom.* New York: McGraw-Hill.

Alberto, P. A., & Troutman, A. C. (2003). *Applied behavior analysis for teachers* (7th ed.). Columbus, OH: Prentice Hall.

Alcohol use. (1989, September 27). *Los Angeles Times,* p. A1.

Alexander, C., & Strain, P. S. (1978). A review of educators' attitudes toward handicapped children and the concept of mainstreaming. *Psychology in the Schools, 15,* 390–396.

Algozzine, B., Christenson, S. L., & Ysseldyke, J. E. (1982). Probabilities associated with the referral to placement process. *Teacher Education and Special Education, 5*(3), 19–23.

Alley, G., & Foster, C. (1978). Nondiscriminatory testing of minority and exceptional children. *Focus on Exceptional Children, 9*(8), 1–14.

Alliance for Technology Access. (n.d.). *Web accessibility.* Petaluma, CA: Author. Retrieved August 28, 2004, from http://www.ataccess.org/rresources/webaccess.html

Allsopp, D. H., Santos, K. E., & Linn, R. (2000). Collaborating to teach prosocial skills. *Intervention in School and Clinic, 35,* 141–146.

Alves, A. J., & Gottlieb, J. (1986). Teacher interactions with mainstreamed handicapped students and their nonhandicapped peers. *Learning Disability Quarterly, 9,* 77–83.

America 2000. (1990). Washington, DC: U.S. Department of Education.

American Academy of Child and Adolescent Psychiatry. (2004). *Teen suicide.* Retrieved October 17, 2004, from http://www.aacap.org/publications/factsfam/suicide.htm

American Academy of Otolaryngoloy. (1995). *Determining if your child has hearing loss.* Retrieved August 12, 2004, from http://www.hearingexchange.com/articles/a-archives/determine.htm

American Association of Colleges for Teacher Education, Commission on Multicultural Education. (1973). No one model American. *Journal of Teacher Education, 24,* 264–265.

American Association on Mental Retardation. (2002). *Mental retardation: Definition, classification, and systems of support* (10th ed.). Washington, DC: Author.

American Diabetes Association. (n.d.). Diabetes symptoms. Retrieved October 2, 2004, from http://www.diabetes.org/for-parents-and-kids/what-is-diabetes/signs-and-symptoms.jsp

American Federation of Teachers. (1996). Retrieved from http://www.aft.org//research/reports/standard/index.htm#Table

American Obesity Association. (2002). *Obesity in youth.* Retrieved October 17, 2004, from http://www.obesity.org/subs/fastfacts/obesity_youth.shtml

American Psychiatric Association. (1994). *Diagnostic and statistical manual of mental disorders* (4th ed.). Washington, DC: Author.

American Psychiatric Association. (2000). *Diagnostic and statistical manual of mental disorders* (4th ed., text revision). Washington, DC: Williams & Wilkins.

American Speech-Language-Hearing Association. (1995, March). Position statement and guidelines for acoustics in educational settings. *ASHA, 37* (Suppl. 14), 15–19.

American Speech-Language-Hearing Association. (1997). *American Speech-Language-Hearing Association answers questions about stuttering.* Retrieved December 13, 1997, from http://www.asha.org/consumers/brochures/stuttering.htm

American Speech-Language-Hearing Association. (n.d.). *Speech and language disorders and the speech-language pathologist.* Rockville, MD: Author.

Andersen, M., Nelson, L. R., Fox, R. G., & Gruber, S. E. (1988). Integrating cooperative learning and structured learning: Effective approaches to teaching social skills. *Focus on Exceptional Children, 20*(9), 1–8.

Andersen, M. L., & Taylor, H. F. (2002). *Sociology: Understanding a diverse society.* Belmont, CA: Wadsworth.

Anderson, S. R., Taras, M., & Cannon, B. O. (1996). Teaching new skills to young children with autism. In C. Maurice, G. Green & S. Luce (Eds.), *Behavioral intervention for young children with autism: A manual for parents and professionals* (pp. 181–193) Austin, TX: PRO-ED.

Aragon, J. (1973). Cultural conflict and cultural diversity in education. In L. A. Bransford, L. M. Baca, & K. Lane (Eds.), *Cultural diversity and the exceptional child* (pp. 24–31). Reston, VA: The Council for Exceptional Children.

Aragon, J., & Marquez, L. (1973). Highlights of Institute on Language and Culture: Spanish-speaking component. In L. A. Bransford, L. M. Baca, & K. Lane (Eds.), *Cultural diversity and the exceptional child* (pp. 20–21). Reston, VA: The Council for Exceptional Children.

Arc, The. (2002). *Information about mental retardation and related topics.* Silver Springs, MD: Author. Retrieved September 18, 2004, from http://www.thearc.org/infomr.html

Archer, A. L. (1992). *Advanced skills for school success.* North Billerica, MA: Curriculum Associates.

Archer, A. L., & Gleason, M. M. (1989). *Design and delivery of lessons.* Paper presented at the annual meeting of the Council for Exceptional Children, San Francisco.

Archer, A. L., & Gleason, M. M. (1994). *Skills for school success.* North Billerica, MA: Curriculum Associates.

Archer, A. L., & Gleason, M. M. (1995). Skills for school success. In P. T. Cegelka & W. H. Berdine (Eds.), *Effective instruction for students with learning difficulties* (pp. 227–263). Boston: Allyn & Bacon.

Archer, A. L., Gleason, M. M., Englert, C. S., & Isaacson, S. (1995). Meeting individual instructional needs. In P. T. Cegelka & W. H. Berdine (Eds.), *Effective instruction for students with learning difficulties* (pp. 195–225). Boston: Allyn & Bacon.

Archer, A. L., Gleason, M. M., & Isaacson, S. (1995). Effective instructional delivery. In P. T. Cegelka & W. H. Berdine (Eds.), *Effective instruction for students with learning difficulties* (pp. 161–194). Boston: Allyn & Bacon.

Arkansas Enterprises for the Blind. (n.d.). *10 rules of courtesy to the blind.* Little Rock: Author.

Artiles, A. J., & Trent, S. C. (1994). Overrepresentation of minority students in special education: A continuing debate. *Journal of Special Education, 27,* 410–437.

Asher, S. R., & Taylor, A. R. (1981). Social outcomes of mainstreaming: Sociometric assessment and beyond. *Exceptional Education Quarterly, 1*(4), 13–30.

Ashton, T. M. (1997). *Making technology work in the inclusive classroom.* Unpublished manuscript, San Diego State University.

Ashton-Coombs, T. M., & James, H. F. (1995). Including all of us: A K–8 bibliography. *California English, 31*(2), 12–13, 26–27.

Association for Retarded Citizens. (n.d.). *The truth about mental retardation.* Arlington, TX: Author.

Atwood, T. (1998). *Asperger's syndrome: A guide for parents and professionals.* London: Jessica Kingsley Publishers.

Autism Society of America. (2004). *What is autism?* Retrieved September 22, 2004, from http://www.autism-society.org/site/PageServer?pagename=whatisautism

Axelrod, S., & Bailey, S. A. (1979). Drug treatment for hyperactivity: Controversies, alternatives, and guidelines. *Exceptional Children, 45,* 544–550.

Axelrod, S., Hall, R. V., & Tams, A. (1972). *A comparison of common seating arrangements in the classroom.* Paper presented at the meeting of the Kansas Symposium on Behavior Analysis in Education, Lawrence.

Baca, L. M. (1998). Bilingualism and bilingual education. In L. M. Baca & H. T. Cervantes (Eds.), *The bilingual special education interface* (3rd ed., pp. 26–45). Upper Saddle River, NJ: Merrill/Prentice Hall.

Baca, L. M., & Almanza, E. (1991). *Language minority students with disabilities.* Reston, VA: The Council for Exceptional Children.

Bacon, E. H., & Schulz, J. B. (1991). A survey of mainstreaming practices. *Teacher Education and Special Education, 14,* 144–149.

Baldwin, A. Y. (1991). Ethnic and cultural issues. In N. Colangelo & G. A. Davis (Eds.), *Handbook of gifted education* (pp. 416–427). Boston: Allyn & Bacon.

Banbury, M. (1987). Testing and grading mainstreamed students in regular education subjects. In A. Rotatori, M. Banbury, & R. A. Fox (Eds.), *Issues in special education* (pp. 177–186). Mountain View, CA: Mayfield.

Barone, T. (1989). Ways of being at risk: The case of Billy Charles Barnett. *Phi Delta Kappan, 71,* 147–151.

Bauer, A. M., & Shea, T. M. (1989). *Teaching exceptional students in your classroom.* Boston: Allyn & Bacon.

Bauwens, J., & Hourcade, J. J. (1989). Hey, would you just LISTEN. *Teaching Exceptional Children, 21*(4), 61.

Becker, W. C., Englemann, S., & Thomas, D. R. (1975). *Teaching 2: Cognitive learning and instruction.* Chicago: Science Research Associates.

Beery, K. E. (1997). *Developmental test of visual-motor integration* (4th ed.). Parsippany, NJ: Modern Curriculum Press.

Bender, W. N., & Mathes, M. Y. (1995). Students with ADHD in the inclusive classroom: A hierarchical approach to strategy selection. *Intervention in School and Clinic, 30,* 226–234.

Berdine, W. H., & Cegelka, P. T. (1980). *Teaching the trainable retarded.* Columbus, OH: Merrill/Prentice Hall.

Berg, F. (1987). *Facilitating classroom listening: A handbook for teachers of normal and hard of hearing students.* Austin, TX: PRO-ED.

Berliner, D. C., & Biddle, B. J. (1995). *The manufactured crisis: Myths, fraud, and the attack on America's public schools.* Reading, MA: Addison-Wesley.

Bess, F., Dodd-Murphy, J., & Parker, R. (1998). Children with minimal sensorineural hearing loss: Prevalence, educational performance, and functional status. *Ear and Hearing, 19,* 339–354.

Bettinger, M. M. (1989). Educating the pregnant teen. *CTA Action, 28*(2), 9.

Biddle, B. J. (1997). Foolishness, dangerous nonsense, and real correlates of state differences in achievement. *Phi Delta Kappan, 79,* 9–13.

Bigby, L. M. (2004). Medical and health-related services: More than treating boo-boos and ouchies. *Intervention in School and Clinic, 39*(4), 233–235.

Biklen, D. (1985). *Achieving the complete school.* New York: Teachers College Press.

Binkard, B. (1985). A successful handicap awareness program—run by special parents. *Teaching Exceptional Children, 18*(1), 12–16.

Blake, K. A. (1981). *Educating exceptional pupils.* Reading, MA: Addison-Wesley.

Blankenship, C., & Lilly, M. S. (1981). Mainstreaming students with learning and behavior problems. New York: Holt, Rinehart & Winston.

Bolt, S. A., & Thurlow, M. L. (2004). Five of the most frequently allowed testing accommodations in state policy: Synthesis of research. *Remedial and Special Education, 25,* 141–152.

Bondy, A., & Frost, L. (2002). *A picture's worth. PECS and other communication strategies in autism.* Bethesda, MD: Woodbine House.

Boning, R. A. (1998). *Specific skill series.* DeSoto, TX: SRA/McGraw-Hill.

Bonjean, L. M., & Rittenmeyer, D. C. (1987). *Teenage parenthood: The school's response.* Bloomington, IN: Phi Delta Kappa Educational Foundation.

Bormuth, J. R. (1968). The cloze readability procedure. *Elementary English, 45,* 429–436.

Bossert, S. T., & Barnett, B. G. (1981). *Grouping for instruction. A catalog of arrangements.* San Francisco: Far West Laboratory for Educational Research and Development. (ERIC Document Reproduction Service No. ED-201–052)

Bowe, F. (2000). *Physical, sensory, and health disabilities: An introduction.* Upper Saddle River, NJ: Merrill/Prentice Hall.

Bower, E. M. (1969). *Early identification of emotionally handicapped children in school* (2nd ed.). Springfield, IL: Thomas.

Braaten, B., & Braaten, S. (1988). Reform: For everyone? *Teaching Exceptional Children, 21*(1), 46–47.

Braaten, S., Kauffman, J. M., Braaten, B., Polsgrove, L., & Nelson, C. M. (1988). The regular education initiative: Patent medicine for behavioral disorders. *Exceptional Children, 55,* 21–27.

Brady, M. P., & McEvoy, M. A. (1989). Social skills training as an integration strategy. In R. Gaylord-Ross (Ed.), *Integration strategies for students with handicaps* (pp. 213–231). Baltimore: Brookes.

Brigance, A. H. (1981). *BRIGANCE® diagnostic inventory of essential skills.* North Billerica, MA: Curriculum Associates.

Brigance, A. H. (1991). *BRIGANCE® diagnostic inventory of early development—Revised.* North Billerica, MA: Curriculum Associates.

Brigance, A. H. (1999). *BRIGANCE® diagnostic comprehensive inventory of basic skills—Revised.* North Billerica, MA: Curriculum Associates.

Brinker, R. P. (1985). Interactions between severely mentally retarded students and other students in integrated and segregated public school settings. *American Journal of Mental Deficiency, 89,* 587–594.

Brolin, D. E. (1986). *Life centered career education: A competency based approach* (rev. ed.). Reston, VA: The Council for Exceptional Children.

Brooks-Gunn, J., & Furstenberg, F. F., Jr. (1989). Adolescent sexual behavior. *American Psychologist, 44,* 249–257.

Brophy, J. E., & Good, T. L. (1986). Teacher behavior and student achievement. In M. C. Wittrock (Ed.), *Handbook of research on teaching* (3rd ed., pp. 328–375). New York: Macmillan.

Brown, L., & Hammill, D. D. (1990). *Behavior rating profile* (2nd ed.). Austin, TX: PRO-ED.

Brown, L., Schwarz, P., Udvari-Solner, A., Kampschroer, E. F., Johnson, F., Jorgensen, J., & Gruenewald, L. (1991). How much time should students with severe intellectual disabilities spend in regular education classrooms and elsewhere? *Journal of the Association for Persons with Severe Handicaps, 16*(1), 39–47.

Brown, M. S., Ilderton, P., & Taylor, A. (2001). Include a student with an attention problem in the general education classroom. *Intervention in School and Clinic, 37*(1), 50–52.

Bruininks, R. H. (1977). *Manual for the Bruininks–Oseretsky test of motor proficiency.* Circle Pines, MN: American Guidance Service.

Bruininks, R. H., Thurlow, M. L., & Gilman, C. J. (1987). Adaptive behavior and mental retardation. *Journal of Special Education, 21*(1), 69–88.

Bruininks, R. H., Woodcock, R. W., Weatherman, R. F., & Hill, B. K. (1996). *Scales of independent behavior—Revised.* Chicago: Riverside Publishing.

Bryan, T. (1997). Assessing the personal and social status of students with learning disabilities. *Learning Disabilities Research & Practice, 12,* 63–76.

Bryan, T. H., & Bryan, J. H. (1977). The social-emotional side of learning disabilities. *Behavioral Disorders, 2,* 141–145.

Bryan, T. H., Pearl, R., Donahue, M., Bryan, J. H., & Pflaum, S. (1983). The Chicago Institute for the Study of Learning Disabilities. *Exceptional Education Quarterly, 4*(1), 1–22.

Bryen, D. N. (1974). Special education and the linguistically different child. *Exceptional Children, 40*(8), 589–599.

Buck, G. H., Polloway, E. A., Smith-Thomas, A., & Cook, K. W. (2003). Prereferral intervention processes: A survey of state practices. *Exceptional Children, 59,* 349–360.

Buffington, D. M., Krantz, P. J., McClannahan, L. E., & Poulson, C. L. (1998). Procedures for teaching appropriate gestural communication skills to children with autism. *Journal of Autism & Developmental Disorders, 28*(6), 535–545.

Bulgren, J. A., & Carta, J. J. (1992). Examining the instructional contexts of students with learning disabilities. *Exceptional Children, 59,* 182–191.

Burron, A., & Claybaugh, A. L. (1977). *Basic concepts in reading instruction* (2nd ed.). Columbus, OH: Merrill/Prentice Hall.

Bush, G. W. (2001). *No child left behind.* Washington, DC: U.S. Department of Education. Retrieved June 1, 2001, from http://www.ed.gov/inits/nclb/index.html

Butler, O. B. (1989). Early help for kids at risk: Our nation's best investment. *NEA Today, 7*(6), 50–53.

Byrom, E., & Katz, G. (Eds.). (1991). *HIV prevention and AIDS education: Resources for special educators.* Reston, VA: The Council for Exceptional Children.

California Governor's Committee for Employment of Disabled Persons. (1990). *Language guide on disability.* Sacramento: State of California, Employment Development Department.

California Teachers of English to Speakers of Other Languages. (1992). *CATESOL position paper on specially-designed academic instruction in English (sheltered instruction).* Retrieved December 16, 1997, from http://www.catesol.org/shelter.html

Campbell, N. J., Dodson, J. E., & Bost, J. M. (1985). Educator perceptions of behavior problems of mainstreamed students. *Exceptional Children, 51,* 298–303.

Campbell, P. H. (1989). Students with physical disabilities. In R. Gaylord-Ross (Ed.), *Integration strategies for students with handicaps* (pp. 53–76). Baltimore: Brookes.

Capuzzi, D. (1988). Adolescent suicide: Prevention and intervention. In J. Carlson & J. Lewis (Eds.), *Counseling the adolescent: Individual, family, and school interventions* (pp. 41–56). Denver: Love.

Carbone, E. (2001). Arranging the classroom with an eye (and ear) to students with ADHD. *Teaching Exceptional Children, 34,* 72–81.

Carlberg, C., & Kavale, K. A. (1980). The efficacy of special versus regular class placement for exceptional children: A meta-analysis. *Journal of Special Education, 14,* 295–309.

Carr, J. E., Nicholson, A. C., & Higbee, T. S. (2000). Evaluation of a brief multiple-stimulus preference assessment in a naturalistic context. *Journal of Applied Behavior Analysis, 33,* 353–357.

Carroll, D. (2001). Considering paraeducator training, roles, and responsibilities. *Teaching Exceptional Children, 34*(2), 60–64.

Cartledge, G., Frew, T., & Zaharias, J. (1985). Social skill needs of mainstreamed students: Peer and teacher perceptions. *Learning Disability Quarterly, 8,* 132–140.

Cartledge, G., & Milburn, J. F. (Eds.). (1986). *Teaching social skills to children: Innovative approaches* (2nd ed.). New York: Pergamon.

Cartledge, G., & Milburn, J. F. (1995). *Teaching social skills to children: Innovative approaches* (3rd ed.). Boston: Allyn & Bacon.

Cartwright, G. P., Cartwright, C. A., & Ward, M. E. (1995). *Educating special learners* (4th ed.). Belmont, CA: Wadsworth.

Castellano, J. A. (2003). *Special populations in gifted education: Working with diverse gifted learners.* Boston: Allyn and Bacon.

Casto, G., & Mastropieri, M. A. (1986). The efficacy of early intervention programs: A meta-analysis. *Exceptional Children, 52,* 417–424.

Caton, H. R. (1993). Students with visual impairments. In A. E. Blackhurst & W. H. Berdine (Eds.), *An introduction to special education* (3rd ed., pp. 313–349). New York: HarperCollins.

Cawley, J. F., Foley, T. E., & Miller, J. (2003). Science and students with learning disabilities: Principles of universal design. *Intervention in School and Clinic, 38,* 160–171.

Cegelka, P. T. (1988). Multicultural considerations. In E. W. Lynch & R. B. Lewis (Eds.), *Exceptional children and adults* (pp. 545–587). Glenview, IL: Scott, Foresman.

Cegelka, P. T. (1995a). An overview of effective education for students with learning problems. In P. T. Cegelka & W. H. Berdine (Eds.), *Effective instruction for students with learning difficulties* (pp. 1–17). Boston: Allyn & Bacon.

Cegelka, P. T. (1995b). Structuring the classroom for effective instruction. In P. T. Cegelka & W. H. Berdine (Eds.), *Effective instruction for students with learning difficulties* (pp. 135–160). Boston: Allyn & Bacon.

Center for Applied Technology. (2003). *Summary of universal design for learning concepts.* Boston: Author. Retrieved August 18, 2004, from http://www.cast.org/udl/index.cfm?i=7

Center for Research on Education, Diversity and Excellence. (2002). *The five standards for effective pedagogy.* Retrieved October 16, 2004, from http://www.crede.ucsc.edu/standards/standards.html

Center for Universal Design. (2004). *Learning about universal design.* Raleigh: North Carolina State University. Retrieved August 18, 2004, from http://www.udeducation.org/learn/index.asp

Centers for Disease Control and Prevention. (2000). *Youth risk behavior surveillance—United States, 1999.* Atlanta, GA: Department of Health and Human Services.

Centers for Disease Control and Prevention. (2001, August 22). *Basic statistics—Cumulative AIDS cases.* Retrieved December 8, 2001, from http://www.cdc.gov/hiv/stats/cumulati.htm

Chalfant, J. C., & Pysh, M. (1989). Teacher assistance teams: Five descriptive studies on 96 teams. *Remedial and Special Education, 10*(6), 49–58.

Chall, J. S. (1967). *Learning to read: The great debate.* New York: McGraw-Hill.

Chall, J. S. (1977). *Reading 1967–1977: A decade of change and promise.* Bloomington, IN: Phi Delta Kappa Educational Foundation.

Chall, J. S. (1983). *Learning to read: The great debate* (updated ed.). New York: McGraw-Hill.

Chall, J. S. (1989). Learning to read: The Great Debate 20 years later—A response to "Debunking the great phonics myth." *Phi Delta Kappan, 70,* 521–538.

Chall, J. S. (2000). *The academic achievement challenge.* New York: Guilford Press.

Chan, S. (1998). Families with Asian roots. In E. W. Lynch & M. J. Hanson (Eds.), *Developing cross-cultural compentence* (2nd ed., pp. 251–354). Baltimore: Brookes.

Chan, S., & Lee, E. (2004). Families with Asian roots. In E. W. Lynch & M. J. Hanson (Eds.), *Developing cross-cultural competence* (3rd ed., pp. 219–298). Baltimore: Brookes.

Charlop, M. H., & Milstein, J. P. (1989). Teaching autistic children conversational speech using video-modeling. *Journal of Applied Behavior Analysis, 23,* 275–285.

Charlop, M. H., & Walsh, M. E. (1986). Increasing autistic children's spontaneous verbalizations of affection: An assessment of time delay and peer modeling procedures. *Journal of Applied Behavior Analysis, 19,* 307–314.

Cheng, L. L. (1991). *Assessing Asian language performance.* Oceanside, CA: Academic Communication Associates.

Chinn, P. C., & Hughes, S. (1987). Representation of minority students in special education classes. *Remedial and Special Education, 8*(4), 41–46.

Christenson, S. L., & Ysseldyke, J. E. (1986). *Academic responding time as a function of instructional arrangements.* Paper presented at the annual meeting of the American Educational Research Association, San Francisco. (ERIC Document Reproduction Service No. ED-271–917).

Clark, B. (2002). *Growing up gifted* (6th ed.). Upper Saddle River, NJ: Merrill/Prentice Hall.

Clark, F. L. (2000). The strategies instruction model: A research-validated intervention for students with learning disabilities. *Learning Disabilities: A Multidisciplinary Journal, 10,* 209–217.

gf ds fgsdfg sdgsfg

Cline, S., & Schwartz, D. (1999). *Diverse populations of gifted students*. Upper Saddle River, NJ: Merrill/Prentice Hall.

Close, D. W., Irvin, L. K., Taylor, V. E., & Agosta, J. (1981). Community living skills instruction for mildly retarded persons. *Exceptional Education Quarterly, 2*(1), 75–85.

Cochran, C., Feng, H., Cartledge, G., & Hamilton, S. (1993). The effects of cross-age tutoring on the academic achievement, social behaviors, and self-perceptions of low-achieving African-American males with behavioral disorders. *Behavioral Disorders, 18,* 292–302.

Cohen, S. B., & Hart-Hester, S. (1987). Time management strategies. *Teaching Exceptional Children, 20*(1), 56–57.

Colangelo, N., & Davis, G. A. (Eds.). (2003). *Handbook of gifted education* (3rd ed.). Boston: Allyn & Bacon.

Colarusso, R. P., & Hammill, D. D. (2003). *Motor-free visual perception test,* (3rd ed.). Novato, CA: Academic Therapy.

Coleman, L. J., & Cross, T. L. (2001). *Being gifted in school: An introduction to development, guidance, and teaching.* Waco, TX: Prufrock Press.

Coleman, M. C. (1986). *Behavior disorders.* Upper Saddle River, NJ: Prentice Hall.

Condon, E. C., Peters, J. Y., & Sueiro-Ross, C. (1979). *Special education and the Hispanic child: Cultural perspectives.* Philadelphia: Temple University, Teacher Corps Mid-Atlantic Network.

Cook, B. G. (2001). A comparison of teachers' attitudes toward their included students with mild and severe disabilities. *Journal of Special Education, 34,* 203–213.

Cook, E. H. (1998). Genetics of autism. *Mental Retardation and Developmental Disabilities Research Reviews, 4*(2), 113–120.

Cooper, P. M. (2003). Effective white teachers of black children: Teaching within a community. *Journal of Teacher Education, 54*(5), 413–427.

Coordinated Campaign for Learning Disabilities. (n.d.). *Starting out.* Retrieved from http://www.focusonlearning.org/startingout2.htm

Corn, A. L., & Webne, S. L. (2001). Expectations for visual function: An initial evaluation of a new clinical instrument. *Journal of Visual Impairment & Blindness, 95,* 110–116.

Correa, V. I., & Heward, W. L. (1996). Special education in a culturally and linguistically diverse society. In W. L. Heward, *Exceptional children* (5th ed., pp. 91–129). Upper Saddle River, NJ: Merrill/Prentice Hall.

Correa, V. I., & Heward, W. L. (2003). Special education in a culturally diverse society. In W. L. Heward, *Exceptional children* (7th ed., pp. 86–119). Upper Saddle River, NJ: Merrill/Prentice Hall.

Council for Exceptional Children. (1993a). *Career education and transition.* Retrieved November 29, 1997, from http://www.cec.sped.org/pp/cec_pol.htm#14

Council for Exceptional Children. (1993b). CEC policy on inclusive schools and community settings. *Teaching Exceptional Children, 25*(4) supplement.

Council for Exceptional Children. (1998). *CEC's comments on the proposed IDEA regulations.* Retrieved February 20, 1998, from http://www.cec.sped.org/pp/regscom.htm

Council for Learning Disabilities. (1993). Concerns about the full inclusion of students with learning disabilities in regular education classrooms. *Journal of Learning Disabilities, 26,* 595.

Cowley, G. (2003, September 8). Autism's gender gap. *Newsweek,* pp. 42–29.

Craig, R., & Howard, C. (1981). Visual impairment. In M. L. Hardman, M. W. Egan, & D. Landau (Eds.), *What will we do in the morning?* (pp. 180–209). Dubuque, IA: Brown.

Cronin, M. E., & Patton, J. R. (1993). *Life skills for students with special needs.* Austin, TX: PRO-ED.

Cropley, A. J., & Urban, K. K. (2000). Programs and strategies for nurturing creativity. In K. A. Heller, F. J. Monks, R. J. Sternberg, & R. F. Subotnik (Eds.), *International handbook of giftedness and talent* (2nd ed., 485–498). Oxford: Elsevier Science Ltd.

Cross, D. P. (1993). Students with physical and health-related disabilities. In A. E. Blackhurst & W. H. Berdine (Eds.), *An introduction to special education* (3rd ed., pp. 350–397). New York: HarperCollins.

Crosscope-Happel, C., Hutchins, D. E., Getz, H. G., & Hayes, G. L. (2000). Male anorexia nervosa: A new focus. *Journal of Mental Health Counseling, 22,* 365–370.

Cuban, L. (1989). The "at-risk" label and the problem of urban school reform. *Phi Delta Kappan, 70,* 780–784, 799–801.

Cuenin, L. H., & Harris, K. R. (1986). Planning, implementing, and evaluating timeout interventions with exceptional students. *Teaching Exceptional Children, 18,* 272–276.

Culatta, B. K., & Culatta, R. (1993). Students with communication problems. In A. E. Blackhurst & W. H. Berdine (Eds.), *An introduction to special education* (3rd ed., pp. 238–269). New York: HarperCollins.

Cullinan, D. (2002). *Students with emotional and behavioral disorders: An introduction for teachers and other helping professionals.* Upper Saddle River, NJ: Merrill/Prentice Hall.

Culross, R. R. (1997). Concepts of inclusion in gifted education. *Teaching Exceptional Children, 29*(3), 24–26.

Cummins, J. (1989). A theoretical framework for bilingual special education. *Exceptional Children, 56,* 111–119.

D'Alonzo, B. J., D'Alonzo, R. L., & Mauser, A. J. (1979). Developing resource rooms for the handicapped. *Teaching Exceptional Children, 11,* 91–96.

D'Antonio, M. (1993, November 21). Sound & fury. *Los Angeles Times Magazine,* 44–48, 60–63.

Dale, E., & Chall, J. S. (1948). A formula for predicting readability. *Educational Research Bulletin, 27,* 11–20.

Dardig, J. C. (1981). Helping teachers integrate handicapped students into the regular classroom. *Educational Horizons, 59,* 124–130.

Davies, S., & White, R. (2000). Self-management and peer-monitoring within a group contingency to decrease uncontrolled verbalizations of children with attention-deficit/hyperactivity disorder. *Psychology in the Schools, 37,* 135–147.

Davis, C. (1980). *Perkins—Binet intelligence scale.* Watertown, MA: Perkins School for the Blind.

Davis, G. A. (2003). Identifying creative students, teaching for creative growth. In Colangelo, N., & Davis, G. A., (Eds.), *Handbook of gifted education* (3rd ed., pp. 311–324). Boston: Allyn and Bacon.

Davis, G. A., & Rimm, S. B. (2004). *Education of the gifted and talented* (5th ed.). Boston: Allyn & Bacon.

Dawson, G., & Watling, R. (2000). Interventions to facility auditory, visual, and motor integration in autism: A review of the evidence. *Journal of Autism and Developmental Disorders, 30,* 415–421.

de Grandpre, B. B., & Messier, J. M. (1979). Helping mainstreamed students stay in the mainstream. *The Directive Teacher, 2*(2), 12.

de Valenzuela, J. S., & Baca, L. (1998). Issues and theoretical considerations in the assessment of bilingual children. In L. M. Baca & H. T. Cervantes (Eds.), *The bilingual special education interface* (3rd ed. pp. 144–166). Upper Saddle River, NJ: Merrill/Prentice Hall.

DeBell, M., & Chapman, C. (2003a). *Computer and Internet use by children and adolescents in 2001: Statistical analysis report.* Washington, DC: U.S. Department of Education, National Center for Education Statistics. Retrieved August 17, 2004, from http://nces.ed.gov/pubsearch/pubsinfo.asp?pubid=2004014

DeBell, M., & Chapman, C. (2003b). *Internet access in U.S. public schools and classrooms: 1994–2002.* Washington, DC: U.S. Department of Education, National Center for Education Statistics. Retrieved August 17, 2004, from http://nces.ed.gov/pubsearch/pubsinfo.asp?pubid=2004011

Decano, P. (1979). Asian and Pacific-American exceptional children: A conversation. *Teacher Education and Special Education, 2*(4), 33–36.

DeLeon, I. G., & Iwata, B. A. (1996). Evaluation of a multiple-stimulus presentation format for assessing reinforcer preferences. *Journal of Applied Behavior Analysis, 29,* 519–533.

Deno, S. L. (1985). Curriculum-based measurement: The emerging alternative. *Exceptional Children, 52,* 219–232.

Deno, S. L. (1987). Curriculum-based measurement. *Teaching Exceptional Children, 20*(1), 41–42.

Deno, S. L., & Fuchs, L. S. (1987). Developing curriculum-based measurement systems for data-based special education problem solving. *Focus on Exceptional Children, 19*(8), 1–16.

Denti, L. G., & Guerin, G. (1999). Dropout prevention: A case for enhanced early literacy efforts. *Clearing House, 72,* 231–237.

Deshler, D. D., & Graham, S. (1980). Tape recording educational materials for secondary handicapped students. *Teaching Exceptional Children, 12,* 52–54.

Dettmer, P. (1994). IEPs for gifted secondary students. *Journal of Secondary Gifted Education, 5*(4), 52–59.

Diana v. State Board of Education. Civ. No. C-70 37 RFP (N. D. Cal. 1970, 1973).

Dismuke, D. (1988). Reducing suicides. *NEA Today, 7*(3), 21.

Division for Learning Disabilities. (1993). *Inclusion: What does it mean for students with learning disabilities?* Reston, VA: Author.

Dolch, E. W. (1953). *The Dolch basic sight word list.* Champaign, IL: Garrard.

Doleys, D. M., & Bruno, J. (1982). Treatment of childhood medical disorders. In A. S. Bellack, M. Hersen, & A. E. Kazdin (Eds.), *International handbook of behavior modification and therapy* (pp. 997–1016). New York: Plenum.

Donaldson, J. (1980). Changing attitudes toward handicapped persons: A review and analysis of research. *Exceptional Children, 46,* 504–514.

Donaldson, J., & Martinson, M. C. (1977). Modifying attitudes toward physically disabled persons. *Exceptional Children, 43,* 337–341.

Donovan, P. (1993). *Testing positive: Sexually transmitted disease and the public health response.* New York: The Alan Guttmacher Institute.

Doorlag, D. H. (1989a). Students with learning handicaps. In R. Gaylord-Ross (Ed.), *Integration strategies for students with handicaps* (pp. 33–52). Baltimore: Brookes.

Doorlag, D. H. (1989b, May). *Getting along better with others: How parents and professionals can improve the social skills of special students.* Paper presented at the Fifth Annual California Parent-Professional Collaboration Conference, San Diego.

Doyle, W. (1986). Classroom organization and management. In M. C. Wittrock (Ed.), *Handbook of research on teaching* (3rd ed., pp. 392–431). New York: Macmillan.

Drabman, R. S., & Patterson, J. N. (1981). Disruptive behavior and the social standing of exceptional children. *Exceptional Education Quarterly, 1*(4), 45–56.

Drew, C. J., Logan, D. R., & Hardman, M. L. (1992). *Mental retardation* (5th ed.). New York: Merrill/Macmillan.

Dunn, L. M. (1968). Special education for the mildly retarded—Is much of it justifiable? *Exceptional Children, 35,* 5–22.

Dunn, R., & Dunn, K. (1978). *Teaching students through their individual learning styles: A practical approach.* Reston, VA: Reston.

Dwyer, K., & Osher, D. (2000). *Safeguarding our children: An action guide.* Washington, DC: U.S. Department of Education, Special Education and Rehabilitative Services.

Dwyer, K, Osher, D., & Warger, C. (1998). *Early warning, timely response: A guide to safe schools.* Washington, DC: U.S. Department of Education, Special Education and Rehabilitative Services.

Dyches, T. T., & Burrow, E. (2004). Using children's books with characters with disabilities. *CEC Today, 10*(6), 13.

Dyer, K. (1989). The effects of preference on spontaneous verbal requests in individuals with autism. *Journal of the Association for Persons with Severe Handicaps, 14,* 184–189.

East, P. L. (1999). The first teenage pregnancy in the family: Does it affect mothers' parenting, attitudes, or mother-adolescent communication? *Journal of Marriage and the Family, 61,* 306–319.

Easterbrooks, S. (1999). Improving practices for students with hearing impairments. *Exceptional Children, 65,* 537–554.

Eaton, M. D., & Hansen, C. L. (1978). Classroom organization and management. In N. G. Haring, T. C. Lovitt, M. D. Eaton, & C. L. Hansen (Eds.), *The fourth R: Research in the classroom* (pp. 191–217). Columbus, OH: Merrill/Prentice Hall.

Eaton, S. B., & Wall, R. S. (1999). A survey of social skills instruction in preservice programs for visual disabilities. *RE:view, 31,* 40–45.

Echevarria, J. (1995). Sheltered instruction for students with learning disabilities who have limited English proficiency. *Intervention in School and Clinic, 30,* 302–305.

Edens, R. M., Murdick, N. L., & Gartin, B. C. (2003). Preventing infection in the classroom: The use of universal precautions. *Teaching Exceptional Children, 35*(4), 62–66.

Edgar, E., & Davidson, C. (1979). Parent perceptions of mainstreaming. *Education Unlimited, 1*(4), 32–33.

Educating refugees: Understanding the basics. (1989). *NCBE Forum, 12*(3), 1, 3.

Edwards, L. L. (1980). Curriculum modification as a strategy for helping regular classroom behavior-disordered students. *Focus on Exceptional Children, 12*(8), 1–11.

Edyburn, D. L. (2000). Assistive technology and students with mild disabilities. *Focus on Exceptional Children, 32*(9), 1–24.

Edyburn, D. L. (2003a). Learning from text. *Special Education Technology Practice, 5*(2), 16–27.

Edyburn, D. L. (2003b). Rethinking assistive technology. *Special Education Technology Practice, 5*(4), 16–22.

Edyburn, D. L. (2004). Key ingredients of an accessible curriculum. *Special Education Technology Practice, 6*(1), 17–22.

Ehly, S. W., & Larsen, S. C. (1980). *Peer tutoring for individualized instruction.* Boston: Allyn & Bacon.

Eiser, L. (1986). "Regular" software for special ed. kids? Yes! *Classroom Computer Learning, 7*(2), 26–30, 35.

Ellett, L. (1993). Instructional practices in mainstreamed secondary classrooms. *Journal of Learning Disabilities, 26,* 57–64.

Elliott, S. N., & Gresham, F. M. (1993). Social skills interventions for children. *Behavior Modification, 17,* 287–313.

Elliott, S. N., Kratochwill, T. R., & Gilbertson, A. (1998). *The assessment accommodation checklist.* Monterey, CA: CTB/McGraw-Hill.

Elmquist, D. L. (1991). School-based alcohol and other drug prevention programs: Guidelines for the special educator. *Intervention in School and Clinic, 27*(1), 10–19.

Emery, R. E. (1989). Family violence. *American Psychologist, 44,* 321–328.

Emmer, E. T. (1981). *Effective management in junior high math classes* (Report No. 6111). Austin: University of Texas, Research and Development Center for Teacher Education.

Emmer, E. T., Evertson, C. M., Sanford, J. P., Clements, B. S., & Worsham, M. E. (1989). *Classroom management for secondary teachers* (2nd ed.). Upper Saddle River, NJ: Prentice Hall.

Englert, C. S. (1984). Measuring teacher effectiveness from the teacher's point of view. *Focus on Exceptional Children, 17*(2), 1–14.

Englert, C. S., & Raphael, T. E. (1988). Constructing well-formed prose: Process, structure, and metacognitive knowledge. *Exceptional Children, 54,* 513–520.

English, K. M. (1995). *Educational audiology across the lifespan: Serving all learners with hearing impairment.* Baltimore: Brookes.

English, K. M. (1997). *Self-advocacy for students who are deaf and hard of hearing.* Austin, TX: PRO-ED.

English, K. M., & Church, G. (1999). Unilateral hearing loss in children: An update for the 1990s. *Language, Speech, and Hearing Services in Schools, 30*(1), 26–31.

Epanchin, B. C. (1987). Anxiety and stress-related disorders. In B. C. Epanchin & J. L. Paul (Eds.), *Emotional problems of childhood and adolescence: A multidisciplinary perspective* (pp. 165–190). New York: Merrill/Macmillan.

Epilepsy Foundation of America. (2000). The Epilepsy Foundation urges caregivers, parents of young children to know the hidden signs of epilepsy. Retrieved October 2, 2004, from http://www.epilepsyfoundation.org/epilepsyusa/media/n110100.cfm

Erickson, R., Ysseldyke, J., Thurlow, M., & Elliott, J. (1998). Inclusive assessments and accountability systems. *Teaching Exceptional Children, 31*(2), 4–9.

Evans, J., & Guevara, A. E. (1974). Classroom instruction for young Spanish speakers. *Exceptional Children, 41,* 16–19.

Evertson, C. M., Sanford, J. P., & Emmer, E. T. (1981). Effects of class heterogeneity in junior high school. *American Educational Research Journal, 18,* 219–232.

Fad, K. S., Ross, M., & Boston, J. (1995). Using cooperative learning to teach social skills to young children. *Teaching Exceptional Children, 27*(4), 29–34.

Falvey, M. A., Grenot-Scheyer, M., & Bishop, K. (1989). Integrating students with severe handicaps. *California State Federation/CEC Journal, 35*(3), 8–10.

Farmer, T. W., & Cadwallader, T. W. (1999). Social interactions and peer support for problem behavior. *Preventing School Failure, 11,* 105–109.

Federal Register. (1999, March 12). Washington, DC: U.S. Government Printing Office.

Feldhusen, J. F. (1989). Thinking skills for the gifted. In J. F. Feldhusen, J. Van Tassel-Baska, & K. Seeley (Eds.), *Excellence in educating the gifted* (pp. 239–259). Denver: Love.

Feldhusen, J. F. (2001). *Talent development in gifted education.* Arlington, VA: The Council for Exceptional Children. (ERIC Clearinghouse on Disabilities and Gifted Education, ERIC EC Digest No. E610).

Feldhusen, J. F., Van Winkle, L., & Ehle, D. A. (1996). Is it acceleration or simply appropriate instruction for precocious youth? *Teaching Exceptional Children, 28*(3), 48–51.

Fenske, E. C., Krantz, P. J., & McClannahan, L. E. (2001). Incidental teaching: A not-so-discrete-trial teaching procedure. In C. Maurice, G. Green and R. M. Foxx (Eds.), *Making a difference: Behavioral intervention for autism* (pp. 75–82). Austin, TX: Pro-Ed.

Fetzer, E. A. (2000). The gifted/learning disabled child: A guide for teachers and parents. *Gifted Child Today, 23*(4), 44–50.

Fiedler, C. R., & Simpson, R. L. (1987). Modifying the attitudes of nonhandicapped students toward handicapped peers. *Exceptional Children, 53,* 342–349.

Finch, A. J., & Spirito, A. (1980). Use of cognitive training to change cognitive processes. *Exceptional Education Quarterly, 1*(1), 31–39.

Fischer, L., & Sorenson, G. P. (1985). *School law for counselors, psychologists, and social workers.* New York: Longman.

Flesch, R. (1951). *How to test readability.* New York: Harper & Row.

Flett, A., & Conderman, G. (2001). Enhance the involvement of parents from culturally and linguistically diverse backgrounds. *Intervention in School and Clinic, 37*(1), 53–55.

Flexer, C., Wray, D., & Ireland, J. C. (1989). Preferential seating is not enough: Issues in classroom management of hearing-impaired students. *Language, Speech, and Hearing in Schools, 20,* 11–21.

Flint, L. J. (2001). Challenges of identifying and serving gifted children with ADHD. *Teaching Exceptional Children, 33*(4), 62–69.

Fonner, K., & Zabala, J. (1997, October). *It really is a small world after all: Sharing knowledge and skill on the Internet.* Paper presented at the Closing the Gap Conference, Minneapolis, MN.

Ford, D. Y., & Harris III, J. J. (1999). *Multicultural gifted education.* New York: Teachers College Press.

Forest, M., & Lusthaus, E. (1989). Promoting educational equality for all students. In S. Stainback, W. Stainback, & M. Forest

(Eds.), *Educating all students in the mainstream of regular education* (pp. 43–57). Baltimore: Brookes.

Forgan, J. W., & Weber, R. K. (2001). Selecting software for students with high incidence disabilities. *Intervention in School and Clinic, 37*(1), 40–47.

Forness, S. R., & Kavale, K. A. (1984). Education of the mentally retarded: A note on policy. *Education and Training of the Mentally Retarded, 19,* 239–245.

Forness, S. R., & Kavale, K. A. (1993). Strategies to improve basic learning and memory deficits in mental retardation: A meta-analysis of experimental studies. *Education and Training in Mental Retardation, 28,* 99–110.

Forness, S. R., Kavale, K. A., Blum, I. M., & Lloyd, J. W. (1997). Mega-analysis of meta-analyses. *Teaching Exceptional Children, 29*(6), 4–9.

Forness, S. R., Kavale, K. A., & Crenshaw, T. M. (1999). Stimulant medication revisited: Effective treatment of children with ADHD. *Reclaiming Children and Youth, 7,* 230–233, 235.

Forness, S. R., Walker, H. M., & Kavale, K. A. (2003). Psychiatric disorders and treatments: A primer for teachers. *Teaching Exceptional Children, 36*(2), 42–49.

Forster, P., & Doyle, B. A. (1989). Teaching listening skills to students with attention deficit disorders. *Teaching Exceptional Children, 21*(2), 20–22.

Foster, S. L., Inderbitzen, H. M., & Nangle, D. W. (1993). Assessing acceptance and social skills with peers in childhood. *Behavior Modification, 17,* 255–286.

Fox, C. L. (1989). Peer acceptance of learning disabled children in the regular classroom. *Exceptional Children, 56,* 50–59.

Foyle, H. C., & Lyman, L. (1990). *Cooperative learning: What you need to know.* Washington, DC: National Education Association.

Franklin, M. E. (1992). Culturally sensitive instructional practices for African-American learners with disabilities. *Exceptional Children, 59,* 115–122.

Freedman, S. W. (1982). Language assessment and writing disorders. *Topics in Language Disorders, 2*(4), 34–44.

Freeman, D., & Freeman, Y. (1988). *Sheltered English instruction.* Washington, DC: ERIC Clearinghouse on Languages and Linguistics. (ERIC Document Reproduction Service No. ED-301–070).

Frost, L. A., & Bondy, A. (1998). *The picture exchange communication system (PECS).* Solana Beach, CA: Mayer-Johnson Co.

Fry, E. (1968). A readability formula that saves time. *Journal of Reading, 11,* 513–516, 575–577.

Fry, E. (1977). Fry's readability graph: Clarifications, validity, and extension to level 17. *Journal of Reading, 21,* 242–252.

Frymier, J., & Gansneder, B. (1989). The Phi Delta Kappa study of students at risk. *Phi Delta Kappan, 71,* 142–146.

Fuchigami, R. Y. (1980). Teacher education for culturally diverse exceptional children. *Exceptional Children, 46,* 634–641.

Fuchs, D., Mock, D., Morgan, P. L., & Young, C. L. (2003). Responsiveness-to-intervention: Definitions, evidence, and implications for the learning disabilities construct. *Learning Disabilities Research & Practice, 18,* 157–171.

Fuchs, D. S., & Fuchs, L. S. (1994). Inclusive schools movement and the radicalization of special education reform. *Exceptional Children, 60,* 294–309.

Fuchs, L. S. (1986). Monitoring progress among mildly handicapped pupils: Review of current practice and research. *Remedial and Special Education, 7*(5), 5–12.

Fuchs, L. S. (1987). Program development. *Teaching Exceptional Children, 20*(1), 42–44.

Furstenberg, F. F., Jr., Brooks-Gunn, J., & Chase-Lansdale, L. (1989). Teenage pregnancy and childbearing. *American Psychologist, 44,* 313–320.

Gable, R. A., Laycock, V. K., Maroney, S. A., & Smith, C. R. (1991). *Preparing to integrate students with behavioral disorders.* Reston, VA: The Council for Exceptional Children.

Gable, R. A., Strain, P. S., & Hendrickson, J. M. (1979). Strategies for improving the status and social behavior of learning disabled children. *Learning Disability Quarterly, 2*(3), 33–39.

Gajar, A., Goodman, L., & McAfee, J. (1993). *Secondary schools and beyond: Transition of individuals with mild disabilities.* New York: Merrill/Macmillan.

Gallagher, J. J. (2003). Issues and challenges in the education of gifted students. In N. Colangelo, & G. A. Davis, (Eds.), *Handbook of gifted education* (3rd ed., pp. 11–23). Boston: Allyn & Bacon.

Gallagher, S. A. (2001). Adapting problem-based learning for gifted students. In F. A. Karnes & S. M. Bean (Eds.), *Methods and materials for teaching the gifted* (pp. 369–394). Waco, TX: Prufrock Press.

Gans, K. D. (1985). Regular and special educators: Handicap integration attitudes and implications for consultants. *Teacher Education and Special Education, 8,* 188–197.

Garcia, R. L. (1978). *Fostering a pluralistic society through multi-ethnic education.* Bloomington, IN: Phi Delta Kappa Educational Foundation.

Garfinkel, B. D., Crosby, E., Herbert, M. R., Matus, A. L., Pfeifer, J. K., & Sheras, P. L. (1988). *Responding to adolescent suicide. A report of the Phi Delta Kappa Task Force on Adolescent Suicide.* Bloomington, IN: Phi Delta Kappa Educational Foundation.

Garrett, M. K., & Crump, W. D. (1980). Peer acceptance, teacher preference, and self-appraisal of social status of learning disabled students. *Learning Disability Quarterly, 3*(3), 42–48.

Gartner, A., & Riessman, F. (1977). *How to individualize learning.* Bloomington, IN: Phi Delta Kappa Educational Foundation.

Gastright, J. F. (1989, April). Don't base your dropout program on somebody else's problem. *Phi Delta Kappa Research Bulletin,* pp. 1–4.

Gay, L. R. (1981). *Educational research* (2nd ed.). Columbus, OH: Merrill/Prentice Hall.

Geary, D. C. (2004). Mathematics and learning disabilities. *Journal of Learning Disabilities, 37,* 4–15.

Gena, A., & Kymissis, E. (2001). Assessing and setting goals for the attending and communicative behavior of three preschoolers with autism in inclusive kindergarten settings. *Journal of Developmental and Physical Disabilities, 13*(1), 11–26.

Gersten, R., & Dimino, J. (1993). Visions and revisions: A special education perspective on the whole language controversy. *Special Education and Remedial Education, 14*(4), 5–13.

Gersten, R., & Jiménez, R. (1998). Modulating instruction for language minority students. In E. J. Kameenui & D. W. Carnine (Eds.), *Effective teaching strategies that accommodate diverse learners* (pp. 161–178). Upper Saddle River, NJ: Merrill/Prentice Hall.

Gersten, R., & Woodward, J. (1994). The language-minority student and special education: Issues, trends, and paradoxes. *Exceptional Children, 60,* 310–322.

Giangreco, M., Cloninger, C., & Iverson, V. (1990). *C.O.A.C.H.—Cayuga-Onondaga assessment for children with handicaps* (6th ed.). Stillwater: Oklahoma State University.

Gibson, A. B., Roberts, P. C., & Buttery, T. J. (1982). *Death education: A concern for the living.* Bloomington, IN: Phi Delta Kappa Educational Foundation.

Gickling, E. E., & Thompson, V. P. (1985). A personal view of curriculum-based assessment. *Exceptional Children, 52,* 205–218.

Gilliam, J. E. (1995). *Gilliam autism rating scale (GARS).* Austin, TX: Pro-Ed.

Gillung, T. B., & Rucker, C. N. (1977). Labels and teacher expectations. *Exceptional Children, 43,* 464–465.

Glass, G. V., & Smith, M. L. (1978). *Meta-analysis of research on class size and achievement.* Boulder: University of Colorado, Laboratory of Educational Research.

Glazzard, P. (1980). Adaptations for mainstreaming. *Teaching Exceptional Children, 13,* 26–29.

Glazzard, P. (1982). *Learning activities and teaching ideas for the special child in the regular classroom.* Upper Saddle River, NJ: Prentice Hall.

Goldman, R., & Fristoe, M. (2000). *Goldman–Fristoe test of articulation—Second edition.* Circle Pines, MN: American Guidance Service.

Goldson, E. (2001). Maltreatment among children with disabilities. *Infants and Young Children, 13*(4), 44–54.

Goldstein, A. P. (1999). *The prepare curriculum: Teaching prosocial competencies.* Champaign, IL: Research Press.

Goldstein, A. P., & McGinnis, E. (1997). *Skillstreaming the adolescent: New strategies and perspectives for teaching prosocial skills.* Champaign, IL: Research Press.

Gollnick, D. M., & Chinn, P. C. (1990). *Multicultural education in a pluralistic society* (3rd ed.). New York: Merrill/Macmillan.

Gollnick, D. M., & Chinn, P. C. (1998). *Multicultural education in a pluralistic society* (5th ed.). Upper Saddle River, NJ: Merrill/Prentice Hall.

Goodman, L. (1978). Meeting children's needs through materials modification. *Teaching Exceptional Children, 10,* 92–94.

Goodwin, M. W. (1999). Cooperative learning and social skills: What skills to teach and how to teach. *Intervention in School and Clinic, 35,* 29–33.

Gordon, T. (1974). *Teacher effectiveness training.* New York: Wyden.

Gorman, C. (2003, July 28). The new science of dyslexia. *Time, 162*(4), 52–57.

Gottlieb, B. (1997). *Coping with chronic stress.* New York: Plenum.

Gottlieb, J., & Leyser, Y. (1981). Facilitating the social mainstreaming of retarded children. *Exceptional Education Quarterly, 1*(4), 57–70.

Graden, J. L., Casey, A., & Christenson, S. L. (1985). Implementing a prereferral intervention system: Part I. The model. *Exceptional Children, 51,* 377–384.

Grady, E. (1992). *The portfolio approach to assessment.* Bloomington, IN: Phi Delta Kappa Educational Foundation.

Graham, S., & Harris, K. R. (1989). Improving learning disabled students skills at composing essays: Self-instructional strategy training. *Exceptional Children, 56,* 201–214.

Graham, S., Harris, K. R., & Reid, R. (1998). Developing self-regulated learners. In R. J. Whelan (Ed.), *Emotional and behavioral disorders: A 25 year focus* (pp. 205–228). Denver: Love.

Graham, S., & Johnson, L. A. (1989). Teaching reading to learning disabled students: A review of research-supported procedures. *Focus on Exceptional Children, 21*(6), 1–12.

Graham, S., & Miller, L. (1979). Spelling research and practice: A unified approach. *Focus on Exceptional Children, 12*(2), 1–16.

Grandin, T. (1995). *Thinking in pictures and other reports from my life with autism.* New York: Vintage Books.

Gray, C. A., & Garand, J. D. (1993). Social stories: Improving responses of students with autism with accurate social information. *Focus on Behavior, 8,* 1–10.

Gray, L. A., & House, R. M. (1989). No guarantee of immunity: AIDS and adolescents. In D. Capuzzi & D. R. Gross (Eds.), *Youth at risk: A resource for counselors, teachers and parents* (pp. 231–263). Alexandria, VA: American Association for Counseling and Development.

Grayson, D. (n.d.). *Facts about blindness and visual impairment.* New York: American Foundation for the Blind.

Green, W. W., & Fischgrund, J. E. (1993). Students with hearing loss. In A. E. Blackhurst & W. H. Berdine (Eds.), *An introduction to special education* (3rd ed., pp. 271–311). New York: HarperCollins.

Gresham, F. M. (1984). Social skills and self-efficacy for exceptional children. *Exceptional Children, 51,* 253–261.

Grieco, E. M., & Cassidy R. C. (2001). *Overview of race and Hispanic origin, Census 2000 brief.* Washington, DC: U.S. Census Bureau. Retrieved June 1, 2001, from http://www.census.gov/prod/2001pubs/c2kbr01-1.pdf

Grosenick, J. K., & Huntze, S. L. (1980). *National needs analysis in behavior disorders: Adolescent behavior disorders.* Columbia: University of Missouri at Columbia, Department of Special Education.

Gross, M. U. M., Sleap, B., & Pretorius, M. (1999). *Gifted students in secondary schools: Differentiating the curriculum.* Sydney: A Gerric Publication.

Grossman, H. J. (Ed.). (1983). *Classification in mental retardation* (1983 revision). Washington, DC: American Association on Mental Retardation.

Grossnickle, D. R. (1986). *High school dropouts: Causes, consequences, and cure.* Bloomington, IN: Phi Delta Kappa Educational Foundation.

Guetzloe, E. C. (1988). Suicide and depression: Special education's responsibility. *Teaching Exceptional Children, 20*(4), 25–28.

Guetzloe, E. C. (1989). *Youth suicide: What the educator should know.* Reston, VA: The Council for Exceptional Children.

Guetzloe, E. C. (1993). Answering the cries for help—Suicidal thoughts and actions. *Journal of Emotional and Behavioral Problems, 2*(2), 34–38.

Guetzloe, E. (1996). Facts pertaining to children and youth with emotional/behavioral disorders. *Council for Children with Behavioral Disorders Newsletter, 10*(2), 4.

Guetzloe, E. (1999). Inclusion: The broken promise. *Preventing School Failure, 43,* 92–98.

Guilford, J. P. (1967). *The nature of human intelligence.* New York: McGraw-Hill.

Gumpel, T. P., & Frank, R. (1999). An expansion of the peer-tutoring paradigm: Cross-age peer tutoring of social skills among socially rejected boys. *Journal of Applied Behavior Analysis, 32,* 115–118.

Guralnick, M. J. (1981). Programmatic factors affecting child-child social interactions in mainstreamed preschool programs. *Exceptional Education Quarterly, 1*(4), 71–92.

Gutstein, S. E., & Sheely, R. K. (2002). *Relationship development intervention with young children.* New York: Jessica Kingsley Publishers.

Hall, L. J., & McGregor, J. A. (2000). A follow-up study of the peer relationships of children with disabilities in an inclusive school. *The Journal of Special Education, 34,* 114–126.

Hall, L. J., & Smith, K. L. (1996). The generalization of social skills by preferred peers with autism. *Journal of Intellectual and Developmental Disability, 21,* 313–330.

Hallahan, D. P., & Kauffman, J. M. (1976). *Introduction to learning disabilities.* Upper Saddle River, NJ: Prentice Hall.

Hallahan, D. P., & Kauffman, J. M. (1988). *Exceptional children* (4th ed.). Upper Saddle River, NJ: Prentice Hall.

Hammill, D. D. (1998). *Detroit tests of learning aptitude* (4th ed.). Austin, TX: PRO-ED.

Hammill, D. D., & Bartel, N. R. (1986). *Teaching students with learning and behavior problems* (4th ed.). Austin, TX: PRO-ED.

Hammill, D. D., Brown, V. L., Larsen, S. C., & Wiederholt, J. L. (1994). *Test of adolescent and adult language* (3rd ed.). Austin, TX: PRO-ED.

Hammill, D. D., & Bryant, B. R. (1998). *Learning disabilities diagnostic inventory.* Austin, TX: PRO-ED.

Hammill, D. D., & Newcomer, P. L. (1997). *Test of language development—3, Intermediate.* Austin, TX: PRO-ED.

Hammill, D. D., Pearson N. A., & Voress, J. K. (1993). *Developmental test of visual perception* (2nd ed.). Austin, TX: PRO-ED.

Hamre-Nietupski, S., McDonald, J., & Nietupski, J. (1992). Integrating elementary students with multiple disabilities into supported regular classes: Challenges and solutions. *Teaching Exceptional Children, 24*(3), 6–9.

Handlers, A., & Austin, K. (1980). Improving attitudes of high school students toward their handicapped peers. *Exceptional Children, 47,* 228–229.

Harley, R. K., & Lawrence, G. A. (1984). *Visual impairment in the schools.* Springfield, IL: Thomas.

Harrington, J. D. (1976). Hard-of-hearing pupils in the mainstream: Educational needs and services. In *Serving hard-of-hearing pupils: Alternative strategies for personnel preparation* (pp. 16–31). Minneapolis: University of Minnesota, Leadership Training Institute/Special Education.

Harvey, S., & Goudvis, A. (2000). *Strategies that work: Teaching comprehension to enhance understanding.* Portland, ME: Stenhouse.

Hasazi, S. B., Furney, K. S., & Hull, M. (1995). Additional preparation for adulthood: Transition planning. In P. T. Cegelka & W. H. Berdine (Eds.), *Effective instruction for students with learning difficulties* (pp. 419–443). Boston: Allyn & Bacon.

Hasselbring, T. S., & Glaser, C. H. W. (2000). Use of computer technology to help students with special needs. *The Future of Children, 10,* 102–122.

Hasselbring, T. S., Goin, L. I., & Bransford, J. D. (1987). Developing automaticity. *Teaching Exceptional Children, 19*(3), 30–33.

Hazekamp, J., & Huebner, K. M. (Eds.). (1989). *Program planning and evaluation for blind and visually impaired students: National guidelines for educational excellence.* New York: American Foundation for the Blind.

Heacox, D. (2002). What do students need? Tiered assignments. In D. Heacox (Ed.), *Differentiating instruction in the regular classroom: How to reach and teach all learners, grades 3–12.* Minneapolis: Free Spirit Press.

Hébert, T. P. (2002). Gifted males. In M. Neihart, S. M. Reis, N. M. Robinson, & S. M. Moon (Eds.), *The social and emotional development of gifted children: What do we know?* (pp. 137–144). Waco, TX: Prufrock Press.

Heflin, L. J., & Bullock, L. M. (1999). Inclusion of students with emotional/behavioral disorders: A survey of teachers in general and special education. *Preventing School Failure, 43,* 103–111.

Helge, D. (1991). *Rural, exceptional, at risk.* Reston, VA: The Council for Exceptional Children.

Hemphill, B. (1997). *Taming the paper tiger.* Washington, DC: Kiplinger Washington Editors.

Henker, B., Whalen, C. K., & Hinshaw, S. P. (1980). The attributional contexts of cognitive intervention strategies. *Exceptional Education Quarterly, 1*(1), 17–30.

Heron, T. E., & Harris, K. C. (1993). *The educational consultant* (3rd ed.). Austin, TX: PRO-ED.

Heron, T. E., & Harris, K. C. (2001). *The educational consultant: Helping professionals, parents, and students in inclusive classrooms* (4th ed.). Austin, TX: PRO-ED.

Heron, T. E., Heward, W. L., & Cooke, N. L. (1980). *A classwide peer tutoring system.* Paper presented at the Sixth Annual Meeting of the Association of Behavior Analysis, Dearborn, MI.

Heward, W. L. (1996). *Exceptional children: An introduction to special education* (5th ed.). Upper Saddle River, NJ: Merrill/Prentice Hall.

Heward, W. L. (2000). *Exceptional children* (6th ed.). Upper Saddle River, NJ: Merrill/Prentice Hall.

Heward, W. L. (2003). *Exceptional children* (7th ed.). Upper Saddle River, NJ: Merrill/Prentice Hall.

Heward, W. L., Courson, F. H., & Narayan, J. S. (1989). Using choral responding to increase active student response. *Teaching Exceptional Children, 21*(3), 72–75.

Heward, W. L., & Orlansky, M. D. (1992). *Exceptional children* (4th ed.). New York: Merrill/Macmillan.

Hill, D. (1989, September/October). Fixing the system from the top down. *Teacher Magazine,* 50–55.

Hiskey, M. (1966). *Hiskey-Nebraska test of learning aptitude*. Lincoln, NE: Union College Press.

Hobbs, N. (1975). *The futures of children*. San Francisco: Jossey-Bass.

Hobbs, N. (1976). *Issues in the classification of children*. San Francisco: Jossey-Bass.

Hocutt, A. M. (1996). Effectiveness of special education: Is placement the critical factor? *The Future of Children, 6*(1), 77–102.

Hodgdon, L. (1998). *Visual strategies for improving communication. Volume 1*. Troy, MI: QuirkRoberts Publishing.

Hodgkinson, H. (1993). American education: The good, the bad, and the task. *Phi Delta Kappan, 74*, 619–623.

Hollinger, J. D. (1987). Social skills for behaviorally disordered children as preparation for mainstreaming: Theory, practice, and new directions. *Remedial and Special Education, 8*(4), 17–27.

Holzberg, C. S. (1991). Sound and image: The world on a disc. *inCider/A1, 9*(11), 30–34.

Horton, L. (1985). *Adolescent alcohol abuse*. Bloomington, IN: Phi Delta Kappa Educational Foundation.

Howell, K. W., Fox, S. L., & Morehead, M. K. (1993). *Curriculum-based evaluation* (2nd ed.). Pacific Grove, CA: Brooks/Cole.

Hughes, C. (1999). Identifying critical social interaction behaviors among high school students with and without disabilities. *Behavior Modification, 23*, 41–60.

Hunt, P., & Goetz, L. (1997). Research on inclusive educational programs, practices, and outcomes for students with severe disabilities. *Journal of Special Education, 31*, 3–29.

Idol, L. (1993). *Special educator's consultation handbook* (2nd ed.). Austin, TX: PRO-ED.

Idol, L., & West, J. F. (1991). Educational collaboration: A catalyst for effective schooling. *Intervention in School and Clinic, 27*(2), 70–78, 125.

Irvine, J. (1990). *Black students and school failure: Policies practices and prescriptions*. New York: Greenwood.

Isaacson, S. L. (1987). Effective instruction in written language. *Focus on Exceptional Children, 19*(6), 1–12.

Israelson, J. (1980). I'm special too—A classroom program promotes understanding and acceptance of handicaps. *Teaching Exceptional Children, 13*, 35–37.

Jackson, N. F., Jackson, D. A., & Monroe, C. (1983). *Getting along with others: Teaching social effectiveness to children*. Champaign, IL: Research Press.

Jacobson, L. (1996, October 11). Falling birthrate leaves experts asking why. *Education Week*, p. 5.

Janesick, V. J. (1995). Our multicultural society. In E. L. Meyen & T. M. Skrtic (Eds.), *Special education and student disability* (4th ed., pp. 713–727). Denver: Love.

Jenkins, J. R., Heliotis, J. D., Stein, M. L., & Haynes, M. C. (1987). Improving reading comprehension by using paragraph restatements. *Exceptional Children, 54*, 54–59.

Jenkins, J. R., & Jenkins, L. (1985). Peer tutoring in elementary and secondary programs. *Focus on Exceptional Children, 17*(6), 1–12.

Joe, J. R., & Malach, R. S. (1998). Families with Native American roots. In E. W. Lynch & M. J. Hanson (Eds.), *Developing cross-cultural competence* (2nd ed., pp. 127–164). Baltimore: Brookes.

Joe, J. R., & Malach, R. S. (2004). Families with American Indian roots. In E. W. Lynch & M. J. Hanson (Eds.), *Developing cross-cultural competence* (3rd ed., pp. 109–139). Baltimore: Brookes.

Johns, M. J., Moncloa, F., & Gong, E. J. (2000). Teen pregnancy prevention programs: Linking research and practice. *Journal of Extension, 38*, 1–4.

Johnsen, S. K. (2004a). Definitions, models, and characteristics of gifted students. In S. K. Johnsen (Ed.), *Identifying gifted students: A practical guide* (pp. 1–21). Waco, TX: Prufrock Press.

Johnsen, S. K. (2004b). Making decisions about placement. In S. K. Johnsen (Ed.), *Identifying gifted students: A practical guide* (pp. 107–131). Waco, TX: Prufrock Press.

Johnson, D. D. (1971). The Dolch list reexamined. *The Reading Teacher, 24*, 455–456.

Johnson, D. W., & Johnson, R. T. (1980). Integrating handicapped students into the mainstream. *Exceptional Children, 47*, 90–98.

Johnson, D. W., & Johnson, R. T. (1984). Classroom learning structure and attitudes toward handicapped students in mainstream settings. In R. L. Jones (Ed.), *Attitudes and attitude change in special education* (pp. 118–142). Reston, VA: The Council for Exceptional Children.

Johnson, D. W., & Johnson, R. T. (1989). Cooperative learning and mainstreaming. In R. Gaylord-Ross (Ed.), *Integration strategies for students with handicaps* (pp. 233–248). Baltimore: Brookes.

Johnson, L. J., & Pugach, M. C. (1990). Classroom teachers' views of intervention strategies for learning and behavior problems: Which are reasonable and how frequently are they used? *Journal of Special Education, 24*, 69–84.

Johnson, R. (1981). *The picture communication symbols: Book I*. Solana Beach, CA: Mayer-Johnson Co.

Johnson, R. (1985). *The picture communication symbols: Book II*. Solana Beach, CA: Mayer-Johnson Co.

Johnson, R. (1992). *The picture communication symbols: Book III*. Solana Beach, CA: Mayer-Johnson Co.

Johnson, R. (1995). *The picture communication symbols guide*. Solana Beach, CA: Mayer-Johnson Co.

Johnston, L. D., O'Malley, P. M., & Bachman, J. G. (2001). Trends in lifetime, annual, and 30-day prevalence of use of various drugs for 8th, 10th, 12th graders, 1991–2001. Monitoring the future national survey results on drug use, 1991–2001: Volume 1—Secondary school students. Ann Arbor: University of Michigan News and Information Services. Retrieved January 3, 2002, from http://www.monitoringthefuture.org

Jones, F. H., & Eimers, R. C. (1975). Role playing to train elementary teachers to use a classroom management "skill package." *Journal of Applied Behavior Analysis, 8*, 421–433.

Jones, F. H., & Miller, W. H. (1974). The effective use of negative attention for reducing group disruption in special elementary school classrooms. *Psychological Record, 24*, 435–448.

Kalyanpur, M., & Harry, B. (1999). *Culture in special education*. Baltimore: Brookes.

Kameenui, E. J., & Simmons, D. C. (1990). *Designing instructional strategies*. New York: Merrill/Macmillan.

Kann, L., Kinchen, S. A., Williams, B. I., Ross, J. G., Lowry, R., Grunbaum, J. A., & Kolbe, L. J. (2000). Youth risk behavior surveillance—United States, 1999. *Journal of School Health, 70*, 271–285.

Kapoun, J. (1998, July/August). Teaching undergrads web evaluation: A guide for library instruction. *College & Research Libraries News, 59*(7), 522–523. Retrieved August 28, 2004, from http://www.library.cornell.edu/olinuris/ref/webcrit.html

Karnes, F. A., & Bean, S. M. (Eds.). (2001). *Methods and materials for teaching the gifted.* Waco, TX: Prufrock Press.

Karnes, M. B., & Johnson, L. J. (1991). Gifted handicapped. In N. Colangelo & G. A. Davis (Eds.), *Handbook of gifted education* (pp. 428–437). Boston: Allyn & Bacon.

Karweit, N. L., & Slavin, R. E. (1981). Measurement and modeling choices in studies of time and learning. *Educational Research Journal, 18*(2), 157–171.

Kauffman, J. M. (1997). *Characteristics of emotional and behavioral disorders of children and youth* (6th ed.). Upper Saddle River, NJ: Merrill.

Kauffman, J. M. (2001). *Characteristics of emotional and behavioral disorders of children and youth* (7th ed.). Upper Saddle River, NJ: Merrill/Prentice Hall.

Kauffman, J. M., Gerber, M. M., & Semmel, M. I. (1988). Arguable assumptions underlying the regular education initiative. *Journal of Learning Disabilities, 21,* 6–11.

Kauffman, J. M., Lloyd, J. W., Baker, J., & Riedel, T. M. (1995). Inclusion of all students with emotional and behavioral disorders? Let's think again. *Phi Delta Kappan, 76,* 542–546.

Kaufman, M. J., Gottlieb, J., Agard, J. A., & Kukic, M. D. (1975). Mainstreaming: Toward an explication of the construct. In E. L. Meyen, G. A. Vergason, & R. J. Whelan (Eds.), *Alternatives for teaching exceptional children* (pp. 35–54). Denver: Love.

Kavale, K. A., & Mostert, M. P. (2003). River of ideology, islands of evidence. *Exceptionality, 11*(4), 191–208.

Keefe, C. H., & Keefe, D. R. (1993). Instruction for students with LD: A whole language model. *Intervention in School and Clinic, 28,* 172–177.

Keller, H. (1965). *The story of my life.* New York: Airmont.

Kellogg, J. B. (1988). Forces of change. *Phi Delta Kappan, 70,* 199–204.

Kennedy, C. H., & Horn, E. M. (Eds.). (2004). *Including students with severe disabilities.* Boston: Allyn & Bacon.

Kennedy, D. M. (1995). Plain talk about creating a gifted-friendly classroom. *Roeper Review, 17,* 232–234.

Kerr, B. A. (1997). Developing talents in girls and young children. In N. Colangelo & G. A. Davis (Eds.), *Handbook of gifted education* (pp. 483–497). Boston: Allyn & Bacon.

Kerr, M. M., & Nelson, C. M. (2002). *Strategies for addressing behavior problems in the classroom* (4th ed.). Upper Saddle River, NJ: Merrill/Prentice Hall.

KIDS COUNT data book: State profiles of child well-being. (2004). Baltimore: Annie E. Casey Foundation.

Kindler, A. L. (2002a). *Survey of the states' limited English proficient students and available educational programs and services, 2000–2001 Summary report.* Washington, DC. National Clearinghouse for English Language Acquisition.

Kindler, A. L. (2002b). *What are the most common language groups for LEP students?* National Clearninghouse for English Language Acquisition. Retrieved October 16, 2004, from http://www.ncela.gwu.edu/expert/askncela/05toplangs.htm

King-Sears, M. E. (1997). Best academic practices for inclusive classrooms. *Focus on Exceptional Children, 29*(7), 1–22.

Kinnaman, D. E. (1992). 2.5 million strong—and growing. *Technology & Learning, 13*(1), 67.

Kirby, D. (1999). Reflections on two decades of research on teen sexual behavior and pregnancy. *Journal of School Health, 69*(3), 89–94.

Kirk, S. A., & Gallagher, J. J. (1979). *Educating exceptional children* (3rd ed.). Boston: Houghton Mifflin.

Kirk, S. A., Kliebhan, J. M., & Lerner, J. W. (1978). *Teaching reading to slow and disabled readers.* Boston: Houghton Mifflin.

Kirk, W. G. (1993). *Adolescent suicide: A school-based approach to assessment and treatment.* Champaign, IL: Research Press.

Kitano, H. (1973). Highlights of Institute on Language and Culture: Asian component. In L. A. Bransford, L. M. Baca, & K. Lane (Eds.), *Cultural diversity and the exceptional child* (pp. 14–15). Reston, VA: The Council for Exceptional Children.

Kitano, M. K. (1989). The K–3 teacher's role in recognizing and supporting young gifted children. *Young Children, 44*(3), 57–63.

Kitano, M. K. (1991). A multicultural educational perspective on serving the culturally diverse gifted. *Journal for the Education of the Gifted, 15*(1), 4–19.

Kitano, M. K., & DiJiosia, M. (2002). Are Asian and Pacific Americans over-represented in programs for the gifted? *Roeper Review, 24*(2), 76–80.

Kitano, M. K., & Pedersen, K. S. (2002). Action research and practical inquiry. Multicultural content integration in gifted education: Lessons from the field. *Journal for the Education of the Gifted, 25*(3), 269–289.

Klein, E. (1989). Gifted and talented. In G. P. Cartwright, C. A. Cartwright, & M. E. Ward (Eds.), *Educating special learners* (3rd ed., pp. 315–341). Belmont, CA: Wadsworth.

Knitzer, J. (1989). *Invisible Children Project: Final report and recommendations of the Invisible Children Project.* Alexandria, VA: National Mental Health Association.

Knoblauch, B., & Sorenson, B. (1998). IDEA's definition of disabilities. Reston; VA: ERIC Clearinghouse on Disabilities and Gifted Education. (ERIC Digest E560)

Koegel, R. L., Koegel, L. K., & Carter, C. M. (1999). Pivotal teaching interactions for children with autism. *School Psychology Review, 28,* 576–594.

Kohl, F. L., Moses, L. G., & Stettner-Eaton, B. A. (1983). The results of teaching fifth and sixth graders to be instructional trainers with students who are severely handicapped. *Journal of the Association for the Severely Handicapped, 8*(4), 32–40.

Kokaska, C. J. (1980). A curriculum model for career education. In G. M. Clark & W. J. White (Eds.), *Career education for the handicapped: Current perspectives for teachers* (pp. 35–41). Boothwyn, PA: Educational Resources Center.

Kokaska, C. J., & Brolin, D. E. (1985). *Career education for handicapped individuals* (2nd ed.). New York: Merrill/Macmillan.

Kollins, S. H., Barkley, R. A., & DuPaul, G. J. (2001). Use and management of medications for children diagnosed with attention deficit hyperactivity disorder (ADHD). *Focus on Exceptional Children, 33*(3), 1–24.

Kolstoe, O. P. (1976). *Teaching educable mentally retarded children* (2nd ed.). New York: Holt, Rinehart & Winston.

Krantz, P. J., & McClannahan, L. E. (1993). Teaching children with autism to Initiate to peers: Effects of a script-fading procedure. *Journal of Applied Behavior Analysis, 26,* 121–132.

Krashen, S. D. (1987). *Principles and practice in second language acquisition.* New York: Prentice Hall.

Kroth, R. (1981). Involvement with parents of behaviorally disordered adolescents. In G. Brown, R. L. McDowell, & J. Smith (Eds.), *Educating adolescents with behavior disorders* (pp. 123–139). Columbus, OH: Merrill/Prentice Hall.

Krouse, J., Gerber, M. M., & Kauffman, J. M. (1981). Peer tutoring: Procedures, promises, and unresolved issues. *Exceptional Education Quarterly, 1*(4), 107–115.

Krug, D. A., Arick, J. R., & Almond, P. J. (1980). *Autism screening instrument for educational planning (ASIEP).* Austin, TX: RO-ED.

Kulik, J. A. (2003). Grouping and tracking. N. Colangelo & G. A. Davis (Eds.), *Handbook of gifted education* (pp. 268–281). Boston: Allyn & Bacon.

Kunisawa, B. (1988). A nation in crisis; The dropout dilemma. *NEA Today, 6*(6), 61–65.

Lambert, N., Nihira, K., & Leland, H. (1993). *AAMR adaptive behavior scale—School* (2nd ed.). Austin, TX: PRO-ED.

Lamers, K., & Hall, L. J. (2003). The response of children with autism to preferred prosody during instruction. *Focus on Autism and Other Developmental Disabilities, 18*(2), 95–104.

Landau, J. K., Vohs, J. R., & Romano, C. A. (1998). *All kids count.* Boston: Federation for Children with Special Needs. Excerpted on LDOnline: http://www.ldonline.org/ld_indepth/assessment/assessment.html

Landi, M. A. G. (2001). Helping students with learning disabilities make sense of word problems. *Intervention in School and Clinic, 37*(1), 13–18, 30.

Lane, K. L. (1999). Young students at risk for antisocial behavior: The utility of academic and social skills interventions. *Journal of Emotional and Behavioral Disorders, 7,* 211–223.

Lapp, D., & Flood, J. (1992). *Teaching reading to every child* (3rd ed.). New York: Macmillan.

Larry P. v. Riles. C-71–2270-RFP (N. D. Cal. 1972), 495 F. Suppl. 96 (N. D. Cal. 1979) Aff'r (9th Cir. 1984), 1983–84 EHLR DEC. 555:304.

Lathrop, A. (1982). The terrible ten in educational programming (My top ten reasons for automatically rejecting a program). *Educational Computer, 2*(5), 34.

Laushey, K. M., & Heflin, J. L. (2000). Enhancing social skills of kindergarten children with autism through the training of multiple peers as tutors. *Journal of Autism and Developmental Disorders, 30*(3), 183–193.

Layton, C. A., & Lock, R. H. (2001). Determining learning disabilities in students with low vision. *Journal of Visual Impairment & Blindness, 95,* 288–298.

Learning Disabilities Association of America. (1993). Position paper on full inclusion of all students with learning disabilities in the regular education classroom. *Journal of Learning Disabilities, 26,* 594.

Leffert, J., & Siperstein, G. N. (2003, Fall). A focus on social skills instruction for students with learning disabilities. *Current Practice Alerts, Alert Issue 9.* Retrieved from http://www.teachingld.org/ld_resources/alerts/

Leinhardt, G., & Pallay, A. (1982). Restrictive educational settings: Exile or haven? *Review of Educational Research, 52,* 557–578.

Leone, P. E., Rutherford, R. B., & Nelson, C. M. (1991a). Juvenile corrections and the exceptional student. Reston, VA: ERIC Clearinghouse on Handicapped and Gifted Children. (ERIC Digest E509)

Leone, P. E., Rutherford, R. B., & Nelson, C. M. (1991b). *Special education in juvenile corrections.* Reston, VA: The Council for Exceptional Children.

Lerner, J. (2003). *Learning disabilities* (9th ed.). Boston: Houghton Mifflin.

Lerner, J. W., Cousin, P. T., & Richeck, M. (1992). Critical issues in learning disabilities: Whole language learning. *Learning Disabilities Research & Practice, 7,* 226–230.

Lerner, J. W., & Lowenthal, B. (1993). Attention deficit disorders: New responsibilities for special educators. *Learning Disabilities: A Multidisciplinary Journal, 4*(1), 1–8.

Lerner, J. W., Lowenthal, B., & Lerner, S. R. (1995). *Attention deficit disorders.* Pacific Grove, CA: Brooks/Cole.

Levine, M. P. (1987). *How schools can help combat student eating disorders: Anorexia nervosa and bulimia.* Washington, DC: National Education Association.

Lewis, R. B. (1980). Performance technologists and the needs of special learners. *NSPI Journal, 19*(4), 20–21.

Lewis, R. B. (1983). Learning disabilities and reading: Instructional recommendations from current research. *Exceptional Children, 50,* 230–240.

Lewis, R. B. (1993). *Special education technology: Classroom applications.* Pacific Grove, CA: Brooks/Cole.

Lewis, R. B. (1997). Changes in technology use in California's special education programs. *Remedial and Special Education, 18,* 233–242.

Lewis, R. B. (1998). Assistive technology and learning disabilities: Today's realities and tomorrow's promises. *Journal of Learning Disabilities, 31,* 16–26, 54.

Lewis, R. B. (2000a). *Final report. Project LITT (Literacy Instruction Through Technology): Enhancing the reading skills of students with learning disabilities through hypermedia-based children's literature.* San Diego, CA: San Diego State University, Department of Special Education. (ERIC Document Reproduction Service No. ED-438–648).

Lewis, R. B. (2000b). Musing on technology and learning disabilities on the occasion of the new millennium. *Journal of Special Education Technology, 15*(2), 5–12.

Lewis, R. B., Ashton, T., & Kieley, C. (1996). Word processing and individuals with learning disabilities: Overcoming the keyboard barrier [Computer software]. In *Eleventh Annual Conference on Technology for People with Disabilities, California State University, Northridge, submitted papers, 1996.* Newport Beach, CA: Rapidtext.

Lewis, R. B., Dell, S. J., Lynch, E. W., Harrison, P. J., & Saba, F. (1987). *Special education technology in action: Teachers speak out.* San Diego, CA: San Diego State University, Department of Special Education.

Lewis, R. B., & Harrison, P. J. (1988, April). *Effective applications of technology in special education: Results of a statewide study.* Paper presented at The Council for Exceptional Children's 66th Annual Convention, Washington, DC.

Lipsky, D. K., & Gartner, A. (1989). *Beyond separate education: Quality education for all.* Baltimore: Brookes.

Lloyd, J. W., & Carnine, D. W. (Eds.). (1981). Foreword to structured instruction: Effective teaching of essential skills. *Exceptional Education Quarterly, 2*(1), viii–ix.

Lloyd, J. W., Crowley, E. P., Kohler, F. W., & Strain, P. S. (1988). Redefining the applied research agenda: Cooperative learning, prereferral, teacher consultation, and peer-mediated interventions. *Journal of Learning Disabilities, 21,* 43–52.

Lloyd, J. W., Kauffman, J. M., Landrum, T. J., & Roe, D. L. (1991). Why do teachers refer pupils for special education? An analysis of referral records. *Exceptionality, 2,* 115–126.

Lloyd, J. W., & Keller, C. E. (1989). Effective mathematics instruction: Development, instruction, and programs. *Focus on Exceptional Children, 21*(7), 1–10.

Loeding, B. L., & Greenan, J. P. (1999). Relationship between self-ratings by sensory impaired students and teacher's ratings of generalizable skills. *Journal of Visual Impairment & Blindness, 93,* 716–727.

Logan, K. R., & Keefe, E. B. (1997). A comparison of instructional context, teacher behavior, and engaged behavior for students with severe disabilities in general education and self-contained elementary classrooms. *JASH, 22,* 16–27.

London, S. B., & Stile, S. W. (1982). *The school's role in the prevention of child abuse.* Bloomington, IN: Phi Delta Kappa Educational Foundation.

Lord, C., Rutter, M., DiLavore, P. C., & Risi, S. (2001). *Autism diagnostic observation schedule: Manual (ADOS).* Los Angeles: Western Psychological Services.

Lovaas, O. I., & Newsom, C. D. (1976). Behavior modification with psychotic children. In H. Leitenberg (Ed.), *Handbook of behavior modification and behavior therapy* (pp. 303–360). Upper Saddle River, NJ: Prentice Hall.

Lovitt, T. C. (1982). What does the direct in directive teacher mean? [Interview with T. C. Lovitt]. *The Directive Teacher, 4*(1), 24–25, 27.

Lowenbraun, S., & Thompson, M. D. (1986). Hearing impairments. In N. G. Haring & L. McCormick (Eds.), *Exceptional children and youth* (4th ed., pp. 357–395). New York: Merrill/Macmillan.

Luckner, J., Bowen, S., & Carter, K. (2001). Visual teaching strategies for students who are deaf or hard of hearing. *Teaching Exceptional Children, 33*(3), 38–44.

Luckner, J. L., & Carter, K. (2001). Essential competencies for teaching students with hearing loss and additional disabilities. *American Annals of the Deaf, 146,* 7–15.

Luetke-Stahlman, B., & Luckner, J. (1991). *Effectively educating students with hearing impairments.* White Plains: NY: Longman.

Luftig, R. L. (1989). *Assessment of learners with special needs.* Boston: Allyn & Bacon.

Lusthaus, E. & Forest, M. (1987). The kaleidoscope: A challenge to the cascade. In M. Forest (Ed.), *More education integration* (pp. 1–17). Downsview, Ontario: G. Allan Roeher Institute.

Lynch, E. W. (1981). *But I've tried everything! A special educator's guide to working with parents.* San Diego, CA: San Diego State University.

Lynch, E. W. (2004a). Conceptual framework: From culture shock to cultural learning. In E. W. Lynch & M. J. Hanson (Eds.), *Developing cross-cultural competence* (3rd ed., pp. 19–39). Baltimore: Brookes.

Lynch, E. W. (2004b). Developing cross-cultural competence. In E. W. Lynch & M. J. Hanson (Eds.), *Developing cross-cultural competence* (3rd ed., pp. 41–77). Baltimore: Brookes.

Lynch, E. W., & Hanson, M. J. (Eds.). (2004). *Developing cross-cultural competence* (3rd ed.). Baltimore: Brookes.

Maag, J. W., & Webber, J. (1995). Promoting children's social development in general education classrooms. *Preventing School Failure, 39*(3), 13–19.

MacArthur, C. A., Graham, S., Haynes, J. B., & DeLaPaz, S. (1996). Spelling checkers and students with learning disabilities: Performance comparisons and impact on spelling. *Journal of Special Education, 30,* 35–57.

MacDuff, G. S., Krantz, P. J., & McClannahan, L. E. (2001). Prompts and prompt-fading strategies for people with autism. In C. Maurice, G. Green, & R. Foxx (Eds.), *Making a difference: Behavioral intervention for autism* (pp. 37–50). Austin, TX: PRO-ED.

Machado, R. E., Belew, A. D., Jans, M., & Cunha, A. (1996). Full inclusion. *SKOLE: The Journal of the National Coalition of Alternative Community Schools, 3*(1), 110–124.

MacMillan, D. L. (1982). *Mental retardation in school and society* (2nd ed.). Boston: Little, Brown.

Madden, N. A., & Slavin, R. E. (1983). Mainstreaming students with mild handicaps: Academic and social outcomes. *Review of Educational Research, 53,* 519–569.

Madsen, C. H., Becker, W. C., & Thomas, D. R. (1968). Rules, praise, and ignoring: Elements of elementary classroom control. *Journal of Applied Behavior Analysis, 1,* 139–151.

Mager, R. F. (1984). *Preparing instructional objectives* (rev. ed.). Belmont, CA: Pitman Learning.

Maginnis, G. (1969). The readability graph and informal reading inventories. *The Reading Teacher, 22,* 534–538.

Maheady, L., Harper, G. F., & Mallette, B. (2003, Spring). A focus on class wide peer tutoring. *Current Practice Alerts, Alert Issue 8.* Retrieved from http://www.teachingld.org/ld_resources/alerts/

Maheady, L., Sacca, M. K., & Harper, G. F. (1988). Classwide peer tutoring with mildly handicapped high school students. *Exceptional Children, 55,* 52–59.

Mainzer, R. W., Deshler, D., Coleman, M. R., Kozleski, E., & Rodriguez-Walling, M. (2003). To ensure the learning of every child with a disability. *Focus on Exceptional Children, 35*(5), 1–12.

Maker, C. J. (2001). DISCOVER: Assessing and developing problem solving. *Gifted Education International, 15*(3), 232–51.

Maker, C. J., & Nielson, A. B. (1996). *Curriculum development and teaching strategies for gifted learners* (2nd ed.). Austin, TX: PRO-ED.

Males, M. (1993). Schools, society, and "teen" pregnancy. *Phi Delta Kappan, 74,* 566–568.

Maloney, M. J., & Klykylo, W. M. (1985). An overview of anorexia nervosa, bulimia, and obesity in children and adolescents. In S. Chess & A. Thomas (Eds.), *Annual progress in child psychology and child development –1985* (pp. 436–453). New York: Brunner/Mazel.

Mandell, C. J., & Fiscus, E. (1981). *Understanding exceptional people.* St. Paul, MN: West.

Manning, M. L., & Baruth, L. G. (1995). *Students at risk.* Boston: Allyn & Bacon.

Manzo, K. K. (1996). Slow progress in reaching goals for 2000 reported. *Education Week, 16*(13), 6.

Markel, G. (1981). Improving test-taking skills of LD adolescents. *Academic Therapy, 16,* 333–342.

Markwardt, F. C. (1998). *Peabody individual achievement test—Revised/normative update.* Circle Pines, MN: American Guidance Service.

Maron, S. S., & Martinez, D. H. (1980). Environmental alternatives for the visually handicapped. In J. W. Schifani, R. M. Anderson, & S. J. Odle (Eds.), *Implementing learning in the least restrictive environment* (pp 149–198). Baltimore: University Park Press.

Martin, E. W. (1974). Some thoughts on mainstreaming. *Exceptional Children, 41,* 150–153.

Martin, J. E., Marshall, J. H., & Sale, P. (2004). A 3-year study of middle, junior high, and high school IEP meetings. *Exceptional Children, 70,* 285–297.

Marttila, J., & Mills, M. (1995). *Knowledge is power.* Bettendorf, IA: Mississippi Bend Area Education Agency.

Mason, S., McGee, G. G., Farmer-Dougan, V., & Risley, T. (1989). A practical strategy for ongoing reinforcer assessment. *Journal of Behavior Analysis, 22,* 171–179.

Masse, L. (2001). Direction of gifted education in the first decade of the 21st century: A step back, continuity, and new direction. *Journal of Secondary Gifted Education, 12,* 170–173.

Mastropieri, M., & Scruggs, T. (2004). *The inclusive classroom: Strategies for effective education* (2nd ed.). Upper Saddle River, NJ: Merrill/Prentice Hall.

Mather, N. (1992). Whole language reading instruction for students with learning disabilities: Caught in the cross fire. *Learning Disabilities Research & Practice, 7,* 87–95.

Mathes, P. G., & Irby, B. J. (1993). *Discussion guide: Teen pregnancy and parenting handbook.* Champaign, IL: Research Press.

Maurice, C. (1993). *Let me hear your voice.* London: Robert Hale.

Maxon, A., Brackett, D., & van den Berg, S. (1991). Classroom amplification use: A national long-term study. *Language, Speech, and Hearing Services in Schools, 22,* 242–253.

Mayer, R. E. (2004). Should there be a three-strikes rule against pure discovery learning? *American Psychologist, 59,* 14–19.

McCabe, M. (2004). Teachers: Spec. ed. students should meet own standards. *Education Week, 33*(17), 20–21.

McCarney, S. B. (1996). *The learning disability evaluation scale.* Columbia, MO: Hawthorne.

McCarney, S. B., & Leigh, J. E. (1990). *Behavior evaluation scale—2.* Columbia, MO: Hawthorne Educational Services.

McClannahan, L. E., & Krantz, P. J. (1999). *Activity schedules for children with autism: Teaching independent behavior.* Bethesda, MD: Woodbine House.

McCoach, D. B., & Siegle. D. (2003). Factors that differentiate underachieving gifted students from high-achieving gifted students. *Gifted Child Quarterly, 47*(2), 144–154.

McCormick, L. (1986). Keeping up with language intervention trends. *Teaching Exceptional Children, 18*(2), 123–129.

McCormick, L. (1990). Cultural diversity and exceptionality. In N. G. Haring & L. McCormick (Eds.), *Exceptional children and youth* (5th ed., pp. 46–75). New York: Merrill/Macmillan.

McDonald, D. (1989). A special report on the education of Native Americans: "Stuck in the horizon" [Special Report insert]. *Education Week, 7*(4), 1–16.

McDonnell, J. (1987). The integration of students with severe handicaps into regular public schools: An analysis of parents' perceptions of potential outcomes. *Education and Training in Mental Retardation, 22,* 98–111.

McGaha, C. G., & Farran, D. C. (2001). Interactions in an inclusive classroom: The effects of visual status and setting. *Journal of Visual Impairment & Blindness, 95,* 80–94.

McGinnis, E., & Goldstein, A. P. (1997). *Skillstreaming the elementary school child: New strategies and perspectives for teaching prosocial skills.* Champaign, IL: Research Press.

McIntosh, R., Vaughn, S., & Zaragoza, N. (1991). A review of social interventions for students with learning disabilities. *Journal of Learning Disabilities, 24,* 451–458.

McLeskey, J., Hoppey, D., Williamson, P., & Rentz, T. (2004). Is inclusion an illusion? An examination of national and state trends toward the education of students with learning disabilities in general education classrooms. *Learning Disabilities Research & Practice, 19*(2), 109–115.

McLoughlin, J. A., & Lewis, R. B. (2005) *Assessing students with special needs* (6th ed.). Upper Saddle River, NJ: Merrill/Prentice Hall.

McNamara, K., & Hollinger, C. (2003). Intervention-based assessment: Evaluation rates and eligibility findings. *Learning Disabilities Research & Practice, 18,* 181–193.

McNergney, R., & Haberman, M. (1988). Dropouts: Time for solutions. *NEA Today, 6*(10), 27.

McWhirter, J. J., McWhirter, B. T., McWhirter, A. M., & McWhirter, E. H. (1998). *At-risk youth: A comprehensive response.* Pacific Grove, CA: Brooks/Cole.

Medley, D. M. (1982). Teacher effectiveness. In H. E. Mitzel (Ed.), *Encyclopedia of educational research* (5th ed., pp. 1894–1903). New York: Free Press.

Meisgeier, C. (1981). A social/behavioral program for the adolescent student with serious learning problems. *Focus on Exceptional Children, 13*(9), 1–13.

Mercer, C. D., & Mercer, A. R. (1989). *Teaching students with learning problems* (3rd ed.). New York: Merrill/Macmillan.

Mercer, C. D., & Mercer, A. R. (1993). *Teaching students with learning problems* (4th ed.). New York: Merrill/Macmillan.

Mercer, C. D., & Mercer, A. R. (2005). *Teaching students with learning problems* (7th ed.). Upper Saddle River, NJ: Merrill/Prentice Hall.

Mercer, C. D., Mercer, A. R., & Bott, D. A. (1984). *Self-correcting learning materials for the classroom.* New York: Merrill/Macmillan.

Mercer, C. D., & Pullen, P. C. (2005). *Students with learning disabilities* (6th ed.). Upper Saddle River, NJ: Merrill/Prentice Hall.

Mercer, J. R. (1973). *Labeling the mentally retarded.* Berkeley: University of California Press.

Meyen, E. L. (1981). *Developing instructional units* (3rd ed.). Dubuque, IA: Brown.

Migliore, E. T. (2003). Eliminating bullying in your classroom. *Intervention in School and Clinic, 38*(3), 172–176.

Miksic, S. (1987). Drug abuse management in adolescent special education. In M. M. Kerr, C. M. Nelson, & D. L. Lambert (Eds.), *Helping adolescents with learning and behavior problems* (pp. 225–253). New York: Merrill/Macmillan.

Miller, A. K., & Chandler, K. (2003). *Violence in U.S. public schools: 2000 school survey on crime and safety.* Washington, DC: U.S. Department of Education, National Center for Education Statistics.

Miller, M. (2003). Students' views of least restrictive environment: A pilot study. *Learning Disabilities, 12,* 85–88.

Mills, C. J. (2003). Characteristics of effective teachers of gifted students: Teacher background and personality styles of students. *Gifted Child Quarterly, 47*(4), 272–281.

Mills, P. J. (1979). Education within the mainstream: Suggestions for classroom teachers. *The Directive Teacher, 2*(2), 16.

Mira, M. P., & Tyler, J. S. (1991). Students with traumatic brain injury: Making the transition from hospital to school. *Focus on Exceptional Children, 23*(5), 1–12.

Monroe, C. R., & Obidah, J. E. (2004). The influence of cultural synchronization on a teacher's perception of disruption: A case study of an African American middle-school classroom. *Journal of Teacher Education, 55*(3), 256–268.

Montague, M. (1992). The effects of cognitive and metacognitive strategy instruction on the mathematical problem-solving of middle school students with learning disabilities. *Journal of Learning Disabilities, 25,* 230–248.

Montague, M., Warger, C., & Morgan, T. H. (2000). Solve it! Strategy instruction to improve mathematical problem solving. *Learning Disabilities Research & Practice, 15,* 110–116.

Montgomery, M. D. (1978). The special educator as consultant: Some strategies. *Teaching Exceptional Children, 10,* 110–112.

Montgomery, W. (2001). Creating culturally responsive, inclusive classrooms. *Teaching Exceptional Children, 33*(4), 4–8.

Morganthau, T. (1986, March 17). Kids and cocaine. *Newsweek,* pp. 57, 59–62, 63, 65.

Morrison, G. M., & Polloway, E. A. (1995). Mental retardation. In E. L. Meyen & T. M. Skrtic (Eds.), *Special education and student disability* (4th ed., pp. 212–269). Denver: Love.

Morrison, W. F., & Omdal, S. N. (2000). The twice exceptional student. *Reclaiming Children and Youth, 9*(2), 103–106.

Morsink, C. V., & Lenk, L. L. (1992). The delivery of special education programs and services. *Remedial and Special Education, 13*(6), 33–43.

Mukherjee, S., Lightfoot, J., & Sloper, P. (2000). The inclusion of pupils with a chronic health condition in mainstream school: What does it mean for teachers? *Educational Research, 42,* 59–72.

Munson, S. M. (1986). Regular education teacher modifications for mainstreamed mildly handicapped students. *Journal of Special Education, 20,* 489–502.

Murdick, N. L., & Petch-Hogan, B. (1996). Inclusive classroom management: Using preintervention strategies. *Intervention in School and Clinic, 31,* 172–176.

Nash, J. M. (2002, May 6). The secrets of autism. *Time, 159*(18), 46–56.

National Advisory Committe on Handicapped Children. (1968). *Special education for handicapped children* [First annual report]. Washington, DC: U.S. Department of Health, Education, and Welfare.

National Center for Education Statistics. (2000). *Dropout rates in the United States: 1999.* U.S. Department of Education: Office of Educational Research and Improvement.

National Center for Education Statistics. (2003). *Dropout rates.* Retrieved October 17, 2004, from http://nces.ed.gov/fastfacts/display.asp?id=16

National Center for Education Statistics. (2004). *The condition of education 2004* (NCES 2004–077). Washington, DC: U.S. Government Printing Office.

National Center for Health Statistics. (1996, December 19). *Teenage birth rates down in a majority of states.* Retrieved November 11, 1997, from http://www.cdc.gov/nchswww/releases/96facts/96sheets/teenbrth.htm

National Center for Learning Disabilities. (2001). *LD at a glance.* Retrieved September 4, 2004, from http://www.ld.org/LDInfoZone/InfoZone_FactSheet_LD.cfm#

National Clearinghouse on Child Abuse and Neglect. (2001). *What is child maltreatment?* Retrieved December 22, 2001, from http://www.calib.com/nccanch/pubs/actsheets/childmal.cfm

National Coalition of Advocates for Students. (1985). *Barriers to excellence: Our children at risk.* Boston: Author.

National Commission on Excellence in Education. (1983). *A nation at risk: The imperative for educational reform.* Washington, DC: U.S. Government Printing Office.

National Committee to Prevent Child Abuse. (1997, April). *Child abuse and neglect statistics.* Retrieved January 10, 1998, from http://www.childabuse.org/facts96.html

National Council of Teachers of Mathematics. (1989). *Curriculum and evaluation standards for school mathematics.* Reston, VA: Author.

National Council of Teachers of Mathematics. (2000). *Principles and standards for school mathematics.* Retrieved August 21, 2003, from http://standards.nctm.org

National Eating Disorders Screening Program. (2001). *Fact sheet on eating disorders.* Retrieved December 21, 2001, from http://www.mentalhealthscreening.org/eat/eat-fact.htm

National Education Goals Panel. (1997). *Commonly asked questions.* Retrieved from http://www.negp.gov/caq/html

National Information Center for Children and Youth with Disabilities. (1997a). *General information about traumatic brain injury: Fact sheet number 4.* Washington, DC: Author.

National Information Center for Children and Youth with Disabilities. (1997b). *Speech and language disorders.* Washington, DC: Author.

National Information Center for Children and Youth with Disabilities. (2001a). *General information about deafness and hearing loss: Fact sheet number 3.* Washington, DC: Author.

National Information Center for Children and Youth with Disabilities. (2001b). *General information about visual impairments: Fact sheet number 13.* Washington, DC: Author.

National Institute of Mental Health. (2001). *Eating disorders: Facts about eating disorders and the search for solutions.* Bethesda, MD: Author.

National Institute on Drug Abuse. (2001). *High school and youth trends.* NIDA Infofax. Retrieved December 23, 2001, from http://www.nida.nih.gov/Infofax/HSYouthtrends.html

National Joint Committee on Learning Disabilities. (1993). A reaction to full inclusion: A reaffirmation of the right of students with learning disabilities to a continuum of services. *Journal of Learning Disabilities, 26,* 596.

National Joint Committee on Learning Disabilities. (1994). *Collective perspectives on issues affecting learning disabilities.* Austin, TX: PRO-ED.

National Research Council. (1997). *Executive summary. Educating one & all: Students with disabilities and standards-based reform.* Washington, DC: National Academy Press.

National Research Council. (2001). *Educating children with autism.* Committee on Educational Interventions for Children with Autism, Division of Behavioral and Social Sciences and Education. Washington, DC: National Academy Press.

National Youth Violence Prevention Resource Center. (2001). Hot topics: Youth suicide. Retrieved December 21, 2001, from http://www.safeyouth.org/topics/suicide.htm

Neal, J., Bigby, L., & Nicholson, R. (2004). Occupational therapy, physical therapy, and orientation and mobility services in public schools. *Intervention in School and Clinic, 39*(4), 218–222.

Neary, T., Halvorsen, A., & Smithey, L. (1991). *Inclusive education guidelines.* Sacramento: California Department of Education, PEERS Project.

Needham, N. (1989). Meet C. Everett Koop: Gruff, tough, and no bluff. *NEA Today, 7*(7), 10–11.

Nelson, C. M. (1988). Social skill training for handicapped students. *Teaching Exceptional Children, 20*(4), 19–23.

Nelson, C. M. (1993). Students with behavioral disorders. In A. E. Blackhurst & W. H. Berdine (Eds.), *An introduction to special education* (3rd ed., pp. 528–561). New York: HarperCollins.

New York State Department of Health Early Intervention Program (1999). *The guideline technical report: Autism/pervasive developmental disorders.* Albany: New York State Department of Health.

Newcomb, M. D., & Bentler, P. M. (1989). Substance use and abuse among children and teenagers. *American Phsychologist, 44,* 242–248.

Newcomer, P. L., & Hammill, D. D. (1997). *Test of language development—3, Primary.* Austin, TX: PRO-ED.

Nietupski, J., Hamre-Nietupski, S., Curtin, S., & Shrikanth, K. (1997). A review of curricular research in severe disabilities from 1976 to 1995 in six selected journals. *Journal of Special Education, 31,* 36–55.

Nirje, B. (1969). The normalization principle and its human management implications. In R. B. Kugel & W. Wolfensberger (Eds.), *Changing patterns in residential services for the mentally retarded* (pp. 231–240). Washington, DC: U.S. Government Printing Office.

Norris, W. C. (1977). Via technology to a new era in education. *Phi Delta Kappan, 58,* 451–453.

Northcutt, L., & Watson, D. (1986). *Sheltered English teaching handbook.* San Marcos, CA: AM Graphics & Printing.

Odom, S. L., McConnell, S. R., & Chandler, L. K. (1994). Acceptability and feasibility of classroom based social interaction interventions for young children with disabilities. *Exceptional Children, 60,* 226–236.

Oehring, S. (1992). Adventures with grandparents. *Instructor, 102*(2), 90, 102.

Office of Civil Rights. (2004). Elementary and Secondary School Survey: 2000. Data retrieved May 24, 2004, from http://205.207.175.84/ocr2000r/wdsdata.html

Ogden, E. H., & Germinario, V. (1988). *The at-risk student: Answers for educators.* Lancaster, PA: Technomic.

Olenchak, F. R., & Reis, S. M. (2002). Gifted students with learning disabilities. In M. Neihart, S. M. Reis, N. M. Robinson, & S. M. Moon (Eds.), *The social and emotional development of gifted children: What do we know?* (pp. 177–191). Waco, TX: Prufrock Press.

Olson, J. L., & Platt, J. M. (1996). *Teaching children and adolescents with special needs* (2nd ed.). Upper Saddle River, NJ: Merrill/Prentice Hall.

Olson, L. (2004). Enveloping expectations. [Special issue: *Quality counts 2004: Count me in.*] *Education Week, 23*(17), 8–21.

Orr, L. E., Craig, G. P., Best, J., Borland, A., Holland, D., Knodel, H., Lehman, A., Mathewson, C., Miller, M., & Pequignot, M. (1997). Exploring developmental disabilities through literature: An annotated bibliography. *Teaching Exceptional Children, 29*(6), 14–17.

Ortiz, A. A. (1988, Spring). Evaluating educational contexts in which language minority students are served. *Bilingual Special Education Newsletter, 7,* 1, 3–4, 7.

Osguthorpe, R. T., & Scruggs, T. E. (1986). Special education students as tutors: A review and analysis. *Remedial and Special Education, 7*(4), 15–26.

Overton, T. (2004). Promoting academic success through environmental assessment. *Intervention in School and Clinic, 39,* 147–153.

Pacchiano, D. M. (2000). A review of instructional variables related to student problem behavior. *Preventing School Failure, 4,* 174–178.

Padrón, Y. N., Waxman, H. C., & Rivera, H. H. (2002). *Educating Hispanic students: Obstacles and avenues to improved academic achievement.* Santa Cruz: Center for Research on Education, Diversity and Education, University of California, Santa Cruz.

Palinscar, A. S., & Brown, A. L. (1988). Teaching and practicing thinking skills to promote comprehension in the context of group problem solving. *Remedial and Special Education, 9*(1), 53–59.

Palmer, D. S., Fuller, K., Arora, T., & Nelson, M. (2001). Taking sides: Parent views on inclusion for their children with severe disabilities. *Exceptional Children, 67,* 467–484.

Pang, V. O., & Park, C. D. (2003). Examination of the self-regulation mechanism: Prejudice reduction in pre-service teachers. *Action in Teacher Education, 25*(3), 1–11.

Parette, H. P., & Petch-Hogan, B. (2000). Approaching families: Facilitating culturally/linguistically diverse family involvement. *Teaching Exceptional Children, 33*(2), 4–10.

Parke, B. N. (1989). *Gifted students in regular classrooms.* Boston: Allyn & Bacon.

Parker, J. P. (1989). *Instructional strategies for teaching the gifted.* Boston: Allyn & Bacon.

Parson, L. R., & Heward, W. L. (1979). Training peers to tutor: Evaluation of a training package for primary learning disabled students. *Journal of Applied Behavior Analysis, 12,* 309–310.

Pasanella, A. L., & Volkmor, C. B. (1981). *Teaching handicapped students in the mainstream* (2nd ed.). Columbus, OH: Merrill/Prentice Hall.

Patrick, J. L., & Reschly, D. J. (1982). Relationship of state educational criteria and demographic variables to school-system prevalence of mental retardation. *American Journal of Mental Deficiency, 86,* 351–360.

Patros, P. G., & Shamoo, T. K. (1989). *Depression and suicide in children and adolescents: Prevention, intervention, and postvention.* Boston: Allyn & Bacon.

Patterson, G. R., DeBaryshe, B. D., & Ramsey, E. (1989). A developmental perspective on antisocial behavior. *American Psychologist, 44,* 329–335.

Pavri, S., & Luftig, R. (2000). The social face of inclusive education: Are students with learning disabilities really included in the classroom? *Preventing School Failure, 45,* 8–14.

Pemberton, J. B. (2003). Communicating academic progress as an integral part of assessment. *Teaching Exceptional Children, 35*(4), 16–20.

Pendarvis, E. D. (1993). Students with unique gifts and talents. In A. E. Blackhurst & W. H. Berdine (Eds.), *An introduction to special education* (3rd ed., pp. 563–599). New York: HarperCollins.

Pendergast, D. E. (1995). Preparing for children who are medically fragile in educational programs. *Teaching Exceptional Children, 27*(2), 37–41.

Pepper, F. C. (1976). Teaching the American Indian child in mainstream settings. In R. L. Jones (Ed.), *Mainstreaming and the minority child* (pp. 133–158). Reston, VA: The Council for Exceptional Children.

Perske, R., & Perske, M. (1988). *Circles of friends: People with disabilities and their friends enrich the lives of one another.* Nashville, TN: Abington.

Peters, W. A. M., Grager-Loidl, H., & Supplee, P. (2000). Underachievement in gifted children and adolescents: Theory and practice. In K. A. Heller, F. J. Mönks, R. J. Sternberg, & R. F. Subotnik (Eds.), *International handbook of giftedness and talent* (2nd ed., 609–620). Oxford: Elsevier Science Ltd.

Phelan, P. (1996). *High interest easy reading: An annotated booklist for middle school and senior high school* (7th ed.). Urbana, IL: National Council of Teachers of English.

Phelps, M. S., & Prock, G. A. (1991). Equality of educational opportunity in rural America. In A. DeYoung (Ed.), *Rural education issues and practice* (pp. 269–312). New York: Garland.

Phi Delta Kappa. (1998). *Fast facts about dropout and completion rates.* Bloomington, IN: Author.

Phi Delta Kappa. (2000). *Fast facts about social promotion & retention.* Bloomington, IN: Author.

Pierce, C. D., Reid, R., & Epstein, M. H. (2004). Teacher-mediated interventions for children with EBD and their academic outcomes: A review. *Remedial and Special Education, 25*(3), 175–188.

Piirto, J. (1999). *Talented children and adults: Their development and education* (2nd ed.). Upper Saddle River, NJ: Merrill/Prentice Hall.

Platt, J. M., & Olson, J. L. (1997). *Teaching adolescents with mild disabilities.* Pacific Grove, CA: Brooks/Cole.

Platt, J. M., & Platt, J. S. (1980). Volunteers for special education: A mainstreaming support system. *Teaching Exceptional Children, 13,* 31–34.

Polloway, E. A., & Patton, J. R. (1993). *Strategies for teaching learners with special needs* (5th ed.). New York: Merrill/Macmillan.

Popham, J. P. (1993). Wanted: AIDS education that works. *Phi Delta Kappan, 74,* 559–562.

Postel, C. A. (1986). Death in my classroom? *Teaching Exceptional Children, 18,* 139–143.

Posth, M. A. (1997, March). Why the Web? *Mac Home Journal,* 36–37.

Prasad, S. (1994). Assessing social interactions of children with disabilities. *Teaching Exceptional Children, 26*(2), 23–25.

Prater, M. A. (2003). She will succeed! Strategies for success in inclusive classrooms. *Teaching Exceptional Children, 35*(5), 58–64.

Prater, M. A. (1994). Improving academic and behavior skills through self-management procedures. *Preventing School Failure, 38*(4), 5–9.

President's Committee for People with Intellectual Disabilities. (2004). *Frequently asked questions.* Washington, DC: Author. Retrieved September 18, 2004, from http://www.acf.hhs.gov/programs/pcpid/

President's Committee on Mental Retardation. (1969). *The six hour retarded child.* Washington, DC: U.S. Department of Health, Education, and Welfare.

President's Committee on Mental Retardation. (1975). *The problem of mental retardation.* Washington, DC: U.S. Department of Health, Education, and Welfare.

Prestia, K. (2003). Tourette's syndrome: Characteristics and interventions. *Intervention in School and Clinic, 39*(2), 67–71.

Prevent Blindness America. (2001). *Signs of possible eye trouble in children.* Retrieved December 11, 2001, from http://www.preventblindness.org/children/trouble_signs.html

Prevent Child Abuse America. (2001). *Total estimated cost of child abuse and neglect in the United States: Statistical evidence.* Chicago: Author.

Prizant, B. M., Wetherby, A. M., & Rydell, P. J. (2000). Communication intervention issues for children with autism spectrum disorders. In A. M. Wetherby & B. M. Prizant (Eds.), *Autism spectrum disorders: A transactional developmental perspective* (pp. 193–224). Baltimore: Brookes.

Puckett, K. S. (2004). Process ACCESS: Field testing an assistive technology toolkit for students with mild disabilities. *Journal of Special Education Technology, 19*(2), 5–17.

Pumpian, I. (1988). Severe multiple handicaps. In E. W. Lynch & R. B. Lewis (Eds.), *Exceptional children and adults* (pp. 180–226). Glenview, IL: Scott, Foresman.

Putnam, J. M. (1992). Teaching students with severe disabilities in the regular classroom. In L. G. Cohen (Ed.), *Children with exceptional needs in regular classrooms* (pp. 118–142). Washington, DC: National Education Association.

Quality Education Data, Inc. (1985). *Microcomputer usage in schools, 1984–1985.* Denver: Author.

Quay, H. C. (1979). Classification. In H. C. Quay & J. S. Werry (Eds.), *Psychopathological disorders of childhood* (2nd ed.). New York: Wiley.

Raison, S. B. (1979). Curriculum modification for special needs at the secondary level. *Education Unlimited, 1*(3), 19–21.

Rankin-Erickson, J. L., & Pressley, M. (2000). A survey of instructional practices of special education teachers nominated as effective teachers of literacy. *Learning Disabilities Research & Practice, 15,* 206–225.

Rapport, J. K. (1996). Legal guidelines for the delivery of special health care services in schools. *Exceptional Children, 62,* 537–549.

Ratleff, J. E. (1989). *Instructional strategies for crosscultural students with special education needs.* Sacramento, CA: Resources in Special Education.

Ray, B. M. (1985). Measuring the social position of the mainstreamed handicapped child. *Exceptional Children, 52,* 57–62.

Recer, P. (1989, June 8). 12% of kids mentally troubled, study says. *Associated Press,* pp. 1–2.

Rees, T. (1992). Students with hearing impairments. In L. G. Cohen (Ed.), *Children with exceptional needs in regular classrooms* (pp. 98–117). Washington, DC: National Education Association.

Reeve, R. E. (1990). ADHD: Facts and fallacies. *Intervention in School and Clinic, 26,* 70–78.

Reeves, M. S. (1988, April 27). "Self-interest and the commonwealth": Focusing on the bottom half. *Education Week,* 14–21.

Reid, D. K., Hresko, W. P., & Swanson, H. L. (Eds.). (1996). *Cognitive approaches to learning disabilities* (3rd ed.). Austin, TX: PRO-ED.

Reid, R. (1996). Research in self-monitoring with students with learning disabilities: The present, the prospects, the pitfalls. *Journal of Learning Disabilities, 29,* 317–331.

Reis, S. M., & Renzulli, J. S. (1985). *Identification of the gifted and talented.* Reston, VA: The Council for Exceptional Children. (Clearinghouse on Handicapped and Gifted Children, ERIC Digest No. 360)

Reis, S. M., Westberg, K. L., Kulikowich, J. M., & Purcell, J. H. (1998). Curriculum compacting and achievement test scores: What does the research say? *Gifted Child Quarterly, 42*(2), 123–129.

Renzulli, J. S. (1978). What makes giftedness? Re-examining a definition. *Phi Delta Kappan, 60,* 180–184.

Renzulli, J. S., & Smith, L. H. (1978). *Learning styles inventory: A measure of student preference for instructional techniques.* Mansfield Center, CT: Creative Learning Press.

Renzulli, J. S., Smith, L., White, A., Callahan, C., & Hartman, R. (2001). *Scales for rating the behavioral characteristics of superior students* (rev. ed.). Manual and nine rating scales. Mansfield Center, CT: Creative Learning Press.

Reschly, D. J., & Lamprecht, M. J. (1979). Expectancy effects of labels: Fact or artifact? *Exceptional Children, 46,* 55–58.

Research and Training Center on Independent Living. (1996). *Guidelines for reporting and writing about people with disabilities* (5th ed.). Lawrence, KS: Author.

Reynolds, C. R., & Bigler, E. D. (1994). *Test of memory and learning.* Austin, TX: PRO-ED.

Reynolds, M. C., & Birch, J. W. (1982). *Teaching exceptional children in all America's schools* (rev. ed.). Reston, VA: The Council for Exceptional Children.

Reynolds, M. C., & Birch, J. W. (1988). *Adaptive mainstreaming* (3rd ed.). New York: Longman.

Reynolds, M. C., Zetlin, A. G., & Wang, M. C. (1993). 20/20 analysis: Taking a close look at the margins. *Exceptional Children, 59,* 294–300.

Rich, H. L., & Ross, S. M. (1989). Students' time on learning tasks in special education. *Exceptional Children, 55,* 508–515.

Richardson, R. C. (2000). Teaching social and emotional competence. *Children & Schools, 22,* 246–251.

Richert, E. S. (2003). Excellence with justice in identification and programming. In N. Colangelo, & G. A. Davis, (Eds.), *Handbook of gifted education* (3rd ed., pp. 146–158). Boston: Allyn & Bacon.

Rieth, H., & Evertson, C. M. (1988). Variables related to the effective instruction of difficult-to-teach children. *Focus on Exceptional Children, 20*(5), 1–8.

Rivera, B. D., & Rogers-Adkinson, D. (1997). Culturally sensitive interventions: Social skills training with children and parents from culturally and linguistically diverse backgrounds. *Intervention in School and Clinic, 33,* 75–80.

Rivera, D. P., & Smith, D. D. (1997). *Teaching students with learning and behavior problems* (3rd ed.). Boston: Allyn & Bacon.

Roberts, R., & Mather, N. (1995). The return of students with learning disabilities to regular classrooms: A sellout? *Learning Disabilities Research & Practice, 10,* 46–58.

Robinson, F. P. (1961). *Effective study.* New York: Harper & Row.

Robinson, S., & Deshler, D. D. (1995). Learning disabled. In E. L. Meyen & T. M. Skrtic (Eds.), *Special education and student disability* (4th ed., pp. 170–211). Denver: Love.

Rockefeller, N. A. (1976, October 16). Don't accept anyone's verdict that you are lazy, stupid, or retarded. *TV Guide,* pp. 12–14.

Rodriguez, R. C., Cole, J. T., Stile, S. W., & Gallegos, R. L. (1979). Bilingualism and biculturalism for the special education classroom. *Teacher Education and Special Education, 2*(4), 69–74.

Roid, G. (2003). *Stanford-Binet intelligence scales, Fifth edition.* Itasca, IL: Riverside Publishing.

Roland, P. (1989, August). A parent speaks to special educators. *Exceptional Times,* p. 3.

Rose, D. H., & Meyer, A. (2002). *Teaching every student in the digital age.* Alexandria, VA: ASCD. Retrieved August 28, 2004, from http://www.cast.org/teachingeverystudent/ideas/tes/

Rose, L. C., & Gallup, A. M. (2001). The 33rd annual Phi Delta Kappa/Gallup poll of the public's attitudes toward the public schools. *Phi Delta Kappan, 83,* 41–58.

Rose, L. C., & Gallup, A. M. (2003). The 35th annual Phi Delta Kappa/Gallup poll of the public's attitudes toward the public schools. *Phi Delta Kappan, 85*(1), 41–56.

Rose, L. C., Gallup, A. M., & Elam, S. M. (1997). The 29th annual Phi Delta Kappa/Gallup poll of the public's attitudes toward the public schools. *Phi Delta Kappan, 79,* 41–56.

Rosenkoetter, S. E., & Fowler, S. A. (1986). Teaching mainstreamed children to manage daily transitions. *Teaching Exceptional Children, 19*(1), 20–23.

Rosenshine, B., & Stevens, R. (1986). Teaching functions. In M. C. Wittrock (Ed.), *Handbook of research on teaching* (3rd ed., pp. 376–391). New York: Macmillan.

Rowland, C., & Schweigert, P. (2000). *Tangible symbol systems.* Portland, OR: OHSU Center on Self-Determination.

Rubin, R. A., & Balow, B. (1978). Prevalence of teacher identified behavior problems: A longitudinal study. *Exceptional Children, 45,* 102–111.

Rueda, R., & Prieto, A. G. (1979). Cultural pluralism: Implications for teacher education. *Teacher Education and Special Education, 2*(4), 4–11.

Ruiz, N. T. (1989). An optimal learning environment for Rosemary. *Exceptional Children, 56,* 130–144.

Rutter, M., LeCouteur, A. L., & Lord, C. (2003). *Autism diagnostic interview revised manual (ADI-R).* Los Angeles: Western Psychological Services.

Ryan, A. L., Halsey, H. N., & Matthews, W. J. (2003). Using functional assessment to promote desirable student behavior in school. *Teaching Exceptional Children, 35*(5), 8–15.

Ryder, R. J., Graves, B. B., & Graves, M. F. (1989). *Easy reading: Book series and periodicals for less able readers* (2nd ed.). Newark, DE: International Reading Association.

Sabornie, E. J., & deBettencourt, L. U. (2003). *Teaching students with mild and high incidence disabilities* (2nd ed.). Upper Saddle River, NJ: Merrill/Prentice Hall.

Sabornie, E. J., & Kauffman, J. M. (1985). Regular classroom sociometric status of behaviorally disordered adolescents. *Behavioral Disorders, 10,* 268–274.

Saddler, B. (2004). 20 ways to improve writing ability. *Intervention in School and Clinic, 39,* 310–314.

Safran, S. P., & Safran, J. S. (1996). Intervention assistance programs and prereferral teams: Directions for the twenty-first century. *Remedial and Special Education, 17,* 363–369.

Sailor, W., Gee, K., & Karasoff, P. (1993). Full inclusion and school restructuring. In M. E. Snell (Ed.), *Instruction of students with severe disabilities* (4th ed., pp. 1–30). New York: Merrill/Macmillan.

Sale, P., & Carey, D. M. (1995). The sociometric status of students with disabilities in a full-inclusion school. *Exceptional Children, 62,* 6–19.

Salend, S. J. (1987). Group-oriented behavior management strategies. *Teaching Exceptional Children, 19*(1), 53–55.

Salend, S. J. (2005). *Creative inclusive classrooms* (5th ed.). Upper Saddle River, NJ: Merrill/Prentice Hall.

Salend, S. J., & Duhaney, L. M. G. (2002). Grading students in inclusive settings. *Teaching Exceptional Children, 34*(3), 8–15.

Salpeter, J. (1988). Answers to your questions about CD-ROM. *Classroom Computer Learning, 8*(6), 18.

Sander, E. K. (1972). When are speech sounds learned? *Journal of Speech and Hearing Disorders, 23*(1), 55–63.

Sarff, L. (1981). An innovative use of free field amplification in regular classrooms. In R. Roesser & M. Downs (Eds.), *Auditory disorders in school children* (pp. 263–272). New York: Thieme Stratton.

Sasso, G., & Rude, H. A. (1988). The social effects of integration on nonhandicapped children. *Education and Training in Mental Retardation, 23,* 18–23.

Scheuermann, B., & Webber, J. (2002). *Autism: Teaching does make a difference.* Belmont, CA: Wadsworth/Thomas Learning.

Schilit, J., & Caldwell, M. L. (1980). A word list of essential career/vocational words for mentally retarded students. *Education and Training of the Mentally Retarded, 15,* 113–117.

Schinke, S. P., & Gilchrist, L. D. (1984). *Life skills counseling for adolescents.* Baltimore: University Park Press.

Schlosser, L. Y., & Algozzine, B. (1980). Sex, behavior, and teacher expectancies. *Journal of Experimental Education, 48,* 231–236.

Schonfeld, D. J., & Quackenbush, M. (2000). Teaching young children about AIDS. *Principal, 79*(5), 33–35.

Schopler, E., Mesibov, G. B., & Hearsey, K. (1995). Structured teaching in the TEACCH system. In E. Schopler & G. B. Mesibov (Eds.), *Learning and cognition in autism* (pp. 243–268). New York: Plenum Press.

Schopler, E., Reichler, R. J., Bashford, A., Lansing, M. D., & Marcus, L. M. (1990). *Psychoeducational profile revised.* Austin, TX: PRO-ED.

Schopler, E., Reichler, R. J., & Renner, B. R. (1988). *The childhood autism rating scale.* Los Angeles: Western Psychological Services.

Schreibman, L., Whalen, C., & Stahmer, A. C. (2000). The use of video priming to reduce disruptive transition behavior in children with autism. *Journal of Positive Behavior Interventions, 2*(1), 3–11.

Schrock, K. (2004). *Kathy Schrock's guide for educators: Critical evaluation tools.* Discovery.com, Discovery School. Retrieved August 28, 2004, from http://school.discovery.com/schrockguide/eval.html

Schubert, M., Glick, H., & Bauer, D. (1979). *The least restrictive environment and the handicapped student.* Dayton, OH: Wright State University.

Schulte, A. C., Osborne, S. S., & McKinney, J. D. (1990). Academic outcomes for students with learning disabilities in consultation and resource programs. *Exceptional Children, 57,* 162–172.

Schultz, J. B., & Torrie, M. (1984). Effectiveness of parenthood education materials for mainstreamed vocational home economics classes. *Journal of Vocational Education Research, 9*(1), 46–56.

Schulz, J. B., & Turnbull, A. P. (1983). *Mainstreaming handicapped students* (2nd ed.). Boston: Allyn & Bacon.

Schumaker, J. B., & Deshler, D. D. (1988). Implementing the regular education initiative in secondary schools: A different ball game. *Journal of Learning Disabilities, 21,* 36–42.

Schumaker, J. B., & Hazel, J. S. (1984). Social skills assessment and training for the learning disabled: Who's on first and what's on second? Part I. *Journal of Learning Disabilities, 17,* 422–431.

Schumaker, J. B., Nolan, S. M., & Deshler, D. D. (1985). *Learning strategies curriculum: The error monitoring strategy.* Lawrence: University of Kansas.

Searcy, S. (1996). Friendship interventions for the integration of children and youth with learning and behavior problems. *Preventing School Failure, 40*(3), 131–134.

Semel, E., Wiig, E. H., & Secord, W. A. (2003). *Clinical evaluation of language fundamentals—Fourth edition.* San Antonio, TX: Psychological Corporation.

Seroussi, K. (2000, February). We cured our son's autism. *Parents, 75*(2), 118–125.

Shames, G. H., & Ramig, P. R. (1994). Stuttering and other disorders of fluency. In G. H. Shames, E. H. Wiig, & W. A Secord (Eds.), *Human communication disorders* (4th ed., pp. 336–386). New York: Merrill/Macmillan.

Shanker, J. L., & Ekwall, E. E. (2000). *Ekwall/Shanker reading inventory* (4th ed.). Boston: Allyn & Bacon.

Shanker, J. L., & Ekwall, E. E. (2002). *Locating and correcting reading difficulties* (8th ed.). Upper Saddle River, NJ: Merrill/Prentice Hall.

Shatz-Akin, T. (1997). DVD comes to the Mac. *MacUser, 13*(7), 74–77.

Shaunessy, E. (2003). State policies regarding gifted education. *Gifted Child Today, 26*(3), 16–21, 65.

Shaywitz, S. (2003). *Overcoming dyslexia.* New York: Knopf.

Shaywitz, S. E., Holahan, J M., Freudenheim, D. A., Fletcher, J. M., Makuch, R. W., & Shaywitz, B. A. (2001). Heterogeneity with the gifted: Higher IQ boys exhibit behaviors resembling boys with learning disabilities. *Gifted Child Quarterly, 15,* 16–23.

Silverman, L. K. (1988). Gifted and talented. In E. L. Meyen & T. M. Socratic (Eds.), Exceptional children and youth: An introduction (3rd ed., pp. 263–291). Denver: Love.

Sheehan, S. (2003, December 1). The autism fight. *The New Yorker,* pp. 76–87.

Shepard, D. H. (1986, November). Special students and regular software. *The Computing Teacher,* 18–19.

Shinn, M. R., & Hubbard, D. D. (1993). Curriculum-based measurement and problem-solving assessment: Basic procedures and outcomes. In E. L. Meyen, G. A. Vergason, & R. J. Whelan (Eds.), *Educating students with mild disabilities* (pp. 221–253). Denver. Love.

Siegel, L. J., & Senna, J. J. (1994). *Juvenile delinquency: Theory, practice and law.* St. Paul: West.

Sierra, V. (1973). Learning style of the Mexican American. In L. A. Bransford, L. M. Baca, & K. Lane (Eds.), *Cultural diversity and the exceptional child* (pp. 42–49). Reston, VA: The Council for Exceptional Children.

Silvaroli, N. J., & Wheelock, W. H. (2003). *Classroom reading inventory* (10th ed.). Boston: McGraw-Hill.

Silver, L. B. (1987). The "magic cure": A review of the current controversial approaches for treating learning disabilities. *Journal of Learning Disabilities, 20,* 498–504, 512.

Simms, R. S., & Falcon, S. C. (1987). Teaching sight words. *Teaching Exceptional Children, 20*(1), 30–33.

Simpson, R. L. (1980). Modifying the attitudes of regular class students toward the handicapped. *Focus on Exceptional Children, 13*(3), 1–11.

Sindelar, P. T. (1987). Increasing reading fluency. *Teaching Exceptional Children, 19*(2), 59–60.

Sirvis, B. (1982). The physically disabled. In E. L. Meyen (Ed.), *Exceptional children and youth* (2nd ed., pp. 382–405). Denver: Love.

Sirvis, B. (1988). Physical disabilities. In E. L. Meyen & T. M. Skrtic (Eds.), *Exceptional children and youth: An introduction* (3rd ed., pp. 387–411). Denver: Love.

Sivin-Kachala, J., & Bialo, E. R. (1996). *Report on the effectiveness of technology in schools, '95–'96.* Washington, DC: Software Publishers Association.

Sklaire, M. (1989). Today's kids face different diseases. *NEA Today, 7*(8), 9.

Slate, J. R., & Saudargas, R. A. (1986). Differences in learning disabled and average students' classroom behaviors. *Learning Disability Quarterly, 9*(1), 61–67.

Slavin, R. E. (1987). *Cooperative learning. Student teams.* Washington, DC: National Education Association.

Slavin, R. E. (1989). Students at risk of school failure: The problem and its dimensions. In R. E. Slavin, N. L. Karweit, & N. A. Madden (Eds.), *Effective programs for students at risk* (pp. 3–19). Boston: Allyn & Bacon.

Slavin, R. E. (1995). *Cooperative learning: Theory, research, and practice* (2nd ed.). Boston: Allyn & Bacon.

Slavin, R. E., Madden, N. A., & Karweit, N. L. (1989). Effective programs for students at risk: Conclusions for practice and policy. In R. E. Slavin, N. L. Karweit, & N. A. Madden (Eds.), *Effective programs for students at risk* (pp. 355–372). Boston: Allyn & Bacon.

Slavin, R. E., Madden, N. A., & Leavey, M. (1984). Effects of cooperative learning and individualized instruction on mainstreamed students. *Exceptional Children, 50,* 434–443.

Smith, D. D. (2001). *Introduction to special education* (4th ed.). Boston: Allyn & Bacon.

Smith, D. D. (2004). *Introduction to special education in an age of opportunity* (5th ed.). Boston: Allyn & Bacon.

Smith, F. (1982). *Writing and the writer.* New York: Holt, Rinehart & Winston.

Smith, R. M., Neisworth, J. T., & Greer, J. G. (1978). *Evaluating educational environments.* Columbus, OH: Merrill/Prentice Hall.

Smith, T. E. C., Finn, D. M., & Dowdy, C. A. (1993). *Teaching students with mild disabilities.* Fort Worth, TX: Harcourt Brace Jovanovich.

Smith, T. E. C., Polloway, E. A., Patton, J. R., & Dowdy, C. A. (1998). *Teaching students with special needs in inclusive settings* (2nd ed.). Boston: Allyn & Bacon.

Smutny, J. F. (2000). *Teaching young gifted children in the regular class-room.* Arlington, VA: The Council for Exceptional Children. (ERIC Clearinghouse on Disabilities and Gifted Education, EC Digest No. 595)

Snell, M., & Brown, F. (1993). Instructional planning and implementation. In M. Snell (Ed.), *Instruction of students with severe disabilities* (4th ed., pp. 99–151). New York: Merrill/Macmillan.

Snider, W. (1988, September 21). Hispanic students require income to remain in school, study finds. *Education Week,* p. 17.

Snow, C. E., Burns, S., & Griffin, P. (Eds.). (1998). *Preventing reading difficulties in young children.* Washington, DC: National Academic Press.

Snyder, H. (2000). *Juvenile arrests: 1999.* Washington, DC: Office of Juvenile Justice and Delinquency Prevention.

Soderberg, L. J. (1988). Educators' knowledge of the characteristics of high school dropouts. *The High School Journal, 71,* 108–115.

Spache, G. (1953). A new readability formula for primary-grade reading materials. *The Elementary School Journal, 53,* 410–413.

Spalding, R. B., & Spalding, W. T. (1986). *The writing road to reading* (3rd ed.). New York: Morrow.

Spear-Swerling, L., & Sternberg, R. J. (2001). What science offers to teachers of reading. *Learning Disabilities Research & Practice, 16*(1), 51–57.

Special needs, common goals. (2004). *Education Week, 33*(17), 7.

Spenciner, L. J. (1992). Mainstreaming the child with a visual impairment. In L. G. Cohen (Ed.), *Children with exceptional needs in regular classrooms* (pp. 82–97). Washington, DC: National Education Association.

Spinelli, C. G. (2004). Dealing with cancer in the classroom: The teacher's role and responsibilities. *Teaching Exceptional Children, 36*(4), 14–21.

Stahl, S. A., & Miller, P. D. (1989). Whole language and language experience approaches for beginning reading: A quantitative research synthesis. *Review of Educational Research, 59,* 87–116.

Stainback, S., & Stainback, W. (1988). Educating students with severe disabilities. *Teaching Exceptional Children, 21*(1), 16–19.

Stainback, S., & Stainback, W. (Eds.). (1985). *Integrating students with severe handicaps into regular schools.* Reston, VA: The Council for Exceptional Children.

Stainback, S., & Stainback, W. (1990a). Inclusive schooling. In W. Stainback & S. Stainback (Eds.), *Support networks for inclusive schooling* (pp. 3–23). Baltimore: Brookes.

Stainback, S., & Stainback, W. (1992). *Curriculum considerations in inclusive classrooms.* Baltimore: Brookes.

Stainback, S., Stainback, W., & Forest, M. (1989). *Educating all students in the mainstream of regular education.* Baltimore: Brookes.

Stainback, S., Stainback, W., & Slavin, R. (1989). Classroom organization for diversity among students. In S. Stainback, W. Stainback, & M. Forest (Eds.), *Educating all students in the mainstream of regular education* (pp. 131–142). Baltimore: Brookes.

Stainback, W., & Stainback, S. (Eds.). (1990b). *Support networks for inclusive schooling.* Baltimore: Brookes.

Stainback, W., Stainback, S., & Froyen, L. (1987). Structuring the classroom to prevent disruptive behaviors. *Teaching Exceptional Children, 19*(4), 12–16.

Stainback, W., Stainback, S., & Wilkinson, A. (1992). Encouraging peer supports and friendships. *Teaching Exceptional Children, 24*(2), 6–11.

State-wide assessment programs. (1998, Spring). Research connections in special education (No. 2). Reston, VA: ERIC/OSEP Special Project, ERIC Clearinghouse on Disabilities and Gifted Education, Council for Exceptional Children.

Steel, E. (1995). AIDS, drugs, and the adolescent. National Institute on Drug *Abuse Research Monograph, 156,* 130–145.

Stephens, K. R. (2000). Gifted education and the law. *Gifted Child Today, 23*(1), 30–37.

Stephens, K. R., & Karnes, F. A. (2000). State definitions for the gifted and talented revisited. *Exceptional Children, 66*(2), 219–38.

Stephens, T. M. (1980). Teachers as managers. *The Directive Teacher, 2*(5), 4.

Stepien, W. J., & Pyke, S. L. (1997). Designing problem-based learning units. *Journal for the Education of the Gifted, 20*(4), 380–400.

Sternberg, R. J. (1991). Giftedness according to the triarchic theory of human intelligence. In N. Colangelo & G. A. Davis (Eds.), *Handbook of gifted education* (pp. 45–54). Boston: Allyn & Bacon.

Sternberg, R. J. (1997). A triarchic view of giftedness: Theory and practice. In N. Colangelo & G. A. Davis (Eds.), *Handbook of gifted education* (2nd ed., pp. 43–53). Boston: Allyn & Bacon.

Sternberg, R. J. (2003). Giftedness according to the theory of successful intelligence. In N. Colangelo & G. A. Davis, (Eds.), *Handbook of gifted education* (3rd ed., pp. 88–99). Boston: Allyn & Bacon.

Sternberg, R. J., & Grigorenko, E. L. (2000). *Teaching for successful intelligence to increase student learning and achievement.* Arlington Heights, IL: SkyLight Professional Development.

Sternberg, R. J., & Grigorenko, E. L. (2002). The theory of successful intelligence as a basis for gifted education. *Gifted Child Quarterly, 46*(4), 265–277.

Stevens, L. J., & Price, M. (1992). Meeting the challenge of educating children at risk. *Phi Delta Kappan, 74,* 18–20, 22–23.

Stevens, R., & Rosenshine, B. (1981). Advances in research on teaching. *Exceptional Education Quarterly, 2*(1), 1–9.

Stitt, B. A., Erekson, T. L., Hofstrand, R. K., Loepp, F. L., Minor, C. W., Perreault, H. R., & Savage, J. G. (1988). *Building gender fairness in schools.* Carbondale: Board of Trustees, Southern Illinois University.

Stone, B., Cundick, B. P., & Swanson, D. (1988). Special education screening system: Group achievement test. *Exceptional Children, 55,* 71–75.

Stowitschek, J. J., Gable, R. A., & Hendrickson, J. M. (1980). *Instructional materials for exceptional children.* Germantown, MD: Aspen Systems.

Strain, P. S. (1981a). Peer-mediated treatment of exceptional children's social withdrawal. *Exceptional Education Quarterly, 1*(4), 93–105.

Strain, P. S. (Ed.). (1981b). *The utilization of peers as behavior change agents*. New York: Plenum.

Strain, P. S., & Kerr, M. M. (1981). *Mainstreaming of children in schools*. New York: Academic Press.

Strickland, B. B., & Turnbull, A. P. (1993). *Developing and implementing individualized education programs* (3rd ed.). New York: Merrill/Macmillan.

Sugai, G., & Lewis, T. J. (1996). Preferred and promising practices for social skills instruction. *Focus on Exceptional Children, 29*(4), 1–16.

Sugai, G. M., & Tindal, G. A. (1993). *Effective school consultation: An interactive approach*. Pacific Grove, CA: Brooks/Cole.

Sullivan, D. (2004). *Major search engines and directories*. Search Engine Watch. Retrieved August 21, 2004, from http://searchenginewatch.com/links/article.php/2156221

Sulzer-Azaroff, B., & Mayer, G. R. (1977). *Applying behavior-analysis procedures with children and youth*. New York: Holt, Rinehart & Winston.

Sulzer-Azaroff, B., & Mayer, R. (1991). *Behavior analysis for lasting change*. Fort Worth, TX: Holt, Rinehart & Winston.

Sunderland, L. C. (2004). Speech, language, and audiology services in public schools. *Intervention in School and Clinic, 39*(4), 209–217.

Sutherland, K. S., & Wehby, J. H. (2001). Exploring the relationship between increased opportunities to respond to academic requests and the academic and behavioral outcomes of students with EBD. *Remedial and Special Education, 22*, 113–121.

Swanson, H. L. (1989). Strategy instruction: Overview of principles and procedures for effective use. *Learning Disabilities Quarterly, 12*, 3–14.

Swanson, H. L., & Cooney, J. B. (1996). Learning disabilities and memory. In D. K. Reid, W. P. Hresko, & H. L. Swanson (Eds.), *Cognitive approaches to learning disabilities* (3rd ed., pp. 287–314). Austin, TX: PRO-ED.

Swift, C. A. (1988). Communication disorders. In E. W. Lynch & R. B. Lewis (Eds.), *Exceptional children and adults* (pp. 318–351). Glenview, IL: Scott, Foresman.

Tarver, S., & Hallahan, D. P. (1976). Children with learning disabilities: An overview. In J. M. Kauffman & D. P. Hallahan (Eds.), *Teaching children with learning disabilities: Personal perspectives* (pp. 2–57). Columbus, OH: Merrill/Prentice Hall.

Taylor, B. A. (2001). Teaching peer social skills to children with autism. In C. Maurice, G. Green, & R. Foxx (Eds.), *Making a difference: Behavioral intervention for autism* (pp. 83–96), Austin, TX: PRO-ED.

Taylor, B. A., & Jasper, S. (2001). Teaching programs to increase peer interaction. In C. Maurice, G. Green, & R. Foxx (Eds.), *Making a difference: Behavioral intervention for autism* (pp. 97–162). Austin, TX: PRO-ED.

Taylor, B. A., Levin, L., & Jasper, S. (1999). Increasing play-related statements in children with autism toward their siblings: Effects of video-modeling. *Journal of Developmental and Physical Disabilities, 11*, 253–264.

Taylor, B. A., & McDonough, K. A. (1996). Selecting teaching programs. In C. Maurice, G. Green, & S. Luce (Eds.), *Behavioral intervention for young children with autism: A manual for parents and professionals* (pp. 63–177). Austin, TX: PRO-ED.

Taylor, O. (1986). Language differences. In G. H. Shames & E. H. Wiig (Eds.), *Human communication disorders* (2nd ed., pp. 385–413). New York: Merrill/Macmillan.

Taylor, S. J. (1988). Caught in the continuum: A critical analysis of the principle of the least restrictive environment. *Journal of the Association for Persons with Severe Handicaps, 13*(1), 41–53.

Technology and the at-risk student. (1988, November/December). *Electronic Learning*, pp. 35–49.

The MetLife Survey of the American Teacher: An Examination of School Leadership. (2003). New York: Author.

Therrien, W. J. (2004). Fluency and comprehension gains as a result of repeated reading: A meta-analysis. *Remedial and Special Education, 25*, 252–261.

Thomas, C. H., & Patton, J. R. (1990). Mild and moderate retardation. In J. R. Patton, M. Beirne-Smith, & J. S. Payne (Eds.), *Mental retardation* (3rd ed., pp. 197–226). New York: Merrill/Macmillan.

Thousand, J. S., & Villa, R. A. (1990). Strategies for educating learners with severe disabilities within their local home schools and communities. *Focus on Exceptional Children, 23*(3), 1–24.

Thurber, D. N. (2001). *D'nealian handwriting cursive connections*. Tucson, AZ: GoodYear Books.

Thurlow, M., House, A., Boys, C., Scott, D., & Ysseldyke, J. (2000). *State participation and accommodation policies for students with disabilities: 1999 update* (Synthesis Rep. No. 33). Minneapolis, MN: University of Minnesota, National Center on Educational Outcomes.

Timar, T. B., & Kirp, D. L. (1989). Education reform in the 1980s: lessons from the states. *Phi Delta Kappan, 70*, 505–511.

Tomlinson, C. A. (2000). *Differentiation of instruction in the elementary grades*. Champaign, IL: ERIC Clearinghouse on Elementary and Early Childhood Education. (ERIC Document Reproduction Service No. ED-443–572)

Tomlinson, C. A. (Winter, 2001). Tiered lessons: What are their benefits and implications? *Gifted Education Communicator*, 37–39.

Tomlinson, C. A., Kaplan, S. N., Renzulli, J. S., Purcell, J., Leppien, J., & Burns, D. (2002). *The parallel curriculum*. Thousand Oaks, CA: Corwin Press.

Tompkins, G. E., & Friend, M. (1986). On your mark, get set, write! *Teaching Exceptional Children, 18*(2), 82–89.

Torgan, C. (2002). Childhood obesity on the rise. *The NIH Word on Health*. Retrieved October 17, 2004, from http://www.nih.gov/news/WordonHealth/jun2002/childhoodobesity.htm

Torgesen, J. K. (1977). The role of nonspecific factors in the task performance of learning disabled children: A theoretical assessment. *Journal of Learning Disabilities, 10*, 27–34.

Torrance, E. P. (1966). *Torrance tests of creative thinking*. Princeton, NJ: Personnal.

Torres, I., & Corn, A. L. (1990). *When you have a visually handicapped child in your classroom: Suggestions for teachers*. New York: American Foundation for the Blind.

Tournaki, N., & Criscitiello, E. (2003). Using peer tutoring as a successful part of behavior management. *Teaching Exceptional Children, 36*(2), 22–29.

Towell, J., & Wink, J. (1993). *Strategies for monolingual teachers in multilingual classrooms.* Turlock: California State University, Stanislaus. (ERIC Document Reproduction Service No. ED-359–797)

Tower, C. C. (1987). *How schools can help combat child abuse and neglect* (2nd ed.). Washington, DC: National Education Association.

Trad, P. V. (1999). Assessing the patterns that prevent teenage pregnancy. *Adolescence, 34,* 221–240.

Tucker, B. F., & Colson, S. E. (1992). Traumatic brain injury: An overview of school re-entry. *Intervention in School and Clinic, 27,* 198–206.

Tur-Kaspa, H., & Bryan, T. (1994). Social information processing skills of students with learning disabilities. *Learning Disabilities Research and Practice, 9,* 12–23.

Turnbull, A., & Turnbull, R. (2001). *Families, professionals and exceptionality: Collaborating for empowerment.* Upper Saddle River, NJ: Prentice Hall.

Turnbull, A. P., & Schulz, J. B. (1979). *Mainstreaming handicapped students.* Boston: Allyn & Bacon.

Turnbull, R., Turnbull, A., Shank, M., & Smith, S. J. (2004). *Exceptional lives* (4th ed.). Upper Saddle River, NJ: Merrill/Prentice Hall.

UCLA/RAND Center for Adolescent Health Promotion. (2003). Bullying in schools pervasive, disruptive and serious. Retrieved July 19, 2004, from http://www.rand.org/health/adolescent/bullying.html

U.S. Census Bureau. (1997). *Population profile of the United States: 1995, Highlights.* Retrieved from http://www.census.gov/population/www/pop-profile/highlgt.html

U.S. Census Bureau. (2000a). *Poverty 1999, graphs.* Washington, DC: Author. Retrieved June 1, 2001, from http://www.census.gov/hhes/poverty/poverty99/povage99.html

U.S. Census Bureau. (2000b). *Profile of general demographic characteristics: 2000.* Washington, DC: Author. Retrieved June 1, 2001, from http://factfinder.census.gov/servlet/BasicFactsServlet

U.S. Census Bureau. (2003). Poverty 2002. Washington, DC: Author. Retrieved June 2, 2004, from http://www.census.gov/Press-Release/www/2003/cb03-153.html

U.S. Department of Education. (1991, September 16). *Memorandum: Clarification of policy to address the needs of children with attention deficit disorders within general and/or special education.* Washington, DC: Office of Special Education and Rehabilitative Services.

U.S. Department of Education. (1996). *Eighteenth annual report to Congress on the implementation of the Individuals with Disabilities Education Act.* Washington, DC: Author.

U.S. Department of Education. (2002). *Twenty-fourth annual report to Congress on the implementation of the Individuals with Disabilities Education Act.* Washington, DC: Author.

U.S. Department of Education, Office of Educational Research and Improvement. (1993). *National excellence: A case for developing America's talent.* Washington, DC: Author.

U.S. Department of Education, Office of Special Education and Rehabilitative Services, Office of Special Education Programs. (2003). *Identifying and treating attention deficit hyperactivity disorder: A resource for school and home.* Washington, DC: Author. Available for downloading at http://www.ed.gov/about/reports/annual/osep/index.html

U.S. Department of Health, Education, and Welfare. (1972). *Education of the gifted and talented.* Washington, DC: Author.

U.S. Public Health Service. (1990). *Healthy people 2000.* Washington, DC: U.S. Government Printing Office.

Utley, C. A., Mortweet, S. L., & Greenwood, C. R. (1997). Peer-mediated instruction and interventions. *Focus on Exceptional Children, 29*(5), 1–23.

Van Riper, C. (1978). *Speech correction.* Upper Saddle River, NJ: Prentice Hall.

Van Tassel-Baska, J. (2001). The role of advanced placement in talent development. *Journal of Secondary Gifted Education, 12,* 126–132.

Van Tassel-Baska, J. (2003). What matters in curriculum for gifted learners: Reflections on theory, research, and practice. N. Colangelo & G. A. Davis (Eds.), *Handbook of gifted education* (pp. 174–183). Boston: Allyn & Bacon.

Vandercook, T., & York, J. (1990). A team approach to program development and support. In W. Stainback & S. Stainback (Eds.), *Support networks for inclusive schooling* (pp. 95–122). Baltimore: Brookes.

Vandercook, T., York, J., & Forest, M. (1989). The McGill Action Planning System (MAPS): A strategy for building the vision. *Journal of the Association for Persons with Severe Handicaps, 14,* 205–215.

Vannatta, R. A. (1997). Adolescent gender differences in suicide-related behaviors. *Journal of Youth and Adolescence, 26,* 559–568.

Vaughn, S. R. (1995, July). *Responsible inclusion for students with learning disabilities.* Paper presented at the conference of the International Academy for Research in Learning Disabilities, Phoenix, AZ.

Vaughn, S., Bos, C. S., & Schumm, J. S. (2003). *Teaching exceptional, diverse, and at-risk students* (3rd ed.). Boston: Allyn & Bacon.

Vaughn, S., & Fuchs, L. S. (2003). Redefining learning disabilities as inadequate response to instruction: The promise and potential problems. *Learning Disabilities Research & Practice, 18,* 137–146.

Vaughn, S., Gersten, R., & Chard, D. J. (2000). The underlying message in LD intervention research: Findings from research syntheses. *Exceptional Children, 67,* 99–114.

Vaughn, S., Linan-Thompson, S., & Hickman, P. (2003). Response to instruction as a means of identifying students with reading/learning disabilities. *Exceptional Children, 69,* 391–409.

Ventura, S. J., & Curtin, S. C. (1999). Recent trends in teen births in the United States. *Statistical Bulletin Metropolitan Insurance Co. 80*(1), 2–12.

Vergason, G. A., & Anderegg, M. L. (1991). Beyond the regular education initiative and the resource room controversy. *Focus on Exceptional Children, 23*(7), 1–7.

Voeltz, L. M. (1980). Children's attitudes toward handicapped peers. *American Journal of Mental Deficiency, 84,* 455–464.

Voeltz, L. M. (1982). Effects of structured interactions with severely handicapped peers on children's attitudes. *American Journal of Mental Deficiency, 86,* 380–390.

Voltz, D. L., Brazil, N., & Ford, A. (2001). What matters most in inclusive education: A practical guide for moving forward. *Intervention in School and Clinic, 37*(1), 23–30.

von Károlyi, C., Ramos-Ford, V., & Gardner, H. (2003). Multiple intelligences: A perspective on giftedness. In N. Colangelo & G. A. Davis (Eds.), *Handbook of gifted education* (3rd ed., pp. 100–112). Boston: Allyn & Bacon.

Wagner, S. (1999). *Inclusive programming for elementary students with autism.* Arlington, TX: Future Horizons, Inc.

Walker, H. M. (1995). *The acting out child: Coping with classroom disruption* (2nd ed.). Longmont, CO: Sopris West.

Walker, H. M., McConnell, S., Holmes, D., Todis, B., Walker, J., & Golden, N. (1983). *The Walker social skills curriculum: The AC-CEPTS* [A Curriculum for Children's Effective Peer and Teacher Skills] *program.* Austin, TX: PRO-ED.

Walker, H. M., Todis, B., Holmes, D., & Horton, G. (1988). *The Walker social skills curriculum: The ACCESS* [Adolescent Curriculum for Communication and Effective Social Skills] *program.* Austin, TX: PRO-ED.

Walker, J. L. (1988). Young American Indian children. *Teaching Exceptional Children, 20*(4), 50–51.

Walsh, J. M., & Jones, B. (2004). New models of cooperative teaching. *Teaching Exceptional Children, 36*(5), 14–20.

Warger, C. L., Tewey, S., & Megivern, M. (1991). *Abuse and neglect of exceptional children.* Reston, VA: The Council for Exceptional Children.

Webb, J. T., & Latimer, D. (1993). ADHD and children who are gifted. *Exceptional Children, 60,* 183–184.

Webster, A., & Roe, J. (1998). *Children with visual impairment: Social interaction, language, and learning.* London: Routledge.

Wechsler, D. (2003). *Wechsler intelligence scale for children—Fourth edition.* San Antonio, TX: Psychological Corporation.

Wehman, P. (1997). *Exceptional individuals in school, community, and work.* Austin, TX: PRO-ED.

Weil, M. L., & Murphy, J. (1982). Instruction processes. In H. E. Mitzel (Ed.), *Encyclopedia of educational research* (5th ed., pp. 890–917). New York: Free Press.

Weiner, J., & Harris, P. J. (1997). Evaluation of an individualized, context-based social skills training program for children with learning disabilities. *Learning Disabilities Research & Practice, 12,* 40–53.

Weinstein, C. S. (1979). The physical environment of the school: A review of research. *Review of Educational Research, 49,* 577–610.

Werts, M. G., Wolery, M., Snyder, E. D., & Caldwell, N. K. (1996). Teachers' perceptions of the supports critical to the success of inclusion programs. *JASH, 21,* 9–21.

Westby, C. E. (1992). Whole language and learners with mild handicaps. *Focus on Exceptional Children, 24*(8), 1–16.

Whelan, R. J. (1995). Emotional disturbance. In E. L. Meyen & T. M. Skrtic (Eds.), *Special education and student disability* (4th ed., pp. 270–336). Denver: Love.

White, K. R., Bush, D., & Casto, G. (1986). Let the past be prologue: Learning from previous reviews of early intervention efficacy research. *Journal of Special Education, 19,* 417–428.

Whitt, J., Paul, P. V., & Reynolds, C. J. (1988). Motivate reluctant learning disabled writers. *Teaching Exceptional Children, 20*(3), 37–39.

Wickstrom, C. D. (2004). Give us the best and brightest, but . . . A historical review of U.S. national policy on education for the highly capable. In D. Boothe & J. C. Stanley (Eds.), *In the eyes of the beholder: Critical issues for diversity in gifted education* (pp. 263–274). Waco, TX: Prufrock Press.

Wiedmeyer, D., & Lehman, J. (1991). "The House Plan" approach to collaborative teaching and consultation. *Teaching Exceptional Children, 23*(10), 7–10.

Will, M. C. (1986a). Clarifying the standards: Placement in a least restrictive environment. *OSERS News in Print, 1*(2), 1.

Will, M. C. (1986b). Educating children with learning problems: A shared responsibility. *Exceptional Children, 52,* 411–415.

Willis, W. O. (2004). Families with African American roots. In E. W. Lynch & M. J. Hanson (Eds.), *Developing cross-cultural competence* (3rd ed., pp. 141–177). Baltimore: Brookes.

Winebrenner, S. (2001). *Teaching gifted kids in the regular classroom* (2nd ed.). Minneapolis: Free Spirit Publishing

Winget, P., & Kirk, J. (1991). *California programs and services for students with serious emotional disturbances.* Sacramento, CA: Resources in Special Education.

Winston, S. (1995). *Stephanie Winston's best organizing tips.* New York: Simon & Schuster.

Winzer, M. A., & Mazurek, K. (1998). *Special education in multicultural contexts.* Upper Saddle River, NJ: Merrill/Prentice Hall.

Witherspoon, J. (1996). The evolving university: No longer virtual. *The Distance Educator, 2*(3), 1, 10–11, 18.

Wolfe, P. S., & Hall, T. E. (2003). Making inclusion a reality for students with severe disabilities. *Teaching Exceptional Children, 35*(4), 56–61.

Wolfensberger, W. (1972). *The principle of normalization in human services.* Toronto: National Institute on Mental Retardation.

Wood, J. W., & Miederhoff, J. W. (1989). Bridging the gap. *Teaching Exceptional Children, 21*(2), 66–68.

Woodcock, R. W., McGrew, K., & Mather, N. (2001). *Woodcock-Johnson III.* Itasca, IL: Riverside.

Woodring, P. (1989). A new approach to the dropout problem. *Phi Delta Kappan, 70,* 468–469.

Woods, M. L., & Moe, A. J. (2003). *Analytical reading inventory* (7th ed.). Upper Saddle River, NJ: Merrill/Prentice Hall.

Woodward, D. M. (1981). *Mainstreaming the learning disabled adolescent.* Rockville, MD: Aspen Systems.

Woodward, J. (2004). Mathematics education in the United States: Past to present. *Journal of Learning Disabilities, 37,* 16–31.

Woolston, J. L. (1999). Combined pharmacotherapy: Pitfalls of treatment. *Journal of the American Academy of Child and Adolescent Psychiatry, 38,* 1455–1457.

Wormeli, R. (2003). *Differentiating instruction: A modified concerto in four movements.* LD Online. Retrieved July 9, 2004, from http://www.ldonline.org/ld_indepth/teaching_techniques/modified_concerto.htm/

Yarber, W. L. (1987). *AIDS education: Curriculum and health policy.* Bloomington, IN: Phi Delta Kappa Educational Foundation.

Yeargin-Allsopp, M., Rice, C., Karapurkar, T., Doernberg, N., Boyle, C., & Murphy, C. (2003). Prevalence of autism in a U.S. metropolitan area. *Journal of the American Medical Association, 289,* 49–55.

York, J., Doyle, M. B., & Kronberg, R. (1992). A curriculum development process for inclusive classrooms. *Focus on Exceptional Children, 25*(4), 1–16.

York, J., & Vandercook, T. (1991). Designing an integrated program for learners with severe disabilities. *Teaching Exceptional Children, 23*(2), 22–28.

York, J., Vandercook, T., MacDonald, C., Heise-Neff, C., & Caughey, E. (1992). Feedback about integrating middle-school students with severe disabilities in general education classes. *Exceptional Children, 58,* 244–258.

Ysseldyke, J. E., Algozzine, B., & Thurlow, M. L. (1992). *Critical issues in special education* (2nd ed.). Boston, MA: Houghton Mifflin.

Ysseldyke, J. E., Thurlow, M. L., Wotruba, J. W., & Nania, P. A. (1990). Instructional arrangements: Perceptions from general education. *Teaching Exceptional Children, 22*(4), 4–8.

Zabel, H., & Tabor, M. (1993). Effects of soundfield amplification on spelling performance of elementary school children. *Educational Audiology Monograph, 3,* 5–9.

Zaragoza, N., Vaughn, S., & McIntosh, R. (1991). Social skills interventions and children with behavior problems: A review. *Behavioral Disorders, 16,* 260–275.

Zentall, S. S. (1983). Learning environments: A review of physical and temporal factors. *Exceptional Education Quarterly, 4*(2), 90–115.

Zentall, S. S., Hall, A. M., & Grskovic, J. A. (2001). Learning and motivational characteristics of boys with ADHD and/or giftedness. *Exceptional Children, 67,* 499–519.

Zigler, E., & Muenchow, S. (1979). Mainstreaming: The proof is in the implementation. *American Psychologist, 34,* 993–996.

Zigmond, N., Jenkins, J., Fuchs, D., Deno, S., & Fuchs, L. S. (1995). When students fail to achieve satisfactorily: A reply to McLeskey and Waldron. *Phi Delta Kappan, 77,* 303–306.

Zirkel, P. A. (1989). AIDS: Students in glass houses? *Phi Delta Kappan, 70,* 646–648.

Zirpoli, T. J., & Melloy, K. J. (2001). *Behavior management: Applications for teachers* (3rd ed.). Upper Saddle River, NJ: Merrill/ Prentice Hall.

Zuniga, M. E. (2004). Families with Latino roots. In E. W. Lynch & M. J. Hanson (Eds.), *Developing cross-cultural competence* (3rd ed., pp. 179–217). Baltimore: Brookes.

Name Index

Subject Index